The
FRUIT & NUT
BOOK

HELENA RADECKA

A
PHOEBE PHILLIPS
EDITIONS
BOOK

The
FRUIT & NUT
BOOK

HELENA RADECKA

SPHERE

SPHERE BOOKS LIMITED
30—32 Gray's Inn Road, London WC1X 8JL

First published in Great Britain by Sphere Books Ltd 1984
Copyright © 1984 Phoebe Phillips Editions
Published in association with Phoebe Phillips Editions

TRADE MARK

SPHERE

Set in Frome, Somerset
Printed and bound in Spain

In memory of my mother, who taught and encouraged me
all her life

CONTENTS

FOREWORD

Every day we are bombarded with publicity celebrating a revolutionary future of electronic technology and modernized industry. Yet, almost unheralded, there has already been a revolution which is transforming our daily lives — the multi-coloured revolution in the supermarkets and fruit stores.

Only a decade ago a winter table setting was brightened with just a few yellows and greens from apples and pears, with the occasional orange or grapefruit and maybe a bowl of walnuts.

Today there is a riot of colour throughout the year, even during the gloomy months of late autumn and winter: ripe mangoes, glowing persimmons, new citrus hybrids, fresh figs bursting with purple flesh, sharp kumquats and crimson cranberries, nuts of every kind, fresh dates — even strawberries from California for Christmas dinner.

In summer the abundance becomes almost overwhelming: all the old favourites are available, plus loganberries and blueberries, rough and smooth avocados, pink-flushed guavas, exotic mangosteens, juicy limes and rich pomegranates... the list is endless and it continues to grow every year.

For once, the marketing chiefs have brought us the perfect package: natural portion control, filled to the brim with vitamins, minerals and fibre — plus a delicious flavour.

There is no moment of the day when we cannot enjoy a piece of fruit, happy in the knowledge that we are satisfying our bodies as well as our appetites.

As if all this were not enough, there are hundreds of other ways to use fruits and nuts — cooked with meats or in vegetarian dishes, blended into superb drinks with or without alcohol, puréed and pounded for sauces, steeped for wines and liqueurs, distilled for remedies, and sliced and chopped to soothe our skins....

This happy revolution, which seems to have brought only pleasure and better health to us all, was reason enough for me to write this book — and is, I hope, reason enough for you to enjoy it.

Such a compendium as this would not have been started without the inspiration of my publisher, Phoebe Phillips Editions, and the encouragement of cooks and cookery writers from all over the world. Many are listed, as they should be, in the bibliography; others are friends and colleagues who have given their time and advice without stint.

There must be a special mention for two researchers who worked tirelessly to gather in the harvest of material: Ursula White and Cecile Landau. My thanks, too, to Hilary Evans who drew the illustrations which decorate the pages, and to Caroline Reeves who designed the book. Tessa Clark has been editor, adviser and arbiter — a burden which she has carried with unfailing good temper and helpfulness.

HELENA RADECKA

INTRODUCTION

The first part of the book is an alphabetical listing of fifty of the more popular fruits and nuts — from almond and apple to tangerine and walnut — that are normally available from most greengrocers and supermarkets.

Each starts with a brief description of the fruit or nut, with information about where it grows, advice on buying, storage and freezing, and hints on preparing it for cooking. This introduction also highlights some of the best-known ways in which it can be combined with other ingredients.

Recipes include health drinks, soups and appetizers, main course dishes, salads, cakes and breads, desserts, pies and puddings — plus preserves and wines and liqueurs as well as non-alchoholic drinks. Suggestions for cosmetics and remedies are also given, often using leaves or blossoms of a particular fruit or nut.

This section is followed by a selection of over thirty unusual fruits and nuts. Many are from the tropics or subtropics and are becoming increasingly available far from their native habitats. There is a short description for identification, followed by information on how the fruit or nut is best used. Some individual recipes are included and, wherever relevant, you are referred to recipes for similar fruits, or to general recipes.

Preserving and Basic Recipes follow, with detailed instructions for jams and jellies, fruit cheeses, pickles and chutneys, etc which can be adapted for different fruits and nuts. There are also the various kinds of pastry, sauces, etc required for some recipes in the main part of the book.

The next section, Nutrition, includes a selection of special diets for people with particular problems as well as weight-watchers, and a vitamin and mineral chart.

For enthusiastic gardeners there is How to Grow Fruits and Nuts with instructions for cultivating tree, bush and stone fruits, vines and cane fruit, perennials, citrus fruit and nuts. Greenhouse and indoor gardening are also included.

Finally, the Menu Planner gives instant suggestions for lunch or dinner parties. The appropriate recipes for each course are listed with their page numbers.

A bibliography and index complete the reference section.

ALMOND

Where would we be in springtime without our glimpse of pink blossom on the delicate branches of almond trees in our gardens and parks? But the juicy nuts we eat are likely to have come from much farther afield. Italy, France and Spain have long been producers and even in the Middle Ages, Spain was doing a roaring trade in these popular sweet nuts.

The tree itself is related to the cherry, plum and peach, and basically — though there are many varieties — there are two kinds; the bitter almond and the sweet. The former yields tiny quantities of prussic acid (refined away before it reaches us) and an oil which is used in cosmetics and to flavour liqueurs. It is the sweet almond which is so familiar in cakes, desserts and pastries. The tree is thought to have originated in the Near East, but is now happily cultivated all around the Mediterranean, in North Africa and the Canary Isles, South Africa, Australia and California.

Almonds can be bought in the shell and keep very well in this state. They can also be bought shelled, whole, split, flaked, ground, slivered or crushed. They are usually ready-blanched, but you can do this easily yourself by putting the shelled whole nuts in a bowl and pouring over boiling water. Leave them to steep for about 15 minutes as the water cools, and the brown skins should rub away easily.

To toast them, spread peeled nuts evenly on a baking sheet and bake in a moderate oven (350°F, 180°C, Mark 4) for 8–10 minutes. Take great care that the nuts do not char.

An easy alternative is to buy almond essence, though when you do, make sure you have the *true* essence of almonds, and not the almond-flavoured substitute which may never have seen a real nut.

Almonds freeze well plain or toasted; don't salt them, but wrap them tightly in foil. They should last for four months if toasted, and up to a year if plain.

Whole shelled nuts can be salted and served with drinks, whole or flaked ones can be scattered over salads. They can be combined with fish, such as trout or plaice and used to make a delicious soup.

Almonds are probably best in dessert specialities. Think of crisp little macaroons, and rich-tasting praline.

Almonds can be added to flour when making pastry cases for flans and pies, though beware of over-handling the mixture. The nuts contain up to fifty per cent oil and the pastry will be heavy if too much of the oil is 'worked out'. Marzipan or almond paste is an essential ingredient of Christmas, wedding and other cakes. It can be bought in handy slabs, and — with a few drops of almond essence added to improve the flavour if you wish — moulded into fruit and novelties to serve as *petits fours*.

More unusually, almonds have long been thought to prevent drunkenness. Plutarch recommended eating them before imbibing, and Gerard says that 'five or six, being taken fasting, do keepe a man from being drunke'.

COSMETICS

Oil of sweet almonds, one of the most important ingredients in cosmetics, is soothing, healing, whitening and nourishing. It can be used on its own as a cleanser or as a softening treatment for rough, red hands, and is especially good for strengthening broken nails and for softening cuticles.

NOURISHING LOTION

An egg beaten up with a dessert-spoon of almond oil makes an excellent nourishing lotion for very dry skin. So does a mixture of almond oil or ground almonds with milk or honey.

Mix well, pat into your face or hands, and leave for 15–20 minutes before rinsing off with tepid water. If you have made a very runny mixture, add it to your bath, and use any extra as a body rub.

FACE MASK

Ground almonds are ideal for adding to a runny ingredient, such as honey or fruit juice, to make a face mask.

For a cleansing paste, mix ground almonds with a little rose, orange-blossom or elder-flower water. Alternatively, combine them with milk or buttermilk to make a soothing and nourishing paste, good for rough or reddened skin.

CHRISTMAS ALMOND SOUP

6 ounces (175 g) whole or ground almonds
2 pints (1·1 litre) creamy milk
One 2 inch (5 cm) cinnamon stick
Sugar
1–2 drops real almond essence (optional)
2–3 tablespoons raisins
6 tablespoons boiled rice (cooked measure)

It is best to blanch, peel and pulverize whole almonds just before they are needed. If you are using ground almonds, put them in a bowl.

In a heavy pan, very slowly bring milk to a rolling boil with the cinnamon stick. Stir in 2 or 3 tablespoons sugar and pour boiling hot over almonds, stirring until smoothly blended. Pour milk mixture back into saucepan. Taste, add a little more sugar and intensify flavour with a drop or two of almond essence if liked. Stir in raisins and cooked rice. Slowly bring to boiling point once more. Discard cinnamon stick and serve soup in a heated tureen.

Serves 4–6.

TROUT WITH ALMONDS

3 ounces (75 g) almonds, blanched
  and slivered
Butter
Juice of 1 small lemon
4 medium-sized trout, gutted
Seasoned flour
1 tablespoon oil
Parsleyed lemon wedges, to serve
  (see method)

Start by preparing the almonds. In a small pan, sauté the almonds in 1½–2 ounces (40–50 g) butter until crisp and a deep golden colour. Stir in lemon juice and keep hot.

Rinse trout and wipe them dry with paper towels. Coat them on all sides in seasoned flour.

In a frying pan large enough to take all the trout side by side in one layer, fry the trout until cooked through and golden brown, about 5 minutes on each side, using 1 tablespoon oil and 1–1½ ounces (25–40 g) butter.

Transfer trout to a heated serving dish. Reheat the pan of almonds if necessary. Pour them over the trout, together with their buttery sauce. Garnish with lemon wedges coated on their cut sides with finely chopped parsley. Serve very hot.

Serves 4.

NOODLES WITH ALMONDS

1 small mild onion, finely chopped
4 ounces (100–125 g) butter
6 ounces (175 g) almonds, peeled and
  slivered
Salt and freshly ground black pepper
Freshly grated nutmeg
Lemon juice
1 pound (450 g) flat ribbon noodles,
  cooked and drained

In a large, deep frying pan or wide saucepan, simmer onion in butter until transparent and golden but not brown. Stir in almonds and fry gently, stirring frequently, until they turn a deep golden colour. Season to taste with salt, freshly ground pepper, a grating of nutmeg and a generous squeeze (about 1 teaspoon) of lemon juice.

Place the hot, cooked noodles in a deep, heated serving bowl. Pour over the sautéed almonds and their buttery juices. Toss well and serve.

Serves 4–6.

PLAICE WITH ALMOND SAUCE

4 ounces (100–125 g) blanched
  almonds, slivered
1½ ounces (35–40 g) butter
3 tablespoons flour
½ pint (300 ml) milk
Salt and freshly ground black pepper
1 tablespoon lemon juice
1 lb (450 g) plaice fillets
Lemon wedges and parsley, to
  garnish

Brown the almonds in 1 ounce (25 g) butter. Add flour and cook gently, stirring, for 1–2 minutes. Add milk gradually to this roux, stirring constantly until the sauce is boiling. Simmer for about 5 minutes. Add salt, pepper and lemon juice. Set aside and keep warm.

Melt the remaining butter. Lay plaice fillets on a greased grill pan, brush with butter, and grill gently without turning until the fish begins to flake.

Put on a warm plate, cover with the almond sauce, and garnish with lemon wedges and parsley.

Serve immediately.

Serves 4.

BUTTERED CELERY AMANDINE

Almonds make the perfect garnish for all kinds of vegetables. This dish goes well with lamb, poultry and lightly cooked fish.

12 crisp stalks celery
Butter
Salt and freshly ground black pepper
2–3 spring onions, white bulbs only,
  thinly sliced
4 ounces (100–125 g) almonds,
  peeled and slivered
4 tablespoons dry or medium sherry

Trim celery stalks and slice them into ½ inch (1·25 cm) pieces. In a heavy pan, melt 2 ounces (50 g) butter until foaming. Stir in celery. Sprinkle with salt and freshly ground black pepper, and sauté gently until celery is golden and each piece is coated with butter, about 5 minutes. Then cover pan and simmer for a few minutes longer until celery is soft but still rather crunchy. Stir in sliced spring onions and cook, uncovered, for 2–3 minutes longer.

In a small frying pan, sauté slivered almonds in 1 ounce (25 g) butter until a rich golden colour, taking great care that they do not burn. (Add a little more butter if it is absorbed too quickly.) Sprinkle with sherry and cook, stirring, for 2 or 3 minutes longer.

To serve, pour celery and its juices into a heated serving dish.

Spoon the browned almonds over the top of the celery, together with their buttery sauce.

Serves 6–8.

CHOCOLATE ALMOND CAKE

A beautifully moist cake, full of flavour, that is equally good served as a dinner dessert or with tea or coffee.

8 ounces (225 g) bitter dark chocolate
2 tablespoons strong black coffee or milk
6 eggs, separated
6 tablespoons caster sugar
4 ounces (100–125 g) ground almonds
Butter and flour, for cake tin
Caster sugar or sifted icing sugar or lightly sweetened whipped cream, to serve

In the top of a double saucepan, combine the chocolate, broken up into small pieces, with the coffee or milk, and melt over simmering water. Beat until smooth. Beat the egg yolks and sugar together lightly. Then grad-ually beat in the melted chocolate and the ground almonds.

In a large bowl that is spotlessly clean and dry, beat the egg whites until they form stiff peaks. With a large metal spoon, carefully fold them into the chocolate almond mixture.

Have ready a deep, loose-bottomed cake tin about 8 inches (20 cm) in diameter, which you have buttered and dusted lightly with flour. Spoon the cake mixture into the tin. Bake in a moderate oven (375°F, 190°C, Mark 5) for 45 minutes, or until the cake is well risen and feels firm and dry to the touch.

Allow the cake to cool and settle before unmoulding it. It may be served either dusted with caster sugar or a sifting of icing sugar, or covered with a layer of *very* lightly sweetened whipped cream.

ALMOND CRESCENTS

4 ounces (100–125 g) ground almonds
4 ounces (100–125 g) caster sugar
½ ounce (15 g) ground rice
¼ teaspoon real almond essence
2 large egg yolks
About 1 ounce (25 g) blanched almonds, finely chopped
Rice paper, for baking sheets

Line 2 large baking sheets with rice paper.

In a bowl, combine ground almonds with caster sugar, ground rice and almond essence. Beat egg yolks lightly with a fork. Pour them over the almond mixture and, using a large wooden spoon or your fingers, work to a paste.

Roll into a thin rope. Cut into 4 inch (10 cm) lengths and roll each length in chopped almonds. Bend into U-shapes and arrange on lined baking sheets.

Bake crescents in a slow oven (325°F, 170°C, Mark 3) for 20 minutes, or until they are firm and almonds are tinged with gold. Cool biscuits and trim off excess rice paper.

ST MARTIN'S ALMOND CROISSANTS

If fresh yeast, which you can some-times buy from a bakery or in a wholefood shop, is unobtainable, use ½ ounce (15 g) dried yeast for the croissant dough, reconstituted ac-cording to the directions on the can or packet.

In Poznań, in Western Poland, these croissants are traditionally baked on St Martin's Day.

1 pound (450 g) plain flour
3 eggs
1 tablespoon sugar
¼ pint (150 ml) milk
1 ounce (25 g) fresh yeast (see above)
2 ounces (50 g) butter, melted and cooled
Beaten egg, to glaze

Almond paste
4 ounces (100–125 g) ground almonds
4 ounces (100–125 g) caster sugar
About 3 tablespoons cream

Sift the flour into a bowl and put it aside to warm gently until needed. In another large bowl (or the bowl of your electric mixer if you have one), beat the eggs with the sugar until fluffy. Stir about 6 tablespoons hot

water into the milk to raise its tem-perature to lukewarm. Crumble the yeast over the top and stir until com-pletely dissolved. Beat the milk mix-ture into the eggs, followed by the melted butter.

With a large wooden spoon, beat in about half of the flour. Then, using your hand, knead in as much as possible of the remaining flour to make a soft yet manageable dough. Continue to knead until dough is smooth and springy, and leaves the sides of the bowl and your fingers quite clean. (This operation can be done quickly and efficiently in an electric mixer fitted with a dough hook.) Roll the dough into a ball. Cover the bowl with a cloth or put it in a large plastic bag and seal opening. Leave to rise in a warm, draught-free place until dough has doubled in bulk, about 2 hours.

Meanwhile, prepare the almond filling. Mix the ground almonds and sugar together, and gradually work in enough cream to make a soft paste. Divide it into 16 pieces.

When dough has doubled its bulk, deflate it with the palm of your hand and knead briefly until smooth again. Divide it in half and work with one

piece of dough at a time. On a lightly floured board, using a lightly floured rolling pin, roll the dough out into a rectangle measuring 12 × 6 inches (30 × 15 cm). With a large, sharp knife, cut it in half lengthwise, then cut each strip across in 4, to make 8 3-inch (7·5 cm) squares.

Lay a square with one of its points facing towards you. Roll a piece of almond paste into a rope about 3½ inches (8·75 cm) long. Lay it on the square of dough slightly up from the point. Fold the point of dough up over it, then roll the square up to the point opposite. Bring the ends round to form a crescent, twisting them once or twice to seal in the roll of almond paste. Transfer the crescent to a baking sheet. Repeat with the re-maining dough and almond paste, making 16 crescents in all.

Leave to rise again until crescents are puffy, about 30 minutes. Then gently brush with lightly beaten egg. Bake for 7 minutes in a moderately hot oven (400°F, 200°C, Mark 6), then lower temperature (to 375°F, 190°C, Mark 5), and continue baking for a further 7 minutes, or until crescents are a rich golden colour. Cool on wire racks.

ALMOND MACAROONS

2 egg whites
4 ounces (100–125 g) ground
*   almonds*
8 ounces (225 g) caster sugar
½ ounce (15 g) ground rice
½ teaspoon vanilla essence
¼ teaspoon real almond essence
Blanched split or shredded almonds,
*   to decorate*
Tasteless oil and rice paper, for
*   baking sheets*

Prepare 2 large baking sheets. Brush them very lightly with oil and line them with rice paper.

In a small bowl, stir egg whites with a fork just enough to break down their gelatinous threads. In another, larger bowl, stir the almonds, sugar and ground rice together. Gradually beat in the egg whites and flavouring essences. Mixture should be of a medium-soft consistency. If necessary, add a few drops of cold water.

Using a pastry bag fitted with a plain, ½-inch (1·25 cm) tube, or dropping the mixture from a small spoon, make little rounds of mixture on the baking sheets, spacing them well apart so they have room to spread. Press a split almond or a pinch of shredded almonds in the centre of each macaroon.

Bake macaroons in a very slow oven (300°F, 150°C, Mark 2) for about 25 minutes, or until they are lightly coloured and feel dry to the touch.

Slip the sheets of rice paper on to a rack to cool.

When macaroons are cold and crisp, crumble off the excess rice paper around sides.

Store in an airtight container.

SWISS ALMOND BISCUITS

When rolling and shaping these little biscuits, keep extra flour down to a minimum.

4 ounces (100–125 g) plain flour
Generous pinch of baking powder
4 ounces (100–125 g) softened butter
4 ounces (100–125 g) ground
*   almonds*
4 ounces (100–125 g) caster sugar
Sieved raspberry jam or other
*   smooth, sharp-flavoured jelly, to*
*   sandwich biscuits*
Sifted icing sugar, to dust biscuits

Sift flour and baking powder into a bowl. Rub in butter. Stir in sugar and ground nuts and work by hand until dough holds together. Roll into a ball and chill lightly, covered, for 1 hour.

On a lightly floured board, using a rolling pin lightly dusted with flour, roll out dough thinly. Stamp out 1 inch (2·5 cm) rounds with a plain pastry cutter. Arrange on baking sheets.

Bake rounds in a slow oven (325°F, 170°C, Mark 3) for about 7 minutes, or until lightly coloured. Allow to cool slightly on baking sheets before transferring to wire cooling racks.

When quite cold, sandwich biscuits with jam or jelly. Dust them with sifted icing sugar. Store in an airtight tin or jar until ready to serve.

MARZIPAN

Traditional Christmas cakes, wedding and christening cakes, as well as Simnel cakes for Easter, would be unthinkable without marzipan or almond paste, made with the purest ingredients – almonds, sugar, eggs and a little flavouring. Synthetic almond essence will ruin it and unless you can get the real thing, which is sometimes stocked in wholefood shops, it is best left out altogether. Some prefer the marzipan to be slightly less sweet and the sugar may be scaled down to, say, 6 ounces (175 g) of each. Whole eggs, egg yolks or just egg whites may be used to moisten the marzipan, plus a little water, or orange-flower water for flavour, if necessary.

8 ounces (225 g) ground almonds
8 ounces (225 g) icing sugar, sifted
8 ounces (225 g) caster sugar
2–3 teaspoons lemon juice
Few drops of real almond essence
2 eggs, lightly beaten (see above)
Orange-flower water (optional)

Mix ground almonds and sugars together in a bowl. Sprinkle with lemon juice and almond essence. Then, with your fingertips, gradually work in the beaten eggs until ingredients combine to form a firm but malleable paste. This will take some time to achieve so keep working the ingredients patiently until they lose their crumbliness and begin to stick together. Only if the eggs are not enough to bind the ingredients together, sprinkle with a little cold water and/or orange-flower water – about a tablespoon.

Roll into a ball and wrap in greaseproof paper or a plastic bag.

ALMOND PRALINE

Use praline in cake fillings, in creams and sweet sauces, or to scatter over ice creams and puddings.

The almonds are usually left unskinned, just wiped with a damp cloth to remove the powder on the surface. However, for a richer flavour they should be blanched, peeled and lightly toasted.

Take an equal weight of sugar to that of nuts. In a heavy pan, carefully melt the sugar in a little water with a squeeze of lemon juice. (For 4 ounces or 100–125 g of sugar, you will need about 4 tablespoons cold water and 1 teaspoon lemon juice.) Heat the syrup, swirling the pan round gently and frequently, until it turns into a deep golden caramel (340°F or 170°C on a sugar thermometer). If the nuts have not been peeled and toasted, they should be stirred into the syrup before it starts changing colour. Otherwise, wait until the caramel is nearly at the right stage. Add the nuts all at once and mix well. Take great care not to let the caramel darken too much at this stage. Like all caramel syrups, it will carry on cooking from the heat of the pan for a minute or two after it has been removed from the stove.

Have ready a large, cold surface (marble is ideal but an ordinary metal baking sheet will do). Rub it all over with a wad of kitchen paper dipped in tasteless, odourless oil (ie, not olive oil).

Scrape the praline out on to the prepared surface and leave until quite cold and hard. With a palette knife, prise the praline off the surface and crush it to a fine powder with a mortar and pestle, or coarsely by breaking it down and rolling it with a heavy rolling pin.

If the praline is not to be used immediately, it should be broken up and stored in pieces in a dry jar which is absolutely airtight to prevent it turning damp and sticky. Then crush or pound it up to the required degree of fineness just before use.

APPLE

Of all the fruits that grow in the temperate world, the apple is the undoubted king. The moist, cool climate seems to bring out all of its sharp flavour in a crisp, juicy texture, and the farther south one goes, the softer and mealier the apples become and the blander their sweetness.

The apple is thought to have originated in the mountains of the Caucasus and its cultivation goes back to the Stone Age, even farther if the story of Adam, Eve and the Tree of Knowledge is to be taken literally. Some think that it was not an apple tree at all that was involved but another fruit, possibly an apricot or a fig, but the majority still come down in favour of the apple.

The Ancient Egyptians cultivated apple trees and the Greeks and Romans knew them well. By the end of the fourth century AD, there were thirty-seven varieties of apple on record. From then on, wherever western civilization went, apples went too – to the New World, to the Antipodes as well as throughout the Old World, to settle wherever the climate and growing conditions suited it. Today, there are well over a thousand varieties of apple in existence but the search for perfection continues unabated. Commercial growers have still to find the perfect apple, one that is a heavy cropper and resistant to disease, of equally good flavour and appearance, unaffected by packing and lengthy transportation.

The apple's versatility cannot be overemphasized. It can be enjoyed at any time of day, in any course of a meal. A fine French cuisine, that of Normandy, relies heavily on apples – fresh, cooked with all kinds of meat, poultry and game, or sliced into large open tarts. The French also have a magnificent apple brandy called Calvados. Americans have apple jack and the British are famous for their cider. Last but not least, there is cider vinegar, which is infinitely preferable to some harsh, inferior potions that go by the name of wine vinegar.

As far as the cook is concerned, apples fall into two main categories, dessert or eating apples, and those suitable for cooking. However, there is no reason why you should not explore the flavours and textures of dessert apples for sauces, pies and other apple dishes as well.

When choosing apples in the store or on a stall, go for fresh, firm fruit with a smooth, shiny skin and good colour. A pale, anaemic colour is usually a sign of immaturity and consequent lack of flavour, which is unlikely to improve, no matter how long you wait. A slightly shrivelled skin could be caused by incorrect or overlong storage. An over-ripe apple, which also tends to be over-size, will be mealy and rather soft to finger pressure, and its flavour will be impaired.

Apples are best frozen as pie slices or purées or apple sauces. Blanch slices in acidulated water and dry or sugar freeze. They can also be dried.

Apples are not just for eating by themselves, for cooking with, or for making wine. They are also very good for you and 'an apple a day keeps the doctor away' is an old saw which is based on scientific fact. Apples, particularly the peel, are rich in vitamins and contain at least six essential minerals, as well as malic acid which is a powerful aid to digestion. A raw apple is good for the teeth and gums and sweetens the breath; eaten last thing at night it will help you to sleep well. Apple pips can be poisonous, but only in considerable quantities – a cupful has been known to be lethal.

APPLE AND ALMOND PACK

This is good for rough skin (on elbows and knees, for instance), and can also be used as a face pack for dry skin.

Peel and grate a firm apple. Add about the same amount of ground almonds, and mix in milk (or cream) until you have a slightly gritty but spreadable paste. Spread the paste on your elbows, knees (or anywhere else with less than smooth skin) or face, and leave to dry. Rub off from arms and legs – preferably over a bath – or wash off from your face with warm water.

APPLE-BASED REMEDIES

A diet of grated apple, in moderation, will often clear up diarrhoea in a couple of days. Use slightly unripe fruit, and peel them first.

Cider vinegar has been hailed as a cure for almost every ill under the sun. Most people are justifiably sceptical about this claim, but it is an excellent blood cleanser and helps to eliminate a vast variety of toxins. Up to two teaspoons in a tumbler of water, two or three times a day, will help digestion and promote energy.

BREAKFAST APPLE SHAKE

2 tart apples, peeled and cored
½ pint (300 ml) milk
Pinch ground cinnamon
1 tablespoon honey
Ice cubes (optional)

Chop the apples and put in the bowl of an electric blender with the milk, cinnamon and honey.

Blend the mixture until smooth and creamy. Serve chilled with ice cubes if desired.

Serves 2–3.

Note: Skimmed milk can be substituted for full fat milk to increase the nutritional value of this drink.

HOT APPLE SOUP

Serve this soup at an informal winter meal instead of the usual mug of hot tomato or oxtail. Use either eating or cooking apples, adjusting the sugar to taste. In fact, if you have an embarrassment of apples stored up for the winter, let your surplus guide your choice.

Potato flour gives the soup a particularly attractive, satiny texture, but if it is difficult to find in your area, cornflour may be used instead.

1½ pounds (700 g) apples
One 2 inch (5 cm) cinnamon stick
Twist of thinly peeled orange rind
1 ounce (25 g) potato flour or cornflour
About ½ pint (300 ml) orange juice
4–6 ounces (125–175 g) sugar
Lemon juice
½ pint (300 ml) hot single cream
Ground cinnamon or cinnamon
*   croûtons, to serve (page 205)*

Wash, quarter and core 1 pound (450 g) apples. Put them in a pan with the cinnamon stick, orange rind and 1 pint (600 ml) water. Bring to the boil and simmer, uncovered, until the apples have disintegrated. Rub the mixture through a sieve, discarding the cinnamon stick and rind. Pour the soup back into the rinsed-out pan.

Blend the potato flour or cornflour smoothly with a few tablespoonfuls of orange juice. Reheat the soup and when it is halfway to the boil, stir in the potato or cornflour paste, together with the remaining orange juice. Sweeten to taste with sugar, bring to the boil, stirring, and simmer gently for 3 or 4 minutes.

Peel and core the remaining apples. Grate them into long shreds on the coarsest side of a grater. If the soup is not to be served immediately, squeeze a little lemon juice over them and toss lightly with a fork.

Just before serving, bring the soup to simmering point. Stir in the grated apples and cream. Taste for sweetness and serve, each portion garnished with either a pinch of cinnamon or a few cinnamon croûtons.

Serves 4.

POLISH HERRING AND APPLE APPETIZER SALAD

A dish to start a couple of days ahead, unless your local delicatessen can offer you herrings that have already been desalted and filleted.

1 pound (450 g) salted herrings
2 tablespoons finely chopped mild
*   onion or shallots*
6–8 tablespoons coarsely chopped,
*   peeled apple*
8 tablespoons thick sour cream
2 tablespoons lemon juice
½ tablespoon sugar
1–2 tablespoons finely chopped
*   parsley, chives or green spring*
*   onion tops, to garnish*

Desalt the herrings for 48 hours as follows. Place them in a large bowl in the kitchen sink and let cold water trickle over them constantly until required; or, alternatively, cover them with cold water and leave them for 48 hours, changing water frequently – several times a day.

Drain the herrings thoroughly. Fillet them, discarding all skin and bones, and cut each fillet into bite-sized pieces. Arrange the pieces in a shallow serving dish.

In a small bowl, mix the onion or shallots and apple with the sour cream, and flavour to taste with lemon juice and sugar. Pour over the pieces of herring and mix lightly but thoroughly to coat them completely. Scatter the top with parsley, chives or spring onion tops and put aside in a cool place for a couple of hours to develop flavours before serving.

Serves 6.

WALDORF SALAD

This salad can be turned into a light main course luncheon dish by mixing in 12–16 ounces (350–450 g) cubed cold roast chicken, pork or ham.

4 red-skinned dessert apples
3–4 tablespoons lemon juice
4–6 stalks celery
2 ounces (50 g) walnuts
4 ounces (100–125 g) raisins
¼ pint (150 ml) thick mayonnaise
*   (page 205)*

Quarter, core and cut the apples into small dice without peeling them. Toss them with lemon juice to prevent discoloration. Halve celery stalks lengthwise if they are thick and slice them thinly. Coarsely chop the walnuts and rinse the raisins, draining them thoroughly.

In a large mixing bowl, combine the apples and their juices with the remaining ingredients. Add mayonnaise and toss lightly until well mixed. Pile into a bowl and serve.

Serves 4–6.

BAKED CHICKEN WITH APPLES

Chicken and apples form the perfect partnership and the addition of dry cider will do much to reinforce the refreshing, sharp flavour. Serve with a potato purée, rice or noodles, and follow with a fresh green salad.

1 roasting chicken, about 3½ pounds (1·6 kilos)
2 ounces (50 g) butter
3 slices lean unsmoked bacon, diced
1½ pounds (700 g) firm, aromatic dessert apples
Salt and freshly ground black pepper
½ pint (300 ml) dry cider

Clean the chicken carefully and cut it into 8 or 9 neat pieces. Dry the joints with paper towels and put them aside until needed.

In a large, heavy frying pan, melt the butter until foaming but not coloured. Add the diced bacon and fry gently until limp and golden but not crisp. With a slotted spoon, drain bacon bits and put aside on a plate until needed.

In the fat remaining in the pan, sauté the chicken joints over moderate heat until a rich golden colour on all sides.

Quarter, core and slice the apples vertically. (I prefer not to peel them, as the skin helps the slices to keep their shape.)

In a heavy, ovenproof casserole with a tight-fitting lid, arrange a third of the apple slices. Lay half of the chicken pieces on top and scatter with half of the bacon pieces. Season lightly with salt and freshly ground black pepper. Repeat with another layer of apples, the remaining chicken joints and bacon pieces, season lightly and top neatly with the remaining apple slices.

Pour the cider into the juices remaining in the frying pan, and over a moderate heat, scrape the bottom and sides of the pan clean with a wooden spoon. Pour the simmering liquid all over the top layer of apples. Cover the casserole tightly and bake in a moderate oven (375°F, 190°C, Mark 5) for 40–45 minutes, or until the chicken is tender. Serve straight from the casserole.

Serves 6.

DOLMEH SIB Persian Stuffed Apples

8–10 large, tart apples
Butter
Ground cinnamon (optional)

Stuffing
5–6 tablespoons yellow split peas
1 Spanish onion, finely chopped
1 ounce (25 g) butter or oil
1 pound (450 g) lean minced beef
½ teaspoon ground cinnamon
Salt and freshly ground black pepper

Basting sauce
4–6 tablespoons cider vinegar
2–3 tablespoons sugar

Start by preparing the stuffing. Boil the split peas in unsalted water until they are very soft, about 30 minutes. Meanwhile sauté the onion in butter or oil until soft and lightly coloured. With a slotted spoon, transfer onion to a plate and in the same fat sauté beef until it changes colour. Return onion to the pan and mix well.

When split peas are soft and almost mushy, drain them thoroughly and mix them with the beef and onion. Sprinkle in the cinnamon and season to taste with salt and freshly ground black pepper. Leave to cool.

Meanwhile, prepare the apples. Wipe them clean with a damp cloth and core them from the stem end to within about ½ inch of the bottom. Core out some of the pulp as well, leaving thick shells firm and unbroken. Chop up the pulp.

Lightly butter a baking dish that will take all the apples in a single layer. Scatter the apple pulp evenly over the dish. Sprinkle with a pinch of cinnamon, if liked, and moisten with a few tablespoons water.

Stuff the apples with a meat mixture and arrange them side by side on the chopped apple pulp. Dot each apple with a flake of butter. Bake in a moderate oven (350°F, 180°C, Mark 4) for 30 minutes.

Prepare a sweet-sour basting sauce for the apples by combining the vinegar and sugar with ¼ pint (150 ml) water. Bring to boiling point, stirring until sugar has melted, and simmer for 1 minute.

Spoon a little boiling sauce into the cavity of each apple. (Any sauce left over may be poured over the chopped apples lining the baking dish.) Continue to bake apples for about 15 minutes longer until they are quite soft. Crush the apple pulp and pan juices together, and serve as a sauce for the apples. Serve hot.

Serves 4–5.

SALADE PARISIENNE (Winter Fruit and Vegetable Salad)

A fresh winter salad to serve with poultry or cheese, or a plate of sliced ham. Prepare shortly before serving.

2–3 large, crisp apples
2 large potatoes, boiled in their jackets
3 bulbs chicory
2 bananas
1 large stalk celery
3 carrots
2 ounces (50 g) nuts, coarsely chopped
2 ounces (50 g) raisins

Dressing
3 tablespoons salad oil
1 tablespoon lemon juice
Pinch of paprika
Salt and freshly ground black pepper

Make the dressing for the salad first. Put the oil, lemon juice, paprika, salt and black pepper to taste in a screw-top jar. Close tightly and shake well to emulsify dressing.

Peel, core and dice the apples, and put them in a large bowl. Peel and dice the potatoes, and add them to the apples. Trim the chicory bulbs. Slice them thinly, together with the bananas and celery, and add them to the bowl. Shred the carrots coarsely and add them. Finally, add the nuts and raisins.

Toss all the ingredients gently with a large kitchen fork until well mixed. Shake the dressing up once more and mix it lightly but thoroughly into the salad. Correct seasoning and chill lightly until ready to serve.

Serves 6.

Note: If you find the salad is rather 'dry', make up some more dressing in the same proportions and add it to the bowl (the exact amount needed will depend on the juiciness of the fruit and vegetables).

FRESH APPLE RELISH

Excellent served with roasts of meat and game, and curried meat dishes. Use well-flavoured, crisp dessert apples such as Cox's for this. Cooking apples would be too sour and uninteresting.

1 pound (450 g) dessert apples
1½–2 tablespoons caster sugar
1 tablespoon crumbled dried
  mint
Cider or white wine vinegar

Peel the apples and grate them coarsely into a bowl containing the sugar, mint and about 3 tablespoons vinegar.

Toss lightly but thoroughly until well mixed (this will prevent the apples discolouring).

Taste and add more sugar or mint if liked, and if necessary pour in a little more vinegar so that apples are thoroughly moistened.

BAKED APPLES

4 large cooking apples
At least 1 ounce (25 g) butter
4–6 ounces (125–175 g) soft brown
  sugar
About 1 teaspoon ground cinnamon
4–6 tablespoons apple juice or cider
Whipped cream, to serve

Quarter, peel and core the apples, and slice them thinly. Butter a baking dish that will hold them comfortably.

In a large bowl, toss the sliced apples with sugar and cinnamon, to taste. Transfer them to the baking dish and moisten with apple juice or cider. Dot the top with small flakes of butter.

Bake apples in a moderate oven (375°F, 190°C, Mark 5) for 30–40 minutes, or until they are a rich golden colour on top and feel soft when pierced with a fork or skewer.

Serve hot or warm, with a bowl of lightly sweetened, chilled whipped cream.

Serves 4–6.

BURGHUL PILAF WITH APPLES AND ALMONDS

A very good side dish to serve with lamb, pork and poultry. If the meat dish is an oven roast, put the pilaf into the oven to cook with it in a tightly covered casserole after the initial frying. Otherwise, cook on top of the stove.

Burghul (cracked wheat) is widely available in Middle Eastern groceries and health food stores as well as from some wholefood stores.

1 large Spanish onion, finely chopped
2 ounces (50 g) butter
5 ounces (150 g) burghul wheat
3 tart, crisp eating apples, peeled,
  cored and diced
¼ teaspoon crumbled dried thyme
¼ teaspoon celery seed
1 tablespoon finely chopped parsley
¾ pint (400 ml) well-flavoured chicken
  stock
Salt and freshly ground black pepper

Almond garnish
6–8 tablespoons slivered blanched
  almonds
2 ounces (50 g) butter

In a large, heavy saucepan or flameproof casserole with a tight-fitting lid, sauté onion in butter until soft and golden. Stir in dry burghul and sauté for a few minutes longer over moderate heat until lightly coloured and aromatic. Add diced apples and continue frying, stirring, until each cube is coated with butter. Sprinkle with dried thyme, celery seed and parsley, and stir in chicken stock.

Bring to boiling point, cover pan tightly and either cook over the lowest possible heat for about 25 minutes until all the stock is absorbed, or bake in a moderate oven (350°F, 180°C, Mark 4) for roughly the same length of time. When burghul is cooked, fluff it up with a fork and correct seasoning with a little salt or pepper if necessary.

Have almonds already sautéed until golden in butter. Serve burghul in a heated bowl with hot almonds and butter poured over the top.

Serves 4–6.

ITALIAN APPLE PANCAKE

2 tablespoons plain flour
Pinch of salt
¼ pint (150 ml) milk
1 tablespoon caster sugar
½ teaspoon vanilla essence
2 tablespoons raisins
2 eggs
2 small dessert apples
Butter, for frying
Sifted icing sugar or caster sugar, to
  serve

First prepare a thin batter by blending the flour and salt smoothly with the milk. Stir in sugar and vanilla essence. Rinse raisins and put aside to drain in a sieve.

Beat eggs lightly in a large bowl and gradually beat in prepared batter. When smoothly blended, stir in drained raisins. Put aside while you quarter, peel, core and slice apples paper-thin. Stir apples into the prepared batter.

Bring out a thick frying pan 7–8 inches (17·5–20 cm) in diameter and a flat plate that is slightly larger. Grease plate lightly all over with butter. In the frying pan, melt a large knob (about 1 ounce or 25 g) butter and when sizzling, tilt pan around so that entire surface is coated.

Pour in batter, making sure apple slices and raisins are evenly distributed in the pan. Cook over low heat until pancake batter has set on top and pancake is a rich golden brown underneath.

Carefully turn pancake out upside down on to the buttered plate. Melt a small knob of fresh butter in the pan and slide the pancake back in to cook and brown the other side over low heat.

Invert pancake on to a heated serving dish.

Dredge with icing sugar or sprinkle with caster sugar and serve immediately, cut in wedges.

Serves 2 as a snack, 4 as a dessert course.

SWISS APPLE TART

The Swiss like to fill these tarts, or *Wähen*, with all sorts of fresh fruit, but the most popular one is made with apples.

One 9 inch (22·5 cm) sweet shortcrust pastry case, pre-baked (page 203)
5–6 firm, tart, dessert apples
2 ounces (50 g) butter
1 teaspoon vanilla essence
3 small eggs
4 ounces (100–125 g) caster sugar
½ pint (300 ml) single cream
Sifted icing sugar, to serve

Peel, core and slice apples thickly. In a large, heavy frying pan, simmer apple slices in foaming butter until they are golden and just tender but not mushy, turning them over gently once or twice with a large spatula. Sprinkle with vanilla and, using the spatula, carefully transfer the slices to the pre-baked pastry case in a neat, even layer.

Beat eggs with sugar until thick and lemon-coloured. Add cream and mix well. Place tart tin back on baking sheet. Cover apples with egg mixture, pouring it in quite slowly over the back of a wooden spoon to avoid disturbing apples.

Return tart to the oven for 30 minutes, or until custard has set, no longer trembles when baking tin is pushed, and is lightly coloured on top. Cool to lukewarm and dust with sifted icing sugar before serving.

Serves 6–8.

APPLE SNOW

A great childhood favourite that – unlike so many others – is equally popular with adults.

About 1½ pounds (700 g) cooking apples, peeled, cored and sliced
3 egg whites
4 tablespoons caster sugar
Whipped cream, to serve

Make a simple, smooth apple purée with the apples and 1 tablespoon of water. When soft, rub them through a fine sieve to break down any lumps. (Taste, and sweeten with a little sugar and flavour with a little lemon juice if liked.) Leave until cold. Then measure off about ½ pint (300 ml) purée.

In a large, clean bowl, beat egg whites until they stand in soft peaks. Gradually beat in caster sugar and continue to beat to a stiff, glossy meringue. Gently fold in measured apple purée.

Spoon into tall glasses and top with swirls of whipped cream.

Serves 4–6.

BARBECUED APPLES

With well-flavoured, firm dessert apples all you need do is first to rinse and dry them thoroughly, and pluck out their stems. Then wrap each apple tightly in a square of heavy-duty foil or a double thickness of ordinary kitchen foil.

While the main course is being eaten, set foil-wrapped apples on the glowing coals. After about 10 minutes turn them over and cook for 10–15 minutes longer on the other side.

Serve hot with brown sugar or syrup and teaspoons for scooping out the pulp.

A more sophisticated way to deal with apples for a barbecue is to stuff them before cooking. First cut squares of foil for them as above and grease the inside of each square with butter. Rinse, dry and core apples, and stuff cavities with a mixture of 1 teaspoon each soft brown sugar, chopped raisins and chopped hazelnuts or walnuts, a generous pinch of finely grated lemon peel and a pinch of ground cinnamon. Pour a teaspoon of rum over each cavity and top with a flake of butter.

Wrap each stuffed apple in its buttered foil. Stand them on a grid over hot coals, and bake until soft, or bake in a moderately hot oven (400°F, 200°C, Mark 6) for 30 minutes.

BAKED RICE AND APPLE PUDDING

A favourite Polish winter dish.

8 ounces (225 g) short-grain rice
1 ounce (25 g) butter
Salt
2 ounces (50 g) raisins
1–2 tablespoons chopped crystallized orange peel
2 pounds (900 g) cooking apples or crisp, tart dessert apples
White or soft brown sugar
1 teaspoon vanilla essence
1 ounce (25 g) butter

Measure the rice in a mug (there should be a mugful) and put it in a pan. Add 3 times the volume (ie about 3 mugfuls) of boiling water, the butter and a generous pinch of salt; stir well and cook very gently with the lid half on the pan until the water has been absorbed and the rice is very soft. Stir in the raisins and peel, cover tightly and put aside while you prepare apples.

Peel, core and slice the apples very thinly into a bowl. Add sugar to taste, sprinkle with vanilla and toss well with a large fork.

Grease a large baking dish generously with some of the butter, and spread base with a third of the rice mixture. Cover with half of the apples, followed by half of the remaining rice, all the remaining apples (and their juices, if any) and the rest of the rice, spreading it out as evenly as possible with the back of your spoon.

Dot the top of the pudding all over with flakes of remaining butter and bake in a moderate oven (350°F, 180°C, Mark 4) for 45–50 minutes, or until surface is crusty and golden brown. Serve hot.

Serves 6.

SOUTHERN APPLE PIE

*About 1 pound (450 g) shortcrust
    pastry for a 2-crust, 9 inch (22·5 cm)
    pie (page 203)*
*1½–2 pounds (700–900 g) tart
    dessert or cooking apples*
Lemon juice (optional)
*4–6 ounces (125–175 g) white or soft
    brown sugar, or half and half*
¼ teaspoon ground cinnamon
⅛ teaspoon grated nutmeg
2 tablespoons plain flour
Pinch of salt
2 ounces (50 g) seedless raisins
½–1 ounce (15–25 g) butter
Caster sugar

Start by lining a pie dish with shortcrust pastry, overhanging the sides a
little, and cutting out a lid to go on top.
Put aside until needed.

Quarter, peel and core apples, and
slice them thinly into a bowl. If they
are not too sour, or are rather old and
tasteless, toss them with a tablespoon of lemon juice. Blend sugar
with spices, flour and salt, and sprinkle over apples. Add raisins and toss
lightly until thoroughly mixed.

Pack apple mixture into pastry-
lined pie dish. Dot surface all over
with flakes of butter.

Lay pastry lid in position. Press all
around sides to seal them, then flute
rim attractively between forefinger
and thumb. Cut slits in top crust.

Bake pie in a hot oven (450°F,
230°C, Mark 8) for 15 minutes, then
reduce heat to moderate (350°F,
180°C, Mark 4), and continue to bake
for 35–40 minutes longer, or until top
crust is a rich golden colour and
apples feel soft when prodded with a
skewer through one of the slits.

Serves 6–8.

APPLE CIDER SAUCE

1 ounce (25 g) butter
3 tablespoons flour
1 pint (550 ml) apple cider, warmed
¼ teaspoon ground cloves
¼ teaspoon ground ginger
Honey or brown sugar

Melt the butter in a saucepan over
gentle heat. Mix in the flour and cook,
stirring, for 1–2 minutes. Slowly stir in
the apple cider and add cloves and
ginger. Bring to the boil, still stirring,
then remove from heat. Sweeten
with honey or brown sugar.

SHERRIED APPLES WITH SPICED NUTS

6 large baking apples
Butter
¼ pint (150 ml) medium sherry
Whipped cream, to serve

Nut stuffing
2 ounces (50 g) butter
3½ ounces (85 g) soft brown sugar
1 teaspoon ground cinnamon
1 tablespoon medium sherry
6–8 tablespoons chopped walnuts

Prepare apples in usual way,
coring them and peeling away about
a third of the skin, starting from the
top.

Prepare nut stuffing by creaming
butter and brown sugar together until
light. Beat in cinnamon and sherry
until thoroughly blended, then stir in
chopped nuts.

Fill apples with nut stuffing. Arrange them side by side in a buttered
baking dish. Pour sherry evenly over
the top.

Bake apples in a moderate oven
(375°F, 190°C, Mark 5), basting frequently with pan juices, for 30–40
minutes, or until they feel soft when
pierced lightly with a skewer.

Serve lukewarm or cold, with a
bowl of whipped cream.

Serves 6.

HOT APPLE CHARLOTTE

*Butter and breadcrumbs for baking
    dish*
12 slices bread
¾ pint (400 ml) milk
2 eggs
1 tablespoon sugar
8 apples, peeled, cored and sliced
*2 tablespoons chopped
    candied peel*
2 tablespoons chopped raisins
3 tablespoons icing sugar, sifted
1 teaspoon vanilla essence

Butter a deep baking dish (a soufflé
dish is ideal) and coat it with breadcrumbs. Toast the bread slices lightly
on both sides until golden but not
browned.

Dip each slice of toast on both
sides in a mixture of milk beaten with
eggs and sugar, and put them aside
on a plate. Mix the apples with the
candied peel, raisins, icing sugar and
vanilla.

Arrange four layers of toast and
three layers of apples in the baking
dish (ie, starting and ending with a
layer of toast). Pour in any remaining
milk mixture.

Bake the charlotte in a moderately
hot oven (400°F, 200°C, Mark 6) for 45
minutes, or until the top is crisp and
golden. Serve hot.

Serves 4–6.

APPLE SAUCES

When making an apple sauce, the first question to ask oneself is how it is to be served and the kind of dish it is intended to complement, whether it is a heavy meat such as roast pork, a light dish of poultry or veal, even a sweet pudding or cake. This will help you to decide the kind of flavour and texture the sauce is to have.

Its texture may be silky-smooth, made with apples that have been cooked in the very minimum of water, or none at all, then rubbed through a sieve, put through a vegetable mill or puréed in an electric blender or food processor. Reheat the thick purée with sugar to taste and beat in a large knob of butter, which will make it even more satiny.

For a less smooth sauce, crush the cooked apples well with a fork, allowing some small pieces to retain their natural texture. And for the most substantial kind of sauce, first dice the peeled, raw apples and sauté them gently in butter until lightly coloured on all sides. Then cover the pan and 'sweat' the apples over very low heat until they are quite soft. Sweeten if necessary, season lightly and if you have some double cream handy, stir in two or three tablespoonfuls to amalgamate with any pan juices.

For an apple sauce to serve four, you will need about 1 pound (450 g) apples. Traditionally, a sauce is made with sour, green cooking apples but often a far more interesting version will result from aromatic dessert apples that cook down well such as Cox's Orange Pippins or Reinettes. Compared with cooking apples, these not only have a richer flavour, but will also retain more shape and texture. Instead of white sugar, sweeten the sauce with a little soft brown sugar, or even better, a tablespoon or two of apple jelly or orange marmalade.

There are many other flavourings with which you can experiment. A small quince cooked and puréed with the apples will transform the flavour of the sauce. Moisten it with a good splash of white wine or cider and let it boil down until it thickens again, or use a few tablespoons of dry white vermouth (a useful alternative when you do not have a bottle of wine already open). A squeeze of lemon juice will balance the sweetness of the sauce.

For a much stronger sauce, beat in a tablespoon or two of grated fresh horseradish or dried horseradish flakes.

Finally, at the other end of the flavour spectrum, a little finely chopped mild onion or shallot sautéed in the butter before adding the pieces of apple, will give the sauce a definite flavour.

Crush the cooked apples. Season with salt, freshly ground black pepper and a pinch of sugar if necessary, and serve hot.

OLD-FASHIONED APPLE BUTTER

This is a good way of using up a surplus of apples from the garden. Any kind is suitable, either one variety or a combination of two or three in equal amounts. Windfalls will do perfectly well and crab apples make an excellent butter. Experiment with different spices to flavour the butter. Cinnamon and cloves are the most popular, but grated nutmeg and ground allspice are also frequently added.

6 pounds (2·7 kilos) apples
2 pints (1·1 litre) sweet cider
Sugar
1½ teaspoons ground cinnamon
½ teaspoon ground cloves

Rinse apples and chop them up. There is no need to peel or core them.

Put them in a preserving pan with cider and barely enough water to cover. Bring to boiling point and simmer the apples until soft and pulpy, stirring occasionally.

Rub contents of pan through a sieve, discarding peels, pips and other debris.

Weigh pulp and return it to rinsed-out pan. Weigh out 12 ounces (350 g) sugar for every pound (450 g) of apple purée.

Bring purée to simmering point, stirring frequently. Add prepared sugar and spices. Stir until sugar has dissolved, then simmer, stirring regularly at an ever-increasing rate as purée thickens to ensure that it does not catch on the bottom of the pan. The butter is ready when no surplus liquid can be seen collecting around the edges of a small mound of purée which you have spooned out on to a saucer.

Pot and cover.

See also page 200.

APPLE CHUTNEY

4 pounds (1·8 kilos) peeled, cored and quartered apples
1 pound (450 g) seedless raisins, chopped
1 pound (450 g) dried dates, pitted and chopped
2 pounds (900 g) brown sugar
4 pints (2·2 litres) brown malt vinegar
2 ounces (50 g) mustard seed
2 ounces (50 g) ground ginger
1 tablespoon salt
¼ ounce (7 g) cayenne pepper, or to taste
½ ounce (15 g) garlic cloves, peeled and very finely chopped

Combine all the ingredients in a preserving pan and mix well. Stir constantly over low heat until sugar has dissolved. Then bring to boiling point and simmer for between 1½ and 2 hours, stirring at an increasing rate as chutney thickens to prevent it scorching on the bottom of the pan.

Pour into a bowl and leave until the following day before potting and covering tightly (page 200).

Fills about 7 jars.

APPLE AND PLUM CHUTNEY

3 pounds (1·4 kilos) prepared apples
3 pounds (1·4 kilos) plums
1 pound (450 g) Spanish onions
2 pints (1·1 litre) brown malt vinegar
2 pounds (900 g) soft brown or demerara sugar
1 pound (450 g) sultanas
1 pound (450 g) currants
1 teaspoon salt
1 teaspoon cayenne pepper
1 teaspoon white pepper
1 teaspoon ground ginger

Peel, core and slice the apples, and weigh them. Stone the plums and cut them into chunks. Peel and chop the onions.

In a large preserving pan or heavy enamelled pan, combine fruit and onions with all the remaining ingredients, and heat gently, stirring, until sugar has melted. Then boil, stirring very frequently, until chutney is thick, about 1 hour.

Cool and when quite cold, pour into jars and cover (page 200).

Fills about 8 jars.

APPLE AND GREEN TOMATO CHUTNEY

1 pound (450 g) green tomatoes
1 pound (450 g) apples, quartered and cored
1 pound (450 g) onions
8 ounces (225 g) sultanas
8 ounces (225 g) brown sugar
1 ounce (25 g) salt
½ ounce (15 g) ground ginger
½ ounce (15 g) cayenne pepper
½ teaspoon ground cloves
1 pint (550 ml) brown malt vinegar

Put tomatoes, apples, onions and sultanas through a mincer, together with brown sugar, and put in a preserving pan. Blend salt and spices smoothly with some of the vinegar. Mix with remaining vinegar, pour into preserving pan and mix well.

Place pan over low heat and stir until sugar has melted and mixture comes to boil. Then boil gently for about 1 hour, stirring more and more frequently as chutney thickens to prevent it catching on the bottom of the pan. Cool.

Pot and cover (page 200).

Fills about 4 jars.

RUSSIAN SOURED APPLES

This is an unusual way of preserving apples for the winter, slightly reminiscent of the way sauerkraut would be made. Russians serve soured apples as an accompaniment for fried breaded escalopes and cutlets of various kinds. The apples should be tart, crisp dessert ones, all of the same medium size and without blemishes. For souring the apples, you will need a large, Victorian-style glazed pot or urn, a round wooden board to fit inside the top of it and a large, smooth stone, scrubbed clean, rinsed with boiling water and wrapped in muslin, to place on top.

10–11 pounds (4·5–5 kilos) apples
About 1 ounce (25 g) fresh blackcurrant leaves
4 ounces (100–125 g) rye flour
4 ounces (100–125 g) sugar or liquid honey
1 teaspoon salt

Wash and drain apples thoroughly. Scrub your pot or urn and line base with a layer of fresh blackcurrant leaves. On this place a layer of apples, fitting them tightly side by side. Cover with more blackcurrant leaves. Continue in this manner until apples have all been packed into pot, ending with a layer of leaves.

Prepare preserving liquor. In a large bowl, work rye flour to a smooth paste with a little cold water. Stirring rapidly, pour in 8 or 9 pints (4·4–5 litres) of boiling water, making sure flour does not go lumpy. Stir in sugar or honey and salt, and put aside until cold.

Pour cold liquor over apples to cover them completely. Then place wooden board on top and weight it down with the muslin-wrapped stone to prevent apples floating to the top. They must at all times remain submerged. Allow apples to marinate in a cool, dry place (such as a garage, outhouse or cellar) for at least 4 weeks before tasting them. They will keep for several months, at least until the following spring. Should mould form on the liquor and turn the stone slimy, skim the liquor, scrub the stone and the muslin separately, and scald them with boiling water.

BOTTLED APPLES IN CIDER

Use windfalls which are too unripe (or badly bruised) to eat raw.

Apples (see above)
Brine made with ½ ounce (15 g) salt to 2 pints (1·1 litre) water

Cider syrup
8 ounces (225 g) sugar
1 pint (550 ml) still cider
Thinly peeled rind of 1 lemon

Start by preparing syrup. Dissolve sugar in 2 pints (1·1 litre) water with cider and lemon rind (use a potato peeler or a small, sharp knife to peel off yellow part of rind as thinly as possible). Stir until sugar has dissolved and bring to boiling point. Remove pan from heat, cover, and leave until quite cold.

Prepare apples. Quarter, peel and core apples, cutting out all bruised and discoloured parts, and drop into brine to prevent discoloration.

Rinse apples thoroughly. Wipe them with a damp cloth or paper towels, and pack tightly into sterilized bottles. Cover with cold syrup and bottle (page 201).

APPLE JELLIES

The colour of an apple jelly depends very much on the apples used. The brighter and riper they are, the darker the jelly will be. Green apples and windfalls make a pale golden jelly that sets well, and windfalls as well as crab apples make good jelly with a sharp, tart flavour. Apart from the more conventional uses, a tablespoon or two of apple jelly may be added to apple sauces to sweeten and flavour them, or it can be eaten with cheese.

All kinds of herb jelly to serve with meat may be made with an apple jelly base – mint jelly to serve with lamb and mutton, sage jelly for pork, and jelly flavoured with bay for ham. The jelly itself should be perfectly clear or, if liked, can be coloured green with a few drops of food colouring. Just before setting point is reached, a little finely chopped fresh mint or a few sage or bay leaves may be stirred in.

6 pounds (2·7 kilos) apples
1 lemon
1 pound (450 g) sugar per pint (550 ml) of juice

Chop up apples but do not peel or core them. Finely grate rind of the lemon, sprinkle it over the apples in a preserving pan and cover with 5 pints (2·7 litres) water. Bring to the boil and cook until apples are very soft and pulpy. Tip the contents of the pan into a jelly bag and allow to drip dry, or leave the apple pulp to drain in a hair sieve.

Measure juice and weigh out 1 pound (450 g) sugar per pint (550 ml).

In the rinsed-out pan, combine the apple juice with the sugar and strain in the juice of the lemon. Bring to the boil slowly, stirring frequently, until sugar has dissolved. Then boil rapidly until setting point is reached, skimming scum from the surface.

Cool slightly, pot and cover.

See also page 199.

APRICOT

Although the apricot is a temperate fruit, it is rare to find fresh apricots at their peak of ripeness in the cooler climates of the north. The main reason for this is that the trees blossom early and an unexpected frost would wipe out the crop. So unless you live in an apricot-growing area, you are unlikely to find them fresh and in an edibly ripe state.

Another problem with fresh apricots is that although they taste best when they have ripened on the tree, once they reach this stage they are extremely perishable, and lengthy transportation over long distances by conventional methods would be sure to spoil them. Consequently, many of the fresh apricots offered in markets were picked when they were still far too hard and immature. Such fruit will never ripen properly and develop its full apricot flavour. The apricots will even start to shrink and shrivel but remain hard and greenish to the end. Unless you can be sure of getting naturally ripened fresh apricots, you would be better advised to concentrate your attention on one of the excellent forms of preserved apricots available, which are many and plentiful – dried, canned or turned into jams, nectars and sweets.

Apricots are thought to have come originally from China but early on they were introduced into the Near East, hence their botanical name, *Prunus armenica*. There their popularity has never waned and apricots appear in all kinds of dishes, from soups to sweets. Since those times, apricots have spread all over the world. They flourish in the warmth of Southern Europe, Australia and California.

Dried apricots are produced in several grades of quality. Finest of all are the large, plump dessert apricots, carefully packed so that they are not squashed out of shape. At the other end of the range are the leathery orange-coloured scraps which can only be used for cooking and chopping or puréeing.

Even if you make most of your own jams and preserves, you will probably have discovered that an apricot preserve is one of the few exceptions worth buying, with dozens of uses in the kitchen. Make sure it contains just apricots and sugar. Then it can either be eaten as it is or spread in layer cakes. You will also need apricot preserve to make an apricot glaze for brushing over open fruit tarts.

Apricots can be halved or sliced then frozen in a syrup made from 1 pound (450 g) sugar to 2 pints (1.1 litres) water; add 2 ounces (50 g) ascorbic acid for each pint (550 ml) syrup. Plunge the whole apricots into boiling water first for about thirty seconds, and peel, stone and halve or slice them.

Apricots can be made into wine and brandy.

They are one of the best natural sources of Vitamin A, especially when dried. Essential for healthy skin and mucous membranes, Vitamin A is also needed for good sight; insufficient amounts can cause night blindness, impair sight and increase susceptibility to colds and other illnesses. Although it is one of the few vitamins which can theoretically build up to toxic levels, this doesn't normally happen if it is taken naturally.

MOISTURIZING MASK

The Vitamin A content of apricots is especially beneficial to dry skins. Either fresh or dried fruit is suitable.

If using fresh apricots, simply remove the stones and mash the fruit; if using dried, soak for an hour or so in water before chopping finely and mashing. Mix the fruit pulp with enough oil (olive, safflower, peanut, avocado or almond) to make a spreadable paste.

Clean your face thoroughly, and pat the paste on, avoiding the area under the eyes. Leave on for about 20 minutes, then wash off gently with warm water.

APRICOT CHICKEN SOUP

¾–1 pound (350–450 chicken joints
Salt
1 chicken stock cube (optional)
4 ounces (100–125 g) short-grain rice, rinsed and drained
6 ounces (175 g) potato, peeled and diced
4 ounces (100–125 g) plump dried apricots, rinsed and cut into strips
Freshly ground black pepper
Ground cinnamon
¼ pint (150 ml) single cream
4 tablespoons finely chopped fresh dill or parsley

Rinse chicken joints and put them in a large pan. Sprinkle with salt and cover with 3 pints (1·7 litres) cold water. Add a crumbled chicken cube if liked at this stage. Slowly bring to boiling point and simmer for 20 minutes. Skim surface clear of any scum and fat.

Stir in rice, diced potato, apricots, and a generous pinch each of freshly ground black pepper and cinnamon. Simmer until the ingredients are quite soft and chicken meat is falling off the bones.

With a slotted spoon, lift out chicken joints. Bone them, sliver meat and return to the soup. Stir in cream. Correct seasoning if necessary. Bring to just below boiling point and serve, each portion sprinkled with chopped dill or parsley.

Serves 6–8.

PORK CHOPS IN APRICOT SAUCE

This is also a good way of preparing chicken joints and is delicious served with brown rice or a fluffy potato purée.

8 ounces (225 g) dried apricots
½ pint (300 ml) dry white wine or cider
6 thick pork chops
Seasoned flour
1 onion, finely chopped
3 tablespoons oil
2 tablespoons soft brown sugar
2–2 tablespoons coarsely chopped blanched almonds or walnuts

Rinse the apricots thoroughly under the cold tap. Put them in a bowl, cover with wine or cider and leave to soak overnight.

The following day, trim pork chops of any excess fat and dust them all over with well-seasoned flour. Remove about a quarter of the apricots from the wine and blend the remainder together with the wine to a smooth purée in an electric blender or food processor. Chop the whole apricots coarsely and stir them into the purée.

In a large frying pan, simmer the onion in half the oil until soft and golden. Remove the onion with a slotted spoon and put aside until needed. Heat the remaining oil in the frying pan and fry the chops, 2 or 3 at a time, until golden brown on both sides. Transfer them to an ovenproof casserole as they are done, making two layers in all and sprinkling each layer with some of the sautéed onion.

Deglaze the pan with 6–8 tablespoons water, stirring and scraping the surface clean with a wooden spoon. Bring to the boil and pour over the chops. Cover with the apricot purée.

Put on the lid and bake in a moderate oven (350°F, 180°C, Mark 4) until chops are quite tender, about 1 hour. For the last 15 minutes of baking time, remove the lid, sprinkle the surface with a mixture of sugar and nuts, and continue baking until sugar has melted and surface is bubbling. Serve from the casserole.

Serves 6.

LAMB AND APRICOT POLO

2 Spanish onions, finely chopped
2 ounces (50 g) butter
2 pounds (900 g) lean boned lamb, cubed
Salt and freshly ground black pepper
½–1 teaspoon ground cinnamon
8 ounces (225 g) plump dried apricots, quartered
6–8 tablespoons seedless raisins
About ¾ pint (400 ml) light chicken (cube) stock
Juice of ½ lemon
1–2 tablespoons apricot preserve, to taste

In a heavy pan or flameproof casserole, sauté onions gently in butter until transparent and lightly coloured. Transfer to a plate with a slotted spoon. In the remaining butter, brown the lamb cubes all over, a portion at a time. Return the onions and all the lamb to the pan. Season lightly with salt, pepper and cinnamon, and stir in the apricots and raisins. Sauté gently for a few minutes longer. Pour in hot chicken stock (or water) to cover. Bring slowly to simmering point, cover the pan and cook gently for about 2 hours until the lamb is tender and the apricots soft and pulpy, adding more stock if it evaporates too quickly.

Half-an-hour before the lamb is ready, flavour to taste with lemon juice and apricot preserve.

Just before serving, correct seasoning, and add a little more cinnamon if liked.

Serves 6.

APRICOT CREAM

8 ounces (225 g) dried apricots, soaked overnight
3 ounces (75 g) granulated sugar.
6–8 tablespoons Madeira
Lemon juice (optional)
2 egg whites
3 ounces (75 g) caster sugar
¼ pint (150 ml) whipping cream

Pour the apricots and their soaking water into a pan. Stir in granulated sugar and 2 or 3 tablespoons more water if necessary so that fruit are barely covered. Bring to boiling point and simmer until apricots are very soft. Drain them thoroughly. Pour cooking juices back into the pan and boil until reduced to a few tablespoons of thick syrup. Stir into apricots and leave until cold.

Add Madeira to apricots and whirl to a smooth, thick purée in an electric blender or food processor. Taste, and blend in a little more sugar, Madeira or a squeeze of lemon juice if liked. The purée should be well flavoured but must remain thick.

Whisk the egg whites until they form soft, floppy peaks when beaters are lifted. Gradually whisk in caster sugar and continue to whisk to a stiff, glossy meringue. Whisk cream lightly.

Fold meringue into apricot purée, followed by whipped cream. Spoon into a glass serving bowl or into individual dishes and chill until ready to serve.

Serves 6.

APRICOT ICE CREAM

8 ounces (225 g) dried apricots,
    soaked overnight
2–3 tablespoons lemon juice
4 eggs, separated
7 ounces (200 g) vanilla-flavoured
    caster sugar
½ pint (300 ml) whipping cream
Thin almond tuiles or sponge finger
    biscuits, to serve

Rinse the apricots thoroughly before leaving them to soak overnight. The following day, simmer them for 10–15 minutes, or until very soft, with more water to cover if necessary. Drain apricots and reserve ¼ pint (150 ml) of the cooking liquid. Pour this into the goblet of an electric blender (or a food processor fitted with the steel blade), add the apricots and blend to a thick, smooth purée. Flavour to taste with lemon juice and blend in the egg yolks, one at a time.

Pour the apricot purée into a heavy pan and cook over gentle heat, stirring constantly, until purée becomes very thick. Take care not to let it come to boiling point or the egg yolks will curdle. (If you feel apprehensive about this, heat the purée in a double saucepan over simmering water, stir-ring constantly, until it thickens.) Pour thickened purée into a large bowl and leave until quite cold.

Whisk egg whites until soft peaks form when beaters are lifted. Then gradually beat in caster sugar ·and continue to whisk to a stiff, glossy meringue. Whisk the cream lightly in a separate bowl until it thickens.

Fold the meringue into the apricot purée, followed by the whipped cream. Taste and flavour with more lemon juice or caster sugar if necessary.

Freeze in an ice cream maker, following manufacturer's instructions. Or pour into ice trays or a large, shallow plastic tray, cover and freeze. Remove the container after about 1½ hours, or when the ice cream has frozen around the edges, and with a fork beat it thoroughly, turning the sides in to the centre. Cover the container and freeze for 3–4 hours longer, or overnight. Transfer the container to the main compartment of the refrigerator about 1 hour before serving.

Serve the ice cream with a dish of crisp biscuits.

Serves 6.

APRICOT ALMOND SWEETS

Use good-quality, plump dried apricots, not the leathery pieces which have often lost a great deal of their flavour. Instead of adding the ground almonds and almond flavouring, the sweetened apricot paste may be left as it is and the sweets decorated with bright green, peeled pistachio nuts. If you do decide to use almonds, be sure to get real almond essence as the artificial one tastes unpleasantly synthetic.

8 ounces (225 g) plump dried apricots
Caster sugar or sifted icing sugar
1 tablespoon ground almonds
    (optional)
1–2 drops almond essence (optional)
Slivered blanched almonds or peeled
    pistachio nuts, to decorate

Wash the apricots and dry them thoroughly. Put them through the fine blade of a meat mincer, or twice if necessary through the coarser blade, to reduce them to a rather coarse paste. Sweeten to taste with sugar and mix in the ground almonds and almond essence if used. Work the paste with your fingertips until ingredients are smoothly blended.

Sprinkle a board lined with greaseproof paper with an even layer of sugar. Roll the apricot paste into marble-sized balls, coat them with sugar and leave to dry and harden overnight.

The following day, decorate each sweet with a few almond slivers or a peeled pistachio nut. Place in little paper cases and serve with after-dinner coffee.

Note: If the apricot paste is too dry to roll into smooth balls, it can be moistened with a few drops of lemon juice or cold water.

APRICOT MERINGUE CAKE

At least 5 oz (150 g) butter
6 egg whites
Pinch of salt
12 ounces (350 g) caster sugar
5 ounces (150 g) plain flour
1 jar (about 1 pound or 450 g) apricot
    jam
Lemon juice (optional)

Meringue
2 egg whites
4 ounces (100–125 g) caster sugar

Start by baking the cake base a day before it is to be served. Grease a deep, loose-bottomed, 8 inch (20 cm) cake tin with butter. Line it with greaseproof paper and butter that lightly as well. In a small, heavy pan, melt 5 ounces (150 g) butter without letting it sizzle and put it aside to cool.

In a large, spotlessly clean and dry bowl, or in the bowl of a large electric mixer, beat the 6 egg whites with a pinch of salt until soft peaks form. Gradually adding sugar, continue to beat to a stiff, glossy meringue. Sift flour and fold into meringue a little at a time alternately with melted butter. Spoon into prepared cake tin. Bake in a moderately hot oven (400°F, 200°C, Mark 6) for 40 minutes, or until cake is well risen and springs back when pressed lightly with a fingertip. Remove cake from the oven, place on a cake rack and leave it to cool in its tin overnight.

The following day, loosen sides of cake by slipping a knife blade round them and carefully turn out cake. Peel off lining paper. With a serrated knife, cut cake horizontally in three.

Put apricot jam in a heavy pan. Taste it and if it is very sweet, sharpen flavour a little with lemon juice. Heat jam slightly so that it will spread more easily.

Place bottom layer of cake on a large baking sheet which has been greased very lightly with butter. Then put layers together again, spreading apricot jam between them and over top and sides of cake as well.

Prepare meringue. Beat egg whites until soft peaks form. Then gradually beat in sugar until stiff and glossy.

Spread meringue all over top and sides of cake. Place cake in a fairly hot oven (425°F, 220°C, Mark 7). Bake for 3 minutes only then, without opening oven door, turn off heat and leave cake until quite cold.

Serves 6–8.

QUICK SAUCE

One 14 ounce (400 g) can apricots in
*   syrup*
About 1 tablespoon sugar
1 teaspoon arrowroot or potato flour
About 1 tablespoon lemon juice
1–2 teaspoons Kirsch, orange liqueur
*   or brandy (optional)*
Icing sugar (optional)

Drain apricots, reserving syrup. Put them in an electric blender or food processor. Sprinkle with sugar and blend to a smooth purée. Pour into a small pan.

Blend arrowroot or potato flour smoothly with 3 or 4 tablespoons reserved syrup and stir into apricot purée, together with the lemon juice. Bring to boiling point and simmer, stirring, for 3 or 4 minutes until sauce has thickened and no longer tastes of raw starch.

If sauce is to be served hot, thin it down with a little more of the reserved syrup if too thick, then taste and add more sugar or lemon juice if liked. If it is to be a cold sauce, let it cool after it has been thickened, then stir in liqueur or brandy if used, and finally adjust sweetness with a little icing sugar (which dissolves most easily) if necessary.

APRICOT WINE

The ingredients listed will produce a medium-dry, white wine. For a sweeter wine, use 3½ pounds (1·6 kilos) sugar and a Sauterne yeast.

4 pounds (1·8 kilos) fresh apricots, or 1
*   pound (450 g) dried apricots*
8 ounces (225 g) chopped sultanas
1 Campden tablet
1 teaspoon Pectozyme
1 teacup cold strong tea
1 nutrient tablet
Burgundy yeast
2½ pounds (1·1 kilos) granulated
*   sugar*

Wash the fruit. If you are using fresh apricots, discard the stones, but do not remove the skin. Chop the fruit into small pieces and place it in the prepared mashing vessel. Add the sultanas, Campden tablet, Pectozyme and 1 gallon (4.5 litres) water. Cover the vessel and then leave it for 24 hours.

Quickly uncover the mashing vessel and add the strong tea, the nutrient tablet and the activated yeast

APRICOT BRANDY

The apricots remaining after the liqueur is drained off are delicious on their own or added to cakes and pies.

2 pounds (900 g) fresh apricots
2 pounds (900 g) granulated sugar
2½ pints (1·4 litres) brandy

Wash the fruit. Halve it and discard the stones. Take a large, wide-neck storage jar, with a screw top (a kilner jar is ideal). It should be thoroughly clean and sterilized (see general instructions for wine making). Arrange the fruit in layers in the jar, sprinkling sufficient sugar to cover over each layer. The fruit should be tightly packed. Screw the top on loosely and leave for 4 days.

Unscrew the lid and add the chopped apricot kernels, if you are using them. Pour sufficient brandy onto the fruit to cover it. Re-seal the jar and leave it for at least 6 months, at room temperature.

Strain off the liquid and siphon it into prepared bottles.

The liqueur may be drunk immediately, but is better if stored for at least 6 months.

Makes 2½ pints (1·4 litres).

(see manufacturer's instructions for quantity and method of use). Replace the lid and leave for 7 days in a warm place (65–75°F or 18–24°C). During this period, stir once a day to ensure that all the fruit is kept moist. Do this quickly and always make sure the vessel is firmly covered at all other times.

Using a fine sieve, strain off the liquid into a clean container. Put the remaining fruit pulp into a linen bag. Seal the bag tightly and squeeze out as much juice as possible into the same container. Stir in the sugar and quickly siphon into a prepared fermentation vessel, filling to within 1 inch (2·5 cm) of the cork. Leave to ferment under an air-lock in a warm place (65–75°F or 18–24°C). This will take approximately 3 weeks.

Rack, store for at least 6 months, and bottle in the usual way. It is advisable to keep this wine for at least a year, before drinking.

See also page 205.

Makes 1 gallon (4·5 litres).

APRICOT JAM

Fruit that is too hard and unripe for eating fresh is perfect for jams.

3½ pounds (1·6 kilos) slightly under-
*   ripe fresh apricots*
Juice of 1 large lemon
1 teaspoon finely grated lemon rind
3 pounds (1.4 kilos) sugar

Wash the apricots, stone them and put them through the coarse blade of a meat mincer. In a preserving pan, combine the apricots with the lemon juice and rind, and stir in the sugar. Leave for an hour or two to allow sugar to draw out the apricot juices. (If there doesn't seem to be enough, you could add up to ¼ pint (150 ml) water.)

Place the pan over low heat and stir frequently until sugar has dissolved. Then raise heat, bring to boiling point and boil rapidly, stirring frequently, until jam has thickened and setting point is reached. Skim off any scum that forms on the surface.

Cool slightly. Pot and cover.

See also page 198.

Fills about 5 jars.

APRICOT GLAZE

A few heaped tablespoons apricot
*   preserve*
Lemon juice
Kirsch or brandy (optional)

Put the preserve into a small pan, taste, and if it seems too sweet, mix in some lemon juice. Add a little boiling water and heat gently, stirring, until runny. If you like, add some Kirsch or brandy to improve the flavour.

Rub the glaze through a sieve, and brush it on your tart, while it is still warm and rather liquid.

AVOCADO

Until the Second World War, few Europeans had seen, let alone tasted, an avocado (also known as an alligator pear). Outside the tropics and subtropics, it was virtually unknown, although it has been cultivated for food since time immemorial. (In Mexico, traces of avocado have been found in excavations said to date back to at least 7,000 years BC.) However, in spite of its long history and culinary importance, cooks are still cautious about preparing it in any other than the most conventional, well-tried ways — with vinaigrette dressing or mayonnaise and seafood, meat or diced vegetables, as a creamy soup or a dip for *crudités* and salty crackers. Occasionally, they may venture into the world of Mexican cooking to try a *guacamole*, but few are aware how wonderful a really ripe avocado tastes when it is turned into a cream or ice cream.

An avocado pear may be small and oval or large and pear-shaped like its namesake. Its skin may be smooth and shiny or leathery and rough, varying from pale green to purple bordering on black. None of this affects its flavour. The flesh of a ripe avocado is always a pale golden green with a buttery texture and a rich, slightly nutty flavour. The skin should be unmarked (it spoils easily if bruised) and the avocado should feel heavy for its size. Once it has ripened, it will yield slightly to gentle pressure when cradled in the palms of your hands.

However, to facilitate transportation, avocados are usually harvested when still rock hard and arrive in the shops in this state. Once they soften they deteriorate rapidly, so it is far safer to buy them hard and ripen them off at home. This will take a few days. Put them in a brown paper bag or a drawer or dark cupboard, and leave them at room temperature until they soften. They can then be held in this state for a few days at the bottom of the refrigerator.

There is only one real drawback to preparing avocados. Uncooked, they will soon turn an unappetizing shade of muddy brown if cut, peeled or puréed and left exposed to the air for any length of time. Discoloration will be slowed down by brushing the surface with lemon or lime juice as soon as it has been cut, but this will last for no more than a few hours. Alternatively, cover the cut surface tightly with plastic wrap and put it in the refrigerator. Treated in this way, an avocado half will keep reasonably well for several days.

A dish made with puréed avocado can also be stored tightly wrapped in the refrigerator. And some people maintain that a purée will stay pale and creamy indefinitely if it is stored with the avocado stone buried in it. But this is a far from reliable measure. The one sure solution to the problem of discoloration is to leave the preparation of an avocado to the very last moment.

Avocados have a high protein and vitamin content, and the pulp and oil are used extensively in beauty preparations for the hair and skin.

NOURISHING CREAM

Avocado oil, one of the most versatile beauty preparations, is obtainable from specialist shops. It can be used on its own as a hair conditioner, or as a cleanser or moisturizer; it blends well with fruit to make packs for dry skin, and revives dry scaly skin when added to bathwater.

Thoroughly blend an egg yolk, a scant teaspoon of avocado oil, a few drops of glycerine and 1 teaspoon of runny honey. Add enough rosewater to make a creamy consistency. Store in the refrigerator.

MOISTURIZER

Because avocados contain so many vitamins, minerals and natural oils, they can be used to make a nourishing moisturizer for dry skins.

Thoroughly mash half an avocado with a little lemon juice and some gently heated almond oil. Apply to the face, and leave for about 20 minutes. Wash off with warm water.

AVOCADO HEALTH DRINK

This is almost a light meal in itself. The avocado is one of the most nutritious fruits, containing a large number of vitamins, minerals and natural oils. The use of an electric blender is essential.

Pulp of 1 large, ripe avocado
Juice and rind of 1 lemon
3 tablespoons honey
½ pint (300 ml) milk
2 tablespoons yoghourt

Put all the ingredients into an electric blender and process until smooth. Taste. Add extra honey or salt, if necessary. If the consistency of the mixture is too thick, add extra milk. Serve chilled in a chilled glass.

Makes 1 large glass.

GUACAMOLE

Guacamole is one of the best-known Mexican contributions to gastronomy. Serve as a dip, with drinks.

1 large, ripe avocado pear
1 ripe tomato
1 tablespoon finely chopped onion
1 tablespoon lemon juice
Salt

Peel avocado. Halve lengthwise, remove the stone and mash the pulp. Peel and seed the tomato, and mix with the avocado pulp. Add onion, lemon juice and salt and blend mixture in an electric blender.

Serves 4–6.

Note: The guacamole can be enriched with 1 tablespoon brewer's yeast and a dash of wheatgerm oil before blending.

AVOCADO DIP

1 large, ripe avocado pear
1 tablespoon lemon juice
1 teaspoon grated onion
½ small clove garlic, crushed
4–6 tablespoons sour cream or
*   natural yoghourt*
1–2 tablespoons thick lemon
*   mayonnaise (page 205)*
Salt and white pepper

Peel and halve avocado, and remove stone. Cut avocado into chunks and place in the goblet of an electric blender. Immediately sprinkle with lemon juice, add remaining ingredients except for salt and pepper, and blend to a smooth cream. Season to taste with salt and white pepper.

Pour into a serving bowl and serve. If dip has to wait for a short time, store the bowl, covered, in the refrigerator.

Serves 4–6, but any number of people if doubled in quantity, and served with other dips.

AVOCADO WITH CREAM CHEESE DRESSING

2 large, ripe avocado pears
Lemon juice

Cream cheese dressing
4 ounces (100–125 g) cream cheese
1–2 tablespoons single cream
1 tablespoon lemon juice or cider
*   vinegar*
1 teaspoon caster sugar
½ teaspoon celery salt

Prepare dressing first so there will be time to chill it lightly before use. Blend cheese smoothly with cream. Beat in remaining ingredients and adjust flavouring to taste. Chill lightly.

Shortly before serving, halve avocados lengthwise and remove stones. Brush cut surfaces carefully all over with lemon juice to prevent discoloration.

Place avocado halves on individual serving dishes. Spoon some of the dressing into hollows and serve, together with remaining dressing in a separate dish.

Serves 4.

STUFFED AVOCADOS

6 large, ripe avocado pears
Lemon juice
Crisp lettuce leaves, to garnish
Lemon mayonnaise (page 205), to
*   serve*

Vegetable stuffing
6–8 tablespoons cooked sweetcorn
6–8 tablespoons cooked green peas
6–8 tablespoons diced cooked green
*   beans*
1 tablespoon finely chopped chives or
*   green spring onion tops*
3–4 tablespoons thick lemon
*   mayonnaise*
Salt and freshly ground black pepper
2–3 drops Tabasco

Peel avocados. Cut them in half lengthwise and remove stones. Brush them all over with lemon juice to prevent discoloration. Lay 2 avocado halves on each of 6 plates lined with crisp lettuce leaves.

Prepare vegetable stuffing. In a bowl, mix sweetcorn, peas and diced green beans together. Add chives or spring onion tops, bind vegetables with mayonnaise and season to taste with salt, freshly ground black pepper and a few drops of Tabasco.

Pile stuffing in cavities of avocados and top each half with a dollop of mayonnaise. Serve immediately.

Serves 6.

CREAMED AVOCADO SOUP

A rich, luxurious soup that will take only minutes to make in an electric blender or food processor.

2 large, ripe avocado pears
About 2 tablespoons lemon juice
1½ pints (900 ml) chilled chicken
*   stock*
Salt and white pepper
Tabasco
¼ pint (150 ml) whipping cream,
*   chilled*
Finely chopped chives, chervil or
*   green spring onion tops, to garnish*

Halve the avocados lengthwise, remove stones and peel them. Cut one half into thin slivers or neat cubes. Brush them carefully all over with about 1 tablespoon lemon juice to stop them discolouring and put aside.

Combine the remaining avocado halves, lemon juice and chicken stock in the goblet of an electric blender or food processor, and blend to a smooth purée. Season to taste with salt, a pinch of white pepper and a few drops of Tabasco. Blend in the chilled cream and pour into a chilled soup tureen. Stir in the reserved avocado slices or cubes and taste for seasoning. Cover and chill until ready to serve.

Serve in chilled soup bowls, each portion garnished with finely chopped fresh herbs.

Serves 4–6.

CHILLED AVOCADO SOUP

3 small, ripe avocado pears
Lemon juice
¼ pint (150 ml) sour cream or thick
    natural yoghourt
½ pint (300 ml) jellied chicken or beef
    stock
4 ripe tomatoes
4 tablespoons finely chopped spring
    onions
Salt
2–3 drops Tabasco
Finely chopped chives or spring
    onion tops, to garnish

Halve avocados lengthwise and remove stones. Peel avocados. Cut one of them into small, neat dice and immediately toss with 1 or 2 tablespoons lemon juice to prevent discoloration. Chop remaining avocados coarsely. In an electric blender or food processor, purée chopped avocados with sour cream or yoghourt until smooth. Gradually blend in stock.

Peel and seed tomatoes. Cut one of them into small cubes and add it to the blended avocado. Chop up remainder and blend into soup.

Pour soup into a large bowl. Stir in cubed avocado and tomato, together with their juices, and finely chopped spring onions. Season to taste with salt, a few drops of Tabasco and a little more lemon juice if liked. Chill well before serving.

This is a thick, rich soup. Serve small portions in chilled soup bowls, garnished with chopped chives or green spring onion tops.

Serves 6.

Note: If you find the soup too thick for your taste, thin it down with a little tomato juice or more stock.

VEAL ROLLS WITH HAM AND AVOCADO

A perfect dish for spring, quite light in itself but also very suitable should the weather turn chilly. Serve with rice or a potato purée and a large, tossed green salad. The best mustard to use for this dish is a coarsely ground brown French mustard such as Moutarde de Meaux, but any spicy French mustard, coarse or smooth, will do very well.

8 small veal escalopes (about 1½
    pounds or 700 g)
8 small slices prosciutto (raw Parma
    ham) or thinly sliced lean cooked
    ham
Coarse French mustard
1–1½ ounces (40 g) butter
6–8 tablespoons chicken (cube) stock
    or dry white wine
1 large, ripe avocado pear
¼ pint (150 ml) thick cream
Salt and white pepper
Sieved hard-boiled egg yolk, to
    garnish (optional)

Trim veal escalopes and pound them out as thinly as possible without tearing them. Trim prosciutto or ham slices to fit escalopes, leaving a narrow border all round. Spread each escalope with ½ to 1 teaspoon French mustard. Top with a slice of prosciutto or ham, roll up tightly and secure each roll with a couple of short wooden toothpicks.

In a deep, heavy frying pan or flameproof casserole with a tight-fitting lid, brown veal rolls all over in butter over moderate heat. Add chicken stock or wine, stirring and scraping surface of pan clean with a wooden spoon. Cover pan tightly and cook gently for 20–30 minutes until veal is quite tender. Give pan a shake now and again so that veal rolls do not stick.

While veal is cooking, peel and stone avocado, and slice it thinly. Remove veal rolls to a heated serving dish. Keep hot. Blend cream into pan juices. Carefully stir in avocado slices and continue to cook for a minute or two longer to heat them through. Taste sauce for seasoning, adding a pinch of salt or white pepper if needed.

Discard toothpicks from veal rolls. Surround them with avocado slices and pour cream sauce over the entire dish. Decorate with sieved hard-boiled egg yolk if used and serve.

Serves 4.

EGGS WITH AVOCADO SAUCE

An unusual and very attractive supper dish that also makes a good appetizer.

8 eggs, hardboiled
2 large, ripe avocado pears
2 teaspoons cornflour
4 tablespoons single cream or
    creamy milk
Salt and white pepper
Few drops of Tabasco
Fried croûtons, (page 205), to garnish

Halve, stone and peel avocados, and either purée them in an electric blender or food processor, or rub through a nylon sieve.

In a medium-sized pan, blend cornflour smoothly with cream or milk. Beat in avocado purée. Bring to boiling point, stirring constantly, and simmer, stirring, for 4 or 5 minutes until sauce has thickened and no longer tastes starchy. Season to taste with salt, white pepper and a few drops of Tabasco.

Shell eggs (hot), cut them in half lengthwise and arrange cut side up on a heated serving dish. Spoon avocado cream sauce over the top, garnish dish with the crisp fried croûtons and serve.

Serves 4 as a supper dish, up to 8 as an appetizer.

AVOCADO SALAD

¼ pint (150 ml) vinaigrette dressing
    made with a mild cider or white
    wine vinegar
Salt and freshly ground black pepper
2 large, ripe avocado pears
Lettuce leaves, to garnish

Pour dressing ingredients into a bowl and season with salt and freshly ground black pepper, beating vigorously to make an emulsion.

Peel avocados, slice them in half lengthwise and remove stones. Cut avocados into long, thin slices or large dice, dropping them into the bowl of vinaigrette as you do so. Mix lightly but thoroughly, making sure that pieces of avocado are coated on all sides with dressing.

Line a serving bowl with crisp green lettuce leaves and pour avocados and their dressing into the centre. Serve immediately.

Serves 6.

AVOCADO PILAF

Serve this unusual pilaf with grilled or roast lamb and poultry. The rice and stock used here are measured in cups as it is the relative volumes that are most important, so be sure to use the same utensil for both.

Rice
1 small onion, finely chopped
2 ounces (50 g) butter
1½ cups long-grain rice
3–4 tablespoons dry vermouth
3½ cups hot, well-seasoned chicken stock

Avocado mushroom garnish
4 ounces (100–125 g) button mushrooms
1½ ounces (40 g) butter
1 medium firm tomato
Generous pinch of dried oregano
Garlic salt and freshly ground black pepper
1 large avocado pear
About 1 tablespoon lemon juice

In a heavy, flameproof casserole which has a tight-fitting lid, sauté the onion gently in butter until soft and transparent but not coloured. Stir in the rice and continue to sauté, stirring, until each grain is shiny and individually coated with butter. Add the vermouth and stock, mix well and bring to boiling point. Cover the casserole. Transfer to a moderately hot oven (400°F, 200°C, Mark 6) and bake for about 20 minutes until the rice has absorbed all the liquid, leaving the grains moist but separate.

Meanwhile, prepare the garnish. Trim and slice the mushrooms, and sauté in 1 ounce (25 g) butter for a few minutes until lightly coloured but still firm. Peel, seed and dice the tomato. Add it to the pan, together with a sprinkling of oregano, garlic salt and black pepper, to taste. Simmer for 4 or 5 minutes longer, making sure tomato does not disintegrate.

While vegetables are simmering, peel, halve, stone and dice the avocado neatly, and toss gently but thoroughly with lemon juice to prevent discoloration. Stir avocado into simmering garnish, remove from heat and put aside, covered.

When ready to serve pilaf, add garnish, together with its juices, and the remaining butter, and toss gently with a large fork until thoroughly mixed. Allow to stand for a minute or two before serving.

Serves 6.

Note: The temperature at which the rice cooks is not crucial. If there are other dishes in the oven requiring a lower temperature, it may take a little longer to absorb the stock but will certainly come to no harm.

AVOCADO LIME CREAM

This is simple and quick to make, and quite sensationally good and pretty, but only when made with very ripe avocados and juicy fresh limes. Lemons would be too harshly acid. Serve in small portions (the cream is rich), accompanied by a dish of *langues de chat* or delicate shortbread biscuits.

2 large, ripe avocado pears
6 tablespoons caster sugar
Juice of 2 limes

Peel avocados. Halve them lengthwise, remove stones and cut avocados into chunks. Put these in an electric blender or food processor. Sprinkle with sugar and lime juice, and whirl to a smooth, creamy purée.

Put purée in a bowl or plastic box and cover tightly. Chill thoroughly until ready to serve.

Serves 3–4.

AVOCADO BUTTER

Use this as you would ordinary butter – as a spread for bread or toast, or as a sauce for grilled or fried fish.

1 large, ripe avocado
Lemon juice (optional)
1 tablespoon oil
1 tablespoon ground cumin, or to taste
1 teaspoon salt
Pinch of cayenne pepper

Halve, stone and peel avocado. Cut into chunks and sprinkle with lemon juice. Mash to a paste with a fork (or purée in an electric blender or food processor) together with remaining ingredients. If you are not using it immediately, pack into a small dish, cover and store in refrigerator.

AVOCADO ICE CREAM

Provided the avocado used is very soft and ripe, this recipe will make an unusual ice cream with a subtle, light flavour and a beautiful, jade-green colour.

1 large, very ripe avocado pear
4 tablespoons fresh lime juice
5 tablespoons caster sugar
¼ pint (150 ml) double cream

Peel and stone avocado, and cut it into chunks. Put them in an electric blender or food processor with lime juice and sugar, and blend to a smooth purée. In a large bowl, beat cream until thick. Gradually beat in avocado purée, and continue to beat until light and fluffy. Taste and beat in a little more lime juice or sugar if necessary, bearing in mind that freezing will modify flavours.

Pour mixture into ice cube trays or a shallow plastic box. Cover with foil or a lid and freeze until ice cream is solid around sides but still soft in the middle.

Scrape ice cream out into bowl again and beat until uniformly smooth and creamy. Then pour it back into container(s) and freeze until firm.

Transfer ice cream to main compartment of refrigerator to soften slightly about 1 hour before serving. Serve small portions with delicate shortbread biscuits.

Serves 6.

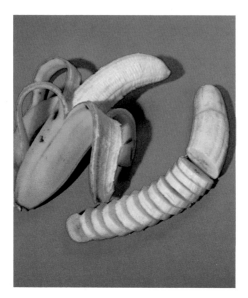

BANANA

Alexander the Great is known to have come across bananas on his travels to India and subsequently, thanks to conquerors and explorers, the banana plant spread throughout the tropical world, both Old and New. In Europe and temperate America, however, bananas were to remain virtually unknown until the 1890s, when the first refrigerated ships were developed to transport them safely over long distances. Today, it would be hard to imagine a fruit stall without a generous supply of bananas.

Of all the fruits we import from the tropics, bananas are one of only a few that should be harvested while they are still green and immature, then allowed to finish ripening *off* the plant. If they are left to ripen fully on the plant, they will develop a rather strong, unpleasant flavour. We, the customers, often make the mistake of using the fruit before it is fully ripe, not realizing that a skin lightly speckled with brown is a sign of ripeness and certainly does not mean that the banana is going bad. In fact, you will often find the best-flavoured and most velvety textured banana inside a skin that is almost black. The best advice would be to buy bananas that are 'unblemished' by all means but then to let them finish ripening and lose any green tints at room temperature (*not* in the refrigerator) before you eat them. The only exceptions are bananas which are going to be cooked (the cooking makes them easy to digest and brings out their flavour). And in markets catering for a West Indian clientele you will come across plantains. These look just like large, hard, green bananas but their sugar content is far lower than that of dessert bananas and they are used exclusively for cooking.

When using bananas, there are only a couple of points to bear in mind. Once it has been peeled and cut up, a banana soon starts turning brown, but this process can be slowed down by sprinkling it with lemon juice or some other acid fruit juice such as orange or grapefruit. The other point to remember when making fruit salads is not to add the bananas too far in advance as prolonged soaking turns them unpleasantly slimy and spongy.

Bananas are not suitable for turning into preserves such as jams, nor are they good frozen, unless they have been made into ice cream. They are delicious made into drinks. Otherwise, the only preserved bananas you are likely to come across are dried ones, which make a rather sticky, sweet snack.

Bananas are exceptionally nutritious, high in proteins, vitamins and minerals. Easily digested, they are ideal for convalescents who are not allowed to eat rich foods, and babies can be given mashed bananas as an introduction to solid food.

HEALTH SHAKE

A standard milk-shake recipe, in which you can use any other fruit. Bananas make a sweet, creamy shake.

½ pint (300 ml) milk
1 large banana (not too ripe), peeled and coarsely chopped
2 tablespoons yoghourt
1 tablespoon honey
Pinch of ground nutmeg

Put all the ingredients into an electric blender and process until smooth. Add extra milk if the consistency is too thick to pour easily. Taste. If a slightly less sweet drink is preferred, stir in a teaspoon of lemon juice. Serve chilled in a chilled glass.

Makes 1 large glass.

FACE PACK

Because of their soft, vitamin-rich flesh, bananas make an excellent moisturizing and nourishing pack for dry skins.

Mash a fresh banana with enough oil (olive, safflower, peanut, avocado or almond) to make a spreadable paste. Clean your face thoroughly then pat the paste over your face and neck, avoiding the area under the eyes. Leave on for about 20 minutes, then wash off very gently with warm water.

BANANA CRISPS

There are several ways of making banana crisps, coming from as far apart as Africa and South America, but they are all quite similar. Either plantains, or hard, unripe bananas with a greenish tinge, are used. Bowls of these are bound to create a sensation at drinks time.

Peel bananas (or plantains) and slice them into rounds about ½ inch (1·25 cm) thick. Drop them into a bowl of iced salted water and let them soak for about 30 minutes. Then drain slices and pat them dry with paper towels.

Heat a pan of vegetable oil to 375°F (190°C). Fry banana slices until crisp and golden. They should be floating freely in the oil. Do not overcrowd the pan or they will clump together. Drain thoroughly on absorbent paper once more and serve very fresh, sprinkled with salt.

In a slightly more elaborate version, the bananas or plantains are fried twice for extra crispness, rather like potato chips. This time, slice them 1½ inches (3·75 cm) thick. Heat the oil to a slightly cooler temperature, at 325°F (160°C). Deep-fry slices for 4 or 5 minutes until they are soft but still very pale. Drain thoroughly and dip in iced salted water as above. Drain again and pat dry.

Lay slices in a single layer, well spaced apart, on a sheet of grease-proof paper and cover with another sheet. With a rolling pin, gently but firmly roll the slices out to a thickness of about ¾ inch (or about 2 cm).

Now heat oil to 375°F (190°C) and fry flattened banana slices briefly until crisp and golden. They will be ready in about 1 minute. Drain thoroughly on crumpled paper towels. Sprinkle with salt and serve.

CHICKEN WITH BANANAS

Serve this Brazilian dish with fluffy white rice and follow with a crisp green salad.

1 roasting chicken, about 3 pounds
*   (1·4 kilos)*
4 tablespoons lemon juice
Salt
2 ounces (50 g) butter
1 medium Spanish onion, very finely
*   chopped*
2 large tomatoes, peeled, seeded and
*   chopped*
⅛ teaspoon sugar
½ pint (300 ml) dry white wine
6 firm, ripe bananas
4 tablespoons vegetable (corn) oil
4 ounces (100–125 g) Parmesan, or
*   half Parmesan and half Gruyère, or*
*   any other good melting cheese,*
*   freshly grated*

Joint chicken into 8 pieces, 2 from each breast and 2 from each leg. On a large platter, rub them with lemon juice and sprinkle with salt.

In a heavy, flameproof casserole, melt 1½ ounces (40 g) butter and add the onion, tomatoes and sugar. (With fresh tomatoes which have little flavour, I also like to add a couple of teaspoons of tomato paste.) Simmer for a minute or two, then add chicken pieces and any lemon juice that might have drained off them, turning them over to coat them in sauce. Simmer, uncovered, for 5 minutes. Then pour in wine and slowly bring to simmering point again. Cover and cook gently until chicken is tender, about 35 minutes.

Meanwhile, peel bananas and halve them lengthwise. In a large, heavy frying pan, brown bananas lightly on both sides in hot oil. Drain pieces well on absorbent paper.

When chicken is cooked through, arrange the pieces of banana on top, cut side down. Sprinkle with grated cheese. (I sometimes use a mixture of grated cheese and stale white breadcrumbs.) Dot with remaining butter, flaked. Place in a moderately hot oven (400°F, 200°C, Mark 6) for 10 minutes, or until topping is bubbling and golden.

Serves 4.

BANANA WALDORF

A variation of the famous American Waldorf apple salad, to be served with savoury main-course meat and poultry dishes.

6 medium tart, red-skinned dessert
*   apples*
3 large, ripe bananas
2 large stalks celery
6–8 tablespoons chopped walnuts
About ½ pint (300 ml) lemon
*   mayonnaise (page 205)*
Lettuce leaves, to garnish

Quarter, core and dice unpeeled apples into a large bowl. Peel bananas, slice them into thin rounds and add them to bowl. Finely chop celery stalks and add them to bowl, together with chopped walnuts. Toss lightly but thoroughly with a large fork.

Add mayonnaise and mix gently until pieces of fruit are individually coated (to protect them from discoloration). Chill lightly before serving. Serve in a bowl lined with crisp green lettuce leaves.

Serves 6.

BANANAS AND ONIONS

An unusual side dish to serve with pork, ham and veal dishes, especially roasts.

4 large, firm bananas
2 Spanish or other sweet, mild onions
1 ounce (25 g) butter
Salt
Lemon juice

Peel bananas and cut into thick rounds. Peel and slice onions thickly, and separate out rings.

In a large frying pan, sauté onions gently in the butter until about half-cooked, ie soft and transparent but not coloured. Add sliced bananas and fry for about 10 minutes longer, turning contents of pan over and over so that banana slices colour on both sides.

Season lightly with salt. Sprinkle with lemon juice and serve hot.

Serves 4.

GRILLED BANANAS

Butter
2 large, firm bananas
3 tablespoons orange juice
1 teaspoon lemon juice
2 tablespoons soft brown sugar
1–2 tablespoons blanched slivered
   almonds, to decorate

Take a heatproof, shallow dish that can go to the table and grease lightly all over with butter. Peel bananas and halve them lengthwise. Arrange in baking dish. Mix orange and lemon juices together, and sprinkle over bananas, turning them to coat them thoroughly on all sides. Sprinkle with sugar and dot with flakes of butter. Grill bananas until sugar has melted and top is bubbling. Then scatter all over with slivered almonds and continue to grill until they are lightly toasted.

Serve hot, straight from the stove.

Serves 4.

BANANES BRÛLÉES

Fold an equal volume of ripe mashed banana, sprinkled with a little lemon juice, into a bowl of whipped double cream and flavour to taste with vanilla essence. The cream will probably need no sweetening if the puréed bananas were really ripe, bearing in mind that there is sugar to come for the topping.

Have the grill pre-heated at maximum and very hot. Spoon cream mixture into a flameproof dish, preferably one without a rim (eg a conventional soufflé dish). Sift a thick layer of soft brown sugar evenly over the top.

Turn grill down to moderate and grill the dish of banana cream until the sugar has melted into a glassy sheet. Leave until cold and hard, and chill until ready to serve.

BANANA CREAM PIE

One 8 or 9 inch (20 or 22·5 cm) rich
   shortcrust pastry case, pre-baked
   (page 203)
3 large, ripe bananas
Juice of 1 large lemon
¼ pint (150 ml) double cream
Angelica sprigs, to decorate (optional)

Cream filling
2 tablespoons plain flour
2 tablespoons cornflour
4 ounces (100–125 g) sugar
Generous pinch of salt
¾ pint (400 ml) milk
3 large egg yolks
½–1 teaspoon vanilla essence
½ ounce (15 g) butter

Start by preparing the cream filling. In a heavy pan, mix the first 4 ingredients together and blend in the milk. Stir over low heat until mixture comes to boiling point, then continue to simmer, stirring constantly, until it thickens and loses any floury taste.

In a bowl, beat egg yolks lightly. Blend in a few tablespoons of the hot milk mixture, then beat back into remaining mixture in pan and stir over low heat until it thickens. Do not let it boil again at this stage as egg yolks may curdle. Remove pan from heat and cool slightly before beating in vanilla and butter. Leave until cold, covered with a disc of greaseproof paper to prevent a skin forming on top.

Peel bananas. Cut them in slices about ¼ inch (6 mm) thick and toss them with lemon juice.

Assemble pie as follows. Spread half of the cream filling in the pre-baked pastry case. Cover surface with banana slices and top with remaining filling.

Whip cream and use it to decorate top of pie. Finish decoration by studding top with small sprigs of candied angelica, if available. Chill lightly for 30 minutes before serving.

Serves 6–8.

BANANAS WITH RASPBERRY SAUCE

4 firm, ripe bananas
1½ ounces (40 g) butter
1 tablespoon soft brown sugar
2–3 tablespoons Grand Marnier or
   other orange liqueur

Raspberry sauce
12 ounces (350 g) frozen raspberries
2 tablespoons Grand Marnier or other
   orange liqueur
About 2 tablespoons icing sugar

Start by preparing raspberry sauce. Leave raspberries at room temperature until partially thawed and softened. Purée in an electric blender or food processor, then rub through a fine nylon sieve, and discard pips. Beat in liqueur and sweeten to taste with icing sugar. Pour sauce into a large jug.

Peel bananas and cut them in half lengthwise. In a frying pan that will hold banana halves in one layer, melt butter. Add sugar and stir over gentle heat until it has melted. Lay bananas in buttery syrup flat side down and fry gently for about 3 minutes. Then turn them over and continue to fry for 3 minutes longer.

Pour raspberry sauce all over bananas and heat through gently. At the same time, warm remaining liqueur in a large metal serving spoon or ladle. When raspberry sauce is hot, put a match to the warmed liqueur and as soon as flames are well established, pour it over the pan. Serve immediately, before flames go out.

Serves 4.

BANANA CHEESE

2 large, ripe bananas
Lemon juice
8 ounces (225 g) curd cheese
About 3 tablespoons
   caster sugar

Peel bananas and slice into thin rounds. Sprinkle with lemon juice to keep them from turning brown. In a bowl, beat cheese until fluffy, using an electric mixer if available. Beat in sugar to taste, a tablespoon at a time.

Gently mix in bananas. Pile into a glass serving dish and chill lightly for about 1 hour before serving.

Serves 4.

BANANA ICE CREAM

Delicious with a sprinkling of chopped nuts, coarsely grated dark chocolate or macaroon crumbs.

3 large, very ripe bananas
4 ounces (100–125 g) sugar
Generous pinch of salt
¾–1 tablespoon fresh lime or lemon juice
1 teaspoon vanilla essence
½ pint (300 ml) double cream
¼ pint (150 ml) single cream

Peel bananas. Pull off and discard any stringy fibres, and cut bananas into chunks. Put them in an electric blender or food processor, together with sugar, salt, lime or lemon juice and vanilla, and whirl to a smooth purée. Taste and add more sugar, lime or lemon juice if necessary, bearing in mind that freezing will modify flavours.

In a large bowl, beat creams together until they thicken but not enough to make the mixture stiff enough to form peaks. Fold in banana purée. Pour mixture into ice cube trays or a shallow plastic box, cover tightly with a sheet of foil or lid, and freeze until ice cream is frozen hard around sides but still soft in the middle.

Scrape ice cream out into a bowl and, using an electric hand whisk if you have one, beat mixture vigorously until it is uniformly smooth and creamy again. Then pour it back into freezing container(s), cover and freeze until firm. Transfer ice cream to main compartment of refrigerator to soften at least 1 hour before serving.

Serve with crisp biscuits.

Serves 4.

SPICED BANANA BREAD

3 ounces (75 g) butter or soft margarine
4 ounces (100–125 g) caster sugar
1 pound (450 g) ripe bananas
1 egg
8 ounces (225 g) flour
2 teaspoons baking powder
1 teaspoon ground cinnamon
½ teaspoon salt
3 tablespoons natural yoghourt

In an electric mixer, if available, beat butter or margarine until creamy. Gradually beat in caster sugar and continue to beat until white and fluffy. Peel and mash bananas smoothly. Beat egg until fluffy. Gradually add banana pulp to creamed butter and sugar, followed by beaten egg, beating vigorously all the time.

Sift flour with baking powder, cinnamon and salt. Lightly mix flour into creamed ingredients alternately with yoghourt to make a soft batter.

Pour batter into a well-greased, large (roughly 9 × 5 inch, or 22·5 × 12·5 cm) loaf tin and bake in a moderate oven (350°F, 180°C, Mark 4) for about 1 hour, or until loaf shrinks away slightly from sides of tin and is firm to the touch and lightly coloured on top. Leave in the tin for about 10 minutes before turning out on to a wire cooling rack. Slice when cold.

ORACABESSA

2 tablespoons crème de banane
1 tablespoon lemon juice
2 tablespoons dark rum
1 tablespoon crushed ice
½ banana, peeled and finely sliced
Lemonade
Maraschino cherries, to decorate

Put the liqueur, lemon juice, rum and ice into a cocktail shaker (a large screw-top jar can be used instead). Shake the ingredients together vigorously. Pour into a tall, chilled glass, place the sliced banana on top and add lemonade to fill. Decorate with maraschino cherries and serve.

Makes 1 large glass.

BANANA DAIQUIRI

4 tablespoons white rum
1 tablespoon crème de banane
1 tablespoon lime juice
½ banana, peeled and chopped
1 tablespoon crushed ice

Put all the ingredients into an electric blender and process until smooth and frothy. Serve in a tulip champagne glass.

Makes 1 glass.

BANANA WINE

Use black or spotted bananas for this sweet, spicy table wine.

3 pounds (1·4 kilos) bananas (with skins)
3½ pounds (1·6 kilos) granulated sugar
1 teaspoon ground cloves
1 teaspoon ground ginger
½ ounce (15 g) citric acid
1 Campden tablet
1 teaspoon Pectozyme
1½ pints (900 ml) strong tea
1 nutrient tablet
Sauterne yeast

Bring 6 pints (3.4 litres) water to boiling point in a large pan. Meanwhile prepare the bananas. Do not remove their skins, but slice them thinly and put into the prepared mashing vessel. Add the sugar, cloves, ginger and boiling water. Stir to dissolve the sugar. When the mixture is cool, add the citric acid, the Campden tablet and the Pectozyme. Cover the mashing vessel tightly and leave for 24 hours.

Uncover and quickly add the strong tea, followed by the nutrient tablet and activated yeast (see manufacturer's instructions for quantity and method of use). Re-cover the mashing vessel and leave in a warm place (65–75°F or 18–24°C) for 10 days. Once a day, quickly remove the cover and push down any fruit that is floating on the surface.

Strain the mixture through a fine sieve into a clean container, extracting as much liquid as possible. It will be a rather cloudy liquid. Siphon this into a prepared fermentation vessel, filling to within 1 inch (2·5 cm) of the cork. Leave to ferment in a warm place (65–75°F or 18–24°C). This will take approximately 5–6 weeks. Leave until there is a good layer of sediment at the bottom, then rack. Store for 6 months, before bottling. Keep for at least a year, before drinking – the longer the better.

See also page 205.

Makes about 7 pints (4 litres).

BLACKBERRY

Blackberries have flourished wild for centuries. Blackberry seeds have even been found in the remains of a Neolithic man dug up in Essex. Possibly because of this, commercial growers have been reluctant to cultivate large fields of blackberry canes, preferring to rely on wild ones. They are late to ripen compared with other soft fruits, starting in late summer.

When you go picking wild blackberries, take a pair of thick gloves to protect your fingers against the thorns, which can be vicious. Some cultivated varieties have had the thorns bred out of them and cultivated berries also tend to be larger, with fewer seeds.

Blackberries should be washed only if necessary. You can eat them raw with plenty of sugar and cream, or instead of cream, flavour them with fresh orange juice. Alternatively, add a handful of shiny fresh berries to a mixed fruit salad, or bake them in a pie or open tart. Mixed with apples or pears, which start coming into season at the same time, they make an excellent Eve's Pudding, topped with sponge and served with a custard sauce or cream. Or why not invent your own version of an English summer pudding, with blackberries and wedges of poached apple instead of the usual soft fruit, and call it autumn pudding? There is also a curious old English sweet called blackberry junket for which sweetened blackberry juice is allowed to stand in a warm atmosphere until it sets to the consistency of a light junket.

Above all, though, blackberries are for making preserves such as jams and jellies, either on their own or in conjunction with apples for their pectin. If you are making jam or jelly with blackberries only, use any standard raspberry recipe but be sure to include plenty of lemon juice for its setting properties.

Whole blackberries can be dry or sugar frozen; or the berries can be pureed and sweetened with caster sugar before freezing.

Medicinally, the valuable parts of the blackberry plant are the roots and leaves (infusions of which help cure dropsy and diarrhoea), although the berries contain some folic acid and Vitamins C and E.

REMEDIES

An infusion of leaves helps to relieve diarrhoea. Put torn or cut up blackberry leaves into a glass, ceramic or stainless steel container. Allow a cup of water to every tablespoon of leaves. Bring the water to the boil, pour it over the leaves, and leave to stand, covered, for 2½–3 hours. Strain. Drink up to a cup a day, a little at a time. (This infusion can also be added to bathwater to bring clearness and vitality to your skin.)

An infusion of the root has much the same properties as that of the leaf, and is also reputed to be good for dropsy. Allow a cup of water to each tablespoon of chopped root, and put in a stainless steel saucepan. Bring to a gentle boil, covered, and simmer for 1–3 hours. Strain and drink as above.

BREAKFAST CRUNCH

Ingredients in this recipe are measured in cups, but you can use any size container provided the proportions remain the same. The quantities below make enough for about 20 servings – which can be stored in an airtight container.

2 cups wheat bran
2 cups rolled oats
1¼ cups sesame seeds
1¼ cups sunflower seeds
1 cup wholewheat or granary flour
½ cup skimmed milk powder
¼ cup brown sugar
½ cup nut oil
Blackberries
Milk (optional)

Mix together the wheat bran, oats, sesame and sunflower seeds, flour, skimmed milk powder, sugar and nut oil and store. Add blackberries, and milk if liked, just before serving.

BLACKBERRY SOUP

This soup is good hot or cold.

1 pound (450 g) blackberries
1½ ounces (40 g) stale bread roll
1 short cinnamon stick
3–4 whole cloves
About 4 ounces (100–125 g) sugar
¼ pint (150 ml) thick cream
Cinnamon croûtons to serve (page 205)

Rinse blackberries and put them in a pan with the sliced bread roll and whole spices. Pour over about 1½ pints (900 ml) hot water and simmer until blackberries are very soft. Add a little more water if it evaporates too quickly. Rub contents of pan through a fine nylon sieve and discard seeds and spices. Sweeten soup to taste and stir in cream. Serve hot or lightly chilled, with a bowl of cinnamon croûtons.

Serves 6.

BLACKBERRY ORANGE MOUSSE

1 pound (450 g) blackberries
Juice and finely grated rind of 1
  orange
4 ounces (100–125 g) caster sugar
½ ounce (15 g) powdered gelatine
½ pint (300 ml) double cream

Put blackberries in a dish. Add orange juice and rind. Sprinkle with sugar, mix well and put aside for a couple of hours to allow sugar to draw out juices. At the same time, soften gelatine by sprinkling it over 3 tablespoons cold water in a cup.

When ready to proceed, rub blackberries and their juices through a fine nylon sieve and discard pips. Dissolve gelatine by standing cup in a bowl of very hot water and stirring until liquid is quite clear. Whisk cream until it stands in soft peaks. Whisk dissolved gelatine into cold blackberry purée, wait until mixture turns syrupy, then fold into whipped cream. Spoon into a serving bowl and chill lightly until softly set.

Serves 4.

BLACKBERRY CUSTARD TART

One 9 inch (22·5 cm) shortcrust pastry
  case, pre-baked (page 203)
1 pound (450 g) blackberries
4 ounces (100–125 g) soft pale brown
  sugar
2 egg yolks
4 teaspoons cornflour
½ pint (300 ml) single cream

Leave pre-baked pastry case to cool still in its tin (preferably one with a removable base).

Toss blackberries and sugar together lightly with a fork. Distribute fruit evenly in pastry case. Beat egg yolks and cornflour together until well blended. Lightly beat in cream. Pour through a sieve over entire surface of tart. Bake tart in a slow oven (325°F, 170°C, Mark 3) for about 30 minutes, or until filling has set. This is best eaten lukewarm or cold.

Serves 6.

BLACKBERRY AND APPLE JAM

By the time autumn comes round, there are not many fresh fruits left for the dedicated jam-maker. This is when blackberries come along, covering woody pathways and lanes.

4 pounds (1·8 kilos) blackberries
1½ pounds (700 g) apples
About 5 pounds (2·25 kilos) sugar

Pick over and if necessary rinse blackberries briefly. Put them in a pan with ¼ pint (150 ml) water and cook gently, stirring and mashing occasionally with a wooden spoon, until blackberries are very soft and pulpy. If you want to remove the blackberry seeds, rub cooked blackberries and their juices through a fine nylon sieve before mixing with the apples.

While blackberries are cooking, peel, core and thinly slice apples. Put them in a separate pan with ¼ pint (150 ml) water and simmer until apples have disintegrated to a pulp, mashing and stirring occasionally.

Combine pulped blackberries and apples, weigh them and pour into a preserving pan. Add the same weight of sugar as there is of mixed fruit. Stir over low heat until sugar has melted. Then raise heat and boil briskly until setting point is reached. Skim off any scum that has collected on the surface towards the end of cooking time.

Cool slightly, pot and cover.

See also page 198.

Fills about 8 jars.

BLACKBERRY WINE

6 pounds (2·7 kilos) blackberries
8 ounces (225 g) chopped raisins
1 Campden tablet
1 teaspoon Pectozyme
1 nutrient tablet
Burgundy yeast
2½ pounds (1·1 kilos) sugar

Remove the stalks and wash the berries thoroughly in a colander under running cold water. Place in the prepared mashing vessel. Add the chopped raisins, the Campden tablet, Pectozyme and 7 pints (4 litres) cold water. Cover the vessel and leave in a warm place (65°F or 18°C) for 24 hours.

Uncover and quickly add the nutrient tablet and the activated yeast (see manufacturer's instructions for quantity and method of use). Recover and leave in a warm place (65–75°F or 18–24°C) for 7 days.

Using a fine sieve strain off the liquid into a clean container. Put the remaining fruit pulp into a linen bag. Seal the bag and press the pulp to extract as much juice as possible. Add this to the strained liquid. Stir in the sugar. Siphon the mixture into a prepared fermentation vessel, filling to within 1 inch (2·5 cm) of the cork. Ferment under an air-lock in a warm, dark place (65–75°F or 18–24°C).

Rack, store for at least 6 months in a dark place, then siphon into dark glass bottles. Mature for 2 years.

See also page 205.

Makes about 7 pints (4 litres).

BLACKCURRANT

It may come as a surprise that, botanically speaking, blackcurrants are more closely related to gooseberries than to the red or white currants one usually associates with them. The history of blackcurrants is a curious mixture of failure and success. Although they are actively discouraged in parts of the United States (on the grounds that blackcurrant bushes are thought to carry a disease that affects pine trees), in the cooler, damper regions of Western Europe there will scarcely be a fruit garden that does not include a few blackcurrant bushes. The peak of their popularity was reached in the last century around Dijon in Burgundy, with the invention of *crème de cassis*, a rich, dark blackcurrant liqueur which is either drunk on its own, added for colour and flavour to fruit salads, creams and sweets, or mixed with chilled white wine, preferably a white Burgundy, to make a refreshing summer drink called *Kir*.

Unless they are very ripe indeed, raw blackcurrants are too astringently sour to eat as they are, but this rather bitter sourness disappears when the fruit is cooked, especially if a little spice is added. All kinds of pies can be made with blackcurrants on their own or mixed with other fruit, such as apples. There are also other puddings that are well worth trying.

Blackcurrants really come into their own for making preserves. Jams and jellies made with blackcurrants are pectin-rich and set without difficulty. In fact, plenty of water must be added, otherwise the jam will set rock-hard before the fruit has had a chance to soften. Blackcurrant juice is bursting with vitamins, especially Vitamin C, and often more suitable than orange juice for young children as it is more easily digested. If you make it yourself, you will be able to control the sweeteners and other additives that go into commercial preparations. Blackcurrants have long been noted for their beneficial effect on sore throats, coughs, feverish colds and tonsillitis.

Blackcurrants should be dry, bright and quite firm to the touch when they come off the bush. Even then, they should be used as quickly as possible. If a basket of ripe, juicy fruit is left overnight, chances are that mould will form and spread like wildfire so that by the following day the fruit will be unfit to use.

Keep fruit on the stalks until you are ready to use it. To remove the stalks, hold a bunch of fruit in one hand and use a fork to strip off the berries.

If at all possible, a surplus of blackcurrants should be stored in the freezer; remove the stalks and pack in freezer bags or rigid cartons. If space is limited, some of your surplus crop may first be puréed by putting ripe fruit through a vegetable *mouli* with a little water, or by blending briefly and rubbing through a sieve to trap seeds and pieces of skin. Then pack in small portions for the freezer. This purée is very strong and will probably need diluting with more water or fruit juice when you come to use it (orange juice goes very well with blackcurrants). Sweeten the purée with icing sugar and use it as a sauce for pudding or a topping for a plain or chocolate ice cream.

BLACKCURRANT JUICE

This is a marvellously pure, healthy drink – rich in Vitamin C and free of any additives – to have in the winter store cupboard. Children are particularly keen on it. For winter coughs and colds, it makes a soothing bedtime drink, diluted with hot water and sweetened with more honey, and in summer all it needs is iced water or soda water or lemonade and ice cubes, to make a refreshing thirst-quencher.

Rinse, drain and strip blackcurrants. Put them in a large pan, cover generously with water and bring slowly to boiling point. Simmer fruit until very soft, crushing and mashing it with a potato masher or a large fork. Alternatively, you can put the contents of the pan through the finest disc of a vegetable mill, but do not liquidize or blend it in any way which could crush the pips and make the juice bitter.

Strain the juice through fine muslin or nylon, squeezing it well to extract as much of the liquid as possible. Sweeten lightly to taste with honey, fruit sugar or plain white sugar.

Have ready individual soda bottles with screw-top caps, thoroughly clean and sterilized in the same way as jars (page 201). Funnel the juice into them, filling the bottles right to the top if the juice is hot, but leaving about 1 inch (2.5 cm) head space for it to expand if it is cold. Screw on caps, not too tightly.

Fit a trivet into the pan in which bottles are to be sterilized or, failing a suitable trivet, line the base with thick cardboard, a folded cloth or several thicknesses of newspaper. Fit bottles side by side in the pan and pour in hot water to come at least three-quarters of the way up sides of bottles. Bring to simmering point and boil gently for 20–25 minutes.

Allow pan to cool slightly. Then, protecting your hands with a cloth, lift out the bottles one at a time and screw the caps down as tightly as possible. When quite cold, store in a dark cupboard.

Note: Raspberries and black cherries make good juice, but use much less water to boil the fruit so that the flavour of the juice will not be too diluted.

BLACKCURRANT PIE

Use rough puff pastry for a blackcurrant (or any other currant) pie. To help avoid the base soaking up too much of the juices before the cornflour has had the opportunity to thicken them, it is a good idea to stand the pie on a baking sheet that was put in the oven to heat up when you switched on.

1¼ pounds (550 g) blackcurrants, washed, drained and stripped
8 ounces (225 g) soft brown sugar
3 tablespoons cornflour
Generous pinch of ground cloves
Pinch of salt
About 1 pound (450 g) pastry for 2-crust 9 inch (22·5 cm) pie (page 203 and above)
½ ounce (15 g) softened butter
Sifted caster or icing sugar and chilled single cream or ice cream, to serve

Place blackcurrants in a colander to allow any final moisture to drip away until you need them.

In a large bowl, mix the sugar, cornflour, cloves and salt together thoroughly. Add the blackcurrants and toss with a large-tined fork until well blended.

Roll the pastry out. Cut out a lid, leaving an overlapping edge all around of about ¾ inch (2 cm), and put aside until needed. With the remaining pastry line the dish, making a similar overlap around the edges. Fill the dish with the blackcurrant mixture and dot with small flakes of softened butter. Moisten the pastry-lined edges of the pie dish with water and fit the pastry lid in position, pressing the edges together with your fingertips and fluting them decoratively. With the tip of a knife, make gashes all over the top to allow steam to escape.

Place the pie dish on the pre-heated baking sheet (see above) and bake in a moderately hot oven (400°F, 200°C, Mark 6) for 45–50 minutes, or until the top of the pie is puffed, crisp and golden.

Cool the pie on a wire rack. Dust with sifted caster or icing sugar and serve lukewarm with a jug of chilled pouring cream or with ice cream.

Serves 6–8.

SPICED BLACKCURRANT PUDDING

A substantial winter pudding with a topping of blackcurrants from the freezer to remind you of summer. Other soft fruits may be used instead. Blueberries are especially good, or raspberries sweetened with sugar.

3 ounces (75 g) frozen blackcurrants, defrosted
1½ ounces (40 g) soft brown sugar
2–3 cloves
Butter or soft margarine

Pudding batter
4 ounces (100–125 g) plain flour
1 teaspoon baking powder
1 teaspoon ground mixed spice
Pinch of salt
2 eggs
4 ounces (100–125 g) softened butter or soft margarine
3 ounces (75 g) caster sugar
Finely grated rind of ½ large orange
2–3 tablespoons milk
2 ounces (50 g) dried currants

Mix the blackcurrants, sugar and cloves together. Spread them over the bottom of a well-buttered pudding basin, crushing lightly with a fork to make an even layer.

To prepare the batter, sift the flour, baking powder, mixed spice and salt together. Beat the eggs until light. Beat the butter or margarine and

POLISH BLACKCURRANT KISIEL

Polish cooks would thicken this simple sweet with potato flour, whereas we would probably find cornflour more easily available. As children, I remember we used to love it thickened with arrowroot for the unusual glutinous quality that it gave.

A simple family Kisiel is best accompanied by a light vanilla custard sauce, but for grander occasions you could scoop it into individual meringue nests and top each portion with pouring cream and a pinch of chopped nuts.

1½ pounds (700 g) fresh or frozen blackcurrants, stripped and rinsed
Sugar
4 tablespoons cornflour
Juice of 1 large orange

sugar together with the orange rind until fluffy. Beat the eggs and flour mixture alternately into the butter and sugar mixture, a few tablespoons at a time, adding a little milk if necessary to soften batter. Beat in the dried currants.

Spoon the batter over the fruit in the pudding basin. Level off the top and make a slight hollow in the middle with the back of the spoon. Cover the basin with foil or a double thickness of greaseproof paper, lightly buttered on the underside, and tie down with fine string. Lower the basin on to a trivet in a pan with boiling water to come halfway up the sides. Cover the pan tightly and steam the pudding gently for 1¼ hours, adding more boiling water if the water in the pan evaporates too quickly.

To serve, turn the pudding out on to a shallow dish and serve accompanied by a jug of lightly sweetened custard sauce or cream.

Serves 4–6.

Note: The pudding may also be cooked in a pressure cooker. Steam in 1¼ pints (700 ml) boiling water for 15 minutes without the pressure gauge, then pressure-cook at low (5 pounds) pressure for a further 25 minutes.

Stew currants, 4½ ounces (130 g) sugar and ¾ pint (400 ml) water together for 10–15 minutes until juices run. Put half of the currants and their juices through an electric blender and return to the pan with the fruit.

Mix cornflour, 4½ tablespoons sugar and 3–4 tablespoons water to a smooth paste. Bring the blackcurrants and their juices to simmering point. Stir in the cornflour mixture; bring to the boil and simmer, stirring, for 3–4 minutes, until the mixture has thickened and lost its opaqueness. Cool slightly and add more sugar if necessary. Blend in the orange juice.

Pour into a decorative dish, cool and serve chilled.

Serves 6–8.

BLACKCURRANT YOGHOURT ICE CREAM

8 ounces (225 g) fresh or frozen
   blackcurrants
Juice of 1 large orange
Finely grated rind of ½ large
   orange
4 ounces (100–125 g) brown sugar
¼ pint (150 ml) double cream
¼ pint (150 ml) natural yoghourt

Strip and rinse fresh blackcurrants. Put fresh or frozen blackcurrants in a pan with 2–3 tablespoons water and cook gently for 10 minutes. Rub fruit through a fine nylon sieve. Add orange juice and sugar, and stir until dissolved.

In a large bowl, beat cream until very thick. Add yoghourt and beat again until mixture is well blended and thick enough to hold impression of the beaters. Gently and thoroughly fold in blackcurrant purée.

Pour mixture into ice cube trays or a plastic box with a lid. Cover with foil or the lid and freeze until ice cream is solid round the sides but still very soft and runny in the middle. Scrape it all out into a bowl and beat until uniformly smooth and creamy again. Then pour the ice cream back into freezing container(s), cover and freeze until firm.

Place in main compartment of refrigerator an hour before serving.

Serves 4–6.

WITCHES' FOAM

A lovely, easy, Scottish sweet; the jam must be of the finest quality.

4 egg whites
4 tablespoons syrupy blackcurrant
   jam (below right)
Sweet wafer biscuits or almond tuiles,
   to serve

Combine egg whites and blackcurrant jam in a bowl. Whisk vigorously until meringue stands in firm peaks. Spoon into individual glass dishes and serve immediately with wafers or tuiles.

Serves 4.

BLACKCURRANT JAM I

A thick, rich jam to serve with bread or scones and butter at tea time. The butter in the jam not only clears away any remaining scum but also keeps the fruit itself soft, and the cloves give it a light touch of unusual flavour.

2½ pounds (1·1 kilos) blackcurrants
3 or 4 cloves
5 pounds (2·2 kilos) sugar
Knob of butter

Rinse and strip the blackcurrants, and put them in a preserving pan with the cloves and 2½ pints (1·4 litres) water. Bring to boiling point and boil for 20 minutes.

Add the sugar and stir over moderate heat until it has dissolved. Then raise heat and boil for a further 20 minutes, or until setting point is reached, skimming scum from the surface as necessary. Turn off the heat and stir in the butter.

Cool slightly, pot and cover.
See also page 198.

Fills about 7 jars.

BLACKCURRANT JAM II

A much lighter, syrupy preserve, delicious spooned over vanilla ice cream or a hot sponge pudding. Very ripe blackcurrants and fruit which has been picked after a rainy spell will take several more minutes of hard boiling to reach setting point. Alternatively, reduce water to ¾ pint (450 ml) per pound (450 g) of fruit.

Per pound (450 g) of blackcurrants:
   14 ounces (400 g) sugar
   1 pint (600 ml) water

Rinse and strip the blackcurrants, and place them in a preserving pan with the sugar and water. Heat very gently until sugar has dissolved and bring to boiling point. Then raise heat and boil *hard* for 7 minutes, or until setting point is reached, skimming off scum as necessary.

Cool slightly. Pot and cover.
See also page 198.

BLACKCURRANT JELLY

This is made in the same way as Redcurrant Jelly, and may be used in similar fashion.

Blackcurrant juice (page 36)
Sugar

Measure the juice and for each pint (575 ml) allow 1 pound (450 g) sugar. In a clean preserving pan combine the two. Heat gently until sugar has dissolved. Then raise heat and boil until setting point is reached, skimming surface clear of scum with a large spoon.

Cool slightly, pot and cover.

See also page 199.

CRÈME DE CASSIS Blackcurrant Liqueur

For this a large glass flagon with a tight-fitting stopper, kept specially for this purpose, is brought out in our kitchen, but any large, wide-necked glass bottles or jars will do just as well. The brandy need not be of special quality—use the cheapest your off-licence can offer. The blackcurrants should be plump and juicy. If they come from the garden, pick a handful of fresh young leaves at the same time and steep them with the fruit. They add a surprising amount of flavour.

Once a liqueur has matured, it has a hundred uses – in its own right, as a flavouring for ice creams, sorbets and puddings of all kinds, but above all for making the refreshing French summer drink called *Kir*. For this a splash of *cassis* is added to a glass of chilled dry white wine, enough to flavour it and turn it pink.

1¼–1½ pounds (575–700 g) ripe
   blackcurrants
1 pound (450 g) sugar
One 2 inch (5 cm) cinnamon stick
2–3 cloves
Blackcurrant leaves (optional)
1 bottle brandy (see above)

Pick over the blackcurrants. Rinse them and shake them dry in a colander. Crush the blackcurrants and sugar together with a fork until juices run, and pack them into a large glass flagon or jar. Add the spices. (If fresh blackcurrant leaves are available, take about half-a-dozen, rinse them, bruise them lightly by crushing them in your hand and add them to the jar.) Top up with brandy. Close tightly.

Leave to mature for a month or so on a sunny windowsill or some similar warm place, giving the flagon a good shake from time to time. After a month, strain the liqueur through a sieve lined with a double thickness of muslin, squeezing the muslin to extract as much liquid as possible.

Funnel the *cassis* into bottles (with tight stoppers) or a large decanter. The liqueur may now be drunk but it will keep indefinitely.

Note: Left-over brandy-steeped fruit can be added to fruit pies, spooned over ice cream or made into a sauce for a steamed pudding.

SOLBAERROM Danish Blackcurrant Rum

A sweet, home-made liqueur, which improves considerably with age.

2 pounds (900 g) blackcurrants
6 blanched almonds
2 pints (1·1 litres) white rum
1½ pounds (700 g) demerara sugar

Wash the fruit, removing any damaged berries. Crush the fruit and blanched almonds and place in a large, wide-neck, screw-top jar (a Kilner jar is ideal). The jar must be clean and sterilized (see instructions for wine-making, page 205). Pour the rum onto the fruit and nuts. Seal the jar and leave in a cool place for a month, stirring daily.

Using a fine sieve, strain off the liquid into a clean container. Put the fruit and nuts into a linen bag. Seal the bag tightly and squeeze out as much juice as possible. Add the juice to the liquid in the container. Stir in the sugar, until dissolved. Bottle the liqueur in clean, sterilized bottles. Cork tightly and leave to mature for at least 6 months, preferably a year.

Makes about 2 pints (1·1 litres).

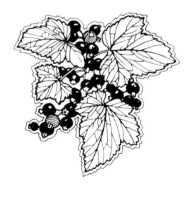

BLUEBERRY

Blueberries, blaeberries, bilberries – not forgetting huckleberries and whortleberries – are all varieties, either cultivated or wild, of the same family of berries, *Vaccinium*.

Throughout Northern Europe, family expeditions into the woods in late summer in search of wild bilberries are almost as popular as mushrooming parties. Growing locations are jealously guarded and the berries are carried home in triumph, to be eaten with sugar and cream, and turned into compotes and other favourites. The berries leave purple stains on the teeth, around the mouth and on the fingers, so it is best to protect yourself by wearing rubber gloves when you pick them.

When the Pilgrim Fathers arrived in America, they found that the Indians were already gathering blueberries in the wild and using them in a variety of ways, both fresh and dried, sweet and savoury. By the middle of the nineteenth century, blueberries were under large-scale cultivation in the woody swamplands of the northern states. Today blueberries are grown commercially in other parts of the world.

Cultivated blueberries are much larger than wild ones, the size of large, mature blackcurrants. When ripe, they are a deep blue-black colour with a noticeable, powdery white 'bloom'. If the berries are being gathered in batches, they can safely be stored in the refrigerator for a week or so until you have enough, provided they are not wet and sticky with juice, or shrivelled. For longer-term storage, the freezer is the answer. Either freeze the berries in the punnets in which they were bought, or spread them out in a single layer on a tray and freeze until rock-hard before storing in cartons or plastic bags. When they are thawed out, the berries will be perfect, down to the bloom and ready for use.

Blueberries can be used in all the ways suitable for blackcurrants, from creams to pies. Or mix a cupful of blueberries into the apples you have sliced up for a pie or crumble. American recipes have a delightful way of adding them to all sorts of scone and cake mixtures, an unusual alternative to the dried currants or raisins one might expect (but before adding the berries, remember to toss them with a little of the flour weighed out for the recipe so that they do not sink to the bottom).

Blueberries may also be turned most successfuly into a liqueur resembling the famous blackcurrant *crème de cassis*, and can be made into decoctions which are good for coughs and head colds.

REMEDIES

This decoction of dried blueberries is good for coughs and head colds.

Use 1 ounce (25 g) of dried berries to 1 pint (550 ml) of water. Put the berries and water into an enamelled saucepan, bring to the boil and simmer, covered, for 10–15 minutes. Strain into a glass or ceramic container and leave to cool. Drink in small quantities (a mouthful or so at a time) up to 2 or 3 cups a day.

A more palatable alternative is Culpeper's recommendation: 'the juice of the berries made into a syrup, or the pulp made into a conserve with sugar'.

Blueberries increase sugar tolerance; the following recipe, which combines them with French beans, is said to lower the blood sugar.

Mix dried pods of French beans (haricots verts) with twice their quantity of dried blueberry leaves. Pour boiling water over in the proportion of 1 pint (550 ml) water to 2 tablespoons of the mixture. Steep for about 20 minutes, strain, and leave to cool. Drink half a cup, three times a day, with the permission of your doctor.

BLUEBERRY SOUP

This refreshing soup is served hot or cold in Scandinavian countries as a dessert. However, with less sugar and a swirl of natural yoghourt on each portion, it makes a delicious summer starter. For a smoother textured soup purée the berries before adding the thickening.

1½ pounds (700 g) fresh blueberries
Juice of ½ lemon
One 2 inch (5 cm) cinnamon stick
Pinch of salt
4 ounces (100–125 g) sugar
4 tablespoons cornflour or arrowroot
¼ pint (150 ml) whipping cream
Thin lemon slices to decorate (if
* serving hot)*

Rinse and drain the blueberries and pick them over to remove any little stems. Put them in a large pan with 3 pints (1.75 litres) water, lemon juice, cinnamon, salt and sugar and bring to the boil. Lower the heat and simmer the berries for about 5 minutes until the berries are just soft.

Remove the cinnamon stick and mix the cornflour or arrowroot to a smooth paste with a cupful of cold water. Stir this into the soup in the pan, and continue stirring until the soup thickens slightly.

Remove the pan from the heat and leave to cool a little while you whip the cream. Pour into individual bowls for serving and decorate with whipped cream.

If serving the soup hot, thin lemon slices make a good extra garnish.

Serves 6.

STEAMED BLUEBERRY PUDDING

This light steamed pudding makes the most of the complementary flavours of lemon and blueberry. Be sure to serve it hot with custard, cream, or lightly soured cream.

As a variation, try making it with wholemeal flour and wholemeal breadcrumbs.

6 ounces (175 g) blueberries
4 ounces (100–125 g) plain flour
2 teaspoons baking powder
Pinch of salt
8 ounces (225 g) fresh white
*   breadcrumbs*
4 ounces (100–125 g) butter or
*   margarine*
4 ounces (100–125 g) sugar
2 eggs
Finely grated rind and juice of 1 lemon
About ¼ pint (150 ml) milk

Pick over the berries, if necessary, to remove any stems, then rinse well and pat dry. Toss in a bag with a little of the flour until the berries are well coated, then set aside. Sift together the rest of the flour with the baking powder and salt, then add the breadcrumbs and mix well. Stir in the blueberries.

In a separate bowl, beat together the butter or margarine and sugar until light and fluffy, then beat the eggs and add them a little at a time, beating well between each addition. Stir in the lemon rind and juice.

Gradually add the flour mixture to the bowl, adding just enough milk to give a soft, dropping consistency. Turn it into a greased 2 pint (1 litre) capacity pudding basin. Cover the top with a layer of well-greased foil or greaseproof paper, pleating it in the centre to allow the pudding to rise. Tie securely with string and put in a steamer, or in a large pan with boiling water halfway up the sides, and steam or boil the pudding for 1–1½ hours. Top up with boiling water as necessary during cooking.

When cooked, turn the pudding out and serve.

Serves 6.

BLUEBERRY CUSTARD FLAN

Cultivated blueberries are usually mild and sweet, so they go well with a rich egg custard.

One 9 inch (22.5 cm) shortcrust pastry
*   case, pre-baked (page 203)*
1½ pounds (700 g) blueberries
3–4 ounces (75–100 g) sugar
3 tablespoons lemon juice
¼ pint (150 ml) rich custard, cooled
*   (page 205)*
Ground allspice
*   or cinnamon*

Rinse the blueberries and pick them over to remove any stalks. Pat dry and mix the berries into the sugar.

Layer the sugared berries in the pastry case and sprinkle with lemon juice. Bake in a moderate oven (375°F, 190°C, Mark 5) for about 10 minutes, until the blueberries are soft but not mushy. Cool.

Pour the custard over the lightly cooked blueberries in the flan. Chill well before serving and sprinkle the top of the flan with a little ground allspice or cinnamon.

Serves 6.

AMERICAN BLUEBERRY PIE

About 1 pound (450 g) rich shortcrust
*   pastry for a deep, 2-crust, 9 inch*
*   (22.5 cm) pie (page 203)*
1¼–1½ pounds (575–700 g)
*   blueberries*
8 ounces (225 g) caster sugar
4 tablespoons flour
Juice of ½ large lemon
½ teaspoon finely grated
*   lemon rind*
Lightly whipped cream, to serve
2 tablespoons caster sugar

Prepare the pastry and cut in half. Roll each piece into a ball, wrap in foil or plastic wrap and chill in the refrigerator for 30 minutes.

Roll one ball of pastry out to make a pastry lid for a deep, round pie dish about 9 inches (22·5 cm) in diameter, giving it a slight overhang. Put aside. Roll out the other ball of pastry more thinly and use it to line the pie dish

with a slight overhang around sides.

In a bowl, combine blueberries with sugar, flour, lemon juice and grated lemon rind, and toss lightly with a fork until well mixed. Pile up in lined pie dish. Fit pastry lid in place and press around sides to seal them.

Trim off excess pastry and decorate edges by crimping or fluting them. Cut a few holes or slits in the top to allow steam to escape.

Bake pie in a hot oven (450°F, 230°C, Mark 8) for 10 minutes. Then turn heat down (to 350°F, 180°C, Mark 4) and continue to bake for 35–40 minutes longer, or until pastry crust is crisp and well coloured.

Serve warm, dusted with 2 tablespoons caster sugar and accompanied by a bowl of unsweetened, lightly whipped cream.

Serves 8.

BLUEBERRY CINNAMON TOASTS

A quick-to-make and quite delicious family dessert.

2 slices white bread
½ ounce (15 g) butter
¼ teaspoon ground cinnamon
2 tablespoons sugar
2 ounces (50 g) fresh or frozen
*   blueberries, thawed*
2–3 tablespoons double cream

Lightly toast the bread on both sides and butter while still hot. Mix the cinnamon with half the sugar and sprinkle over both toast slices. Put one slice into the bottom of an individual serving dish and cut the other one diagonally into quarters.

Crush half the blueberries with the rest of the sugar and layer over the toast in the dish. Sprinkle the whole berries on top, then arrange the triangles of cinnamon toast around the sides.

Pour over the cream and serve immediately.

Serves 1.

BLUEBERRY CREAM

This delicious old American recipe is suitable for wild or cultivated blueberries.

5–6 ounces (150–175 g) blueberries
½ pint (300 ml) whipping cream
Sugar

Whip the cream lightly and add sugar to taste. Fold the blueberries into the cream, and serve with more sugar for people to help themselves.

Serves 2.

BLUEBERRY LOAF CAKE

Serve this for tea, or with your morning coffee – or try it as one of the dishes in a selection for brunch.

4 ounces (100–125 g) fresh or frozen
    blueberries
4 ounces (100–125 g) butter
6 ounces (175 g) soft brown sugar
2 eggs
½ teaspoon vanilla essence
8 ounces (225 g) plain flour
2 teaspoons baking powder
Pinch of salt
About ⅓ pint (200 ml) milk

Pick over fresh berries to remove any stems, then rinse and pat dry. Frozen berries do not need to be thawed.

Soften the butter, add the sugar and beat until the mixture is soft and fluffy. Beat the eggs and gradually add them to the mixture, beating well between each addition. Continue to beat until the mixture is well combined – about 2 minutes by hand but only seconds if using a food processor. Add the vanilla essence.

Toss the blueberries in a little of the flour and set aside. Sift the rest of the flour into a basin with the baking powder and salt. Stir into the egg mixture alternately with the milk until the batter is smooth. Lastly, stir in the blueberries.

Lightly grease a loaf tin measuring about 9 × 5 × 3 inches (23 × 13 × 75 cm) and spoon the batter into the tin. Bake in a moderate oven (350°F, 180°C, Mark 4) for about an hour, or until a skewer inserted into the centre comes out clean.

Turn the loaf out on to a wire rack and leave to cool.

BLUEBERRY DROP SCONES

6 ounces (175 g) blueberries
6 ounces (175 g) plain flour
1 tablespoon caster sugar
½ teaspoon baking powder
½ teaspoon bicarbonate of soda
½ teaspoon cream of tartar
¼ teaspoon salt
About ½ pint (300 ml) milk
1 egg
1 ounce (25 g) butter, melted and
    cooled
1 teaspoon vanilla essence
Oil or fat, for frying pan
Warmed golden syrup and butter, to
    serve

Rinse blueberries in a colander and shake off excess moisture.

Prepare drop scone batter. Sift the next 6 ingredients together and put them in an electric blender or food processor. Pour in about half the milk and break in the egg. Switch on and blend until smooth. Gradually blend in enough of remaining milk to make a creamy batter that is thick enough to drop heavily from a spoon. Finally, blend in melted butter and vanilla essence.

In a bowl, pour batter over blueberries and mix lightly but thoroughly.

Heat a heavy griddle or frying pan and brush or rub with a wad of paper dipped in oil or smeared with margarine or white vegetable fat (not butter, which might burn).

Drop tablespoonfuls of blueberry batter on to hot pan, spacing them well apart so they can spread slightly. Bake over low heat until surface of scones is covered in bubbles and they are golden brown on the underside. Then loosen each scone with a broad spatula or fish slice, flip it over and bake until well risen and golden brown on the other side.

Keep scones warm in a folded napkin until they are all ready. Serve warm with plenty of butter and golden syrup.

Serves 4.

BLUEBERRY BUCKLE

American country cooking contains a variety of fruit dishes with delightful names such as grunts and humps and buckles. A buckle is traditionally made with blueberries, but when blueberries are scarce, try making one with another soft berry fruit such as blackcurrants or raspberries. A buckle makes a lovely change for a late Sunday breakfast with plenty of cream and a pot of coffee.

8 ounces (225 g) blueberries or other
    soft fruit
8 ounces (225 g) plain flour
2½ teaspoons baking powder
¼ teaspoon salt
4 ounces (100–125 g) white vegetable
    fat
6 ounces (175 g) caster sugar
1 egg, well beaten
About ⅓ pint (200 ml) milk

Cinnamon topping
2 ounces (50 g) plain flour
½ teaspoon ground cinnamon
4 ounces (100–125 g) sugar
2 ounces (50 g) butter

Rinse blueberries and shake them dry in a large sieve or colander. Sift flour, baking powder and salt together. Beat vegetable fat until creamy. Gradually add sugar and continue to beat until fluffy. Beat in egg, a tablespoon at a time. Add sifted flour alternately with milk to make a smooth, soft batter, but not too soft, otherwise topping will sink without trace. Pour batter into a greased, 9 inch (22·5 cm) square, deep baking tin.

Prepare topping. Sift flour and cinnamon into a bowl. Stir in sugar. Rub in butter to make a crumbly mixture. If you have a food processor, this can be done in seconds. Simply load all the ingredients into the bowl and blend until thoroughly mixed and crumbly.

Scatter blueberries evenly over batter and crumble topping over the surface.

Bake buckle in a moderate oven (350°F, 180°C, Mark 4) for 45–50 minutes, until it is well risen, a rich golden colour on top and firm to the touch.

Serve fresh and warm from the oven, with a jug of chilled cream.

Serves 6.

BLAEBERRY JAM

A traditional Scottish jam. Blueberries are called blaeberries in Scotland.

7 pounds (3·2 kilos) blaeberries
   (blueberries or bilberries)
1 pound (450 g) thin red rhubarb
   stalks
5 pounds (2·25 kilos) sugar
Knob of butter or margarine
   (optional)

Pick over the blaeberries, removing any stems or other debris, and if necessary rinse briefly · with cold water. Shake dry in a large sieve or colander. (It will probably be easiest to deal with the berries a batch at a time, draining them thoroughly and tipping them out into a wide, shallow dish or a large bowl).

Wipe rhubarb stalks clean. Trim them and cut into 1 inch (2·5 cm) lengths.

Put rhubarb in a preserving pan. Add a few tablespoons of cold water and the sugar, and stir over low heat until sugar has melted. Then raise heat, bring to boiling point and boil briskly for 10 minutes, stirring frequently.

Add blaeberries and continue to boil until setting point is reached, stirring and skimming off scum as it forms on the surface. Remove pan from heat and if liked, stir in a knob of butter or margarine to disperse any remaining scum.

Cool slightly. Pot and cover.
See also page 198.

Fills about 8 jars.

BLUEBERRY CHEESE

Fruit cheeses are sweetened fruit purées, cooked to remove the moisture content. When cool, they set solid. Slice or cut into fingers, but never spread.

2 pounds (900 g) blueberries
1½ pints (900 ml) water
Juice of 1 lemon
2 pounds (900 g) sugar

Wash the fruit in a colander under running, cold water. Remove any stalks and damaged berries, and put the fruit in a thick saucepan. Cover with water, bring to the boil quickly, lower the heat and simmer gently until the fruit is soft. Using a fine sieve, strain the contents of the pan. Discard the liquid.

Return the fruit pulp to the pan, add the lemon juice and simmer over a very low heat, until no liquid is noticeable. Remove from the heat.

Warm the sugar in another saucepan. Gradually add it to the fruit purée, stirring constantly to dissolve. Return the pan to the heat. Raise the heat slightly. Stirring constantly, continue to cook until the mixture is thick enough for a spoon to leave an impression when pressed into it. Pot and cover (page 200).

To use, turn out of the jar whole and slice. Serve with game, poultry or even bread and cheese.

BLUEBERRY LIQUEUR

This liqueur closely resembles *crème de cassis*.

The brandied fruit that remains should never be thrown away. It's delicious, and can be added to the fruit filling for mince pies, spooned over ice cream, or can be diluted, then thickened with a little cornflour, to serve as a sauce for a steamed pudding or fruit pie.

1 pound (450 g) blueberries
8 ounces (225 g) sugar
One 2 inch (5 cm) cinnamon stick
2–3 cloves, or small piece dried
   ginger root, bruised
Brandy

Crush the blueberries roughly with a fork, and mix in the sugar. Pack into a glass flagon (any bottle or jar with a wide neck will do), with the cinnamon and cloves or ginger. Fill the flagon with brandy and stopper it tightly.

Leave to mature on a sunny windowsill for at least a month, shaking frequently. After a month, strain the liqueur through a sieve lined with a double thickness of muslin, squeezing the muslin to extract as much liquid as possible. Funnel the liqueur into bottles (with tight stoppers) or a large decanter. The liqueur can be drunk straightaway or can be kept indefinitely.

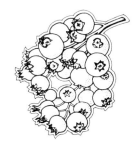

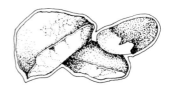

BRAZIL NUT

Brazil nuts are in fact edible seeds. The tree on which they grow is – unsurprisingly – a native of Brazil, but is also found in Venezuela, Chile and parts of Africa, if not on the same scale. Almost the entire Brazilian production is gathered from trees in the forests of the Amazon valley.

The broad-leaved evergreen trees grow to a great height. The fruits – each about the size of a man's head and weighing between 2 and 4 pounds (900 g and 1·8 kilos) – are produced on the upper branches, and the weight of the nuts causes them to fall as they ripen. Between twelve and twenty-two triangular nuts are tightly packed in each kernel, clustered like the segments of an orange. Their shells are extremely hard, and difficult to open without cracking the white kernel. It is often simpler and more economical to buy Brazils ready shelled – one pound (450 g) of nuts in the shell will provide about 7 ounces (200 g) of kernels. When buying in the shell, avoid nuts that rattle; this indicates age, and the nut will probably have shrunk and become dry, sharp and virtually uneatable.

The best season for the nuts is between November and February, which is why they are traditionally eaten at Christmas.

Brazils are delicious with poultry, add texture to salads, and can be dipped in rich plain chocolate to make chocolate Brazils. Like other nuts they are a good source of protein in vegetarian diets.

The Brazil has one of the highest fat contents of any nut – 66 per cent – and is 14 per cent protein. It is also a valuable source of several nutrients including calcium, iron and Vitamin B.

WATERCRESS, BRAZIL NUT AND ORANGE SALAD

This light, tangy salad is a good accompaniment to fish or poultry.

2 bunches watercress
2 large oranges
4 ounces (50 g) shelled
   Brazil nuts

Dressing
1 tablespoon wine vinegar
1 tablespoon lemon juice
6 tablespoons olive oil
1 tablespoon yoghourt
1 garlic clove, finely chopped
Pinch of ground cinnamon
Salt and freshly ground black pepper

Soak the watercress in a bowl of cold water for 1 hour, then wash thoroughly in a colander under cold, running water. Trim off any unwanted parts. Dry thoroughly in kitchen paper or in a salad spinner and place in a large serving bowl.

Peel the oranges. Make sure there are no traces of white pith left. Cut into thin slices and add to the serving bowl. Slice the nuts in half lengthwise. This is easier if you immerse them first in boiling water for a few minutes.

Add to the serving bowl, and leave in a cool place.

Put all the ingredients for the dressing into a small screw-top jar. Replace the lid tightly and shake vigorously. Taste, and adjust the seasoning if necessary. Leave dressing in the jar in a cool place. Just before serving, shake the dressing to mix thoroughly and pour it over the salad. Toss, and serve.

Serves 4.

BRAZIL NUT BAKE

Oil or butter
7 ounces (200 g) fine breadcrumbs
8 ounces (225 g) Brazil nuts, shelled
   and finely chopped
6 large tomatoes, peeled and coarsely
   chopped
3 tablespoons soya flour
3 tablespoons rolled oats
3 fluid ounces (75 ml) tomato juice
1 teaspoon dried basil
1 teaspoon dried thyme
Salt and freshly ground black pepper

Grease a 1 pound (450 g) loaf tin liberally with oil or butter. Coat the inside of the tin with 2 ounces (50 g) of the breadcrumbs, pressing them down very firmly.

Put the chopped nuts into a large bowl. Add the tomatoes, the remaining breadcrumbs, soya flour and oats. Mix well together with a wooden spoon. Add the tomato juice, herbs, and salt and pepper to taste. Blend in thoroughly with a wooden spoon. Turn the mixture into the prepared tin. Press well down and bake in a moderate oven (375°F, 190°C, Mark 5) for 50 minutes, until firm to touch.

Allow to cool slightly before turning out onto a warm plate.

Slice and serve hot or cold, with a spicy tomato sauce (home made, if possible).

Serves 4–6.

DUCK WITH BRAZIL NUTS AND BANANAS IN ORANGE SAUCE

1 large, oven-ready duck, 5–6 pounds
  (2·3–2·7 kilos)
2–2½ pints (1·1–1·4 litres) fresh
  orange juice
2 teaspoons finely grated orange
  rind
Bouquet garni (2 sprigs parsley, 1
  sprig thyme, 1 bay leaf)
Salt and freshly ground black pepper
3–4 firm bananas
6–8 tablespoons flaked Brazil nuts
  (see method)
4 tablespoons orange liqueur or
  brandy (optional)
1 tablespoon cornflour

Wash and dry duck both inside and out. In a flameproof casserole into which duck will fit comfortably, bring about 1½ pints (900 ml) orange juice to boiling point with the grated orange rind, bouquet garni, a generous pinch of salt and a grinding of pepper. Lower duck into simmering juice and cook gently with the lid half-on for 1 hour, turning duck several times.

Drain orange stock into a bowl. Place well-drained duck on a rack in a roasting tin. Sprinkle bird with more salt and pepper, and place in a hot oven (450°F, 230°C, Mark 8) for 30 minutes to colour and crisp its skin.

While duck is roasting, skim every scrap of fat from bowl of orange stock. Measure out a generous pint (600 ml) of stock through a sieve and put it aside. Peel bananas and cut them into 2 inch (5 cm) chunks. Flake Brazil nuts by whittling them down individually with a small, sharp knife. (Twelve large nuts should be enough.)

Pour another ¾ pint (400 ml) fresh orange juice into roasting tin, scraping up any crusty bits from bottom and sides of tin.

Add bananas, rolling them over so they are thoroughly coated, and stir in orange liqueur or brandy, if used. Baste duck thoroughly. Reduce oven to moderate (350°F, 180°C, Mark 4) and continue to roast duck for 30 minutes longer, or until it is quite tender, basting frequently.

Transfer duck and bananas to a heated serving platter, and keep hot. Skim any fat from pan juices. Pour in all but 3 or 4 tablespoons reserved orange stock and bring to boiling point, stirring and scraping bottom and sides of roasting tin clean with a wooden spoon. Pour contents of tin into a saucepan.

Blend remains of reserved orange stock smoothly with cornflour. Stir into saucepan and simmer, stirring, until sauce has thickened. Stir in flaked Brazil nuts, correct seasoning if necessary and simmer, stirring occasionally, for a few minutes longer.

Spoon some sauce over duck and serve remainder in a separate, heated sauce boat.

Serves 4.

NUTTY BUTTER BISCUITS

Butter
8 ounces (225 g) shelled Brazil nuts
3 tablespoons caster sugar or soft
  pale brown sugar
4 ounces (100–125 g) plain flour
Pinch of salt
1 teaspoon vanilla essence
Sifted icing sugar, to decorate

Start by greasing 2 or 3 large baking sheets lightly with butter. Chop nuts finely by hand or blend them coarsely in an electric blender or food processor. Add sugar, flour and salt, and mix thoroughly.

Cream 5 ounces (150 g) butter until pale and fluffy, and beat in vanilla essence. Stir in nut mixture with a wooden spoon, working ingredients until thoroughly blended.

Between the palms of your hands, shape paste into balls the size of a marble. Arrange them on prepared baking sheets. Bake in a moderate oven (375°F, 190°C, Mark 5) for 10 minutes, or until only lightly coloured.

Dredge a sheet of greaseproof paper or a large, flat plate with sifted icing sugar.

Roll hot biscuits in icing sugar until coated on all sides and cool on a wire rack.

CHOCOLATE BRAZILS

1 pound (450 g) dipping (couverture)
  chocolate
1 pound (450 g) Brazil nuts, shelled

Put the nuts on a baking tray and roast in a slow oven (325°F, 170°C, Mark 3), until the skins become flaky and parched. Remove from the oven, peel off the skins, wash the nuts and dry on kitchen paper. Put 1 inch (2·5 cm) of water into a thick saucepan and bring to the boil. Remove from the heat. Break the chocolate into small pieces and place these in a bowl that will sit securely over the hot water in the pan, without the water touching the bottom of the bowl. Put the bowl of chocolate over the steaming water, and melt. Use a sugar thermometer to check the temperature of the chocolate. It should never exceed 120°F (49°C). Cover the bowl to keep the heat in. Lift the lid off the bowl at intervals and stir the chocolate with a wooden spoon. When the chocolate has melted completely, remove the lid. Stir until the consistency is creamy and smooth.

Place the sugar thermometer in the chocolate and leave until the temperature has fallen to 110°F (43°C). At this temperature the chocolate should be of the right consistency for coating. To check this, pick up a small amount between the thumb and forefinger. The chocolate should set almost immediately. If it remains liquid, cool and test again.

Place the nuts on a tray by the side of the bowl of chocolate. Line another tray, placed on the other side of the bowl, with waxed paper. Drop one nut at a time into the melted chocolate. Use a fork to submerge and turn the nut, so that it is completely covered. Lift out on a fork, tapping the fork on the side of the bowl to remove excess chocolate. Hold the fork over the tray lined with waxed paper and angle the fork so that the chocolate Brazil nut slides off. Make sure the chocolate nuts are well spaced on the tray. Leave for about an hour, until the chocolate is completely hard, before eating.

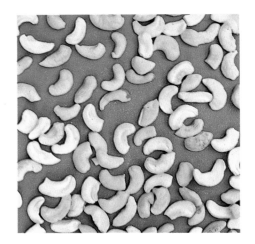

CASHEW NUT

The cashew nut is the fruit of the cashew, cadju or acaju tree, and a relation of the mango. Early explorers in South America brought it back with them and were responsible for its arrival in Africa and Asia. Today it is extensively cultivated in India and East Africa – Mozambique and Tanzania are big exporters, especially to the United States.

One of nature's stranger growths, it consists of a large fleshy apple below which hangs the true fruit, a kidney-shaped, olive-coloured single nut. The kernel, the part we eat, is encased in a dark rind containing an extremely acrid juice, and a smooth, grey, tough outer layer.

An edible oil produced from the cashew is said to equal olive oil for cooking.

In the tropics cashews are eaten raw, or roasted and added to sweet and sour vegetable dishes. Cashews are familiar in Indian and Chinese restaurant dishes in the West and are available in most vegetarian food shops.

At home cashews are easily blanched for cooking, or can be roasted and lightly salted and stored in an airtight tin or jar in a cool place.

They are an unusual addition to casseroles and fish dishes, and can also be used to make a delicious butter.

Cashews are rich in protein, Vitamin B and minerals, especially magnesium, with a high proportion of unsaturated fatty acid and almost no cholesterol. They contain an extremely caustic oil, cardol, which is driven off in roasting. It has been successfully applied to corns and warts, as well as to ringworms.

The cashew apple has a pleasant acid taste, and is used in the West Indies and Brazil to make an alcoholic beverage sometimes known as *kaju*. The Brazilians also use it for making vinegar and jam.

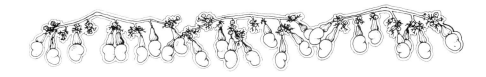

NUT AND SEED DRINK

Quantities for the main ingredients in this recipe are measured in cups. The size of the containers can vary, provided ratios remain the same and the amounts of honey and soya milk powder are increased or decreased in proportion.

1/4 cup sunflower seed kernels
3/4 cup cashew nuts
3 dessertspoons honey
3/4 teaspoon soya milk or skim milk powder
Salt, to taste.

Put the sunflower seed kernels, cashew nuts and 1 cup of cold water in the bowl of an electric blender. Leave to soak for about 15 minutes, then blend until smooth.

Add the remaining ingredients and 2 cups of cold water to the mixture and blend until smooth. Chill.

Serves 3.

BAKED FISH WITH CASHEW STUFFING

Use either one large fish, such as a salmon trout or red mullet for four people, or one small fish – rainbow trout or whiting – per person. Start preparing the dish well in advance; the fish must marinate for several hours.

8 tablespoons olive oil
Juice of 2 lemons
1 clove garlic, crushed
Salt and freshly ground black pepper
1 large or 4 small fish, gutted and washed
Butter
1 large onion, chopped
1 large green pepper, seeded and thinly sliced
4 ounces (100–125 g) cashew nuts
2 tablespoons chopped parsley
Lemon slices, to garnish

Make a marinade by blending together 4 tablespoons of the oil, the lemon juice, crushed garlic, salt and pepper in a dish large enough to take the fish. Add the fish, cover well with the marinade and leave for 4 hours. After 3½ hours, pre-heat the oven to moderately hot (400°F, 200°C, Mark 6). Butter another baking dish, large enough to take the fish in a single layer.

Heat the remaining oil in a frying pan. Add the onion and fry gently until soft, then add the sliced pepper and cashew nuts. Cook, stirring continuously, until the pepper is soft. Remove the pan from the heat and add half the chopped parsley. Add salt and pepper to taste. Blend the contents of the pan together well, to form the stuffing.

Fill the centre of each fish with an equal portion of the stuffing. Close up the opening. Put the fish into the prepared baking dish and cover with the marinade. Bake for 30 minutes, until the flesh parts easily from the bone. Baste with the marinade, if necessary while cooking, to keep the fish moist. Transfer the cooked fish to a warm serving dish. Garnish with the lemon slices and the remaining parsley.

Serves 4.

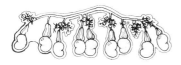

CHICKEN WITH CASHEW NUTS IN HOISIN SAUCE

Most of the ingredients are available in specialist Chinese food shops and delicatessens.

2 large Chinese mushrooms
1 whole uncooked chicken breast
1 tablespoon dry sherry
1 teaspoon plain flour
2 tablespoons corn oil
½ teacup bamboo shoots, cut into 1 inch (2·5 cm) pieces
6 water chestnuts, diced
2 tablespoons Hoisin sauce
½ teacup unsalted, raw cashew nuts

Soak the mushrooms in warm water for about 20 minutes. Meanwhile remove the skin and bones from the chicken and discard. Cut the meat into 1 inch (2·5 cm) cubes. In a medium bowl blend together the sherry and flour. Add the chicken, make sure it is well covered by the marinade, and leave for at least 10 minutes. When the mushrooms are soft, dry on kitchen paper and slice across into sections about ⅛ inch (3 mm) thick.

Heat the oil in a wok (or large, good quality frying pan) over a high heat. When the oil starts to sizzle, add the cubed chicken and stir continuously for about 2 minutes or until the chicken is white (When stir-frying, it is essential to stir throughout the cooking process, otherwise the food will burn.) Keep stirring and add the mushrooms, bamboo shoots and water chestnuts. Cook for a further minute.

Sprinkle on the Hoisin sauce, mix in well and stir the mixture over the heat for another 3 minutes. Add the cashew nuts and stir well in. Serve immediately with fried rice or Chinese noodles.

Serves 2.

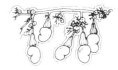

VEAL AND CASHEW NUT CASSEROLE

3 pounds (1·4 kilos) stewing veal
Salt and freshly ground black pepper
2 ounces (50 g) butter
2 tablespoons oil
1 large Spanish onion, finely chopped
2 plump cloves garlic, crushed
1 large tomato, peeled, seeded and diced
8 ounces (225 g) cashew nuts
½ pint (300 ml) tomato juice
1 teaspoon flour
2 teaspoons Worcestershire sauce

Remove any sinews, fat etc, and cut veal into bite-sized cubes. Season all over with salt and pepper.

In a large, heavy, flameproof casserole, melt butter in oil. Brown veal cubes all over in hot fat, a portion at a time, transferring them to a plate with a slotted spoon as you do so. In fat remaining in casserole, gently fry onion and garlic until limp and lightly coloured. Stir in tomato and continue to fry, stirring, until mushy.

Add veal cubes and cashew nuts. Pour in tomato juice and mix well. Bring to simmering point, cover casserole and cook gently for 1 hour, or until veal is almost done. Occasionally stir veal and turn cubes over.

Blend flour smoothly with Worcestershire sauce. Stir it into sauce and simmer uncovered, stirring frequently, for 20–30 minutes longer, until veal is tender and sauce is thick and reduced. Correct seasoning and serve with plain boiled rice.

Serves 6–8.

CASHEW NUT BUTTER

Nut butters are usually very popular with children. Make a small quantity at a time and keep in the refrigerator in a sealed container. Cashew nuts need very little added oil.

Nut butters can be blended with chopped fruit or vegetables (celery, green pepper, raisins, grated carrot), to make a variety of delicious spreads.

8 ounces (225 g) unsalted, raw cashew nuts
Sunflower oil
Salt

Put the nuts, a teacupful at a time, into a electric grinder or food processor. Grind until they are the consistency of flour, then transfer to a medium bowl. Repeat until all the nuts are ground, then add the oil, drop by drop, and blend into the ground nuts with a wooden spoon. (This can be done more efficiently in an electric blender with a hole in the top.) Continue adding oil and blending until a thick paste forms. Taste the mixture and add salt if desired.

Pack the nut butter into a small, clean jar or other container. Seal and store in the refrigerator.

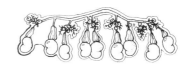

CHERRY

Cherries are native to Asia Minor, their very name deriving from Cerasus, the ancient city where Europeans first came across them. Since then, migratory birds have helped to spread cherries to most parts of the temperate world.

The arrival of the season's first cherries is a sure sign that summer has arrived. They are eaten fresh or cooked in all kinds of compotes, pies, cakes and puddings. A large proportion of the crop is used to make delectable jams and syrups, or canned. They are also preserved in brandy or *eau-de-vie* for special occasions and used to make spirits and to flavour all sorts of liqueurs based on brandy, gin, even whisky. Maraschino liqueur is flavoured with cherries but Kirsch is probably the most famous of all, a clear, colourless spirit from Switzerland and the Black Forest, with a light, bitter almond flavour that goes superbly with all kinds of fruit from pineapple to strawberries.

The colour of ripe cherries runs from golden streaked with red to deep, purple-black. There are also white Queen Anne cherries and a variety that stays a pale green colour even when fully ripe and sweet. Basically, cherries can be divided into two categories – sweet cherries, which can be light- or dark-fleshed, and are either eaten raw or cooked, and sour or 'tart' cherries such as the famous Morellos, which are used primarily for pies and preserves, and for making liqueurs. Dukes or Royal cherries are a cross between the two.

When the season ends, switch to canned cherries by all means but do check first if they have been pitted or not. Pitting cherries can be a tedious job, although a cherry-stoner is a time-saving gadget that can double up as an olive-stoner. Check, too, when buying dried cherries (available in some wholefood stores) whether they have been pitted. Reconstituted overnight in a bowl of water, then simmered in a light sugar syrup, they make a lovely compote or topping for ice cream.

To prepare cherries for cooking, rinse them first if necessary, then take off the stems. Remove the pits over a large bowl to catch any juices that might escape, dropping the cherries into the bowl as you do so.

Whole cherries can be dry or sugar frozen; stem, wash and dry them first. Freeze stoned ones in a sugar syrup made from 1 pound (450 g) sugar to 2 pints (1.1 litres) water. Allow ½ teaspoon ascorbic acid for every pint (550 ml) syrup.

REMEDIES

The bark of the wild black cherry tree is well known as a remedy for coughs and colds, and it is traditionally combined with coltsfoot to cure fever as well as coughs and bronchitis.

The bark should be dried in the shade, not in the sun as is usual with most plants.

Put 2 tablespoons dried wild or sour cherry bark and 2 tablespoons dried coltsfoot leaves or flowers in an enamel or stainless steel saucepan. Bring 1 pint (600 ml) water to the boil, pour it over the mixture, and simmer very gently for 15–20 minutes. Strain. Sweeten to taste with honey and allow to cool. Take up to half a cup, 3 or 4 times per day. Children can take half that dosage.

Cherry trees also yield a gum which has soothing properties similar to those of gum arabic, and may be substituted for it in various recipes. Culpeper says this gum 'dissolved in wine, is good for a cold, cough and hoarseness of the throat; mendeth the colour in the face, sharpeneth the eye-sight, provoketh appetite, and helpeth to break and expel the stone.'

CHERRY STALK TEA

This recipe was once well known as a diuretic. The stalks can be of wild cherry or of the sour Morello cherry.

Pour 1 pint (600 ml) boiling water over 1 tablespoon dried stalks and steep for 10–15 minutes, before straining and cooling. Drink lukewarm, a mouthful at a time, up to 3 or 4 cups per day.

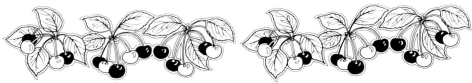

ICED CHERRY SOUP

When fresh cherries are not in season, canned fruit may be used, provided they are pitted and packed either in water or a very light syrup.

1½ pounds (700 g) sour black cherries
  (see above)
6 ounces (175 g) granulated sugar
One 3 inch (7·5 cm) cinnamon stick
1 tablespoon potato flour or cornflour
¼ pint (150 ml) double cream
Caster sugar (optional)
Lemon juice (optional)
4–6 tablespoons cherry brandy

Stem and pit fresh cherries.

In a large saucepan, dissolve granulated sugar in about 1½ pints (900 ml) water. Add the cinnamon stick, bring to boiling point and boil gently for about 5 minutes. Then add the cherries and their juices, and continue to simmer until they have softened, about 30 minutes.

Blend the potato flour or cornflour smoothly with 2 or 3 tablespoons cold water. Stir into the poached cherries and simmer, stirring, until soup is slightly thickened and has lost its opaque, floury look. Discard the cinnamon stick.

Take a large cupful of the cherries and their liquid, and purée smoothly in a food processor or electric blender. Return purée to the soup and leave until quite cold. Blend in cream. Then taste and adjust flavours, adding caster sugar and a few drops of lemon juice, if necessary. Chill until ready to serve.

Just before serving, stir in a few tablespoons of cherry brandy, to taste. Serve in chilled soup bowls.

Serves 6–8.

Duck with Cherries

4 pound (1·8 kilo) duck, cleaned, and
    giblets
Salt
3 carrots, peeled and sliced
1 small onion, chopped
1 garlic clove, crushed
1 teaspoon dried marjoram
1 teaspoon dried basil
1 wine glass red wine
Freshly ground black pepper
Sugar
½ pound (225 g) Morello cherries

Season the duck, by rubbing the skin and the inside of the carcass with salt. Put to one side, in a large casserole dish.

Arrange the carrots, onion and giblets around the duck. Sprinkle the garlic, marjoram and basil over it. Pour in the wine and about ½ pint (300 ml) water, and add salt, pepper and sugar to taste. Cover the casserole and bake in a moderate oven (350°F, 180°C, Mark 4) for 2 hours or until the duck is tender.

Remove the casserole from the oven. Uncover and pour off the liquid and vegetables into a large saucepan. Put the duck on to a plate and set aside to cool. Heat the contents of the saucepan over a high flame until reduced by half. Strain off the liquid into a small bowl and chill in the refrigerator for 1 hour. Discard the vegetables.

Meanwhile, stem and pit the cherries and put into a medium bowl.

Take the chilled liquid out of the refrigerator. The fat content should form a layer on the surface. Remove this. Reheat the remaining liquid until not quite boiling. Pour over the cherries and chill in the refrigerator until the sauce has turned to jelly. Remove from the refrigerator, turn out of the bowl and slice. Serve the duck cold, surrounded by slices of the jellied sauce in which the cherries are embedded.

Serves 4.

Cherry Compote

If you are feeling extravagant, stir a tablespoon or two of cherry brandy into the syrup at the very end. Serve the compote with chilled pouring cream. A plate of almond macaroons is also nice but not really necessary.

2 pounds (900 g) sweet black cherries
10–12 ounces (275–350 g) sugar
One 3 inch (7·5 cm) cinnamon stick
3–4 cloves
Spirals of orange and lemon rind

Stem and pit the cherries.

Place remaining ingredients in a large, wide pan or flameproof casserole. Pour in a generous pint (600 ml) of water and bring to boiling point over moderate heat, stirring until sugar has dissolved. Simmer for 5 minutes to make a syrup.

Drop cherries and their juices into simmering syrup and poach gently until they are just tender, about 10 minutes. With a slotted spoon, transfer cherries to a serving bowl.

Boil remaining syrup briskly for about 5 minutes to thicken it slightly. Strain over cherries. Cool and chill before serving.

Serves 6.

Cherry Lamb Mayonnaise

12 ounces (350 g) ripe, sweet cherries,
    red or black
1 pound (450 g) lean, cold roast lamb,
    sliced ½ inch (1·25 cm) thick
3–4 stalks celery
6–8 tablespoons chopped, lightly
    toasted almonds
About ¼ pint (150 ml) thick lemon
    mayonnaise (page 205)
Salt and freshly ground black pepper
Crisp lettuce leaves, to garnish

Stem and pit the cherries. Trim any visible fat from lamb. Cut it into ½ inch (1·25 cm) cubes and add to cherries. Trim celery stalks. Dice them and add to bowl, together with chopped almonds. Mix in enough mayonnaise to bind ingredients together, tossing lightly with a large fork, and season to taste with a little salt and freshly ground black pepper.

Line 4 individual plates with lettuce leaves and pile salad on top.

Serves 4.

Cherry Breadcrumb Pudding

12 ounces (350 g) ripe cherries
5 ounces (150 g) brown breadcrumbs
Finely grated rind of 1 lemon
3 ounces (75 g) caster sugar
½ pint (300 ml) single cream
4 eggs, separated
Butter, for pudding basin

Cherry sauce
4 ounces (100–125 g) ripe cherries
2 ounces (50 g) sugar
Juice of 1 lemon
Red food colouring
1–2 tablespoons cherry brandy or
    orange liqueur (optional)

To make pudding, first stem and pit the cherries. Add breadcrumbs, grated lemon rind and sugar to the bowl with the cherries, and toss with a fork until thoroughly mixed.

Bring cream to just below boiling point and pour over breadcrumb mixture. Mix lightly and cool to lukewarm.

Meanwhile, in separate bowls, first beat egg whites until they stand in peaks, then with the same whisk, beat egg yolks until creamy. Stir egg yolks into bowl of breadcrumb mixture and finally fold in egg whites.

Spoon mixture into a large, well-buttered pudding basin. Cover with a double thickness of greaseproof paper or foil buttered on the inside and tie down with string. Steam pudding as usual for 1 hour, or until it has risen and is firm to the touch.

While pudding is steaming, prepare a simple cherry sauce. Pit cherries, working over a small pan and dropping them into it as you do so. Add sugar, lemon juice and about ⅓ pint (200 ml) water. Bring to boiling point, stirring until sugar has dissolved, and simmer for 15–20 minutes, or until cherries are very soft. With a fork, crush them slightly to release juices. Intensify colour with 1 or 2 drops of red food colouring and, if liked, flavour to taste with a little cherry brandy or orange liqueur.

When pudding is ready, turn it out on to a heated serving platter and pour cherry sauce over and around it.

Serves 6–8.

CHERRY PIE

For this, the best cherries to use will, naturally, be pie cherries, the kind that often grow in the garden and are just too astringent to eat raw. Use them for making pies such as this one, for jams and other preserves. Ice cream makes a lovely accompaniment for a cherry pie.

About 1 pound (450 g) rough puff pastry for a 2-crust, 8–9 inch (20–22·5 cm) pie (page 203)
1¼ pounds (575 g) pie cherries
4–5 drops almond essence
About 10 ounces (275 g) sugar, or to taste
5 tablespoons plain flour
½ ounce (15 g) butter
Caster sugar, to decorate

Roll out about half of the pastry to make a lid. Put aside. Roll out remaining pastry rather more thinly and use it to line base and sides of dish with a slight overhang.

Stem and pit the cherries, and put them in a bowl. Sprinkle with almond essence. Blend sugar and flour together, and toss with cherries. Pile cherries in pastry-lined dish and dot all over with tiny flakes of butter. Moisten pastry edges lightly with water, fit pastry lid in position and seal the two together, pressing lightly and fluting edge neatly. Cut a few gashes in pastry lid to allow steam to escape.

Bake pie in a hot oven (450°F, 230°C, Mark 8) for the first 15 minutes. Then lower heat to moderate (350°F, 180°C, Mark 4) and continue to bake for 30 minutes longer, or until pastry lid is crisp, puffed and golden. Strew pie with caster sugar and allow to cool to lukewarm before serving.

Serves 6–8.

Bigarreau.

CHERRY CHEESECAKE

This can be made with either cottage or curd cheese, but whichever one of these is used must first be well drained in a sieve or squeezed dry wrapped in muslin; and cottage cheese must also be rubbed through a sieve to make it smooth. Make the cheesecake the day before you propose to serve it to give it time to 'settle'.

Biscuit crust
4 ounces (100–125 g) wholemeal biscuits, finely crushed
1 tablespoon caster sugar
1 ounce (25 g) butter, melted

Cheese mixture
1 pound (450 g) curd or cottage cheese (see above)
6 ounces (175 g) caster sugar
3 eggs
Finely grated rinds of 1 lemon and 1 orange
4 tablespoons double cream or sour cream
1½ tablespoons self-raising flour, sifted

Cherry topping
Two 14 ounce (400 g) cans pitted black cherries in syrup
Lemon juice
1 teaspoon arrowroot, potato flour or cornflour

Prepare biscuit crust. Mix crushed biscuit crumbs, sugar and butter together. Press firmly and evenly over the base of a loose-bottomed, 7–8 inch (17·5–20 cm) cake tin.

To prepare cheese mixture, beat the well-drained curd or sieved cottage cheese with sugar until fluffy (in an electric mixer if available). Add eggs one at a time, beating well between each addition. Beat in grated orange and lemon rinds, and then cream. Beat until blended. Finally, lightly but thoroughly fold in flour.

Spoon cheese mixture into biscuit-lined baking tin and place in a moderately hot oven (400°F, 200°C, Mark 6). After 10 minutes, turn oven down (to 300°F, 150°C, Mark 2) and continue to bake for 1½ hours longer, or until cheese filling is risen and firmly set. Allow to cool. Then chill for several hours, preferably overnight.

The following day, prepare cherry topping. Drain cherries thoroughly and arrange them closely on top of cheesecake. Measure 5 tablespoons of their syrup into a small pan. Sharpen flavour to taste with a little lemon juice. Heat gently while you blend arrowroot smoothly with another tablespoon of cherry syrup. Stir into hot syrup. Bring to boiling point and simmer, stirring, until translucent and thickened. Cool. Spoon over cherries. Put back in refrigerator to set.

To serve, run a knife blade round sides of cheesecake and carefully unmould it on to a flat dish.

Serves 8.

CLAFOUTIS

The texture of a clafoutis should be a cross between a baked custard and a pancake, soft but firm enough to unmould when cold.

3 tablespoons plain flour
Pinch of salt
3 tablespoons vanilla-flavoured caster sugar (page 205)
2 eggs
1 egg yolk
1 tablespoon light vegetable oil
½ pint (300 ml) milk
1 pound (450 g) ripe black cherries
Butter
Sifted icing or caster sugar, to decorate

Sift flour, salt and sugar into a bowl, and make a well in the centre. Add the eggs and egg yolk, and work them into the flour with a wooden spoon to make a smooth paste. Beat in the oil. Then gradually add the milk, beating vigorously to make a smooth, light batter. Put aside to rest while you prepare the fruit.

Generously butter a tart tin or oven-proof porcelain dish about 10 inches (25 cm) in diameter. Stem and pit the cherries and spread evenly in the dish. Cover them with the batter, pouring it over the back of a spoon to avoid disturbing them. Dot the top with a few tiny flakes of butter.

Bake clafoutis in a moderate oven (350°F, 180°C, Mark 4) for 40–45 minutes, or until a knife blade slipped through to the bottom comes out clean.

Serve warm from the dish, dusted with sifted sugar. Alternatively, the clafoutis may be unmoulded and served lukewarm or cold, in wedges like a pie.

Serves 6–8.

EASY KIRSCH GÂTEAU

3 ounces (75 g) plain flour
1 ounce (25 g) cornflour
3 eggs
6 ounces (175 g) caster sugar
1 tablespoon Kirsch
Butter, for baking tins
Grated dark chocolate, to decorate

Cherry filling
One 15 ounce (425 g) can black
  cherries in syrup, pitted
4 tablespoons sugar
2 tablespoons Kirsch

Kirsch cream
½ pint (300 ml) whipping cream
2 teaspoons caster sugar
2 tablespoons Kirsch

Butter two 8½ inch (21 cm) layer cake tins thoroughly. Line bases with buttered greaseproof paper. Sift flour and cornflour together 3 times.

Have eggs at room temperature and break them into a large bowl. With mixer at moderate speed, beat eggs until thick and fluffy. Gradually beat in sugar and continue to beat vigorously until mixture leaves a momentary trail on the surface when beaters are lifted. Beat in Kirsch and finally fold in flour mixture. Distribute evenly between prepared cake tins. Bake in a moderate oven (350°F, 180°C, Mark 4) for 20–25 minutes until layers are well risen and very lightly coloured. Allow tins to cool on cake racks for 5 minutes before loosening sides and turning cakes out of tins. Leave until quite cold.

To prepare the cherry filling, drain syrup from cherries into a small pan. Add sugar, stir over low heat until dissolved, then boil until reduced to 8 or 9 tablespoons. Cool to lukewarm, stir in Kirsch and leave until cold.

To prepare the Kirsch cream, whisk cream until thick. Add sugar and Kirsch, and continue to beat until cream holds its shape.

To assemble gâteau, lay one cake layer on a large, flat serving dish and spoon more than half of the cherry syrup over it. Spread with half of the cream and scatter evenly with cherries, pressing them in lightly. Soak underside of other cake layer with remaining syrup and quickly lay it on top, saturated side down. Spread with remaining cream. Sprinkle evenly with grated chocolate and chill thoroughly before serving.

Makes 12 portions.

CHERRIES IN BRANDY

For this you will need plump, ripe Morello cherries, brandy (one of the least expensive ones from the off-licence or supermarket will do perfectly well), sugar and a great deal of patience to resist opening the jar and sampling the cherries while they are maturing. This will take a minimum of 8 weeks but the longer they are left, the better they will be.

Choose perfect cherries that still have their stalks attached. With a pair of scissors, trim the stalks down to about ¾ inch (2 cm). Wipe the cherries clean by rolling them gently between the folds of a damp cloth. (Do not rinse them unless absolutely necessary.)

Pack the cherries into a tall, wide-mouthed glass jar that has a tight-fitting lid, tapping the jar gently on the table from time to time to 'settle' the cherries so that you can fit in as many as possible.

Fill the jar with brandy, covering the cherries completely. Close the jar tightly and put it away for a minimum of 3 weeks, preferably longer, say 4.

Open the jar and spoon in enough sugar to come halfway up the sides. Then screw down the lid again and shake the jar gently until the sugar has dissolved. Put the jar of cherries away in a cool, dark cupboard for a further 8 weeks (or longer), frequently giving it a good shake.

The cherries are best served in small glasses, 5 or 6 to a glass, with some of the brandy poured over them.

CHERRY JAM

½ pound (225 g) redcurrants
3 pounds (1·35 kilos) ripe Morello
  cherries
3 pounds (1·35 kilos) sugar

Rinse the redcurrants and strip off any stalks. Place in a pan with a few tablespoons of water over low heat until juices run. Then continue to cook gently, mashing occasionally, until redcurrants are soft and pulpy.

Meanwhile, stem and pit the cherries over a bowl to catch any juices.

Rub the redcurrants through a fine nylon sieve and return purée to the rinsed-out pan. Add the pitted cherries and their juices, slowly bring to boiling point and simmer gently until cherries have softened.

Add sugar and continue to cook gently, stirring frequently, until sugar has dissolved. Then raise heat and boil rapidly until setting point is reached, skimming as necessary.

Cool slightly. Pot and cover.

See also page 198.

Fills about 5 jars.

CHESTNUT (SWEET)

The sweet chestnut tree, which grows up to 115 feet (35 metres) high and bears creamy flower 'candles' in spring, was originally from southern Europe. The nuts fall to the ground in green casings covered with prickly spines, and must not be confused with their inedible relative, the horse chestnut.

The sweet chestnut is cultivated in Spain, Italy and France, and is used in soups, stews, sauces and stuffings. Whole (shelled) chestnuts combine well with Brussels sprouts, while Mont Blanc is one of the world's classic desserts.

To peel chestnuts, make a small nick in the flat side of their shells, and roast them in a moderately hot oven for six to eight minutes; or put them on top of the stove in a pan of cold water just to cover, and bring the water to the boil. As soon as the water is bubbling briskly, take the pan from the heat and peel off the shells and inner skins. This is easier to do while they're hot, but remember to hold them in a cloth. Don't allow them to continue boiling, or they will turn floury and be impossible to peel.

It may be easier to buy dried nuts. Put these in a basin and pour over boiling water, then leave them to soak for up to twenty-four hours. If you do not need whole nuts, use cans of purée. Be sure you know which you are buying – the sweetened or the unsweetened variety.

To freeze chestnuts, remove every scrap of skin. Blanch them, then plunge them into cold water before patting dry and freezing in polythene bags.

Sweet chestnuts contain more starch and less fat than most other nuts, which is why they are so easily ground into flour, and are rich in Vitamins B and C. Their leaves and bark are also useful medicinally.

CREAM OF CHESTNUT SOUP

½ pound (225 g) chestnuts
1 ounce (25 g) butter
1 tablespoon oil
2 carrots, thinly sliced
1 small parsnip, thinly sliced
1 small stalk celery, thinly sliced
1 large potato, peeled and sliced
¾ pint (400 ml) well-flavoured chicken
   stock
½ pint (300 ml) single cream
Salt
3–4 tablespoons dry sherry
Crisp croûtons, to garnish

Peel and skin the chestnuts, and chop them into small pieces.

In the large pan, heat butter and oil together, and sauté carrots, parsnip and celery for 2–3 minutes. Cover pan and 'sweat' vegetables for about 10 minutes longer until they soften slightly. Add the chestnuts and potato. Cover with chicken stock, bring to boiling point and simmer with the lid half on until chestnuts and vegetables are disintegrating, about 45 minutes. Add a splash of hot water if liquid in pan evaporates too quickly.

Purée the contents of the pan in an electric blender or put them through a vegetable mouli. Return purée to rinsed-out pan. Reheat gently, blending in the cream smoothly with a wire whisk. Do not allow soup to boil again at this stage.

Season with salt and flavour to taste with sherry. Serve immediately with a bowl of croûtons to scatter over the top.

Serves 4–6.

REMEDIES

Chestnut leaves are traditionally believed to be good for coughs.

Infuse 1 ounce (25 g) fresh or dried leaves (picked in early summer) in a pint (600 ml) boiling water. Allow to cool, and drink one cupful three times a day, or use as a gargle.

To cure diarrhoea, boil 1 ounce (25 g) crushed wood or bark in a pint (600 ml) water for 2 minutes only; strain and take 2 or 3 cupfuls a day.

CHESTNUT STUFFING

2 pounds (900 g) chestnuts, skinned
   and peeled
Stock
4 ounces (100–125 g) butter, melted
4 ounces (100–125 g) breadcrumbs,
   white or wholemeal
1 pound (450 g) sausagemeat
1 tablespoon chopped parsley
Salt and freshly ground black pepper

Put the chestnuts in a saucepan with just enough stock to cover. Simmer gently over low heat until they are cooked through and almost dry.

Rub the chestnuts through a sieve into a bowl and mix well with the breadcrumbs, sausagemeat, parsley and salt and pepper.

Note: These quantities are enough for a 12–14 pound (5–6 kilo) turkey.

CHICKEN WITH CHESTNUTS

Serve the casserole with floury, plain-boiled potatoes or a creamy potato purée.

One 3–3¼ pound (1·4–1·5 kilo) roasting chicken, jointed
2–3 slices unsmoked streaky bacon
2 tablespoons light cooking oil
1 Spanish onion, finely chopped
1 large clove garlic, crushed
4 ounces (100–125 g) button mushrooms, sliced
Salt and freshly ground black pepper
1 teaspoon crushed dried rosemary
½ teaspoon dried thyme
¼ pint (150 ml) Marsala or medium sherry
6–8 tablespoons chicken stock
1 can peeled whole chestnuts, about 10 ounces (285 g) drained weight
1 ounce (25 g) butter

Cut bacon into small dice. In a heavy, flameproof casserole, fry bacon gently with 1 tablespoon oil until fat runs.

Stir in onion and sauté gently until soft and golden. Stir in garlic and mushrooms, and sauté for 2–3 minutes longer, taking care garlic does not burn, as this would make it bitter. Cover and put aside.

Heat the other tablespoon of oil in a large, heavy frying pan and fry chicken pieces, a few at a time, until golden brown on all sides. Transfer to the casserole, giving each piece of chicken a generous sprinkling of salt and freshly ground pepper as you do so. When all the chicken pieces have been dealt with, sprinkle them with rosemary and thyme, and mix well with the onion and mushrooms. Pour over Marsala or sherry.

Rinse out frying pan with chicken stock, stirring and scraping surface clean with a wooden spoon, and pour into casserole. Bring to simmering point, cover and cook gently for 15 minutes.

Meanwhile drain chestnuts thoroughly. In the same frying pan, toss them lightly in butter, taking care butter does not brown too much.

Stir chestnuts and all their butter into casserole. Cover again and continue to cook gently for 15–20 minutes, or until chicken pieces are quite tender.

Correct seasoning if necessary and serve.

Serves 4.

CAUCASIAN LAMB

2 pounds (900 g) lean leg of lamb steaks
1½ ounces (40 g) butter
2 large Spanish onions, finely chopped
Salt and freshly ground black pepper
About ¾ pint (400 ml) chicken (cube) stock
1 pound (450 g) chestnuts, peeled and skinned
Juice of 1 lemon
Finely chopped parsley, to garnish

Have the lamb steaks sliced across the grain. Trim off all fat and gristle, and cut meat into about 12 pieces. With a meat mallet or rolling pin moistened with water, pound meat out thinly.

In a heavy, flameproof casserole with a tight-fitting lid, brown meat on

CHESTNUT SAUCE

A good sauce for chicken and turkey. Use stock in which you have boiled a fowl or skimmed juices from the roasting tin, supplemented with stock made with a cube.

1 ounce (25 g) butter
2 tablespoons flour
½ pint (300 ml) cooking juices and chicken (cube) stock (see above)
½ pound (225 g) chestnuts, peeled, skinned and chopped
Salt
½ teaspoon sugar
Generous pinch of ground cinnamon (optional)

In a heavy pan, melt the butter. Blend in the flour with a wooden spoon and cool gently, stirring, until mixture turns a rich golden colour and has a nutty aroma. Gradually add cooking juices and stock, beating vigorously to prevent lumps forming. When sauce is smooth and simmering gently, stir in the chestnuts. Season lightly with salt. Add sugar and a pinch of cinnamon if liked, and continue to cook gently for 15–20 minutes, stirring occasionally. Correct seasoning and serve hot.

both sides in butter, a portion at a time to avoid overcrowding the casserole. Stir in onions and season generously with salt and freshly ground black pepper. Add a few tablespoons of the stock, stirring and scraping bottom of casserole clean with a wooden spoon. Cover tightly and cook gently.

Add chestnuts to casserole, together with remaining stock. Mix well, cover and continue cooking gently until meat and chestnuts are quite tender.

Five minutes before the end of cooking time, stir lemon juice into stew. Correct seasoning if necessary and transfer to a heated serving dish. Garnish with parsley, and serve.

Serves 4–6.

MONT BLANC

1 pound (450 g) chestnuts
Salt
8 ounces (225 g) sugar
¼ pint (150 ml) whipping cream
2 tablespoons brandy or ½ teaspoon vanilla essence

Peel and skin the chestnuts. In a pan, cover them with water and add a pinch of salt. Bring to boiling point and simmer for 45–60 minutes until they are quite soft. Drain the chestnuts thoroughly. Using a potato masher, mash them to a purée together with the sugar and a pinch of salt. Press the purée through a potato ricer, mouli or sieve, allowing it to fall lightly on to a plate.

Beat the cream until it thickens and forms very soft peaks, flavouring it with brandy or vanilla, and a little more sugar to taste if liked.

Spoon the cream over the mound of chestnut purée. Serve immediately.

Serves 4.

COCONUT

Man has to take the responsibility for moving many food crops around the world, but the coconut is one of the few which has taken an active part in its own propagation. Because of its buoyancy and the hardness of its protective shell, the coconut has from time immemorial drifted thousands of miles across both Indian and Pacific oceans, taking root where it was carried ashore – and where it felt happy to be. It still grows best near the sea, but it will also grow inland if it has the company of humans. A nineteenth-century traveller to Sri Lanka was heard to remark that 'the natives have a superstition that the cocoa-nut will not grow out of the sound of a human voice, and will die if the village where it formerly thrived becomes deserted.'

We are all familiar with pictures of the coconut palm, with its tall, slender, leaning trunk and its impudent crown of giant leaves – some up to 20 feet (over 6 metres) in length – sheltering the nuts the tree bears every year.

Experts tend to argue as to whether the coconut originated in India or Malaysia – but as far away as West Africa, it is one of life's staple foods. (The Ibo tribe fringing the Niger river have very special prayers for peace, prosperity, health and lots of coconuts.) But the coconut is far more than a food. Besides the refreshing coconut water, the sugary sap from the young flower branches is tapped and drunk fresh, or fermented into 'toddy' – a wine with the alcoholic strength of beer. Toddy, in its turn, can be distilled into 'arrack', a spirit at least as potent as brandy. Copra, from the dried flesh inside the nut, is used in cosmetics, and coconut oil can be used in cooking.

Coconut is perhaps most familiar to us as the fresh, whole nut, or in its desiccated form. Shredded coconut, often lightly and deliciously toasted, is familiar as an ingredient of sweet desserts. Think of little coconut macaroons, familiar from childhood, crusty on the outside and moist and chewy in the middle, or steaming coconut puddings to cheer the family on a winter's day, and the perennially popular pink-and-white coconut ice.

When buying a whole coconut, pick one that feels heavy for its size, hold it to your ear and give it a gentle shake. There should be plenty of water splashing about inside. To open it, pierce two of its brown eyes and pour out the water from inside. Put it, eyes down, on a hard surface and give it a blow with a hammer. Once it has split or broken into small pieces, the creamy white flesh inside can be scraped out and stored. Left-over coconut can be shredded or grated, moistened with a little coconut water and packed into small containers for freezing (up to 6 months).

Coconuts are very nutritious, especially if they are fresh when they contain appreciable amounts of minerals, particularly potassium, and vitamins. The oil is used in cosmetics and sun-tan lotions.

NECK CREAM

Coconut oil has many cosmetic uses. This recipe will prevent wrinkles, and is also a firming, nourishing neck cream.

Put 1 part beeswax, 2 parts lanolin and 6 parts coconut oil into a double boiler. Melt, beat well, and remove from the heat. Add 4 parts camomile infusion a little at a time, as if making mayonnaise.

SUNTAN LOTIONS

Coconut oil is very effective in promoting a rich, even tan. It can be used on its own, or mixed with olive or sesame oil (both of which are also good tanning agents) to give a better consistency – it solidifies unless the weather is very warm. A few drops of bergamot essence can also be added for an even deeper tan, as well as for its scent, but take care: it is very potent, and not suitable for sensitive skins.

A less sticky suntan lotion can be made in the same way as the neck cream, using 1 part lanolin to 1 or 2 parts coconut oil and 2 or 3 parts rosewater (or diluted cider vinegar).

COCONUT MILK

When recipes call for coconut milk or cream, they do not mean the watery liquid you hear slopping about inside when you shake a fresh coconut, but a creamy milk, made as follows.

In the goblet of an electric blender or food processor, place a cupful of finely chopped fresh coconut meat and pour over a cupful of boiling water. Blend or process until the two are reduced to a thick and rather rough purée. Alternatively, shred coconut meat on the coarse side of a cheese grater and put it in a bowl. Cover with an equal volume of boiling water and leave to soak for 30 minutes.

Strain through a fine sieve or a colander lined with muslin, gathering up sides and wringing muslin to extract every drop of moisture.

The first 'pressing' results in a thick, creamy liquid. For a thinner version put contents of muslin bag in a small pan, cover with another portion of water, cold this time, and slowly bring to boiling point. Remove from heat and leave to soak for another 30 minutes before squeezing liquid out as above.

If fresh coconuts are not available, you can use desiccated shredded coconut instead. Or you can use creamed coconut which comes in slabs or packets from Oriental grocery stores. About 4 ounces (100–125 g) soaked in water will produce a thicker liquid, while about 1 ounce (25 g) soaked in water will produce a thinner one.

FISH AND COCONUT CURRY

This fairly mild curry is popular in South India and Sri Lanka. Use ghee (clarified butter), available at most Indian grocers, if possible. It is the best fat for Indian cooking, because it can be heated to a high temperature without burning.

8 fluid ounces (225 ml) coconut milk (see opposite page and method)
4 large cod steaks
1 teaspoon turmeric
Salt
2 ounces (50 g) ghee or butter (see above)
2 small onions, sliced
2 green chillies, chopped
½ inch (1.25 cm) piece of root ginger, peeled and sliced
Juice of 1 lemon
2–3 tablespoons yoghourt

Prepare coconut milk, following the method described on the opposite page, up to the 'first pressing' stage.

Wash the fish steaks and dry them on kitchen paper. Mix the turmeric and 1 teaspoon salt together in a small dish. Rub the mixture all over the fish. In a thick frying pan, heat the ghee (or butter). Add the fish and fry over a medium heat for a few minutes on each side. Take the fish out of the pan and set to one side.

Add the onions, chillies and ginger to the pan and cook until the onions are light brown. Stir in half the coconut milk and cook for a further minute.

Put the fish steaks back into the pan. Pour over the remaining coconut milk. Bring to the boil. Cover the pan and simmer the contents gently over a low heat for 15 minutes or until the fish is cooked. Uncover the pan and stir in the lemon juice. Taste the sauce and season to taste. Remove the pan from the heat, stir in the yoghourt. Return to the heat for a few minutes, but do not allow the sauce to boil. Serve with boiled rice.

Serves 4.

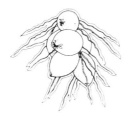

CHICKEN IN SPICED COCONUT SAUCE

6 ounces (175 g) desiccated shredded coconut
1 pint (500 ml) milk
One 3½ pound (1·6 kilo) roasting chicken, jointed
Peanut oil
2 Spanish onions, finely chopped
1 large clove garlic, crushed
¼ teaspoon each ground cinnamon, ginger and sharp (hot) paprika or cayenne
⅛ teaspoon ground cloves
2–3 teaspoons soya sauce
Salt and freshly ground black pepper
2–3 ounces (50–75 g) roasted peanuts, chopped

This coconut milk is richer than the one described on the opposite page. In a small pan, combine coconut with milk. Slowly bring to boiling point and simmer for 5 minutes. Then draw pan off heat and cool to lukewarm. Strain contents of pan through a sieve lined with muslin, wringing out as much milk as possible. Put aside.

In a large, flameproof casserole, brown chicken joints on all sides in 2 or 3 tablespoons peanut oil, removing them to a plate as you prepare them. When they are all done, pour off all oil remaining in casserole, leaving behind any brown bits, add 2 tablespoons fresh oil and sauté onions and garlic gently until transparent and golden but not charred. Sprinkle in spices and fry, stirring, for a minute or so longer. Mix in soya sauce and prepared coconut milk. Season lightly with salt and freshly ground black pepper.

Return chicken joints to casserole, spooning sauce over them so they are quite submerged. Cover and cook very gently for about 30 minutes. Then stir in chopped peanuts, taste for seasoning and continue cooking for 15 minutes longer, or until chicken is quite tender.

Serve with a bowl of rice.

Serves 4.

Note: Do not waste coconut left behind after preparing milk. Spread it out on a baking sheet to dry for 2–3 hours in a cool oven (250°F, 130°C, Mark ½), raking it over with your fingers from time to time.

Then use it to sprinkle over iced cakes and plain ice cream, or to decorate candies.

COCONUT RICE

A traditional accompaniment, delicious with European-style meat and especially poultry dishes, as well as the hot Indian curries which it was originally intended to accompany. Use basmati rice, a delicate, long-grained rice available in Indian stores and some delicatessens. Failing that, ordinary long-grain rice will do perfectly well. It will not need pre-soaking like basmati rice, but can take more liquid, say ½ cup more. Measurements are given in cups as relative volumes are more important than weights.

1 cup basmati or long-grain rice
1 tablespoon oil
½ ounce (15 g) butter
3 whole cloves
3 whole cardamom pods, lightly
*   crushed*
2–2½ cups coconut milk
*   (see page 54)*
1 teaspoon salt
3–4 tablespoons toasted shredded
*   coconut, to garnish*

Wash the rice under the cold tap until the water runs clear. If using basmati rice, place it in a bowl with cold water to cover and leave it to soak for at least 30 minutes before draining it thoroughly.

In a heavy pan with a tight-fitting lid, heat the oil and butter together until foaming. Add the cloves and cardamom pods, and swirl the pan round over moderate heat until the aroma begins to rise and the spices seem to puff out, about 3 minutes.

Add the rice and stir over moderate heat until each grain is separate and golden, and shiny with melted fat. Draw the pan from the heat and cool slightly before pouring in the coconut milk — 2 cups if using basmati rice, 2½ cups for plain, long-grain rice. Add salt and stir well.

Bring to boiling point. Stir well with a fork once more. Reduce the heat to a bare simmer, cover pan tightly and cook gently for 15 minutes, undisturbed. Most of the liquid will have been absorbed, leaving the rice grains rather moist.

Switch off the heat. Gently fluff the rice grains up with a fork. Clamp on the lid again and leave to stand for 10–15 minutes longer.

To serve, pile the rice in a heated serving dish. Scatter toasted shredded coconut over the top.

Serves 3–4.

COCONUT CREAM PIE

A rich pie, best served in a pre-baked pastry shell made of shortcrust, or a meringue case. If making a meringue, use the 3 egg whites left over from the cream filling and 3 ounces (75 g) caster sugar; to prepare the base and shape the case, follow the instructions in Coconut Meringue Case, below.

1 pre-baked shortcrust pastry
*   (page 203) or meringue case*
*   8 or 9 inches (20 or 22.5 cm)*
*   in diameter*
Whipped cream and shredded
*   coconut, to decorate*

Coconut cream filling
4 tablespoons cornflour
5 ounces (150 g) sugar
¼ teaspoon salt
1 pint (550 ml) creamy milk
3 egg yolks
1 teaspoon vanilla essence
½ ounce (15 g) butter
4 ounces (100–125 g) dessicated
*   shredded coconut*

Prepare coconut cream filling first. In the top of a double saucepan, blend cornflour smoothly with sugar, salt and milk. Bring to boiling point over direct heat, stirring constantly, and simmer for 2 or 3 minutes until sauce is thick and smooth.

In a bowl, beat egg yolks lightly. Beat in a few tablespoons of the hot cornflour sauce, then beat back into rest of sauce. Fit top of pan over simmering water and stir until sauce is smooth and has thickened again. Take care not to let sauce come to boiling point at this stage, or egg yolks may curdle. Lift off top part of pan. Beat in vanilla, butter and coconut. Pour into a bowl and leave until cold, stirring occasionally to prevent a skin forming on top.

Fill pastry shell or meringue case with cream filling and chill lightly. Serve decorated with whipped cream and sprinkled lightly with coconut.

Serves 6–8.

COCONUT MERINGUE CASE

Filled with whipped cream and decorated with fruit, this makes a delightful sweet that will serve 6 to 8 people. Or the same mixture may be shaped into individual meringues with 2 large spoons, dried out in the oven on prepared baking sheets and sandwiched with whipped cream.

Tasteless oil
2½ ounces (65 g) fresh or desiccated
*   shredded coconut*
3 tablespoons sifted icing sugar
3 egg whites
⅛ teaspoon salt
¼ teaspoon cream of tartar
6 ounces (175 g) caster sugar
1 teaspoon vanilla essence

Start by preparing baking equipment. A meringue case is baked on a baking sheet lined with greaseproof paper that has been marked with an 8 or 9 inch (20 or 22.5 cm) circle with a pencil and brushed very lightly with oil. Or it may be baked in a pie dish similarly greased with oil (just enough to prevent meringue sticking).

In a small bowl, toss the coconut with icing sugar until strands are individually coated. Put aside. In a large, spotlessly clean and dry bowl, beat egg whites with salt until foamy. Add cream of tartar and continue to beat until very soft peaks form. Then beat in caster sugar, a couple of tablespoons at a time, and continue to beat to a stiff, glossy meringue. Beat in vanilla essence. Sprinkle sugared coconut over the top and gently but thoroughly fold it in, using a large, metal spoon.

Shape meringue into a neat nest on baking sheet, following pencil guideline on greaseproof paper, or pile into pie dish and smooth out bottom and sides with the back of a spoon, shaping sides so they extend about an inch above the rim of the dish.

Bake meringue case in a very slow oven (300°F, 150°C, Mark 2) for about 1 hour or until it is a light golden colour and firm to the touch. Loosen meringue case while still lukewarm, then leave until quite cold on the baking sheet or in the pie dish before transferring to a flat serving dish, filling and decorating.

STEAMED COCONUT PUDDING

2 ounces (50 g) desiccated shredded
    coconut
½ pint (300 ml) milk
2 ounces (50 g) butter
2 ounces (50 g) caster sugar
2 eggs, separated
2 ounces (50 g) soft white
    breadcrumbs
2 ounces (50 g) cake crumbs
½ teaspoon vanilla essence
Butter, for pudding basin
Orange or lemon custard sauce, to
    serve (page 205)

In a pan, cover coconut with milk. Bring to boiling point and simmer for 10–15 minutes. Cool.

Meanwhile, beat butter until creamy. Beat in sugar and continue to beat until light and fluffy. Beat in egg yolks, one at a time. With a wooden spoon, mix in the bread and cake crumbs, the coconut and milk mixture, and vanilla. Beat egg whites until stiff but not dry and fold them into pudding.

Pour mixture into a well-buttered pudding basin. Cover with a double thickness of greaseproof paper or foil buttered on the underside. Tie down securely with string. Stand basin on a trivet in a pan with boiling water to come halfway up sides, cover tightly and steam for at least 1 hour, or until pudding is well risen and firm.

Turn out on to a heated serving platter. Coat with a hot orange or lemon custard sauce and serve.

Serves 4–6.

COCONUT SAUCE

2 ounces (50 g) unsalted butter
4 ounces (100–125 g) caster sugar
2 egg whites
3–4 tablespoons desiccated
    shredded coconut
Lemon juice
Vanilla essence

Beat butter until light and creamy. Add sugar gradually, beating vigorously until mixture is very pale and fluffy. Beat egg whites until they stand in stiff peaks. Fold them into the creamed mixture, together with coconut. Flavour with lemon juice and vanilla essence.

Spoon butter into a glass serving dish and chill until firm.

LEMON COCONUT CREAMS

These sweets are quick, simple and foolproof to make, providing you use a sugar thermometer to determine the temperature.

1 ounce (25 g) butter
12 ounces (350 g) sugar
6 tablespoons evaporated milk
Juice and grated rind of 1 lemon
6 ounces (175 g) desiccated
    shredded coconut

Line a large baking tray with waxed paper. In a thick-bottomed saucepan, melt the butter over a low heat. Stir in the sugar, 3 tablespoons cold water, the evaporated milk, and grated lemon rind. Bring to the boil slowly and continue to boil, stirring frequently until the temperature is 240°F (115°C). Remove the pan from the heat. Leave to cool.

When cold, add the lemon juice to the mixture, and beat until creamy. Shape the mixture into balls about ¾ inch (2 cm) in diameter. Put the coconut into a small bowl. Roll the balls in the coconut, and arrange on the prepared baking tray. Leave in a cool place for several hours.

COCONUT ICE

A favourite British sweet.

Butter
¼ pint (150 ml) milk
2 pounds (900 g) sugar
8–10 ounces (225–275 g) desiccated
    shredded coconut
1 teaspoon vanilla essence
Red food colouring

Grease an 8 inch (20 cm) square baking tin with butter. Put aside until needed.

In a heavy pan, mix milk with ¼ pint (150 ml) water. Add sugar and 1 ounce (25 g) butter, and heat gently, stirring, until they have dissolved. Bring to boiling point. Cover pan and simmer for 2 minutes. Then remove lid and boil gently for 7–10 minutes longer, stirring frequently, until temperature of liquid reaches 240°F or 115°C on a sugar thermometer (soft-ball stage).

Draw pan off heat. Add coconut and vanilla, and beat vigorously with a wooden spoon until mixture is thick and creamy. Pour half of the mixture into the buttered baking tin. Tint the remaining mixture pale pink with a few drops of red food colouring (for safety's sake, administer a drop at a time on a matchstick until the right shade is reached). Pour it out evenly over the white layer of coconut ice, if necessary levelling it out with the back of a spoon.

When ice is setting but not hard yet, mark it into about 60 1 inch (2.5 cm) squares with the point of a sharp knife.

Leave until quite cold before cutting along the marks to divide cubes completely.

COCONUT MACAROONS

A cheaper alternative to pure almond macaroons. To pursue the deception, flavour the mixture with a few drops of real almond essence instead of vanilla.

4 ounces (100–125 g) desiccated
    shredded coconut
4 ounces (100–125 g) caster sugar
2 teaspoons plain flour or cornflour
2 egg whites
½ teaspoon vanilla essence
Rice paper, for baking sheets

In a bowl, stir coconut, sugar and flour together until well mixed. Whisk egg whites until they hold soft peaks and mix lightly with dry ingredients. Sprinkle in vanilla (or almond) essence while you are mixing.

Drop large teaspoonfuls of coconut mixture, well spaced apart, on baking sheets lined with rice paper. Bake in a slow oven (325°F, 170°C, Mark 3) for 20–30 minutes, until macaroons are lightly coloured and firm to the touch.

Cool on a wire rack. When cold, crumble off excess rice paper around sides of each macaroon. Store in an airtight box or jar.

Makes 12–24, depending on size.

CRANBERRY

Although varieties of cranberry are to be found growing wild in cool, swampy areas all over Europe, Asia and North America, only the large, bright red berry native to North America, *Vaccinium macrocarpon*, has become an important culinary fruit. In America, it has been cultivated commercially on an ever-increasing scale for nearly 200 years.

When the first settlers arrived in America in the sixteenth century, they found that the local Indians had long been using the cranberries they gathered in the wild in a variety of ways. They added the berries to pemmican, a nutritious and long-lasting sausage of sun-dried chopped venison or bear meat and fat, which early North American explorers included in the provisions they carried on long journeys; and mixed them into succotash, a dish of fresh broad beans and sweetcorn, which is still an American favourite today. Cranberries were used to treat arrow wounds and added to poultices, while cranberry juice was used as a dye with which to decorate their rugs and blankets. The Indians quickly introduced the settlers to this marvellously versatile fruit and showed them where and when to look for it. So it is quite possible that cranberries accompanied the first Thanksgiving turkey as they do to this day.

European cranberries are smaller and darker in colour than the American variety, and are used to make sauces and relishes very similar to the American ones. The British often serve cranberries with the Christmas turkey, preferably cold on Boxing Day, whereas the Continentals use the sauce to accompany meat dishes of all kinds, especially game.

Fresh European cranberries are rarely to be found in British shops. At best, you may come across jars of cranberry sauce imported from Eastern Europe. Otherwise, the market is dominated by cranberries imported from the United States – fresh, frozen and preserved in the form of sauces, jellies and juice. The cranberries sold fresh in autumn and winter are almost invariably in excellent condition, plump, bright and dry. They also freeze perfectly in their punnets or plastic bags.

Cranberries are far too sour and astringent to eat without sugar, but with generous sweetening they become deliciously tart. Chopped up raw, or cooked, they may be used on their own or matched with other flavours and textures such as oranges or apples and almonds or walnuts.

The colour of cranberries is so brilliant, their flavour so sharp and penetrating, that just a small amount will go a long way. They can be used to make dips, sorbets and ice creams. Or try chopping up a handful of berries and add them to pancake batter, a scone dough, or the batter for a rich fruit cake in place of some of the dried fruit.

Cranberries contain a significant amount of Vitamin C.

SKIN BLEACH

This mixture helps to bleach reddened skins, freckles and fading suntans.

Take a good handful of fresh cranberries, crush them, and mix with enough buttermilk to make a not too runny paste. Spread this on the affected part and leave for 15—20 minutes. You may need to cover it with a cloth to keep it in place. Wash off with lukewarm water.

As buttermilk has an astringent effect, you will probably need to apply a moisturizer if you have a dry skin.

CRANBERRY AND TURKEY PIE

1 ounce (25 g) butter
1 ounce (25 g) plain flour
¼ pint (150 ml) chicken stock
¼ pint (150 ml) milk
12 ounces (350 g) turkey meat, cut into small pieces
8 ounces (225 g) mushrooms, cleaned and sliced
2 stalks celery, cleaned and chopped into 1 inch (2·5 cm) lengths
8 ounces (225 g) fresh cranberries
3 tablespoons medium sherry
4 fluid ounces (100 ml) single cream
Juice of 1 lemon
8 ounces (225 g) rough puff pastry (page 203)
1 egg, lightly beaten

Melt the butter in a large, thick saucepan, and stir in the flour to form a smooth paste. Gradually pour in the chicken stock and milk, stirring continuously to form a smooth sauce. Cook over a low heat until the sauce begins to thicken. Remove from the heat and add the turkey, mushroom slices, celery and cranberries. Now pour the sherry, the cream and lemon juice into the saucepan. Stir the mixture and heat gently, without boiling. Leave over a low heat to keep warm, but do not allow to boil.

Grease a large ovenproof pie dish. Roll out the pastry on a floured board until about ⅛ inch (3 mm) thick. Transfer the contents of the saucepan to the prepared ovenproof dish. Cover with the pastry. Brush the pastry with the beaten egg. Bake in a hot oven (425°F, 220°C, Mark 7) for 30 minutes or until the pastry is brown, and serve immediately.

Serves 4—6.

CRANBERRY STUFFING

An unusual and delicious stuffing that will be enough for a 10 pound (4·5 kilo) turkey, a goose, 2 large ducks or a crown roast of pork. You will need about 8 ounces (225 g) day-old bread that has been trimmed of crusts.

1 pound (450 g) cranberries
4 ounces (100–125 g) butter
6 ounces (175 g) sugar
About 8 ounces (225 g) trimmed day-old bread cubes (see above)
2 teaspoons crumbled dried marjoram
Salt and freshly ground black pepper
2 tablespoons finely chopped parsley
Scant ½ pint (300 ml) pure orange or apple juice

Rinse cranberries. Shake them dry in a colander and put them through a meat mincer.

In a large, preferably wide pan, melt butter without letting it sizzle or colour. Add minced cranberries. Cook gently for 5 minutes, stirring frequently. Stir in sugar and continue cooking over low heat for a few minutes longer, stirring until sugar has dissolved.

Stir in bread cubes, turning them over to coat them individually with cranberry sauce. Sprinkle with marjoram and season generously with about 2 teaspoons salt and a grinding of black pepper.

Finally, stir in parsley, sprinkle with fruit juice, and cook gently for 5 minutes, stirring frequently.

Allow to cool, then use the stuffing as required.

CRANBERRY FLUFF

1½ pounds (700 g) fresh or frozen cranberries, thawed
1 pound (450–500 g) sugar

Pick over berries, if using fresh ones, and rinse well. Pat dry. Put them into a blender or food processor with the sugar and work to a fine-textured purée. With a blender, you may have to do this in batches. Turn the purée into a bowl and leave for 3–4 hours to set.

Serve with crisp wafer biscuits.

Serves 6.

CRANBERRY DIP

For serving with fresh fruits.

3 ounces (75 g) full-fat cream cheese
¼ pint (150 ml) natural yoghourt
2 ounces (50 g) cranberry sauce or cranberry orange sauce (page 61)

Beat the cream cheese until softened, then beat in the yoghourt until smooth. Stir in cranberry sauce or cranberry orange sauce to taste.

Serves 4.

CRANBERRY ORANGE COMPOTE

This refreshing mixture may either be served with the main course or spooned over ice cream or cake and eaten for dessert.

2 pounds (900 g) cranberries
2 large, thin-skinned oranges
Sugar
4 tablespoons orange liqueur or brandy

Rinse and drain cranberries. Scrub 1 orange under the cold tap but leave it unpeeled. Peel the other one, stripping off every scrap of white pith (discard peel and pith). Cut both oranges up. Pick out and discard all the pips.

Put cranberries and oranges through a meat mincer. In a bowl, mix them together with sugar to taste and orange liqueur or brandy. Cover bowl and chill for several hours before serving.

CRANBERRY FROSTING

2 ounces (50 g) butter, softened
1 egg yolk
2 tablespoons cranberry jelly
½ teaspoon vanilla essence
4 ounces (100 g) icing sugar

In a small bowl, combine the softened butter with all the other ingredients. Beat until smooth and thick. Use to decorate sponge cakes or buns.

CRANBERRY RELISH

8 ounces (225 g) fresh cranberries
8 ounces (225 g) sugar
1 small, thin-skinned orange
½ small lemon
1 small, sharply flavoured apple

Rinse cranberries and drain them thoroughly in a colander. Cut the orange into chunks, removing the pips, and cut the end off the lemon half, removing any pips. Quarter and core the apple.

Put all the ingredients through the coarse blade of a meat mincer. Mix them together in a bowl, spoon into a large, screw-top jar, and store in the refrigerator for at least 24 hours.

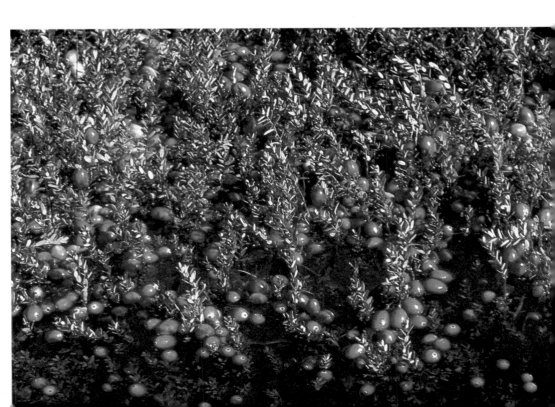

CRANBERRY TART

From *The Cook's Oracle* by Dr Kitchener (1823).

'Take Swedish, American, or Russian Cranberries, pick and wash them in several waters, put them into a dish, with the juice of half a Lemon, a quarter of a pound of moist (ie unrefined soft brown) or pounded Loaf (granulated) Sugar, to a quart of Cranberries. Cover it with Puff or Tart (rich shortcrust) Paste, and bake it three quarters of an hour; if Tart Paste is used, draw it from the oven five minutes before it is done, and ice it,* return it to the oven, and send it to table cold.'

*The following instructions are given for icing fruit tarts, puffs or pastry:

'Beat up in a half pint mug the White of two Eggs to a solid froth; – lay some on the middle of the pie with a paste brush, – sift over plenty of pounded Sugar, and press it down with the hand, – wash out the brush, and splash by degrees with Water till the Sugar is dissolved, – and put it in the oven for ten minutes, and serve it up cold.'

CRANBERRY SORBET

This refreshing sorbet makes a change from the more usual flavours, but it is no coincidence that orange juice is added to complement the tart cranberry flavour. If you find the juicy purée too sweet, sharpen it with a little lemon juice before freezing.

8 ounces (225 g) fresh or frozen cranberries
8 ounces (225 g) sugar
One 3 inch (7.5 cm) cinnamon stick
1/4 pint (150 ml) orange juice
1 teaspoon gelatine
1 large egg white
A little whipped cream to decorate
Thin orange slices to decorate

Pick over the cranberries, if using fresh ones, then rinse well. Put in a saucepan with 1/3 pint (200 ml) water. If using frozen berries, use a little less water. Bring to the boil and simmer the cranberries until soft, then purée in a blender or food processor and return them to the pan.

Add the sugar, cinnamon and orange juice and bring to the boil. Boil without stirring for 5 minutes. Remove the cinnamon stick.

Dissolve the gelatine in 1½ tablespoons cold water, then stir it into the hot juice in the pan and continue stirring until the spongy gelatine dissolves completely. Take the pan off the heat and allow to cool, then chill.

Beat the egg white until stiff, then fold this into the chilled purée. Turn the mixture into a container and cover with foil. Freeze until slushy.

Remove and beat well to break up the ice crystals, then cover again and freeze until firm.

About 15 minutes before serving, transfer the sorbet to the main compartment of the refrigerator to soften a little. Serve decorated with whipped cream or thin orange slices.

Serves 4.

CRANBERRY LAYER DESSERT

Another Scandinavian special. The rich taste of the dark rye bread contrasts well with the cranberries, and would also complement a mixture of raspberries and redcurrants.

1 pound (450 g) fresh or frozen cranberries, thawed
4 tablespoons lemon juice
4–5 ounces (125–150 g) caster sugar
4 ounces (125 g) dark rye bread
½ pint (300 ml) whipping cream

Pick over berries, if using fresh ones, then rinse well under cold running water. Dry well on kitchen paper. Make sure frozen ones are thoroughly thawed, if using these.

Put the berries in a pan with the lemon juice and cook over moderate heat for about 10 minutes. Stir in sugar to taste and allow the berries to cool completely.

Crumble the rye bread, or use a blender or food processor to make it into breadcrumbs. Whip the cream until it holds soft peaks. In 4 individual glasses, arrange the cranberry sauce, crumbs and whipped cream in layers, sprinkling a few breadcrumbs over the top.

Decorate with a swirl of whipped cream and chill well before serving.

Serves 4.

CRANBERRY PARFAIT

This luscious dessert is popular in Finland, where cranberries abound. You can also use raspberries or strawberries. If using frozen fruit, remember to thaw them first.

2 egg yolks
5 ounces (150 g) icing sugar
5 ounces (150 g) cranberries
Just under ¾ pint (400 ml) double cream
A little extra whipped cream to decorate (optional)

In a bowl, beat together the egg yolks and sugar until the mixture is foamy. Purée the cranberries in a blender or food processor and whisk into the mixture. Adjust sweetness.

Whisk the cream until it holds soft peaks, then fold this into the cranberry mixture until coloured an even pink.

Rinse out a 2 pint (1 litre) metal mould in cold water, then pour in the parfait mixture. Freeze for at least 8 hours, or overnight.

To unmould the parfait, dip the outside of the mould in hot water for about 20 seconds, then invert it on to a serving dish. Decorate with whipped cream, if liked.

Serves 4–6.

SIMPLE CRANBERRY SAUCE

Recipes for a basic cooked cranberry sauce are two a penny. This one is very simple, but if you substitute red wine or port for the water, the sauce will be superb.

½ pound (225 g) sugar
¼ pint (150 ml) water (see above)
1 pound (450 g) fresh cranberries

Dissolve the sugar in the water over low heat, and then add the cranberries. Simmer, stirring frequently and very gently, until the skins all pop (with a snap rather like the famous rice cereal when milk is poured over it) after about 7 minutes.

CRANBERRY ORANGE SAUCE

A Christmas preserve to make ahead of time and store in the refrigerator or freezer, ready to brighten up the cold turkey that almost inevitably appears on the table on Boxing Day. It will keep for up to a month in the refrigerator, several months if stored in the freezer.

7 ounces (200 g) sugar
½ pint (300 ml) fresh orange juice
12 ounces (350 g) cranberries
1 teaspoon finely grated
  orange rind

In a heavy pan, dissolve the sugar in orange juice over low heat, stirring. Add the cranberries and grated orange rind, and bring to the boil, stirring. Simmer, covered, for a few minutes until the cranberries pop open and soften.

Pour into a jar (for the refrigerator) or a carton (for the freezer). Cover tightly and store in the refrigerator (see above).

APPLE CRANBERRY SAUCE

Delicious with any dish of roast poultry, and an economical way of making a few cranberries go a long way.

8 ounces (225 g) peeled, cored sour
  apples, thinly sliced (prepared
  weight)
8 ounces (225 g) fresh or frozen
  cranberries
8 ounces (225 g) sugar

Combine all the ingredients in a heavy pan. Add about ¼ pint (150 ml) water and slowly bring to boiling point, stirring until sugar has dissolved.

Cover pan and cook gently for 10–15 minutes longer until cranberry skins have burst and fruits are pulpy.

Pour into a bowl. Cool slightly. Then whisk until well blended and fluffy.

Serve cold.

CRANBERRY ALMOND SAUCE

An interesting combination of textures and flavours. Store for, say, a month in the refrigerator.

1 pound (450 g) cranberries
1 pound (450 g) sugar
¼ pint (150 ml) fresh orange juice
6–8 tablespoons blanched slivered
  almonds
Finely grated rind of 1 small orange

Rinse cranberries in a colander and shake them dry. In a large, heavy saucepan (or a small preserving pan), mix cranberries, sugar and orange juice, and sprinkle with 5 or 6 tablespoons water. Stir over low heat until sugar dissolves, then raise heat to moderate, bring to boiling point and boil, stirring frequently, for about 5 minutes until cranberries pop open. Skim surface clear of scum and stir in almonds and orange rind.

Allow to cool, stirring occasionally. Pot, cover and store in the refrigerator or freezer (see above).

CRANBERRY PARTY PUNCH

A sparkling, non-alcoholic party punch.

8 ounces (225 g) sugar
1½ pints (900 ml) cranberry juice
1¼ pints (750 ml) orange juice
¼ pint (150 ml) lemon juice
2¼ pints (1.25 litres) ginger ale
2 lemons
Ice cubes for serving

Make a sugar syrup by dissolving the sugar in ¼ pint (150 ml) water in a heavy-based pan. Stir from time to time until the sugar is dissolved, then set aside to cool.

Mix together the cranberry juice, orange juice, lemon juice and chill until ready to serve. Just before serving, pour in the ginger ale and sweeten to taste with the sugar syrup. Thinly slice the lemons and float the slices on top of the punch. Put in some ice cubes and serve.

Makes about 20 glasses.

CRANBERRY CANDY

You can use any soft fruit that you like in this Italian recipe.

1 pound (450 g) fresh cranberries
2 ounces (50 g) black grapes
1 pound (450 g) demerara sugar

Line a tin about 15 inches (37·5 cm) square and 3 inches (7·5 cm) deep with greaseproof paper. Oil the surface of the paper lightly.

Wash the fruit in a colander under cold running water. Discard any stalks or damaged berries. Put the cranberries and grapes into a bowl, and crush with a wooden spoon. Press this pulp through a fine sieve to remove the pips and skins. Put the remaining pulp in a thick saucepan, and cook over a medium heat for 30–40 minutes, stirring occasionally, until it has the consistency of thick jam. Leave on one side.

In another saucepan, dissolve the sugar in 6 fluid ounces (175 ml) water over a low heat. Bring to the boil, stirring frequently and cook until the syrup reaches a temperature of 310°F (154°C) on a sugar thermometer. Drop a little of the syrup into a bowl of iced water. Remove immediately. This sample should snap firmly into two when bent. If it does not, heat the syrup a few more degrees and test again, until the test sample snaps firmly into two.

Remove the syrup from the heat, stir in the fruit pulp, return the pan to the heat and cook the mixture gently, stirring constantly, until the surface appears to cloud over. Pour into the prepared tin and leave to set, in a cool place. When almost set, mark out into squares. When set, turn out of the tin and break into separate pieces.

DATE

One of the first foods eaten by man, dates are still a staple in the diet of desert nomads and play an important part in many Arab dishes.

Date palms may well have grown in the Garden of Eden. They have been found in the tombs of the pharaohs and the cultivation of date palms is depicted on Assyrian murals. To the Muslim, the date palm is 'the tree of life' which was fashioned by God out of the dust left over after the creation of Adam. Dates were introduced into California by the Spanish in the second half of the eighteenth century and have flourished there ever since.

Fresh ripe dates are delicious eaten on their own as a snack, just as they are, or with soft white cream cheese. Or try halving them lengthwise, stoning them and adding them to a fresh mixed fruit salad. However, remember that unless you are simply snacking on fresh dates, it is always a good idea to peel off their papery outer skins as these are hard and have an unpleasant, acrid taste.

Dried dates, with which most people are far more familiar, are produced in a variety of forms. The finest quality are large specimens, carefully packaged side by side in rectangular, rounded-end boxes with tiny white plastic forks to help extract them. Smooth and plump, they are barely distinguishable from fresh dates until you taste them. Although they have none of the cloying sweetness normally associated with dried dates, they are rather sweeter than the fresh fruit.

Next come the dates which have been stoned and dried whole but are less carefully packed in large cartons. These may be stuffed and eaten whole, sliced into winter vegetable and fruit salads, or chopped and mixed with other dried fruits in substantial puddings, breads and cakes. You will find that dates go well with most other fruits, particularly orchard and citrus fruits which need sweetening. These dried dates should not be confused with the dried olive-sized fruits known as red dates or jujubes which you will find in Oriental stores and which are used in Chinese cooking to flavour both savoury and sweet dishes.

Finally, slab dates are cheapest of all. These are fine for cooking and baking but must always be carefully examined for stray pieces of broken stone.

Dates are rarely used in preserves or as a flavouring base for liquors. One strong date liqueur called *sirop* was described by someone who tasted it as 'the strongest and most dreadful drink ever invented'.

Especially when dried, dates are among the most nutritious of fruits, high in potassium and folic acid. They are also an excellent restorative and energy-giving food for anyone recovering from a debilitating illness.

The 1837 edition of the *London Encyclopaedia* records that the male flowers, if eaten when still tender and sprinkled with a little lemon juice, are 'provocative'.

DATE AND WALNUT SPREAD

A delicious – and healthy – spread for wholemeal bread.

8 ounces (225 g) stoned dates
2–3 teaspoons lemon juice
2 ounces (50 g) walnuts

Chop the dates very finely, or work to a paste in a blender. Heat gently in a pan with the lemon juice and ¾ pint (400 ml) water until thick. Cool a little, then chop and add the walnuts. Store in a screw-topped jar.

MOROCCAN DATE SALAD

A good buffet dish or starter. You can use a mild herb vinegar instead of orange-flower water, though the latter gives the authentic taste.

1 crisp lettuce
3 oranges
2 ounces (50 g) stoned dates
2 ounces (50 g) fresh walnuts
½ teaspoon ground cinnamon

Dressing
2 tablespoons lemon juice
1–2 tablespoons caster sugar
2 tablespoons orange-flower water
  (see above)

Wash the lettuce, removing any bruised outer leaves. Shred the remainder and arrange in the bottom of a salad bowl. Peel the oranges and slice them thinly across the segments into circles. Arrange these over the shredded lettuce. Finely chop the dates and walnuts and sprinkle over the top.

Whisk together the lemon juice, sugar and orange-flower water and pour over the salad. Sprinkle with cinnamon and serve.

Serves 6.

KOREAN RICE WITH DATES

Use fine Chinese or Indian basmati rice for this dish. It is also very good made with brown rice, although it will absorb more water (say 2 cups) and take longer to cook. The ingredients are measured in cups to ensure that the right proportion of dry ingredients to liquid is maintained. This rice goes beautifully with poultry or lamb.

1 cup rice (see above)
¼ cup plump dried dates
Salt

In a large sieve, rinse rice under the cold tap until water runs clear. Leave aside to drain for about 1 hour.

Cut each date lengthwise in four and remove stones.

In a heavy pan with a tight-fitting lid, combine rice, quartered dates, a generous sprinkling of salt and 1¼ cups water. Leave to soak for 30 minutes.

Bring to boiling point, stir well, lower heat to a bare simmer and cover pan tightly. Cook for 15 minutes. Then, without touching lid, let pan stand for about 15 minutes longer before fluffing up rice with a fork and serving.

Serves 3–4.

DATES WITH CREAM

2 tablespoons tasteless vegetable oil
8 ounces (225 g) stoned fresh (or very plump dried) dates
8 fluid ounces (225 ml) chilled double cream
2 tablespoons coarsely chopped pistachio nuts

In a large, heavy frying pan, heat oil, and add dates. Sprinkle with a tablespoon of water and fry, stirring, just long enough to heat dates through and evaporate water.

Whip cream very lightly, just enough to thicken it without making it stiff enough to hold its shape. Stir in chopped pistachio nuts.

With a slotted spoon, place hot dates in a serving dish. Pour cream and nuts over dates and serve.

Serves 4–6.

STEAMED DATE PUDDING I

A perfect pudding for a chilly winter's day. Serve it with a sauce, vanilla custard, clear lemon or sherry sauce. A wedge of left-over pudding should be wrapped in foil and reheated in a moderate oven (350°F, 180°C, Mark 4) for 20–30 minutes before serving with some more sauce.

8 ounces (225 g) plump
*   dried dates*
6 ounces (175 g) plain flour
2 teaspoons baking powder
Generous pinch of salt
Butter
3 ounces (75 g) caster sugar
2 eggs, lightly beaten
Juice and finely grated rind
*   of 1 small lemon*
6–8 tablespoons milk

Pit dates and cut them into small pieces (about the size of sultanas). Sift flour, baking powder and salt together. Put aside until needed.

Cream 4 ounces (100–125 g) butter with the sugar until fluffy. Add eggs, a few tablespoons at a time, alternating them with a tablespoon or two of the flour to prevent mixture curdling.

Beat well between each addition. Beat in lemon juice and grated lemon rind.

Fold in flour mixture alternately with enough milk to make a dropping batter. Finally, fold in dates.

Spoon batter into a large, well-buttered pudding basin. Level batter off and make an indentation in the middle with the back of your spoon. Cover bowl with a double thickness of greaseproof paper or with foil, well buttered on the underside. Tie down with fine string. Place on a trivet or rack in a pan with boiling water to come about halfway up sides. Cover tightly and steam in simmering water for about 1½ hours, or until pudding is light-textured and well risen, topping up level of water with *boiling* water as it evaporates.

Turn pudding out on to a heated serving platter and serve hot with the sauce of your choice.

Serves 6–8.

Note: If you wish to steam the pudding in a pressure cooker, follow manufacturer's instructions.

CHINESE DATE PANCAKES

10–12 pancakes about 9 inches
    (22·5 cm) in diameter (page 92)
1¾ pounds (800 g) plump dried dates
3 teaspoons sesame oil
About 8 ounces (225 g) sugar
Peanut or corn oil, for frying

Fry pancakes and keep them soft and warm under a large plate or wrapped in foil.

Rinse dates. Put them in a bowl and steam in a covered pan over simmering water for 15 minutes. Cool. Remove stones and take off as much of the hard outer skins as possible. Cut dates up and blend to a paste in an electric blender or food processor.

In a large frying pan, heat sesame oil. Add date paste and sugar to taste, and cook over low heat, stirring constantly, for about 7 minutes.

Spread each pancake with date paste. Fold them in half and fry in a little oil until a rich golden colour on both sides.

Cut in strips and serve.

Serves 6.

DATE SQUARES

2 ounces (50 g) walnuts
3 ounces (75 g) wholemeal biscuits
½ teaspoon baking powder
Generous pinch of salt
3 eggs
4 ounces (100–125 g) soft dark brown
    sugar
½ teaspoon vanilla essence
6 ounces (175 g) dates, pitted and
    chopped
Butter, for baking tin

In a food processor or electric blender, grind the walnuts finely. Tip them into a bowl and put them aside. In the same way, grind the biscuits to a fine meal. (Alternatively, put the biscuits in a plastic bag and crush them with a rolling pin until reduced to powdery crumbs.) Mix crumbs well with baking powder and salt.

Beat eggs until fluffy and lemon-coloured. Gradually add sugar, beating vigorously, and vanilla essence. Fold in biscuit mixture, followed by ground walnuts and dates.

Pour mixture into a large, square, buttered, baking tin and bake in a moderate oven (350°F, 180°C, Mark 4) for 30 minutes, or until the surface is lightly coloured and feels firm.

Allow the slab to cool in its tin before cutting it in 4, and each quarter into 4 squares.

DATE BREAD

A good, basic loaf which freezes well. Add a handful of chopped walnuts to vary the texture, or half a teaspoon of mixed spice.

2 ounces (50 g) butter
6 ounces (175 g) soft brown sugar
1 egg
8 ounces (225 g) plain flour
½ teaspoon salt
1 teaspoon bicarbonate of soda
4 ounces (100–125 g) stoned dates

In a pan over moderate heat, melt the butter and sugar in ¼ pint (150 ml) water. Stir, then take off the heat and allow to cool. Beat the egg and stir in the cooled butter and sugar mixture.

Sift the flour into a bowl with the salt and bicarbonate of soda. Make a well in the centre and pour in the liquid ingredients. Add the dates and mix well until the batter is smooth. Pour into a greased 2 pound (900 g) loaf tin and bake in a moderate oven (350°F, 180°C, Mark 4) for 50–60 minutes. Test the centre with a skewer – if it comes out clean, the date bread is ready to be turned out on to a wire rack to cool.

CHOCOLATE DATE CAKE

For this American cake you will need a large, tubular cake tin about 9 inches (22·5 cm) in diameter. However, if you cannot get hold of one of these, the cake may be baked in 2 large layer cake tins, then sandwiched and covered with cream. If liked, the cake may also be decorated with a sprinkling of coarsely grated bitter chocolate or with whole stoned plump dried dates.

3 tablespoons plain flour
2 tablespoons unsweetened cocoa
    powder
1 teaspoon baking powder
4 eggs, separated
8 ounces (225 g) caster sugar
1–2 tablespoons fresh orange
    juice
6 ounces (175 g) stoned dried dates,
    chopped
6 ounces (175 g) walnuts, chopped
Pinch of salt
Butter, for cake tin
½ pint (300 ml) double or whipping
    cream

Sift flour with cocoa and baking powder. Beat egg yolks and sugar together until thick and fluffy. Beat in a tablespoon of orange juice. Sift flour and cocoa mixture again over the surface, and with a large metal spoon, lightly fold it in, together with a little more orange juice if necessary to make a light, creamy batter. Fold in chopped dates and walnuts until thoroughly mixed.

Beat egg whites with a pinch of salt until stiff but not dry. Gently fold into cake batter. Immediately spoon batter into cake tin or tins that have been thoroughly greased with butter. Bake in a slow oven (325°F, 170°C, Mark 3) until cake is well risen, lightly coloured on top and has shrunk away slightly from sides of tin. This will take 35–45 minutes.

Allow cake to 'settle' for 15 minutes before turning out on a wire rack. Leave until quite cold before covering and/or sandwiching cake with lightly sweetened whipped cream and decorating it if liked (see above).

MARZIPAN DATES

Choose top-quality dried dessert dates, the kind that come neatly packed in pretty, oblong wooden boxes with rounded ends. Carefully slit each date down one side, remove stones and replace them with a piece of marzipan. Lightly press the dates back into shape. Finally, roll each date in caster sugar.

For chocolate dates, you will need a 3½ ounce (90 g) bar of good-quality dark dessert or cooking chocolate. Break the chocolate into the top of a double saucepan or a bowl fitted snugly over a pan of simmering water, and heat gently just long enough to melt the chocolate. Beat in a knob of butter.

When chocolate is smooth, using two forks, coat each stuffed date with chocolate, allowing excess to drip back into the pan. Leave to cool and harden on a rack over a baking sheet to catch any drips, or on a sheet of non-stick paper. When dry, arrange the dates in little paper cases.

MOROCCAN STUFFED DATES

A variation on the familiar theme of dates stuffed with marzipan. Afterwards, instead of being coated with caster sugar, they are sometimes dipped in thick syrup, then rolled in sugar and allowed to dry before serving.

1 pound (450 g) dried dessert dates
8 ounces (225 g) almonds
About 4–5 tablespoons caster sugar
2–3 tablespoons orange-flower water
Caster sugar, to decorate

Carefully slit dates down one side and remove stones. Blanch and peel almonds and toast them in the oven, spread out on a baking sheet, shaking sheet and stirring them frequently so that they brown evenly. Allow almonds to cool.

In an electric blender or food processor, grind almonds finely. Stir in sugar to taste and gradually add enough orange-flower water to make mixture hold together. (This may take some time, as when making an ordinary marzipan.)

Stuff stoned dates with small rolls of orange marzipan and lightly press them shut again. Roll dates in caster sugar and serve in little paper cases.

RUM DATES

Plump dried dessert dates
Rum
Blanched almonds or shelled walnuts
Sifted icing sugar

Slit dates down one side and carefully remove stones.

Select a large, wide-necked bottle with a good lid. Pour in rum to come about a quarter of the way up. Then pack in stoned dates to fill bottle about three-quarters full. Close bottle tightly, lay it on its side and allow dates to macerate in the rum for about 3 months. Every day or so, roll the bottle round to keep the dates wet with rum.

Empty the bottle out into a sieve set over a bowl to catch the remains of the rum. Pat dates lightly with kitchen towels to remove any excess rum. Stuff each date with an almond or a piece of walnut in place of the stone and lightly press shut again.

Roll dates in sifted icing sugar and pack in a clean, dry glass jar or box. When serving the dates (they make a lovely *petit four* with after-dinner coffee), stick a wooden toothpick in each one.

DATE SWEETENER

A liquid counterpart to date 'sugar', from *Fruit and Vegetables in Particular* by Rita Greer who, when faced with the daunting task of devising a diet for her husband that was not only sugar-free but restricted in almost every other way imaginable, produced not one but three books of delicious food.

1 pound (450 g) packet cooking dates (ie slab dates)

Put the date slab on a cutting board and, using a large kitchen knife, cut into thin slices. Put into a medium saucepan with 1 pint (550 ml) cold water and bring to the boil. Simmer for 10 minutes, stirring from time to time. Allow to cool. Beat with a wooden spoon until you have a smooth, thick sweetener. Spoon into screw-top jars and store in the refrigerator. Keep for up to a week and use as required.

Use in cake-making, for mixing with fruit juice, adding to soups, stews, casseroles and anything which doesn't need a dry sweetener. If you prefer to liquidize the sweetener it needs only a 5-second whizz.

Although cooking dates are supposed to be stoned, very often little fragments remain and sometimes even whole stones. The quickest way to locate these is to search the cooled mixture with clean fingers.

DATE 'SUGAR'

Over the past few years, refined white cane and beet sugars have been subjected to a great deal of criticism as 'empty calories' with no nutritional value. Brown sugar is only marginally better, provided it is not just white sugar that has been dyed brown. Date sugar, on the other hand, is pure dried fruit ground whole, an unrefined natural sweetener that behaves and looks very much like soft brown sugar.

Store it in an airtight and moisture-proof jar as it will quickly absorb any moisture in the air and turn unmanageably sticky and lumpy.

1 pound (450 g) unstoned dried dates

Stone the dates, cutting each one in quarters, and arrange the pieces in one layer on a large, ungreased baking sheet. Dry the dates out in a very cool oven (250°F, 130°C, Mark ½) until they are rock hard. This will take several hours, anything up to a whole day or night, depending on the quality of the dates. Switch the oven off, leave the door ajar and allow dates to cool to room temperature.

Drop the pieces of date, a few at a time, on to the whirling blades of an electric blender or food processor, and blend until they are reduced to a fine powder. Store as directed above.

Makes about 8 ounces (225 g).

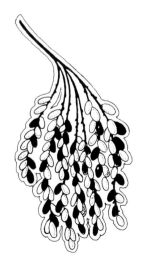

FIG

From the Mediterranean to the West Coast of America, figs flourish in warm regions. They will even grow reasonably well and produce fruit as far north as Scotland, albeit under glass, but their native home is probably the Middle East. Indeed, the botanical name of the variety *Ficus carica* comes directly from the ancient region of Caria in Asia Minor.

In the classical world, figs were cultivated with enthusiasm. They are known to have been a staple in the diet of the Spartans. Remains of dried figs have been found in Pompeii, and both the ancient Greeks and Romans respected their alleged aphrodisiac properties. The Romans fed figs to the geese they kept to warn them when invaders threatened their city. They introduced this custom to the Gauls, and in this are said to lie the origins of *foie gras*, the great French delicacy, made with the livers of force-fed geese.

Figs can be green, brown or purple-black when they are ripe, depending on the variety. But to be at their best, they must be very ripe indeed, which can be awkward as figs cannot be ripened off the tree and ripe figs do not travel well. A fig is ready to be picked when a drop of nectar collects in its 'eye', opposite the stem end, and the fruit feels quite soft when gently pressed. If the figs are not to be eaten at once, they are best stored in the bottom of the refrigerator.

Fresh figs may be eaten on their own or matched with other flavours as appetizers or sweets. The Italians traditionally accompany them with Pecorino, a hard ewe's milk cheese which is rather like Parmesan. Experiment with other cheeses such as a mixture of cream cheese and mild, soft Gorgonzola or Dolcelatte, moistened if necessary with a little thick cream. Beat this mixture together until light and smoothly blended, and spread it over the cut surfaces of fresh figs which have been halved lengthwise. You will need three or four large, juicy fig halves per person for an appetizer. Another excellent partnership is that of ripe figs and paper-thin slices of *prosciutto* (raw Parma ham). A less expensive dish for breakfast is fresh, ripe figs with crisp-grilled unsmoked bacon and a good grinding of black pepper.

For those who cannot sample the fresh fruit, there are always plenty of preserved ones, in particular canned figs, which are quite close to fresh poached ones and can in many cases be used in their place, and dried figs. Drying figs alters them radically, toughening their skins and making the seeds inside hard and gritty. Both white and black figs are dried. The black are less easily available and somewhat less sweet than white ones, but are full of flavour. Like most other dried fruit, they are graded by quality. Cellophane packets of large, moist, dried figs pressed in neat rows and topped with a bay leaf come from Izmir (Smyrna) in Turkey. These are delicious to eat as a snack by themselves, but the moisture left in them means they easily start to ferment and turn inedible. It is far better to buy fully dried, whole figs from a wholefood shop. If you rinse off any white powder from the surface, snip off the hard stem ends and soak overnight in cold water, you'll find they can often be eaten just as they are. Or after soaking, simmer them in the water for 30–40 minutes until very soft and plump. Sweeten the water with sugar or honey as desired and cool before serving. Occasionally, too, you will find small boxes of figs preserved in honey, and crystallized Chinese figs, both of which are delicious.

Sweet, ripe figs, peeled or unpeeled, can be frozen whole with or without sugar; first remove the stems. Alternatively, crush and sugar freeze them. In either case, you will need to sprinkle the fruit with lemon juice.

FIG POULTICE

Long known for their laxative properties, figs were also used as 'emollient cataplasms' or soothing poultices, for external application to boils, ulcers, carbuncles and the like.

Originally they were roasted, but today the simplest method would be to wrap fresh figs loosely in foil and bake in a medium to hot oven (375–425°F, 190–220°C, Mark 5–7) for 15–20 minutes. Cut in half and cool. Apply to the part to be treated, holding it in place with a piece of cloth if necessary.

Alternatively, boil the figs in as little water as possible, then mash to make a paste. Cool, and apply as above.

FIG APPETIZER

12 fresh figs
8 ounces (225 g) cream cheese
4 tablespoons double cream
A little lemon juice
12 crisp lettuce leaves
Paprika or a little cayenne for
  sprinkling

Trim the stalks from the figs and cut each one into quarters almost through to the base. Beat the cream cheese with the cream and lemon juice and spoon or pipe into the centre of the figs. Arrange each fig on a lettuce leaf and sprinkle with paprika or a little cayenne.

Serves 6.

ITALIAN FIGS WITH SALAMI

This is an appetizer which should be served only when the best, sweet, ripe figs (either white or black) are available.

Per person:
3 ripe figs
About 1 ounce (25 g) Italian salami, sliced

Chill the figs in the refrigerator for several hours before serving. Or, if time is short, drop them into a bowl of water and ice cubes until they are very cold indeed, then drain them and pat them dry. Carefully skin salami slices.

Just before serving, peel the outer skin from each fig and slash a deep cross through the top (stem end) to expose the red flesh and seeds.

Arrange the figs and salami on separate platters so that each guest can help himself.

Note: If salami is not available, the figs are also delicious eaten with raw Parma ham (*prosciutto*) or raw Westphalian ham, sliced paper-thin.

KHOSHAF
Syrian Fruit Salad

This refreshing fruit salad can be made with any combination of dried fruits, including figs. Prepare two days in advance.

4 ounces (100–125 g) dried figs
2 ounces (50 g) dried apricots
2 tablespoons raisins
2 tablespoons blanched almonds
2 tablespoons pine nuts (optional)
1 tablespoon honey

Wash all the dried fruit carefully in a colander under cold running water. Put into a large bowl, cover with cold water and place the bowl in the refrigerator for 48 hours.

Remove the bowl from the refrigerator. Stir in the nuts and honey. When the honey has dissolved, taste the liquid and add further honey if desired. Serve chilled.

Serves 4.

FIG AND ORANGE COMPOTE

This makes a good winter dessert, when the variety of fresh fruit available is limited. Prepare well in advance.

8 ounces (225 g) dried figs
1 tablespoon honey
3 large oranges
1 tablespoon liqueur (Cointreau or Grand Marnier)
Unsweetened whipped cream

Wash the figs in a colander under cold, running water, then leave to soak in a pan of cold water for 3 hours. Put the pan over a low heat, add the honey and cook the figs gently in the soaking water, until just soft. Do not overcook. Remove from the heat, lift out the figs using a slotted spoon and place in a bowl.

Return the pan to the heat and boil the liquid rapidly until it starts to thicken forming a syrup. Pour this honey syrup over the figs and leave to cool.

Thirty minutes before serving, peel the oranges, removing all traces of pith. Cut into thin slices and arrange in a serving dish, with the figs and syrup. Pour in the liqueur. Serve slightly chilled, with the whipped cream.

Serves 4.

FIGGY PUDDING

This traditional pudding was eaten on Mothering Sunday, and in many parts of the country figs were always in demand on Palm Sunday. Serve this one with a sherry-flavoured white sauce, or corn syrup.

6 ounces (175 g) dried figs
3 ounces (75 g) butter
3 ounces (75 g) soft brown sugar
Grated rind of 1 lemon
3 ounces (75 g) plain flour
2 ounces (50 g) fresh breadcrumbs
1 ounce (25 g) ground almonds
Pinch of mixed spice
1 teaspoon baking powder
1 egg
3 tablespoons sherry
A little milk

Soak the figs overnight, if necessary, then drain and chop, removing any stalks.

Soften the butter, beat in the sugar and lemon rind until the mixture is light and fluffy, then fold in the flour, breadcrumbs and almonds. Add the mixed spice and baking powder and stir to mix.

Beat the egg until foamy, then add to the mixture with the sherry and just enough milk to make a soft, dropping consistency. Pour or spoon the mixture into a well-greased 1½ pint (900 ml) capacity pudding basin and cover with buttered foil or greaseproof paper, leaving a pleat in the centre to allow the pudding to rise. Tie securely with string.

Steam in a steamer, or in a large pan half-filled with boiling water, for 2–3 hours, topping up with hot water during cooking.

Turn out and serve while hot.

Serves 4.

FIG AND APPLE CRISPY BAKE

8 ounces (225 g) dried figs
4 large cooking apples, peeled, cored and thinly sliced
2 tablespoons wheatgerm
4 tablespoons honey
4 tablespoons sunflower oil
3 ounces (75 g) mixed nuts, chopped
Yoghourt

Wash the figs in a colander under cold, running water. Put about 1 inch (2·5 cm) of water in a medium saucepan. Bring to the boil. Add the figs. Cover the pan and cook over low heat for 5 minutes. Remove from the heat. Strain off the liquid and discard. Cut the steamed figs into small pieces.

Grease a baking dish. Arrange the apple slices and chopped figs in the prepared baking dish. Mix the wheatgerm, honey, oil and nuts in a bowl, and sprinkle this mixture over the fruit. Bake in a moderate oven (350°F, 180°C, Mark 4) for 30 minutes, and serve hot with yoghourt.

Serves 4–6.

FIGS AND ICE CREAM

8 large, ripe, fresh figs
4–6 tablespoons light rum
4 scoops vanilla ice cream
Coarsely grated dark chocolate, to serve

Carefully wash figs and pat them dry with paper towels. Snip off any remaining stems. Quarter each fig vertically and lay them cut side up in a deepish platter or wide bowl. Sprinkle with rum. Cover bowl and chill figs for at least 2 hours, gently turning them over a couple of times.

When ready to serve, put a scoop of ice cream in each of 4 individual glass dishes and surround with figs and their liquor. Sprinkle scoops of ice cream generously with chocolate. Serve immediately.

Serves 4.

FIGS AND PEACHES IN CREAM

A delightfully extravagant sweet that shows the fruits off to advantage.

4 large ripe peaches
¼ pint (150 ml) white wine
2 tablespoons sugar
1 vanilla pod, split lengthwise
4 large ripe figs (about ½ pound or 225 g)
About 2 tablespoons lemon juice
¼ pint (150 ml) double cream
About 1 tablespoon vanilla-flavoured caster sugar (page 205)
Flaked blanched pistachio nuts or toasted flaked almonds, to decorate

Peel the peaches one at a time as follows. Drop a peach into boiling water for 60 seconds, or just long enough to loosen the skin. Then gently lift the peach out with a slotted spoon and holding it in the folds of a large kitchen towel to protect your fingers, carefully peel off the skin. Cut each peach in half vertically and remove the stone.

In a wide pan, combine the wine, sugar and vanilla pod. Bring to simmering point and cook gently for 5 minutes. Drop the peach halves into the simmering syrup and carefully turn them round once or twice to make sure they are thoroughly coated. Then remove the pan from the heat and leave the peaches to cool in the syrup.

Meanwhile, peel the figs, halve them vertically and brush them all over with lemon juice. Add them to the peaches in their syrup, tucking the figs under the peach halves if necessary to make sure they are totally submerged. Leave the fruit in the syrup until ready to serve.

Assemble each portion on a small flat dish as follows. Lay 2 peach halves on it, stoned side up, and cover with 2 fig halves, cut side up.

Whisk the cream lightly and sweeten to taste with vanilla-flavoured caster sugar. Top each portion with dollops of whipped cream and decorate with pistachio nuts or almonds.

Eat with small dessert knives and forks.

Serves 4.

FIGS IN BRANDY

Fresh figs are not always readily available, but if you keep a can of figs in syrup on your shelf, you'll be able to rustle up this quick dessert when unexpected guests call. It's just as good (some say even better) if fresh figs are used and the brandy and sherry are replaced by orange juice.

3 tablespoons brandy
2 tablespoons sherry
1 tablespoon grated orange rind
¼ teaspoon ground cinnamon
One 1 pound 15 ounce can (about 900 g) figs in syrup
1 ounce (25 g) toasted almonds

Heat the brandy and sherry in a pan with the orange rind and cinnamon, but do not allow it to boil.

Drain the figs, reserve the syrup and arrange the figs in a single layer in a serving dish. Pour over the hot brandy sauce, adding about 3 tablespoons of the reserved syrup. Set aside for at least an hour.

Just before serving, sprinkle with toasted almonds.

Serves 4.

FIG JAM

2 pounds (900 g) green figs
Sugar
1 teaspoon finely grated lemon rind
2–3 tablespoons lemon juice

Trim the stalks from the figs, then put the figs in a large bowl and pour over enough hot water to cover them. Leave the figs to soak for about 3 minutes.

Drain them and chop each one into small chunks. Weigh the fruit and put into a large, heavy-based pan with their equal weight in sugar. Add the lemon rind and the juice, then cook over low heat, stirring from time to time, until a clear syrup forms. Thin it down with a little water if the mixture becomes too thick.

Take the pan off the heat and let the jam cool completely before pouring it into clean dry jars for sealing and labelling.

Store in a cool, dry place.
See also page 198.

Fills about 3 jars.

GRANDMOTHER'S FIG AND WALNUT PRESERVE

Although I never tasted the original myself, my mother has more than once described the wonderful fig preserve which Grandmother in Istanbul used to prepare specially for my father. If you have access to a supply of fresh figs, it is well worth using some of them up for this preserve. In Turkey, it would be eaten with a glass of water or a small cup of black Turkish coffee.

2 pounds (900 g) fresh figs
Small shelled walnuts
1¾ pounds (800 g) sugar
1 tablespoon lemon juice

Wash figs and pat each one dry individually. Cut off any remains of stem and with the point of a knife, dig a small hole quite deeply into the stem end. With the tip of your forefinger, push a shelled walnut quite deeply down inside the fig. Repeat with remaining figs, stuffing each one with a walnut.

In a large pan, preferably enamelled, combine sugar and lemon juice with ¾ pint (400 ml) water, and bring to boiling point, stirring until sugar has dissolved. Simmer syrup for a few minutes, then add stuffed figs. Bring to boiling point slowly once more. Remove from heat, cover and leave overnight.

The following day, simmer figs in syrup until softened and swollen but not broken or burst. With a slotted spoon, lift figs out of syrup and pack them quite tightly in sterilized jam jars. Simmer syrup to thicken it if necessary and pour over figs, covering them completely.

Cover jars with lids or papers as you would jam (page 199).

Fills about 4 jars.

Note: In another version of this preserve from the same part of the world, the figs are pricked lightly all over with a fork and dipped in brandy before they are cooked in syrup, presumably to help keep them from turning mouldy.

SPICED FIG PRESERVE

A useful, chutney-like preserve that can be made at any time of the year. Serve it with plain roast poultry, the 'paler' meats such as lamb, and game dishes of all kinds.

1 pound (450 g) dried figs
¾ pint (400 ml) cider vinegar
1¼ pounds (575 g) white or soft
  brown sugar
2 tablespoons whole cloves
Twist of orange peel
1 cinnamon stick (2–3 inches
  or 5–7·5 cm)

The day before you plan to make the preserve, rinse the figs thoroughly under the cold tap and cover them with lukewarm water. Leave to soak overnight.

The following day, combine the remaining ingredients in a heavy, enamelled pan. Stir in ¼ pint (150 ml) water and bring to boiling point over low heat, stirring with a wooden spoon until sugar has dissolved. Continue to simmer gently while you finish preparing figs.

Cut off and discard tough, knobbly stem ends from figs, then halve them or cut them in quarters if they are very large.

Add figs to the simmering syrup and continue to cook for about 1 hour longer, stirring more frequently as the mixture thickens in case it should stick to the bottom of the pan.

Discard orange peel and cinnamon stick. Pot in hot, clean jars. Allow to cool, then cover (page 200).

Fills about 2 jars.

DULCE DE HIGOS
Candied Figs

This will be particularly useful for anyone who has a tree with figs which have not had a chance to ripen – a common hazard in an uncertain temperate climate.

1½ pounds (700 g) green (unripe) figs
1 tablespoon salt
1½ pounds (700 g) sugar

Scrape figs with a pumice stone. Place them in a pot with 1½ pints (900 ml) water and the salt. Bring to boiling point, remove from heat and allow to stand for about 30 seconds. Repeat this procedure 4 times (5 times in all). Drain and wash figs thoroughly in 2 or 3 changes of warm water.

Remove stems from figs and make a little cross cut in the stem end of each fig.

In a large pan, dissolve sugar in ½ pint (300 ml) water and bring to boiling point over low heat. Add figs and simmer gently for 10 minutes. Let them stand in syrup for 24 hours. Repeat this procedure another 2 times (3 times in all), by which time figs should be transparent.

Store in boxes, tins or jars.

FIG BONBONS

8 ounces (225 g) moist, dried figs
3 ounces (75 g) roasted almonds
4 ounces (100–125 g) sugar

Mince the figs, either in a mincer or, preferably, in a food processor, to form a thick paste. Chop the almonds finely. Put the minced figs and chopped almonds into a bowl and knead together by hand.

Line a tray with waxed paper. Put the sugar in a bowl. Pinch off small pieces of the fig and almond mixture and form into balls about 1 inch (2·5 cm) in diameter. Roll the fig balls in the sugar to coat them and place on the prepared tray. Leave to stand for 15 minutes until the sugar is partly absorbed. Roll each sweet once more in the sugar to coat and return to the tray. Leave for at least an hour before eating.

GOOSEBERRY

Like their botanical cousins, blackcurrants, gooseberries grow best in a cool climate. In Europe, they have been cultivated since the early Middle Ages, and the British, who grow particularly fine gooseberries, have immortalized them in the form of pies, and above all, in English gooseberry fool.

The French liking for a sharp gooseberry sauce with fatty fish such as mackerel is shown by their name for the berries, *groseilles à maquereau.*

Gooseberries can be used for cooking when they are still far too hard and sour to eat raw. In England, the first gooseberry pie traditionally used to be served at Whitsun, which falls some time in May. This is intentional. Immature green gooseberries contain far smaller, and consequently less troublesome, seeds than ripe ones. Also, their pectin and acid content are at their peak at this time, so they make easy jams and jellies either on their own or in conjunction with other fruits which may not be as rich in natural pectin.

The berries will be ready by the time elderflowers come into bloom, and this has given rise to an exceptionally successful combination of flavours — that of gooseberries and the faint, aromatic flavour of elderflowers, reminiscent of muscat grapes. But take care not to overdo this flavouring. One or two heads of blossom wrapped in a square of muslin, tied with fine string and suspended in a pan of jam or jelly while it cooks, are enough.

The gooseberry season lasts for many weeks from the time the first green berries appear on the bush ready for cooking. When it is over, you can switch to excellent preserved fruit in cans or bottled, or from the freezer. Whole gooseberries are best frozen dry, in bags; wash, dry, top and tail them first. Alternatively, the berries can be puréed and frozen.

GOOSEBERRY STUFFING

2 ounces (50 g) green gooseberries
1 medium onion
1 ounce (25 g) butter, melted
3 ounces (75 g) fresh white
  breadcrumbs
1 tablespoon chopped fresh herbs —
  thyme, parsley or sage
Salt and freshly ground black pepper
2 tablespoons chicken stock

Top and tail the gooseberries and wipe them. Peel and finely chop the onion and sauté it in the melted butter until transparent. Chop and add the gooseberries. Cook until soft, then stir in the breadcrumbs and herbs. Season with the salt and pepper and bind with stock.

Note: Use this to stuff pork — chops or joints — as well as duck, turkey or chicken.

ELIZA ACTON'S GOOSEBERRY SAUCE

'Cut the stalks and tops from half to a whole pint of quite young gooseberries, wash them well, just cover them with cold water, and boil them very gently indeed, until they are tender; drain and mix them with a small quantity of melted butter, made with rather less flour than usual (ie a *beurre manié*). Some eaters prefer the mashed gooseberries without any addition; others like that of a little ginger. The best way of making this sauce is to turn the gooseberries into a hair-sieve to drain, then to press them through it with a wooden spoon and to stir them in a clean stewpan or saucepan over the fire with from half to a whole teaspoonful of sugar, just to soften their extreme acidity, and a bit of fresh butter about the size of a walnut. When the fruit is not passed through the sieve it is an improvement to seed it.'

As usual, Miss Acton has come up with a perfect formula, this time for gooseberry sauce. Follow the second version starting 'The best way of making this sauce'. Well-drained, puréed gooseberries do not need thickening with flour.

Personally, I have never warmed to the idea of eating gooseberry sauce with grilled mackerel, classic though the combination may be. Instead, I sweeten it slightly more (exactly how much sugar you add will depend on the ripeness of the gooseberries, but keep them sharp), and serve it with roast poultry or a heavy meat such as pork.

GOOSEBERRY PIE

*1–1¼ pounds (450–550 g) slightly
under-ripe gooseberries*
*About 1 pound (450 g) rough puff or
shortcrust pastry for a 2-crust, 8 or
9 inch (20 or 22·5 cm) pie (page
203)*
*4–5 ounces (125–150 g) white or soft
brown sugar*
4 tablespoons plain flour
1½–2 ounces (40–50 g) butter
Creamy milk or egg wash

Top, tail and rinse gooseberries,
and drain them thoroughly. Allow
to drip dry in a colander while you roll
out pastry. Cut a top for pie dish, then
line with remaining pastry.

In a bowl, toss gooseberries with
sugar and flour, and pile them into the
lined pie dish. Dot with flakes of
butter. Moisten edges lightly with
water. Place pastry lid in position and
press sides down gently with your
fingertips to seal them. Flute or crimp
edges neatly and make a few gashes
in top crust to allow steam to escape.
Brush with creamy milk or egg wash.

Bake pie in a hot oven (450°F,
230°C, Mark 8) for 10 or 15 minutes.
Then lower heat to moderate (350°F,
180°C, Mark 4) and continue to bake
for about 30 minutes longer, or until
pastry crust is crisp and richly coloured, and a gooseberry prodded
with a skewer feels soft.

Serves 6–8.

Note: Egg wash consists of an egg
yolk lightly mixed with a couple of
tablespoons of cream or milk.

ENGLISH GOOSEBERRY FOOL

Do you crush or purée the fruit for a
gooseberry fool? Modern recipes
usually advise you to rub the cooked
berries through a sieve or purée them
in an electric blender, but as Jane
Grigson points out in her book *Good
Things*, the word 'fool' comes from
the French *fouler*, to crush.

Frozen green gooseberries make
an excellent fool.

*1 pound (450 g) hard green
gooseberries*
1½–2 ounces (40–50 g) butter
Sugar
½ pint (300 ml) whipping cream

Top and tail the gooseberries, and
put them in a pan with the butter
buried among them. Moisten with 2
tablespoons water. Cover pan tightly
and cook gently, shaking pan occasionally, until gooseberries are soft
and have turned a golden green
colour. Crush them lightly with a fork
once or twice during cooking.
Sweeten to taste and put aside.

In a large bowl, whisk cream until it
stands in soft, floppy peaks. With a
large metal spoon, fold in the
gooseberries and their juices. Pile
into a large glass bowl and chill
thoroughly before serving. Serve accompanied by a dish of delicate biscuits such as almond tuiles, *langues
de chat* or even wafers.

Serves 4–6.

GOOSEBERRY ORANGE FOOL

*1 pound (450 g) under-ripe
gooseberries*
About 3 ounces (75 g) sugar
*Finely grated rind and juice of 1
orange*
Knob of butter (optional)
*½ pint (300 ml) thick custard sauce
(page 205)*
¼ pint (150 ml) double cream

Rinse gooseberries. Top and tail
them, and put them in a pan with
sugar, orange rind and juice, and
butter if used. Cover tightly and stew
gently until gooseberries are very
soft. Then either purée gooseberries
and their juices in an electric blender
or food processor, or crush them to a
pulp with a fork. Cool to lukewarm
and beat into custard sauce, which
has also been cooled. Taste and add
a little more sugar if liked. Leave until
quite cold.

Whisk cream to soft peak stage and
fold in gooseberry custard. Spoon
into stemmed glasses and chill lightly
before serving. Serve accompanied
by a dish of sponge finger biscuits.

Serves 4–6.

GOOSEBERRY CHARLOTTE

3 ounces (75 g) fresh breadcrumbs
1 ounce (25 g) ground almonds
2 teaspoons grated lemon rind
2 ounces (50 g) sugar
*About 1 pound (450 g) bottled or
lightly poached gooseberries,
drained*
2 ounces (50 g) butter

Mix together breadcrumbs, almonds, rind and sugar. Arrange in
layers in a buttered ovenproof dish,
alternating with drained gooseberries
and finishing with a layer of crumbs.
Dot with butter and bake in a moderate oven (350°F, 180°C, Mark 4) for
about an hour. Serve with cream.

Serves 4.

GOOSEBERRY SOUFFLÉ

1 pound (450 g) green gooseberries
4 ounces (100–125 g) sugar
4 eggs
2 ounces (50 g) caster sugar
½ pint (300 ml) double cream
½ ounce (15 g) gelatine
Green colouring (optional)

Wash and poach the gooseberries in ¼ pint (150 ml) water with sugar to taste until tender. Purée in a blender or food processor, then rub through a sieve. You should have about ½ pint (300 ml).

Butter a 6 inch (15 cm) diameter soufflé dish and tie a band of buttered foil or greaseproof paper to stand 3 inches (7.5 cm) above the rim.

Separate the eggs, beat the yolks with the caster sugar and purée until the mixture thickens, then lightly whip half the cream and fold it in.

Dissolve the gelatine in 5 tablespoons water over low heat, add the colouring, if using, and stir into the soufflé mixture. Lastly, whip the egg whites until stiff and fold into the soufflé. Leave to set.

Remove the paper collar and decorate with the rest of the cream, stiffly whipped, to serve.

Serves 4–6.

GOOSEBERRY COMPOTE WITH ICE CREAM

Make a simple gooseberry compote. First top and tail hard green gooseberries. Drop them into a syrup made of 8 ounces (225 g) sugar dissolved in ½ pint (300 ml) water, and simmer until tender but not broken or mushy. Allow berries to cool in the syrup. (When fresh gooseberries are not in season, you could, of course, poach some frozen ones or just use a can of gooseberries in syrup.)

Taste poached berries and sweeten them with a little more sugar if necessary.

Serve in tall sundae glasses. At the bottom put a few tablespoons of poached gooseberries. On them put a large scoop of plain vanilla ice cream. Decorate with a generous swirl of very lightly sweetened whipped cream and finally sprinkle with chopped nuts – either green pistachio nuts or lightly toasted blanched almonds.

GOOSEBERRY JAM I

Hard, immature green gooseberries have the advantage of containing much smaller seeds than mature, soft ones, but you will find it quicker to make jam with them if they are softened in water before the sugar is added. A rich, thick gooseberry jam makes a delicious spread for a plain, sponge layer cake or hot, buttered scones.

2 pounds (900 g) hard, green
*   gooseberries, rinsed, topped and*
*   tailed*
2 pounds (900 g) sugar
Knob of butter or soft margarine
*   (optional)*

In a preserving pan, simmer gooseberries in ½ pint (300 ml) water, mashing occasionally with a potato masher or a large wooden spoon, for 10–15 minutes, until the gooseberries are very soft and mushy. Remove from the heat.

Stir in the sugar until quite melted. Return the pan to the heat and boil briskly until setting point is reached, stirring occasionally and skimming scum from the surface as necessary. Stir in the small knob of butter or margarine at the last moment to clear away any remaining scum.

Cool slightly. Pot and cover.
See also page 198.

Fills about 6 jars.

GOOSEBERRY RASPBERRY JAM

You do not need a large amount of raspberries but their presence is quite unmistakable. Unlike most gooseberry preserves, this one calls for fruit which is quite ripe and well coloured.

3 pounds (1·4 kilos) ripe
*   gooseberries*
8 ounces (225 g) raspberries
2 pounds (900 g) sugar

Rinse, top and tail gooseberries, and put them in a preserving pan. Stir in raspberries. Heat gently, stirring and mashing with a large wooden spoon or a potato masher, until juices run. Then raise heat and boil fruit until

GOOSEBERRY JAM II

Ripe gooseberry jam is preferred by many people for its aromatic perfume, which can be improved upon even more if you use a strip of orange or tangerine peel. Those who find the seeds troublesome should rub the hot jam through a fine-meshed sieve before potting it.

2 pounds (900 g) ripe gooseberries,
*   rinsed, topped and tailed*
2 pounds (900 g) sugar
Strip of dried orange or tangerine peel
*   (optional)*
Knob of butter or soft margarine
*   (optional)*

In a preserving pan, combine the gooseberries with ¼ pint (150 ml) water, the sugar and strip of peel, if used. Cook over moderately low heat, stirring occasionally, until sugar has melted and gooseberries are soft. Then raise heat and boil briskly until setting point is reached, skimming foam from the surface. Remove peel and stir in the knob of butter if liked, to disperse any remaining scum. Strain through a sieve if desired (see above). Pot and cover.

See also page 198.

Fills about 6 jars.

soft and pulpy, about 15 minutes, stirring occasionally.

Rub contents of pan through a fine sieve. Discard seeds etc, and return purée to the rinsed-out pan. Bring to boiling point and simmer purée until it thickens, about 30 minutes, stirring frequently.

Add sugar, stir over low heat until quite dissolved, then raise heat and boil briskly, stirring frequently, for 10–15 minutes, or until setting point is reached. Skim any scum from the surface if necessary.

Pot and cover.
See also page 198.

Fills about 6 jars.

POLISH GOOSEBERRY PRESERVE

If you thought all you could make with gooseberries are thick jams and jellies, this lovely preserve of translucent whole gooseberries suspended in a golden syrup will make you think again. It takes some time to make, but it is well worth putting away a batch for Christmas gifts.

2 pounds (900 g) green (unripe) gooseberries
2 pounds (900 g) sugar

Top and tail gooseberries. Rinse them in a colander and shake them dry.

In a preserving pan or large saucepan, make a syrup with sugar and about ½ pint (300 ml) water, stirring over low heat until sugar has dissolved. Simmer for a few minutes. Remove from heat and stir in gooseberries. Leave for several hours. Then return pan to low heat and bring slowly to just below boiling point. Remove from heat and leave overnight in a cool place.

The following day, bring contents of pan to just below boiling point over low heat once again, only this time maintain this steady, low temperature for several hours until the gooseberries are soft and translucent but not in danger of losing their shape. During this time, on no account stir the gooseberries with a spoon for fear of crushing them. Instead, gently swirl the whole pan round from time to time to keep them on the move. Take care, too, that they never come to a pronounced boil. As the gooseberries soften, they become very fragile and either stirring or boiling could break them up. Towards the end of cooking time, skim the surface clear of any scum.

Cool the preserve for 10–15 minutes, pot and cover (page 199).

Fills about 4 jars.

SPICED GOOSEBERRY ORANGE PRESERVE

4 pounds (1·8 kilos) slightly under-ripe gooseberries
2 oranges
4 tablespoons orange liqueur
3 pounds (1·4 kilos) sugar
½ teaspoon ground cinnamon
Generous pinch (about ⅛ teaspoon) each freshly grated nutmeg and ground cloves
Fresh orange juice (see method)

Rinse the gooseberries thoroughly; top and tail them. With a potato peeler or a small, sharp knife, peel the oranges very thinly, avoiding any of the bitter white pith. Sliver the peel finely. Put it in a small pan, cover with cold water and bring slowly to boiling point. Boil for 1 minute, then drain the peel thoroughly and put it in a small bowl. Stir in the orange liqueur and leave to macerate for 1 hour.

Meanwhile, put the gooseberries in a preserving pan with about ½ pint (300 ml) water and boil for 15–20 minutes, just long enough to soften skins, mashing fruit lightly with a potato masher or a large wooden spoon or mallet.

Stir in the sugar and spices. Squeeze the peeled oranges and make up to ¾ pint (400 ml) with fresh orange juice. Stir juice into the gooseberries and cook over low heat, stirring, until sugar has dissolved. Then raise heat to moderate and continue to cook, stirring frequently, until the preserve is rather thick. Skim off any scum on the surface.

Finally, stir in the slivered orange peel and any remaining liqueur, bring back to boiling point and boil gently for 15 minutes. Stir frequently at this stage or the preserve may catch on the bottom of the pan.

Cool. Pot and cover (page 199).

Fills about 8 jars.

GOOSEBERRY CHUTNEY

2 pounds (900 g) green (unripe) gooseberries
About 1½ pints (900 ml) brown malt vinegar
1 pound (450 g) slab dates
1 pound (450 g) raisins
1 Spanish onion
2 ounces (50 g) preserved (crystallized) ginger
2 pounds (900 g) soft brown or demerara sugar
1½ ounces (40 g) salt
1 teaspoon cayenne pepper

Rinse, top and tail the gooseberries, and put them through a meat mincer. In a large, heavy, preferably enamelled pan, cover gooseberries well with vinegar. Bring to boiling point and simmer until soft.

Meanwhile, put the dates and raisins through the mincer, and finely chop the onion and ginger. Add sugar, salt and cayenne pepper to the gooseberries, and stir until sugar has dissolved. Finally, add all the remaining ingredients and boil, stirring frequently, until chutney is very thick, about 45 minutes.

Allow to cool completely before potting and covering.

See also page 200.

Fills about 6 jars.

MRS MARSDEN'S GRAND RECIPE FOR GOOSEBERRY WINE (1843)

'4 quarts of berries to a gallon of pure soft water

'Crush the gentlemen, pour the water upon them cold. Let them reside in the tub 3 days. Poke them up and stir them very often with a long pole, then strain the liquor through a sieve, but do not squeeze the berries. Add 3½ lbs of lump sugar to each gallon of liquor. When well dissolved barrel it and allow it to work, which it will, I say months, until cleared. Add liquor to keep it full. Then (when clear) bung it up well and in 6 months bottle it with new fresh corks and seal them.

'*Note:* The berries must be all nicely picked, free from stalk or flower, cleaned and ripe . . .'

GRAPE

The grape was probably one of the first fruits seriously cultivated by man. The Bible tells how Noah planted a vineyard when he decided to settle down and become a 'husbandman'. He must also have devised a way of making wine and it was not long before he discovered the effects of over-indulgence in fermented grape juice (wine). Ever since then, men have enthusiastically been growing grapes and turning them into wine.

Grapes are thought to have originated somewhere near the Caspian Sea. Fossils of recognizable vine leaves show just how old the plant is. The Ancient Egyptians certainly knew grapes and used them to make wine 6,000 years ago, followed by the Greeks and Romans who developed viticulture to a high degree. Then, as they colonized Western Europe, the Romans planted vines wherever the conditions would support them, in France and as far north as the Rhineland, even in southern Britain. In the British Isles, viticulture was practised on quite a large scale, first by the Roman colonizers and then by the monks until a change in the climate forced them to abandon it. As European culture spread, grapes spread with it and today there is hardly a corner of the globe that has not been colonized by the grape.

Both dessert and wine grapes can be eaten, black, red or white. Grapes are one of the few fruits which cannot be judged by sniffing them. Size and flavour do not always go hand in hand, and the only sure way of finding out is to taste one. Grapes should be plump and juicy when you bite into them, highly coloured and firmly attached to the bunch. If you have the chance – and a good-tempered greengrocer – give the bunch a sharp shake. If it 'shatters', shedding grapes all over the place, it is no longer fresh.

Store grapes on a plate in a cool room or at the bottom of the refrigerator. Like strawberries, they should be washed quickly just before serving and drained on a soft, dry cloth. If you do not want to damage the 'bloom' on a handsome bunch of black hothouse grapes, serve them as they are and place a bowl of chilled water on the table so that each person can rinse his own.

A handsome bunch of chilled grapes makes a refreshing finale to an elaborate meal, either on its own or on top of a bowl of mixed fresh fruit. Provide a pair of grape shears so that each person can snip off a small cluster. Small green or white seedless grapes are very good in savoury dishes, and black or white varieties, seedless or with the seeds removed, are excellent in all sorts of salads, and with poultry and fish dishes. Grapes make good preserves.

The best-known product associated with grapes is, of course, wine. This has always been recommended – in *reasonable* quantities – as a cordial: it will stimulate your appetite, revive and invigorate you, and also help you to relax, and sleep. Brandy is admitted to be medicinal even by those who dislike it. Wine mulled with spices (cinnamon, cloves, nutmeg) and sweetened with honey rather than sugar makes an excellent nightcap. Teetotallers may drink plain, unfermented grape juice to help insomnia; again, honey rather than sugar is best if sweetening is necessary.

A significant portion of the world's annual grape crop of roughly 50 million tons is dried to make raisins, sultanas or 'white raisins', and currants. As with most other dried fruit, you can choose between naturally sun-dried varieties and fruit treated with chemicals and preservatives such as mineral oil. The method used is clearly stated on the label.

Store raisins, sultanas and currants in tightly stoppered jars. If they have dried out too much, plump them up in boiling water for an hour before use. They will also be delicious soaked overnight in brandy, sherry or orange liqueur, or just orange juice. Another way to restore moisture to very dry fruit is to steam it, covered, in a sieve over simmering water for 15 to 20 minutes.

Mixed with nuts these dried fruits make excellent snacks. They can be used in salads, with meats and in rice dishes, or added to breads, and rich fruit cakes – a fine way to bring summer into the winter kitchen.

Nutritionally, grapes are most valuable in their dried form. Besides being rich in energy, they contain significant amounts of copper, necessary for the assimilation of iron.

LOTION

This is an old recipe for removing freckles, tan and/or sunburn. It makes an acid face bleach, milder than lemon.

Moisten a bunch of unripe green grapes in water (ripe ones work less well). Sprinkle with a mixture of 1 tablespoon powdered alum and 1 teaspoon salt. Wrap grapes in brown paper, and bake in hot ashes or slow oven for 15 minutes. Squeeze juice of grapes and wash face with the liquid. Allow to dry for 15 minutes, then wash off with tepid water.

A similar extract of green grapes can be used as a tonic suitable for all types of skin.

For really oily skin, white wine is a marvellously astringent cleanser and toner.

ROAST PHEASANT WITH GRAPE STUFFING

1 oven-ready roasting pheasant, about 3 pounds (1·4 kilos) or a little more
3 ounces (75 g) butter
8 juniper berries
¼ teaspoon crumbled dried thyme
Salt and freshly ground black pepper
1 pound (450 g) seedless green grapes
4 ounces (100–125 g) mixed nuts, coarsely chopped
2 slices fat salt pork or unsmoked fat bacon

Wipe pheasant clean with a damp cloth both inside and out, and pluck out any stray pin feathers with a pair of tweezers. In a small pan, melt butter without letting it sizzle. Crush juniper berries with the flat side of a knife blade and stir them into the butter, together with thyme, a teaspoon of salt and a generous grinding of pepper. Brush bird with juniper butter both inside and out. Reserve remaining butter.

Prepare stuffing. Strip grapes from their stalks and rinse well in a colander. Place half of them in a bowl and crush to a pulp with a fork. Stir in remaining grapes and the nuts, and pour over remaining juniper butter. Toss until well mixed. Stuff tightly into pheasant (the stuffing will shrink in cooking as the grapes collapse). Skewer opening shut and truss bird. Lay slices of salt pork or unsmoked fat bacon over breast of pheasant. Place in a roasting tin, on a roasting rack if you have one.

Roast pheasant in a fairly hot oven (425°F, 220°C, Mark 7) for the first 15 minutes. Then baste with pan juices, lower heat to moderate (350°F, 180°C, Mark 4) and continue to roast for 35–40 minutes, or until pheasant is tender, basting regularly with pan juices.

Remove salt pork or bacon, trussing skewers and strings from pheasant and transfer it to a heated serving dish. Skim fat from pan juices and rinse the pan out with a splash of water (or, even better, wine), stirring and scraping pan clean with a wooden spoon. Serve in a separate heated sauceboat with the pheasant.

Serves 2–3.

DUCKLING VÉRONIQUE

After sole and chicken, duckling is an obvious candidate for preparing Véronique-style, with grapes.

1 oven-ready duckling, about 5 pounds (2·3 kilos)
½ teaspoon freshly ground black pepper
½ teaspoon freshly grated nutmeg
1 tablespoon oil
½ ounce (15 g) butter
½ pint (300 ml) port
2 tablespoons redcurrant jelly
8 ounces (225 g) black grapes

Quarter the duckling and cut away as much fat as possible. Wash and dry the pieces, and rub them with a mixture of salt, pepper and nutmeg.

In a heavy, flameproof casserole that has a tight-fitting lid, heat the oil and butter together until sizzling, and over a moderate heat fry the pieces of duckling until the fat runs and the duckling is a rich, golden brown colour on all sides. Take the duckling out of the casserole.

Pour off all the fat from the casserole. Pour in the port, stirring and scraping the bottom clean with a wooden spoon. Stir in the redcurrant jelly. Bring slowly to simmering point, and add the duckling pieces. Cover the casserole and cook gently for 1 hour, or until the duckling feels tender when pierced with a skewer.

Meanwhile, wash and drain the grapes. Halve them and remove pips.

When the duckling is tender, transfer the pieces to a deep, heated serving dish. Keep hot. Skim the pan juices of all remaining fat and add the grapes. Simmer, uncovered, for 5–10 minutes longer, or until the juices are well reduced, stirring frequently. Taste for seasoning and adjust if necessary. Spoon over the pieces of duckling and serve.

Serves 4.

QUAIL WITH GRAPES

6 dressed quails
Salt and white pepper
2 ounces (50 g) butter
Chicken stock
3–4 ounces (75–100 g) seedless green grapes
¼ pint (150 ml) dry white wine

Wipe the quails with a damp cloth and season them both inside and out with salt and white pepper. In a heavy, flameproof casserole wide enough to take all the quails in one layer, brown the birds all over in hot butter.

Moisten with 2 or 3 tablespoons stock, cover the casserole tightly and cook gently for 15 minutes, turning quails once or twice.

Add grapes and wine, bring back to simmering point, cover and cook over low heat for 15 minutes longer, or until quails are tender. Serve from the casserole.

Serves 6.

CHICKEN AND GRAPE SALAD

1½ pounds (700 g) cooked chicken
¼ pint (150 ml) thick mayonnaise (see
    page 205)
4 tablespoons thin cream or top of
    milk
2 tablespoons cider vinegar
1 shallot, finely chopped, or 1
    tablespoon very finely chopped
    mild onion
½ sweet red pepper, cored, seeded
    and finely diced
2 stalks celery, diced
1 pound (450 g) green grapes
Salt and white pepper
Pinch of sugar (optional)
Lettuce leaves, to serve
Coarsely chopped blanched
    almonds, to garnish

Skin the chicken and dice it.

In a large bowl, thin down the mayonnaise by beating in the cream or milk and vinegar. Stir in the chicken, shallot or onion, red pepper and celery. If seedless grapes are used, rinse and drain them thoroughly, separate them and add them to the bowl whole. Otherwise, first rinse them, halve them and remove pips. Mix all the ingredients lightly but thoroughly, and season to taste with salt, white pepper and a pinch of sugar if liked.

Serve on a bed of crisp lettuce leaves, garnished with coarsely chopped almonds.

Serves 6.

AUSTRIAN GRAPE TART

Both green and black dessert grapes may be used for this tart, or a combination of the two. The latter can look most spectacular if you arrange them in concentric circles, alternating the colours. Or, mark the tart into six equal sections and cover them alternately with black and green grapes.

9 ounces (250 g) plain flour
Pinch of salt
6 ounces (175 g) butter
3 ounces (75 g) caster sugar
Finely grated rind of ½ lemon
1½ ounces (40 g) ground almonds
1 egg yolk, lightly beaten
2 tablespoons lemon juice

Filling
1 egg white
3–4 ounces (75–100 g) apricot
    preserve
Maraschino liqueur or Kirsch
    (optional)
1 pound (450 g) dessert grapes
Chopped toasted almonds, to
    decorate

Make the rich pastry first. Sift the flour and salt into a bowl. Lightly rub in the butter until the mixture resembles fine breadcrumbs. Stir in the sugar, lemon rind and ground almonds until well mixed. Knead lightly to a dough with the egg yolk and lemon juice, adding a tablespoon or two of iced water if necessary. Roll into a ball. Wrap in greaseproof paper or plastic wrap and leave in the refrigerator to 'rest and ripen' for 1 hour.

If dough is too hard to shape when it comes out of the refrigerator, let it soften at room temperature. Then roll it out thinly and use it to line a large tart tin with a removable base. With a fork, beat the egg white just enough to break down its gelatinous threads and brush it lightly all over the bottom of the unbaked pastry shell. Prick lightly all over with a fork (held upright to avoid gashing the pastry). Bake 'blind' for 8–10 minutes in a moderately hot oven (400°F, 200°C, Mark 6), then lower heat to moderate (350°F, 180°C, Mark 4) and bake for a further 15 minutes, or until pastry is cooked but only very lightly coloured.

Make an apricot glaze by thinning the preserve down with 1 or 2 tablespoons boiling water. Flavour to taste with a little Maraschino liqueur or Kirsch, if liked.

While the pastry shell is still quite warm, brush the base with a thin coating of apricot glaze. Cool.

Meanwhile, rinse the grapes, dry them and neatly gouge out pips. Green grapes should also be peeled. Arrange the grapes closely side by side in the tart shell. Reheat the remaining glaze if necessary until liquid again and brush it over the grapes. Finally, sprinkle the centre of the tart with a few chopped almonds.

Serves 6.

SWEDISH GRAPE JELLY WITH VANILLA CREAM

The quality of vanilla you use to flavour the cream mixture is very important. Failing real vanilla essence, sweeten the cream with vanilla-flavoured caster sugar (page 205).

1 ounce (25 g) powdered gelatine
6 tablespoons sugar
1 bottle medium white wine
2–3 tablespoons Madeira or sweet
    sherry
12 ounces (350 g) small black grapes,
    halved and seeded

Vanilla cream
4 egg yolks
4 tablespoons caster sugar
¾ pint (400 ml) double or whipping
    cream
1 teaspoon vanilla essence (see
    above)

In a cup, sprinkle the gelatine over 4 tablespoons cold water, and leave to soak. Meanwhile, dissolve the sugar in 6–8 tablespoons water in a large pan, and bring to boiling point. Remove from the heat.

Next, place the cup containing the soaked gelatine in a pan of very hot water and stir until the gelatine has dissolved and the liquid is quite clear. Combine with the cooling sugar syrup and mix well. Cool.

Stir in wine and Madeira or sherry, and taste for sweetness, adding a little more sugar and Madeira or sherry if necessary – the liquid should be quite strongly flavoured as it loses some of its sweetness on setting.

When the mixture is very syrupy and on the point of setting, layer it with the grapes in a large (about 3 pint or 1·7 litre) mould, and chill until firmly set.

Meanwhile, prepare the vanilla cream. Whisk the egg yolks and sugar together until very thick and lemon-coloured. In another large bowl, whisk the cream lightly until soft, floppy peaks form. Fold the egg mixture into the whipped cream, together with the vanilla. Chill lightly until ready to serve.

Turn the grape jelly out on to a flat serving dish and serve with the vanilla cream in a separate bowl.

Serves 6–8.

GRAPES IN SOUR CREAM

Seedless white grapes
Soft brown sugar, sifted
Thick sour cream or natural yoghourt

Small seedless white grapes are the best for this. Large ones which have pips must first be cut in half and have the pips removed. Rinse and drain grapes thoroughly before de-pipping them. Lay them in a glass serving bowl. Sprinkle with a generous layer of brown sugar and spread with sour cream or natural yoghourt beaten until smooth.

According to another version, about 1½ pounds (700 g) seedless grapes are mixed lightly but thoroughly with ½ pint (300 ml) sour cream and about 4 ounces (100–125 g) sifted brown sugar, or to taste. Chill well before serving and serve accompanied by a dish of delicate sweet biscuits.

Serves 6.

GRAPES IN VINEGAR

A delicious and unusual accompaniment for cold poultry, ham or pork, from Georgia in the Soviet Union.

½ pint (300 ml) cider vinegar
4 ounces (100–125 g) soft brown sugar
6 cloves
One 2 inch (5 cm) cinnamon stick
Generous pinch of salt
1 pound (450 g) small seedless green grapes

In an enamelled pan, combine the first 5 ingredients with ½ pint (300 ml) water. Bring to a steady, rolling boil and boil for 10 minutes.

Rinse the grapes. Strip them from their stalks and drop them into the marinade. Simmer for 10–15 minutes longer, depending on size.

Bottle in a perfectly clean, screw-top jar and leave for at least a few days to allow flavours to mature before serving, the longer the better.

CITRUS GRAPE CONSERVE

For this conserve, which comes from the United States, the citrus fruits must all be thin-skinned, otherwise the result could be rather bitter.

2 pounds (900 g) seedless green grapes
1 large orange
2 large lemons
2 small limes
2 pounds (900 g) sugar
2 tablespoons small seedless raisins
4–6 tablespoons coarsely chopped walnuts (optional)

Strip grapes from their stalks and rinse them in a colander. Scrub citrus fruits under the cold tap. Quarter them, pick out pips with the point of a knife and chop the fruit into small pieces. Put chopped fruit in a preserving pan with about ¾ pint (400 ml) water. Bring to boiling point and simmer for 10–15 minutes.

Stir in grapes, sugar and raisins, and cook over low heat, stirring constantly, until sugar has dissolved. Then continue to simmer for a further 45 minutes, or until mixture is thick and has reached setting point, stirring occasionally and skimming off any scum on the surface.

Add walnuts, if used. Mix well with the conserve, pot and cover.

See also page 199.

Fills about 5 jars.

RED GRAPE WINE

This is a dark, Burgundy type wine, which improves considerably with age, and it is a good accompaniment to game or red meat. Use only the best quality grapes. It is important to ferment and store in a dark place to preserve the rich red colour.

10 pounds (4·5 kilos) black grapes
1 Campden tablet, crushed
Burgundy yeast
1½ pounds (700 g) granulated sugar

Remove the stalks and any damaged or over-ripe fruit. Place in a colander and wash thoroughly under cold, running water. Put the grapes in a prepared mashing vessel. Add the crushed Campden tablet. Cover and leave for 24 hours.

Quickly remove the cover and add the activated yeast (see manufacturer's instructions for quantity and method of use). Replace the cover and leave the vessel in a warm place (65–75°F or 18–24°C) for 7 days.

Using a fine sieve, strain off the liquid into a clean container. Put the fruit pulp into a linen bag. Seal the bag and press hard. It should be possible to obtain almost a gallon (4·5 litres) of juice (a small press or an electric fruit juice extractor is useful). Add this juice to the strained liquid. Stir in the sugar and quickly siphon into a prepared fermentation vessel, filling to within 1 inch (2·5 cm) of the cork. Ferment under an air-lock, in a dark, warm place (65–75°F or 18–24°C).

Leave until a good layer of sediment has formed on the bottom of the fermentation vessel. Rack, store for a minimum of 6 months, and siphon into dark glass bottles. Keep for a minimum of 1 year, and 2 years for a full-bodied wine.

See also page 205.

Makes about 1 gallon (4·5 litres).

GRAPE JUICE

If you do not feel like going into wine production, you can make your own grape juice instead.

Use ripe black grapes for the best colour and flavour. Rinse them, strip off their stalks and put them in a pan. Then lightly crush the fruit with a potato masher or just with the palm of your hand so that the skins burst to expose the pulp and pips. Cover with cold water and boil gently until the pulp softens and the pips begin to float loose. Pour the contents of the pan into a jelly bag or a large sieve lined with a double thickness of muslin, and allow the juice to drip out, squeezing the bag at the end to extract every last drop.

The juice will keep, bottled, for several weeks in the refrigerator, or you can freeze it, or sterilize it in bottles. Dilute with water.

See also Syrups, page 202.

WHITE GRAPE WINE

This is a sweet, white dessert wine. Use only undamaged, good quality fruit. There should be no need to add water; sufficient juice can be extracted from the crushed fruit pulp (an electric juice extractor is useful).

10 pounds (4·5 kilos) small seedless grapes
1 Campden tablet, crushed
Juice of 2 lemons
1 pound (450 g) granulated sugar
Sauterne yeast

Remove the stalks and place the fruit in a colander. Wash thoroughly under cold, running water, removing any damaged grapes. Transfer to the prepared mashing vessel. Add the crushed Campden tablet and the lemon juice. Cover the vessel and leave for 24 hours.

Using a fine sieve, strain off any liquid into a clean container. Put the fruit pulp in a linen bag. Seal the bag tightly and press out as much juice as possible from the pulp. It is possible, by pressing hard, to extract nearly 1 gallon (4·5 litres) of juice. Stir in the sugar and the activated yeast (see manufacturer's instructions for quantity and method of use). Quickly siphon into a prepared fermentation vessel, filling to within 1 inch (2.5 cm) of the cork. Ferment under an air-lock in a warm place (65–75°F or 18–24°C).

Rack, store for at least 3 months and bottle. Keep for a minimum of 6 months before drinking.

See also page 205.

Makes about 1 gallon (4·5 litres).

Black Hamburgh.

Buckland Sweetwater.

Black Alicante.

Raisins, Sultanas, Currants

CAUCASIAN LAMB PILAU WITH RAISINS

Use the same cup or mug to measure out the rice and stock.

1–1½ pounds (450–700 g) lean boned lamb
1 medium Spanish onion
2 medium carrots
2 cups (mugs) long-grain rice
4 ounces (100–125 g) raisins
1 ounce (25 g) butter
1 tablespoon oil
1 teaspoon ground cinnamon
Salt and freshly ground black pepper
3 cups (mugs) hot chicken (cube) stock (or water)

Wipe lamb clean and cut it up into small pieces. Coarsely chop the onion and cut the carrots into matchsticks. In a large sieve, wash rice under cold running water until water runs clear. Rinse raisins in warm water in another sieve. Put both aside to drain.

In a large, flameproof casserole with a tight-fitting lid, sauté lamb in a mixture of butter and oil until richly browned all over. Season generously with cinnamon, salt, and freshly ground black pepper. Add onion and carrots, and sauté for a few minutes longer, scraping bottom of casserole clean with a wooden spoon. Stir in half the rice, level the surface and scatter raisins evenly over the top. Cover with remaining rice, levelling it out with your spoon. Pour hot stock or water over the entire surface. Then, using the handle of your wooden spoon, bore deep holes all over rice so stock can run easily right to the bottom of casserole.

Slowly bring to simmering point, cover tightly and cook over the lowest possible heat for 30–40 minutes, or until liquid is all absorbed, meat is cooked and rice grains are tender and separate.

Shortly before serving, carefully mix all the ingredients together. Allow to stand, covered, for 10 minutes before serving.

Serves 6.

CHICKEN WITH RAISIN STUFFING

1 large roasting chicken, about 4 pounds (1·8 kilos), with giblets
Salt
3 carrots, cut into chunks
2 stalks celery, with tops, cut into chunks
1 medium-sized onion, stuck with 2 cloves
3 black peppercorns
2 allspice berries
Bouquet garni (2 sprigs parsley, 1 sprig thyme, 1 bay leaf)
Butter
8 ounces (225 g) raisins, washed and drained
2 ounces (50 g) mild, clear honey
Generous pinch of ground cinnamon

Wash chicken thoroughly both inside and out. Wash all giblets. Put chicken and giblets except liver (which tends to make stock bitter) in a large pot. Sprinkle with a tablespoon of salt. Pack vegetables, spices and bouquet garni around bird. Cover with water and very slowly bring to boiling point. Skim any scum from surface and simmer for 30 minutes, or until chicken is half-cooked. Then lift it out on to a plate, draining back all stock from its cavity into pot. Place chicken in a roasting tin. Let stock with giblets carry on simmering for at least 30 minutes longer before switching off heat.

In a frying pan, melt 1½ ounces (40 g) butter and fry raisins for a few minutes, turning them over so they are individually coated. Stir in honey, add a pinch of cinnamon and salt, to taste, and moisten with 3 or 4 tablespoons chicken stock. Simmer, stirring frequently, until stock is absorbed.

Stuff cavity of chicken with raisin mixture and skewer opening shut. Truss bird and lay breast side up in roasting tin. Coat bird all over with about 3 ounces (75 g) melted butter and sprinkle with salt.

Roast chicken in a moderately hot oven (400°F, 200°C, Mark 6) for 45 minutes, or until it is crisp and golden brown, and juices run clear when leg is pierced with a fork through the thickest part close to the body. Baste occasionally with pan juices and a little more stock if necessary while chicken is roasting. Serve hot.

Serves 6.

MAZUREK CYGAŃSKI
Polish Fruit and Nut Pastry

A traditional Polish Easter pastry. The exact combination of fruit that goes into it depends on the family's preference and the cook's whim, but dried dates, figs and/or apricots, finely slivered or chopped, are often included as well. I remember as a child during the war in Scotland, when dried fruit was scarce and nuts rarely seen, my mother in desperation supplemented the fruit she had with a large bar of coarsely chopped fruit and nut milk chocolate. Everyone loved it and a bar of chopped chocolate has been included in the family version ever since. The fruit mixture is sometimes baked on a sweet shortcrust pastry base that has first been lightly baked 'blind', but I prefer it on rice paper (which can be bought from any good stationers).

3½ ounces (90 g) sultanas
3½ ounces (90 g) raisins
3½ ounces (90 g) currants
4 egg yolks
1 whole egg
7 ounces (200 g) caster sugar
3 ounces (75 g) candied mixed peel, diced
3½ ounces (90 g) blanched almonds, chopped
3½ ounces (90 g) plain flour, sifted
Rice paper, for baking sheet

Pick over and rinse dried fruit, and dry on a clean kitchen cloth. Using an electric mixer if available, beat egg yolks, egg and sugar together until pale and fluffy. Put dried fruits in a bowl. Add candied peel and chopped nuts, and toss with a fork until well mixed. Add a couple of tablespoons of sifted flour and toss lightly until pieces are individually coated.

Sift remaining flour once more over beaten eggs and sugar, and mix it in gently, followed by fruit and nuts. Pour out on to a large baking sheet which you have lined with rice paper, overlapping edges where they meet and bringing the paper slightly up at the sides.

Bake in a moderate oven (350°F, 180°C, Mark 4) for 30 minutes, or until top feels firm to the touch. Cool to lukewarm before cutting into individual rectangles with a very sharp or serrated knife. Allow to cool completely on the baking sheet.

GERTIE'S CHRISTMAS PUDDING

The longer a fruit pudding matures, the richer it becomes; a Christmas pudding should be prepared at least three months ahead.

The following recipe makes one 2 pound (900 g) pudding, ample for six or seven post-turkey-and-trimmings adults and two children. Or you can double the ingredients, make two puddings and put one by for the following Christmas or, as some people do, for Easter.

Butter, for pudding basin
1½ pounds (700 g) mixed dried fruit
4 ounces (100–125 g) diced candied peel
1 small cooking apple
1 small lemon
4 ounces (100–125 g) soft dark brown sugar (if it is not very dark, add 1 teaspoon coffee essence)
5 ounces (150 g) shredded beef suet
1 ounce (25 g) ground almonds
1 ounce (25 g) fresh white breadcrumbs
3 ounces (75 g) plain flour
1 teaspoon mixed spice
Pinch of salt
2 large eggs
3 tablespoons black treacle
3 tablespoons brown ale
3 tablespoons brandy

Butter a 2 pound (900 g) pudding basin. Cut discs of greaseproof paper, one to fit the bottom of the basin and one for the top of the pudding. Butter those as well. Fit the bottom disc in position and put the other one aside.

Pick over and rinse dried fruit if necessary, and dry it on a kitchen cloth. Put fruit in a large mixing bowl with the candied peel. Peel, core and finely chop the apple, and add it to the bowl. Finely grate the lemon rind and add it together with the strained juice of the lemon. Stir in brown sugar, shredded suet, ground almonds and breadcrumbs. Sift in flour, mixed spice and salt, and mix well.

Beat eggs. Pour over contents of bowl. Add treacle, brown ale and brandy, and continue to mix batter to a soft, dropping consistency.

Spoon mixture into prepared pudding basin. Level off top and lay the second disc of greaseproof in position, buttered side down. Cover basin with greaseproof paper and foil, or a double thickness of either, tying them in position with thin string.

In a steamer, or standing on a trivet in a large, covered pan with boiling water to come halfway up sides of basin, steam pudding for 4–5 hours. Top up pan with more *boiling* water as it evaporates. Cool pudding in its basin and store well-wrapped in a cool, dry cupboard.

On Christmas Day, steam or boil pudding as above for another 4 hours.

SELKIRK BANNOCK

¾ ounce (20 g) dried yeast
2 ounces (50 g) caster sugar
1 pound (450 g) strong white flour
2 teaspoons mixed spice
Pinch of salt
2 ounces (50 g) butter
2 ounces (50 g) lard
¼ pint (150 ml) lukewarm milk
   (optional)
6 ounces (175 g) sultanas
4 ounces (100–125 g) raisins
2 ounces (50 g) currants
2 ounces (50 g) chopped mixed peel
Finely grated rind of ½ lemon
Butter, for baking sheets and to glaze
   bannocks

Reconstitute the yeast in ¼ pint (150 ml) water with 1 teaspoon of the weighed sugar, following directions on the can or packet.

Meanwhile, sift flour, mixed spice and salt into a large bowl, and rub in fats until mixture resembles fine breadcrumbs. Stir in remaining sugar. Make a well in the centre, pour in frothy yeast mixture, together with another ¼ pint (150 ml) lukewarm water (or use milk if preferred) and knead to a soft, springy dough.

Add dried fruit, mixed peel and lemon rind, and continue to knead until they are well dispersed and dough is shiny and springy again. Roll into a ball, cover bowl and leave to rise in a warm place until dough has doubled in bulk, about 2 hours.

Deflate dough. Knead lightly until smooth again and divide in half. Shape into 2 balls. Place each ball on a greased baking sheet and with the palm of your hand press it down lightly into a round. Cover and leave to rise until doubled in bulk again.

Bake bannocks on racks fitted just above centre in a moderate oven (375°F, 190°C, Mark 5) until firm and a rich golden colour, about 25 minutes.

As soon as the bannocks come out of the oven, rub them liberally all over with a butter paper or brush them with melted butter. Cool on a wire rack and store in an airtight tin. They will actually improve in flavour as they mature over the next couple of days and will stay fresh for a long time, provided they are properly stored. If they become stale, they will be delicious eaten sliced and toasted and spread liberally with butter.

IRISH FRUIT CAKE

Butter, for cake tin
10 ounces (275 g) raisins
6 ounces (175 g) sultanas
4 ounces (100–125 g) currants
2 ounces (50 g) chopped mixed peel
Finely grated rind of 1 lemon
2 ounces (50 g) glacé cherries
2 ounces (50 g) almonds, blanched
   and peeled
10 ounces (175 g) plain flour
2 teaspoons ground mixed spice
Pinch of salt
8 ounces (225 g) softened butter
8 ounces (225 g) soft brown sugar
3 large eggs
About ¼ pint (150 ml) Guinness

Start by preparing a deep, round and preferably loose-bottomed cake tin 7 or 8 inches (17·5 or 20 cm) in diameter. Grease it lightly with butter, lining base and sides with greased greaseproof paper.

Rinse and drain the dried fruit thoroughly, and roll it over a clean cloth to dry. Then put fruit in a large bowl. Add the chopped peel and grated lemon rind. Quarter the cherries and add them as well. Finely chop the almonds, add them to the bowl, and toss with a fork until ingredients are well mixed.

Sift flour, mixed spice and salt into another bowl. Take a few tablespoons of this mixture and toss it with the mixed dried fruit – this will help to keep the fruit evenly suspended throughout the cake, pre-venting it sinking to the bottom.

Using an electric mixer if available, beat butter and sugar together until light and creamy. In another bowl, beat eggs until thick and lemon-coloured. Beat a couple of heated tablespoons of the flour mixture into creamed butter and sugar, followed by all the eggs, adding them gradually and beating well between each addition. With a large metal spoon, fold in remaining flour and all the fruit, together with about half of the Guinness to make a soft batter.

Spoon batter into prepared cake tin. Level off the top and make an indentation in the middle. Bake cake in a slow oven (325°F, 170°C, Mark 3) for 1 hour. Then lower heat (to 300°F, 150°C, Mark 2) and continue to bake for about 1½ hours longer until cake is firm to the touch in the middle and a thin skewer pushed right down through the middle to the bottom comes out feeling dry to the touch. Should top of cake brown too quickly, cover top of tin with brown paper or a double thickness of greaseproof.

Allow cake to cool in its tin for 10 minutes before turning it out on to a wire cooling rack. Then, when it is barely lukewarm, turn cake over and peel off greaseproof paper from the bottom. Prick base all over with a sharp fork or skewer and soak it with about 4 more tablespoons Guinness, spooning it on gradually. Leave until cold before wrapping and storing.

IRISH SPICED FRUIT LOAF

8 ounces (225 g) sultanas
8 ounces (225 g) raisins
5 ounces (150 g) currants
10 ounces (275 g) soft pale brown
   sugar
½ pint (300 ml) strong hot tea
Butter and flour, for loaf tins
10 ounces (275 g) plain flour
2 teaspoons ground mixed spice
2 teaspoons baking powder
2 large eggs

Rinse sultanas, raisins and currants thoroughly, and shake or pat off all excess moisture. Put in a large bowl. Stir in sugar and cover with hot tea. Cover bowl and soak overnight.

The following day, start by greasing 2 small loaf tins with butter and dusting them with flour, tapping out excess. Sift flour, mixed spice and baking powder together (any bran left in the sieve when sifting a wholemeal flour should be mixed in as well). Beat eggs until light and fluffy.

Beat flour mixture and eggs alternately into basin of fruit, about one-third at a time. When thoroughly mixed, divide between prepared loaf tins, levelling off tops.

Bake loaves in a slow oven (325°F, 170°C, Mark 3) for about 1½ hours, or until loaves are well risen and firm to the touch, and a thin skewer pushed right down to the bottom through the middle comes out clean and dry.

Cool loaves in their tins for 5 minutes before turning them out on to wire cooling racks. When quite cold, slice and serve with fresh butter.

DUNDEE CAKE

This traditional Scottish fruit cake with its topping of whole almonds is an excellent standby to have in the cake tin as it keeps so well. People who find the classic Christmas cake too rich and heavy will happily have a slice of this one instead.

Melted butter, for baking tin
10 ounces (275 g) plain flour
½ teaspoon ground mixed spice
Pinch of salt
8 ounces (225 g) butter
8 ounces (225 g) caster sugar
Finely grated rind of ½ orange and ½
    lemon
½ teaspoon vanilla essence
5 eggs
8 ounces (225 g) sultanas
6 ounces (175 g) seedless raisins
6 ounces (175 g) currants
4 ounces (100–125 g) chopped mixed
    peel
2 ounces (50,g) glacé cherries,
    quartered
2 ounces (50 g) ground almonds
2 ounces (50 g) blanched almonds,
    finely chopped
1–2 tablespoons milk

Topping
1 egg white
2 ounces (50 g) whole blanched
    almonds

Brush a deep 8 inch (20 cm) cake tin with melted butter. Line the base and sides with greaseproof paper, and brush with melted butter as well.

Sift the flour, mixed spice and salt together. Using an electric mixer if available, cream the butter, sugar, grated rinds and vanilla until light and fluffy. Add the eggs one at a time, together with a tablespoon of flour to prevent batter curdling, beating well after each addition. Fold in the remaining flour, followed by the dried fruit, mixed peel, glacé cherries, the ground and chopped almonds, and milk as necessary to help mix the batter. Spoon batter into the prepared tin and smooth off the top.

Prepare the topping. With a fork, beat the egg white lightly just enough to break down the gelatinous threads. Dip the whole almonds in egg white and arrange them on top of the cake in close, concentric circles, covering the surface completely.

Bake the cake in a moderate oven (350°F, 180°C, Mark 4) for 30 minutes. Then reduce the temperature (to 325°F, 170°C, Mark 3) and continue to bake for about 2 hours longer, or until cake is richly coloured on top and a skewer pushed right through the centre down to the bottom comes out clean.

Remove cake from the oven and allow it to stand for 10–15 minutes before removing it from the tin and leaving it to cool completely on a wire rack.

FÜRSTENBROT Swiss Rusks

5 eggs
9 ounces (250 g) caster sugar
9 ounces (250 g) plain flour, sifted
9 ounces (250 g) sultanas
9 ounces (250 g) unpeeled almonds,
    split or coarsely chopped
½ ounce (150 g) ground cinnamon
Pinch of salt
Butter, for baking tin

Using an electric mixer if available, beat the eggs and sugar together until white and fluffy. Gradually beat in the flour, a little at a time. Stir in the sultanas, almonds, cinnamon and salt until thoroughly mixed.

Pour the batter into a large, buttered, oblong loaf tin and bake in a moderate oven (375°F, 190°C, Mark 5) for 45 minutes, or until well risen, golden and firm to the touch. Allow the cake to remain in the tin for 24 hours, preferably standing on a wire rack and covered lightly with a cloth.

The following day, using a very sharp or serrated knife, cut the loaf into thin slices. Arrange them side by side on wire racks (or on the grids of a cooling oven) and let them dry out completely until they are crisp and golden.

Store in an airtight tin.

RAISIN WINE

This is a sweet, white wine. For a drier wine, use 2 pounds (900 g) of currants and 2 pounds (900 g) raisins, with only 2¾ pounds (1·3 kilos) sugar. The rice gives the wine 'body'. Never ferment on the raisins and rice – only on the juice.

4 pounds (1·8 kilos) raisins
Grated rind and juice of 1 orange
1 pound (450 g) uncooked rice
3 pounds (1·4 kilos) granulated sugar
Juice of 1 lemon
1 Campden tablet
1 teaspoon Pectozyme
1 nutrient tablet
Wine yeast

Put the raisins in a colander and wash under the cold tap. Pour 1 gallon (4.5 litres) water into a large preserving pan and bring to the boil. Add the raisins and orange peel. Lower the heat and simmer for 20 minutes. Strain off the liquid, using a fine sieve and return it to the pan. Heat until just boiling. Add the rice and simmer over a low heat for 5 minutes.

Put the sugar into the prepared mashing vessel. Strain the hot liquid on to the sugar and stir to dissolve it. Leave to cool, until the temperature falls to 65°F (18°C). Add the orange and lemon juices, the Campden tablet and Pectozyme. Stir, and cover the vessel. Leave in a warm place, (65–75°F or 18–24°C) for 24 hours. Add the nutrient tablet and activated yeast (see manufacturer's instructions for quantity and method of use). Quickly siphon into a prepared fermentation vessel, filling to within 1 inch (2·5 cm) of the cork. Ferment under an air lock in a warm place (65–75°F or 18–24°C).

When fermentation is complete, rack, store and bottle in the usual way. Do not store the wine for less than 3 months. Keep in the bottle for a year, if possible, before drinking.

See also page 205.

Makes about 1 gallon (4·5 litres).

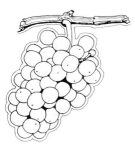

GRAPEFRUIT

A native of the West Indies, the grapefruit is believed to be the only important citrus fruit to have originated outside Asia. It was identified as a distinct species in 1830 and commercial cultivation began in Florida fifty years later. But it was not until the twentieth century that it began to gain worldwide popularity, when it joined the orange as the most marketed citrus fruit. Today it is available throughout the year, imported from different countries at different times.

The grapefruit tree is said to be named from the clusters of young fruit that, with a little imagination, seem to resemble grapes. Today's big producers and exporters are in Florida and California (the United States currently produces seventy-five per cent of the world's crop), the West Indies, Central America and South Africa – the most prominent variety is Marsh's Seedless. There is also a Texan variety with pinkish pulp.

Buy large, firm fruit, with fine-grained skins, that are heavy for their size. Lighter ones will be pithy and less juicy. A big specimen can weigh as much as ¾ pound (350 g) while small ones (not to be neglected) can be just 6 ounces (175 g).

Grapefruit can be served simply cut in half crossways with the pips removed, or grilled with sugar. It gives a special bitter-sweet sharpness to salads, combines well with oranges and lemons in marmalade, and gives a special tang to sorbets.

Half an average grapefruit provides an adult with his minimum daily Vitamin C requirement, and the fruit also contains most other nutrients except fat and Vitamin D. Segmented, canned fruit and juice both retain useful amounts of Vitamin C.

Grapefruits freeze well, either whole, segmented or as juice. The fruit should keep for about eight months; the juice for four months.

GRAPEFRUIT FLOWER WATER

Less well known than its orange-flower counterpart, grapefruit-flower water is equally kind to the skin, and can be used as a soothing and toning lotion.

You will need a large enamel saucepan with a slightly domed lid and a non-plastic handle (plastic will spoil the scent), a small heat-resistant bowl, a non-metallic rack or trivet, some small smooth pebbles, ice – and grapefruit flowers and leaves.

Put the pebbles on the bottom of the pan and cover them with grapefruit flowers and leaves. Now put the bowl on the rack in the centre of the pan. Add a little water – enough to cover the flowers and leaves to stop them from burning, but not so much that it will dilute the scent.

Put the saucepan lid on and bring the water to the boil. When it boils, turn the lid over and fill it with ice. The steam will rise, meet the cold lid, condense, and run off into the bowl. Don't boil the water for more than 5 or 10 minutes.

The lotion can be used on its own, but won't keep long. To preserve it, and make a simple eau-de-toilette, add 20 per cent ethyl alcohol. For a face lotion, add 15 per cent glycerine to the mixture to counteract the astringent effect of the alcohol.

GRILLED GRAPEFRUIT

An easy and invariably popular appetizer. Allow ½ grapefruit per portion, plus an extra one for every 4 fruit used. Slice them in half crosswise and scoop out sections, leaving behind pith and membranes, and working over a bowl to catch juices. Use a special serrated grapefruit knife for this or a sharp-edged teaspoon, and be careful not to puncture grapefruit shells. Gently squeeze remaining juice into bowl. With a pair of scissors, snip out all remaining pieces of membrane and fibre from shells.

Place a half-shell per person in grill pan. Fill with grapefruit sections and some of the juices. Sprinkle thickly with soft brown sugar and dot with flakes of butter.

Set pan so tops of grapefruit are about 5 inches (12·5 cm) from source of heat and grill until sugar has melted and is caramelized, and grapefruit underneath is heated through (10–15 minutes). Serve hot.

GRAPEFRUIT AND CARROT SALAD

2 grapefruit
4 fresh young carrots
Crisp green lettuce leaves
6–8 tablespoons coarsely chopped toasted peanuts
2 tablespoons peanut oil
Salt and freshly ground black pepper
Pinch of sugar (optional)
1–2 tablespoons finely chopped parsley

Peel grapefruit and cut out segments, working over a dish to catch juices and picking out pips with the point of your knife as you come across them. Squeeze out juice remaining in grapefruit piths into dish. Scrub or scrape carrots clean under cold running water and grate them coarsely.

Assemble salad in a large serving bowl (or in individual bowls) as follows. Line bowl with torn lettuce leaves. On this bed place grapefruit segments. Top with grated carrots and scatter with chopped peanuts.

In a cup or small bowl, beat the grapefruit juices you have saved with peanut oil. Season to taste with salt, freshly ground black pepper and a pinch of sugar, if liked. Pour dressing over salad and sprinkle with chopped parsley.

Chill briefly before serving.

Serves 6–8

MINTED GRAPEFRUIT SORBET

12 ounces (350 g) sugar
Thinly peeled rind of 1
*   grapefruit and 1 lemon*
¾ pint (400 ml) pure
*   grapefruit juice*
¼ pint (150 ml) pure lemon juice
1 large egg white
Pinch of salt

To serve and decorate
Chilled fresh grapefruit segments
Icing sugar (optional)
Chilled Crème de Menthe
Sprigs of fresh mint

In a large pan, stir sugar with 1¼ pints (900 ml) water over low heat until dissolved. Add grapefruit and lemon rinds (best peeled off with a potato peeler). Bring to boiling point and simmer for 5 minutes. Remove from heat, cool and stir in grapefruit and lemon juices. Leave until cold.

Strain sweetened juice into ice cube trays or a large, shallow box, cover with foil or a lid and freeze in the ice-making compartment of your refrigerator or in a freezer until solid around sides but still slushy, like wet snow, in the middle.

Scrape sorbet out into a bowl and beat vigorously with a fork, or an electric hand whisk if available, to break up any large ice crystals which may have formed.

When uniformly slushy, pour back into container(s), cover and freeze to the same state again. Beating and refreezing once more will ensure a smoother texture, but if time is short, this second stage may be omitted.

When ready to proceed, whisk egg white with the pinch of salt until stiff but not dry. Then scrape sorbet out into a bowl again and beat vigorously until slushy once more. Stir in beaten egg white until texture is uniform, and pour sorbet back into container(s). Cover and freeze until firm.

Transfer sorbet to main cabinet of refrigerator to soften slightly and develop flavours about 1 hour before it is served. To serve, scoop a ball of sorbet into each individual glass or bowl. Surround with 4 or 5 grapefruit segments, skinned, seeded and sweetened with a little icing sugar if liked. Pour a tablespoonful of Crème de Menthe over the ball of sorbet and decorate with a small sprig of fresh mint. Serve immediately.

Serves 6.

CRANBERRY GRAPEFRUIT COMPOTE

Make this in late autumn and winter, when fresh cranberries are in the shops, or use frozen cranberries.

8 ounces (225 g) sugar
8 ounces (225 g) cranberries
3 large grapefruit, peeled and
*   sectioned*

In a saucepan, stir sugar with ½ pint (300 ml) water over low heat until sugar has dissolved. Then bring to boiling point and boil hard for 5 minutes. Add cranberries and simmer until their skins pop, 5–10 minutes. Cool and chill thoroughly.

Prepare grapefruit halves and divide between 6 glass bowls. Spoon cranberries and syrup over the top and serve.

Serves 6.

MIXED FRUIT MARMALADE

An easy preserve to make. Admittedly, its preparation is spread out over three days, but it will take only a few minutes of your time after the initial preparation of the fruit.

1 large grapefruit
1 large sweet orange
1–2 lemons
1 large sour apple
Sugar
Knob of butter or margarine (optional)

The first day. Cut the grapefruit, orange and lemon in half horizontally. Squeeze out their juice and pick out all the pips. Cut the peels in pieces. Quarter, core and peel the apple. Put the citrus peels and apple through the coarse blade of a meat mincer. Stir in the fruit juices. Measure volume and add three times the volume in cold water. Cover.

The second day. Pour fruit and juices into a preserving pan. Bring to boiling point and boil hard for 1 hour.

The third day. Measure the contents of the preserving pan. Heat gently while you measure out an equal volume of sugar. Add sugar to the pan and stir over moderate heat until sugar has dissolved. Boil for about 1 hour, or until setting point is reached, skimming off any scum as it rises to the surface. A small knob of butter or margarine stirred in at the last minute will clear any remaining cloudiness from the syrup.

Cool slightly. Pot and cover.
See also page 198.

Fills about 3 jars.

HAZELNUT

Hazelnuts are part of the same family as the cobnut and filbert. In Scandinavian folklore, the tree was dedicated to the god Thor, and the king's symbolic staff was made from its wood. Forked hazel twigs are used, to this day, in water-divining.

Hazelnuts have been eaten since earliest times. There are records of their having been collected for food by Stone Age man, and references to them in the works of Theophrastus, the Greek philosopher, and Pliny, the Roman chronicler.

Today, they grow throughout Europe where the male catkins herald spring with their bright yellow anthers. In Britain they are particularly common in the county of Kent. However, this corner of England cannot satisfy the home demand and the nuts are imported from several sources including France, Italy, Spain, Turkey and Armenia.

Hazelnuts can usually replace walnuts and almonds in cakes and pastries, and can be served salted as snacks. They can be lightly roasted in a moderate oven (350°F, 180°C, Mark 4) for 10–15 minutes depending on their size, until they are a golden brown. They can also be browned under the grill. Their thin brown skins will rub off easily but, during roasting, they should be watched and stirred to avoid over-cooking and uneven colouring. Like all nuts, hazels quickly turn rancid. Once cooled after roasting, they should be stored in an airtight container in a cool place.

Ideally hazelnuts should be left in their shells for storing. They can also be frozen successfully. For recipes that call for ground hazelnuts, it is best to break them up in a small hand-rotary cheese mill to avoid extracting too much oil. Be careful, and handle them lightly during mixing to ensure that the oil does not separate out, making the mixture too heavy. If you use an electric grinder, make sure you don't reduce the nuts to a powder. If they are to be added to flour and sugar, grind all three ingredients together in a blender or food processor to keep the nuts as dry as possible. But make sure this is done rapidly. They should not be worked too long. It obviously makes sense to grind only the amount of nuts necessary for a particular recipe.

Add ground hazelnuts to biscuit and cake mixtures, decorate cakes with whole nuts, and caramelize them as an accompaniment to ice cream and after-dinner coffee.

Hazelnuts are high in protein and unsaturated fat, as well as in mineral salts and vitamins (especially calcium, Vitamin E and folic acid) and are recommended for heart complaints, and also anaemia (which can be associated with lack of both folic acid and Vitamin E). Finally, an old recipe in Oxford's Ashmolean Museum gives hazel buds as an ingredient in an unguent which enables the user to see fairies!

HAZELNUT AND CHERRY SALAD

An unusual salad that combines two contrasting textures. It is good with cold poultry or game.

2½ pounds (1·1 kilos) hazelnuts,
    shelled, roasted and skinned
2 pounds (900 g) ripe Morello cherries,
    stoned

Dressing
6 tablespoons sunflower oil
1 tablespoon wine vinegar
1 tablespoon orange juice
1 tablespoon yoghourt
¼ teaspoon ground cinnamon
Salt and freshly ground black
    pepper

Place the nuts in a chilled salad bowl. Add all the cherries, except about six. Leave the bowl covered in the refrigerator.

Place all the ingredients for the dressing in a screw-top jar. Squeeze as much juice as possible from the remaining cherries, by crushing them with your fingers, into the jar. Screw the lid on tightly and shake the jar vigorously to mix. Chill the jar of dressing in the refrigerator for at least an hour. Just before serving, shake the dressing again before pouring over the cherries and nuts.

Serves 6.

COUGH REMEDY

For a persistent cough, pound hazelnuts with two or three times their weight of honey, and a little lemon juice, to make a perfectly smooth paste. Make this into pastilles, or dilute with hot water.

LOTION

For an astringent, stimulating yet soothing, lotion for greasy skin boil 1 ounce (25 g) dried hazel leaves in 1 pint (600 ml) water for 20–30 minutes. This lotion can also be used for raw, chapped hands.

HAZELNUT SOUFFLÉ

3 ounces (75 g) hazelnuts, shelled,
  roasted and skinned
2 ounces (50 g) butter
1½ ounces (40 g) plain flour
½ pint (300 ml) hot milk
2 ounces (50 g) sugar
4 eggs, separated

Start by chopping hazelnuts. Put aside until needed. Line a soufflé dish with greaseproof paper, so that the paper extends 3 inches (7·5 cm) above the top of the dish. Grease the paper well and coat lightly with some sugar.

Melt the butter in a thick-bottomed saucepan. Remove from the heat, add the flour, and stir to form a paste. Gradually pour on the milk, stirring constantly, to form a smooth liquid. Return the pan to the heat, and stirring continuously, cook the sauce until it begins to thicken.

Remove the pan from the heat, stir in the sugar, then beat in the egg yolks, one by one. Add the chopped nuts to the mixture.

In a small, clean bowl whisk the egg whites until very stiff. Fold this into the mixture in the pan, then turn into the prepared soufflé dish. Bake in a moderately hot oven (400°F, 200°C, Mark 6) for 5 minutes, then lower the over temperature (to 375°F, 190°C, Mark 5) and continue cooking for another 20–25 minutes, until the soufflé is brown and well risen. Serve immediately.

Serves 4.

NUSSTORTE

Make this rich cake for a special occasion.

6 eggs
6 ounces (175 g) sugar
6 ounces (175 g) flour, sifted
4 ounces (100–125 g) butter, melted
Few drops vanilla essence

Filling
1 pound (450 g) hazelnuts, shelled,
  roasted and skinned
1½ pints (900 ml) double cream
6 ounces (175 g) caster sugar

Icing
8 ounces (225 g) icing sugar
3–4 tablespoons water

Line and grease a 10 inch (25 cm) round cake tin.

Put 1 inch (2·5 cm) of water into a small saucepan and bring it to the boil. Lower the heat. In a bowl that fits securely in the pan, over the hot water, whisk the eggs and sugar together until thick and creamy. Remove the bowl from the heat. Carefully fold in the flour and melted butter. Add the vanilla essence. Stir well, then pour the mixture into the prepared tin. Bake in a moderate oven (350°F, 180°C, Mark 4) for 45 minutes, until firm and golden. A knife slipped into the centre should come out clean.

Remove from the oven and cool until the cake has shrunk away from the side of the tin. Remove the cake from the tin and cool on a wire rack. When cold, slice across into 3 equal layers.

To make the filling, chop all but 6 of the roasted nuts finely (you may use an electric grinder for this but be careful that the nuts are not reduced to a powder). In a medium bowl, whip the cream until thick. Add two-thirds of the ground nuts and the caster sugar. Blend together well. Spread this between the cake layers, sandwiching them together. Put the assembled cake on a serving plate.

In a small bowl, mix the icing sugar and water until smooth. Spread this icing over the top and sides of the cake, with a palette knife. While the icing is still wet, sprinkle the remaining ground nuts onto the sides of the cake. Decorate the top with the reserved whole nuts. Let the cake stand in a cool place for a few hours, before serving.

HAZELNUTS IN CARAMEL

Shell the hazelnuts, and roast and peel them if you want to bring out their nutty flavour.

Oil a large marble slab or a couple of baking sheets with tasteless oil. Arrange the nuts on the prepared surface in little heaps, each of which should be enough to make an individual mouthful.

For every pound (450 g) of shelled nuts allow about 1 pound (450 g) sugar. In a heavy pan, melt the sugar with a few tablespoons of cold water and a generous squeeze of lemon juice. Over low heat, swirl the syrup round steadily until it turns a rich golden colour. Immediately remove the pan from the heat and pour a spoonful or so of syrup over each heap of nuts so that they are completely coated and held together. Leave them to cool and harden. Then carefully prise each sweet free with a round-bladed knife or a small palette knife.

Store in an airtight jar.

HAZELNUT BISCUITS

These biscuits are quick and simple to prepare and store well in an airtight container.

1 pound (450 g) hazelnuts, finely
  ground
2 eggs
2 tablespoons honey
Pinch salt
Few drops vanilla essence

Line a baking tray with greaseproof paper. Oil the paper well.

Put all the ingredients in a large bowl and blend into a paste with a wooden spoon.

Cover the bowl and place in the refrigerator for 1 hour.

Remove and roll the paste into small balls, about ¾ inch (2 cm) in diameter. Place these on the prepared baking tray, spacing well. Bake in a slow oven (325°F, 170°C, Mark 3) for about 15 minutes until golden brown. They should still be slightly soft to touch.

Leave the biscuits to cool, before eating (or storing).

KIWI FRUIT

The kiwi fruit, or Chinese gooseberry, is native to the Yangtse valley in eastern China where it grows, like the grape, on a type of vine. The Chinese version is smaller and more prickly than the cultivated New Zealand variety.

Hairs on the greenish-brown skin should be rubbed off before the fruit is eaten; or take off the skin with a sharp knife or potato peeler. Leave the fruit in boiling water for 30 seconds if the peel is difficult to remove at first. A ripe specimen feels soft and gives slightly when lightly pressed. Under-ripe fruits continue to ripen off the vine – put them in a polythene bag with an apple or two, or a banana, both of which give off ethylene gas which helps to ripen the kiwis. They should be ready to eat – after an airing – in a few days, and keep well in the refrigerator once ripe.

You can cut the unpeeled fruit in half and scoop out the soft flesh with a teaspoon; or peel it, slice it very thinly across the core, and use it in salads, fritters, or as a garnish for meat dishes. Its taste and texture goes well with fruit-filled meringues and whipped cream to make that well-known antipodean speciality, Pavlova. Like many other exotic and tropical fruits, it makes delicious and refreshingly different ice creams.

Kiwi fruit contains an enzyme, actinidin, which prevents it from setting with gelatine, unless the fruit has been cooked first. The same enzyme makes the fruit an effective tenderizer for meat.

Kiwis can be frozen whole (rub the hairs off the skin first), as thick slices, in syrup made from 8 ounces (225 g sugar) to 1 pint (550 ml) water, layered with sugar, or as purée.

They have a very high concentration of Vitamin C – higher than either blackcurrants or citrus fruit – and are therefore excellent for invalids and convalescents. Peel them immediately before serving – exposure to the air causes vitamin loss.

KIWI CHICKEN SALAD

1 or 2 celery sticks
Small bunch of spring onions
1 small pale green crisp lettuce
1 pound (450 g) cooked chicken
2 ounces (50 g) button mushrooms
4 kiwi fruit
1–2 tablespoons flaked almonds
A sprinkling of bean shoots

Dressing
5 tablespoons soured cream
5 tablespoons mayonnaise (page 205)
2 teaspoons lemon juice
Salt and freshly ground black pepper

Wipe, trim and chop the celery. Do the same with the spring onions, chopping them finely. Wash and shred the lettuce. Pile into a salad bowl.

Dice the chicken, removing any skin, then thinly slice the button mushrooms and add these to the salad with the chicken.

Peel and thinly slice the kiwi fruit and arrange over the salad with the almonds and bean shoots.

Make the dressing by whisking the soured cream into the mayonnaise and sharpening it with lemon juice. Season well with salt and pepper and chill both salad and dressing before serving.

Serves 6.

AUCKLAND STEAK

Four 8 ounce (225 g) pieces fillet or lean sirloin steak
1 ripe kiwi fruit, peeled and halved
2 ripe kiwi fruit, peeled and sliced, to garnish
Oil

Pre-heat the grill to high. Rub each piece of steak well with the halved kiwi fruit to impregnate it with the juice. Brush each steak lightly with oil. Grease the bars of the grilling rack.

When the grill is red hot, place the prepared steak on the grilling rack in the grill pan, and cook for 1 minute on each side to brown. Then reduce the heat slightly and cook, turning the steaks every 2 minutes, until cooked to taste.

Place the steaks on a warm serving dish and garnish with the sliced kiwi fruit.

Serve immediately.

Serves 4.

GRACE'S PAVLOVA

A classic foil for kiwi fruit, a Pavlova is also delicious served with any other fresh, acid fruit such as raspberries.

3 egg whites
9 ounces (250 g) caster sugar
2 teaspoons white wine or cider vinegar
1 teaspoon vanilla essence
1 rounded teaspoon cornflour
2 tablespoons boiling water
Whipped cream and peeled, sliced kiwi fruit, to decorate

Mark a 9 inch (22.5 cm) circle on a sheet of greaseproof paper. Use it to line a lightly greased baking sheet and dampen it with cold water.

Place all the first 6 ingredients in a bowl and beat until thick, white and fluffy. Meanwhile, pre-heat the oven to cool (300°F, 150°C, Mark 2).

Pile the meringue on the lined baking sheet and with the back of a large spoon, shape it into a 'nest', hollowed out in the centre. Bake for 10 minutes, then turn off the heat and leave it in the oven without opening the door for at least 1 hour, preferably overnight.

When ready to serve, transfer the meringue to a serving platter, fill it with whipped cream and decorate generously with fruit.

Serves 6–8.

KIWI ICE CREAM

6 kiwi fruit
5 ounces (150 g) caster sugar
3 eggs
½ pint (300 ml) double cream

Peel the kiwi fruit and mash well with half the sugar. Set aside for 15 minutes.

Separate the eggs and whisk the yolks with the remaining sugar in the top of a double boiler, or in a heat-proof bowl over a pan of hot water, until thick and mousse-like. Allow this to cool.

Beat the egg whites until stiff and fold into the cooled egg mixture with the mashed fruit. Whip the cream until stiff and fold this into the mixture. Turn into a metal tray and freeze quickly until the edges of the mixture are frozen, then beat it well and freeze again until firm.

Serves 4–6.

KIWI FRITTERS

Most of the preparation for these can be done in advance. They then only take a few minutes to cook. The crisp, dry batter makes a nice contrast to the fleshy, tangy fruit centre.

4 ounces (100–125 g) plain flour
1 teaspoon salt
1 egg
¼ pint (150 ml) milk
8 ripe kiwi fruit
Oil for deep frying
Caster sugar and lemon juice, to garnish

Sift the flour and salt into a bowl and make a well in the centre. Put the egg and half the milk in the well and, mixing from the centre, work the mixture into a thick batter. Gradually stir in the remaining milk and beat until the batter is smooth. Put on one side. Wash, peel and slice the kiwi fruit in slices ⅓ inch (8 mm) thick.

Heat the oil in a deep frying pan until sizzling. Holding each slice of kiwi fruit on a fork, dip into the batter, coating the fruit well, then plunge into the hot fat. Fry a few slices at a time, until they are golden brown. Put the fritters, as they come out of the pan, onto a layer of kitchen paper to drain off surplus fat. Then transfer to a warm serving dish and keep warm in a low oven until all the fritters are cooked. Sprinkle with caster sugar and lemon juice before serving.

Serves 4.

KIWI FRUIT CHUTNEY

12 ripe kiwi fruit
3 medium onions, peeled and finely chopped
1 lemon, sliced
4 ounces (100–125 g) raisins, chopped
¾ pint (400 ml) cider vinegar
12 ounces (350 g) demerara sugar
5 tablespoons coarsely chopped preserved ginger
1 teaspoon ground ginger
Salt
¼ teaspoon cayenne pepper

Wash the kiwi fruit, then peel and put them in a preserving pan. Add the rest of the ingredients. Stir well and bring to the boil. Turn down the heat to very low and simmer the contents of the preserving pan gently, stirring frequently, until a smooth pulp is obtained. This should take about 1½ hours.

Cool, pot and cover (page 200).

Fills about 5 jars.

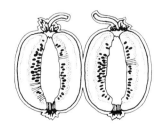

KUMQUAT

The name kumquat (or cumquat) comes from the Chinese word *chin chu*, which appropriately enough means 'golden orange'. These little natives of South West China have been cultivated there for over 1,000 years but were not seen in the western world until relatively recently. The small evergreen shrub from which they come has glossy, dark green leaves and flowers of the purest white, later succeeded by little miniature 'golden oranges'. At formal dinners in the Far East, guests are invited to pick fresh kumquats straight from dwarf trees which decorate the tables. These ornamental shrubs are popular, as focal points, with landscape gardeners.

The kumquat is usually oval, and brilliantly coloured. The thin, aromatic skin tastes sweet, though the segmented fruit inside tends to be more acid. Buy unbruised fruits with a slight sheen on the skin. Store them in a cool, dry place and eat within a week.

Kumquats can be peeled and eaten like oranges, or sliced and eaten whole, rind and all. They are delicious simmered in a syrup, cooled, and served with a vanilla ice cream. Use them instead of oranges in a fruit salad, make them into a marmalade, or candy them.

Packed in foil or polythene bags after open-freezing, kumquats will keep in the freezer for up to two months; packed in rigid containers and covered with a cold sugar syrup (about 8 ounces or 225 g sugar to 1 pint or 550 ml water), they will freeze satisfactorily for up to twelve months. Thaw them overnight in the refrigerator, or for three hours at room temperature. And try canned kumquats if fresh ones are not available.

MELON AND KUMQUAT SALAD

An unusual blend of flavours and textures.

4 small melons (ogen or charentais)
12 candied or fresh kumquats
8 fresh or canned lychees, halved and stoned
12 glacé cherries, halved
4 tablespoons Kirsch or Cointreau

Slice the tops from the melons and scoop out the flesh. Cut in small dice.

Discard the seeds and scoop out the flesh with a melon baller, or dice it. Set aside.

Quarter the kumquats and mix in a bowl with the melon cubes, lychees and cherries and sprinkle with liqueur. Leave to macerate for 15 minutes, then pile the fruits into the melon cups. Chill for about an hour before serving.

Serves 4.

KUMQUATS IN BRANDY

A tangy dessert to serve with ice cream. And there's no need to use the very best brandy ...

2 pounds (900 g) fresh kumquats
1 pound (450 g) caster sugar
About ¾ pint (400 ml) brandy

Wipe the fruit and remove any stalks. Make a small cross with a sharp knife in the base of each one.

Put the sugar in a heavy-based pan or a preserving pan with 1 pint (550 ml) water and stir over medium heat until the sugar has completely dissolved. Bring this syrup to the boil, add the kumquats and boil, uncovered, for about 15 minutes until the fruit is almost transparent. Lift out

the fruit with a slotted spoon and put into clean, dry warm jars. Set aside until needed.

Continue to boil the syrup in the pan until it is thick, and a temperature of 212°F (100°C) is registered on a sugar thermometer. Take great care that the boiling syrup does not splash out of the pan.

Turn off the heat, let the syrup cool a little and then strain it. Stir in an equal amount of brandy.

Pour the brandy syrup into the jars to cover the fruit and leave until the syrup is completely cold. Cover, seal and label and store for at least 4 months before using.

Top up the jars with brandy from time to time.

KUMQUAT BATH

Enclose a small handful of fresh or dried kumquat flowers, leaves and rind, in a bag made of muslin, cheesecloth or fine cotton. If the mixture is dried, make the bag big enough to allow for expansion. Either infuse the bag (like an outsize teabag) in boiling water and pour the result into the bath, or simply hang the bag under the hot tap. It can be used two or three times before being discarded.

KUMQUAT MARMALADE

This has a sharper flavour than orange marmalade.

2 pounds (900 g) kumquats
Sugar

Wash the kumquats thoroughly in a colander under cold running water. Do not peel, but slice finely. Put the sliced kumquats into an enamel saucepan, cover with about 2 pints (1.1 litres) water and leave overnight.

Put the pan on the heat and bring the contents to the boil. Lower the heat and simmer gently for 1 hour. Cover the pan and again leave overnight.

The next day, measure the quantity of kumquat pulp and liquid from the pan, then return to the pan and add 1½ pounds (700 g) sugar to each pint (550–600 ml) of liquid and pulp. Dissolve the sugar by stirring the mixture over a gentle heat. Increase the heat and boil rapidly, until setting point is reached. Cool, pot and cover.

Keep for several months, at least, before using.

See also page 198.

Fills about 6 jars.

CANDIED KUMQUATS

These sweets are delicious any time, but try them as a mid-afternoon treat, served with lemon or mint tea, or with coffee after dinner.

½ pint (300 ml) rosewater
8 ounces (225 g) sugar
8 ounces (225 g) kumquats (about 2 dozen)

Line a baking sheet with waxed paper. Wash the kumquats thoroughly in a colander, under cold, running water. Do not peel or divide.

Put the rosewater and sugar into a thick saucepan and bring to the boil. Remove from the heat. Add the kumquats and stir. Return to the heat and heat to boiling point, then reduce the heat and simmer for 30 minutes. As soon as the sugar begins to caramelize (it will turn light brown), remove the pan from the heat. Lift out the kumquats on a spoon, allowing most of the syrup to drain off, and place, spacing well, on the prepared tray.

Put the tray of kumquats in the refrigerator for 15 minutes. Then peel the kumquats off the waxed paper and store in an air-tight container.

KUMQUATS IN SYRUP

Kumquats are usually available in early summer, at the same time as mangoes, papayas and other exotics. Although they are quite expensive, a few small jars of these pretty little fruits put away at this time will make unusual and attractive Christmas gifts.

2 pounds (900 g) kumquats
2 tablespoons bicarbonate of soda
2 pounds (900 g) sugar

Wash kumquats in warm water. Put them in a large bowl and pour on bicarbonate of soda dissolved in a few tablespoons of cold water. Then stir in 2 pints (1.1 litres) boiling water (or more, to cover) and leave until cold. Drain in a colander and rinse thoroughly. This preliminary step will help to soften the rinds of the fruit.

With a thin skewer or the tines of a sharp fork, prick each kumquat in 2 or 3 places to prevent it bursting. Place them in a preserving pan and add just enough boiling water to cover. Simmer fruit until soft, about 15 minutes. Then lift them out of the pan with a slotted spoon and put them back in the (rinsed-out) bowl.

Add sugar to cooking water and stir over low heat until it dissolves. Then raise heat and boil syrup for 10–15 minutes to thicken it slightly. Carefully replace kumquats in pan and boil them until soft and translucent. Remove pan from heat and leave kumquats to soak in syrup overnight.

The following day, bring kumquats just to boiling point once more. Pack fruit in hot, sterilized glass jars, fill to the brim with syrup, cover and seal as you would jam (page 199).

Fills about 3 jars.

SPICED KUMQUATS

This recipe also works well with tangerines, or any of the small fruit of the orange family. (You'll need about 16 tangerines for this quantity of pickle.) Good with game and poultry, it should be ready after about three months.

2 pounds (900 g) kumquats
½ teaspoon bicarbonate of soda
One 3 inch (7.5 cm) cinnamon stick
½ inch (1 cm) piece fresh root ginger
12 allspice berries
12 cloves
½ pint (300 ml) white wine vinegar
1¼ pounds (600 g) soft light brown sugar

Wipe the fruit and remove any pieces of stalk. Pierce each fruit with the prongs of a fork in several places so that the pickling liquid can penetrate.

Put the fruit in a large, heavy-based pan, or a preserving pan with water to cover. Add the bicarbonate of soda and bring to the boil. Boil for about 5 minutes.

Put the cinnamon, ginger, allspice berries and cloves into a piece of muslin or cheesecloth and tie them firmly inside. Add this to the pan along with the vinegar, then cover and simmer for 10–12 minutes.

Remove the bag of spices and lower the heat under the pan. Add the sugar and stir over gentle heat until completely dissolved. Bring to the boil and simmer covered for another 15 minutes. Lift the fruit from the liquid with a slotted spoon and pack into clean, dry sterilized jars.

Continue to simmer the liquid for another 10 minutes, then cool a little before pouring into the jars to cover the kumquats. Seal, label and store in a cool dry place.

See also page 200.

Fills about 3 jars.

LEMON

Lemons can be used in every kind of dish, from savoury soups to desserts, as both flavouring and garnish. And slices of lemon may well have appeared before the start of the meal itself, floating in pre-dinner drinks. Their usefulness does not end here. Lemon juice is used to acidulate water in which slices of food such as apples are soaked to prevent them turning brown when exposed to the air, or it can be brushed directly over cut surfaces that would otherwise discolour rapidly. On pale meats such as chicken or rabbit, lemon juice acts as a mild, harmless bleaching agent. It also makes a fine alternative to mild wine or cider vinegar, far preferable to the harsh malt variety for mayonnaises and salad dressings. Finally, always have a squeezed-out lemon half on a soap dish by the kitchen sink. Rub it on your hands to kill any odours left after handling strong-smelling foods like fish or garlic.

The original home of the lemon is thought to be south-eastern Asia. From there it gradually came west until in about AD 1,000 the Arabs introduced it into the Mediterranean region. To begin with, it was only used medicinally, but gradually its culinary importance took precedence. Today, large quantities of lemons are grown all over the world.

Choosing lemons is easy once you know what to look for. Like all citrus fruit, a juicy specimen will feel heavy for its size. The deeper yellow its colour, the less acid it is likely to be. Examine the skin, too. Thin-skinned fruit is usually finely textured. A thick skin often looks lumpy and is deeply pock-marked. Avoid hard-skinned lemons (which are probably old and may be rather dry inside) and any which have soft, spongy patches (they are probably already decaying inside and will soon turn mouldy all over).

Lemon juice and grated rind are constantly used in the kitchen, often in very small amounts. When only a few drops of juice are called for, there is no need to cut a whole lemon in half. Simply use a thick needle or sharp skewer to puncture the skin at one end in several places, and squeeze the whole fruit until drops of juice run out. If you need to squeeze out a whole fresh lemon, its juice will run more freely if you first soften the fruit by rolling it over a hard surface under the palm of your hand.

Never waste the zest, even if it is not to be used immediately. Grate it off *before* halving and squeezing the fruit and store it in a tightly covered container in the freezer. Use it straightaway in its frozen state when you need a pinch for a recipe.

Invariably, however, there will be times when a lemon half, both rind and juice, is left over. It can be stored for two or three days in the door of the refrigerator, the cut surface tightly sealed with plastic wrap. (A whole lemon whose skin has been grated off should be kept in the same way.)

Finally, a good way of making the most of lemon chunks that might otherwise go to waste is to cut them in slices or wedges, arrange them in one layer on a baking sheet (so they are not touching) and freeze them hard. The pieces of lemon can then be tied up in a plastic bag ready to add, still frozen, to drinks, instead of fresh lemon and ice cubes.

Lemons are almost as valuable medicinally as they are in cooking, and are also used cosmetically in a number of ways.

COSMETICS

Lemon juice is a powerful natural bleach, and soothes the skin as well as whitening it. Instead of throwing out old lemon halves, rub them on roughened and discoloured elbows. A lemon juice rinse is a very effective hair lightener, especially if you dry your hair in the sun. It also makes a good setting lotion.

LOTIONS

These lotions are easy to make and take advantage of the soothing and whitening properties of lemons.

For a toning and cleansing lotion, roughly chop one or two lemons, put them in an enamel or earthenware pan, press to extract the juice, cover with milk and bring very gently to the boil. Turn off the heat, allow to cool, strain, and add a little glycerine – just enough to give a pleasant consistency.

The following lotion will bleach dingy skin, sunburn and freckles, and will whiten and soften rough hands. Simply shake together roughly equal parts of lemon juice, glycerine and rosewater. Some people prefer less glycerine.

REMEDIES

For a sore throat, squeeze the juice of a lemon, or chop it roughly and simmer it in water for about 20 minutes to make a lemony liquid. In either case, when mixed with honey, hot water, and whisky or vodka, it makes a soothing toddy that helps fight infection.

Lemon juice is a natural antibiotic, tonic, diuretic and restorative. A teaspoonful in a glass of warm water, taken first thing in the morning, promotes regularity; cleanses and generally tones up the system, and helps digestion. It is not usually recommended in cases of gout or rheumatism because of its acidity, but an infusion of the leaves can be substituted. This also helps to induce sleep, and has been used to bring down fevers in illnesses such as typhoid.

Lemon peel is also good for fevers as it helps induce sweating.

AVGOLEMONO
Greek Egg and Lemon Soup

In Greece, this classic soup is often based on other stocks including meat, especially lamb, or fish.

6 tablespoons rice
2½ pints (1.4 litres) well-flavoured
  chicken stock
2 egg yolks
About 3 tablespoons lemon juice
Thin slices of lemon and finely
  chopped parsley, to garnish

Rinse the rice in a sieve under the cold tap. Cover with cold water and leave to soak for 15 minutes.

Meanwhile, bring chicken stock to simmering point. Drain rice thoroughly, stir it into the stock and cook gently until tender, about 15 minutes. Remove pan from the heat.

In a bowl, beat egg yolks and lemon juice together thoroughly. Gradually beat in a ladleful of the hot stock and slowly pour the mixture back into the remaining soup, stirring constantly.

Reheat gently, stirring and taking great care that the soup does not come to the boil, or the egg yolks will curdle. Taste and flavour with more lemon juice, if liked. The soup should be very sharp and lemony.

Serve immediately, each portion garnished with a thin slice of lemon and a sprinkling of chopped parsley.

Serves 6.

VEAL IN LEMON PARSLEY SAUCE

A light summer dish that is quick and elegant.

6 thin slices veal escalope
Seasoned flour
2 ounces (50 g) butter
1 tablespoon olive oil
Juice of 1 large lemon
2–3 tablespoons finely chopped
  parsley

Pound each escalope out with a dampened mallet and cut it into small squares. Dust on both sides with seasoned flour.

In a large frying pan, heat 1 tablespoon olive oil and 1 ounce (25 g) butter, and brown veal quickly on both sides. Remove veal from the pan. Pour off remaining fat and add 1 ounce (25 g) fresh butter. When this has melted, stir in the lemon juice and parsley. Stir over low heat until well mixed.

Return veal to the pan. Mix well until thoroughly hot and coated with buttery juices, and serve immediately.

Serves 6.

BAKED FISH WITH LEMON SOUR CREAM SAUCE

Serve the fish with rice, puréed potatoes or hot crusty bread and a tossed green salad.

Butter
1 thin-skinned lemon
1 mild, medium onion
1½ pounds (700 g) small white fish
  fillets, cod or haddock
Salt and freshly ground black pepper
8 fluid ounces (225 ml) sour cream
  (see right)
¼ teaspoon sweet paprika
1 teaspoon coarse French mustard (eg
  Moûtarde de Meaux)

Grease a large, flat baking dish lightly with butter. Cut lemon horizon-tally into thin slices, discarding end pieces which are mostly rind and pith. Pick out pips as you come across them and discard these as well. Cut onion into paper-thin slices. Arrange lemon and onion rings in baking dish in alternating, overlapping rows. Lay fish fillets on top in a single layer. Sprinkle them lightly all over with salt and freshly ground black pepper, and dot with a few flakes of butter. Cover dish with a sheet of foil and bake fish in a moderately hot oven (400°F, 200°C, Mark 6) for 20 minutes, or until it can be flaked with a fork.

While fish is in the oven, switch on grill so that it will be thoroughly hot when needed. Blend sour cream with paprika, mustard and a pinch of salt.

Uncover fish. Pour sour cream mixture over the entire surface, spreading it out evenly. Immediately grill fish about 3 inches (7.5 cm) from source of heat until surface is lightly coloured. Serve immediately.

Serves 4.

Note: Sour cream is becoming more widely available, but if you cannot find it, substitute half plain yoghourt and half double cream, lightly beaten, or use yoghourt on its own, beaten until smooth.

LEMON AND ARTICHOKE SALAD

An unusual way to use lemons, this luxury salad is perfect with grilled fish. Use tinned artichoke hearts.

3 large juicy lemons
3 teaspoons salt
10–15 tinned artichoke hearts
4 ounces (100–125 g) whole roasted almonds
1 teaspoon honey
2 tablespoons olive oil
Juice of 1 large lemon

Wash the lemons, under cold running water, but do not peel or cut. Place them in a saucepan. Add the salt and enough water to cover, and bring to a boil over a medium heat. Continue to cook until the fruit starts to soften, then remove from the heat and drain. Leave the lemons to cool.

When the lemons are cold, slice thinly and throw into a chilled salad bowl. Halve the artichoke hearts and add them to the lemons. Add the roasted almonds, the honey and the oil. Leave in a cold place until ready to serve (do not prepare more than 2 hours in advance). Just before serving, toss and sprinkle the lemon juice over the salad.

Serves 4.

LEMON HERB BUTTER

This makes a delicious stuffing for a whole baked fish, or it can be dotted liberally on freshly steamed vegetables, just before serving.

4 ounces (100–125 g) butter, softened
Juice and rind of 1 lemon
1 tablespoon finely chopped fresh parsley
1 teaspoon finely chopped fresh chives
½ teaspoon each finely chopped fresh basil and fresh chervil

Mash all the ingredients together in a bowl, or use an electric blender. Mix thoroughly. Use immediately or place in sealed container and store in the refrigerator until needed.

BAKED LEMON PUDDING

A deliciously tart pudding with which to round off a substantial family meal. As it bakes, it separates into two distinct layers – a light, spongey topping, with a rich, smooth sauce underneath that is reminiscent of lemon curd.

3 eggs, separated
Finely grated rind and juice of 2 large lemons
8 ounces (225 g) caster sugar
Butter
4 tablespoons flour
½ pint (300 ml) milk
Pinch of salt

Beat egg yolks and lemon rind together until light. Gradually add sugar, beating vigorously. If mixture becomes too stiff to absorb all the sugar, thin it with some of the lemon juice, then beat in remaining sugar, followed by remaining lemon juice, and continue to beat until white and fluffy. Beat in a tablespoon of melted butter.

Sift the flour on to the lemon mixture, a tablespoon at a time, and gently stir it in. Gradually stir in the milk.

In a large bowl, beat the egg whites with a pinch of salt until they form stiff peaks.

Using a large metal spoon, lightly and gradually fold lemon mixture into the beaten egg whites.

Pour mixture into a large, buttered baking dish and bake in a moderate oven (350°F, 180°C, Mark 4) for 35–40 minutes, or until pudding feels springy to the touch and is a rich golden colour.

This is at its best warm.

Serves 4–6.

LEMON PANCAKES

I have made these pancakes with unbleached white flour, which gave them the silkiest, most delicate texture I can remember. The final touch of frying the filled pancakes is not, strictly speaking, necessary but when some of the sugary lemon spills out over the hot pan, it caramelizes on the pancakes and makes them deliciously crisp.

4 ounces (100–125 g) plain flour (see above)
Pinch of salt
1 egg
¼ pint (150 ml) milk
1 tablespoon oil
Soft pale brown sugar
Lemon juice
Butter

Start by preparing pancake batter. Sift flour and salt into a bowl, and make a well in the centre. Break in the egg. Dilute milk with ¼ pint (150 ml) water. Working with a large wooden spoon, break up the egg and gradually work it into the flour, slowly adding diluted milk as you do so. When batter is smooth and free of lumps, beat in oil. Put aside to 'rest' for 1 hour before frying pancakes.

When ready to fry pancakes, heat your pancake (or omelette) pan (about 7 inches or 17.5 cm in diameter), and quickly brush surface with a butter paper or a wad of kitchen paper dipped in oil. Pour in just enough batter to coat base of pan, pouring back any excess left over after a thin layer has set on surface of pan. (Scrape off 'trail' left on side of pan by pancake batter when pouring excess out.)

When pancake is lightly coloured on the underside, loosen edges all round with a spatula and flip it over. Colour on the other side, then turn out on to an upturned soup plate and cover with a folded tea towel to keep pancake soft and moist. Stack pancakes on top of one another as you prepare them.

When time comes to serve pancakes, scatter each one with brown sugar and sprinkle with lemon juice, leaving a border of about 1 inch (2.5 cm) clear around sides. Fold pancake in four.

In a large, heavy frying pan, melt a large knob of butter. When foaming, arrange a single layer of folded pancakes in pan and fry steadily until crisp and golden. Turn pancakes over and fry on other side, adding a little more butter as needed.

Serve hot, sprinkled with a little more sugar and lemon juice if liked.

Serves 4–6.

SUSSEX POND PUDDING

A traditional English steamed suet pudding with a buttery filling of lemon and brown sugar. The lemon rind does, however, sometimes remain tough even after prolonged steaming. To avoid this, first freeze the lemon hard, then allow it to thaw out again before use.

8 ounces (225 g) plain flour
2 teaspoons baking powder
Pinch of salt
4 ounces (100–125 g) shredded suet
Milk and water, mixed
Butter, for pudding basin

Filling
4 ounces (100–125 g) butter
4 ounces (100–125 g) soft brown sugar
1 large, thin-skinned lemon, frozen and thawed (see above)

To make pastry, sift flour, baking powder and salt into a bowl, and stir in suet with a fork until thoroughly mixed. Then add enough milk diluted half and half with water to make a softish dough.

Butter a medium-sized pudding basin. Take a quarter of the dough and roll it out on a lightly floured board to make a 'lid' for the basin. Put aside. Roll out remaining dough and line the basin with it.

To make filling, slice the butter thickly and place half of it in a bowl, together with half of the sugar. Prick the lemon all over with a sharp skewer, and place it on top. Cover with the remaining butter and sugar. Fit the pastry lid on top and press well to seal it to pastry on sides of basin.

Cover top of basin loosely with foil or a double thickness of greaseproof paper and tie firmly around sides with string. Place basin on a trivet in a large pan. Pour in boiling water to come halfway up sides of basin, cover tightly with a lid and boil gently for 3½–4 hours, topping up pan with more boiling water as necessary.

To serve, turn pudding out on to a deepish serving dish to catch the buttery sweet sauce that flows out of it. Serve each portion with a piece of lemon.

Serves 6–8.

Note: The pudding will take an hour to cook in a pressure cooker at 15 pounds pressure.

LEMON CHEESECAKE

8 ounces (225 g) curd cheese
3 eggs, separated
4 ounces (100–125 g) caster sugar
¼ pint (150 ml) sour cream
Juice and finely grated rind of 2 large lemons
½ teaspoon vanilla essence
3 tablespoons flour
1 ounce (25 g) candied orange peel, diced
1 ounce (25 g) raisins

Beat the cheese until smooth and creamy. Beat in the egg yolks one at a time. Then, beating vigorously, gradually add the sugar, followed by the sour cream, lemon juice and vanilla essence. Sift flour over the surface of the mixture, folding it in gently, together with the lemon rind, candied orange peel and raisins.

In a large bowl, beat egg whites until stiff but not dry. Using a large metal spoon, carefully fold cheese mixture *into* the beaten egg whites. Spoon mixture into a well-buttered, 8 inch (20 cm), springform cake tin. (Failing a springform tin, use an ordinary deep cake tin, butter it, line the bottom with a disc of greaseproof paper and butter this as well.)

Bake the cheesecake in a slow oven (325°F, 170°C, Mark 3) for 1 hour, or until it feels firm to the touch and is lightly coloured on top. Switch off the oven and without opening the oven door, allow the cheesecake to stand for an hour. Then open the oven door and cool it for a further 30 minutes. Remove the cheescake from the oven, let it stand until quite cold and chill it thoroughly before unmoulding.

Makes 8 wedges.

LEMON MERINGUE PIE

One 8 or 9 inch (20 or 22.5 cm) shortcrust pastry case, pre-baked (page 203)

Filling
5 tablespoons cornflour
Generous pinch of salt
About 6 ounces (175 g) sugar
6–8 tablespoons fresh lemon juice
3 egg yolks
Finely grated rind of 1 lemon
½ ounce (15 g) butter

Meringue
3 egg whites
Pinch of salt
6 tablespoons caster sugar
1 teaspoon lemon juice or vanilla essence

Leave the baked pastry case in its baking tin (preferably one with a removable base).

In a heavy pan, stir cornflour with salt and 4 ounces (125 g) sugar until well mixed. Gradually stir in ¾ pint (400 ml) hot water and bring to the boil over high heat, stirring constantly. Lower heat and simmer for 3–4 minutes, stirring frequently, until mixture is thick and smooth, and no longer tastes floury. Remove pan from heat.

Beat egg yolks with remaining 2 ounces (50 g) sugar. Slowly beat in several tablespoons of the hot corn-flour sauce, then pour the egg mixture into the pan of cornflour sauce, beating or stirring vigorously with a wooden spoon. Place the pan over low heat and cook gently for a few minutes longer, stirring constantly, until sauce thickens again. Remove from the heat, beat in grated lemon rind and butter, and cool to luke-warm. Taste and add a little more lemon or sugar if you like.

Make a meringue. Whisk the egg whites with a pinch of salt until they form very soft, floppy peaks. Add half of the sugar, a tablespoon at a time, whisking vigorously until mixture is stiff and glossy. Finally, fold in the remaining sugar and the lemon juice or vanilla.

Pour the cooled lemon filling into the pastry case. Cover with meringue, spreading it right to the pastry rim so that the filling is sealed in (this will help prevent the meringue shrinking back while it is in the oven). Flick up the surface of the meringue in rough peaks with the tip of a knife blade.

Bake the pie in a slow to moderate oven (325–350°F, 170–180°C, Mark 3–4) for 15–20 minutes, or until the surface of the meringue feels firm to the touch and the tips of the peaks are lightly coloured. Serve lukewarm.

Serves 6–8.

LEMON SOUFFLÉ

1 tablespoon unflavoured powdered
   gelatine
3 eggs, separated
6 ounces (175 g) caster sugar
Finely grated rind and strained juice of
   3 large lemons
¼ pint (150 ml) double cream

Sprinkle gelatine over 3 or 4 table-spoons cold water in a cup and leave to soften for a few minutes. When mixture turns hard and stiff, stand cup in a small pan of very hot water and stir until gelatine has dissolved and liquid is quite clear. Allow to cool to room temperature.

In a heatproof bowl, work egg yolks with sugar and beat in lemon rind and juice. Fit bowl snugly over a pan of simmering water, and beat over gentle heat until mixture is thick and fluffy. Remove bowl from pan and continue beating for a few minutes longer to cool it. Then slowly whisk in dissolved gelatine.

Whisk egg whites to a firm snow. In another bowl, carefully whisk cream until thick and floppy but not stiff. Fold cream into lemon mixture, fol-lowed by egg whites. Spoon into a serving bowl and chill until firm.

Serves 6.

FRESH LEMON JELLY

A citrus-sharp finish to a heavy meal. Serve decorated with frosted grapes and accompanied by a bowl of lightly sweetened whipped cream.

Finely pared rind of 2 lemons
One 2 inch (5 cm) cinnamon stick
2–3 cloves
3 tablespoons powdered unflavoured
   gelatine
6 ounces (175 g) sugar
½ pint (300 ml) fresh lemon juice

In a pan, cover the lemon rind, cinnamon stick and cloves with ½ pint (300 ml) cold water. Slowly bring to boiling point, remove from heat and leave to 'infuse', covered, for 15 minutes.

Meanwhile, sprinkle gelatine over 6 tablespoons water taken from a mea-sured pint. Leave to soften for 10 minutes, then place container in a bowl of hot water and stir until gela-tine has dissolved and liquid is quite clear.

Stir into infused lemon liquid, which should still be warm.

Add sugar and stir until dissolved. Finally, stir in lemon juice and the rest of the measured pint of water. Strain into a large (2½–3 pint or 1.4–1.7 litre) jelly mould and when quite cold, chill in the refrigerator until firmly set. Turn out and serve.

Serves 6.

SYLLABUB

A famous old English sweet, as served at the Sharrow Bay in Ullswa-ter, described by the AA as Britain's 'most beautifully situated hotel'.

1 orange
1 lemon
1½ ounces (40 g) caster sugar
¼ pint (150 ml) double cream,
   preferably Jersey
½ wine glass dry sherry
Peeled pistachio nuts, to decorate

Finely grate the rinds and squeeze the juice of the orange and lemon into a large bowl. Add the sugar and stir until dissolved. Add the cream and sherry, and whisk slowly (prefer-ably with a hand whisk) until syllabub is thick.

Pile in a glass serving bowl or in individual, tall, stemmed glasses (wine glasses, for example). Spike with pistachio nuts and serve ac-companied by a dish of shortbread fingers.

Serves 4.

LEMON ICE CREAM

An easy recipe for a very special ice cream that makes a deliciously re-freshing end to a meal.

Juice and finely grated rind of 1
   medium lemon
7 ounces (200 g) caster sugar
¾ pint (400 ml) single cream

Blend lemon juice, grated lemon rind and sugar together until they are syrupy. Gradually blend or beat in cream. Taste and add a little more lemon juice or sugar if necessary, bearing in mind that freezing will weaken flavours.

Pour mixture into a freezing tray, cover with a lid or a sheet of foil and freeze until mixture has solidified around sides and is thick and mushy in the middle.

Scrape out into a bowl and beat thoroughly to break down any large ice crystals. When mixture is smooth and creamy, quickly pour back into freezing containers, cover and freeze until solid.

Transfer to main cabinet of re-frigerator for about 1 hour to soften slightly before serving.

Serves 4.

Mazurck Cytrynowy
Polish Easter
Lemon Bars

One 9 inch (22.5 cm) tart shell or large
*   rectangular pastry base, pre-baked,*
*   made with shortcrust pastry using*
*   8 ounces (225 g) flour (page 203)*
4 large, thin-skinned lemons
8 ounces (225 g) caster sugar
1 pound (450 g) ground almonds
1½ pounds (700 g) granulated sugar

Peel the lemons, scraping off white pith, and slice them horizontally, discarding pips. In a deep, wide dish, sprinkle the slices with caster sugar and put aside for at least 1 hour to allow sugar to dissolve.

In a heavy pan, mix together the almonds, sugar, the syrup from the lemons and 3 tablespoons water. Stir over low heat until it becomes a smooth paste.

Arrange lemon slices neatly on the pastry base. Cover them evenly with the almond mixture and place in a slow oven (325°F, 170°C, Mark 3) for 20 minutes, or until top feels dry.

Cool slightly before cutting into bars with a sharp knife.

Serves 8.

Lemonade

This recipe makes a concentrate to serve diluted with an equal part of water and chilled with ice cubes.

1 pound (450 g) sugar
3 oranges
6 large lemons

In a heavy pan, dissolve sugar in 1 pint (550 ml) water over low heat. Bring to the boil, then remove from heat and leave to cool.

Meanwhile, grate enough rind from the oranges to make 2 tablespoons. Add it to the cooling syrup together with the squeezed juice of the oranges and lemons, and mix well. Leave for 1 hour.

Strain through a muslin-lined sieve. Pour into a stoppered bottle or jug and store in the refrigerator. It will keep for a few days.

Makes about 2½ pints (1.4 litres).

Lemon Curd

Use a double saucepan for the curd, or improvise one by fitting a bowl over a pan of simmering water.

4 juicy, thin-skinned lemons
4 eggs
4 ounces (100–125 g) unsalted butter,
*   softened*
12 ounces (350 g) sugar

Finely grate the lemon rinds, taking care to get rid of any bitter white pith. Squeeze lemon juice and put it through a strainer. Beat eggs until well mixed and foamy.

In the top of your double boiler, combine lemon rind and juice, softened butter and sugar, and stir occasionally over simmering water until butter has melted. Strain in the beaten eggs, stirring vigorously to blend all the ingredients thoroughly. Continue to stir over simmering water until the curd is smooth, thick and creamy, about 20 minutes. It will be very hot, but do not let it boil, or the eggs will curdle.

Pour the curd into small, hot, clean jars and allow to cool before covering as you would jam and storing in the refrigerator (page 199). It will keep for a maximum of 8 weeks.

Fills about 3 jars.

Lemon Marmalade

This marmalade can be melted and poured over pudding.

12 juicy, thin-skinned lemons
2 pounds (900 g) sugar

With a potato peeler, peel the lemons very thinly so that you take only the coloured zest. Cut it into thin, long slivers.

Squeeze the lemons. Collect all the pips, tie them up in a muslin bag and put them in a preserving pan with 2 pints (1.1 litre) cold water. Leave to soak for at least 2 hours.

When ready to make the marmalade, add the lemon juice and shredded zest to the pan with the soaking pips, bring to the boil and boil briskly for 20 minutes. Stir in the sugar and cook gently, stirring, until it has dissolved. Then raise the heat again and boil until setting point is reached.

Remove the bag of pips. Pour marmalade into hot, sterilized jars and cover as usual.

See also page 198.

Fills about 4 jars.

LIME

If the only lime you ever tasted was in the form of a cordial in a bottle, you would be forgiven for thinking that these fruits are grossly overrated. In fact, if you ever have the opportunity of tasting a fresh one, take it. Limes may look like small, mean-looking lemons with tough green skins and green-tinged pulp, but the taste of their juice is quite remarkable. The flavour is not unlike that of lemons, but more subtle and slightly sweeter.

Limes are thought to be native to southern Asia and to have been brought to the Middle East and the Mediterranean by the Arabs in the tenth century, but nowadays they are cultivated all over the subtropical world. The West Indies and Mexico are the world's principal suppliers.

It has been known for a long time that they are a particularly rich source of Vitamin C and contain about one-third more citric acid than lemons. They also keep well. For these reasons they were carried on long sea voyages by British seafarers in order to prevent scurvy, caused by a lack of Vitamin C in the diet. Hence the nickname 'limeys' for British sailors.

Similar rules apply whether choosing lemons or limes, the only major difference being that the latter are always thin-skinned. Look for heavy fruits that are bright green in colour. Once they start turning yellow, they lose much of the sharpness that people find so appealing. But do not be put off by brown scald marks on the skin. The pulp and juice inside are probably still fresh and edible.

In cooking of all kinds, from marinades for fish and poultry to desserts and preserves, limes play as diverse a role as lemons. Both the juice and rind are used. Try substituting them wherever you would normally use lemons to add a new accent to cooking.

Like lemons, limes can be cut in slices or wedges for freezing. Put them in one layer on a baking tray so that they are not touching.

Cosmetically and medicinally, limes are as useful as lemons.

SEVICHE Mexican Fish Appetizer

All kinds of fish may be prepared in this manner.

1½ pounds (700 g) fillets of sole, skinned (see method)
About ¼ pint (150 ml) fresh lime or lemon juice

Dressing
6 tablespoons olive oil
2 medium tomatoes, peeled, seeded and diced
2 canned hot green chilli peppers, rinsed, seeded and chopped (but see method)
1 small mild onion, finely chopped
2 tablespoons finely chopped parsley
½ teaspoon chopped oregano
Salt and freshly ground black pepper

Ask your fishmonger to skin fish fillets for you or do it yourself as follows. Lay a fillet on its skin with the pointed (tail) end towards you. With a sharp knife cut fish from skin at the pointed end, going far enough to allow you to get a good grip on the skin. Then turn fillet over and pull skin sharply so it rips off in one piece, holding fish down with the other hand.

Cut skinned fillets into thin strips and lay them out evenly in a deep glass or porcelain dish. Pour over lime juice, adding some more if necessary to cover fish completely. Cover dish and leave to marinate in the bottom of the refrigerator for 3–4 hours, or until strips have lost their translucent, raw look and have turned opaque. Turn fish strips several times while they are marinating to ensure they are constantly coated in lime juice.

Prepare dressing. Assemble all the ingredients in a bowl and stir gently until thoroughly mixed. If you are not afraid of quite a fiery sauce, leave some of the seeds in the peppers. On the other hand, if hot green chilis are not available, a dash or two of Tabasco may be substituted.

Shortly before serving, drain fish thoroughly. Mix gently with dressing and chill lightly until ready to serve.

Serves 6.

Note: A garnish of sweet, mild onion rings, slices of peeled and stoned avocado or whole green olives is sometimes used.

ASTRINGENT OR FRICTION

Limes are the most acid of all citrus fruits and this recipe uses an extract of the leaves and flowers in pure alcohol to make an effective astringent for greasy skin or a friction rub for the scalp.

Put about a cup of alcohol in a glass jar and add a generous amount of lime flowers and leaves. (Lime flowers in recipes generally refer to the linden, but the citrus lime is used in this recipe.) Steep for a week, strain, discard the flowers and leaves, and put a fresh batch in the strained alcohol. Repeat three or four times, or until the extract smells strongly of citrus. Dissolve half a teaspoon of simple tincture of benzoin in a quarter of a cup of witch-hazel, and add to the extract (these are both astringent, and the benzoin is also a preservative).

GRILLED CHICKEN WITH LIME MARINADE

If you are worried that the bits of onion in the marinade could burn under the grill and impart a bitter flavour, strain the marinade before use. Prepare it at least 24 hours before you need it; it will keep for several days in the refrigerator.

One 3 to 3¼ pound (1·4–1·6 kilo) chicken, jointed

Marinade
6–8 tablespoons fresh lime juice
5 tablespoons peanut or corn oil
2 tablespoons finely chopped spring onion, white part only
2 tablespoons soft brown sugar
1 teaspoon finely grated lime rind
1 large clove garlic, crushed
Salt and freshly ground black pepper

Start by preparing the marinade. Combine all the ingredients in a screw-top jar and shake well until sugar has dissolved. Place in the refrigerator until needed.

The following day, wipe the chicken joints clean with a damp cloth or paper towels and prick them all over with a fork. Lay them in a single layer in a large dish and coat generously on all sides with marinade (strained if you prefer, see above). Cover the dish, place at the bottom of the refrigerator and leave to absorb flavours for several hours, turning joints occasionally.

When ready to cook the chicken, drain the joints, brushing off any stray pieces of onion. Reserve the marinade for basting the chicken. Pre-heat the grill.

Arrange chicken joints on the rack of the grill pan and grill for 30–40 minutes until cooked through and coloured on all sides, turning frequently and brushing with the reserved marinade. The joints should be juicy but the juices will run clear when the chicken is pierced with a fork.

Serve with a large green salad.

Serves 4.

LIME SORBET

For ¼ pint (150 ml) lime juice you will need to squeeze 5 or 6 limes, depending on their size and how juicy they are. If you do not have enough of them, you can make it up with a *small* proportion of lemon juice.

¼ pint (150 ml) fresh lime juice (see above)
12 ounces (350 g) sugar
A few drops of green food colouring
1 egg white

Squeeze lime juice, pour it into a jug and chill until ready to use it.

In a pan, dissolve sugar in 1¼ pints (700 ml) water and bring to boiling point. Simmer for 2 or 3 minutes. Remove from heat and allow to cool, stirring occasionally. Stir in chilled lime juice and tint syrup green with a few drops of food colouring. Pour into a shallow plastic box which has a lid or into ice cube trays, cover with the lid or with a sheet of foil and freeze until slushy, like wet snow.

When ready to proceed, first beat egg white to soft peak stage – it should not be too stiff. Turn the frozen lime syrup out into a bowl and beat it thoroughly to break down any large ice crystals. Then beat in egg white, pour back into freezing containers, and freeze until mushy again.

Sorbet can now be frozen until semi-firm and served, but if there is time, its texture will be even smoother if you turn it out into a bowl and beat it up vigorously once more before re-freezing it.

Serves 6.

CANDIED LIMES

12 juicy limes
10 ounces (275 g) sugar

Brush limes under cold running water, using a stiff brush (a wire one is best). Slash each one vertically from top to bottom in two or three places. Place limes in a large bowl of cold water to cover and leave to soak for 3 days. Change water every morning and evening, gently squeezing out water from limes between the palms of your hands each time you do so.

On the fourth day, make a syrup with the sugar and ¼ pint (150 ml) water. Bring to boiling point, add well-drained limes and simmer for 15 minutes. Remove pan from heat and leave, covered, until the following day. Repeat boiling and cooling twice more, once a day over the next 2 days, by which time limes should be soft and translucent. If not, carry on simmering a little longer on the third day.

Pack limes tightly into sterilized, screw-top jars (page 201), pour over syrup and screw down lids. Store as you would jams or other preserves.

Fills about 2 jars.

LIME CURD

An unusual alternative to lemon curd.

1 whole egg
2 egg yolks
5 tablespoons sugar
5 tablespoons fresh lime juice
3 ounces (75 g) softened butter, diced

In a heatproof bowl, beat the whole egg and egg yolks lightly with the sugar and lime juice. Fit the bowl over a pan of simmering water, add the butter and stir over low heat until the butter has melted and the curd is smooth and thick, about 20 minutes. Make sure that the water does not touch the bottom of the bowl, and that the curd does not boil, or the eggs will scramble.

Pour into small, hot, clean jars. Cover as you would jam (page 199), allow to cool and store in the refrigerator.

Fills about 1 jar.

LYCHEE

Lychees – usually the canned variety – have long been familiar to lovers of Chinese food. Sweet, fragrant and juicy, with a refreshing, slightly acid after-taste, canned lychees are delicious, but the fresh fruit is infinitely more so.... No wonder a Chinese poet of long ago, when exiled to Canton in Southern China, wrote that 'lychees could reconcile anyone to living in eternal banishment.' His average daily consumption was recorded as being a mere 300; stouter stomachs were known to take up to 1,000, so popular was the lychee with the ancient Chinese court. The fruit has been cultivated in China for over 2,000 years and the Chinese have identified over fifty varieties.

The fresh fruits need to be peeled from their brittle brown skins and are pearly and translucent rather than opaque. The flesh is crisp, and they are so good in their natural state that it seems a pity to cook them. Their light, fragrant taste goes perfectly with traditional Chinese ingredients like chicken and almonds, and duck.

Fresh lychees keep well for up to three months in the refrigerator, and they can be frozen in a cold sugar syrup (8 ounces or 225 g sugar to 1 pint or 550 ml water) for up to twelve months. They are rich in Vitamin C, with a high sugar content.

LYCHEE AND ALMOND CHICKEN

1 tablespoon vegetable oil
2 ounces (50 g) blanched almonds
2 large celery stalks, coarsely chopped
3 spring onions, thinly sliced
12 ounces (350 g) cold chicken meat, diced
½ teaspoon ground ginger
1 tablespoon soya sauce
½ tablespoon cornflour
8 ounces (225 g) lychees in syrup (see opposite; use at least ½ pint or 300 ml syrup)

Heat the oil in a large frying pan or wok until smoking slightly. Add the almonds, celery and spring onions. Cook, stirring constantly, until the almonds begin to brown. Add the chicken and cook, still stirring, for a further 5 minutes.

Lower the heat, add the ginger and pour over the soya sauce and half the lychee syrup. Keep stirring the mixture, over a low heat, for 2 minutes. Remove from the heat.

In a small bowl blend the cornflour and the remaining lychee syrup and pour this into the pan. Return the pan to the heat and cook, stirring constantly, until the sauce thickens. Stir in the lychees and serve on boiled rice.

Serves 4.

LYCHEE PORK

This Chinese dish originates in Fukien province, where lychees grow in abundance. Traditionally the surface of the pork is cut with a criss-cross pattern to resemble the skin of a ripe lychee.

10 ounces (275 g) lean fillet of pork
2 tablespoons cornflour
1 teaspoon salt
1 pound (450 g) fresh lychees
6 tablespoons vegetable oil
1 large onion, finely sliced
¼ pint (150 ml) chicken stock
1 tablespoon soya sauce
3 teaspoons sugar
2 teaspoons vinegar
2 teaspoons sesame oil
2 tablespoon medium sherry

Turn the oven to its lowest setting.

Slice the pork into small pieces about 1½ inches (3·75 cm) long by 1 inch (2·5 cm) wide and about ½ inch (6 mm) thick. Using a sharp knife, mark one surface of the pork slices with a criss-cross pattern. On a plate, mix half the cornflour and the salt. Coat each slice of pork lightly with this mixture and leave on one side. Peel the lychees. Remove the stones, wash under cold, running water and set on one side.

Heat the oil in a large frying pan or wok until it smokes slightly. Add the pork and fry, stirring constantly, for 3–4 minutes. Then arrange the pork, criss-cross surface down in the pan, and allow to cook for a further 2 minutes. Remove the pork from the pan and keep warm.

Pour any excess oil out of the pan. Add the chopped onion and fry stirring constantly for 2 minutes. Stir in the stock, soya sauce, sugar, vinegar, sesame oil and sherry. Remove the pan from the heat.

In a small bowl, blend the remaining cornflour with 3 tablespoons water. Add this to the contents of the pan and return to the heat. Cook gently until the sauce thickens, then add the pork and lychees. Allow to boil and keep cooking, while stirring, for a further 2 minutes. Serve immediately on boiled rice or noodles.

Serves 4.

LYCHEE AND PINEAPPLE PORK

Here's an 'authentic' Chinese recipe all the way from San Francisco! I like to fry the pork first to make sure it is well cooked, then finish it off in the sauce in the pan. The Chinese would add ½ teaspoon of monosodium glutamate to the sauce, but since this is now a controversial subject in the West, I leave this decision to you.

18 fresh lychees or a 14 ounce (400 g)
    can lychees
One 14 ounce (400 g) can pineapple
    slices
1 medium green pepper
1 egg
1 pound (450 g) pork fillet
About 6 ounces (175 g) flour
Salt
Oil for frying
1 teaspoon soya sauce
4 ounces (100–125 g) sugar
3 tablespoons tomato purée or
    ketchup
Scant ¼ pint (150 ml) white vinegar
Freshly ground black pepper
2 tablespoons cornflour

Peel the lychees if using fresh ones and remove the stones, otherwise drain the can, discarding the juice. Drain the can of pineapple slices, reserve the juice and cut the pineapple slices into chunks. Remove core and seeds from the pepper and cut into ¾ inch (2 cm) squares. Beat the egg. Cut the pork into neat ½ inch (1 cm) cubes and dip these into the beaten egg until thoroughly coated on all sides.

Sift the flour into a bowl with about a teaspoon of salt. Add the pork and toss until well coated. Heat the oil in a deep-fat fryer and fry the pork cubes for 6–8 minutes, until browned, then drain well on kitchen paper.

In a wok or frying pan, mix the soya sauce with the sugar, tomato purée or ketchup, vinegar and 4 tablespoons of the reserved pineapple syrup. Bring to the boil and season with salt and pepper.

Stir the cornflour into 3 tablespoons water to make a smooth paste, then gradually stir this into the mixture in the wok or pan. Cook, stirring, until the sauce thickens, then add the pork, lychees, pineapple pieces and green pepper. Stir-fry over a high heat until all the ingredients are very hot and well mixed together.

Serve at once with plain boiled rice.

Serves 4.

TROPICAL FRUIT SALAD

This is an expensive dessert, but worth it for a special occasion. It is foolproof to make, but always impressive.

1 fresh mango
1 large banana
1 small pineapple
1 pound (450 g) fresh ripe lychees
4 ounces (100–125 g) sugar
1 pint (550 ml) Kirsch

Peel and slice the mango. Arrange the slices in a medium serving bowl. Peel and slice the banana into thick, ¼ inch (6 mm) chunks. Add these to the bowl. Remove the outer skin and core of the pineapple and cut across into ¼ inch (6 mm) slices. Add these to the fruit in the bowl. Peel the lychees, remove the stones and wash under cold, running water. Arrange the lychees on top of the other fruit.

In a small saucepan, mix the sugar and ¼ pint (150 ml) water. Place the pan over low heat and stir until the sugar dissolves. Continue cooking until the syrup boils, then lower the heat and simmer for 10 minutes. Remove the pan from the heat, allow the syrup to cool, then stir in the Kirsch. Pour this mixture over the fruit. Place the bowl in the refrigerator, and leave for at least 1 hour before serving.

Serves 4–6.

LYCHEES IN SYRUP

Fresh lychees appear infrequently in Western fruit shops and do not keep long. So when available, set some aside for preserving in syrup.

4 ounces (100–125 g) sugar
1½ pounds (700 g) fresh lychees

Place the sugar and ½ pint (300 ml) water in a medium saucepan and gently bring to the boil, stirring until the sugar has dissolved. Leave to boil for 15–20 minutes until the syrup starts to thicken slightly. Remove the pan from the heat.

Peel each lychee, but do not remove the stone. Wash under cold running water and add to the cooling sugar syrup.

Pot, cover and seal.

Fills about 3 jars.

MANGO

The mango is one of the best and most popular of tropical fruits. The tree on which it grows flourishes in the hot, humid climate of India, its native home, but it has been introduced into countries including Brazil, Kenya and, most recently, Israel. Many cultivars have been developed, of which one of the most famous is the Indian Alphonso. The fruits vary in shape, size and colour, from rather flat, yellowish-green specimens weighing about 8 ounces (225 g) to large, round, rosy-red ones that weigh well over a pound (450 g). Mangoes travel well and, like bananas, are often picked before they are fully ripe and allowed to ripen in cold storage while being shipped.

When choosing a mango, look for one that yields slightly to finger pressure. If the fruit is hard and unyielding, leave it to soften at room temperature for a few days then store in the refrigerator until ready to serve.

All mangoes are dealt with in the same way, whatever their shape and size. First, peel the skin off thinly with a sharp knife. Alternatively, mark the whole skin in segments like an orange and carefully peel them back with your fingers. Then cut away the large, flat stone from the flesh. To do this, slice down one side with the knife blade as close to the stone as possible, then repeat on the other side. Finally trim off any remaining flesh.

The flavour of a ripe mango has been described as a cross between a peach and a melon with gingery undertones. It is sweet and powerfully aromatic, and needs no accompaniment apart from a sprinkling of lime or lemon juice. Cubes of diced mango make an unusual addition to a fresh fruit salad, or it can be turned into a variety of delightful mousses, creams and ice creams.

Canned fruit in syrup and mango purée can be substituted when fresh mangoes are out of season. You may also be able to find dried fruit, imported from the Far East. And no curry dinner would be complete without a dish of mango chutney.

Mangoes are very high in Vitamin A – less so than carrots, but more so than apricots.

MANGO AND PORK SALAD

Serve this Thai dish with rice as part of a main course, or as an appetizer. The dried salted shrimps and fish sauce may be bought from a Chinese food store or delicatessen.

2 large, unripe green mangoes, peeled and stoned
1 teaspoon salt
1 ounce (25 g) lard
1 tablespoon finely chopped shallot
2 cloves garlic, finely crushed
6 ounces (175 g) lean pork, finely chopped
1 tablespoon dried salted shrimps, pounded
1 tablespoon roasted peanuts, partly pounded
1 tablespoon fish sauce
1 teaspoon sugar
Salt and freshly ground black pepper
1 red chilli, finely shredded

Shred the mangoes into long, even strips, place in a bowl and sprinkle with the salt. Leave for 15 minutes, then wash the mango thoroughly in a colander, under cold running water, to remove all traces of the salt. Put the washed fruit into a large salad bowl.

In a frying pan, heat the lard until smoking. Add the shallot and garlic and cook until lightly browned. Add the pork to the pan and fry until crisp on the outside. Using a slotted spoon, remove the shallots, garlic and pork from the pan, dry on kitchen paper and set on one side to cool.

Add the shrimp, peanuts, fish sauce and sugar to the hot fat and stir well. Cook for 5 minutes, then remove the pan from the heat and set to one side for the contents to cool.

Just before serving, add the fried ingredients to the mango in the large bowl, mix well and season to taste. Sprinkle the shredded chilli on top.

Serves 4–6.

REMEDIES

In parts of India and Bangladesh, dried mangoes, with milk, are often given to invalids and convalescents. They are also preserved in mustard oil and served during a meal as an aid to digestion.

Small, very unripe mangoes stewed in water to a soup-like consistency are reputed to be calming and strengthening to the nerves and stimulating to the appetite.

HAM AND MANGO MAYONNAISE

4 ounces (100–125 g) thinly sliced prosciutto (raw Parma ham) or 6 ounces (175 g) thickly sliced cooked ham
1 medium ripe mango
3–4 slices pineapple, fresh or canned
8 ounces (225 g) small seedless green grapes
1 crisp, tart eating apple
1 large, ripe banana
4–5 tablespoons thick cream
4–5 tablespoons lemon mayonnaise (page 205)
Milk (optional)
Salt
Crisp green lettuce leaves, to garnish

If using *prosciutto*, shred it into ribbons and gently separate them out. Cooked ham slices should have all excess fat trimmed off and then be cut into thin strips about 1½ inches (3·75 cm) long.

Prepare fruit shortly before assembling and serving the salad. Peel mango and slice flesh off the stone. Cut it into thin strips. Cut pineapple slices into small wedges and strip grapes from their stalks. Peel, core and dice apple. Peel and slice banana thinly crosswise.

In a large mixing bowl, whip cream until it thickens and begin to hold its shape. If mayonnaise is very thick, dilute with a few drops of milk before folding it into whipped cream. Gently fold in *prosciutto* or ham and all the prepared fruit, tossing lightly with a fork until each piece of fruit is individually coated. Taste and season with a sprinkling of salt if necessary. (Ham and mayonnaise may have already made salad salty enough.)

Pile salad into a bowl lined with lettuce leaves. Serve immediately.

Serves 4.

Note: You can substitute ½ pound (225 g) – or more – skinned and slivered cold roast chicken for the ham. You may also need a little more dressing and seasoning.

MANGO AND GINGER ICE CREAM TART

A dinner-party special that should not be assembled until the last moment to avoid the danger of the pastry going soggy.

Prepare the pastry and bake the tart shell well in advance on the day it is to be served, so that it is quite cold when you fill it.

1 deep 8 inch (20 cm) rich shortcrust pastry case, pre-baked (page 203)
3 large, ripe mangoes
4–5 tablespoons finely chopped preserved ginger in syrup
3 tablespoons ginger syrup
2–2½ pints (1·1–1·4 litres) vanilla ice cream
4–6 tablespoons finely chopped toasted blanched almonds

Peel mangoes, slice flesh off the stone in lengthwise slices, and place in a dish. Scatter with chopped ginger, moisten with syrup and mix gently to coat slices all over. Cover dish and allow mangoes to macerate for several hours until needed.

Do not assemble tart until just before serving. If pastry case is still in its tin, unmould it on to a flat serving dish. With a large serving spoon, scoop up large curls of ice cream and arrange them in pastry shell. Arrange slices of mango neatly on top. Cover with syrup and juices which have run from the fruit, and sprinkle with chopped almonds. Serve immediately.

Serves 8.

MANGO SORBET

5 ounces (150 g) sugar
¾ pound (350 g) mango purée, fresh or canned
1–2 tablespoons lime or lemon juice

In a heavy pan, dissolve sugar in ¼ pint (150 ml) water over low heat. Bring to boiling point and boil hard for 6–8 minutes. Cool.

Combine the syrup with the mango purée and sharpen flavour with lime or lemon juice, bearing in mind that flavours tend to be modified by freezing. Pour into ice cube trays or a

MANGO MOUSSE

Cans of mango purée are usually stocked by Indian food stores but if fresh mangoes are available, use them instead. You will need 2 or 3 large ones which are very ripe and soft. Peel them, cut them off their stones and blend the pulp to a purée with the ginger, lime or lemon juice and sugar to taste. Individual portions of mousse may be decorated with swirls of more whipped cream, or slices of mango.

One 16 ounce (450 g) can mango purée (see above)
1 teaspoon ground ginger
About 4 ounces (100–125 g) sugar
1–2 tablespoons lime or lemon juice
1 tablespoon powdered gelatine
½ pint (300 ml) double cream

Pour mango purée into a bowl and blend in ginger, followed by sugar and lime or lemon juice to taste. Purée should be strongly flavoured. If using a purée of fresh mangoes that has turned out rather fibrous, rub it through a fine nylon sieve.

Sprinkle gelatine over 2 or 3 tablespoons cold water in a cup and let it soak for 10 minutes. Then stand cup in a pan of hot water and stir until gelatine has dissolved and liquid is quite clear. Cook, then beat into mango purée. Leave until syrupy but not set.

In a large bowl, beat cream until it thickens and forms very soft peaks. With the same beaters, beat the mango purée once more until smooth and light. Fold it lightly but thoroughly into cream. Divide between individual glasses and chill until set. Serve plain or decorated with more cream and fruit (see above).

Serves 6.

plastic box, cover with foil and freeze.

When the sorbet has solidified around the sides, scrape it out into a bowl and beat well to break down any large ice crystals. Pour back into the container and return to the refrigerator. Repeat once more, then freeze until solid.

About 30 minutes before serving the sorbet, transfer the container to the main compartment of the refrigerator to allow it to soften slightly.

Serves 4–6.

MANGO CREAM

A rich, quickly made dessert from Central America.

2 ripe mangoes, peeled, stoned and
   chopped
1 orange, peeled and sectioned
1½ ounces (40 g) icing sugar, sifted
¼ pint (150 ml) double cream, stiffly
   whipped
4 ounces (100–125 g) pecan nuts,
   shelled, roasted and coarsely
   chopped

Combine the mangoes, orange sections and sugar in a large bowl. Mix the fruits to a pulp using a potato masher or, preferably, an electric blender. Fold in the whipped cream and pecan nuts. Serve chilled in tall glasses.

Serves 6.

MANGOES IN SYRUP

1 pound (450 g) sugar
6 large ripe mangoes
1 teaspoon vanilla essence

In a large, wide pan, dissolve sugar in ¾ pint (400 ml) water and simmer for about 30 minutes until reduced to a thick syrup. If any scum forms on the surface, skim it off with a slotted spoon.

With a sharp, thin-bladed knife, peel mangoes and cut flesh from stones in lengthwise strips.

Stir vanilla into syrup. Drop in mango slices and cook over the lowest possible heat until mango is practically transparent but not disintegrating and syrup is very thick and reduced to about a quarter of its original volume.

Cool mangoes in syrup and chill thoroughly before serving.

Serves 6–8.

MANGO FOOL CRÉOLE

2 ripe mangoes
3 tablespoons lime juice
2 tablespoons clear honey
¼ pint (150 ml) whipping cream

Peel the mangoes, discard the stones and chop the flesh of one mango into neat dice. Sprinkle with half the lime juice and set aside.

Put the flesh of the second mango in a blender with the rest of the lime juice and the honey and blend to a smooth purée. Whip the cream until stiff, then fold into the mango purée with a metal spoon, leaving it streaky.

Stir the diced mango into the purée and put in a serving dish. Chill for about 1 hour before serving.

Serves 6.

MANGO SAUCE

This sweet sauce, from the Caribbean island of St Kitts, is delicious with cold meats or served as a dessert with sponge fingers and whipped cream.

3 almost ripe mangoes, peeled,
   stoned and chopped
4 ounces (100–125 g) demerara sugar
½ teaspoon ground ginger
½ teaspoon ground cinnamon
Pinch of salt

Place the mangoes and ½ pint (300 ml) water in a saucepan, and bring to the boil over a medium heat. Cover and simmer gently until the fruit is soft. Stir in the remaining ingredients, then cook uncovered, stirring occasionally, for 10 minutes, until the sauce is thick. Serve hot or cold

MANGO RELISH

1½ pounds (700 g) green mangoes,
   peeled, stoned and coarsely
   chopped
2 pints (1·1 litre) vinegar
2 ounces (50 g) demerara sugar
3 ounces (75 g) salt
4 teaspoons mustard powder
10 large garlic cloves, crushed
4 ounces (100–125 g) root ginger,
   peeled and finely chopped
Pinch cayenne pepper
4 ounces (100–125 g) raisins
3 teaspoons turmeric

Put the mangoes and ¼ pint (150 ml) water into a saucepan. Bring to the boil, then simmer gently until the fruit is reduced to a pulp. Add the vinegar, sugar and salt, stir and continue to simmer for a further 5 minutes, until the sugar is completely dissolved. Remove the pan from the heat. Stir in the rest of the ingredients, and mix well.

Return the pan to the heat and bring to the boil, stirring continuously. Turn the heat down very low and allow the mixture to simmer, stirring occasionally, for about 2½ hours, until well reduced. Remove from the heat. Allow to cool slightly, pot and cover. Keep for a week in a warm place, then store in a cool, dry place for at least 1 month before serving.

See also page 200.

Fills about 3 jars.

DRIED MANGO CHUTNEY

This is a spicy chutney rather than a pungent one, and is made with the dried mangoes available from Indian and Chinese grocers.

8 ounces (225 g) dried mangoes
4 ounces (100–125 g) stoned dates
1 pound (450 g) small onions or
    shallots
Grated rind and juice of 2 lemons
About 1 inch (2.5 cm) fresh root ginger
1 teaspoon salt
1 pint (550 ml) white vinegar
½ teaspoon chilli powder
1 inch (2.5 cm) cinnamon stick
1 pound (450 g) soft brown sugar

Slice the mango pieces and put them in a bowl with water to cover. Leave to soak overnight.

Drain them and place in a large saucepan. Chop the dates and peel and chop the onions or shallots. Put them into the pan with the mango, add the lemon rind and juice and grate the ginger over. Add the rest of the ingredients except the sugar and bring to the boil, stirring from time to time. Lower the heat under the pan and simmer for about 30 minutes, stirring occasionally to prevent it sticking to the pan.

Now stir in the sugar and continue stirring until it dissolves completely. Bring the chutney back to the boil and boil for about 15 minutes, or until it has thickened.

Remove the cinnamon stick and pour the chutney into clean, dry, sterilized jars and seal and label. Store in a cool dry place for up to 3 months. Leave it to mature for 3 weeks before opening.

See also page 200.

Fills about 3 jars.

FRESH MANGO CHUTNEY 1

2 green mangoes
1 medium onion
1 green chilli pepper
Handful fresh coriander leaves
Salt

Peel the mangoes and coarsely chop the flesh. Peel and chop the onion and chop the chilli pepper.

Wash and chop coriander leaves.

Put all in a blender with salt and 2 tablespoons water and blend to a smooth paste.

Serves 4.

FRESH MANGO CHUTNEY 2

2 green mangoes
1 green chilli pepper
1 teaspoon salt
2 tablespoons chopped fresh mint
1½ teaspoons sugar

Peel the mangoes and coarsely chop the flesh. Chop the chilli pepper. Put into a blender with the remaining ingredients and blend.

Serves 4.

MANGO TEA

1 fresh, ripe mango, peeled, stoned
    and coarsely chopped
1 tablespoon sugar
Juice of 1 lemon

Rub the chopped mango through a fine sieve or put into a blender to purée. Place the purée in a tall, heat-proof jug, add the sugar and lemon juice, and stir well.

Heat ½ pint (300 ml) water to boiling point in a small saucepan or kettle and pour onto the ingredients in the jug. Stir and cover.

If you want a hot drink, leave to stand for 5 minutes, stir well, then strain and sieve. Alternatively, leave until cool, then place in the refrigerator to chill. When ice-cold, strain into tall chilled glasses.

Serves 2.

MANGOADE

This cooling drink from Jamaica makes an unusual non-alcoholic beverage for a summer garden party.

2 ripe mangoes, peeled, stoned and
    coarsely chopped
2 ounces (50 g) sugar
Grated rind of 1 orange
¾ pint (400 ml) orange juice
¼ pint (150 ml) lime juice

Purée the mangoes by rubbing through a fine sieve into a large bowl. Place the sugar, ¾ pint (400 ml) water and orange rind in a small saucepan. Stir over a low heat until the sugar has dissolved, then remove from the heat and leave on one side to cool.

Slowly add the orange juice, the lime juice and the sugar syrup to the mango purée in the bowl, stirring constantly to blend. Alternatively blend the mango and the liquid together in an electric blender. Pour the mangoade into a tall jug and refrigerate for several hours before serving, with ice, in tall chilled glasses.

Serves 6.

MELON

Melons are gourds, the sweetest and most succulent members of the family which embraces cucumbers, marrows, pumpkins and watermelons. Wherever they originated – the experts toss up between Asia and Africa – it is certain that they have been eaten and enjoyed by man for over 4,000 years. They are clearly shown in ancient Egyptian wall paintings of the time of the Pharaohs, and the Roman Emperor Tiberius decreed that they should be served to him every day. The Arabs take the credit for introducing them to southern Spain, while the French king Charles VIII brought them from Naples to France in the Middle Ages.

The familiar honeydew, oval-shaped and with dark green or yellow ridged flesh, varies in sweetness and is often a good bet for serving as a starter with caster sugar, and powdered ginger to add a little tang of spice. The cantaloup (a group of melons rather than one specific type) takes its name from the Cantalupo region not far from Rome. A type of musk melon, it is smaller and rounder than the honeydew, with pinky-orange flesh and a pinkish skin with pale green stripes. Serve these halved (if large-ish), or with the tops sawn off like a cap, and the seeds hollowed out. The little charentais, also a member of the cantaloup family, is delicious if caught at maximum ripeness. The ogen, with sweet, pale green flesh and yellow-and-green-striped skin like a football jersey, is named after the kibbutz on which it was developed. The gallia is a rival of the charentais and the lavan has creamy-coloured skin and succulent pale flesh.

One of the tests for ripeness, whatever the type, is to lift the melon to your nose and *sniff* for fragrance. A ripe melon smells sweet, feels heavy for its size and – the time-honoured double-check – the skin should give if pressed lightly at the stalk end; too soft, and it's over-ripe.

Melons make splendid baskets when scooped out and filled with other fruits for serving. Cut smaller ones with a serrated edge and fill with melon water ice or raspberries, with which the melon has a delicate affinity. Melons can make a welcome appearance in salads too. They will freeze for up to a year if the flesh is cut in cubes or scooped in balls, and layered with sugar, but the texture is somewhat woolly when thawed.

If serving fresh, melons are best when lightly chilled; too cold, and their full flavour is lost. Always wrap cut melons in foil or plastic wrap, otherwise their aroma will permeate everything else in the refrigerator.

Melons, especially cantaloups, are rich in minerals and vitamins.

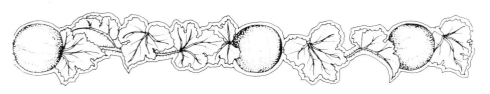

REMEDIES

Melon juice, often mixed with rose-water and a little sugar, is used as a remedy for fevers in the East.

The seeds have been used for dropsy, congestion of the liver, and strangury (painful retention of urine) and other urinary tract conditions.

COSMETICS

For a skin-brightening face mask, pound equal parts of melon, cucumber, pumpkin and gourd seeds, and mix with water to make an emulsion.

Melon juice will cleanse, soothe and nourish dry skin; that of cantaloups, in particular, is an excellent moisturizer.

It can be used on its own or mixed with a little honey. To loosen dead, flaky skin combine a little almond oil with juice and rub into your face.

CHILLED MELON SOUP

I have tried several recipes for melon soup, but this one, which came from Jane Grigson's column in the *Observer* Colour Supplement several years ago, is my favourite.

1½ pounds (700 g) melon pulp (see method)
5 ounces (150 g) sugar
8 fluid ounces (225 ml) dry white wine
Juice of ½ lemon
¼ pint (150 ml) sour cream
Icing sugar (optional)

Start by dissolving sugar in 1 pint (600 ml) water. Bring to boiling point, stirring until sugar has dissolved, and simmer for 4 minutes. Cool.

Halve melon and scrape out seeds and fibrous pulp. Take off melon peel and cut flesh into chunks. To obtain 1½ pounds (700 g) melon pulp, you will have to start with a melon which weighs about 2¼ pounds (1 kilo).

In a blender or food processor purée melon pulp, gradually adding the wine and sugar syrup to taste. If the melon is very sweet, use less syrup and add extra water. Finally, blend in lemon juice and sour cream. Taste and adjust flavours with a little more lemon juice, sugar syrup (or icing sugar) if liked. Serve chilled.

Serves 6.

Note: When I can, I use fresh limes, instead of lemons.

KANG KUNG

This is a hot, spicy soup from Cambodia. The dried shrimps, fish sauce and mushrooms are available from specialist Chinese foodstores.

4 ounces (100–125 g) dried shrimps
6 dried Chinese mushrooms
1 large, ripe honeydew melon
3 pints (1·7 litres) chicken stock
2 tablespoons fish sauce
6 thin slices of fresh root ginger
1 teaspoon cayenne pepper
2 tablespoons dry sherry

Put the dried shrimps in a small bowl. Cover with water that has just boiled and leave the shrimps to soak overnight, then drain.

The next day, put the dried mushrooms in another small bowl. Cover with boiling water and leave for 40 minutes. Drain the mushrooms, discarding the liquid. Slice thinly. Cut the melon into quarters. Remove the seeds and cut off the rind. Chop the flesh into small pieces.

Put the stock, fish sauce, ginger, cayenne pepper, mushrooms and shrimps in a large saucepan. Heat quickly to boiling point, then lower the heat and simmer for 30 minutes. Lift out the ginger, using a slotted spoon, and discard. Add the melon and simmer for a further 5 minutes. Remove the pan from the heat and stir in the sherry. Return the pan to the heat and cook until almost boiling (do not boil). Serve hot.

Serves 6.

AVOCADO AND MELON COCKTAIL

An unusual, refreshing start to a rich meal.

1 large, ripe honeydew melon
2 large, ripe avocado pears
Juice of 1 large lemon
Sprigs of fresh mint, to garnish

Cut the melon in half and remove the seeds. Then quarter the melon, remove the rind and cut the flesh into approximately ½ inch (1·25 cm) chunks. Place these in a salad bowl, together with any juice.

Cut the avocados in half, remove the stones, then peel and cut the flesh into thin slices.

Put these on a plate and pour the lemon juice over them. Leave for 2 minutes, then add to the melon in the salad bowl.

Toss all the ingredients together, and place in the refrigerator to chill for at least 30 minutes. Serve in individual glasses, garnished with sprigs of fresh mint.

Serves 4.

MELON AND CUCUMBER SALAD

This refreshing salad goes well with grilled lamb or pork.

1 medium cucumber
Juice of 1 large lemon
2 teaspoons salt
1 small, ripe honeydew melon

Dressing
10 tablespoons olive oil
5 tablespoons white wine vinegar
Juice of 1 small lemon
½ teaspoon salt
½ teaspoon freshly ground black pepper
1 tablespoon clear honey

Peel the cucumber, slice thinly and spread the slices out on a plate. Pour over the lemon juice, sprinkle with salt, and leave for 30 minutes.

Cut the melon in half, and scoop out the seeds. Cut off the rind and chop the flesh into small chunks. Place in a chilled salad bowl.

Drain any liquid off the cucumber slices, and add the cucumber to the melon. Leave in the refrigerator while preparing the dressing.

Put all the ingredients for the dressing in a large screw-top jar. Shake vigorously and place in the refrigerator to chill. Just before serving, shake the jar of dressing to mix the contents well, and pour over the cucumber and melon. Toss and serve.

Serves 4–6.

PROSCIUTTO WITH MELON

An inspired partnership of fruit and meat, Italian style, this dish is child's play to put together – but its success depends entirely on the quality of the ingredients used. The *prosciutto* (raw air-dried ham from Parma) should be moist and ruby-red, cut in paper-thin slices. Admittedly, it is expensive, in the smoked salmon class, but only a very small amount is needed per portion.

Failing authentic, fresh *prosciutto*, try serving the melon with Westphalian ham, which is easier to find in good delicatessen stores, and rather less expensive.

The melons, too, should be selected with care. Use 2 slices of juicy, ripe cantaloup (¼ melon) or ½ ogen per portion. When fresh ripe figs are in season, substitute them for the melon, allowing 3 average-sized ones per serving.

Per portion:
2 slices cantaloup or ½ ogen melon (see method)
2–3 large, paper-thin slices (about 2 ounces or 50 g) prosciutto
Lettuce leaves, to garnish (optional)
Freshly ground black pepper (optional)

Several hours before the dish is to be prepared, put the whole melons in the refrigerator so they will come to the table well chilled.

Shortly before serving, assemble the dish. If using a cantaloup melon, slice it vertically in eight. Scrape out seeds and fibres, then with a sharp, pliable knife, carefully cut away the flesh in one piece, close to the rind. Lay 2 wedges, still on their rinds, on each individual plate. Prepare ogen melons in the same way, allowing ½ melon per serving. Alternatively, slice ogen in half horizontally. Scrape out seeds and fibres. Then, using a melon baller or a small spoon with a round bowl (eg a measuring teaspoon), scoop out neat balls of melon and return them to their half-shells.

Arrange slices of *prosciutto* on a separate plate lined with a few lettuce leaves to prevent the ham sticking to it, or crumple 2 or 3 slices attractively over the top of each piece of melon.

Have the peppermill on hand for those who like to eat the melon sprinkled lightly with pepper. Serve well chilled.

BAKED SPICED MELON

Even the most experienced shopper can buy a melon that is never going to ripen sweetly enough to serve raw. The only solution is to cut one's losses and treat it as a vegetable. This produces a surprisingly fine accompaniment for poultry, pork, and even the more strongly flavoured game dishes and curries.

Melon
Salt
Ground cinnamon or
    allspice
Freshly grated nutmeg
Lemon juice
Soft brown sugar
Butter

Halve melon, scrape out seeds and peel off skin. Cut melon flesh into large (about 1 inch or 2·5 cm) cubes. Season lightly with salt, a sprinkling of cinnamon or allspice and a grating of nutmeg. Squeeze a little lemon juice over the melon, sweeten to taste with soft brown sugar and toss lightly with a fork until well mixed. Spread melon cubes out evenly in a shallow, buttered baking dish and dot with flakes of butter.

Bake in a moderate oven (350°F, 180°C, Mark 4) for 20–30 minutes, or until melon is soft and juicy.

Serve hot.

MELON STUFFED WITH FRUITS

All kinds of fruit may be served in a melon shell. This recipe, and the three that follow, are variations on the theme.

1 large, ripe melon
12 ounces (350 g) strawberries,
    hulled, or raspberries
8 ounces (225 g) redcurrants
8 ounces (225 g) ripe red or black
    cherries, pitted
3–4 large, ripe peaches, peeled and
    cubed
Caster sugar or sifted
    icing sugar

Shave a thin slice from one end of the melon to give it a secure base. Take a thick slice from the other end (cutting about one-quarter of the way down) to expose the seeds inside. Scrape out all the seeds and fibres. Using a melon baller or a teaspoon with a round bowl, scoop out as much flesh as possible into a bowl. Add the strawberries, redcurrants, cherries and peaches.

Sweeten to taste, mixing gently to avoid crushing the fruit.

Pile the fruit into the melon shell. Replace the melon 'lid' and seal the melon in foil or plastic wrap. Chill well before serving on a shallow dish.

Serves 4–6.

MELON WITH RASPBERRIES

Melon and raspberries go well together. Serve this simple but spectacular presentation as either an appetizer or dessert.

1 pound (450 g) fresh or frozen
    raspberries, defrosted
Caster sugar
Lemon juice
2 teaspoons powdered gelatine
1 ripe honeydew melon

Put aside about a quarter of the best raspberries and rub remainder through a fine nylon sieve, discarding seeds. Measure ½ pint (300 ml) raspberry purée into a pan. Sweeten and flavour to taste with lemon juice – the exact amount of sugar and lemon juice you need will depend on the flavour of the raspberries in the first place. The purée should be sweet and sharp, as melon is quite bland.

In a cup, sprinkle gelatine over 4 or 5 teaspoons water and leave for 10 minutes to soften. Then dissolve gelatine by standing cup in a pan or bowl of hot water and stirring until it has melted and liquid is quite clear. Warm the pan of raspberry purée to more or less the same temperature as that of the dissolved gelatine – this is important, because if the gelatine is much warmer than the purée when the two are combined, the gelatine may set too fast and be unpleasantly 'ropey'. Blend the two thoroughly. Cool and chill until syrupy and on the point of setting.

Meanwhile, cut the melon in half lengthwise and scrape out seeds, fibres and a little of the pulp to make room for raspberries and jelly. Stir reserved raspberries into syrupy purée, and divide between melon halves. Chill until jelly is firmly set.

To serve, heat the blade of a large knife thoroughly by dipping it in boiling water. Wipe it dry and carefully slice each melon half in three lengthwise. Then take another large, sharp knife and cut the melon flesh free of its rind. Serve each wedge of melon sitting on its rind, accompanied by a small knife and fork.

Serves 6.

MELON À LA SCHEHEREZADE

This extravagant melon 'basket' was created by Alice B. Toklas's mother.

1 ripe cantaloup melon
1 ripe, but firm, peach
Two ½ inch (1·25 cm) thick slices of fresh pineapple
1 banana
2 ounces (50 g) fresh strawberries
2 ounces (50 g) fresh raspberries
1 tablespoon caster sugar
¼ pint (150 ml) dry non-vintage champagne
1 tablespoon Kirsch
1 tablespoon Maraschino
1 tablespoon Crème de Menthe
1 tablespoon grenadine syrup

Wash the outside of the melon, then slice off the stem end. Scoop out as much of the flesh as possible, leaving the outer casing intact. Pour out any juice into a large bowl, and put this on one side.

Cut the melon flesh into small chunks. Peel and slice the peach thinly. Remove the core from the pineapple and chop into chunks, about the same size as those of the melon. Peel and slice the banana across thinly. Put all this fruit into a bowl.

Remove the stalks from the strawberries and raspberries and wash gently. Add to the rest of the fruit. Sprinkle the fruit with caster sugar and leave until it has dissolved, then pack the fruit into the melon case.

Add the champagne, Kirsch, Maraschino, Crème de Menthe and grenadine syrup to the bowl of melon juice. Mix well and pour onto the fruit inside the melon. Place in the refrigerator overnight. Serve the fruit from the melon casing.

Serves 2.

MELON WITH PORT

Allow a thick slice cut from a large, ripe, sweet melon or half a small one, for example an ogen, gallia or charentais, per person.

Clean out seeds and fibres, and either pierce flesh deeply all over with a fork or gash it at intervals with a spoon to allow port to seep right in. Lay on individual dishes or in small bowls and spoon 2 or 3 tablespoons port over each portion. Allow to macerate for an hour before serving.

MELON WITH BLACKCURRANTS

Both fruits are easily available in the early autumn and complement each other well.

2 small, ripe cantaloup melons
½ pound (225 g) blackcurrants
3 tablespoons sugar
1 tablespoon vodka
Fresh mint leaves, to decorate

Place the melons in the refrigerator to chill. Wash the blackcurrants in a colander under cold, running water, removing any stalks and damaged fruit. Place in a small pan, with the sugar and just enough water to cover.

Cook over moderate heat until boiling, then lower the heat and simmer for 4 minutes. Remove the pan from the heat and allow to cool. Taste and add more sugar if desired. Purée the blackcurrants by rubbing through a fine sieve. (Using an electric blender will not remove the seeds and the purée will still have to be sieved to remove them.) Stir in the vodka.

Take the melons out of the fridge and cut across in half. Scoop out the seeds and fill the cavity with the blackcurrant purée. Garnish with mint leaves and serve.

Serves 4.

MELON WATER ICE

4 ounces (100–125 g) sugar
1 small, ripe honeydew melon
Juice of 1 large lemon
1 egg white

Put the sugar and ½ pint (300 ml) water into a small saucepan. Place over a moderate heat and stir until the sugar dissolves. Bring to the boil and boil for 10 minutes. Remove from the heat and set this syrup on one side to cool.

Cut the melon in half. Remove the pips and scoop out the flesh, reserving any juice. Purée this (with the juice) by pushing through a fine sieve or preferably using an electric blender. Stir the melon purée into the cooked syrup. Add the lemon juice and mix well.

Place this mixture in a freezing tray and place in the freezer or the ice compartment of a refrigerator at its lowest setting. Leave for 1 hour. Then whip the egg white until stiff. Empty the half-frozen melon mixture into a bowl and beat it well until slushy. Fold in the stiff egg white.

Pour this mixture back into the freezing tray and return to the freezer. Freeze the water ice until solid (about 2–3 hours).

Serves 4.

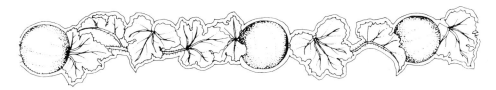

BAKED MELON ALASKA

This dish is easy to make but does need a little careful pre-planning. Have ready a wooden baking board covered with foil (both are poor conductors of heat). Pre-heat the oven well in advance and have the melon ready and thoroughly chilled before you embark on the final stages.

If you want to make the Alaska even more spectacular, press half an empty egg shell deep into the top of the meringue just before it goes into the oven. Then, as you are going to serve it, fill the shell with brandy, rum or Kirsch, allowing just a little to trickle down the sides. Put a match to the alcohol and serve the Alaska as soon as flames are well established.

1 large, ripe melon
Lemon or lime juice
4 egg whites
¼ teaspoon cream of tartar
Generous pinch of salt
4 ounces (100–125 g) caster sugar
Mixed fruit-flavoured and vanilla ice
   creams to fill melon
Sifted icing sugar

Carefully peel off rind of melon. Lay melon on one side and cut off a thin slice so melon will lie steady. Then turn melon over and, from the side opposite to the slice, cut another slice, deep enough to expose seeds. Carefully scoop out seeds and fibres. Sprinkle cavity with lemon or lime juice. Put the 'lid' back on, wrap melon tightly in foil or plastic wrap and chill thoroughly in refrigerator.

Pre-heat oven to very hot (450°F, 230°C, Mark 8). Beat egg whites with cream of tartar and salt until soft peaks form when beaters are lifted. Gradually beat in caster sugar and continue to beat to a stiff, glossy meringue.

Lay melon on prepared board. Lift off and discard 'lid' (for the purposes of this dish). Fill melon to the brim and over with scoops of ice cream of different flavours and colours. Cover entirely with meringue, working quickly and flicking up surface all over with a broad knife blade. Dust thickly with sifted icing sugar.

Bake Alaska for about 5 minutes until meringue tips and tinged with brown and surface of meringue feels dry to the touch. Serve immediately, cut across in thick slices or wedges.

Serves 6.

WATERMELON

No one who has ever seen them, stacked in piles on a stall or by the roadside, their dark green skins contrasting so vividly with the crisp, bright reddish pink of their glistening flesh, can fail to have been impressed by watermelons. Whether or not it is this association with sun and heat, the watermelon is somehow a happy fruit, one huge slice resembling the grin of a joyful child – perhaps the joyful child who is doing his best to sell them to you ...

Redolent of sun and heat they may be but, amazingly in so much dryness, they manage to come up ninety-two per cent water – a natural refresher just where they are most needed, especially if you can negotiate the seeds. In Hungary and the USA, they have managed to grow seedless varieties, but these wouldn't be appreciated in Greece, where the seeds are dried and sold on the streets, nor in southern China, where dried and toasted watermelon seeds are eaten by the handful and considered a great delicacy.

Rumour has it that in West Africa the fruits are gathered and thrown in heaps until they ferment, thus making the seeds easier to get at for grinding into meal and making into bread. A special, large-seeded variety has been cultivated for the purpose. As well as water, the huge fruits yield valuable minerals and the seeds, cooking oil.

The watermelon is prized wherever it is found for its immensely refreshing qualities. In the USA, where it is widespread in the southern states, they have grown monsters of 40 pounds (18 kilos); luckily, the ones we see in shops are more manageable – from 3–5 pounds (1·5–2·3 kilos). If choosing one, try and give the candidate a surreptitious thump – if it's ripe and ready, it should sound dull, flat and somehow heavy. This means its juice and flavour are at their peak. We don't often see the ones with the mottled grey skins, or those with whitish yellow flesh, and they certainly would not make the attractive table centrepiece that can be contrived from a ripe, green-skinned watermelon if it is carved out into a basket shape, complete with handle, and the flesh cubed, chilled and put back with a selection of fresh soft fruits such as strawberries, kiwi fruits, melon scooped into balls, orange segments, slices of nectarine or peach and perhaps a lychee or two. If the fruit has been prepared first and macerated in a little white wine with a generous splash of brandy or orange liqueur, the dessert moves into the millionaire class. And for an extra touch of elegance (which costs almost nothing) serve the melon basket on a bed of crushed ice.

Like melons, watermelons freeze well if they are layered in sugar but, also like melons, the flavour can be disappointing.

Medicinally, the watermelon shares many of the qualities of the other melons. Its juice is also given as a remedy for fevers; its seeds too are nutritious and medicinal and have been used against worms. If used for a facial treatment, watermelon is more suitable for normal skins than for very dry or very greasy ones.

It is often recommended as an ideal ingredient in a slimming diet, since it is exceptionally low in calories but comparatively high in vitamins and minerals, especially potassium.

CHILLED WATERMELON SOUP

4 pounds (1·8 kilos) ripe
   watermelon
1 pint (550 ml) sweet white wine
About 3 tablespoons sugar
1 teaspoon ground allspice
Finely grated rind of 1 large lemon
   (about 4 teaspoons)
½ pint (300 ml) chilled sour cream or
   thick plain yoghourt

Quarter and peel watermelon, and cut it into small chunks, picking out and discarding as many of the large, black seeds as you can find.

Put watermelon chunks and any of their juices that have escaped in a pan. Pour over wine, stir in sugar, allspice and grated lemon rind, and simmer until watermelon is very soft and pulpy, about 20 minutes, stirring and mashing occasionally with a wooden spoon.

Rub soup through a fine nylon sieve into a large bowl and discard fibres and any seeds left behind in sieve. Taste purée and add a little more sugar if necessary. Conversely, if flavour is very strong, purée may be diluted with a little water. Cool and chill thoroughly.

Shortly before serving, beat sour cream with a few tablespoons of chilled watermelon purée until smooth and liquid. Blend smoothly with remaining purée and return to refrigerator until ready to serve.

Serve small portions in chilled soup bowls.

Serves 6.

AMARGOSO SALAD

This dish from the Philippines makes a good starter to a Western-style meal, or a satisfying light lunch, served with thin buttered slices of wholemeal bread.

8 ounces (225 g) watermelon flesh,
   de-seeded and thinly sliced
8 ounces (225 g) prawns, cooked and
   shelled
2 large firm red tomatoes, peeled and
   sliced
2 hardboiled eggs, finely chopped

Dressing
3 tablespoons wine vinegar
½ teaspoon salt
2 teaspoons sugar
¼ teaspoon freshly ground black
   pepper

Boil about ¼ pint (150 ml) water in a medium saucepan. Drop in the melon slices, return to the boil and cook for a minute. Remove the pan from the heat, drain off the water, and place the melon in a serving bowl. Add the prawns, tomatoes and chopped egg. Leave the bowl in the refrigerator to chill.

Put all the ingredients for the dressing in a large screw-top jar. Seal the jar, shake vigorously and place in the refrigerator to chill.

Just before serving, shake the jar of dressing again, pour over the salad, and toss.

Serves 4 as a starter or part of a meal. Serves 2 as a complete lunch.

GUYANAN WATERMELON

This tangy, refreshing Caribbean dessert is a good finale to a heavy dinner.

1 watermelon, weighing about 3
   pounds (1·4 kilos)
3 tablespoons caster sugar
¼ pint (150 ml) white rum
3 large, juicy oranges

Lie the melon on its side and cut a large slice off the top. Scoop out the flesh keeping the melon skin intact, and reserving any juice. Cut the flesh into small chunks, discarding the seeds. Keep the melon case.

Put the melon chunks and juice into a large bowl. Sprinkle over with sugar and pour on the rum. Peel the oranges, removing all the pith and divide into segments. Add to the melon mixture. Pile the fruit mix into the melon case. Place in the refrigerator and chill for at least 1 hour before serving.

Serves 6.

WATERMELON PICKLE

About 3 pounds (1·4 kilos)
   watermelon rind
Brine (see method)

Syrup
¾ pint (400 ml) cider vinegar
1½ pounds (700 g) sugar
1 long (3–4 inch or 7·5–10 cm)
   cinnamon stick, in 2 or 3 pieces
1 teaspoon whole cloves
1 teaspoon allspice berries
1 small lemon, thinly sliced
½ orange, thinly sliced

Cut away green skin from one side of watermelon rind and red flesh from the other. Cut rind that remains into 1 inch (2·5 cm) squares. Put them in a large bowl and cover with brine, made by dissolving 4 tablespoons salt in 1½ pints (900 ml) water. Leave to soak overnight.

The following day, drain rinds and rinse thoroughly with cold water. Place in a large pan, cover with fresh water and bring to boiling point. Simmer, covered, for 20–30 minutes until rind is barely tender and turning translucent.

While rind is simmering, prepare syrup. In a large, stainless steel or enamelled pan, combine vinegar with sugar and ¾ pint (400 ml) water. Stir over low heat until sugar has melted. Tie spices up loosely in a square of muslin and add them to the pan, together with slices of orange and lemon. Bring to boiling point and simmer slowly, uncovered, for 20 minutes.

Drain watermelon rind and add it to the syrup. Bring to boiling point and cook gently, uncovered, until rind is soft and clear, about 30 minutes.

With a slotted spoon, lift squares of rind out of syrup and pack them into hot, clean glass jars. Strain boiling hot syrup over them to cover, leaving ⅛ inch (3 mm) head space. Seal jars, cool, and store in a cool, dry cupboard for several weeks.

See also page 200.

Fills about 3 jars.

NECTARINE

The nectarine is a smooth-skinned variety of peach with a distinctive flavour that has been described as something like a cross between a peach and a plum. Its devotees could argue that its sweet and rich juice must indeed be nectar – the drink of the gods. Like the apricot, it tastes best when, heavy with juice, it is ready to fall off the tree at the lightest touch.

Known to man for 2,000 years, this natural mutation from the peach family is said to have originated in China, coming westwards via Persia and the old spice routes and reaching Europe in the sixteenth century. Occasionally, to prove its parentage, a smooth-skinned nectarine appears on a peach tree and vice versa.

Nectarines are at their best, when fully ripe and freshly picked; unfortunately, they rarely reach the shops in that condition. But do not be deterred – choose soft, full, unblemished fruits that feel heavy for their size. Though they do not ripen satisfactorily once off the tree, they will soften nicely if left in a warm room for a few days.

Nectarines can be used instead of peaches in any recipes that use the latter – in casseroles with chicken, flambéed in brandy, or baked. Their great advantage is that they do not need peeling and the flesh holds its shape better when lightly cooked. If made into a purée and frozen – use about 4 ounces (100–125 g) sugar to every pound (450 g) of fruit – you can have a taste of summer out of season. Thaw the purée, swirl it into stiffly whipped Chantilly cream, and top with freshly toasted almonds. The purée will keep in the freezer for up to 12 months. Nectarines can also be sliced (remove the stone), sprinkled with sugar, and frozen for the same length of time.

Sun-dried nectarines may be found in health food shops (the fruit is low in calories and a good source of Vitamins A and C and natural fibre), and can be chopped and added to cakes with other dried fruit such as apricots.

CHICKEN WITH NECTARINES

A light and delicate summer main course that is quickly made and needs only a bowl of plain cooked rice as an accompaniment. Substitute small, firm peches for nectarines if the latter are not available.

*1 small roasting chicken, 2½–3
    pounds (1·1–1·4 kilos), jointed
1 ounce (25 g) butter
1 tablespoon olive oil
Salt and freshly ground black pepper
Generous pinch each of crushed dried
    rosemary and thyme
¼ pint (150 ml) medium dry white
    wine
¼ pint (150 ml) strong chicken (cube)
    stock
1 tablespoon cornflour
3–4 nectarines, peeled and sliced (see
    above)
6–8 tablespoons coarsely chopped
    cashew nuts
Pinch of sugar (optional)
Lemon juice (optional)*

Wipe chicken joints dry. In a wide, flameproof casserole, melt butter in oil and fry chicken joints until golden brown on all sides. Sprinkle them all over with salt, freshly ground black pepper and a generous pinch each of rosemary and thyme. Try and pack all the chicken joints in a single layer in the casserole, skin side up, or arrange them so that leg joints are on the bottom and breast joints on top. Moisten with wine and chicken stock. Bring to simmering point. Cover and cook gently for about 30 minutes, until chicken is tender, turning joints once or twice.

Remove chicken from casserole with a slotted spoon and keep hot. Blend cornflour with 2 or 3 tablespoons cold water, stir into pan juices and simmer gently until thickened and no longer floury. Gently stir in sliced nectarines and nuts. Correct seasoning with more salt or pepper, a pinch of sugar and a squeeze of lemon juice if liked.

Return chicken joints to casserole and spoon sauce, nectarine slices and cashew nuts over them. Reheat gently for 2–3 minutes longer and serve immediately.

Serves 4.

Note: You can transform this dish and give it an oriental accent by leaving out the lemon juice and flavouring the sauce with a good dash of soya sauce instead.

SUGARED NECTARINES

A lovely accompaniment for poultry, pork, ham and bacon. Use firm nectarines that are not quite ripe or juicy enough to eat as they are.

*4 firm nectarines
1½ ounces (40 g) butter
3 tablespoons soft brown sugar
1–2 tablespoons lemon juice*

Cut nectarines in two lengthwise and remove stones. Then, without peeling them, slice each half lengthwise as you would peaches.

In a heavy frying pan, melt butter. Stir in sugar and continue to cook, stirring, until it melts and turns syrupy. Add nectarine slices, turning them over to coat them in syrup, and cook gently until heated through and lightly glazed. Finally, sprinkle with lemon juice. Serve immediately.

Serves 4.

BAKED NECTARINES

8 ripe nectarines
Lemon juice
12 ounces (350 g) sugar
Long strip of orange rind
Long strip of lemon rind
8 whole cloves

Peel nectarines as you would tomatoes, first dropping them in boiling water for a minute to loosen skins. When peeled, place in a bowl of water acidulated with lemon juice.

Make a syrup by dissolving sugar in ½ pint (300 ml) water. Add strips of orange and lemon rind (peeled off with a potato peeler), bring to boiling point and simmer for 10 minutes.

Drain nectarines. Pat dry with paper towels and stick a clove in the stem end of each one. Arrange them side by side on their stem ends in a deep baking dish. Pour over boiling syrup. Bake in a moderate oven (350°F, 180°C, Mark 5), basting frequently with syrup, until nectarines are soft when pierced with a skewer but not mushy, 20–30 minutes.

Remove baking dish from oven. Allow nectarines to cool in their syrup, occasionally spooning syrup over them. Chill well before serving. Serve in some of the syrup, accompanied by a jug of thick pouring cream.

Serves 4.

NECTARINE LIQUEUR

2½ pounds (1·1 kilos) nectarines
2 pounds (900 g) granulated sugar
2½ pints (1·4 litres) vodka

Wash the fruit. Halve and discard the stones. In a large wide-neck storage jar with a screw top (cleaned and sterilized, page 201), pack the nectarines tightly in layers, sprinkling sufficient sugar to cover over each layer. Replace the top, but do not screw on tightly, and leave for 4 days.

Drain off the resultant syrup and store in the refrigerator in a tightly covered bowl. Pour the vodka over the nectarines in the jar, to cover the fruit. Re-seal the jar and leave it for 2 weeks at room temperature.

Strain off the liqueur, stir in the nectarine syrup and pour into clean, sterilized bottles. Keep for 3 months.

Makes 2½ pints (1.4 litres).

FLAMBÉED NECTARINES

Easy culinary pyrotechnics can be demonstrated with all kinds of fruits such as bananas, peaches or cored pears as well as nectarines. If you want to carry out the operation at the dining table, you will need a chafing dish.

4–6 large, ripe nectarines
4 ounces (100–125 g) butter
5 ounces (175 g) soft light brown sugar
2 tablespoons lemon juice
5 tablespoons brandy

Peel nectarines but keep them whole.

In a chafing dish (or a flameproof casserole if working on the kitchen stove), melt butter until foaming but not coloured. Stir in sugar and lemon juice, and cook over moderate heat, stirring, until sugar has dissolved. Add nectarines and cook gently, uncovered, for a few minutes, turning them with a spoon and rolling them over to coat them in buttery syrup.

In a large kitchen ladle or small pan, heat brandy gently. Set a match to it and when flames are burning strongly, pour all over pan of nectarines. Allow flames to die down and serve.

Serves 4–6.

NECTARINE MARMALADE

If you are lucky enough to have a surplus of nectarines (they should not be too ripe and need not be of the best table quality), this is a lovely, subtly flavoured preserve.

2 pounds (900 g) nectarines
2 thin-skinned oranges
Juice of 1 lemon
About 1½ pounds (700 g) sugar

Peel, halve and stone nectarines. Scrub oranges under cold running water. Dry them and cut off, and discard, the peel of one of them. Chop up nectarines and both oranges, discarding any pips as you come across them. Put fruit through the coarse blade of a mincer.

With a cup or mug, measure minced fruit into a preserving pan and add the same volume of sugar (ie the same number of cupfuls). Add lemon juice and slowly bring to boiling point, stirring constantly with a large wooden spoon until sugar has dissolved. Then raise heat and boil briskly, stirring occasionally, until setting point is reached. Towards the end of cooking time, skim surface clear of scum. Pot and cover.

See also page 198.

Fills about 6 jars.

OLIVE

Both green (young) and black (mature) olives were widely enjoyed by the Greeks and Romans. Their remains have been found in Egyptian tombs, and the Cretans built up a thriving olive trade around 3,500 BC. The gnarled trees with their small, silvery leaves grow all around the Mediterranean area, where they are extensively cultivated – not least for their oil. The trees grow slowly, are not considered fully productive and at their best until they are between fifty and seventy-five years old – and can survive for centuries.

As with humans, the older the olive, the more wrinkled the skin. The flesh of the black olive is naturally softer, which is why the green varieties lend themselves better to stuffing. They can now be bought, stuffed with all kinds of exciting things, in packets, cans or jars, or loose in brine from delicatessens. You can stuff them yourself if you first remove the stone by slitting them down one side. (If you don't intend to stuff them, pit the olives by making a smaller cross-cut across the top.)

Three main types of olive are cultivated – two for the table (the larger queens and the smaller manzanillas) and a bitter little green variety for its highly flavoured oil. The green-tinged *huile vièrge*, or first pressing, should be kept for use in mayonnaise and salad dressings. Cook with it only if you must. You can cheat (and economize) by adding four or five well-drained olives to a jar of bland salad oil, topping up with oil and/or olives as necessary until you get the flavour you prefer.

Alone or with other ingredients, olives make excellent appetizers to serve with drinks. They add piquancy to salads; and a distinctive taste to casseroles and stews. Add them towards the end of the cooking time, or taste and texture will vanish leaving only their bitterness. Tapénade, an olive spread from Provence, is often called the caviare of vegetables. Anything labelled *niçoise* on a menu should have a touch of the olive, traditionally and authentically the small, black ones.

Olives can be frozen out of their brine for up to six months, but last very well in the refrigerator. If an opened jar develops a white mould on top, the brine is oxidizing; the olives are perfectly edible if rinsed.

Olive oil is valued medicinally for its soothing, healing and nourishing properties.

OLIVE CHEESE BALLS

An unusual savoury to have with drinks. To make the olives easy to handle, spear each one with a wooden toothpick or cocktail stick.

3 ounces (75 g) cream cheese
4 tablespoons finely grated Cheddar cheese
About 3 tablespoons double cream
A few drops of Worcestershire sauce or Tabasco
18–24 pimento-stuffed green olives
4 ounces (100–125 g) almonds, blanched and finely chopped

In a bowl, work first 4 ingredients to a smooth, thick paste (use an electric blender or food processor if you have one). Coat each olive completely with cheese paste and roll it in finely chopped almonds. Impale each olive on a cocktail stick and chill until firm before serving.

Note: Instead of chopped almonds, try rolling the coated olives in ground almonds which have first been toasted to a light golden colour, or in sesame seeds.

OLIVE OIL HAIR TREATMENT

Olive oil is wonderfully nourishing for dry hair, and can also be used to counteract dandruff and to treat hair damaged by sun and salt water.

Warm a little oil to about blood heat. Massage it very thoroughly into your scalp. Cover your hair with a warm towel or bath cap and leave as long as possible before washing out.

GARLIC OLIVES

1 large can large black or green olives in brine
6 tablespoons olive oil
3–4 fresh, plump cloves garlic, finely chopped or crushed
½ teaspoon dried oregano

Empty the can of olives into a large, screw-top jar, draining off brine and reserving ¼ pint (150 ml) of it in a jug or bowl. With a fork, beat remaining ingredients into brine. Pour over olives. Screw down lid and shake gently until well mixed. Olives should be submerged in marinade.

Leave in the refrigerator for at least 24 hours to absorb flavours before serving, drained, with drinks.

OLIVE CHEESE PASTRIES

5 ounces (150 g) plain flour
½ teaspoon salt
½ teaspoon baking powder
4 ounces (100–125 g) butter, diced
1 egg yolk
6–8 tablespoons milk
4 ounces (100–125 g) mild Cheddar
  cheese, grated
24–36 green or black olives or a
  mixture of the two, pitted and
  halved

Start by preparing the pastry. Sift flour, salt and baking powder into a bowl. Rub in butter until mixture resembles fine breadcrumbs. Beat egg yolk lightly and sprinkle it over bowl, together with enough milk to make a dough. Roll dough into a ball, wrap it in plastic or foil and chill for 1 hour.

On a lightly floured board with a rolling pin dusted with flour, roll dough out into a rectangle ¼ inch (1·25 cm) thick. (Let it soften at room temperature for a little while if it comes out of the refrigerator too hard to handle.) Sprinkle rectangle with grated cheese, fold in two and roll out into a ¼ inch (1·25 cm) thick rectangle once more. Repeat folding and rolling yet again. This time, roll pastry out rather more thinly.

With a plain 2 inch (5 cm) pastry cutter, stamp out 24 circles of dough. On each circle place 2 or 3 pitted olive halves and fold circle in half over olive filling. Seal edges thoroughly. Arrange pastries on baking sheets and bake in a fairly hot oven (425°F, 220°C, Mark 7) for 12–15 minutes, or until pastries are golden. Cool for a few minutes and serve hot.

Note: If you have a bottle of Tabasco, shake a tiny drop over the olive filling before folding each pastry in half.

CHEESE AND OLIVE PÂTÉ

A very simple pâté with a rich taste. If the olives are very salty and you have no time to soak them first, use fewer — and add 2 tablespoons chopped parsley instead.

4 ounces (100–125 g) butter
8 ounces (225 g) Ricotta, or full-fat
  cream cheese
4 ounces (100–125 g) mild blue
  cheese
1 garlic clove, crushed
4 ounces (100–125 g) green olives (see
  above)
Freshly ground black pepper

Soften the butter and beat into the Ricotta or cream cheese, then beat in the blue cheese, and blend in the garlic. Finely chop the olives — discarding the stones. Beat the finely chopped olives into the pâté and season with pepper.

Chill for about an hour before serving with hot toast.

Serves 8.

OLIVE AND SALAMI SALAD

Quick and simple to prepare, this is a good starter to an Italian-style dinner. It also makes a delicious snack at any time.

4 ounces (100–125 g) salami, thinly
  sliced
4 ounces (100–125 g) black olives,
  pitted
1 small onion, finely chopped
2 tablespoons olive oil
2 teaspoons wine vinegar
1 teaspoon coriander seeds, crushed
1 teaspoon finely chopped basil

Arrange the slices of salami around the edge of a serving plate. Put the olives in a small bowl with onion, olive oil, vinegar and coriander. Toss well and spread across the centre of the serving plate. Place the plate in the refrigerator for 30 minutes to chill. Just before serving, sprinkle with chopped basil.

Serves 4.

PROVENÇAL TAPÉNADE

Although this savoury paste takes its name from *tapéno*, the Provençal word for the capers it contains, olives predominate. Use a food processor or an electric blender to reduce the ingredients to a smooth purée in seconds. Failing one of these invaluable gadgets, you will have to make the *tapénade* in the time-honoured way, first pounding the ingredients together in a mortar, then rubbing the paste through a sieve.

The paste can be stored for a couple of weeks in the refrigerator, poured into a screw-top jar and covered with a thin film of oil (beat this in before using the paste). It makes a fine spread for fresh country bread, washed down with rough red wine. Or you can dress hot pasta with it, or beat it into hard-boiled egg yolks and stuff them back into the egg whites to eat as an appetizer.

2 ounces (50 g) pitted black olives
1 ounce (25 g) drained canned
  anchovy fillets, coarsely chopped
1 ounce (25 g) drained canned tuna,
  flaked
1 ounce (25 g) drained bottled capers
1 small, ripe tomato, peeled, seeded
  and coarsely chopped
1 teaspoon coarse French mustard
Olive oil
Freshly ground black pepper or
  Tabasco

Assemble the first 6 ingredients in a food processor or electric blender and whirl to a smooth, homogenous paste (see left). Gradually blend in about 6 tablespoons olive oil. Taste and season generously with freshly ground black pepper or a few drops of Tabasco. Purée will already be salty enough.

Store in the refrigerator.

ITALIAN PEPPER AND OLIVE APPETIZER

Prepare this salad at least 4 hours in advance to give it a chance to develop flavours, and serve it as part of an Italian antipasto platter. In a screw-top jar, the ingredients covered with olive oil to prevent them drying out, this salad will keep in the refrigerator for a couple of weeks. For a really dramatic colour effect, use bright red or yellow peppers, or a mixture of the two.

4–5 ounces (125–150 g) black olives, pitted
4 large sweet red or yellow peppers
2 large plump cloves garlic, finely chopped or crushed
About 6 tablespoons olive oil
Salt

If olives have been packed in brine, rinse them in cold running water *before* pitting them.

Peel peppers as follows. Put them under a hot grill and turn them over regularly until their skins blister, burst and blacken. Then, with your fingers, rub and peel off skins under running water. (If preferred, you can spear each pepper on a fork and turn it over an open gas flame to blister the skin.) Cut peppers in half. Remove cores and rinse out seeds. Then slice peppers into long, narrow ribbons.

In a serving dish, gently mix olives with peppers. Make a dressing by shaking olive oil in a screw-top jar with garlic and a pinch of salt. Pour over peppers and olives. Allow to marinate for a minimum of 4 hours before serving, gently turning ingredients over from time to time.

OLIVE AND RABBIT STEW NIÇOISE

This dish is a speciality of the region around Nice.

3 tablespoons olive oil
2 large onions, finely chopped
2 garlic cloves, crushed
4 large or 8 small joints of rabbit
2 ounces (50 g) butter
1 ounce (25 g) plain flour
1 pint (600 ml) chicken stock
½ pint (300 ml) white wine
1 tablespoon tomato purée
1 teaspoon dried tarragon
1 teaspoon dried rosemary
4 ounces (100–125 g) green olives, pitted
4 tablespoons Madeira
Sprigs of parsley

Heat the olive oil in a large frying pan. Lower the heat, add the onions and garlic, and fry for 5 minutes. Then add the rabbit joints and cook, turning, until the meat is well browned. Remove the pan from the heat and set on one side.

Melt the butter in a large, heavy casserole, over a low heat, and stir in the flour to form a thick paste. Remove from the heat, and stir in the stock, wine, tomato purée and herbs. Mix well to make a smooth sauce. Add the rabbit, onions, garlic and oil from the frying pan. Stir and return the casserole to the heat.

Cover and cook slowly, stirring occasionally, for 30 minutes. Then add the olives. Stir and cook for a further 30 minutes, until the rabbit is tender.

Just before serving, stir in the Madeira. Garnish with the parsley, and serve hot, with boiled potatoes and a green salad.

Serves 4.

BEEF AND OLIVE STEW

1½ pounds (700 g) stewing beef
2–3 tablespoons olive oil
2 medium onions, chopped
4 tomatoes, quartered
2 ounces (50 g) black or green olives, stoned
2 carrots, diced
1 aubergine (optional)
½ teaspoon dried thyme
Salt and freshly ground black pepper
2 garlic cloves, chopped
¾ pint (400 ml) red wine

Cut the beef into neat cubes and fry in the hot oil until browned. Add the onion and fry until golden, then stir in the tomatoes, olives and carrot pieces. Slice and add the aubergine, if using, and continue frying for a few minutes, stirring to prevent the vegetables sticking to the pan.

Add the thyme, salt and pepper and garlic, then pour in the wine. Turn down the heat to very low, press a piece of greaseproof paper on the surface of the stew, cover the pan with a lid and stew very, very gently for about 3 hours until the beef is tender.

Serves 4.

BRAISED DUCK WITH OLIVES

4 pound (1.8 kg) duckling
1 ounce (25 g) butter
1 medium onion, finely chopped
1 glass port
1 teaspoon paprika
½ pint (300 ml) chicken stock
Bouquet garni
Salt and freshly ground black pepper
2 large tomatoes
12 large green olives
1 tablespoon flour

Melt the butter in an ovenproof casserole and brown the duck all over.

Tip away any excess fat, add the onion and cover and cook until the onion is transparent. Pour in the port and cook until reduced by half, then add the paprika and cook for about 2 minutes.

Pour in the stock, add the bouquet garni and salt and pepper. Cover the casserole and cook over low heat for about 45 minutes, or until the bird is cooked through. If cooking in the oven, it should be moderate (350°F, 180°C, Mark 4).

Peel, slice and deseed the tomatoes. Stone the olives and cut the flesh into shreds. Blanch in boiling water for about 5 minutes, then drain and leave covered with cold water.

Take the duck out of the pot and remove the bouquet garni. Skim off excess fat and stir in the flour. Bring to the boil, still stirring, then add the tomatoes and drained olives, and return to the boil. Adjust the seasoning. Divide the duck into 4 portions and serve with the sauce.

Serves 4.

NOODLES WITH TOMATOES, CHEESE AND OLIVES

This is a superb side dish to accompany simple meat dishes such as fried veal escalopes or chicken.

1 pound (450 g) flat ribbon noodles
Salt
1–2 ounces (25–50 g) butter, coarsely cut up
6–8 ounces (175–225 g) fresh Mozzarella cheese, cubed
4 tablespoons finely grated Parmesan cheese
2 ounces (50 g) plump black olives, pitted and sliced

Tomato sauce
1 medium Spanish onion, finely chopped
1 ounce (25 g) butter
2 tablespoons olive oil
2 tablespoons concentrated tomato paste
1 large (14 ounce or 400 g) can Italian peeled tomatoes
1 teaspoon crushed dried oregano
Salt and freshly ground black pepper
Pinch of sugar

Start by boiling noodles in salted water and draining them thoroughly. While noodles are cooking, prepare a simple tomato sauce as follows. In a pan, sauté onion in butter and oil until soft and golden. Stir in tomato paste and fry gently for 2 or 3 minutes longer, stirring. Pour in the whole can of tomatoes with its juices and about one-third of a can of water, and bring to boiling point, stirring and mashing tomatoes to a pulp with your spoon. Add oregano and season lightly with salt, a grinding of black pepper and a pinch of sugar. Continue to simmer sauce for about 15 minutes longer until reduced and slightly thickened. Correct seasoning if necessary, bearing in mind saltiness of olives and cheese that are to come.

To serve, pile hot drained noodles in a large, heated serving bowl. Add bits of butter, the cubed Mozzarella and 2 tablespoons grated Parmesan. Toss until thoroughly mixed. Pour simmering tomato sauce over the top and sprinkle with sliced olives and remaining Parmesan. Give the noodles a final good toss and serve very hot.

Serves 4–6.

TUNA OLIVE MAYONNAISE

Two 7 ounce (200 g) cans tuna in oil
2 ounces (50 g) pitted black or stuffed green olives, chopped
2 boiled potatoes, peeled and diced
1 small mild onion, finely chopped
2 tablespoons finely chopped parsley
About ¼ pint (150 ml) mayonnaise (page 205)
Salt and freshly ground black pepper
Crisp green lettuce leaves, to garnish

Drain cans of tuna, empty fish into a bowl and flake it with a fork. Add the next 4 ingredients and toss lightly but thoroughly. Fold in mayonnaise, adding a little more if necessary to bind ingredients creamily. Taste and season with a pinch of salt if necessary and a good grinding of black pepper. Chill lightly.

Serves 4.

OLIVE AND FENNEL SALAD

A Mediterranean salad that is a complete meal in itself.

2 large potatoes
Salt
1 large bulb fennel
1 small can anchovies
1 large green pepper
1 head chicory
1 small can artichoke hearts
24 black olives
3 hard-boiled eggs

Dressing
10 tablespoons olive oil
5 tablespoons wine vinegar
Juice of 1 small lemon
½ teaspoon salt
½ teaspoon freshly ground black pepper
½ teaspoon dry mustard
½ teaspoon sugar

Put all the ingredients for the dressing in a screw-top jar and shake.

Peel the potatoes and cut into small pieces. Boil in salted water, until just tender. (They must not be too soft.) Cut the potato pieces into approximately ¼ inch (6 cm) cubes. Place in a salad bowl. Shake the jar of dressing and pour over the potatoes.

Cut the leafy top off the fennel. Divide the bulb. Slice and wash in a colander under cold, running water and dry on kitchen paper. Drain the oil from the anchovy fillets. Cut open the pepper, seed and core it, and slice finely. Wash, divide and chop up the chicory. Drain the artichoke hearts. Add the fennel, anchovy fillets, pepper, chicory and artichoke hearts to the bowl.

Pit the olives and quarter the hard boiled eggs. Toss the salad and garnish with the olives and eggs.

Serves 2–4.

ORANGE

The evergreen orange tree, with its dark, glossy leaves and scented blossom, is probably the best known of all the citrus family. China is thought to be the home of the sweet orange and India the home of the bitter variety. The species has a number of synonyms, but all oranges share the name *hespiridium*, from the Roman goddess Hesperides, who was thought to have brought the orange across the seas to Italy.

Goddess- or sailor-borne, the first arrival was the bitter orange, an ornamental shrub with sour, inedible fruit. The flowers and leaves are very aromatic, with a heady, lasting scent which can carry for miles. A mature tree can yield up to 60 pounds (27 kilos) of blossom in a season. The white flowers are traditionally used in wedding bouquets and pot pourri mixtures, and orange-flower water — much beloved of French and English pastrycooks as a flavouring for cakes and dessert pastries — is used in cosmetics as well. The rind of the bitter orange is also valuable, providing *neroli*, or orange oil, and is used in many orange-flavoured liqueurs, such as Curaçao and Grand Marnier.

The sour Seville orange was traditionally brought to Spain by the Moors, who forbade any unbeliever to taste one until he was converted to Islam. The juice was thought to be an aid to digestion, and today the Spanish groves are a picturesque but highly commercialized industry. Seville oranges, small and sharply flavoured, are favourites for the traditional English marmalade. They can be combined with their cousins in the citrus family — grapefruit or tangerines — to produce delicious variations on the marmalade theme (see page 83). The bergamot orange is a separate cultivar; its special contribution is the oil that is processed from the rind and used in cosmetics and perfumes.

The sweet orange found its way across Europe first with the Romans and then with the Portuguese East Indian traders in the fifteenth and sixteenth centuries. Spanish ships on their way to colonies in the New World were required to carry orange seeds and young trees for the new plantations. Today, there are huge orange groves in North Africa, Israel, Florida and California. In the tropics, the fruit stays green.

Although there are many individual varieties, sweet oranges fall mainly into three categories: blondes or normal oranges, the most common; smaller blood oranges, their darker flesh flecked with reddish spots which may indeed tint the entire fruit; and navel oranges, with a prominent growth at the stem end — often an entire, miniature, undeveloped orange in itself. The navel has become the most popular orange for eating raw as it peels easily and can be divided into segments with the fingers.

The rind or zest contains enough oil to intensify any orange flavour in a dish. Rub the rind with a cube of sugar to absorb the oil, and add the crushed cube to the other ingredients. The peel can be candied for use in cakes, and any of the sweet or bitter oranges can be stuck with cloves and powdered with orris root to make sweet-smelling pomanders.

Orange segments (with all the pith removed) can be sugar frozen; use 8 ounces (225 g) caster sugar for every pound (450 g) of fruit. Freeze Seville oranges whole in plastic bags. Grated peel can also be frozen.

As everyone knows, oranges are full of Vitamin C — one sweet orange supplies the average adult with enough of this important vitamin for one day. They also have valuable cosmetic properties. Orange-flower water soothes the skin, and orange oil is an important constituent in many creams and perfumes.

REMEDIES

Long before the importance of Vitamin C was understood, oranges, especially the bitter variety, were used for various medicinal purposes.

True orange-flower water, made from essence of orange flowers, is an excellent sedative. An infusion of dried orange flowers, though not so potent, is still effective, as are infusions and decoctions of the leaves.

The distilled oil of orange blossom is said to have a hypnotic effect when inhaled.

SKIN LOTION

Orange-flower water is a soothing skin lotion, and not as astringent as lemon. Make a distillation (see page 82), or add a few drops of essential oil of orange flowers (also called oil of neroli) to some distilled water. This will improve after a week or two, but will not keep indefinitely. Mix with glycerine – about 1 part glycerine to 3 or 4 of orange-flower water – to make a gentle toning lotion.

ORANGE-FLOWER BATH OIL

It is easy to make your own orange-flower bath oil, given a reasonable supply of sunlight.

Put the flowers (the leaves can be added too) into a glass jar and pour enough oil to cover them. Any unscented oil is suitable; olive oil is often recommended and almond oil, though expensive, is superb. A little wine or cider vinegar – a tablespoon to ½ pint (300 ml) – will help preserve it. Seal the jar and stand it in a sunny place for 2–3 weeks, shaking it twice a day. Strain the oil and repeat with fresh flowers. The process may need repeating 2 or 3 times before the oil is strongly enough scented.

POMANDER

Exotic-smelling pomanders perfume clothes and keep away moths.

Mark an orange into quarters, and use a knitting needle to make holes all over the skin, leaving enough space at the quarter marks to tie a ribbon around the orange. Press cloves firmly into the holes.

Now put the pomander in a paper bag with powdered orris root, which will 'fix' the spicy fragrance, and shake it until well covered. Then store it in a warm, dry, dark place, still in its bag, for a fortnight or so to dry out. Tie a pretty ribbon round it and make a loop for hanging it up.

DUCKLING WITH ORANGE

In France, this dish is called *à la bigarade* after the small, bitter Seville oranges which are used in its preparation – their flavour being uniquely suitable for a fatty bird like duck. But the Seville orange season, which comes in the middle of winter, is a very short one. So if you would like to prepare this dish at other times of the year, it's a good idea to stock up with a supply of Seville oranges in the freezer.

1 oven-ready duckling, about 5
    pounds (2·3 kilos)
2 ounces (50 g) butter
Salt and freshly ground black pepper
3 Seville oranges
2 lemons
¼ pint (150 ml) dry white vermouth
2 large, sweet oranges
1 tablespoon sugar
1 tablespoon wine vinegar
½ tablespoon cornflour
2 tablespoons orange liqueur
    (optional, see method)
2 tablespoons redcurrant jelly
1 tablespoon orange marmalade,
    preferably Seville
Thin slices of sweet orange and
    watercress sprigs, to garnish

In a flameproof roasting tin, brown duckling all over in foaming butter, taking care butter does not burn. When bird is uniformly crisp and brown all over, sprinkle it with salt and freshly ground black pepper.

Roast duckling in a moderate oven (350°F, 180°C, Mark 4) for 45–60 minutes, or until juices run clear when a skewer is pushed into the thickest part of the leg, closest to the breast. Baste regularly with pan juices and take care not to overcook duck as this will make it dry and tasteless.

While duck is roasting, peel Seville oranges with a potato peeler, taking only the coloured rind (*no pith*). Cut rind into fine, hair-thin strips. Put them in a pan with plenty of water to cover, bring slowly to boiling point, drain thoroughly and put aside until needed. Then cut oranges in half, squeeze out all their juice and strain into a large, wide-necked jug. Squeeze juice from lemons and strain into jug. Stir in dry vermouth.

Peel sweet oranges and, working over jug to catch juices, cut out segments. Remove pips with the point of your knife. Squeeze all remaining juices from orange piths into jug.

When duckling is done, transfer it to a heated serving dish. Return it to the switched-off oven with the door left slightly ajar to keep hot while you finish garnish and sauce.

In a small, heavy pan, swirl sugar and vinegar together over moderate heat until sugar melts and turns into a rich golden caramel. Immediately pour in contents of jug, stirring until caramel has dissolved. Then add prepared orange segments and poach gently for 5 minutes. With a slotted spoon, lift orange segments out and arrange them carefully around duckling.

Pour off all but 1 or 2 tablespoons of fat from roasting tin. Pour in citrus syrup and slowly bring to boiling point, stirring and scraping bottom and sides of pan clean with a wooden spoon.

Blend cornflour smoothly with orange liqueur (or use water if you have no liqueur available). Stir into roasting tin and simmer for 2 or 3 minutes, stirring, until sauce is slightly thickened and no longer cloudy. Stir in blanched orange zest, redcurrant jelly and orange marmalade, simmering until melted. Season generously with salt and freshly ground black pepper.

Spoon some of the sauce over duckling and pour remainder into a heated sauceboat. Decorate dish with paper-thin slices of fresh sweet orange and sprigs of watercress. Serve with sauce.

Serves 4.

MOROCCAN SPICED LAMB WITH ORANGE

A richly flavoured dish which needs only a bowl of plain boiled or steamed rice as an accompaniment.

3–3½ pounds (1.4–1.6 kilos) lean
    lamb, cubed
1 teaspoon ground cinnamon
½ teaspoon ground cloves
Salt
4 tablespoons peanut or corn oil
2 Spanish onions, finely chopped
1 clove garlic, finely chopped
A 2 inch (5 cm) piece of fresh ginger
    root, peeled and finely chopped
2–3 sprigs parsley
1 sprig thyme
¼ pint (150 ml) dry white wine
Finely grated rind and juice of 2–3
    oranges
Freshly ground black pepper
1 teaspoon flour
1 teaspoon French mustard

Sprinkle cubes of lamb with a mixture of cinnamon, cloves and 2 teaspoons salt, turning them round to coat them on all sides. In a heavy, flameproof casserole over moderate heat, fry spiced lamb cubes, a portion at a time, in about half the oil until golden brown on all sides, transferring them to a plate with a slotted spoon as they are done.

In the remaining oil, sauté finely chopped onions with garlic and ginger until soft and golden. Return lamb to casserole. Add parsley and thyme sprigs tied together in a bouquet, and mix well. Moisten with wine and orange juice, and stir in grated orange rind. Finally, stir in about ½ pint (300 ml) water and season generously with freshly ground black pepper. Slowly bring to simmering point. Stir once more, cover and cook very gently until lamb is tender, about 45–60 minutes.

Blend flour and mustard smoothly with 2 or 3 tablespoons water. Stir into casserole. Mix well with sauce and bring to simmering point once more. Cook gently, stirring frequently, until sauce has thickened.

Discard herb bouquet. Correct seasoning with more salt or freshly ground black pepper if necessary and serve.

Serves 6–8.

ORANGE ONION SALAD

Delicious with roast or grilled lamb and pork, either hot or cold. Use a very sharp knife or one with a serrated blade for slicing the oranges.

4 juicy, sweet oranges
1 large, mild (Spanish or red) onion
Salt and coarsely ground black
   pepper
Olive oil
Lemon juice or white wine or cider
   vinegar (optional)

Peel oranges, removing every scrap of white pith, and slice them thinly crosswise, working on a board to catch any juices. Pick out pips with the tip of your knife and place the orange slices and their juices in a large, shallow dish.

Slice onion thinly. Separate it into rings and place them in a colander. Slowly pour over them a kettleful of boiling water (this is for the benefit of those who find raw onion trouble-some). Shake off excess moisture and leave onion until quite cold.

Gently mix onion and orange slices together. Sprinkle to taste with salt and coarsely ground black pepper, and moisten with a few tablespoons of olive oil. Taste the salad and if it is too sweet, sharpen its flavour with a squeeze of lemon juice or a few drops of wine or cider vinegar.

Serves 4.

ORANGE AND CARROT SALAD

The orange-flower water, which gives this salad rather an Arab accent, can be bought in Greek, Middle Eastern and Indian groceries, and is often stocked by chemists.

5–6 fresh young carrots
Juice of 1 lemon
1 tablespoon orange-flower water
2–3 teaspoons caster sugar, or to
   taste
Salt
2 oranges

Scrub or scrape carrots clean, and grate them coarsely. In a serving bowl, combine lemon juice with orange-flower water, sugar and a pinch of salt, stirring until sugar has dissolved. Peel oranges. Working over bowl to catch any juices, cut out orange segments. Pick out orange pips as you come across them, and halve segments crosswise if they are large. Add them to bowl. Squeeze out any remaining juice from orange pith into bowl.

Add grated carrots to bowl, and toss lightly but thoroughly with a fork. Correct seasoning with a little more sugar or salt. Chill lightly.

Serves 6.

THAI ORANGE AND PORK SALAD

A light, main-course salad for lunch.

4 large, sweet oranges
1 crisp head lettuce
4–6 ounces (125–175 g) lean raw
   pork, trimmed
1 plump clove garlic, crushed
2 tablespoons peanut or other
   cooking oil
1 tablespoon finely chopped peanuts
1 teaspoon sugar
2 tablespoons dark soya sauce
Pinch of monosodium glutamate
Pinch of paprika
Salt and freshly ground black pepper
Finely chopped parsley, chives or
   spring onion tops, to garnish

Peel and segment oranges, work-ing over a plate to catch any juices and discarding pips as you come across them. Take lettuce apart. Wash and pat leaves dry individually. Lay them, torn up if they are large, on a serving platter. Arrange orange sec-tions on top and sprinkle with any juices you have saved. Put aside while you prepare dressing.

Cut pork into small, thin strips, dis-carding any fat or gristle as you come across it.

In a large frying pan, sauté garlic in oil until golden but not burned (this could make it bitter). Add pork strips and stir-fry until lightly coloured all over. Stir in chopped peanuts and continue to stir-fry for a minute or two longer. Sprinkle with sugar, soya sauce and 2 tablespoons water. Mix well. Season with monosodium glutamate and paprika, and a little ordinary salt and/or freshly ground black pepper to taste if liked. Con-tinue to stir-fry for a few minutes longer until pork is thoroughly cooked and sauce reduced.

Pour hot contents of pan over oranges and lettuce. Sprinkle with chopped parsley, chives or spring onion tops. Serve cold.

Serves 4.

ORANGE AND DATE SALAD

Serve this salad with the heavier kinds of meats such as pork and roast duckling.

4 ounces (100–125 g) dried dates
3 tablespoons salad oil
1 tablespoon lemon juice
Salt
2 juicy oranges
Lettuce leaves and finely chopped walnuts, to garnish

Cover dates with boiling water and leave to soften and plump up for about 10 minutes. Then drain dates thoroughly, stone them and cut into small pieces. In a bowl, beat oil and lemon juice together with a pinch of salt. Add dates and toss with a fork until well mixed.

Peel oranges, removing every scrap of white pith. Cut them horizontally into thin slices, picking out and discarding pips as you come across them.

Line a serving platter or bowl with lettuce leaves. Arrange orange slices on them and spoon dates and dressing over the top. Sprinkle with a few chopped walnuts and serve.

Serves 4–6.

MEXICAN ORANGE SALAD

4–6 sweet oranges
1 large, green cooking apple
Salt
Cayenne pepper
Lettuce leaves, to garnish

Peel oranges. Strip off every scrap of white pith, and segment the oranges, working over a bowl to catch juices. Cut each section in two or three, removing and discarding pips as you come across them. Place in the bowl together with all the juices.

Peel, core and dice the apple, and add it to the bowl. Mix gently but thoroughly and season to taste with salt and cayenne pepper.

Serve on a bed of crisp green lettuce.

Serves 4–6.

BEETROOTS IN ORANGE SAUCE

Beetroots and orange are natural partners, and this dish makes a fine accompaniment for heavier meats such as pork, and game – especially in winter, when the choice of green vegetables can be limited.

1½ pounds (700 g) beetroots, trimmed and peeled
¼ pint (150 ml) orange juice (juice of 2 small oranges)
Juice of ½ small lemon
1–1½ ounces (25–40 g) softened butter
1 teaspoon soft brown sugar
Salt
1 tablespoon cornflour
2 tablespoons dry sherry

Shred the beetroots on the coarsest side of a grater and put them in a pan together with the orange and lemon juices, butter, sugar and a sprinkling of salt. Mix well. Push a sheet of greaseproof paper down on to the surface and cook gently until beetroot is soft, about 15 minutes.

In a small bowl, dissolve cornflour in a mixture of sherry and 1 tablespoon water. Pour into the pan of beetroot, stirring, and continue to cook, stirring constantly, until sauce has thickened and cleared.

Correct seasoning and serve.

Serves 4–6.

GLAZED CABBAGE À L'ORANGE

This is an unusual vegetable dish, especially good with pork.

1 large, juicy orange
1 small white cabbage
1 Spanish onion, finely chopped
2 ounces (50 g) butter
6–8 tablespoons chicken (cube) stock
Salt and freshly ground black pepper
2–3 tablespoons currants (optional)
1–2 tablespoons soft brown sugar

Grate orange rind finely. Then peel orange and cut out segments. Discard any pips and cut each segment in 2 or 3. Work over a dish to catch all the juice which may drip out and add orange segments to dish. Quarter, core and shred cabbage finely. Put it in a colander and slowly pour a kettle of boiling water over it. Shake off as much water as possible and put aside until needed.

In a heavy, flameproof casserole or saucepan, sauté onion gently in butter until soft and golden. Stir in shredded cabbage and continue to sauté for a minute or two longer until shreds are coated with butter. Mix in grated orange rind. Moisten with chicken stock and any juice that has drained from orange segments. Season to taste with salt, grind in some pepper, cover and cook gently until cabbage has softened, about 20 minutes. Then mix in pieces of orange and currants, if used, and sprinkle with sugar. Correct seasoning with a little more salt or freshly ground black pepper. Continue to cook gently, stirring frequently, until sugar has melted and is beginning to look slightly caramelized.

Keep hot, covered, until ready to serve.

Serves 4–6.

ORANGE RICE WITH ALMONDS

Pages have been written about the cooking of rice, each nation seemingly devoted to its own method of boiling, steaming or baking. My own favourite method is the way in which Turkish pilaus are made: the raw grains are first fried until thoroughly coated with fat and very lightly coloured. Then *twice the volume* of boiling or very hot liquid is poured in (carefully, because it will spatter and sizzle alarmingly). When the bubbling has subsided, give the rice a good stir, clamp on the lid and leave the pot undisturbed over the lowest possible heat for 15–20 minutes, until all the liquid has been absorbed, leaving the surface dotted with tiny craters. And that's it.

Orange rice goes especially well with poultry dishes and ham.

1 teaspoon whole coriander seeds
1 medium-sized onion, finely chopped
3–4 stalks celery, diagonally sliced
4 ounces (100–125 g) butter
1 tablespoon finely grated orange rind
2 cups (about ¾ pound or 350 g) long-grain rice
2 cups (about ¾ pint or 400 ml) each well-flavoured chicken stock and fresh orange juice
Salt
Sautéed slivered almonds, to garnish

In a mortar, crush coriander seeds finely with a pestle. Put aside.

Choose a large, heatproof casserole with a tight-fitting lid. In it, fry the onion and celery gently in half the butter until quite soft but only lightly coloured. Add the crushed coriander seeds, orange rind and the remaining butter, and when this has melted, stir in the rice. Cook gently, stirring, until each grain is coated with butter. Then add chicken stock, orange juice and salt, to taste. Bring to boiling point, stirring, then lower heat to a bare simmer, cover tightly and cook for 20 minutes, or until rice grains are tender and all the liquid has been absorbed.

Heap rice into a heated dish.

Sprinkle sautéed almonds over the top and serve.

Serves 6–8.

GINGERED ORANGE RICE

A most unusual and subtly flavoured dish of rice that makes a fine accompaniment for roast poultry, ham and pork or lamb chops. Use the same cup for liquids and rice.

1½ ounces (40 g) butter
1 medium onion, finely chopped
1 cup long-grain rice
Finely grated rind of 1 orange
½ teaspoon ground ginger
½ cup fresh orange juice
1½ cups well-flavoured chicken (cube) stock
Finely chopped parsley, to garnish

In a heavy pan, melt butter and fry onion gently until soft and golden. Stir in rice and continue to fry, stirring, until each grain is shiny with butter and lightly coloured. Stir in orange rind and ginger, mix well and fry for a minute or two longer. Remove pan from heat and cool slightly.

Stir in orange juice and chicken stock. Bring to boiling point, stir once and lower heat to a bare simmer. Cover pan tightly and cook gently for 15–20 minutes (without lifting the lid once) until all the liquid is absorbed and rice grains are fluffy and separate. Garnish with parsley.

Serves 4.

ORANGE SOUFFLÉ PUDDING

A dish of thin, delicate almond biscuits makes a delicious accompaniment for this sweet.

1 tablespoon unflavoured powdered gelatine
4 eggs, separated
6 ounces (175 g) caster sugar
Finely grated rinds of 1 orange and 1 lemon
Juice of 3–4 oranges
Juice of 1 lemon

Sprinkle gelatine over 3 or 4 tablespoons cold water in a small cup. Then, when the gelatine has absorbed the water and set, stand the cup in a pan of hot water, stirring until the liquid is clear. Allow to cool to room temperature.

In a large bowl, whisk the egg yolks, sugar and grated rinds together until thick and fluffy. Stir the gelatine into the orange and lemon juices, then gradually whisk into the egg yolk mixture. Leave until syrupy.

Whisk the egg whites until stiff but not dry. Fold them gently into the mixture. Spoon it into a serving bowl and chill until set.

Serves 6.

BOODLE'S ORANGE FOOL

There are many versions of this famous sweet, which was created by Boodle's, a London club founded in 1763.

4 stale rectangular sponge cakes
Finely grated rind and juice of 2 oranges and 1 lemon
3 tablespoons caster sugar, to taste
½ pint (300 ml) double cream
Crystallized orange segments and unsweetened whipped cream, to decorate

Cut the sponge cakes into long, thin strips and arrange them over the base of a glass serving bowl.

In a small bowl, mix the grated rind and juice of the oranges and lemon with the sugar, and stir until it has dissolved. Beat the cream until thickened but not stiff, and gradually beat in the sweetened fruit juice. Pour over the strips of sponge cake. Chill for several hours in the refrigerator.

Serve decorated with unsweetened whipped cream and crystallized orange segments.

Serves 4–6.

PETITS POTS DE CHOCOLAT À L'ORANGE

Oranges have a remarkable affinity for chocolate and their flavour will add magic to any chocolate confection. This dish comes from Robert Carrier's restaurant in Islington – a sweet that has become justly famous.

In the original version, the rind of an orange is first grated, then blended with the juice, which has been squeezed separately. However, provided the orange has a very thin skin and thus little white pith, which would make the sweet bitter, you can save time and trouble by blending the whole orange, minus any pips, to a smooth pulp.

The recipe below makes ample for four. For six portions, simply increase the number of eggs to three.

4 ounces (100–125 g) good-quality
dark, bitter chocolate
1 ounce (25 g) unsalted butter
2 thin-skinned oranges
Grand Marnier, Curaçao or brandy
2 eggs, separated

Break the chocolate up into the top of a double saucepan, and add the butter. Cut 1 orange into chunks, saving juice; remove pips and blend orange finely; add its juice and blend the two together thoroughly. Add to the chocolate. Stir over hot water until chocolate has melted and mixture is smooth. Remove top of pan, cool slightly and stir in 1 tablespoon orange liqueur or brandy.

In a bowl, whisk egg yolks until fluffy. Strain in the chocolate mixture, whisking constantly. Whisk egg whites until stiff but not dry and fold into the chocolate mixture. Pour into individual little pots, custard cups or soufflé dishes; allow to become quite cold and chill until ready to serve.

Just before serving, cut 2 large, thin slices from the centre of the second orange. Quarter them by making two crosswise cuts through each slice and lay two quarters point to point on top of each portion to make a bow-tie shape. Finally, pour a little more liqueur over the surface of each pot, just enough to make it look glossy.

Serves 4.

ORANGES IN MARSALA

7 sweet, juicy, thin skinned
oranges
¼ pint (150 ml) Marsala
2 tablespoons lemon juice
8 ounces (225 g) sugar

With a potato peeler, peel off the coloured rind of 4 of the oranges as thinly as you can. With a small, sharp knife, shave off any white pith which may have come off as well. Slice rind into matchstick strips. Drop them into a small pan of cold water, bring to boiling point and drain thoroughly.

In a measuring jug, combine Marsala with lemon juice. Strain in the juice of 1 orange and make up to ½ pint (300 ml) with water. Pour into a heavy pan, add sugar and bring to boiling point, stirring until sugar has dissolved. Stir in blanched strips of rind and simmer, stirring occasionally, until strips are translucent and syrup has thickened and is reduced by about one-third. Add a little more boiling water if it appears to be reducing too quickly. Pour into a wide-necked jug. Cool and chill until ready to serve.

Peel remaining 6 oranges, slicing away every scrap of bitter white pith and the tough membrane beneath it. Then, working on a board or plate to catch any juices, lay each orange on its side and with a sharp knife, slice it horizontally. Pick out any pips and reassemble each orange, sticking a couple of long cocktail sticks or toothpicks right down from top to bottom to hold slices in position.

Arrange re-formed oranges side by side in a glass bowl. Stir juices that escaped when you were cutting them into the syrup. Pour syrup over oranges and top each one with a little bundle of caramelized orange rind. Return to refrigerator until ready to serve. Serve with dessert knives and forks.

Serves 6.

CRÊPES SUZETTE

These pancakes in orange liqueur sauce were named by Edward VII after his pretty young dinner companion, when a pan of *crêpes au liqueur* with which they were being served accidentally burst into flames.

For the pancakes use the batter given for Lemon Pancakes on page 92, making them no more than 5 or 6 inches (12·5 or 15 cm) in diameter.

12–16 small, thin pancakes
4 ounces (100–125 g) unsalted butter
6 tablespoons caster sugar
Finely grated rind of 1 large orange
6 tablespoons fresh orange juice
1 teaspoon lemon juice
5 tablespoons Curaçao or Cointreau
2 tablespoons brandy

Prepare pancakes in advance and stack them on an upturned soup plate under a cloth to keep them soft and pliable. The orange butter may also be made in advance and stored in the refrigerator until needed.

Cream butter and gradually add 5 tablespoons caster sugar, beating vigorously until mixture is white and fluffy. Beat in grated orange rind, then slowly beat in orange and lemon juice, followed by 2 tablespoons of the orange liqueur. Do not worry if butter looks curdled at this stage. Scrape it all out into a bowl and chill until you are ready to use it.

Fry pancakes in orange butter either in a large, heavy frying pan, preferably one with rounded sides so pancakes will slip out easily, or in a chafing dish at the table. First place the remaining orange liqueur and the brandy in a small pan, ready to heat up and set alight when needed. Next, melt orange butter in frying pan. Place the first pancake flat in the bubbling hot butter, submerging it totally, then fold it in four and push it to one side. Repeat with remaining pancakes. Then distribute them all evenly over surface of pan and allow to bubble gently while you proceed to the final stage.

Sprinkle pancakes with remaining tablespoon of caster sugar. Gently heat pan of brandy and liqueur, and when fumes start rising, carefully put a match to it. As soon as flames are well established, pour all over pancakes. Take pan from the heat and keep shaking it gently and spooning buttery syrup over pancakes until flames die out. Serve immediately.

Serves 4–6.

ORANGE CHEESE BREAD

The flavour of this tea bread improves tremendously if it is left to mellow for 24 hours before serving.

12 ounces (350 g) plain wholewheat
   flour
2 ounces (50 g) soft dark brown sugar
1 teaspoon ground cinnamon
½ teaspoon salt
¼ teaspoon bicarbonate of soda
8 ounces (225 g) cottage cheese
Finely grated rind of 1 orange
1 teaspoon vanilla essence
1 egg
1 ounce (25 g) fresh yeast or ½ ounce
   (15 g) dried yeast
6 tablespoons orange juice
3 ounces (75 g) raisins
Margarine, for loaf tin

Stir the flour, sugar, cinnamon, salt and soda together until well mixed. Rub the cottage cheese through a sieve into another bowl and beat in the orange rind and vanilla essence. Beat the egg until foamy. Dissolve fresh yeast in orange juice (if using dried yeast, follow packet directions).

Make a well in the centre of the flour mixture. Add all the remaining ingredients except the raisins and margarine, and knead vigorously until the dough tends to leave the sides of the bowl clean (it will still be very sticky). Work in the raisins so they are well distributed throughout the dough. Cover the bowl with a cloth and leave the dough to rise until doubled in bulk.

Grease a 2 pound (900 g) loaf tin with margarine. Deflate the dough, knead lightly and transfer it to the loaf tin, which it will half-fill. Cover the tin with a cloth and leave the dough until doubled in bulk again. Then bake bread in a moderate oven (375°F, 190°C, Mark 5) for 35 minutes, or until it is well risen and a thin skewer pushed through the centre feels dry to the touch.

Let the loaf cool in its baking tin, lying on its side on a cooling rack. Then remove the tin and let the loaf cool completely, still on its side, before storing (till the following day if possible).

ORANGE WALNUT CAKE

4 ounces (100–125 g) walnuts
3 tablespoons plain flour
1 teaspoon baking powder
Generous pinch of salt
1 medium orange
4 eggs, separated
5 ounces (150 g) caster sugar
3 tablespoons melted butter
Walnut halves, to decorate

Chocolate icing
4 ounces (100–125 g) bitter dessert
   chocolate
2 tablespoons melted butter

Grind the walnuts finely in a blender or food processor. (Do not use a meat mincer, which tends to make the nuts too oily.) Mix the ground nuts thoroughly with the flour, baking powder and salt. Grate the rind of the orange finely and mix into the flour mixture.

Beat egg yolks until thick and lemon-coloured, then gradually beat in 3½ ounces (90 g) caster sugar. Fold in the walnut mixture, followed by the juice of ½ the orange.

In another bowl, whisk the egg whites until they form soft, floppy peaks. Gradually add the remaining sugar, whisking constantly to make a stiff meringue. With a large metal spoon, fold meringue into yolk mixture.

Spoon cake mixture gently into a well-buttered, deep 8 inch (20 cm) cake tin. Bake in a moderate oven (350°F, 180°C, Mark 4) for 40 minutes, or until the cake is a rich golden colour, feels firm when pressed lightly and has shrunk away slightly from the sides of the tin. Allow the cake to cool in its tin on a rack for 10 minutes before turning it out on to the rack and leaving it until cold.

To make chocolate icing, break the chocolate into small pieces. Put it in a heatproof bowl, stand the bowl in simmering water and leave until chocolate has melted, stirring frequently. Beat in the butter and continue to beat until smooth.

Spread icing over top and sides of cake with a broad-bladed knife. Decorate with walnut halves. Leave until icing has become dry to the touch.

ORANGE AND ALMOND CAKE

This cake, with its pure orange flavour, comes from Claudia Roden's *Book of Middle Eastern Food*. As Mrs Roden points out, the texture of the cake will depend on how long it stays in the oven. For a cake with a moist, pudding-like texture (which I like to serve as a dessert with lightly whipped cream), give it less time. If you want it to turn out firmer and drier, increase the baking time. In any case, have a look at it after 30 minutes. The cake will not go any flatter if the oven door is opened while it is baking.

Butter and flour, for cake tin
2 large oranges
6 eggs
8 ounces (225 g) caster sugar
8 ounces (225 g) ground
*   almonds*
1 teaspoon baking powder

Start by buttering and flouring a cake tin about 8 inches (20 cm) in diameter, preferably one with a removable base.

Rinse oranges and boil them in water to cover for about 2 hours until very soft. If you have a pressure cooker, this will take only 30 minutes at 15 pounds pressure. Lift oranges out of pan, cool them and cut them into large pieces, picking out and discarding pips. Then pulp oranges, skins and all, in an electric blender or food processor, or by putting them through a sieve.

In a large bowl (preferably the bowl of an electric mixer if available) beat eggs until fluffy. Beating constantly, gradually add sugar. Gently stir and fold in ground almonds, baking powder and orange pulp. When thoroughly blended, pour into prepared cake tin.

Bake cake in a moderately hot oven (400°F, 200°C, Mark 6) for about 45 minutes (see above). Allow cake to cool in its tin before turning it out.

ORANGE SHORTBREAD

2 ounces (50 g) soft brown sugar
3½ ounces (90 g) soft margarine
Finely grated rind of 1 large orange
5 ounces (150 g) unbleached plain
*   flour*
1 ounce (25 g) cornflour
1 teaspoon baking powder

If you have a food processor, put all the ingredients in it together, switch on, and your ball of dough will be ready in a couple of minutes.

Otherwise, cream the sugar with the margarine and the finely grated orange rind. Sift the flour, cornflour and baking powder together, and combine with the sugar mixture to make a firm dough. Roll into a ball, wrap in plastic and chill for 1 hour.

Dust a board and your rolling pin *very* lightly with flour and roll the dough out about ⅛ inch (3 mm) thick. Stamp out biscuits with a 2 inch (5 cm) pastry cutter and carefully, with a spatula, transfer them to lightly greased baking sheets. Prick each biscuit two or three times with the tines of a fork.

Bake the biscuits in a moderate oven (350°F, 180°C, Mark 4) for 25 minutes, or until a rich golden colour. Allow them to cool a little on the baking sheets before transferring to wire racks. When quite cold, store in an airtight tin or jar.

ORANGE SWEETMEATS

2 large thin-skinned oranges
8 ounces (225 g) sugar
1 centre slice lemon
2 tablespoons Grand Marnier,
*   Curaçao or brandy (optional)*

Wash the oranges and dry them thoroughly. Carefully strip off the peel from each orange in eight sections. If the white pith is thick, shave it down with a sharp knife. Roll the peels up tightly and thread them side by side to make a 'necklace', using a large needle and a length of strong thread. Tie the ends of thread together.

In an enamelled pan, cover the necklace of rinds with cold water and bring to a rapid boil. Drain and repeat twice more. The third time, continue to boil gently until the peels are quite soft, 10–15 minutes. Drain thoroughly and pat dry with paper towels.

Rinse the pan and in it dissolve the sugar in ½ pint (300 ml) water, together with the lemon slice. Stir in the liqueur or brandy, if used. Skim off scum if necessary. Add the rinds and simmer gently until they are very soft and the syrup is thick, 20–30 minutes. Cool in the pan, covered.

Remove the lemon slice, unthread the orange rolls and pack them into a glass jar. Pour over the syrup, cover the jar and store in a cool, dark cupboard.

CANDIED PEEL

There is a great difference — in flavour, texture *and* price — between peels candied at home and those prepared commercially for the supermarket. Home-candied peels are well worth having all year round but are particularly useful made in autumn, in time for Christmas baking.

Use either strips of orange peel, taken off lengthwise in quarters or sixths, or squeezed-out halves, cut into large pieces. If the peels have a thick layer of white pith attached, this should be left, but squeezed-out halves must first be parboiled for several minutes, then drained and scraped clean of the remains of pulp and other debris with a small, sharp spoon.

Put the peels in a pan, cover with water and simmer until quite tender, which will take about 1½ hours. Top up with more water as it evaporates.

Drain peels thoroughly, reserving water. Measure water, pour it back into the pan, and for every ½ pint (300 ml) add 8 ounces (225 g) sugar. If there is not enough syrup to cover the peels comfortably, more may be made with tap water and sugar in the same proportions. Stir over low heat until sugar is dissolved. Then raise heat, bring syrup to boiling point and add peels. Make sure they are all thoroughly coated with syrup and put aside till the following day.

The second day, bring syrup to boiling point again and simmer for 5 minutes.

The third day, simmer peels until they are translucent, the syrup is very thick and nearly all of it has been absorbed. Lift out pieces of peel on to a wire rack lined with greaseproof paper. Cover lightly with another sheet of greaseproof paper and leave to dry in a warm, airy place. Take advantage of a cooling oven whenever it is available (a temperature of about 100°F or 210°C will be suitable) to help speed up the drying process.

Store candied peels in an airtight box or screw-top jar. Should they dry out too much and become impossibly tough to chop up for use, they can be softened again by soaking them for a short time in boiling water.

TRADITIONAL MARMALADE

In *The Feill Cookery Book*, published in 1907 by Messrs McNaught & Sinclair of Glasgow, the following recipe for marmalade was contributed by Messrs M. Campbell & Son, Preserve Makers, of 15 Hartington Place, Edinburgh. Although the recipe is well over 70 years old, nothing seems to have changed in the world of marmalade making.

7 bitter (Seville) oranges
8 pints water
7 pounds sugar

'Wash the oranges in warm water and scrape off black specks, if any. Then with a very sharp knife cut the oranges across in thin slices right through skin and pulp. The pips will fall out and they should be placed in a basin. Then re-cut the slices so that the pieces of peel are not too long; these should then be placed in a basin. Add the 8 pints of cold water; place the pips in a muslin bag and let them soak in the water with the peel for 24 hours. Then place all together in a preserving pan and boil for 1½ hours without the sugar (when it has boiled for about 1 hour take out the bag of pips). Now add the sugar and boil for another ½ hour, fill up the pots and cover when cold.'

SAUCE MALTAISE

This orange-flavoured Hollandaise sauce is a classic accompaniment for hot poached asparagus. Originally, it was made with blood oranges but ordinary ones will do very well. The amount yielded by the recipe below will be enough to dress about 1½ pounds (700 g) asparagus and serve 4–6 people.

3 egg yolks
1–2 tablespoons lemon juice
Salt and white pepper
6 ounces (175 g) unsalted butter
Finely grated rind of ½ orange
Juice of 1 small orange

In the top of a double saucepan, or a bowl that fits snugly over (*not* in) a

ORANGE MARMALADE

It is almost worth borrowing, or even investing in, a pressure cooker for this recipe alone. It not only cuts the preparation time dramatically but also makes the best orange marmalade I know. Three pounds (1·4 kilos) fruit is the maximum I would use at a time in a large pressure cooker.

If you cannot find the time to make marmalade during the few weeks that Seville oranges are on the market, but do have a freezer, freeze a supply of oranges, tied up in a plastic bag, until you are ready. They will keep perfectly for up to a year (I once used oranges that were 2 years old most successfully). Thaw them completely before use (overnight, at room temperature, is best), then use them in the same way as fresh fruit.

2 pounds (900 g) Seville oranges
2 lemons
4 pounds (1·8 kilos) sugar
Small knob of butter or margarine (optional)

Scrub the oranges and lemons thoroughly under the cold tap. Pack them in a pressure cooker with 1 pint (550 ml) water, bring to 15 pounds pressure and cook for 15 minutes if oranges are very large, only 10 minutes if smaller. Reduce pressure.

Open the cooker and lift out the fruit with a slotted spoon. When they are cool enough to handle, cut them in half and with a sharp-edged teaspoon scrape all the pulp, pith and seeds out of the peels into a bowl. Stir this back into the water remaining in the cooker and boil hard for 10 minutes.

Meanwhile, slice the peels in half again lengthwise and cut them into matchstick strips.

Strain the boiled liquid through a fine sieve. For a crystal-clear jelly, line the sieve with double-thick muslin and allow as much liquid as possible to drip through without squeezing or pressing through any pulp. However, if this is not important, press the pulp lightly against the sides of the sieve with the back of a wooden spoon to extract as much liquid as possible. Pour it back into the cooker.

Add sugar and stir with a wooden spoon over low heat until dissolved. Stir in shredded peel and boil briskly until setting point is reached. A small knob of butter or margarine stirred in at the last moment will take care of any scum.

Cool for 5 minutes and pour hot into hot, dry jars. Cover immediately and leave until quite cold before storing.

See also page 198.

Fills about 7 jars.

pan of simmering water, beat egg yolks with a tablespoon each of lemon juice and water, a good pinch of salt and a generous dash of white pepper.

Divide butter into 10 or 12 cubes and leave on a plate to soften slightly without turning oily.

Fit top of double saucepan or bowl over simmering water. Drop in the first piece of butter and beat lightly by hand with a wire whisk until it is incorporated into egg yolks. Beat in one or two more pieces of butter in the same way, taking great care that sauce does not overheat, or it will curdle. If it looks in any danger of separating, immediately lift the top container off and quickly beat in a tablespoon of cold water to lower the temperature of the sauce slightly, beating vigorously until it is quite smooth again.

With the pan off the heat, continue to beat in butter, a piece at a time. Then flavour sauce with grated orange rind and thin it down slightly with orange juice. Finally, taste and adjust flavour of sauce with more salt, white pepper or orange juice as desired.

Keep sauce hot until ready to serve by standing it over hot (*not* boiling) water. Give it an occasional stir, paying particular attention to the bottom and corners of the pan.

Serve sauce in a heated sauceboat.

Serves 4–6.

BISHOP

This is a form of mulled wine. When claret is used instead of port it is called 'Cardinal'. When champagne is used, it is known as 'Pope'.

1 large orange
1 tablespoon whole cloves
½ teaspoon ground cinnamon
½ teaspoon ground cloves
½ teaspoon allspice
1 blade mace
½ ounce (15 g) root ginger, peeled and finely chopped
2 pints (1·1 litre) non-vintage port
3 ounces (75 g) granulated sugar
Juice of 1 lemon
Nutmeg

Pre-heat the oven to cool (250°F, 120°C, Mark ¼). Stud the orange all over with the whole cloves. Place on a baking tray and cook in the oven for about 1 hour.

Then, put all the spices and ½ pint (300 ml) water in a medium saucepan. Bring to the boil and simmer until the water is reduced by half. In a separate large saucepan, heat the port until almost boiling.

Remove from the heat. Strain the spiced water through a fine sieve onto the port. Add the baked orange. Return the pan to the heat and cook slowly for 10 minutes, but do not allow to boil.

When ready to serve, put the sugar and lemon juice in a punch bowl. Pour over the hot, spiced port. Stir and grate some nutmeg over the surface. Serve hot, by ladling into warm glasses.

Serves 6.

ORANGEADE

Make large quantities of this cooling drink to store in the refrigerator, ready to be served chilled with ice on hot summer days.

8 ounces (225 g) sugar
Grated rind and juice of 2 large oranges
Juice of 1 lemon
Soda water
Orange slices, to decorate

Place the sugar and 1½ pints

ORANGE WINE

The combination of Seville and sweet oranges gives this sweet, dessert wine a tangy 'bite'.

6 Seville oranges
6 sweet oranges
1 pound (450 g) sultanas, chopped
1 teaspoon Pectozyme
1 nutrient tablet
Sherry yeast
3 pounds (1·4 kilos) sugar

Heat 1 gallon (4·5 litres) water to boiling point. Meanwhile peel the oranges, keeping the peel thin and avoiding the pith. Chop the peel finely, and place in the prepared mashing vessel. Add the sultanas, then pour on the boiling water. Stir, then cover and leave to cool to a temperature of 65–75°F (18–24°C).

Squeeze the juice from the oranges into the mashing vessel, add the Pectozyme, nutrient tablet and activated yeast (see manufacturer's instructions for quantity and method of use). Cover the mashing vessel tightly and leave in a warm place (65–75°F or 18–24°C) for 6 days.

Uncover the vessel, strain off the liquid through a fine sieve, into a sterilized container. Stir in the sugar and siphon into a fermentation vessel.

Ferment under an air-lock. When a good layer of sediment has formed on the bottom of the vessel, rack, then store for at least a year before bottling. Keep for a further year before drinking.

See also page 205.

Makes about 1 gallon (4·5 litres).

(900 ml) water in a pan. Heat gently, stirring, until the sugar dissolves, but do not boil. Pour into a 2 pint (1·1 litre) jug. Add the rind and juices to the jug, stir, cover and leave to stand in a cool place for 3 hours. Strain off the rind and chill in the refrigerator until wanted.

To serve, two-thirds fill a tall chilled glass then top up with soda water and ice.

Decorate each serving with a thin slice of orange.

ORANGE GIN

Use Seville oranges for this recipe — the sweet variety make rather a flat, sickly liqueur. Select fruit with an unblemished skin — only the peel is used.

1 pound (450 g) sugar
4 Seville oranges
2 lemons
2 pints (1·1 litre) gin

Make a syrup by dissolving the sugar in ½ pint (300 ml) water and boiling for 15 minutes. Leave to cool. Meanwhile peel the fruit thinly, making sure that no pith is taken off with the peel. Chop the peel and place in a large wide-neck storage jar with a screw top (a large Kilner jar is ideal). Pour on the sugar syrup and gin. Screw the lid firmly onto the jar.

Shake gently and leave for 2 weeks at room temperature.

Unscrew the lid, strain off the liqueur and bottle it. Keep for at least 6 months, preferably longer, before drinking.

Makes about 2¼ pints (1·25 litres).

BUCK'S FIZZ

A perfect celebratory drink.

1 part fresh orange juice
2 parts non-vintage champagne

Chill the champagne and the orange juice by placing in the refrigerator for at least 2 hours before you wish to use them. Just before serving, pour the ingredients into a chilled jug. Stir well and serve in tulip shaped champagne glasses.

PAPAYA

The papaya, also called a tree melon or paw paw, grows throughout the tropics of both the Old and New Worlds, from India to South America. It is known to have been cultivated by the Aztecs and Mayas, perhaps the first people to do so. Even though you may never have seen, let alone tasted, a fresh papaya, the chances are you have eaten meat tenderized with the proteolitic enzyme *papain* which is extracted from the fruit.

Papayas do not look particularly inviting – a cross between small, oval melons and large dumpy pears of a faded green colour. This changes dramatically once the fruit is cut open to reveal its brilliant coral or golden flesh and hundreds of shiny black seeds. These should all be scraped out with a teaspoon as they can taste quite peppery.

A ripe papaya yields slightly to pressure when squeezed gently between the palms of the hands and its skin feels soft. But unripe papayas are also edible. In the West Indies, they are treated as a vegetable and served cooked. If the fruit you have is ripe but still too hard to eat, leave it for a day or two in a warm airing cupboard, or wrapped in a brown paper bag in the kitchen, to soften.

CLEANSER AND TONERS

Papaya is used to 'tenderize' the skin, in cosmetic face masks and lotions. It also makes a very effective occasional treatment for removing dead skin and freshening and bleaching the complexion. Pat on a little juice very gently: don't leave on more than 5 minutes before removing with lukewarm water.

FRIED PAPAYA

An unusual accompaniment that is delicious served with ham or bacon. Use firm, slightly under-ripe fruit that will not go mushy in the frying pan.

1 large papaya
1 ounce (25 g) butter
1 tablespoon lemon juice

Peel papaya and cut it horizontally into slices about ½ inch (1·25 cm) thick. Scrape out black seeds.

In a large, heavy frying pan, melt butter. When it is foaming, lay papaya rings in it in one layer and fry until heated through and lightly coloured, about 1 minute on each side. Sprinkle with lemon juice and serve immediately.

Serves 4.

PAPAYA STRAWBERRY APPETIZER

2 large, ripe papayas, chilled
Fresh lime or lemon juice
6 ounces (175 g) medium strawberries
Icing sugar

Halve papayas lengthwise and clear out all the black seeds with a sharp teaspoon. Brush cut surfaces all over with lime or lemon juice. Lay halves on 4 individual glass dishes.

Clean or quickly rinse strawberries and hull them. They should all be of the same size; if there are large ones among them, halve or quarter them. Pile strawberries into papaya cups and sift icing sugar over the top.

Serves 4.

DULCE DE PAPAYA VERDE
Candied Green Papaya

This interesting recipe comes from *Good Food From Mexico* by Ruth Watt Mulvey and Luisa Maria Alvarez. As the authors say in their introduction to the recipe, this is 'one of the most elaborate and one of the best ways' of preparing unripe papaya.

4 tablespoons slaked lime (food pure)
½ medium-sized green papaya
About 1 pound (450 g) sugar
2–3 fig leaves

Soak lime in about 3 pints (1·7 litres) water for 1 hour. Allow it to settle, then strain it out through muslin. Pour water back into bowl. Peel papaya, cut it into 2 inch (5 cm) squares, drop it into the lime water overnight.

The following day, remove papaya, wash and simmer lightly in fresh water to cover for about 10 minutes. Cool. Press the pieces of papaya gently between thumb and forefinger to remove all excess moisture.

Boil together sugar and ¾ pint (400 ml) water, stirring, until sugar is dissolved and syrup forms a thread. Add papaya and fig leaves. SImmer gently over very low heat for about 20 minutes. Remove papaya pieces to a serving dish. Chill thoroughly. Although it has a somewhat candy-like quality, this sweet is served as a dessert, to be eaten with a fork.

Serves 6.

PAPAYA MILKSHAKE

1 small, ripe papaya
6 tablespoons coconut milk (page 54)
Juice of 2 large limes
Grated rind of 1 large lime
2 ounces (50 g) sugar
4 tablespoons crushed ice
Lime slices, to decorate

Peel the papaya, then cut it in half and remove the seeds. Chop the flesh coarsely and place in an electric blender. Add all the remaining ingredients except the lime slices, and blend until smooth and creamy. Pour into tall, chilled glasses and serve, decorated with a slice of lime.

Makes 3 large glasses.

PASSION FRUIT

Varieties of passionflower vine (*Passiflora*) flourish in South America, the West Indies, South Africa, Australia and along the shores of the Mediterranean. The best-known variety also called grenadilla (or granadilla), is purplish-black and wrinkled when ripe, with small edible seeds surrounded by an aromatic yellow pulp. Other fruits have orange or yellow skins.

It is generally eaten raw – just cut the fruit in half and scoop out the flesh with a teaspoon. Or the flesh can be added to cocktails, fruit punches, or other fruit juices. Beat it into whipped cream or ice cream for a refreshing and subtly different fruit fool or sundae, or use it in fruit salads.

The fruit keeps well in a freezer, but should be eaten before the skin becomes too thin and wrinkled or the flavour will not be at its best. The flesh alone will freeze for up to a year: before freezing, add half its weight in sugar then leave to stand, stirring occasionally, until the sugar is dissolved.

The passionflower plant has a long and respectable history as a sedative.

PASSION WHIP

1 small papaya
½ pint (300 ml) double cream
4 small passion fruit
½ teaspoon vanilla essence
1 teaspoon ground mace

Halve the papaya and discard the seeds. Scoop out the flesh, place in large bowl, and beat into a foamy purée.

In another bowl, whip the cream until stiff then gently fold this into the papaya purée. Mix together well and set on one side.

Cut the passion fruit in half and scoop out the flesh. Push through a fine sieve and fold into the cream and papaya mixture. Stir in the vanilla essence and mace, then turn the mixture into a serving dish. Chill in the refrigerator for at least 1 hour before serving.

Serves 4.

PASSION CURD

6 small passion fruit
4 ounces (100–125 g) butter
8 ounces (225 g) sugar
3 eggs, beaten

Halve passion fruit and scoop out flesh. Sieve to remove seeds.

In a large, thick-bottomed saucepan, melt the butter over a low heat. Remove from the heat and stir in the sugar. Return the pan to the heat and stir continuously until the sugar dissoves. Then stir in the passion fruit and the beaten eggs, mixing thoroughly. Allow the mixture to simmer gently until it starts to thicken, stirring occasionally. Remove from the heat and cool slightly.

Pot and seal (page 199).

Fills about 3 jars.

ORANGE PASSION PIE

One 8 or 9 inch (20 or 22·5 cm) sweet shortcrust pastry case, pre-baked in a deep pie dish (page 203)
10 large passion fruit
2 teaspoons powdered gelatine
juice of 1 lemon
2 eggs, separated
1 tablespoon brandy
2 large oranges
Unsweetened whipped cream, to serve

Halve the passion fruit. Scoop out the flesh and pass through a fine sieve. Set aside.

Put the gelatine in about 5 tablespoons warm water and stir until the gelatine dissolves.

Whisk the lemon juice and egg yolks together well in another bowl that will fit into a small saucepan to make a double boiler. Boil about 1 inch (2.5 cm) of water in the saucepan, then lower the heat and place the bowl (not touching) over the simmering water. Stir the mixture constantly until it begins to thicken. Remove the bowl from the heat and stir the gelatine into the thickened egg and lemon mixture. Add the brandy and passion fruit, blending well. Leave this mixture to cool.

Beat the egg whites until stiff and gently fold them into the cold passion fruit mixture. Peel the oranges, removing any pith, and divide into segments. Fold these into the passion fruit mixture and spoon into the cooked pastry case. Place the pie in the refrigerator to chill for at least 1 hour, then serve with unsweetened whipped cream.

Serves 4–6.

PEACH

For hundreds of years, the succulence of ripe peaches has been a source of inspiration for artists, ranging from decorators of Chinese porcelain to great European still-life painters. Peaches are thought to be native to China, where they were cultivated 4,000 years ago, but early in their history they were introduced into Europe via Persia. The Romans called them Persian plums. Peaches were brought to the New World by Spanish conquerors in the sixteenth century. Over the next 300 years, they were taken all over the world, flourishing wherever they found a suitable climate, and today the cultivation of peaches is second in popularity only to that of apples.

There are two main types, 'clingstone' and 'freestone', with a few in-between varieties known as 'semi-clingstone' and 'semi-freestone'. Most peaches have yellow flesh. White-fleshed ones are far rarer and considered to have the finest flavour. Because they are so prone to decay, peaches are usually picked when they are still in a hard-mature state. Such fruit will take several days to ripen at home. However, if they have been picked too soon, they will shrivel up without ripening, and have rubbery, tasteless flesh. Soft peaches must be used as quickly as possible as decay spreads very fast. Fine, ripe fruits are best eaten just as they are. If they are hard, you may prefer to poach them in a light sugar syrup.

To peel peaches, pour boiling water over a few fruits at a time, and leave for 1 or 2 minutes to loosen their skin. Then, hold each peach in a soft kitchen cloth and strip off its skin. If this is done with care, faint markings of colour will remain on the surface of the peeled fruit. Halve the peaches lengthwise and remove stones.

Once the season starts, fresh peaches are cheap and plentiful throughout the summer months. This is the time to indulge in exciting soups, sweets and ice creams. Use them to garnish baked ham and roast duckling, instead of other fruits such as pineapple, oranges or cherries. For a slimming summer salad serve peeled and stoned peach halves stuffed with cottage cheese on a bed of crisp lettuce.

Canned peaches, either halves or slices, make a very good substitute for fresh fruit. Or use dried peaches, preferably sun-dried fruit that has not been treated with chemicals, for winter puddings and fruit salads.

Peel and stone peaches before freezing. Brush halves or slices with lemon juice and use a syrup made from 1 pound (450 g) sugar to every pint (550 ml) water.

Peach juice is soothing and diuretic – and an excellent moisturizer.

PEACH DRINK

Pack the goblet of an electric blender with chopped ripe peaches, and blend to a purée. Blend in a carton of natural yoghourt, and dilute to taste with crushed ice.

COSMETICS

Peach juice is an excellent moisturizer, and peach kernel oil, like its close relatives almond oil and apricot kernel oil, is much used in cosmetics as it has a wonderful moisturizing, nourishing and healing effect on the skin. It is also excellent for massage. As it is unscented, it mixes well with perfumed essential oils, for use in aromatherapy or simply as a fragrance.

For a very quick, unfussy, pick-me-up for tired or rough skin, put a few drops of peach kernel oil into an eggcup and add a very little witch-hazel. Mix together with your fingers and pat gently on your face, stroking until it is absorbed. It leaves the skin feeling smooth and silky, and is particularly good for the neck.

CHILLED SUMMER PEACH SOUP

For this soup, the fruit must be sweet and aromatic, bordering on the over-ripe. Serve with a dollop of sour cream or lightly whipped sweet cream, if desired.

2–2½ pounds (900 g–1·1 kilos) sweet ripe peaches
8 tablespoons sugar
Finely grated rind of ½ lemon
½ pint (300 ml) white wine (medium), or still cider
Icing sugar and lemon juice (optional)

Peel peaches. Cut them in half lengthwise and remove stones. Slice peaches thinly. Crack open 6 peach stones, take out kernels and chop them finely.

In a large pan, make a light syrup with the sugar, lemon rind, chopped peach kernels and 1½ pints (900 ml) water. Simmer for 5 minutes, then add about half of the sliced peaches and simmer until very soft but not mushy. Meanwhile, put remaining peaches in a glass serving bowl. Pour over wine or cider.

When poached peaches are tender, allow slices to cool in their syrup. Then pour peaches and syrup into the bowl and mix lightly but thoroughly with uncooked peaches and wine. Taste and sweeten with a little sifted icing sugar or flavour with a squeeze of lemon juice if liked. Serve very cold.

Serves 4–6.
Note: To decorate the soup and make it more colourful, dot the bowl with some ripe red strawberries or raspberries, or float a glossy green leaf on the surface of the soup.

PEACH DUMPLINGS

An old American favourite from the Deep South to serve warm with pouring cream for Sunday supper.

6 ripe peaches
8 ounces (225 g) sugar
One 2 inch (5 cm) cinnamon stick
Twist of orange peel
6 ounces (175 g) plain flour
1½ teaspoons baking powder
Generous pinch of salt
1 ounce (25 g) lard, butter or white vegetable fat
Milk
Chilled pouring cream, to serve

Peel peaches. Halve them lengthwise and remove stones.

In a wide, heavy pan with a tight-fitting lid, dissolve sugar in ½ pint (300 ml) water, adding cinnamon stick and orange peel (use only the coloured part). Stir over low heat until sugar melts, and bring syrup to simmering point.

Lower peach halves into simmering syrup. Push a sheet of greaseproof paper down over them to prevent syrup evaporating too much and simmer until they are almost tender but still very firm. If peaches are ready before they are needed, leave them to cool in the syrup and bring to simmering point again just before adding dumplings.

Sift flour, baking powder and salt into a bowl, and rub in fat until mixture resembles fine breadcrumbs. Stir in enough milk to make a dough that is soft but still holds its shape. Stop mixing as soon as this stage is reached as overhandling will make dumplings tough.

Shape dumplings as follows. Dip a metal tablespoon into simmering syrup. Shake it free of excess syrup, take a rounded spoonful of dough at a time and drop it on top of simmering peaches. Repeat with remaining dough, dipping spoon in syrup each time so dough will not stick to it. Cover pan tightly and simmer undisturbed for about 15 minutes until dumplings are light and airy, and they are no longer sticky and moist to the touch.

Cool to lukewarm, uncovered, and serve peaches, dumplings and syrup together in soup bowls, accompanied by a jug of pouring cream.

Serves 6.

PEACH MERINGUE PIE

For those with a sweet tooth, this is sheer self-indulgence. It is based on a great American favourite, the Angel Pie.

Meringue
4 egg whites
¼ teaspoon cream of tartar
8 ounces (225 g) caster sugar

Peaches and cream filling
4 egg yolks
4 ounces (100–125 g) caster sugar
Pinch of salt
Finely grated rind and juice of 1 large lemon
½ pint (300 ml) double cream or ¼ pint (150 ml) each double and single cream, mixed
4–5 ripe peaches

Prepare the meringue shell well in advance. The preceding day will probably be the most convenient. First, line a baking sheet with silicone paper or a sheet of greaseproof paper lightly brushed with a wad of kitchen paper dipped in tasteless oil. On the lining paper, mark a circle 9 inches (22·5 cm) in diameter as a guide for the shell.

In a large bowl that is spotlessly clean and dry, whisk egg whites until just frothy. Sprinkle with cream of tartar and whisk to soft peak stage. Then gradually whisk in sugar and continue to whisk to a stiff, glossy meringue.

Shape meringue into a 9 inch (22·5 cm) nest, either using a piping bag fitted with a large, plain nozzle, or in a far simpler (and less messy) way as follows. With a tablespoon, scoop up balls of meringue and place them around sides of circle. Then fill the centre of the circle with more meringue and with the back of your spoon, smooth it out to form a nest. Finally, if you like, rough up the surface (neatly and regularly) with a skewer or the prongs of a large kitchen fork.

Let the meringue shell dry out in a cool oven (275°F, 140°C, Mark 1) for at least 1 hour, or until it is hard and brittle, and very lightly tinged with gold. Then turn off the oven, leaving the meringue in it for several hours or overnight to cool completely.

Prepare cream filling. In the top of a double saucepan, beat egg yolks just enough to mix them and make them foamy. Lightly beat in sugar, salt and the grated lemon rind and juice. Fit top of pan over simmering water and stir constantly until mixture is very thick and creamy. Take care not to let it boil or egg yolks will curdle. Cool, giving it an occasional stir to prevent a skin forming on top.

Whisk cream until it stands in light, floppy peaks. Put aside about 4 large tablespoonfuls in a small bowl or cup for decoration. Gently but thoroughly fold remainder into cream filling. Chill lightly.

Peel and stone peaches, and slice them lengthwise. Pick out about 8 of the best slices for decoration.

Assemble the meringue pie as follows. Peel off lining paper and lay meringue case on a large, flat serving dish. Spread evenly with a thin layer of cream filling. Cover closely with slices of peach. Then spread remaining filling over the top. Decorate with reserved peach slices and dollops of whipped cream. Chill lightly until ready to serve but serve as soon as possible.

Serves 8.

PEACH SALAD

This makes a simple and good sweet on its own, but can also be served with creamy vanilla ice cream or simply a jug of chilled pouring cream.

4 large, ripe peaches
Juice of 1 large lemon
2 ounces (50 g) caster sugar
1–2 tablespoons coarsely chopped, skinned and toasted hazelnuts, or toasted flaked almonds

Peel peaches. Cut them in half lengthwise and remove stones. Crack stones open, remove kernels and chop them finely. In a small bowl, stir lemon juice and sugar together until sugar has melted. Stir in chopped peach kernels.

Slice peaches into a glass serving bowl. Pour sweetened lemon juice over slices and turn them gently until coated on all sides. Sprinkle with nuts and chill before serving.

Serves 4.

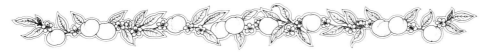

PEACH PARFAIT

A quickly prepared summer sweet, which can be made in advance.

The parfait can be stored in the ice-making compartment of a refrigerator for up to 2 days (longer in a freezer) before use.

4 large ripe peaches
4 ounces (100–125 g) sugar
Pinch of salt
3 egg yolks, beaten well
¼ pint (150 ml) whipping cream

Peel peaches. Remove the stones and chop the fruit into small pieces, then push these through a fine sieve (or use a blender) to make a purée.

Place ¼ pint (150 ml) water, sugar and salt in the top of a double boiler or in a basin over a pan of boiling water. Cook, stirring constantly until the sugar dissolves. Then add the beaten egg yolks. Continue beating the mixture as it cooks over the hot water, until it thickens (do not allow to boil). Then beat in the peach purée and cook for a further 2 minutes, stirring constantly. Remove the pan from the heat and stand the basin containing the mixture in a bowl of cold water. Whisk for a few minutes as it cools.

In another bowl, whip the cream until it is light and airy, but not stiff, then fold this into the peach mixture. Pour into a freezing tray and freeze. This should take about 3 hours, and the parfait does not need stirring during this time.

Serves 4–6.

PEACH AND ALMOND TART

This tart is made with fresh peaches but a large can of peach halves or slices, well drained of syrup, may be used instead.

One 8 or 9 inch (20 or 22·5 cm) shortcrust pastry case, pre-baked (page 203 and method)
1 pound (450 g) fresh, ripe peaches (see above)
3 eggs
4 ounces (100–125 g) ground almonds
4 ounces (100–125 g) icing sugar, sifted
Flaked almonds, to decorate (optional)

Bake the case very lightly, just long enough to set the pastry without colouring it. Leave the pastry case in its tin or flan ring on a baking sheet.

Peel peaches. Cut them in half lengthwise, remove stones and either leave them in halves or cut each half into 6 or 8 slices, depending on size. Arrange peaches neatly in case.

Beat eggs until fluffy. Gently fold in ground almonds and icing sugar until thoroughly mixed. Pour evenly over peaches and sprinkle with a few flaked almonds if available. Bake tart in a moderate oven (375°F, 190°C, Mark 5) until filling is set and a rich golden colour, about 30 minutes. Serve lukewarm or cold.

Serves 6.

ITALIAN STUFFED PEACHES

There are many versions of this classic. This one is simple and good.

4 large firm ripe peaches
2 ounces (50 g) amaretti or macaroons
1 ounce (25 g) almonds, blanched and peeled
4 tablespoons caster sugar
1 tablespoon unsweetened cocoa powder
4–6 tablespoons white wine
Butter, for baking dish
Chilled pouring cream, to serve (optional)

Cut peaches in half lengthwise and remove stones. Break stones open, remove kernels and chop them finely. Place in a bowl. Hollow out peach cavities slightly to make room for filling. Chop up scooped-out pulp and add to bowl. Crumble amaretti or macaroons and stir them into bowl.

Split 4 of the almonds in half and reserve for decoration. Chop remainder finely and add to bowl. Stir in 3 tablespoons sugar and the cocoa powder. Moisten with 2 or 3 tablespoons wine and work to a paste.

Stuff each peach cavity with some of the paste, rounding it up and smoothing it over with a knife blade. Arrange peach halves side by side in a lightly buttered baking dish. Sprinkle them with remaining sugar and top each half-peach with an almond flake. Moisten with remaining wine.

Bake peaches in a moderate oven (375°F, 190°C, Mark 5) for 25–30 minutes, until peaches have softened and mounds of stuffing are crisp and crusty on top.

Serve 2 peach halves per person while they are still very warm, accompanied by chilled, unsweetened pouring cream if liked.

Serves 4.

GRILLED PEACHES

A good way to use peaches that are too hard to eat raw.

Halve and stone peaches. Lay the halves on a baking sheet, cut side up; sprinkle with brown sugar, dot with flecks of butter, and grill for 5–7 minutes until the butter and sugar have caramelized into a bubbling brown topping.

Serve hot with chilled cream.

PEACHES IN BRANDY

This preserve may be something of a luxury but a few jars prepared and stored away at the height of the season when peaches are at their cheapest and best will make very acceptable gifts when Christmas comes round.

The peaches may either be sliced, as in the recipe below, or left in halves. In the latter case, however, it is a wise precaution to check that the necks of the jars you plan to use are wide enough for the peaches to slip through without bruising.

Any leftover poaching syrup is very good used (diluted with white wine or water, if necessary) for poaching other fresh fruit such as apples.

2 pounds (900 g) ripe, unblemished
  peaches
8 ounces (225 g) sugar
About ¼ pint (150 ml) brandy

Peel the peaches, halve them verti-cally and remove stones. Cut each peach half into 6 or 8 thin slices.

In a wide, shallow pan, dissolve sugar in 1 pint (550 ml) water to make a light syrup. Drop the peach slices into the simmering syrup and poach gently until just cooked and still very firm. With a slotted spoon, transfer slices to hot, clean jars.

Boil syrup briskly until thickened and reduced to about one-third of the original amount. Strain it through a fine sieve. Measure out about ¼ pint (150 ml) and stir in an equal amount of brandy.

Drain off any syrup that has accumulated in the jars of peaches. Then slowly pour in brandied syrup, wait a few minutes for it to 'settle', and top up with more, covering the peaches completely.

Cover jars as usual and store in a cool, dry cupboard. Leave for several weeks before tasting to allow flavours to develop.

PEACH AND STRAWBERRY CLARET CUP

The type of fruit used with the peaches can be varied according to availability. This combination gives a cool, refreshing summer drink, ideal for a barbecue or outdoor party.

2 ripe peaches
6 ounces (175 g) strawberries
½ pint (300 ml) brandy
2 pints (1·1 litre) red wine
Soda water
Peach slices, to decorate

Peel, halve and stone the peaches. Cut the halves into thin slices and place in a medium sized bowl. Husk and wipe the strawberries, removing any damaged fruit. Cut in half and add to the peaches. Pour the brandy over the fruit and leave for 3 hours, stirring occasionally.

Pour the brandied fruit into a punch bowl or large glass jug. Add the wine and some ice. Leave in a cool place, until just before serving. Dilute to taste with soda water and decorate with the peach slices.

Serves 10.

PEACH PICKLE

1 pound (450 g) dried peaches
2 Spanish onions
8 ounces (225 g) seedless raisins
8 ounces (225 g) sugar
1 tablespoon salt
2 teaspoons ground ginger
1 teaspoon powdered mustard
1 pint (550 ml) white malt vinegar

Rinse peaches thoroughly and put them in a bowl. Cover with 1 pint (550 ml) boiling water and leave to soak overnight.

The following day, pour contents of bowl into a large, enamelled, stain-less steel or aluminium pan.

Parboil onions for 2 minutes. Drain thoroughly, chop finely and add to peaches, together with raisins and sugar. In a cup, blend salt, ginger and mustard powder smoothly with some of the vinegar. Pour into pan, together with remaining vinegar, and mix well. Bring to boiling point over low heat, stirring until sugar has dissolved. Then simmer for about 1 hour, stirring frequently to prevent mixture catching on bottom of pan as it thickens. Take care not to mash peaches up as you stir them. They should become very soft but stay intact.

Pour into clean glass jars. Allow to cool before covering as for jam.

See also page 200.

Fills about 4 jars.

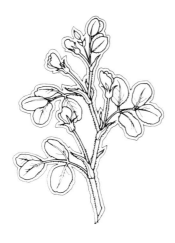

PEANUT

The peanut, also known as the ground nut or monkey nut, is thought to be native to South America and to have been taken to West Africa by Portuguese traders in the sixteenth century. It subsequently spread to the Dutch East Indies, India and China. There are many different varieties and sizes, but the peanut we know is grown in most hot countries.

Roasted and salted peanuts are popular snacks in the west, while in Africa the nuts are used in soups and stews. In Malaysia and Indonesia, peanuts are used in the rich sauce for a *satay* (or *saté*) dish – pieces of meat or chicken marinated in a soya sauce mixture, then threaded on skewers, grilled and served with a luscious peanut sauce. Then there is that American favourite, peanut butter, invented by a doctor from St Louis. Spread on slices of crusty fresh bread, it combines the moist consistency of ordinary butter with the nutrition and bulk of a meat or fish paste.

Peanuts are sold unroasted in their shells, shelled and unroasted, roasted without salt, and roasted and salted. Freeze-drying and salting, a more recent development, makes the nuts less sticky to handle. Roughly chopped, roasted and unsalted nuts can be sprinkled on fruit salads and ices. They can also be added to fudge.

Peanut oil is used for deep-frying and general cooking, in a bland-tasting salad dressing and, commercially, for making margarine. It keeps well if stored in cool conditions.

The high protein content of peanuts makes them a more than adequate meat substitute in vegetarian diets. One ounce (25 g) of shelled, roasted peanuts contains slightly more protein than one egg or one ounce (25 g) of cheese – and compares favourably in price. Peanuts also have a high fat content, some carbohydrate, calcium and iron, and are a good source of Vitamin B.

PEANUT SOUP

This thick, spicy soup from the Caribbean island of St Kitts may be served either hot or chilled.

4 ounces (100–125 g) roasted,
    unsalted peanuts
2 pints (1·1 litres) chicken stock
Salt and freshly ground black pepper
Few drops of Tabasco or chilli sauce
¼ pint (150 ml) double cream
1 tablespoon Angostura bitters
4 tablespoons dry sherry
Croûtons (page 205) or chopped fresh
    chives, to garnish

Place the peanuts and 2 tablespoons of the chicken stock in an electric blender, or use a pestle and mortar to make into a thick paste. Put paste into a large saucepan. Gradually add the rest of the stock, stirring to avoid lumps. Season with salt and pepper to taste, add the Tabasco or chilli sauce and stir well.

Place the pan over a moderate heat and bring the contents to the boil, stirring occasionally. Lower the heat and allow to simmer gently for 15 minutes. Remove the pan from the heat and stir in the cream. Return the pan to the heat and cook soup, stirring constantly, but do not allow to boil. Just before serving, stir in the Angostura bitters and sherry. If serving hot, garnish each portion with croûtons. Otherwise, chill thoroughly and sprinkle some finely chopped chives over each serving.

Serves 6.

PEANUT OIL HAND CREAMS

Mix a little peanut oil with an equal quantity of kaolin or Fuller's earth, and a beaten egg yolk. Rub into your hands.

For a protective and nourishing barrier cream, combine equal quantities of beeswax, cocoa butter and peanut oil in the top of a double boiler. Heat until the wax and cocoa butter have melted. Beat well to amalgamate and allow to cool, beating frequently to prevent the mixture from separating.

PEANUT PORK

2 pounds (900 g) lean pork belly
3 tablespoons peanut oil
4 ounces (100–125 g) roasted
    peanuts, very finely chopped or
    ground
4–6 tablespoons soya sauce
Generous pinch of hot ground chilli
    pepper or cayenne

Cut pork up into bite-sized cubes. In a flameproof casserole, brown pork cubes all over in oil, a portion at a time if necessary to avoid overcrowding casserole. Stir in peanuts, soya sauce and hot pepper. Cover casserole tightly and cook gently until pork is quite tender, about 1 hour, stirring frequently and adding a little water if casserole is very dry. Taste for seasoning and serve.

Serves 6–8.

GHANAIAN CHICKEN IN PEANUT SAUCE

This flavoursome stew is locally known as 'Chop'. Serve it like a curry with plain boiled rice, mango chutney and sliced bananas or plantains as accompaniments.

1 3½ pound (1·6 kilo) chicken
6 ounces (175 g) fresh peanuts
½ pint (300 ml) coconut milk
   (page 54)
2 tablespoons peanut oil
1 medium onion, finely chopped
3 large tomatoes, skinned, de-seeded
   and chopped
1 garlic clove, crushed
Salt and freshly ground black pepper
½ teaspoon paprika (optional)
¼ teaspoon ground nutmeg
4 hardboiled eggs, shelled

Joint the chicken into pieces and set aside. Purée the peanuts in a blender or food processor with ¾ pint (300 ml) boiling water. Transfer the purée to a saucepan and simmer gently for about 5 minutes, until the sauce is thick but still liquid. Stir in the coconut milk and set aside.

Heat the oil in a large frying pan and fry the chicken joints until golden brown on all sides. Remove them from the pan with a slotted spoon and set aside. Fry the onion until golden brown, then add the tomatoes and garlic and cook for 2–3 minutes until pulpy, stirring from time to time to prevent the tomato from sticking. Stir in the peanut sauce and season with salt, pepper and the spices.

Bring the sauce to the boil, return the chicken pieces to the pan and simmer, uncovered, for 30–40 minutes, until the chicken pieces are very tender. Stir from time to time.

Five minutes before the end of cooking time, add the hardboiled eggs and spoon over enough sauce to cover them. Serve when the eggs are heated through.

Serves 4–6.

GADO-GADO

2 medium potatoes, peeled, boiled
   and thinly sliced
6 ounces (175 g) white cabbage, finely
   shredded
2 large carrots, peeled, sliced into
   julienne strips, and blanched
8 ounces (225 g) green beans,
   blanched
8 ounces (225 g) bean sprouts,
   washed
1 small cucumber, peeled and diced
6 ounces (175 g) spinach, washed,
   boiled and coarsely chopped
2 large onions, thinly sliced and fried
2 hard-boiled eggs, sliced

Sauce
8 ounces (225 g) roasted, unsalted
   peanuts
2 tablespoons peanut oil
1 small onion, finely chopped
2 cloves garlic, crushed
3 large green chillies, seeded and
   chopped
1 teaspoon brown sugar
Juice of 2 lemons
½ pint (300 ml) coconut milk
   (page 54)
1 teaspoon salt

Prepare the sauce first. Grind the peanuts with a little water to a thick paste in an electric blender or with a pestle and mortar. Leave to one side. Heat the oil in a frying pan until sizzling, then add the onion, garlic and chillies, and cook until slightly browned. Stir in the peanut paste, sugar and lemon juice, and cook for a further minute, stirring constantly. Add the coconut milk, ¼ pint (150 ml) water and the salt. Mix well and allow the mixture to boil. Lower heat and let the sauce simmer, stirring occasionally, until thick and smooth, but still of pouring consistency. Taste, and adjust seasoning with more sugar and salt if necessary. Pour into a small serving bowl or sauceboat and leave to cool.

Just before serving, arrange the prepared vegetables on a large serving platter with the fried onions sprinkled on top. Garnish with slices of hard-boiled egg.

Serves 4. Each person takes a portion of the vegetables, and tops them with a spoonful of the sauce.

CHINESE AUBERGINES IN PEANUT SAUCE

To give this dish an authentic Chinese flavour you will need fresh ginger root and Oriental sesame oil, which is a dark golden brown colour and has a rich, nutty flavour. It is sold in bottles in Chinese groceries and should be used in small amounts mainly as a flavouring, and not a frying, medium.

One 1–1½ pound (450–700 g)
   aubergine
2 cloves garlic, finely chopped
1 slice fresh ginger root, finely
   chopped
2–3 tablespoons peanut or corn oil
2 tablespoons crunchy peanut butter
Salt
½ teaspoon Oriental sesame oil (see
   above)

Peel the aubergine and cut it into large cubes.

In a wok or a large, heavy frying pan with a lid, stir-fry the garlic and ginger in oil for ½ minute, taking care that the garlic does not burn, or it will taste bitter. Add the aubergine cubes and stir-fry for about ½ minute longer.

Blend peanut butter and ½ teaspoon salt with ¼ pint (150 ml) cold water. Stir into aubergine, bring to boiling point, cover and simmer for 6–8 minutes, or until aubergine is tender but not mushy. Correct seasoning with a little more salt if necessary.

Sprinkle with sesame oil, mix well and serve.

Serves 4.

PEANUT BRITTLE

Toast the shelled peanuts lightly and rub off their skins.

Prepare an oiled surface as for a praline (page 13). Then make a rich golden caramel. Stir in the nuts and mix well to distribute them evenly throughout the caramel.

Scrape out on to the oiled surface and if necessary lightly press flat with the back of your spoon.

Leave the slab of brittle to cool and harden before breaking it into pieces.

PEANUT MACAROONS

Peanut oil (optional)
6 ounces (175 g) roasted peanuts
¼ teaspoon salt
1 large egg white
3 ounces (75 g) soft brown sugar, sifted
½ teaspoon vanilla essence

Line 2 or 3 baking sheets with rice paper or use greaseproof paper and grease lightly all over with peanut oil.

Chop the roasted peanuts to a coarse meal by hand, in an electric blender or by putting them through a mincer fitted with a coarse blade. Sprinkle with salt and put aside.

In a large bowl, beat the egg white until it forms soft peaks. Gradually beat in the sifted brown sugar, followed by vanilla essence. Fold in the prepared peanuts.

Arrange heaped teaspoonfuls of the mixture about 1 inch (2·5 cm) apart on the prepared baking sheets. Bake in a slow oven (325°F, 170°C, Mark 3) for 15–20 minutes, or until macaroons are firm to the touch, slightly puffed and lightly coloured.

Crumble off excess rice paper surrounding macaroons and place on a wire cooling rack. Or use a broad palette knife to lift macaroons from greaseproof paper and transfer them to the cooling rack.

INDIAN PEANUT CHUTNEY

This is an unusual chutney to serve with Indian dishes.

4 ounces (100–125 g) roasted peanuts
1 tablespoon finely chopped fresh ginger root
¼ pint (150 ml) plain yoghourt
1 teaspoon sugar
1 teaspoon ground coriander
Salt and cayenne pepper

Put the peanuts, fresh ginger root, yoghourt, sugar and coriander in the goblet of an electric blender or in a food processor. Season with about ½ teaspoon each salt and cayenne pepper. Blend ingredients to a paste. Taste cautiously – chutney will be hot – and add a little more sugar, salt or cayenne if liked.

Spoon into a screw-top jar and store in the refrigerator until ready to serve with an Indian-style meal. The chutney will keep for several days in the refrigerator.

Note: Failing a blender or food processor for grinding the nuts to a paste, a very good chutney can be made with natural coarse-ground peanut butter from a health food shop or wholefood store. This contains no additives apart from a little sea salt, so cut salt by about half.

PEANUT SKILLET SCONE

A last-minute inspiration for teatime on a Sunday afternoon. You will need a deep, heavy frying pan with a lid.

6 ounces (175 g) 81% wholewheat flour
2 teaspoons baking powder
Pinch of salt
2 tablespoons smooth peanut butter
1 teaspoon soft brown sugar
Milk or plain yoghourt, to mix
Peanut or corn oil

Sift flour, baking powder and salt into a bowl – add bran to the flour mixture if it has stayed behind in the sieve. Rub in peanut butter as you would ordinary butter or margarine. Stir in the sugar. With a large, rounded knife blade, stir in enough milk or plain yoghourt (or a mixture of the two, diluted if necessary with a little water) to make a soft dough.

Brush a large frying pan very lightly with a wad of paper dipped in oil and put it on to heat gently, standing it on a wire or asbestos mat for extra protection if it is not very thick.

Turn the scone dough out on to a lightly floured board. Knead it very briefly until smooth, and pat it into a circle that fits the pan – use the lid as a rough guide if necessary.

Drop the round of dough into the frying pan. Pat it out evenly with the palm of your hand if necessary and with the blade of a knife or spatula dipped in flour, mark it into 8 or 10 wedges. Heat the lid until very hot. Fit it on the pan and cook over very low heat for about 20 minutes, or until the scone is lightly browned and crisp underneath, and feels dry to the touch on top.

Gently turn the scone out on to a large, lightly oiled plate and slip it back upside-down into the pan. Continue to cook uncovered until underside of scone is crisp and well-coloured, about 15 minutes longer.

Cool on a wire rack. Serve warm with butter and syrup or jam.

PEAR

The first pears were the small, hard and green fruits of the wild pear tree, which can still be found growing all over Europe and as far east as the Himalayas, and are the ancestors of all the varieties developed since. By Roman times Pliny, that tireless compiler of botanical information, could list thirty-eight varieties of pear and today there are over 3,000, of which only a few, admittedly, are widely cultivated.

Pears, apples and quinces all belong to the same family and can be used together or substituted for each other most successfully.

Like apples, pears can be divided into cooking and eating varieties, and perry (cider) pears. Different varieties mature at different times of the year. One of the best known is the tender, juicy Williams, known as the Bartlett pear in the United States. This develops from pale green to golden yellow when ripe. It can either be eaten as it is or poached in syrup or wine and served warm or cold with thick, chilled cream. Then there is the Conference pear, elongated, thin, and a hard, gritty green, which keeps and cooks well. Finest of all for eating is the Comice pear, which is sweet, aromatic, buttery and tender.

A ripe eating pear yields slightly to finger pressure at the stem end. But pears are best bought before they are completely ripe and left to ripen at home at room temperature. A good trick is to leave them in a brown paper bag together with a ripe apple, which seems to trigger off the ripening process. Cooking pears have a smoother texture if they are picked before they are ripe as their texture tends to coarsen if they ripen on the tree.

A juicy, ripe dessert pear needs no accompaniment or cooking. However, pears that seem unpleasantly hard will be far better if they are first poached briefly in a light sugar syrup with a vanilla pod and a twist of lemon rind or a cinnamon stick.

Pears must be brushed with lemon juice or dropped into a bowl of acidulated water as soon as they have been peeled, as cut surfaces discolour rapidly. A firm cooking pear should be quartered and cored just like an apple, but if it is very soft and ripe all you need do is cut it in half, scoop out the nest of seeds with a pointed teaspoon, then pick out the fibres that run up towards the stem.

The simplest way to preserve pears is to bottle them in light syrup. They are also delicious bottled in spiced vinegar, and turned into preserves. They can be peeled, cored and quartered or sliced, and frozen in a light sugar syrup made from 8 ounces (225 g) sugar to 1 pint (550 ml) water, but they tend to discolour badly when thawed, so quite a lot of lemon juice must be added. Dried pears can be bought in wholefood stores and occasionally whole crystallized pears are included in a box of crystallized fruits.

Medicinally, pears are diuretic and mildly laxative, and infusions of their leaves and flowers help restore bruised or infected tissue.

HAND OR FOOT BATH

Boil 3½ pints (2 litres) water and leave until lukewarm. Add 4 handfuls of fresh pear leaves and/or flowers, cover to protect from dust, and leave to infuse for 4–5 hours. Just before bathing your feet or hands, boil another 3½ pints (2 litres) water, let it stand for 5 minutes, add the original preparation to it and re-heat. Do not boil. Use for not more than 8 minutes.

PEAR SOUP

6 soft, ripe, dessert pears
Lemon juice
¾ pint (400 ml) dry white wine
4 ounces (100–125 g) caster sugar, or
*   to taste*
¼ pint (150 ml) double cream
¼ pint (150 ml) single cream

Peel, halve and core the pears, and scoop out about 18 balls with a melon baller. Sprinkle them with lemon juice and toss lightly to prevent discoloration. Put them aside.

Cut the remaining pears into chunks and put them in a blender with the remaining ingredients. Blend until smooth. Check for sweetness and chill thoroughly.

Serve with pear balls.

Serves 6.

PEAR AND CHEESE SALAD

This is delicious on its own as a light main course or served as an accompaniment to cold roast poultry or ham.

½ pint (300 ml) thick home-made
    mayonnaise (page 205)
Single cream or creamy milk
    (optional)
1 pound (450 g) Emmenthal cheese,
    diced
3 large, ripe, dessert pears, cored and
    diced
6 ounces (175 g) small seedless
    grapes
2 stalks celery, chopped or thinly
    sliced
3–4 ounces (75–100 g) walnuts,
    coarsely chopped
Salt
Crisp lettuce leaves, to garnish

Put mayonnaise in a large mixing bowl and if necessary thin it down to easy mixing consistency with a tablespoon or two of cream or creamy milk. Add the cheese, pears, grapes, celery and walnuts, and mix or toss gently until they are all coated with mayonnaise. Correct seasoning with a little salt if necessary. Serve in a bowl lined with lettuce leaves.

Serves 6.

PEARS, BEANS AND

A traditional German dish from Holstein. The unexpected combination of ingredients works surprisingly well. I like to serve it as a late-summer supper dish, made with fresh fruit and vegetables from the garden.

1 pound (450 g) small, ripe pears
2 pounds (900 g) French beans
About 12 ounces (350 g) smoked
    streaky bacon in one piece
Salt and freshly ground black pepper
Finely chopped parsley, to garnish

Wash pears. Remove stalks but leave fruit whole and unpeeled. Wash beans. Trim off ends and break beans into halves or thirds, depending on size. Cut slab of bacon into

CHEESE GRILLED PEARS

An unusual accompaniment for a hot meat dish such as pork, ham or grilled chicken.

3 slices fat unsmoked bacon
4 ripe, round dessert pears
½ green pepper
2 ounces (50 g) butter
4 tablespoons fine stale breadcrumbs
4 tablespoons freshly grated
    Parmesan

Remove rinds from bacon and grill or fry slices until they are crisp.

Halve the pears lengthwise and core them. Pat the cut surfaces dry and immediately brush them with the drippings from the bacon.

Seed the pepper, remove every scrap of white pith, and dice the flesh finely. In a frying pan, melt the butter. Stir in the diced pepper, breadcrumbs, Parmesan and crumbled bacon, and fry gently over a moderate heat for 2 or 3 minutes.

When ready to serve, arrange the pear halves cut side up in a grill pan. Grill them under moderate heat for 10 minutes, or until they yield slightly to pressure. Spread the cheese mixture evenly over each cut surface, filling the cored cavities as you do so. Continue to grill for 3 or 4 minutes longer until the coating is bubbling and crisp on top.

Serves 6–8.

BACON

large (roughly ¾ inch or 2 cm) cubes.

In a large, flameproof casserole with a tight-fitting lid, sauté bacon cubes gently in butter until they are coloured on all sides and their own fat is running. Stir in beans and pour over about ¾ pint (400 ml) boiling water. Sprinkle with salt and freshly ground black pepper. Lay pears on top.

Bring casserole to simmering point. Cover tightly and cook gently, undisturbed, for about 1 hour until beans and pears are quite tender but not mushy. Top up with a little more water if it evaporates too quickly.

Serve sprinkled with finely chopped parsley.

Serves 4.

CURRIED PEARS

A tasty accompaniment for all kinds of poultry and meat dishes, especially ham.

4 firm, ripe pears
Butter
4 tablespoons soft brown sugar
4 teaspoons curry powder
4 tablespoons chopped hazelnuts or
    other nuts

Wipe pears clean. Halve them lengthwise and scoop out cores, seeds and fibres with a sharp teaspoon, leaving them unpeeled. butter a large, shallow baking dish and arrange pear halves in it, cored side up.

Prepare filling. Blend sugar with curry powder and moisten with 2 ounces (50 g) melted butter. Mix in chopped nuts. Divide evenly between pear halves, pressing filling firmly into hollows.

Bake pears in a moderate oven (350°F, 180°C, Mark 4) for 30 minutes, or until they feel tender when prodded with a skewer. Serve lukewarm.

Serves 4 or 8, depending on their size and your taste.

PEARS IN CREAM

8 firm pears
6–8 tablespoons soft brown sugar
4 ounces (100–125 g) butter
½ pint (300 ml) double cream
3–4 tablespoons milk
3 tablespoons Kirsch
Toasted flaked almonds, to decorate

Peel the pears, quarter them and cut out cores. In a wide, shallow pan or deep frying pan, arrange the pieces in a single layer. Sprinkle with sugar and cover with pieces of butter. Place the pan over moderate heat and cook, shaking the pan gently at frequent intervals, until the sugar has melted and turned into a syrupy caramel.

Add the cream mixed with the milk and Kirsch, and bring to a gentle boil. Let it simmer for a few minutes, shaking the pan frequently, until the sauce thickens.

Pour into a serving dish. Sprinkle with toasted flaked almonds and serve lukewarm.

Serves 6.

SPICED PEAR PIE

A truly old-fashioned family pie. All sorts of spices may be used as a flavouring instead of the nutmeg and cinnamon mixture. Ginger is a great favourite, added in the form of ½ teaspoon ground dried ginger or finely grated fresh ginger root, but if you use it, leave out the orange.

About 1 pound (450 g) rough puff
pastry for a 2-crust 8 or 9 inch (20 or
22·5 cm) pie (page 203)
1½ pounds (700 g) pears
Juice of 1 small lemon
6–7 ounces (175–200 g) granulated
or soft pale brown sugar
4 tablespoons plain flour
¼ teaspoon freshly grated nutmeg
¼ teaspoon ground cinnamon
Generous pinch of salt
Finely grated rind of ½ orange
2 tablespoons orange juice
½–1 ounce (15–25 g) butter
Caster sugar, to decorate

Roll out about half of the pastry and cut out lid for pie, allowing an extra ½ inch (1·25 cm) all round the border. Put aside. Roll out remaining pastry and use it to line an ovenproof pie dish, again with an overlap.

Quarter pears lengthwise. Peel and core them, and slice them about ½ inch (1·25 cm) thick into a bowl. Sprinkle pears with lemon juice, turning them over so they are coated all over to stop them turning brown. In another bowl, blend sugar with flour, spices, salt and grated orange rind. Sprinkle pears with orange juice, followed by the spiced sugar mixture, and mix gently until pieces of pear are evenly coated.

Pile pears in pastry-lined pie dish and dot surface with flakes of butter. Moisten rim of pastry lightly with cold water and fit lid in position. Press lightly to seal edges, then flute or crimp edges neatly all round. Make a few slits or gashes in lid to allow steam to escape.

Bake pie in a hot oven (450°F, 230°C, Mark 8) for the first 10–15 minutes. Then lower temperature (to 350°F, 180°C, Mark 4) and continue to bake pie for about 30 minutes longer, or until it is puffed and golden brown on top, and a piece of pear prodded with a skewer through one of the slits in the lid feels soft.

Remove pie from the oven. Dust generously with caster sugar and cool to lukewarm. Serve with a custard sauce or pouring cream.

Serves 6.

PEARS IN BUTTERSCOTCH SAUCE

Delicious but definitely not for the calorie-conscious.

Juice of 1 lemon
4 ounces (100–125 g) sugar
One 2 inch (5 cm) cinnamon stick
4 firm, round pears
4 scoops vanilla ice cream

Butterscotch sauce
4 ounces (100–125 g) butter
8 ounces (225 g) soft brown sugar
¼ pint (150 ml) single cream
½ pint (300 ml) double cream

Start by preparing a light syrup with 1 pint (550 ml) water, the lemon juice, sugar and cinnamon stick. Bring to boiling point, stirring until sugar has dissolved, and allow to simmer while you prepare pears.

Peel pears. Halve them lengthwise and scoop out 'threads', cores and seeds with a small, sharp spoon. Immediately slip pear halves into simmering syrup. Push a sheet of greaseproof paper down over the top and poach pears gently until they feel quite tender when pierced with a skewer. Allow pears to cool in their syrup and chill lightly in syrup until ready to proceed.

To make butterscotch sauce, melt butter, without letting it sizzle or colour, in a heavy pan. Stir in sugar and, when it has melted, gradually beat in single cream, followed by double cream. Simmer, stirring, for a few minutes until sauce is thick and smooth. Keep hot. If sauce should thicken too much while it is waiting, thin it down again by beating in some of the pear syrup or some more cream if available.

To serve, put a scoop of vanilla ice cream in each of 4 individual glass dishes. Lay 2 poached pear halves on each ball of ice cream and pour some hot butterscotch sauce over the top. Serve remaining sauce in a separate sauceboat.

Serve immediately.

Serves 4.

Note: Some people like to indulge themselves even further by topping each portion with a swirl of unsweetened whipped cream and a pinch of chopped nuts.

PEARS IN CHOCOLATE SAUCE

Also known by the grander name of Poires Belle Hélène. Ideally, soft and juicy ripe pears should be used, in which case they will not need preliminary poaching. If pears are rather hard and woody, first poach them in sugar syrup flavoured with a thin strip of lemon peel and either a piece of vanilla pod or a little vanilla essence, then chill them thoroughly before assembling portions.

6 ripe, round pears (see above)
Lemon juice
6 scoops (about 1 pint or 550 ml)
vanilla ice cream

Chocolate sauce
6 ounces (175 g) bitter dessert
chocolate
1½ ounces (40 g) butter, softened
¼ pint (150 ml) whipping cream, or
half double and half single cream
Vanilla essence, to taste, or 1
tablespoon brandy or rum

Do not start this dish too far ahead of time unless the pears have to be poached and chilled first (see above). If not, peel, halve them lengthwise and core them, dropping them into a bowl of cold water acidulated with lemon juice as you do so to prevent them turning brown while they wait.

Prepare chocolate sauce next. Break chocolate into the top of a double saucepan. Add butter and stir over simmering water until chocolate has melted and is smoothly blended with butter. Beat in cream a little at a time. When sauce is smooth, place top part of pan over direct heat, bring sauce to boiling point, stirring constantly, and simmer, stirring, for 2 or 3 minutes.

Remove from the heat and flavour to taste with a few drops of vanilla essence, or with a tablespoon of brandy or rum.

Assemble individual portions as follows. Drain pear halves and lightly pat them dry with paper towels. Put a large ball of ice cream in each of 6 glass dishes. Press half a pear to opposite sides of each ball of ice cream pointed ends up, and mask with warm chocolate sauce. Serve immediately.

Serves 6.

PEARS IN RED WINE

Use firm, hard pears for this. Conference pears which are ripe but still hard are probably the best. Instead of using red food colouring for the syrup, you can tint it most attractively and at the same time enrich its flavour by adding a few tablespoons of *creme de cassis* (blackcurrant liqueur) or redcurrant jelly. If you are afraid that the pears are not too flavoursome in themselves, dig a whole clove into the rounded (blossom) end of each one. Instead of red wine, port or sherry may be used for poaching the pears, but you will have to adjust the sugar, depending on the sweetness of the wine.

This is an ideal dish to leave overnight in the slow oven of a solid-fuel cooker, or to cook on low in an electric slow-cooker, in which the pears will take about 6 hours to soften.

6 hard pears
Lemon juice
8 ounces (225 g) sugar
One 2 inch (5 cm) cinnamon stick
2 cloves
2 thin strips orange peel
2 thin strips lemon peel
¾ pint (400 ml) red wine
Red food colouring (optional, see above)
Unsweetened whipped cream

Peel the pears, keeping them whole and leaving their stalks intact. As you prepare them, drop them into a large bowl of cold water acidulated with lemon juice to prevent them turning brown.

In a heavy pan, preferably enamelled, dissolve sugar in ¼ pint (150 ml) water. Add cinnamon stick, cloves and strips of orange and lemon peel. Stir in wine, bring to boiling point and simmer for 10 minutes.

Choose a deep, flameproof casserole or pan that will hold the pears upright in a single layer without letting them topple over. Pour over the boiling wine syrup. Cover tightly and either cook over the lowest possible heat or transfer to a slow oven (325°F, 170°C, Mark 3). Cook pears until they feel soft when pierced with a skewer, basting tops occasionally with syrup if necessary. They will take anything from 30 minutes to well over 1 hour, depending on ripeness.

With a slotted spoon, transfer pears to a wide, shallow dish. Boil syrup down rapidly to a medium-light coating consistency. When cooled slightly and spooned down the side of a pear, it should give it an attractive reddish gleam. If the colour of the syrup does not seem bright enough, intensify it with 2 or 3 drops of red food colouring.

Spoon the hot syrup over the pears and continue to baste them several times until they are quite cold. Then chill until ready to serve, with unsweetened, lightly whipped cream.

Serves 6.

BAKED PEARS WITH ORANGE

4 cooking pears
4 ounces (100–125 g) sugar
Long strip of orange peel
Strained juice of 1 orange
4–6 tablespoons Curaçao or other orange liqueur
Whipped cream or pouring cream, to serve

Peel and quarter pears lengthwise, and cut out cores. Lay pears in a wide, shallow, ovenproof casserole with a lid.

In a small pan, dissolve sugar in ¼ pint (150 ml) water over low heat. Add the strip of orange peel, bring to simmering point and pour over pears. Cover casserole and bake in a moderate oven (350°F, 180°C, Mark 4) until pears feel tender when pierced with a skewer, about 30 minutes. Stir in orange juice and allow to cool.

When pears are quite cold, transfer them to a serving bowl with a slotted spoon. Discard the strip of orange peel. Flavour the syrup remaining in the casserole with orange liqueur to taste and pour over pears.

Serve chilled with unsweetened whipped cream or a jug of chilled pouring cream.

Serves 4.

PEAR MARMALADE

5 pounds (2·25 kilos) pears
About 4 pounds (1·8 kilos) sugar
1 vanilla pod, split

Peel and core the pears. Cut them in chunks and put them in a preserving pan. Cover generously with boiling water and boil until pears are soft. Then drain, reserving cooking water. Weigh cooked pears and allow 1 pound (450 g) sugar to every pound (450 g) of fruit pulp.

Put sugar in a preserving pan with about ¼ pint (150 ml) pear water for every pound (450 g) of sugar, and slowly bring to the boil, stirring frequently until sugar has dissolved and skimming off scum from the surface. Add cooked pears and vanilla pod, and boil until setting point is reached, skimming towards the end.

Cool slightly and remove vanilla pod. Pot and cover.

See also page 198.

Fills about 5 jars.

Favourite Fruits and Nuts

PEAR AND APPLE PRESERVE

An unusual, lightly spiced jam that is not only delicious eaten with hot buttered toast or scones but also very good for flavouring and sweetening puddings, especially good spread over baked bread pudding. Apart from that, the jam is an excellent way of using up windfalls and surplus fruit from the garden.

2 pounds (900 g) pears
2 pounds (900 g) cooking apples
Juice and finely grated rind of 2 lemons
½ ounce (15 g) whole cinnamon sticks
3–4 whole cloves
4 pounds (1·8 kilos) sugar
Knob of butter (optional)

Quarter, peel and core the pears and apples, cut them into chunks and sprinkle them with lemon juice to prevent them turning brown.

In a small pan, boil the cinnamon sticks and cloves in 1 pint (550 ml) water for 30 minutes. Strain the water into a preserving pan. Stir in the sugar and heat gently, stirring, until sugar has dissolved.

Add the prepared fruit and all its juices, and the finely grated lemon rind, and bring to the boil. Cook rapidly, skimming off any scum as it forms on the surface, until setting point is reached. Finally, stir in a knob of butter if necessary to clear the jam completely.

Cool slightly. Pot and cover.
See also page 198.

Fills about 4 jars.

BOTTLED PEARS IN CIDER

Hard, ripe pears such as Conference pears are bottled in cider syrup in the same way as apples (see page 21). The only difference is that pears look best if they are left whole, preferably with a short length of stem intact. They are then packed tightly into prepared jars. You will manage to fit in the largest number of pears per jar if you stand the bottom row tightly side by side, stems up, followed by a row with stems pointing downwards, and so on until jar is full. Cover with syrup and bottle as usual (page 201).

PRESERVED PEARS

Hard dessert pears are the best for this simple preserve, which makes a good accompaniment for all kinds of meat, poultry and game.

2 pounds (900 g) sugar
¾ pint (400 ml) white malt vinegar
6 pounds (2·7 kilos) hard pears

In a preserving pan, or a large, preferably enamelled, saucepan, dissolve the sugar in the vinegar over a low heat.

Peel pears but leave them whole. Place them in vinegar syrup. Cover with a sheet of greaseproof paper and simmer very gently until pears feel soft when pierced with a fine skewer or toothpick. If they are not submerged in syrup, baste frequently and carefully turn them over.

When pears are done, draw pan to the side of the stove, cover and allow to stand for 15 minutes (this is to preserve the colour of the fruit). Then pack pears in jars, pour in syrup to within ⅛ inch (3 mm) of the brim and cover tightly.

Fills about 10 jars.

PEARS IN BRANDY

These jars of preserved pears should be prepared at the beginning of October, when pears are in their best condition. They have to be left macerating in syrup and brandy for about three months, which means they will be ready for sampling at Christmas and New Year. Eat them as a sweet with their syrup and chilled, thick, unsweetened cream.

Choose the best, unblemished, ripe pears you can find for this. Williams and Conference pears are both very good, although very different in texture. Quarter pears lengthwise. Peel and core them, and pack them into sterilized jars with screw-top lids.

Make a sugar syrup, allowing 8 ounces (225 g) sugar to every ½ pint (300 ml) water, and simmer for 5 minutes. Cool slightly, then pour over pears to come about one-third of the way up jars. Top up jars with brandy (the cheapest stocked by your local off-licence). Screw on lids, then gently invert jars a few times to mix brandy with sugar syrup.

Store jars away in a cool, dark cupboard for at least 3 months before you taste them. The sugared brandy in which they have been preserved can be drunk as a sweet liqueur or used to add flavour to light sweets and fruit salads. You may also like to experiment with other kinds of alcohol, such as Kirsch.

PECAN

The pecan is a native of the United States and a relatively late addition to the store-cupboards of cooks in other parts of the world. The Indians, who were the first to discover its virtues, used to take supplies of roasted nuts on hunting expeditions and grind them and add them to stews. Its name comes from the Creek and Algonquin word *paccan*, meaning 'nut having hard shell to crack'; in fact, the shells vary considerably in thickness. The thinner-shelled varieties are naturally the most popular.

Two American presidents have gone on record as enthusiasts – some of the trees planted by George Washington in his lovely garden at Mount Vernon more than 150 years ago are still flourishing, and Thomas Jefferson arranged to send many hundreds of pecan nuts to his gardening friends in France. Pecans are now also cultivated in Australia, Israel and South Africa.

The nuts are sold shelled, either salted or roasted and should be stored in a sealed jar so that they don't turn rancid. Pecans are particularly oily. When fried, they should be taken off the heat before they turn too brown, or they will continue cooking in their own internal fat.

Pecans are mostly used in cakes and pastries – pecan pie is a famous traditional recipe in the American South – and can be substituted for walnuts, their close relative.

The nuts contain useful amounts of protein and Vitamin A – and less useful amounts of calories (125 to 1 ounce or 25 g).

MEAT LOAF WITH PECAN STUFFING

An unusual variation on the traditional minced beef loaf. Serve with a spicy tomato sauce.

1 pound (450 g) minced beef
4 ounces (100–125 g) green pepper, seeded and finely chopped
2 small onions, finely chopped
1 teaspoon salt
1 tablespoon Worcestershire sauce
12 ounces (350 g) wholemeal breadcrumbs
½ pint (300 ml) milk
2 eggs
2 ounces (50 g) butter
2 large sticks celery, coarsely chopped
Freshly ground black pepper
½ pint (300 ml) stock
4 ounces (100–125 g) shelled pecan nuts, coarsely chopped

Grease a 2 pound (900 g) loaf tin.

In a large mixing bowl, blend the minced beef, green pepper, onions, salt, Worcestershire sauce, half the breadcrumbs, milk and one of the eggs. Mix thoroughly. Place *half* this mixture in the bottom of the prepared loaf tin.

In another bowl, mix together the remaining egg, the butter, the rest of the breadcrumbs, the celery, pepper, stock and chopped pecans. Spread this pecan stuffing on top of the meat mixture in the loaf tin.

Put the remaining meat mixture on the top of the pecan stuffing, and smooth over the top with a knife. Bake in a moderate oven (350°F, 180°C, Mark 4) for 1 hour, until firm and well browned. Allow to cool slightly before turning out of the tin, then slice and serve with a hot, spicy, tomato sauce, and vegetables.

Serves 6.

OLD-FASHIONED AMERICAN PECAN PIE

About 8 ounces (225 g) shortcrust pastry for a 9 inch (22·5 cm) pastry case (page 203)

Filling
6–8 ounces (175–225 g) pecan kernels
1 pound (450 g) soft pale brown sugar
3 tablespoons plain flour
¼ teaspoon salt
¼ pint (150 ml) milk
1½ teaspoons vanilla essence
3 eggs
3 ounces (75 g) butter, melted

Line a 9 inch (22·5 cm) pie dish or deep tart tin with shortcrust pastry and crimp rim attractively.

Cover unbaked pastry with pecan kernels, arranged closely in concentric circles.

In a bowl or large jug, blend sugar with flour and salt. Heat milk to boiling point and with a wooden spoon or hand whisk, beat it vigorously into sugar mixture. Beat in vanilla essence.

Beat eggs lightly. Gradually beat them into filling mixture, followed by the cooked, melted butter. Pour sugar filling gently over pecans, taking care not to disturb them.

Bake pie in a hot oven (450°F, 230°C, Mark 8) for the first 15 minutes, then turn heat down (325°F, 170°C, Mark 3) and continue to bake for about 45 minutes longer, or until filling is set and crusty on top, and pastry rim looks crisp and a rich golden colour. Cool to lukewarm before serving.

Serves 8.

PECAN CHERRY CAKE

3 ounces (75 g) pecans
3 ounces (75 g) glacé cherries
3 eggs, beaten
6 ounces (175 g) butter
6 ounces (175 g) caster sugar
8 ounces (225 g) self-raising flour
Pinch of salt
1–2 tablespoons milk or whisky

Roughly chop the pecans; rinse and dry, then halve the cherries.

Beat together the butter and sugar until light and fluffy, then whisk in the beaten eggs a little at a time, beating well between each addition.

Sift together the flour and salt and toss the pecans and cherries in 2 tablespoons of this, then fold in the rest of the flour a third at a time. Lastly, add the pecans, cherries and milk or whisky and stir lightly.

Turn the mixture into a greased, lined cake tin, 7 inches (18 cm) in diameter, and bake in a moderate oven (350°F, 180°C, Mark 4) for 1–1¼ hours, or until a skewer inserted into the centre of the cake comes out clean.

PECAN BISCUITS

4 tablespoons clear honey
4 tablespoons sunflower oil
2 eggs, beaten
2 tablespoons milk
½ teaspoon salt
½ teaspoon dried fennel seeds, crushed
1 pound (450 g) wholemeal flour
8 ounces (225 g) shelled pecan nuts, coarsely ground
6 ounces (175 g) seedless raisins, chopped

Grease a large baking tray.

In a large mixing bowl, blend the honey, oil and eggs thoroughly. Gradually stir in the milk, then add the salt and crushed fennel seeds. Mix together the flour, nuts and raisins in another bowl. Then fold this bowlful carefully into the wet ingredients, to form a stiff dough. If the dough is too thick add a little more milk and if too sticky add a bit more flour.

Turn the dough onto a floured board, and roll out until about ¼ inch (6 mm) thick. Using a floured pastry cutter, cut out discs about 2 inches (5 cm) in diameter, and arrange these on the prepared baking tray. Bake in a moderate oven (350°F, 180°C, Mark 4) for 15 minutes or until golden-brown. They will be slightly soft to touch, hardening as they cool.

PECAN BALLS

Serve these small balls with ice cream – they're particularly good with either vanilla or chocolate flavours.

4 ounces (100–125 g) butter
2 tablespoons caster sugar
1 teaspoon vanilla essence
4 ounces (100–125 g) pecans
4 ounces (100–125 g) plain flour
2 ounces (50 g) icing sugar

Beat together the butter, sugar and vanilla essence until light and fluffy. Grind the pecans as finely as you like, or finely chop them. Stir the chopped nuts into the butter mixture. Sift the flour into the mixture and work to a stiff paste.

Roll into about 30 small balls and place them on greased baking sheets.

Bake in a moderate oven (350°F, 180°C, Mark 4) for about 12 minutes, then sift the icing sugar over and continue baking for about 5 minutes just to glaze.

Cool on a wire rack and store in an airtight container.

CREAMY PECAN NOUGAT

3 egg whites
1½ pounds (700 g) sugar
8 ounces (225 g) glucose
1½ pounds (700 g) shelled pecans, chopped
A few drops of vanilla essence

Prepare a large baking tin, about 15 inches (37·5 cm) square and about 1 inch (2·5 cm) deep, by lining with rice paper. In a large bowl whisk the egg whites until stiff.

Place 6 ounces (175 g) of the sugar and ¼ pint (150 ml) water in a small saucepan. Put the pan over a moderate heat and stir until the sugar dissolves. Bring to the boil and allow to cook until the temperature reaches 250°F (120°C). (Use a sugar thermometer to determine this, or drop a small sample of the syrup into a saucer of cold water. It should harden immediately and be very brittle.) Remove the pan from the heat.

Pour the hot syrup onto the egg whites, beating all the time. Leave on one side.

Put the remaining sugar, another ¼ pint (150 ml) water and the glucose in a saucepan, over a moderate heat. Stir until the sugar and glucose dissolve, then allow to boil until the temperature reaches 260°F (125°C). Remove the pan from the heat. Pour the hot glucose and sugar syrup onto the egg white mixture, stirring constantly. Then fold in the pecan nuts and vanilla essence. Allow to cool.

Turn the mixture into the prepared baking tin. Press down well and smooth over the surface with a knife. Put another piece of rice paper on top then a wooden board on top to weigh the nougat down. Leave overnight. The next day, remove the board, turn out the nougat and cut into squares. Store the squares in an airtight container ready for use.

SAVOURY PECAN ROLLS

Serve these with creamy soups.

Slice a close-textured brown or wholemeal loaf (a few minutes in the freezer will make this easier). Butter generously and trim away crusts. Sprinkle with chopped pecans and grind over a little coarse salt. Roll up from the short end, stopping and cutting halfway. You should get 2 or 4 from each bread slice – depending on size.

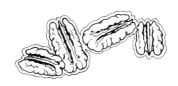

PERSIMMON

Just when you think you have had the best of summer's offerings, a mysterious fruit, looking like a rather squashed yellow tomato, begins to come on to the market. This is the persimmon, also known by the more romantic names of Sharon fruit or fruit of Sharon.

Persimmons were originally cultivated widely in China and Japan. Nowadays they are grown all over the temperate world, in the United States and especially throughout the southern Mediterranean. Several different species of different shapes and sizes are grown, some smooth and round, some pendulous and faintly ribbed, seeded or seedless.

The actual fruit is a berry, which matures and ripens in late autumn, often after the first frosts, when most of the leaves have withered and fallen off the tree. In some places it is thought that a touch of frost actually helps the fruit to ripen, but this varies according to species. But persimmons must be completely ripe before they can be eaten. Until then, their high tannic content, which gradually disappears as they ripen, literally sets the teeth on edge. Once the fruit is fully ripe, however, it becomes sweet and aromatic, with a delightful, jelly-like texture.

This state of edible ripeness lasts for only a short time, and is followed rapidly by deterioration. Because of this, persimmons are usually sold before they are ripe enough to eat. Left at home at room temperature, it will be several days before they are ready. Admittedly, they will seem less attractive on the surface and look decidedly squashy and discoloured, but this is as they should be.

Ripe persimmons are very good to serve raw on their own at breakfast. Slit the skin and ease it back to expose the pulp, which can be scooped out with a small spoon. The puréed pulp also makes an interesting alternative to apple sauce with meat and poultry. Persimmons freeze very well, either as whole fruits or a purée; just put them in the freezer.

Finally, persimmons are also excellent sliced and eaten with other fruit such as pineapple or added to mixed seasonal fruit salads. If you want to spark them up with a little alcohol, rum and Kirsch are particularly good.

The persimmon's medicinal properties are appreciated by both the Chinese and the American Indians. The former dry the calyx and use it as a remedy for fevers, etc, and a tea rich in Vitamin C can be made from the leaves.

REMEDIES

As might be expected, both the Chinese and the American Indians have long appreciated the medicinal qualities of the persimmon.

The Chinese use the dried calyx as a remedy for fevers, coughs, colds, catarrh and asthma: infused with crushed, dried ginger and a few cloves, it will help cure hiccups.

The American Indians make a tea from the leaves (dried are better than fresh) which is pleasant tasting and high in Vitamin C.

PERSIMMON FLUFF

3 ripe persimmons
1 tablespoon powdered gelatine
4 ounces (100–125 g) sugar
3 tablespoons lemon juice
1 teaspoon vanilla essence
2 egg whites
Pinch of salt
¼ pint (150 ml) whipping cream

Stem and cut persimmons in halves or quarters. Scoop out pulp and rub it through a fine nylon sieve to trap seeds. Measure purée. There should be 8 fluid ounces (225 ml) or a little more — up to, say, ½ pint (300 ml).

In a cup, sprinkle gelatine over 4 tablespoons cold water and leave to soften. At the same time, in a heavy pan, stir sugar with another 4 tablespoons water over low heat until dissolved. Place cup of softened gelatine in a pan of very hot water and stir until quite clear and liquid. Blend dissolved gelatine with hot syrup and add lemon juice. Cool slightly and mix thoroughly with persimmon purée and vanilla. Mixture should be strongly flavoured. Add more lemon juice or sugar (preferably icing or caster sugar) if necessary. Leave until cold, then chill until syrupy and on the point of setting.

Beat egg whites with a pinch of salt until stiff but not dry. Beat cream separately until it thickens and stands in floppy peaks.

Finally, beat persimmon purée until light and frothy.

Fold cream into persimmon purée, followed by stiffly beaten egg whites. Pile into a glass serving bowl and chill until set. Serve with delicate sweet biscuits.

Serves 6–8.

PERSIMMON ICE CREAM

For this recipe use large, sweet persimmons that are so ripe they are like jelly.

3 large, ripe persimmons (see above)
About 6 tablespoons caster sugar
2 tablespoons lemon juice
½ pint (300 ml) double cream
¼ pint (150 ml) single cream

Stem and cut persimmons in half. Scoop out pulp and rub it through a nylon sieve, eliminating seeds. Sweeten pulp and flavour with lemon juice. Remember that freezing weakens flavours and a large amount of cream still has to be added, so flavour of pulp should be quite pronounced. Add sugar or lemon juice if necessary.

Mix creams together and beat just enough to thicken them. Mix lightly with persimmon pulp. Pour into ice-cube trays or a wide, shallow box. Cover tightly with foil or a lid, and freeze ice cream until it is solid around sides but still soft in the middle.

Scrape ice cream out into a bowl and, using an electric hand mixer if available, beat vigorously until mixture is quite smooth and creamy again. Pour back into container(s), cover and freeze until firm.

Transfer to main cabinet of refrigerator to soften slightly and allow flavours to develop, about 1 hour.

Serves 4–6.

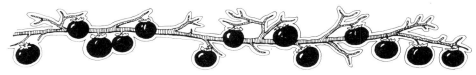

PERSIMMON WATER ICE

Persimmons have a very high water content, yet freeze very well. This must be the easiest, quickest water ice in the world.

Take ripe persimmons and put them in the freezer, just as they are or in the form of a pulp. Freeze them hard, then thaw very slightly before serving.

The freezing process breaks down any remaining traces of tannic acid, leaving the iced fruit perfectly sweet and mellow.

PERSIMMON PIE

Persimmons can be used to make a deliciously different pie filling. Be sure though to select fruit that is ripe and juicy.

One 9 inch (22·5 cm) shortcrust pastry
  case, pre-baked (page 203)
3 ripe persimmons
6 ounces (175 sugar
Juice and grated rind of 1 lemon
½ teaspoon ground cinnamon
Unsweetened whipped cream

Wash the persimmons, remove the stems, quarter and scoop out the pulp. Rub the pulp through a fine sieve (or place in a blender) to form a purée. Meanwhile, prepare a syrup by dissolving the sugar in ¼ pint (150 m) water and boiling this mixture for 15 minutes. Add the sugar syrup, lemon rind and juice and cinnamon to the persimmon purée, and blend thoroughly.

Fill the pastry case with the fruit mixture and top with whipped cream.

Chill before serving.

Serves 6.

TRADER VIC'S PERSIMMONS WITH RUM

4 large, ripe persimmons
6 tablespoons rum (medium or dark)
2 ounces (50 g) soft light brown sugar
4 tablespoons sour cream

Pull off persimmon stems and cut each persimmon in half lengthwise. Arrange 2 halves, cut side up, on each of 4 individual plates. Sprinkle them with rum and sugar, and spoon sour cream over the top. Serve with small spoons with which to scoop out the pulp.

Serves 4.

Note: If sour cream is not available, top the persimmon halves with a little fresh plain yoghourt, beaten with a fork until smooth.

REMEDY

Bromeline, the enzyme that makes pineapple good to eat after a rich meal, is also useful in other ways. To remove warts, either rub them with the juice, or put a piece of fruit over the wart and hold in place with a bandage or piece of cloth.

CUTICLE SOFTENER

Pineapple's 'digestive' or softening action is utilized in this cuticle lotion.

Combine 2 tablespoons fresh pineapple juice with 2 tablespoons egg yolk and ½ teaspoon cider vinegar. Soak nails for half an hour.

PINEAPPLE AND BANANA DRINK

A welcome change from the usual breakfast glass of orange or grapefruit juice.

¾ pint (400 ml) unsweetened
pineapple juice
1 large ripe banana
Grated nutmeg

Chill the pineapple juice thoroughly. Peel the banana and slice it into chunks. In an electric blender, whirl the two together until smooth.

Divide between 6 small glasses. Sprinkle each glass with a tiny pinch of nutmeg and serve immediately.

Serves 6.

PINEAPPLE

Of all the fruits that came to us from the tropics of the New World, pineapples are undoubtedly among the finest. Christopher Columbus is thought to have found them on the island of Guadeloupe in the early 1490s. In an attempt to give people in Europe some idea of the flavour of this magnificent new fruit, one of his crew described its taste as a combination of melon, wild strawberries, raspberries and apples.

For centuries pineapples were a symbol of great luxury. Their exotic form apppears sculpted in the stonework of grand houses, but only kings and the cream of the aristocracy could hope to taste the fruit itself. In Europe, the first home-grown pineapple was offered to Charles II of England by the Duchess of Cleveland in 1672. Not to be outdone, the gardeners of Louis XIV succeeded in growing pineapples in the hothouses at Versailles. This situation remained unchanged until the end of the nineteenth century, when canning techniques were perfected. Indeed, the canning of pineapples has been one of the great success stories of this process, so much so that, faced with a choice between the unripe fresh fruit and the canned version, even growers actually preferred the latter. Today, canned pineapple is available in a variety of forms: sliced and cored, cubed, cut in sticks or crushed, packed in a light syrup or its own natural juice. We have had crystallized or candied pineapple pieces for a long time and cartons of pure pineapple juice are almost as popular as the ubiquitous orange and grapefruit. It is excellent drunk on its own, lightly chilled, or as a fruit cocktail mixed with other juices. Fresh pineapples are also widely available.

A ripe, fresh pineapple will be very fragrant and heavy with juice, with a crown of spiky green leaves that are fresh and unwithered, and offer little resistance when you tug at them with your fingers. Under its tough, horny skin, a ripe fruit yields slightly to finger pressure. Turn it over and examine its underside closely for brown spots; this is where decay usually starts.

When the pineapple is cut open, its golden flesh has a hard, woody core running lengthwise through the centre. This becomes tough and quite inedible as the fruit ripens, and must be cut out of halved or quartered fruit, or stamped out of slices with a small, plain, round cutter.

A fresh pineapple can be served on the half- or quarter-shell, or peeled and cut in pieces. For the former, first rinse and dry the fruit, together with its crown of leaves. With a sharp, pointed knife cut it in half from middle to base. Then turn the pineapple round and finish halving it, cutting through the crown of leaves. Finally, cut the flesh from the shell, leaving the latter about ½ inch (1·25 cm) thick.

To peel a pineapple, first tug out the tuft of leaves at the top, holding them together tightly (this tuft makes an attractive house plant if you trim any stray pineapple flesh from the bottom and root it in a flowerpot of potting compost or even ordinary garden soil). With a serrated knife take a thin slice from the top and bottom of the pineapple so that it will stand steady. Then, holding it firmly on its base, cut off the skin as far as the middle in thick, downward slices. Turn it upside down and peel off the rest of the skin in the same way. With the point of your knife, gouge out all the little brown 'pines' that remain. Then halve, quarter or slice the pineapple and core it as usual.

Pineapples are best frozen dry; peel them and cut into slices or chunks.

Fresh ripe pineapple is delicious eaten as it is with a sprinkling of sugar and a few drops of Kirsch. Fresh uncooked pineapple contains an enzyme (*bromeline*) which has a digestive effect similar to that of the better known *papain* in papayas, though not so strong. This makes it an excellent fruit to eat raw at the end of a rich meal – cooking will destroy the enzyme. But pineapple can be served at any stage of a meal. Serve pineapple chunks on cocktail sticks with cheese with drinks, thread them on to skewers with pieces of chicken and squares of green pepper to make colourful kebabs, and add them, fresh, candied or canned, to cakes and sweets of all kinds. Don't forget, though, that the *bromeline* will prevent any food recipes ,containing gelatine from setting (you will have to cook the pineapple first).

CHICKEN WITH PINEAPPLE CHINESE STYLE

This may not be an authentically Chinese dish but it is quite delicious nevertheless, and should be served with plain boiled rice.

1 chicken, about 2½ pounds (1·1 kilos)
5 tablespoons soya sauce
1 tablespoon dry sherry
About 1 pint (550 ml) peanut or corn oil
1 can (15½ ounce or 440 g) pineapple rings in natural juice
1 large onion
2 tablespoons raisins
½ tablespoon sesame oil
1 tablespoon cornflour

Wash the chicken and pat it dry both inside and out. Lay it in a deep dish. Rub it all over with a mixture of soya sauce and sherry, and pour the remainder over the top. Leave the chicken to marinate in this mixture for about 1 hour, turning it occasionally.

In a heavy casserole that will hold the chicken comfortably, heat 1 inch (2·5 cm) oil. While the oil is heating, drain the chicken thoroughly, reserving the marinade. When the oil is hot enough to sizzle when a few drops of water are shaken into it, lay the chicken in the hot oil, lower the heat and fry until golden brown all over. Meanwhile, drain the pineapple rings, reserving the juice, and cut each ring into 10 chunks. Chop the onion into slightly smaller chunks.

When the chicken is well coloured, transfer it to a plate. Pour off all but 3 tablespoons oil and fry the onion chunks for 30 seconds, stirring and scraping the bottom and sides of the casserole with a wooden spoon.

Stir in the reserved marinade and pineapple juice. Turn the chicken over in this mixture, cover the casserole and simmer for 30 minutes, or until the chicken is very tender, turning it occasionally.

Remove chicken from casserole and cut the meat into chunks. Keep warm. Add pineapple and raisins to casserole, and simmer for 5 minutes. Stir in the sesame oil and cornflour blended with 1 tablespoon cold water, and simmer, stirring, for 2 or 3 minutes until sauce has thickened and is no longer cloudy.

Return the chicken to the casserole. Reheat gently and serve.

Serves 4.

ROAST PINEAPPLE

A delicious and unusual way of presenting a fresh pineapple hot. It is said to originate with the Indians of North America.

1 fresh pineapple
2 tablespoons liquid (clear) honey

Shorten pineapple leaves if necessary. Slice it in half lengthwise from top to bottom and with the point of a knife score the flesh deeply criss-cross fashion. Lay the pineapple halves in a baking dish and spoon a tablespoon of honey over each half

Roast the pineapple in a moderately hot oven (400°F, 200°C, Mark 6) for 20–30 minutes until bubbling on top. Cut each pineapple half in 2 or 3 lengthwise, depending on size, and serve hot.

Serves 4–6.

Note: Another good topping for the pineapple is a sprinkling of soft brown sugar and a few flakes of butter. Roast until bubbling.

FRUIT IN A BLANKET

One of Robert Carrier's brilliantly simple recipes, created by accident when he forgot to grill a dish of crème brûlée which was waiting in the refrigerator, ready for a dinner party.

3 large, thin-skinned oranges
3 slices fresh pineapple
Orange juice and Kirsch
1 pint (550 ml) double cream
½ pound (225 g) soft brown sugar

Carefully peel the oranges, stripping off all the white pith, and slice them thinly crosswise, discarding any pips. Quarter the pineapple slices. Arrange the fruit in overlapping slices in a deep, wide serving dish. Sprinkle with orange juice and Kirsch, to taste.

Whisk the cream until soft peaks form. Pile it on the fruit and smooth it out evenly with a spatula. Sprinkle top evenly with a layer of sugar about ⅛ inch (3 mm) thick. Chill until ready to serve.

Serves 6.

PINE AND APPLE SALAD

3 slices fresh pineapple
4 crisp dessert apples
2 tablespoons lemon juice
4 tablespoons dry or medium sherry
3–4 tablespoons caster sugar
2 tablespoons flaked or slivered toasted almonds, to decorate

Slice off skin from pineapple slices. Cut out central cores if woody, and cut pineapple into individual bite-sized chunks. Place in a bowl. Quarter, core and peel apples, dice them and add them to bowl. Sprinkle with lemon juice and toss until apples are thoroughly coated to prevent discoloration. Sprinkle with sherry and sugar to taste. Toss again and allow to stand for a little while before serving with toasted almonds sprinkled over the top.

Serves 6.

PINEAPPLE CREAM

An unusual recipe to find in a Victorian cookery book, making use of even the peelings of what was a precious fruit. From Mrs Bowman's New Cookery Book (1867).

'Boil the rind of a pine-apple, cut in pieces, in a quarter of a pint of milk for half an hour (add more milk if it all evaporates too quickly); then strain it, and add a pint of thick cream, three ounces of sugar, and a teaspoonful of lemon-juice (or a little more, to taste); thicken for ten minutes over the fire, and when cool, whisk into froth, and fill glasses.'

PINEAPPLE AMBROSIA

3 ounces (75 g) desiccated coconut
Caster sugar
1 ripe pineapple, about 2 pounds
  (900 g)
4 sweet, juicy oranges

In a bowl, moisten coconut shreds with ¼ pint (150 ml) hot water and put aside to soak for 30 minutes. Then drain off excess moisture in a sieve, squeezing shreds as dry as possible. Toss with 3 or 4 tablespoons caster sugar.

Cut off leafy crown of pineapple. With a razor-sharp, pointed knife, peel pineapple and cut out the brown 'pines'. Working on a board or plate to catch any juices, lay pineapple on its side and slice it thinly. Cut out core.

Peel oranges and cut away the tough membrane under the skin and the white pith. Again working on a board or plate, lay each orange on its side and slice thinly. Discard any pips.

Arrange a layer of pineapple slices in a large glass bowl. Sprinkle with sugared coconut. Follow with a layer of orange slices and more sugared coconut. Continue until all the fruits have been used up, ending with the remaining coconut. Sprinkle with pineapple and orange juices.

Cover the bowl and chill lightly for a couple of hours before serving.

To serve, place the pineapple crown on top.

Serves 4–6.

PINEAPPLE JELLY

Another recipe from Mrs Bowman's *New Cookery Book.* Obviously the author had discovered that raw pineapple contained an enzyme (if that is how she would describe it) that prevents setting unless it is first boiled. Use ordinary powdered gelatine instead of the isinglass, following the usual procedure of first softening it in a few tablespoons of cold water. Taste the juice and dilute it with less water if its flavour is too weak.

'Cut a fresh pine in slices; cover them with powdered sugar, and leave them a few hours; then pour off, and strain to obtain a pint of the syrup (the juice will flow more readily if the pineapple is first crushed in an electric blender or food processor – or you could start with a can or pack of unsweetened pineapple juice, sweetened to taste). Dissolve an ounce of isinglass in a pint of water and clarify it; pour it over the syrup and simmer five minutes over the fire; add a glass of Curaçao, and pour into a mould shaped like a pineapple. It will require to be very carefully turned out, and will then be very elegant.'

PINEAPPLE UPSIDE-DOWN CAKE

A spectacular cake, simple to make once you know how.

Butter
3 ounces (75 g) soft pale brown sugar
1 large can (16 ounces or 450 g)
  pineapple rings, or about 8 slices
  fresh pineapple, cored
6–8 tablespoons desiccated coconut
  or 8 glacé cherries (see method)

Cake batter
6 ounces (175 g) butter
6 ounces (175 g) caster sugar
6 ounces (175 g) plain flour
1½ teaspoons baking powder
Pinch of salt
3 eggs
½–¾ teaspoon real almond essence
Milk (optional)

Start by preparing a baking tin. Grease a deep 8 or 9 inch (20 or 22·5 cm) square tin all over with butter. Line base with a square of baking parchment or greaseproof paper and grease that as well. In a small, heavy pan, melt 4 ounces (100–125 g) butter without letting it sizzle. Add soft brown sugar and stir vigorously with a wooden spoon. Butter and sugar may to some extent remain separate. Pour this mixture into the prepared baking tin and spread it out evenly with the back of your spoon. Put aside while you finish topping and make the cake.

Cut each slice of pineapple in four. Arrange wedges in rows on sugar topping in tin. Sprinkle thickly with desiccated coconut and any remaining pineapple juice (if using canned pineapple, sprinkle coconut with a couple of tablespoons syrup from the can). Alternatively, arrange whole pineapple rings over base of baking tin and plug the cored-out middle of each ring with a glacé cherry.

To make cake, cream butter and sugar together until fluffy. Sift flour with baking powder and salt. Beat eggs until light and lemon-coloured. Beat a good tablespoon of flour mixture into the butter and sugar, then gradually add beaten eggs, beating well between each addition. Beat in almond essence. Fold in remaining flour to make a soft, dropping batter. If it is very stiff, you can thin it down a little with 2 or 3 tablespoons milk. Spoon batter into cake tin and level off top with your spoon.

Bake cake in a moderate oven (350°F, 180°C, Mark 4) for about 45 minutes, or until a skewer pushed down through middle of cake feels dry to the touch. Leave to cool for 5 minutes. Then slip a knife blade round sides of cake to loosen them if necessary, place a large, flat serving platter on top and invert cake tin on to it. Carefully remove tin and peel off lining paper if still attached.

Serve lukewarm, with a bowl of very lightly sweetened whipped cream if desired.

Serves 8.

PINE-APRICOT JAM

An unusual jam specially for city-dwellers, who may not have access to large quantities of conventional soft fruits but are more likely to find good-quality fresh pineapples going cheap in the local street market or supermarket. The apricots need not be high-quality plump ones.

1 medium, ripe pineapple
1 pound (450 g) dried apricots
Juice of 3 lemons
1 tablespoon finely grated lemon rind
4 pounds (1·8 kilos) sugar

Working on a board or over a plate to catch all the juices, carefully peel pineapple. Quarter it lengthwise, cut out woody core and chop pineapple into small pieces. Drain off all the juices into a measuring jug.

Cut dried apricots in pieces and wash them thoroughly in cold water.

Put in a bowl. Pour in pineapple juice made up to 1 pint (550 ml) with water, plus another 2 pints (1·1 litres) water, and soak overnight.

The following day, pour contents of bowl into a preserving pan. Stir in lemon juice and rind, bring to boiling point and simmer until apricots are quite soft. If pieces of pineapple are on the large side, shred them with a sharp knife or by whizzing briefly in an electric blender or food processor. Stir into the apricots, followed by the sugar, and continue to stir over low heat until sugar has quite dissolved. Then raise heat, bring to boiling point and boil briskly until setting point is reached. Towards the end of cooking time, skim surface clear of scum.

Pot and cover as usual.

See also page 198.

Fills about 6 jars.

CRYSTALLIZED PINEAPPLE CHUNKS

1 large, ripe, firm pineapple
1½ pounds (700 g) granulated sugar
4 ounces (100—125 g) caster sugar

Peel the pineapple and cut across into slices about ½ inch (1·25 cm) thick. Cut each slice in half, remove the core and then divide the remaining fruit into approximately ½ inch (1·25 cm) cubes. Place the cubes in a medium saucepan, and pour boiling water over to cover.

Place the pan over a moderate heat and cook gently until the pineapple is just tender. Remove the fruit, using a slotted spoon, and place it in a large bowl.

Drain off ½ pint (300 ml) of the cooking water into another pan (discard the remainder). Stir in 6 ounces (175 g) of the granulated sugar and bring this mixture to the boil, stirring frequently. Remove from the heat and pour the syrup over the pineapple. Cover the bowl with a cloth and leave for 24 hours.

After 24 hours, drain off all the syrup into a small saucepan. Add 2 ounces (50 g) granulated sugar, stir to dissolve, bring the mixture to the boil and pour back over the pineapple in

the bowl. Re-cover the bowl and leave for a further 24 hours. Repeat this last process 5 times more. Then repeat once using 3 ounces (75 g) sugar, and leave the fruit to soak in the syrup for 48 hours. Finally, dissolve 3 ounces (75 g) sugar in the drained syrup, bring the mixture to the boil, and pour over the pineapple. Leave the fruit to soak for 4 days. Uncover the bowl and discard any liquid.

Line a baking tray with waxed paper. Arrange the crystallized pineapple chunks on the tray. Turn the oven to its lowest setting. Place the tray of crystallized fruit in the oven for 2—3 hours, until the chunks are dry, turning the fruit several times.

When the fruit is dry, put the caster sugar in a small bowl. Bring about 1 pint (600 ml) water to the boil in a medium saucepan. Plunge each chunk, one at a time, on the end of a fork into the boiling water. Remove immediately, shake off any excess water and dip the fruit in the caster sugar to coat. Return the fruit chunks to the lined baking tray. Leave for several hours, before eating or storing in a sealed glass jar.

PINA COLADA

An unusual, refreshing drink from Puerto Rico.

Per person:
8 ounces (225 g) fresh pineapple
2 fluid ounces (50 ml) light rum
2 fluid ounces (50 ml) thick coconut milk (page 54)
1 tablespoon crushed ice
1 Maraschino cherry, to decorate

Crush the pineapple to extract the juice, preferably in an electric juice extractor (or use an electric blender), then strain off the juice from the pulp. Place the juice, rum, coconut milk and ice in an electric blender and blend thoroughly. Pour into a tall, chilled glass, decorate with cherry, and serve.

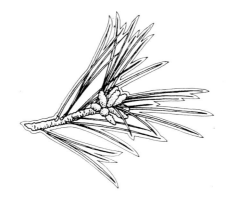

PINE NUT

Although the seeds of several pines are edible, the pine nuts sold in delicatessens and specialist shops come mainly from the stone pine, a familiar and picturesque constituent of the Mediterranean coastal landscape with its dark green umbrella-shaped crown, cracked scaly bark and huge glossy brown cones. Since Roman times it has been widely planted along the Mediterranean coast from Spain to the Lebanon.

Pine nuts (also known as pine kernels and Indian nuts) have been used in Italy for centuries — at least since the first century AD. Called *pignoli, pinoli* or *pinocchio*, depending on the region, the nuts are traditionally used in soups, stews and ragoûts, and as a basic ingredient in that fragrant basil and garlic sauce for pasta called *pesto*.

In Spain, particularly in the Balearics, they are minced, chopped, or ground to a paste to flavour sauces; and in France, where pine nuts are known as *pignons*, they are occasionally used in the cooking of Provence in the south, and the Landais.

Pine nuts are high in protein and fat, and comparatively low in carbohydrates. Because of their high fat content they soon turn rancid and should be used quickly. Store them in a cool place in an airtight jar.

PINE NUT SOUP

8 ounces (225 g) pine nuts
¾ pint (450 ml) creamy milk
½ pint (300 ml) chicken stock
2 spring onions, thinly sliced
1 sprig mint
Pinch of ground coriander
Salt and freshly ground black pepper
Finely chopped parsley and/or
  chives, to garnish

In a large, heavy pan, combine pine nuts with milk, chicken stock, spring onions and mint. Season with coriander and a pinch each of salt and freshly ground black pepper. Bring to boiling point and simmer with the lid half on, stirring occasionally, until nuts are very soft, 25–30 minutes. Discard mint sprig.

Rub contents of pan through a sieve or the medium disc of a vegetable mill, or purée in an electric blender or food processor. Return to pan and correct seasoning. (If flavour of soup is too strong, dilute with a little more milk.)

Either serve soup hot or allow it to cool, then chill thoroughly before serving, garnished with finely chopped fresh parsley and/or chives. Serve in small portions as soup is very rich.

Serves 4–5.

PINE ESSENCE

For a glorious-smelling addition to your bath, fill a muslin, fine cotton or cheesecloth bag with pine needles. Infuse the bag in boiling water and pour the liquid into the bath, or simply hang the bag under the hot tap.

This essence is good for the skin and heart, and generally stimulating to the system.

PINE AND HERB PILLOW

To make a fresh-smelling herb pillow, crush together two parts dried pine needles, one part each dried rosemary (or lavender) and dried lemon balm, and a pinch of powdered orris root. Enclose the mixture in a linen or cambric case.

LEBANESE RAGOUT WITH PINE NUTS

Pine nuts transform this stew. If they are not available, substitute coarsely chopped skinned hazelnuts or walnuts. In winter, when fresh tomatoes have little flavour, use a couple of 14 ounce (400 g) cans of Italian peeled tomatoes instead.

About ½ teaspoon ground cinnamon, sprinkled over the fried meat before the pine nuts are added, is a typically Middle Eastern touch.

Serve with plain boiled rice.

1 pound (450 g) lean lamb
2–2½ pounds (900 g–1·1 kilo) ripe
  tomatoes (see above)
1 large Spanish onion, chopped
1 large plump clove garlic, crushed
2 ounces (50 g) butter
1 ounce (25 g) pine nuts
Salt and freshly ground black pepper
Pinch of sugar (optional)
Finely chopped parsley, to garnish

Wipe meat clean and cut it into small, bite-sized cubes, trimming off any fat or gristle. Peel, seed and coarsely chop fresh tomatoes. If using canned tomatoes, you need only cut them up and with them use some of the juices from the can.

In a large, heavy pan or flameproof casserole, sauté onion and garlic in butter until soft and golden. Add lamb and sauté over moderate heat until lightly browned on all sides. Stir in pine nuts and continue to sauté for a minute or two longer.

Stir in tomatoes. Season to taste with salt, freshly ground black pepper and a pinch of sugar if you think tomatoes need it. Slowly bring to simmering point and cook gently until meat is tender and sauce is reduced. Sprinkle with parsley.

Serves 4.

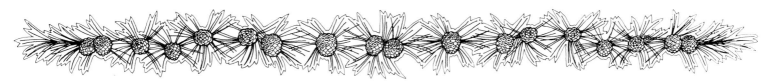

MEXICAN CHICKEN WITH PINE NUTS

1 roasting chicken, 2½–3 pounds
(1·1–1·4 kilos)
Salt
2 ounces (50 g) pine nuts
4 ounces (100–125 g) butter
2 tablespoons flour
6 tablespoons dry sherry
1 tablespoon ground cinnamon
2 tablespoons sugar
4 tablespoons raisins
4 tablespoons blanched almonds,
slivered

Quarter chicken, carefully removing any lumps of fat from body cavity. Put chicken joints in a pan with just enough salted water to cover and cook gently, covered, until chicken is tender. This will take 45 minutes or more, depending on the quality of the chicken.

Meanwhile, grind pine nuts finely in an electric blender or food processor. In a small pan, melt 3 ounces (75 g) butter and sauté ground nuts until a rich golden colour.

Drain chicken pieces, reserving cooking liquor, and return them to the pan. Cover and keep hot.

Melt remaining butter in a small pan. Stir in flour and cook, stirring constantly, to a golden brown, nutty *roux*. Gradually add ½ pint (300 ml) reserved chicken liquor, stirring vigorously to prevent lumps forming. Bring to simmering point, stirring. Add nuts and their butter, the sherry and cinnamon mixed with sugar. Mix well and bring to simmering point once more. Pour over chicken pieces and cook gently, covered, for 15–20 minutes longer.

Finally, stir in raisins and slivered almonds. Taste for seasoning, adding a little more salt if necessary. Simmer for 5 minutes and serve.

Serves 4.

PESTO ALLA GENOVESE
Italian Basil and Pine Nut Sauce

A magnificently flavoured cold sauce. It can be used as a dressing for pasta and *gnocchi* (dumplings), but they must be really hot for the sauce to release its full fragrance. Italians often stir a tablespoon or two of *pesto* into a pot of minestrone shortly before ladling it out.

If you have some of this precious sauce left over, it will keep best in a screw-top jar, covered with a layer of oil and stored in the refrigerator.

4 plump cloves garlic, peeled
About 2 ounces (50 g) pine nuts
1 large bunch fresh basil (30–40 large
leaves)
½ teaspoon coarse sea salt
1 heaped tablespoon each crumbled
or coarsely grated Parmesan and
Pecorino cheese, or 2 heaped
tablespoons Parmesan
6–8 tablespoons olive oil

Coarsely chop garlic cloves and pine nuts, and put them in a large mortar. Pound with a pestle until well mixed and broken down into a coarse paste.

Strip basil leaves from their stalks and either tear them into shreds or snip them up with scissors. Add basil to mortar with a sprinkling of salt (to help preserve its colour) and continue to pound until all the ingredients are reduced to a thick purée. Then add cheeses, pounding vigorously until smooth. The Pecorino makes the sauce more piquant; all Parmesan gives a more mellow flavour.

Next, replace the pestle with a wooden spoon and gradually beat in olive oil, a spoonful at a time, as though you were in the latter stages of making a mayonnaise. Sauce should be creamy, thick and smooth. Allow it to stand for a little while before use.

Note: An electric blender or food processor will save a great deal of time and effort. Have the ingredients ready, chopped up as above. Pour the oil into the goblet of the blender first, and with the machine turned to its lowest speed, add the remaining ingredients and blend to a smooth, creamy sauce.

ITALIAN SPINACH WITH PINE NUTS

2 pounds (900 g) fresh spinach
2 ounces (50 g) small raisins
2 ounces (50 g) butter
2 tablespoons olive oil
1 clove garlic
2 ounces (50 g) pine nuts
Salt
Freshly grated nutmeg

Wash spinach leaves in several changes of cold water, ripping out any hard ribs or thick stems as you come across them. Pack leaves into a pan (the water left clinging to them after washing will be enough to moisten them). Cook, tightly covered, until mound has collapsed and spinach is soft. While spinach is cooking, cover raisins with hot water and allow to soak and swell until needed.

When spinach is ready, turn the leaves out into a sieve or colander and with the back of a wooden spoon, press out excess moisture. If spinach leaves are large, slice them into wide ribbons.

In a deep frying pan or wide, flameproof casserole, melt butter in oil. Peel garlic clove, bruise it lightly and add it to the foaming butter. Fry over moderate heat until garlic clove is a rich golden colour. Do not let it burn or it will impart a bitter flavour.

Discard garlic clove. Add spinach, drained raisins and pine nuts to butter, mix well and cook gently, stirring, for 5 minutes, or until thoroughly hot. Season to taste with salt and a grating of nutmeg, and serve.

Serves 4.

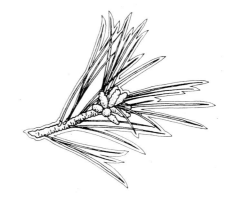

PISTACHIO

The mild-flavoured, green pistachio kernel in its pinky-red skin wrapped in a smooth white shell, is reputed to have been a favourite of the Queen of Sheba. A member of the same family as the cashew, its original home was in the warmer parts of central Asia, where it flourished in rugged mountain terrain, accessible only to goats and agile human beings. Immensely valuable to man's survival during the bitter winters, it became the subject of blood feuds amongst the nomadic tribes of Northern Persia and Afghanistan.

The Roman chronicler Pliny tells us that pistachio trees were brought to Rome by Lucius Vitellus, the Governor of Syria, in the first century AD, and they are now found all over the Middle East and around the Mediterranean. More recently, they have been planted in California, Texas and Arizona.

Pistachios are sold roasted and salted in their shells, and also as unsalted kernels. The former are for nibbling with drinks, the latter are intended for cooking. In general, the greener the kernel, the better the quality of the nuts and though they are expensive, they will keep for a long time in a tightly sealed jar. Pistachio essences and extracts can sometimes be used instead of the nuts.

To skin pistachio nuts, put them in boiling water and soak for a few minutes, then drain and add some cold water. The skins will come off when you rub each nut between your forefinger and thumb.

Pistachios appear time and time again in the incredibly rich and sweet pastries of the Middle East. They make an attractive decoration for our rather more puritan Anglo-Saxon cakes and desserts, and are firm favourites with French pastry-cooks. They are also used in one of the most delicious of all ice creams.

Like all nuts, pistachios pack a very concentrated amount of goodness into a small space. They are particularly rich in potassium.

PORK AND PISTACHIO PÂTÉ

1 pound (450 g) pork belly
4 ounces (100–125 g) streaky bacon
12 ounces (350 g) pig's or lamb's liver
1 medium onion or 2 shallots,
    chopped
2 cloves garlic
Salt and freshly ground black pepper
3 tablespoons brandy
2–3 ounces (50–75 g) shelled
    pistachio nuts
2 bay leaves, to garnish

Remove any rind and bone from the pork belly and take the rind off the streaky bacon. Mince together the pork, bacon, liver and onion. Crush the garlic with a little salt and stir into the mixture, then season with salt and pepper and stir in the brandy.

Add the pistachio nuts and mix in well so they are as evenly distributed as possible. Transfer the mixture to a 1½ pound (700 g) capacity loaf tin and smooth the top. Arrange the bay leaves on top and cover with a foil lid.

Put the loaf tin into a roasting tin and half-fill with boiling water. Cook in a moderate oven (375°F, 190°C, Mark 5) for about 1½ hours.

Remove from the oven and loosen the lid, but do not remove it. Leave overnight with weights on top.

Serve as a starter, or with a mixed or green salad for lunch.

Serves 8.

PISTACHIO RICE SALAD

This refreshing side salad is the perfect foil for cold roast meat or poultry – especially chicken, turkey or pork.

10 ounces (275 g) long grain rice
3 ounces (75 g) shelled pistachio nuts,
    halved if liked
3 ounces (75 g) currants

Dressing
6 tablespoons oil
2–3 tablespoons vinegar
Salt and freshly ground black pepper
½ teaspoon ground cinnamon

Cook the rice in twice its volume of boiling salted water for 10–12 minutes, then drain and rinse with hot water. Leave it to drain, then spread the rice on a flat serving dish to cool.

To make the dressing, whisk together the oil and vinegar until the dressing is cloudy. Season with salt, pepper and cinnamon.

Mix the pistachios and currants into the cooled rice and add the dressing. Adjust seasoning and serve.

Serves 4–6.

BAKLAVA

The best baklava I ever tasted was baked by Mme Nelly Douek for the party to celebrate the Bar-mitzvah of her grandson Simon. It had been stuffed with pistachio nuts and was quite memorable. Fortunately, Mme Douek's recipe for baklava is given in *A Book of Middle Eastern Food*, written by her daughter, Claudia Roden.

Filo pastry can be bought in boxes of ½ and 1 pound (225 and 450 g) from Greek and Turkish food stores. Once the packet has been opened, it must be used as soon as possible, especially on a warm day, as it quickly dries out and becomes brittle. For the same reason, it is a good precaution to keep any unused sheets of pastry rolled up in a damp cloth until you get to them.

1 pound or 450 g (about 24 sheets) filo
   pastry (see above)
8 ounces (225 g) unsalted butter
8 ounces (225 g) shelled pistachio
   nuts
2 tablespoons caster sugar

Syrup
8 ounces (225 g) sugar
1 tablespoon lemon juice
1 tablespoon orange-flower
   water

Start by preparing the syrup and have it chilling lightly in the refrigerator before you proceed with the pastry. Dissolve the sugar in ¼ pint (150 ml) water together with the lemon juice. Bring to boiling point and simmer until it thickens enough to coat the back of a spoon. Stir in orange-flower water and simmer for 2 minutes longer. Pour into a jug, leave until cold and chill until ready to use.

Melt the butter without letting it sizzle and leave to cool. With a pastry brush, coat the base and sides of a large, deep baking dish, round or square, with melted butter. I often use a deep, rectangular roasting tin, but it is really up to you.

Fit half of the pastry sheets into the baking dish one after the other, brushing each sheet with melted butter and folding over the sides neatly if necessary to make them fit the dish. Do not worry if some of the pastry sheets tear. Simply fit them

together again and brush them with butter.

Mix the nuts and sugar together, and spread evenly over the pastry-lined dish. Cover with the remaining sheets of pastry, brushing each one with melted butter as before. When you get to the final sheet of pastry, which should be perfectly whole, gently fold it *under* the pastry like a bed sheet. Brush the surface with melted butter. With a sharp-pointed knife, cut the pastry diagonally into individual lozenges.

Bake the baklava in a moderate oven (350–375°F, 180–190°C, Mark 4–5) for 30 minutes. Then turn the heat up (to 450°F, 230°C, Mark 8) and continue to bake for 15 minutes longer, or until the pastry is crisp and puffed, and a light golden colour.

As soon as you take the dish of baklava from the oven, pour all the chilled syrup over the entire surface. Leave to cool.

When quite cold, run your knife blade down along the original lines between the pastry lozenges to make sure they are separated and lift out as many as you need on to a serving platter. The remainder may be left in the baking dish, covered with plastic wrap or foil.

PISTACHIO ICE CREAM

4 ounces (100–125 g) pistachio nuts,
   skinned
1 ounce (25 g) almonds, blanched
1½ pints (900 ml) milk
12 ounces (350 g) caster sugar
8 egg yolks
½ pint (300 ml) single cream

Place the nuts and a little of the milk in an electric blender and blend to a thick paste. Put the paste in a large mixing bowl.

In a saucepan, bring the rest of the milk to the boil, over a high heat. Remove the pan from the heat and gradually pour the hot milk on to the nut paste, stirring to mix well. Cover and leave for 20 minutes.

Beat the sugar and egg yolks together until thick and creamy. Slowly mix in the milk and nut mixture, stirring until smooth. Put into a thick-bottomed saucepan, place over a low heat and cook, stirring until thick. Remove the pan from the heat, allow to cool, then stir in the cream.

Pour the mixture into a freezing tray and place in the freezer or the ice-compartment of a refrigerator turned to its lowest setting, for 1 hour.

Then tip the contents of the freezing tray into a large mixing bowl and beat well. Pour back into the freezing tray and freeze until solid.

Serves 4–6.

PLUM

Plums, both wild and cultivated, are to be found in a great variety of shapes, sizes and colours throughout the temperate world on both sides of the Atlantic.

Every region has its favoured varieties, depending on climate. In the British Isles, for example, the Victoria, which was discovered in a Sussex wood in the early 1840s, is considered to be the supreme dessert plum. Although its flavour is not the finest, this golden-fleshed fruit can always be depended on to crop heavily under orchard conditions in Britain. Greengages are considered to have the finest flavour. Most dessert plums with a greenish-golden skin can boast a gage in their ancestry.

All dessert varieties can be cooked, but not all cooking plums can be eaten raw as they are usually rather dry, with a sharp, uninteresting flavour. Cooking transforms this. Most European cooking plums are descended from the wild blackthorn or sloe and the myrobalan or cherry plum, a native of Western Asia, with bright, juicy but rather tasteless red or yellow fruit. One of the finest species cultivated for jam-making is the damson. This small, oval plum with a dark blue skin is far too astringent to eat raw but makes superb preserves. Another excellent plum for eating and baking is the *Zwetschen*, a small, purple fruit with bronze flesh, which is in season for only a few weeks in late summer. And if you can find Mirabelles, do try them. These cherry-sized, golden plums are very good to eat raw and also make delicious compotes and fruit tarts.

Like pears, plums are best bought slightly under-ripe and taken home to finish ripening at room temperature. Fruit for making jams should be used before it is quite ripe. Ripe dessert plums are soft, yield slightly to finger pressure and have a delicious, light scent.

Plums make delicious chutneys, and can also be preserved in the freezer. Use ripe, stoned and skinned fruit (the skins are liable to toughen in freezing) and freeze them covered in sugar syrup made from 1 pound (450 g) sugar to 2 pints (1·1 litres) water to avoid discoloration as they thaw.

But by far the most popular way of preserving plums is in the form of prunes. Only the best plums are used, preferably 'freestone' ones (like peaches, plums can be either 'freestone' or 'clingstone'). They are sold both pitted and unpitted.

There are dozens of ways to serve prunes. They range from hot cocktail titbits, wrapped in strips of bacon, speared on to metal skewers or cocktail sticks and grilled until the fat runs, to juicy little after-dinner sweets, the pits replaced with a roll of almond paste, either plain, or flavoured with a little orange liqueur or Kirsch. Prunes can also be cooked with meats in casseroles, with vegetables, chopped into grated winter vegetable salads, or turned into sweets of all kinds.

Prunes are well known as an effective but gentle natural laxative. They also stimulate the appetite, are good for sluggish livers, and help to clear the skin.

HEALTH DRINK

Per person:
½ cup prunes, soaked overnight
2 tablespoons skimmed milk powder

Drain the prunes and remove stones. Chop, and put in the bowl of an electric blender with 1 cup water and the skimmed milk powder.

Blend until smooth and creamy.

CHILLED PLUM SOUP

1½ pounds (700 g) ripe plums
3 ounces (75 g) sugar, or to taste
One 4 inch (10 cm) cinnamon stick
1 small, juicy orange, thinly sliced
2 slices lemon
½ bottle dry red wine
½ pint (300 ml) single cream

Rinse the plums, remove any stalks and put them in a pan with the sugar, cinnamon stick, orange and lemon slices (from which you have picked out and discarded any pips). Pour in the wine and ½ pint (300 ml) water. Bring to boiling point, cover and simmer gently until plums are very soft.

Discard cinnamon stick, orange and lemon slices, and rub the contents of the pan through a fine sieve into a bowl. If using an electric blender, stone the plums first, then pass the puréed plums through a fine sieve to trap any remaining pieces of skin. Allow to cool, then taste for flavour, adding a little more sugar or lemon juice if necessary. (If the purée is very thick at this stage, it may also be thinned down with a little fresh orange juice or water.) Chill very thoroughly. Just before serving, blend in the cream.

Serve in chilled soup bowls, garnished to taste (see below).

Serves 6.

Note: There are several ways of garnishing this soup – with a light sprinkling of finely grated orange rind or a pinch of ground cinnamon, a dollop of thick cream or, most luxurious of all, a swirl of very lightly sweetened whipped cream flavoured with orange liqueur.

PLUMS IN CREAM

1 pound (450 g) sweet plums
½–1 ounce (15–25 g) butter
2–4 tablespoons white or soft brown
    sugar, or to taste
Generous pinch of ground
    cinnamon
Small pinch of ground cloves
4 tablespoons thick cream

Rinse and dry plums, cut them in half lengthwise and remove stones. In a large, heavy frying pan, melt ½ ounce (15 g) butter (or enough to coat surface of pan). Lay plums in pan, cut side up, in a single layer. Sprinkle with sugar and spices, to taste. Fry plums gently, shaking pan and carefully turning plums over from time to time with a spatula, until flesh is a deep golden colour but plums are far from mushy and still retain their texture. Add a little more butter to the pan if necessary.

Spoon cream over plums. Mix lightly to blend with pan juices. Serve hot or cold.

Serves 4.

FRESH PLUM COMPOTE

4–5 ounces (125–150 g) sugar
Twist of orange or lemon rinds, or
    one 2 inch (5 cm) cinnamon stick
Lemon juice
1 pound (450 g) ripe plums

Make a syrup by dissolving sugar in 1 pint (550 ml) water with the orange or lemon rind, or cinnamon stick. Simmer for 15 minutes. Cool to lukewarm and flavour with lemon juice.

Wash plums. Cut them in half and remove stones. Then cut each half in two or three, depending on size. Put them in a bowl.

Pour syrup over prepared plums and allow to stand for at least 30 minutes before serving.

Serves 4.

PLUM COMPOTE WITH RED WINE SYRUP

An extravagant compote, lovely served with thick, chilled cream.

1½ pounds (700 g) firm plums
Juice of 1 large orange
6 ounces (175 g) soft pale brown
    sugar
½ pint (300 ml) red wine
Finely grated rind of ½ large orange

Rinse plums. Halve them lengthwise and remove stones. In a bowl, sprinkle plums with orange juice.

In a saucepan, preferably a wide, enamelled one, slowly dissolve sugar in red wine. Add grated orange rind and simmer for 10 minutes. Then stir in plums and their juices, cover pan and cook gently until plums are soft but not disintegrating. Cool plums in their syrup, then chill until ready to serve.

Serves 4–6.

PACZKI   Polish Doughnuts

If you do not have any homemade plum preserve, excellent ones from Eastern Europe can be bought quite inexpensively.

A ½ ounce (15 g) dried yeast may be used instead of fresh yeast, reconstituted according to directions on the can or sachet.

1 pound (450 g) plain flour
Pinch of salt
4 eggs
3 ounces (75 g) caster sugar
Finely grated rind of 1 orange
1 ounce (25 g) fresh yeast
    (see above)
About ¼ pint (150 ml) lukewarm
    milk
1–2 tablespoons dark rum or 2
    teaspoons vanilla essence
3 ounces (75 g) butter, melted and
    cooled
Thick plum preserve (page 154)
About 3 pounds (1·4 kilos) pure lard,
    for deep-frying
Thick rum-flavoured water icing

Sift flour and salt into a large bowl, or the bowl of your electric mixer, and put it in a warm place to heat gently until needed. In another bowl, beat eggs and sugar together until light and fluffy. Towards the end, beat in grated orange rind.

Dissolve yeast in ¼ pint (150 ml) lukewarm milk.

Make a well in the warmed flour. Pour in dissolved yeast, beaten eggs and sugar, and knead ingredients vigorously to make a smooth and soft, elastic dough that leaves the sides of the bowl and your fingers quite clean. Use a little more milk if necessary. Finally, add rum or vanilla essence and gradually incorporate melted butter.

Roll dough into a ball. Cover bowl or slip it into a plastic bag so dough will not dry out, and leave it in a warm place to double in bulk. This may take about 2 hours or longer as the dough is rather rich.

Meanwhile, spread 2 large trays with clean kitchen cloths and dust them with a little extra flour. In a large, wide pan, in which doughnuts are to be fried, melt lard without letting it sizzle. Put aside.

When doughnut dough has doubled its bulk, deflate it with the palm of your hand and knead until smooth.

To shape doughnuts, break off a piece of dough the size of a small apple, roll it into a ball, then flatten it out, not too thinly, on the palm of one hand. Place a rounded teaspoon of plum preserve in the middle and close the dough up over it. This must

be done very carefully as otherwise the doughnuts might burst open while frying. As an extra precaution, pinch off a small piece of dough from the join so that the surface is quite smooth. Lay doughnuts on floured cloth, spaced apart slightly to allow for their rising. Cover with another cloth and allow to double in bulk once more. This time it should take less than half the time. When doughnuts are rising and starting to look puffy, very carefully turn each one over on to the other side with floured fingertips.

Reheat lard until a cube of bread dropped into it turns crisp and golden brown within 60 seconds. Carefully float 3 or 4 doughnuts in lard and fry steadily until they have turned a rich golden colour on the underside, 2 or 3 minutes. Then gently flip them over to fry and colour the other side. The doughnuts will rise above the level of the oil when you turn them, forming a pale ring round the middle.

As soon as doughnuts are cooked, lift them out of lard with a slotted spoon and drain on paper towels. Then, while still hot, brush tops all over with icing and place on prepared dish to cool.

These are best eaten very fresh, preferably still just warm.

RITA'S PLUM CAKE

A doubly-useful recipe; it can be served with whipped cream as a dessert or with coffee or tea.

2 pounds (900 g) Zwetschen plums
1 egg
1 egg yolk
6 ounces (175 g) caster sugar
¼ teaspoon vanilla essence
5 ounces (150 g) softened butter or soft margarine
4 tablespoons sour cream
8 ounces (225 g) self-raising flour
Granulated sugar, to decorate

Rinse the plums in a colander. Shake off excess moisture. Halve and stone them, and put aside.

In a large bowl, beat the egg, egg yolk and sugar until fluffy and lemon-coloured. Add vanilla and butter or margarine, and continue to beat until smoothly blended. Beat in sour cream.

With a wooden spoon, beat in flour a little at a time to make a stiffish batter. Depending on the type of flour used, a little more or less may be needed.

Spread the batter evenly in a 10 × 12 inch (25 × 30 cm) baking tin or ovenproof dish. Arrange the plum halves in rows on top.

Bake in a moderate oven (375°F, 190°C, Mark 5) until the cake mixture has risen up between the plums and is a rich golden colour, about 1 hour.

Remove from the oven. Sprinkle sugar generously over the surface and leave to cool completely before cutting into rectangles and removing from baking tin with a broad-bladed spatula.

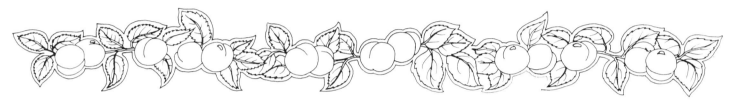

POWIDŁA ZE ŚLIWEK Polish Plum Preserve

2½ pounds (1·1 kilos) plums, Zwetschens if possible
8 ounces (225 g) sugar

Rinse plums and pick off any stems. Slit them in half and remove stones, dropping plums into a heavy, flameproof casserole or pot as you do so. If stones are difficult to remove, just leave them in and chop up the plums as they will in any case have to be rubbed through a sieve once they are cooked.

To cook plums, first either heat them gently with a few tablespoons of water, tightly covered, on top of the stove until juices begin to flow, or heat covered casserole in a slow oven (or on the floor of a hotter one) to start juices off. Then place casserole over a low heat and cook, stirring and mashing occasionally with a wooden spoon, until plums are very soft and mushy.

Rub plums and their juices through a sieve or put through a vegetable mouli and return purée to the casserole. Stir in sugar over moderate heat. When it has melted, continue to simmer purée, stirring, until it is very thick and reduced, and begins to come away from the sides of the casserole.

Spoon or pour hot plum purée into sterilized earthenware pots or glass jam jars. Heatproof earthenware pots of preserve may then be put in a hot oven for a few minutes to 'set' the surface before covering and sealing pots as for jam (page 199).

Fills about 5 jars.

PICKLED PLUMS

7 pounds (3·2 kilos) plums
3 pounds (1·4 kilos) brown sugar
2 pints (1·1 litres) brown (malt) vinegar
½ ounce (15 g) each mace, cloves, cinnamon sticks and ginger root

Rinse plums and prick all over with a darning needle or sharp-tined fork.

In a large pan, combine sugar with vinegar and spices. Bring to boiling point, stirring until sugar has dissolved, and simmer for 10 minutes. Then drop in plums and allow to simmer for a further 15 minutes.

Lift plums out of spiced vinegar with a slotted spoon and pack into clean glass jars. Bring vinegar back to boiling point. Strain through a sieve into jars, covering plums and filling jars completely. Cool and cover. Mature for at least a month.

See also page 200.

Fills about 7 jars.

PLUM CHUTNEY

Ripe Victoria plums make very good chutney.

2½ pounds (1·1 kilos) plums
1 pound (450 g) raisins
½–¾ pint (300–400 ml) brown malt
   vinegar
½–¾ pound (225–350 g) brown or
   white sugar
3 whole cloves garlic, peeled
1 ounce (25 g) salt
1 ounce (25 g) in all of ground ginger,
   cinnamon and allspice
½ ounce (15 g) mustard seeds,
   bruised

Rinse plums, stone them and cut them into chunks. Rinse raisins in a colander and leave to drain.

In a large, heavy pan (an enamelled pan is best, but care must be taken as chutney tends to scorch as it thickens), combine vinegar with all remaining ingredients and bring to the boil, stirring until sugar has dissolved. Add plums and raisins, and simmer until tender, stirring frequently. If chutney is still rather thin, continue to cook, stirring constantly, until the desired consistency is reached.

Leave until quite cold before potting and covering.

See also page 200.

Fills about 4 jars.

PLUM BRANDY

2 pounds (900 g) dark red plums
2 pounds (900 g) demerara sugar
2½ pints (1·4 litres) brandy

Remove any stalks and leaves from the fruit. Wash in a colander under cold, running water, then halve, removing stones.

In a large, wide neck, screw-top storage jar (a large Kilner jar is ideal) arrange the plums in layers, covering each layer with a generous coating of sugar. Add sufficient brandy to cover the fruit. Seal the jar tightly and leave it for 6 months at room temperature.

The liqueur is now ready to strain off and bottle. Keep in the bottle for at least 6 months before drinking.

Makes 2½ pints (1·4 litres).

Damsons and Greengages

DAMSON CHEESE

The finest of all traditional fruit 'cheeses' is made with damsons. It is served in thick slices with cold poultry or game, or as a dessert.

3 pounds (1·4 kilos) damsons
3 pounds (1·4 kilos) sugar
Finely grated rind of 1 orange
   (optional)

Rinse damsons and pull off any stems. Put fruit in a preserving pan with barely enough water to cover and simmer until very soft and pulpy. Alternatively, at this stage, damsons may be cooked in the oven. Place them in an ovenproof casserole, cover and leave in a very cool oven (250°F, 130°C, Mark ½) for several hours until juices have run from the fruit and flesh is very soft.

Put damsons through a food mill or rub through a sieve. Return pulp to preserving pan. Stir in sugar and grated orange rind, if used. Allow sugar to dissolve and mixture to come to boiling point, then continue to cook and stir until cheese is thick enough to hold the impression of the stirring spoon. Scrape the bottom of the pan regularly.

When very thick, pour into suitable jars or bowls and cover.

See also page 200.

PICKLED DAMSONS

The following recipe comes from *The Dumfriesshire Cookery Book*, first published in Dumfries, Scotland, by the Courier Press in 1935.

3½ pounds (1·6 kilos) damsons
1½ pints (900 ml) brown malt vinegar
1½ pounds (700 g) sugar
½ ounce (15 g) cinnamon sticks
   (snapped in half if very long)
6–8 cloves

Wipe damsons and prick all over with a fork. Place in a large bowl.

In an enamelled or stainless steel pan, boil vinegar, sugar, cinnamon and cloves together, stirring until sugar has dissolved. Pour over damsons and leave for 24 hours.

The following day, pour off vinegar and spices, and again boil them up and pour over damsons. Allow to stand for another 24 hours.

On the third day, pour entire contents of bowl into pan and boil all together for 15–20 minutes. Pack damsons into glass jars, strain vinegary liquid over them to cover them completely and allow to become quite cold before covering.

See also page 200.

Fills about 4 jars.

CANDIED GREENGAGES

A Victorian sweetmeat which is still great fun to prepare. Serve some candied greengages on a dish of after-dinner petits fours, or use them to decorate a fruit cake.

The greengages should be slightly under-ripe and rather firm, gathered on a dry day, according to the original recipe, with the stalks left on.

1 pound (450 g) greengages (see above)
¼ teaspoon bicarbonate of soda
1½ pounds (700 g) sugar
Sifted caster sugar, to finish

Rinse greengages. With a darning needle or a thin skewer, prick a few holes in each greengage near the stalk. In a pan, cover greengages with cold water and slowly bring to boiling point. Immediately remove pan from heat, cover and leave until the following day.

Return pan to heat. Add bicarbonate of soda, but this time remove from the heat before water reaches boiling point. With a slotted spoon, transfer greengages to a large bowl of cold water. Then place them in a large sieve or colander and leave to drip dry.

Dissolve sugar in a teacup of water and allow to boil steadily for a few minutes. Drop in greengages, bring back to boiling point and simmer for 5 minutes. Pour contents of pan into a bowl and leave for 24 hours.

The following day, drain all the syrup back into the pan. Bring to boiling point once more. Place greengages back in syrup and simmer 5 minutes.

Repeat on 4 successive days, making it 5 times in all that the greengages have been boiled in sugar syrup. After the final boiling, lift greengages out of syrup with a slotted spoon, place in one layer in a sieve or colander and leave to dry in a warm, airy place. Old cookery books suggest leaving the greengages to dry in the sun or near the fire but a cool oven with the door left ajar is not only more convenient but also rather more reliable.

Roll greengages in sifted caster sugar before putting in paper cases and packing in an airtight box.

LEEK AND PRUNE APPETIZER

8 ounces (225 g) whites of leek
12 plump prunes, soaked overnight
2 tablespoons round-grain (pudding) rice
1½–2 tablespoons sunflower oil
Generous pinch of ground cinnamon (optional)
Salt and freshly ground black pepper
Lemon wedges, to serve

Wash the leeks carefully. Trim off stem ends and slice leeks into 1 inch (2·5 cm) lengths. Place them in a wide, shallow, flameproof pan in a single layer if possible. Add the prunes. Sprinkle in the rice, oil and the cinnamon, if liked, and season with salt and a generous grinding of black pepper. Pour in ½ pint (300 ml) hot water. Bring to boiling point. Cover tightly and cook gently for about 20 minutes, or until all the ingredients are cooked through but the dish is still rather moist. Pour into a shallow serving dish and allow to cool.

Serve lukewarm or cold, garnished with lemon wedges.

Serves 4.

PRUNE AND BACON SKEWERS

Excellent served hot on a tray of cocktail appetizers. Tamari almonds (lightly toasted almonds seasoned with soya sauce), which can sometimes be found in wholefood stores, make a very good and original alternative to the plain salted almonds with which the prunes are stuffed in this recipe.

24 large plump prunes, soaked overnight
24 salted almonds (see above)
8 slices smoked streaky bacon, de-rinded
Butter

Drain prunes and pat them dry with paper towels. With a sharp knife, slit each prune carefully down one side, remove the stone and replace it with an almond. Pat back into shape.

With the back of a knife, stretch and spread out each slice of bacon as thinly as possible. Cut it in 3 crosswise. Wrap each prune in a piece of bacon and secure it with a short wooden cocktail stick.

In a large frying pan, fry the prunes gently in a little butter until the bacon fat has run and is transparent, and the prunes are hot through. Drain well on paper towels and serve hot.

CAUCASIAN CHICKEN WITH PRUNES

1 roasting chicken, 3–3¼ pounds (1·4–1·5 kilos), jointed
Salt and freshly ground black pepper
3 tablespoons oil
2 large Spanish onions, very thinly sliced
½ pound (225 g) plump prunes, soaked overnight
1 teaspoon whole coriander seeds
¼ teaspoon crumbled dried thyme
Generous pinch of paprika
3 tablespoons finely chopped dill
2 tablespoons finely chopped parsley

Wipe the chicken joints dry with paper towels and season generously with salt and freshly ground black pepper. In a heavy, heatproof casserole, brown the chicken joints all over in oil, a portion at a time. Then return them all to the casserole, mix in the shredded onions and add just enough boiling water to half-cover the contents of the casserole (¼ pint or 150 ml, or perhaps a little more). Cover the casserole and simmer very gently for 30 minutes.

Meanwhile, drain the soaked prunes and remove pits. In a mortar, combine coriander seeds with thyme and paprika, and crush them finely with a pestle.

When chicken and onions have cooked for 30 minutes, add the prunes, the crushed coriander mixture, finely chopped dill and parsley. Mix well to distribute prunes and seasoning evenly. Cover the casserole again and continue to cook gently for a further 40 minutes, or until both the chicken and prunes are very tender, and the sauce is thick and reduced.

Correct seasoning with a little more salt or pepper if necessary. Serve from the casserole.

Serves 4–6.

ROAST PORK WITH PRUNES

2½–3 pounds (1·1–1·4 kilos) lean loin of pork in one piece (6 chops)
16–20 plump prunes, pitted
1 teaspoon ground ginger
Salt and freshly ground black pepper
1 Spanish onion, peeled
1 small, thin-skinned orange
1 tart green apple, quartered and cored
1 tablespoon cooking oil
Still cider or apple juice (optional)
1 tablespoon cornflour

Have bone cut out of pork joint. Remove rind and some (about half) of the fat under it. With a large metal skewer or similar instrument that is strong and not too pliable (a knife-sharpening steel, for example, is very good), make a hole right through the middle of the lean, round chop of the meat. If necessary, enlarge the cavity with the steel or the handle of a wooden spoon. Push in prunes tightly one after the other to make a row of them side by side. Tie the joint tightly in shape with thin string in 4 or 5 places along its length. Rub it all over with ginger and season generously with salt and freshly ground black pepper.

Lay pork joint in a roasting tin, fat side up. Cut onion, orange and apple into large chunks, and toss them with oil and a sprinkling of cider, apple juice or water. Arrange chunks of onion and fruit around pork.

Roast pork in a fairly hot oven (425°F, 220°C, Mark 7) for the first 20 minutes to brown it, then lower heat (400°F, 200°C, Mark 6) and continue to roast until pork is thoroughly done, about 1 hour longer. Baste regularly with pan juices, more cider or apple juice, or water.

Transfer meat to a heated serving platter and remove strings.

Pour contents of roasting tin through a sieve into a saucepan, pressing with a spoon to extract as much juice as possible. Deglaze tin with a few tablespoons of water, scraping any crusty bits loose with a wooden spoon, and add them to pan. Skim excess fat from the surface. Blend cornflour smoothly with a little water and use as much as you need to thicken sauce. Correct seasoning with more salt and black pepper. Pour into a heated sauce boat and serve with meat.

Serves 6.

STEAMED PRUNE PUDDING

10 large juicy prunes, soaked overnight
Butter or soft margarine, for pudding basin
1 ounce (25 g) soft brown sugar

Pudding batter
4 ounces (100–125 g) unbleached plain flour
1 teaspoon baking powder
4 ounces (100–125 g) soft margarine or softened butter
3 ounces (75 g) caster sugar
2 eggs, lightly beaten
¼ teaspoon almond essence
1–2 tablespoons milk

With a sharp knife, cut the prunes in half lengthwise and remove stones. Grease a pudding basin, put in the sugar and smooth it out evenly over the bottom of the basin with the back of a spoon. Arrange halved prunes evenly on top. Cut a double thickness of greaseproof paper to cover the top of the basin with a generous overlap and grease lightly on one side. Put aside until needed.

To make the pudding batter, sift the flour and baking powder into a bowl. In another bowl, beat the margarine or butter and sugar together until white and fluffy. Beat in about half of the eggs, followed by 2 or 3 tablespoons flour mixture, the remaining eggs, flour and almond essence. Finally, beat in a little milk if necessary to make a soft batter that drops easily from the spoon.

Pour the batter into the prepared basin. Level off the top and make a slight hollow in the centre. Cover with the greaseproof paper, buttered side down, and tie round the sides with fine string.

Lower the basin into a pan with boiling water to come halfway up its sides, cover the pan tightly and steam gently for 1¼ hours, adding a little more *boiling* water if and when necessary.

To serve, turn pudding out and serve accompanied by a jug of lightly sweetened custard sauce or cream.

Serves 4–6.

PRUNE SAUCE

8 ounces (225 g) plump, dried prunes, soaked overnight
2–3 plump cloves garlic
Salt and freshly ground black pepper
Sharp (hot) paprika
About ¼ pint (150 ml) stock (cube) or water
2 tablespoons finely chopped parsley
2 tablespoons finely chopped fresh dill

Drain soaked prunes, reserving liquid, and stone them. In a small pan, cover stoned prunes with soaking water, adding a little fresh water if necessary to make sure prunes are covered, and simmer until they are quite soft and water has almost all evaporated.

Meanwhile, crush garlic to a paste with ¼ teaspoon salt.

Pour prunes and their juices into the container of an electric blender or food processor. Add garlic, its salt, a grinding of black pepper and a generous pinch of sharp paprika. Blend smoothly, gradually adding enough stock (poultry or beef cube, depending on the meat it is to be served with) or water to make a thick, creamy sauce.

Pour sauce back into pan. Stir in chopped parsley and dill, and correct seasoning if necessary. Bring to boiling point, stirring. Pour into a bowl and serve cold.

PRUNE LIQUEUR

Macerate a handful of prunes in a small carafe of vodka or gin, sweetened with 2 or 3 tablespoons sugar. Leave for a few weeks, swirling the carafe round occasionally.

Pour off the vodka or gin into liqueur glasses.

POMEGRANATE

With its leathery yellow skin and hundreds of seeds encased in juicy, ruby-red kernels (arils), the pomegranate is a curious fruit which you either love or dislike intensely. The shrub-like tree on which it grows originally came from tropical Asia but for a long time it has been cultivated throughout the Mediterranean region and the Middle East. Today it also grows quite happily in suitably warm areas in other parts of the world.

For thousands of years, pomegranates have been a symbol of wealth, prosperity and fertility. They are mentioned in ancient myths as a fruit favoured by the gods; the Romans nicknamed them 'apples of Carthage', and according to Jewish tradition pomegranates were – and still are – served at the New Year as a symbol of prosperity. Christian cultures have adopted similar customs. At the New Year, Greek children hurl whole pomegranates at their friends' houses 'for luck'.

Pomegranates come into season in autumn but will keep fresh in cold storage for several months and can be bought in perfect condition throughout the winter. Don't worry if the skin is hard as wood; the kernels inside will be fresh and juicy. The seeds inside the kernels and the pith are both extremely bitter. To enjoy fresh pomegranates, cut the fruit open with a knife (a serrated blade will go through the tough skin more easily), then break it into pieces and scoop out the kernels with a teaspoon. Or roll a pomegranate over a hard surface until the kernels are squashed, then cut a small plug out of the skin so that the juice can be sucked out.

Whole kernels make a pretty garnish for almost everything; hot and cold meats, fresh fruit salads, even a cheese board can be studded with balls of cream cheese rolled in the kernels.

POMEGRANATE JUICE

A refreshing pre-lunch or pre-dinner drink. Follow the instructions below to extract juice for cooking, but don't add sugar, etc.

2 ripe pomegranates
Fresh lemon or lime juice
Icing sugar

Cut the pomegranates in half, and squeeze the halves in a strainer-juicer as you would an orange. Alter-natively, place the kernels in a fine-meshed nylon sieve and crush them firmly with the back of a wooden spoon. Take care not to bruise the seeds themselves as they will release an unpleasantly bitter flavour.

Pour juice into a jug. Sharpen flavour with lemon or lime juice and stir in icing sugar, to taste.

Put 2 or 3 tablespoons crushed ice in a glass. Top up with chilled pomegranate juice, stir once and serve.

REMEDIES

Infusions made from pomegranate flowers or rind can be used to make compresses to stop bleeding, douches for vaginal discharges, and gargles for mouth ulcers and sore throats. The juice is cooling and refreshing in cases of fever.

COSMETICS

To darken hair, apply an infusion of pomegranate flowers or bark. The astringent juice is good for oily skin, but will stain if left on for too long.

LIVER IN POMEGRANATE SAUCE

1½ pounds (700 g) calf's or lamb's
*   liver*
Flour
3–4 tablespoons oil
Generous pinch each of dried
*   crumbled thyme and rosemary*
Salt and freshly ground black pepper
3 tablespoons pomegranate juice
*   (see above)*
Finely chopped parsley, to garnish

Have the liver cut in thin slices on the slant. Alternatively, buy the liver in one piece. Remove any outer membrane and with a very sharp knife, cut the liver diagonally into large, thin slices. Dust each slice lightly with flour on both sides.

In a large, heavy frying pan with a lid, brown the slices of liver in hot oil, a portion at a time, keeping them hot as you do so. Return all the slices to the pan. Sprinkle them with thyme and rosemary, and season with salt and freshly ground black pepper. Moisten with pomegranate juice, cover the pan and cook gently for 1 or 2 minutes until the liver is done.

Transfer the liver to a heated serving dish. Pour over pan juices, sprinkle with finely chopped parsley and serve immediately. Plain steamed or boiled potatoes make the best accompaniment.

Serves 4–6.

CHICKEN AND POMEGRANATE SYRUP

Chicken and pomegranates are a favoured combination in the Caucasus and the Near East.

Two 2 pound (900 g) chickens
¼ pint (150 ml) natural yoghourt or
 sour cream
Salt and freshly ground black pepper
2 Spanish onions
Fresh lettuce leaves and parsley
 sprigs, to garnish
Pomegranate syrup (see right)

Split chickens in half lengthwise and firmly press them as flat as possible with the heel of your hand. Wipe pieces clean with a damp cloth and prick skin all over with the tines of a fork or a sharp skewer. Mix yoghourt or sour cream until smooth and season generously with salt and freshly ground black pepper. Brush all over chicken pieces. Lay them on a large, flat dish and allow them to marinate for an hour or so before cooking them. At the same time, peel onions, slice them and separate into rings. Sprinkle with salt, rubbing it in gently.

When ready to cook chicken, lay pieces flat on a rack and grill over hot coals or under a pre-heated, moderate grill, turning and brushing occasionally with remaining yoghourt. In all, it will take about 20 minutes on each side before juices run clear.

Meanwhile, rinse onion rings and press them dry between sheets of absorbent kitchen paper or the folds of a cloth.

Lay chicken halves skin side up on a heated serving platter. Garnish with lettuce leaves and sprigs of parsley. Strew chicken with prepared onion rings. Serve with a bowl of pomegranate syrup for each person.

Serves 4.

POMEGRANATE SYRUP

This syrup has many different uses — with charcoal-grilled meats, as a topping for plain vanilla ice cream or one of the lighter sponge puddings, or simply drunk well diluted with iced water, milk or fizzy lemonade.

Juice of 6 large pomegranates (see
 Pomegranate Juice opposite)
3 ounces (75 g) sugar

Strain the pomegranate juice into an enamelled or stainless steel saucepan. Stir in sugar and bring to boiling point over low heat, stirring constantly until sugar dissolves. Then raise heat and boil briskly, stirring frequently, until syrup has thickened and is well reduced. Skim off any scum from surface with a slotted spoon as you would from jam. Cool slightly.

Funnel syrup into a hot, dry bottle and screw down cap. Store in the door of the refrigerator or any similar cool, dark place.

See also page 202.

POMEGRANATE WATER ICE

An unusual, refreshing ice, for which it is essential to use only ripe fruit.

Juice of 4 large ripe pomegranates
 (see Pomegranate Juice left)
Juice of 1 lemon
4 ounces (100–125 g) sugar

Strain the pomegranate juice through a fine sieve. This should give about ¾ pint (400 ml) juice. Add the lemon juice.

Put the sugar and ½ pint (300 ml) water in a small, thick bottomed pan, and bring to the boil over medium heat, stirring frequently. Simmer for 10 minutes, then remove from the heat and allow to cool. When the syrup is cold, stir it into the fruit juice. Mix well and taste. Adjust the sweetness if desired, remembering that it will taste less sweet when frozen. Pour the mixture into a shallow freezing tray and freeze for 1 hour. Remove from the freezer, tip into a bowl, and beat for 1 minute.

Return to the tray and freeze for 3–4 hours more until solid. Serve alone or with other fruit, topped with pouring cream.

Serves 4.

GRENADINE

When pomegranates are plentiful — usually in the autumn — you can make your own version of grenadine.

Measure 6 cups each fresh pomegranate kernels and granulated sugar into a bowl. Mix well, cover and leave for 24 hours.

The following day, pour the mixture into a heavy saucepan and very slowly bring it to boiling point, stirring and mashing the kernels gently with a spoon or wooden kitchen fork. Take care not to bruise the seeds. Strain the syrup through a fine nylon sieve, pressing the kernels gently to extract as much juice as possible, and pour it into tightly stoppered hot, dry bottles.

QUINCE

A dish of ripening quinces will fill a room with the most unbelievable fragrance. The cooked fruit is just as powerfully flavoured. You will need only a few slices to transform the taste of a dish made with apples or pears.

The fruit is thought to have come from Western Asia and the Eastern Mediterranean, where it is still widely used for all kinds of dishes from meat stews to sweetmeats and preserves. Today, however, quinces also grow freely throughout the warmer regions of the temperate world.

Quinces were familiar to the Greeks and Romans, who dedicated them to Venus as a symbol of love, happiness and fruitfulness, and used their blossoms as a symbolic decoration for the bridal chamber. But although they were widely known and the beauty of their blossoms was especially admired, the fruits themselves never achieved overwhelming popularity. One exception was in Portugal, where they were used to make a preserve or jam.

Quinces should be gathered in the autumn before they are quite ripe and left to finish ripening indoors. Some people maintain that the flavour will be improved if the fruit is left on the tree until after the first frost. Freshly picked quinces are covered in a white down, just as if they had been packed in cotton wool. This should be rubbed off gently with a damp cloth.

A raw quince is quite inedible, but cooking softens the flesh and turns it a deep golden, rosy colour with a firm, rather gritty texture. Some people claim that pear-shaped specimens keep best and apple-shaped ones cook even better, but there is little to choose between them. The flesh discolours rapidly as soon as it has been cut and exposed to the air, so unless they are to be used immediately, peeled or sliced quinces should be kept in a bowl of water acidulated with lemon juice to preserve their colour. Another point to bear in mind when making preserves is that over-cooking will turn the pieces rock-hard. Should this happen, the simplest solution is to use the preserve to sweeten other fruit pies and sauces. This will soften them.

Quinces can be frozen in a syrup made from 8 ounces (225 g) sugar to 1 pint (550 ml) water; peel, core and quarter or slice them first.

The pips and peels of quinces are very rich in pectin and make easy jams and jellies, either on their own, or mixed with other fruit such as apples and pears. Excellent preserves can also be made with the fruit of the japonica, a relative of the quince.

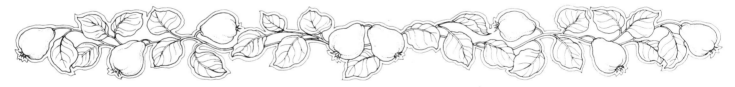

COSMETICS

Quinces are used in many different countries for care of the hair — to increase growth, to cure baldness, to give body and to revive. Women in ancient Greece used a mixture of quince juice and privet to dye their hair golden.

Quince seeds have the useful property of turning to jelly when mixed with boiling water. In this classic recipe for a deep-cleansing clay mask, they not only soften the skin but also make the mask easy to remove.

Mix a teaspoon of quince seeds, dissolved in a little boiling water, with 4 tablespoons fullers' earth, 1 tablespoon lanolin, and enough rosewater to make a paste. Apply to the face and leave for 20 minutes before rinsing off.

CHICKEN WITH QUINCE STUFFING

1 roasting chicken, 3–3½ pounds
   (1·6 kilos)
Salt and freshly ground black pepper
Corn or sunflower seed oil
1 pound (450 g) quinces
Lemon juice
4 ounces (100–125 g) raisins
1–1½ ounces (25–40 g) softened
   butter

Wash the chicken both inside and out, and wipe it dry with paper towels. Season generously both inside and out, brush all over with a tablespoon of oil and put aside for 30 minutes while you prepare the stuffing.

Peel, quarter and core the quinces, and cut them into small chunks, dropping them immediately into a bowl of water acidulated with lemon juice to prevent them turning brown. When they are all prepared, drain well and pat free of excess moisture with paper towels.

Mix the quince chunks with the raisins and butter. Stuff the cavity of the chicken with this mixture and skewer or sew the opening up. Truss the chicken.

In a heavy, heatproof casserole that has a tight-fitting lid, brown the chicken all over in 3–4 tablespoons oil, ending up with the chicken on its back. Moisten with a few tablespoons of hot water, cover the casserole tightly and cook over very low heat for 1 hour, or until the chicken is tender, turning it over once or twice and adding a little more hot water from time to time if necessary.

Serve with fluffy boiled rice.

Serves 4–6.

CAUCASIAN STUFFED QUINCES

4 ounces (100–125 g) shelled, skinned
   chestnuts
1 pound (450 g) lean lamb, minced
8 tablespoons finely chopped fresh
   dill
Salt
8 medium quinces
2 ounces (50 g) butter
Sugar to taste
About ¾ pint (400 ml) beef stock

To make stuffing, boil chestnuts for 15 minutes until softened. Drain them, chop them up and mix them with minced lamb, dill and salt, to taste.

Cut a ½-inch (1·25 cm) slice from the stem end of each quince and reserve it for the 'lid'. With an apple corer, scoop out cores to within ½ inch (1·25 cm) of the bottom, then scoop out some of the pulp to leave a shell ⅓ to ½ inch (8–10 mm) thick. (If quinces have uneven bases which prevent them from standing upright, it is a good idea to shave a thin slice off the bottom before hollowing out the quinces so they will stand steady.)

Stuff quince shells with meat mixture and cover with reserved lids. Butter the bottom of a large, flameproof casserole that will hold the quinces side by side with little room to spare. Fit them into casserole. Sprinkle with sugar and dot with remaining butter.

Pour in beef stock. Cover and simmer for 50–60 minutes, or until quinces are tender, adding a little more stock if it evaporates too quickly. Lift quinces out of casserole with a slotted spoon. Serve, moistened with some of the pan juices.

Serves 4.

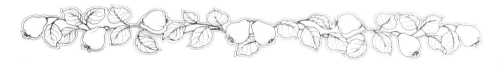

QUINCE COMPOTE

This exquisite compote, golden tinged with red, is delicious served either with roast poultry and meats, especially pork and lamb. Or it is very good as a dessert with chilled whipped or clotted cream.

4 quinces
Lemon juice
8 ounces (225 g) sugar
Thinly peeled strips of orange and
   lemon rind

Quarter, peel and core quinces, and slice each piece in 3 lengthwise. Drop into a bowl of water acidulated with lemon juice to prevent them going brown before they are all prepared.

In a wide pan, combine sugar with ¾ pint (400 ml) water, the orange and lemon rinds, and bring to boiling point, stirring until sugar has dissolved. With a slotted spoon, transfer slices of quince from bowl of water to syrup. Sprinkle with 2 or 3 teaspoons more lemon juice. Simmer until quince slices have turned a translucent, rosy pink and feel soft when poked with a thin skewer.

Allow to cool in syrup before serving.

Serves 4–6.

JAPONICA JAM

Many gardeners are unaware of the excellent jams and jellies that can be made with the fruit of the ornamental quince.

2 pounds (900 g) japonica fruit
Sugar
1 teaspoon ground cloves

Wash the japonicas, cut them up and put them in a preserving pan with about 3½ pints (2 litres) water. Bring to boiling point and boil until fruit is very soft and pulpy.

Rub the fruit through a sieve or vegetable mill. Weigh it and return it to the rinsed-out pan with ¾ pound (350 g) sugar to every pound (450 g) of pulp, and the ground cloves. Stir over gentle heat until the sugar has dissolved, then boil hard until setting point is reached.

Cool slightly, pot and cover.
See also page 198.

Fills about 5 jars.

QUINCE JELLY

One of the most beautiful jellies of all, a clear golden pink in colour, with a unique aroma and flavour, quince jelly goes particularly well with pork, veal and poultry.

Wash the quinces under the cold tap and chop them up into large chunks. Cut out the cores and seeds as you come across them, and tie them up in a muslin bag. Put the quinces and bag of cores etc, in a large pan. Cover with water and boil until very soft and pulpy.

Tip the contents of the pan into a jelly bag and leave suspended above a bowl to drip dry. Measure juice and weigh out a pound (450 g) of sugar per pint (550 ml) of juice. Pour them into a preserving pan. Stir over low heat until sugar has dissolved, then raise heat and boil until setting point is reached, skimming surface until it is quite clear of scum.

Cool slightly, pot and cover.
See also page 199.

QUINCE RATAFIA

First, wipe your quinces clean with a damp cloth. Then grate them, peels, pips and all, into a large bowl, cover tightly and leave for 3 days. They will go rather black, but this is normal. Then squeeze the grated quinces through muslin or press through a fine sieve to extract as much juice as possible. With a teacup, measure this liquid into a glass flagon and mix in an equal volume of brandy (or vodka). Then, for every cupful of mixed liquid add a quarter-cup of granulated sugar and a whole clove. Drop in a cinnamon stick snapped in two, cover the flagon, and shake it well to dissolve the sugar.

Leave the ratafia to mature and mellow for at least 6 weeks before tasting it, then strain it through muslin once more and re-bottle it. Drink this precious liqueur on its own in small glasses, or use it to flavour other sweets and fruit salads.

RASPBERRY

If you have ever caught your clothes on the thorns of a wild raspberry, it will hardly surprise you to learn that raspberries belong to the rose family or *Rosaceae*. They grow wild in rocky woodlands throughout Europe from the British Isles and Scandinavia right across to Greece and Anatolia. In the south, people are still content to gather berries in the wild, but as early as the end of the Middle Ages northern gardeners had begun cultivating raspberries in their kitchen gardens. The fruit thrives in a cool, damp climate. When European plants were introduced into America, it was found that they were not suitable for the dry, hot conditions that prevailed there, and an indigenous native species had to be used instead.

The fragile, thimble-shaped berries ripen to various shades of red, ranging from scarlet to purple, almost black. There are also clear golden varieties. Raspberries vary greatly in size. The smallest of all are wild ones, which are full of pips; many people are prepared to tolerate this, claiming that their flavour is finer than that of any cultivated fruit.

The berries are ripe when they are brightly and evenly coloured, and slip easily off their hulls. Ideally, they should be used as soon as they have been picked as they rapidly turn mouldy. When buying them, take a look at the bottom and sides of the punnet if you can for signs of dampness, which indicate that the contents are over-ripe, leaking and stale.

Raspberries should never be washed unless absolutely necessary and then given only the lightest of sprays with water. If they are not to be used immediately, they may be stored in the bottom of the refrigerator before cleaning, but bring them out well in advance of serving.

Fine raspberries need no accompaniment apart from a sprinkling of sugar. You can also serve them with lightly whipped cream flavoured with orange liqueur or Kirsch, or with dollops of vanilla ice cream.

For special occasions, toss them with sugar, finely grated orange rind and juice, pile them into hollowed-out orange cups and decorate with sprigs of fresh mint.

Raspberries go well with many other fruits, in particular strawberries, peaches, apricots, pineapple and melon. The combinations are endless. Mix whole raspberries with crushed or shredded pineapple and serve with almond macaroons. Marinate raspberries and cantaloupe melon balls in orange liqueur, pile them into hollowed-out melon shells and serve lightly chilled. Alternatively, sieve the raspberries to make a purée and serve with a bowl of strawberries or a dish of lightly chilled, peeled ripe figs. Raspberry purée is also a feature of Nouvelle Cuisine.

Raspberries are rich in Vitamin C. They are also rich in pectin and so make very good jam. They can also be bottled, turned into juice or vinegar. But by far the best way of preserving them is in a freezer. Whole berries will come out looking as fresh as the day they were picked. For best results, freeze them on a baking sheet in a single layer before packing them into cartons or bags; if space is limited, purée them first. This gives you the opportunity to use up any squashed or crumbled fruit. Sweeten the purée lightly before it goes into the freezer but be prepared to adjust the flavour with more sugar before using it.

REMEDIES

Raspberries are renowned for their beneficial effects on women in child-birth; raspberry leaf tea is said to help prevent miscarriage, ease labour pains, speed delivery and help the uterus to contract after labour. A juice made by steeping raspberries and sugar together in a lidded glass container is excellent for preventing colds.

RASPBERRY SHRUB

This traditional drink is refreshing and cooling if you have a fever. It is also said to be good for the heart.

Fill a bowl (not of metal or plastic) with fresh ripe raspberries and pour over enough wine or, preferably, cider vinegar to cover. Let it stand for 3 or 4 days, stirring from time to time. Strain into a saucepan and sweeten to taste – roughly a pound (450 g) sugar to each pint (550 ml) liquid (or you may prefer to use honey). Bring to the boil and let it simmer for 20–30 minutes, skimming off any scum that rises. Allow to cool. The addition of a wine glass of brandy to each pint (550 ml) liquid will help preserve it. Pour into clean bottles and cork tightly. Dilute with water to taste.

BERRY SOUP

This is a refreshing starter for lunch or dinner on a hot summer's day.

1 pound (450 g) mixed berries:
   raspberries, strawberries,
   blackberries etc, as available
¾ pint (400 ml) single cream
1¼ pints (700 ml) milk
½ pint (300 ml) thick sour cream
About 2 ounces (50 g) caster sugar
Lemon juice
Ice cubes and sugared croûtons
   (page 205), to serve

Rub the fruits through a fine sieve or vegetable mouli, or purée them in an electric blender and then sieve out the seeds.

Blend the cream, milk and sour cream together with the puréed fruit. Sweeten to taste, and if necessary intensify the flavour with a little lemon juice.

Chill the soup until ready to serve. Serve in a large tureen with a few ice cubes floating in it to keep it chilled throughout the course, and accompanied by a bowl of sugared croûtons to sprinkle over each portion.

Serves 8.

SUMMER PUDDING

In putting together the medley for a summer pudding, think in terms of about 3 pounds (1·4 kilos) fruit or a little more to pack a 2 pint (1·1 litre) pudding basin, half of them raspberries, or a mixture of raspberries and a small punnet of very ripe loganberries. The cherries are there for texture as well as flavour, but don't worry if there are none to be had – just use more berries and currants.

1½ pounds (700 g) raspberries or
    mixed berries (see above)
12 ounces (350 g) ripe sweet cherries,
    stemmed and pitted
8 ounces (225 g) blackcurrants,
    stalked
8 ounces (225 g) redcurrants, stalked
6–8 ounces (175–225 g) caster sugar
White bread (see method)
Thick chilled cream, to serve

Gently mix the fruit and sugar together in a bowl. If it is a warm day, let the bowl stand for an hour or two in a sunny spot to help the sugar draw out the juices from the fruit and soften them. But if time and weather are against you, you can achieve the same effect by warming the mixture very gently on top of the stove or in a cool oven for 10–15 minutes.

Meanwhile, cut slices of bread a good ¼ inch (6 mm) thick and trim off their crusts. Cut a round to fit the bottom of the basin, then line the sides with fan-shaped pieces, butting them together as closely as possible.

Pile the fruit into the basin, pressing gently but firmly as you go, until it is level with the top after a final light pressing. Save all the excess juices to touch up any pale patches when the pudding is turned out.

Cover the pudding with more slices of bread. Place a *flat* plate that just fits inside the rim of the basin on top, or use a thick cardboard template cut to measure and sealed in plastic wrap. Weight it down and chill until the following day.

Serve turned out, the top decorated with a representative selection of whole fruits, accompanied by a jug of chilled cream.

Serves 6–8.

RASPBERRY ORANGE CREAM

6 ounces (175 g) sugar
Long strip of orange rind
1½ pounds (700 g) fresh or thawed
    frozen raspberries
2 tablespoons Curaçao, Cointreau or
    Grand Marnier
Lemon or lime juice and sifted icing
    sugar (optional, see method)
¾ pint (400 ml) double cream
Toasted flaked almonds, to decorate

Dissolve sugar in ½ pint (300 ml) water. Add strip of thinly peeled orange rind. Bring to boiling point and boil hard until syrup has thickened and is reduced by about half. Leave until cold, then fish out orange rind and discard it.

Rub raspberries through a fine nylon sieve. Blend in orange syrup and orange liqueur. Taste purée. Flavour should be sharp and sweet. If necessary, it may be intensified with a squeeze of lemon or lime juice or sweetened further with a little sifted icing sugar.

In a bowl, beat cream until it stands in very soft peaks. Gradually beat in raspberry purée. Spoon into individual stemmed glasses.

Sprinkle each glass with just a pinch of toasted flaked almonds and chill the glasses very thoroughly before serving.

Serves 6.

FROZEN RASPBERRY CREAM

A simple sweet, light and refreshing, to serve with delicate almond meringues or tuiles.

Use fresh or frozen raspberries for the purée. One pound (450 g) of fresh berries makes about ¾ pint (400 ml) purée. Sweeten it lightly to taste with icing sugar.

½ pint (300 ml) lightly sweetened
    raspberry purée (see above)
3–4 tablespoons Framboise
    or Kirsch
2 large egg whites
Pinch of salt
About 3–4 tablespoons caster sugar
¾ pint (400 ml) double cream

Flavour the raspberry purée with Framboise or Kirsch and put aside until needed.

In a large, clean, dry bowl, beat the egg whites with a pinch of salt until they form soft, floppy peaks when beaters are lifted. Gradually adding 3 tablespoons sugar, continue to beat to a stiff, glossy meringue. In a separate bowl, beat cream until it is thick but not buttery.

Fold egg whites into whipped cream, followed by raspberry purée. Taste and add a little more sugar if needed to sweeten.

Pour mixture into a freezer tray or plastic bowl. Cover with a lid or a sheet of foil. Freeze until firm.

Transfer the container to the main compartment of the refrigerator about 1 hour before serving to soften slightly.

Serves 6.

RASPBERRY YOGHOURT ICE CREAM

Simply delicious and rather less fattening than a conventional ice cream made with cream only or an egg and cream custard.

8 ounces (225 g) fresh or frozen
   raspberries
Juice of 1 large orange
Finely grated rind of ½ large
   orange
4 ounces (100–125 g) soft pale
   brown sugar
¼ pint (150 ml) double cream
¼ pint (150 ml) natural yoghourt

If using frozen raspberries, mix them with the orange juice and grated orange rind, and leave until quite thawed. Otherwise, mix fresh raspberries with orange juice and rind just before use.

Rub fruit through a fine nylon sieve to make a purée. Add sugar and stir until dissolved.

In a large bowl, beat cream until very thick. Add yoghourt and beat again until mixture is well blended and thick enough to hold impression of the beaters. Gently and thoroughly fold in raspberry purée. If small lumps of cream remain unblended, you can break them down most easily by stirring with a small wire whisk.

Pour mixture into ice cube trays or a plastic box with a lid. Cover with foil or the lid and freeze until ice cream is solid round the sides but still very soft and runny in the middle.

Scrape it all out into a bowl and beat until uniformly smooth and creamy again. Then pour the ice cream back into freezing container(s), cover and freeze until firm.

Place in main compartment of refrigerator an hour before you plan to serve ice cream so that it has time to soften very slightly and develop its full flavour.

Serves 4–6.

RASPBERRY MOUSSE

Either fresh or frozen raspberries may be used to make this mousse, but if using frozen fruit allow a few ounces more to make up for the weight lost when the juice drains off during thawing.

1 pound (450 g) fresh raspberries or
   1¼ pounds (575 g) frozen
   raspberries
½ ounce (15 g) powdered gelatine
½ pint (300 ml) double cream
4 tablespoons caster sugar
4 eggs, separated
4 ounces (100–125 g) almond
   macaroons
Whipped cream and whole
   raspberries, to decorate

If using frozen raspberries, thaw them in a sieve set over a bowl to allow any juices to drip away. Then, in a food processor or blender, purée fruit. Press purée through a fine nylon sieve and discard pips. Put aside. Sprinkle gelatine over 2 or 3 tablespoons water (or the juice that drained from the thawing raspberries) in a cup and allow to soften, then solidify. Stand cup in a small pan of very hot water and stir until gelatine has dissolved and liquid is quite clear. Cool to lukewarm.

In the top of a double saucepan, or a heatproof bowl that will fit snugly over a pan of simmering water, beat cream, sugar and egg yolks together until fluffy and well blended. Fit pan over simmering water and continue to beat until custard has thickened. Remove pan from lower container and continue beating lightly until custard has cooled to lukewarm. Then stir in dissolved gelatine and raspberry purée until thoroughly blended. Allow to cool until syrupy but not set, stirring occasionally to prevent a skin forming on top.

Beat egg whites until they form soft peaks and fold them into the cold raspberry custard. Crush macaroons to crumbs (in a plastic bag with a rolling pin is easiest) and fold them in as well.

Spoon mousse into a glass serving bowl and chill until quite set. Serve decorated with swirls of whipped cream and a few whole raspberries.

Serves 6.

RASPBERRY ALMOND MERINGUE

This delicious dessert, with its unusual combination of flavours, uses frozen raspberries. Make sure they are unsweetened.

8 ounces (225 g) almonds
8 ounces (225 g) caster sugar
4 egg whites
Pinch of salt

Raspberry filling
12 ounces (350 g) frozen
   unsweetened raspberries
1–2 tablespoons caster sugar
½ pint (300 ml) whipping cream

Dampen a large baking sheet slightly and line it with a sheet of greaseproof paper marked with a circle 9 inches (22·5 cm) in diameter.

In an electric blender or food processor, grind the dry (unblanched) almonds finely. Mix thoroughly with the caster sugar. In a large, clean, dry bowl, beat the egg whites with a pinch of salt until stiff but not dry. Using a large metal spoon, gently but thoroughly fold in the ground almonds and sugar. Spread the meringue evenly over the circle marked on the greaseproof paper, building up the sides slightly.

Bake the meringue in a slow oven (325°F, 170°C, Mark 3) for 1 hour, or until it feels firm and dry when you touch it, and is lightly coloured. Leave until cold, then peel off the paper and transfer the meringue case to a large, flat serving dish.

Take about a dozen of the best raspberries. Place them on a plate in a single layer and leave to thaw in the refrigerator. These will be used to decorate the meringue. Sprinkle remaining raspberries with sugar. Place them in a large sieve fitted over a bowl and leave to thaw in the refrigerator. Beat the cream until firm but not buttery.

Shortly before serving, assemble the meringue. Fill the case with thawed raspberries. Cover with whipped cream and decorate with remaining whole raspberries.

Serves 8–12.

RASPBERRY TART WITH CREAM

From Mrs Bowman's *New Cookery Book* (1867).

'Fill the tart-dish with fresh raspberries, and less than a quarter of the weight in fine sugar; cover with a thin paste; bake half or three quarters of an hour, according to size; take it out of the oven, raise the cover, beat up the yolks of two eggs well, and mix with half a pint of cream and a tablespoonful of sifted sugar; pour this over the fruit, restore the crust, and return it to the oven for five or six minutes. Strew sugar over the crust, and serve hot or cold.'

RASPBERRY SAUCE

A simple, delicious sauce with a thousand uses. You can pour it over fresh strawberries, peaches and practically any other fruit, or serve it with ice cream.

1 pound (450 g) fresh or thawed
frozen raspberries
Lemon juice
Icing sugar

Rub raspberries through a fine nylon sieve and discard seeds. Beat in lemon juice and icing sugar to taste (2 or 3 tablespoons of each should be enough) and chill lightly until ready to serve.

RASPBERRY JAM

Raspberries
Their weight in sugar

In a preserving pan, over low heat, cook raspberries with sugar until sugar has dissolved and juices run, stirring and mashing frequently with a potato masher or a wooden mallet. Then raise heat and boil briskly until setting point is reached, skimming off scum until surface is clear.

Cool slightly. Pot and cover as usual.

Note: To make a smooth jam free of pips that is particularly useful for tarts and for sandwiching sponge cakes, first heat the raspberries without sugar until the juices run and the berries are very mushy, then rub them through a fine sieve. Discard pips, return purée to the pan and proceed as above.

RATAFIA DE FRAMBOISE
Raspberry Liqueur

Raspberries produce a rich, fruity, deep pink liqueur. Use firm, undamaged berries.

2 pounds (900 g) ripe, fresh
raspberries
3 pints (1·7 litres) vodka
2 pounds (900 g) granulated sugar

Pick over and wash the fruit, then crush the berries slightly. Pack into a large, wide necked, screw-top jar (a Kilner jar is ideal) and pour over the vodka. Seal the jar and leave to stand in a cool place for 1 month, shaking occasionally.

At the end of this time, make a syrup by dissolving the sugar in 1 pint (550 ml) water and boiling for 15 minutes. Open the jar containing the fruit and alcohol and strain off the liquid through a fine sieve into a clean bowl, pressing the fruit to extract as much juice as possible. Stir the sugar syrup into the fruit liqueur. Bottle and leave for 6 months before drinking.

Makes about 3½ pints (2 litres).

RASPBERRY REDCURRANT JAM

The Victorian cookery book from which this recipe is taken boasts that 'the addition of the currant-juice is a very great improvement to this preserve'.

To every pound (450 g) of raspberries:
1 pound (450 g) sugar
¼ pint (150 ml) redcurrant juice
(page 166)

In a preserving pan, crush the raspberries to a pulp with a potato masher or a wooden spoon. Bring to boiling point slowly, raise heat and boil for 15 minutes. Stir in sugar and redcurrant juice, and when sugar has dissolved, continue to boil the jam for about 30 minutes longer, or until setting point is reached, skimming surface until it is free of scum.

Cool slightly, pot and cover.
See also page 198.

RASPBERRY ACID

The following recipe, written on a scrap of paper, was found acting as a bookmark in my copy of *The London Art of Cookery*, published in 1783. It can also be made with strawberries.

'Put 12 lbs of fruit into a pan. Pour over them 2 quarts of spring water previously acidulated with 5 oz of tartaric acid. Let them remain 24 hours then strain them taking care not to bruise the fruit. To each pint of clear liquor add 1 lb & a ½ of loaf sugar finely pounded (use caster sugar, which will dissolve more easily than granulated), stir it frequently and when quite dissolved bottle the syrup. The whole process must be cold and the bottles kept uncorked for some days as the liquor generally ferments a little.'

Exactly the same recipe, contributed by a Mrs Campbell of Inverneill, appears in *The Feill Cookery Book*, published in Glasgow in 1907. Mrs Campbell adds: 'It is useful as a beverage mixed with water and also for flavouring creams and jellies.'

RASPBERRY RHUBARB JAM

The recipe and method are exactly the same as for Raspberry Redcurrant Jam, except that instead of redcurrants, 1½ pounds (700 g) rhubarb stalks, trimmed and cut into 1 inch (2·5 cm) lengths, are used. The fruit need not be sieved or puréed unless the raspberry pips are going to be very troublesome.

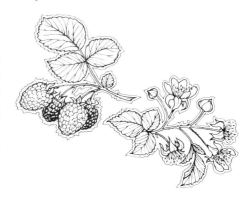

REDCURRANT, WHITECURRANT

To all intents and culinary purposes, there is nothing to choose between redcurrants and whitecurrants, except that the latter lack the red pigment and are possibly slightly sweeter. On the whole, however, both are too sour to eat raw on their own, rather like blackcurrants, though they do not have the characteristic strong aroma of blackcurrant fruit and leaves, which some people find unpalatable.

Red- and whitecurrants are native to the northern hemisphere. They have long been a cultivated garden fruit but will happily grow wild and produce fruit in woods and hedgerows, particularly near water. Unlike blackcurrants, they do not need a rich soil.

Add redcurrants to fresh vegetable and fruit salads in small amounts — too many could make a dish too sharp. Sprays of glazed redcurrants, sparkling like precious stones, make an enchanting decoration for a bowl of fruit or a cake, a sweet or a fruit tart.

For many people, especially anyone who wears dentures, redcurrants have one great drawback. Their pips are numerous, tiny and hard, and become even harder when the fruit is cooked. My mother tells the story of painstakingly seeding redcurrants one by one with a pin for many hours. At the end she had no more than a pot of preserves to show for her trouble — but they *were* unforgettable preserves. Even if you are not prepared to go to those lengths, it may still be worth while eliminating the seeds by rubbing the cooked fruit through a fine sieve. Failing that, console yourself with the thought that some people actually enjoy biting on the seeds!

Redcurrant jellies are traditional with roasts of lamb, poultry, and game birds. They also make an excellent glaze rather along the lines of an apricot glaze, for brushing over pastries, cakes and open fruit tarts.

Otherwise, you can dry or sugar-freeze red- and whitecurrants whole, juice them, or mix them with other fruit.

Redcurrants contain much less Vitamin C than blackcurrants, but are also good for fevers.

REDCURRANT JUICE

Redcurrant juice diluted with water or soda water makes a delightfully refreshing drink, ideal for invalids and convalescents.

Rinse redcurrants, strip them from their stalks and put them in the top of a double saucepan or in a heatproof jar or jug standing in a pan of simmering water.

Add enough water to show at the top of the currants. Heat steadily until juices have run from the fruit, mashing lightly once or twice with a fork. Then strain through a very fine sieve or a colander lined with muslin, pressing lightly to extract as much juice as possible.

The juice can be used in water ices and for jellies. If you have made a large quantity, it is worthwhile bottling and sterilizing it (page 202) for storing.

REDCURRANT AND CARROT SALAD

A deliciously refreshing summer salad to serve with a plate of cold meat, or perhaps poultry. For the best effect, the fruit and vegetables should be garden-fresh.

4 ounces (100–125 g) redcurrants, stemmed and rinsed
4 large, crisp carrots, coarsely grated
2–3 teaspoons caster sugar
Juice of 1 lemon
Lettuce leaves, to garnish

In a mixing bowl, toss the currants, carrots, sugar and lemon juice together until well mixed. Taste for flavouring.

Arrange in a bowl lined with crisp lettuce leaves and serve.

Serves 4–6.

Note: A few drops of light soya sauce may add a welcome accent, or some may prefer a little Tabasco, to taste.

REDCURRANT AND HONEY FOOL

An unusual — but very successful — combination of flavours.

1 pound (450 g) redcurrants, stemmed and rinsed
4 ounces (100 g) honey
Sugar (optional)
½ pint (300 ml) cream, whipped
Lemon juice

Put the redcurrants in a casserole with the honey and just enough water to moisten. Cook, covered, in a moderate oven (350°F, 180°C, Mark 4) until redcurrants are tender. Rub through a nylon sieve and add sugar if necessary.

Fold the purée into the whipped cream and flavour with lemon juice, to taste.

Spoon into individual glass dishes and chill well before serving.

Serves 4.

AUSTRIAN REDCURRANT TART

One 8 or 9 inch (20 or 22·5 cm) rich shortcrust pastry case, pre-baked (page 203).

Redcurrants
10–12 ounces (275–350 g) redcurrants, stemmed
2 ounces (50 g) sugar

Meringue
2 egg whites
Pinch of salt
3–4 ounces (75–100 g) caster sugar

Dissolve sugar in about ¼ pint (150 ml) water – or just enough to 'take' redcurrants. Bring to boiling point, drop in redcurrants and simmer gently for a few minutes. Lift fruit out with a slotted spoon, draining thoroughly. Boil the syrup rapidly until it is well thickened. Cool and pour over fruit.

When ready to assemble tart, make a meringue. Whisk egg whites with salt until they form soft, floppy peaks when beaters are lifted. Gradually beat in half of the sugar and continue to beat until meringue is stiff and glossy. Fold in remaining sugar with a large metal spoon.

Spread the redcurrant mixture evenly over the tart shell and cover with meringue, spreading it right to the pastry rim to seal the filling in. Flick up the meringue decoratively all over with a knife blade.

Return tart to a slow oven (325°F, 170°C, Mark 3) and bake for 25–30 minutes, or until meringue is very lightly coloured and feels crisp and firm. Serve lukewarm or cold.

Serves 4–6.

REDCURRANT WATER ICE

1 pint (550 ml) redcurrant juice (see opposite page and method)
8 ounces (225 g) sugar
Juice of ½ lemon
Icing sugar (optional)
2 egg whites
Whipped cream and sweet wafer biscuits, to serve

Simmer at least 1 pound (450 g) redcurrants, and strain juice as described on the opposite page.

Prepare sugar syrup by dissolving sugar in 1 pint (550 ml) water. Bring to boiling point and simmer for 10–15 minutes, skimming off any scum that forms on the surface.

Stir in lemon juice and allow the syrup to cool.

Combine 1 pint (550 ml) each redcurrant juice and sugar syrup, and adjust flavour with more sugar or lemon juice. Pour into ice cube trays or shallow plastic boxes, cover with foil or lids and place in the freezing compartment of a refrigerator, or in a freezer. Freeze until the water ice is solid around the edges. The time this takes will depend on the size of the containers and the depth of the ice mixture.

When ice is sufficiently frozen, beat egg whites until stiff but not dry. Scrape all the ice mixture (both frozen and liquid) into another bowl and beat vigorously with a whisk or fork to break down any large ice crystals and make the mixture smooth again. Fold into beaten egg whites.

Pour the mixture back into container(s), cover and freeze until firm, several hours; or leave overnight if preferred.

An hour before serving, transfer container(s) to the main body of the refrigerator in order to allow ice to soften a little.

Serve with swirls of whipped cream (also frozen hard if liked) and/or sweet wafer biscuits.

Serves 8–10.

RODGROD MED FLODE Scandinavian Fruit Mould

A similar dish is prepared in Germany, where it is known as *Röte Grütze*. The Scandinavians serve it with cream, whereas the Germans prefer a cold custard sauce or simply milk. Any soft summer fruits may be used to make the pudding but the combination below is one of the best.

1½ pounds (700 g) ripe redcurrants, stemmed
12 ounces (350 g) raspberries
About 12 ounces (350 g) sugar
3 ounces (75 g) cornflour
1 teaspoon vanilla essence

In a large, enamelled pan, cover the fruits with ¾ pint (400 ml) cold water. Bring slowly to boiling point and simmer for about 10 minutes, or until fruits are very soft, stirring and mashing occasionally with a wooden spoon. Rub contents of pan through a fine nylon sieve.

Pour the purée back into the rinsed-out pan and sweeten to taste. Blend cornflour smoothly with about ⅓ pint (200 ml) cold water. Stir it into the fruit purée and simmer, stirring, for 3–4 minutes until the pudding is thick and smooth, and has lost its cloudy appearance and its taste of raw starch. Cool slightly and flavour with vanilla.

Rinse a large (roughly 3 pint or 1·7 litre) mould out with cold water and shake away excess. Pour in the pudding. Cool and chill until mould is firmly set, about 2 hours.

Loosen edges of mould with the tip of a knife. Invert on to a shallow serving dish and gently but firmly shake out the pudding. Serve accompanied by a jug of pouring cream, cold custard sauce or milk.

Serves 6.

REDCURRANT JELLY

Redcurrant jelly is a classic accompaniment for roast lamb and poultry, with a thousand-and-one other uses in the kitchen, for both savoury and sweet dishes.

Prepare the redcurrant juice following the instructions on page 166. However, there is no need to stalk the fruit, and do not try to squeeze the juice through the jelly bag or muslin-lined sieve – simply leave it for as long as necessary.

Measure the juice and for each pint (550 ml) allow 1 pound (450 g) sugar. In a clean preserving pan, combine the two. Heat gently until sugar has dissolved. Then raise heat and boil until setting point is reached, skimming surface clear of scum with a large spoon.

Cool slightly, pot in small jars and cover.

See also page 199.

ELIZA ACTON'S REDCURRANT JELLY

This recipe, which is entitled 'Superlative Red Currant Jelly' in Eliza Acton's *Modern Cookery* of 1845, makes a fine, sharp jelly with the minimum of fuss and trouble. With the addition of lemon juice, it is a very easy way of making a few pots of jelly with redcurrants from the freezer (I have successfully used fruit that was over a year old). As Miss Acton claims, the jelly is 'of the finest possible flavour', and it will set firmly provided the currants are not too ripe and the growing season has been a dry, sunny one. The timing is spot on for frozen as well as fresh fruit, but the latter does not need the help of lemon juice.

2 pounds (900 g) frozen redcurrants
2 pounds (900 g) sugar
Juice of 1 large lemon

Put the frozen redcurrants in a bowl (after weighing them) and leave to thaw overnight. The following day, add sugar and with a potato masher or a large fork, mash lightly to burst the currants. Pour into a preserving pan and bring to boiling point over a low heat, stirring and mashing constantly. Stir in lemon juice, raise heat and boil rapidly for exactly 8 minutes, by which time it will have reached setting point on a thermometer. Stir constantly and skim off any scum (there will be less with frozen fruit than with fresh).

Strain jelly through a fine nylon sieve, pressing pips and skins against sides of sieve with the back of a large wooden spoon to extract as much jelly as possible. Pour hot into hot, sterilized jars and cover immediately. Leave until cold before storing. When it is cold, the jelly will be spoonable but not set rock hard.

See also page 199.

CUMBERLAND SAUCE

This is a spicy sauce for serving with poultry and game.

4 ounces (100–125 g) redcurrants
2 ounces (50 g) sugar
½ teaspoon finely chopped shallots
Juice and grated rind of ½ orange
*   and ½ lemon*
¼ pint (150 ml) port
½ teaspoon mustard powder
Pinch of cayenne pepper
¼ teaspoon ground ginger

Wash the redcurrants thoroughly in a colander, under cold running water. Discard any stalks and damaged berries. Put redcurrants in a saucepan with ¼ pint (150 ml) water, and cook gently over a low heat to soften the fruit.

Strain off the liquid through a fine sieve into another pan. Put the fruit pulp in a linen bag. Seal the bag tightly and squeeze to extract as much juice as possible on to the liquid already in the pan. Stir in the sugar until dissolved. Cook over a low heat until syrupy.

Add the shallots, orange and lemon juices and rinds, the port, mustard, cayenne and ginger to the fruit syrup. Mix together well and serve hot or cold.

REDCURRANT AND MINT SAUCE

This is a variation of the traditional mint sauce to serve with cold roast lamb.

2 tablespoons redcurrant jelly
1 tablespoon finely chopped fresh
*   mint*
Juice and finely grated rind of
*   ½ orange*

Put the redcurrant jelly in a bowl and break it into small pieces with a wooden spoon. Add the chopped mint, orange juice and rind. Mix together thoroughly and chill before serving.

GLAZED REDCURRANTS

Egg white
Sprays of redcurrants
Caster sugar

Lightly mix the egg white with a fork, just enough to break down any gelatinous threads. Coat each spray. Allow excess egg white to drip off, then coat the wet sprays with caster sugar. Gently lay them on sheets of greaseproof paper to dry off for 15 minutes before use.

REDCURRANT AND MUSTARD SAUCE

A German sauce to serve with ham and bacon.

2 tablespoons redcurrant jelly
½ teaspoon mustard powder
Red wine

Put the redcurrant jelly into a bowl and mash it with a wooden spoon until it has a smooth jam-like consistency. Stir in the mustard powder. Gradually add red wine until the sauce has the consistency of pouring cream. Serve hot.

RHUBARB

Rhubarb is a leaf stem or stalk botanically, but to the Western cook it is a fruit, and a grossly underrated one at that. In cool, damp climates, rhubarb will flourish like a weed – possibly one of the reasons why it has so often been treated with disdain. Not so in Asia Minor, one of the areas put forward as its original home (the other one is farther east, possibly in Tibet). Persian cooks have invented a variety of delicious *koreshtha* in which meats such as beef are partnered with rhubarb to make sharp, sour sauces to serve with rice.

Rhubarb is thought to have reached Europe in the fourteenth century. Europeans were interested in its medicinal properties but rather slow to exploit its culinary potential. They acknowledged its importance as the first fresh fruit of the year ('spring fruit' was one of the names by which it was known), but tended to think of it as a mere substitute for what was to come later. Rhubarb sauce was an excellent accompaniment to fatty fish such as mackerel, but abandoned for gooseberry sauce as soon as the berries came into season. The sweet rhubarb dishes that are so popular today – compotes, pies, crumbles and preserves – are comparatively late arrivals. Writing in the mid-Victorian period, Mrs Beeton describes rhubarb as a newcomer which was practically unknown twenty years earlier.

Look for stalks which are neither too thick, nor thin and spindly. They should be firm and full of juice, and snap crisply in two when you bend them. Another, more discreet way of testing is to puncture the stalk with your thumbnail. If it is fresh, the juice will run out. Avoid stalks that flop and are flabby – they are also stale – and any that are over-thick or split.

Rhubarb benefits from being partnered with other flavours, especially orange, and spices such as cinnamon and ginger. It goes well with most other garden fruit and can be used to bulk them out if necessary. Remember, though, that cooking quickly reduces it to a pulp and will have to be very brief indeed if you want pieces to retain their shape.

Unless the stalks are forced or very young, they are bound to have developed a few 'strings', but these are easy to locate and strip away as you cut up a stalk. Do not risk leaving them as they can be unpleasantly pithy when cooked. To prepare rhubarb for most recipes, wash and trim the stalks, stripping off any strings or tough fibres. Chop the stalks into ½–1 inch (1·25–2·5 cm) lengths. However crisp and juicy the leaves may look, they must never be eaten as they contain poisonous oxalic acid.

To freeze rhubarb, wash, trim and chop the stalks and plunge into boiling water for a minute. It can be sugar frozen (and packed in polythene, not aluminium, bags) or frozen in a syrup made from equal quantities of sugar and water. Rhubarb purée can also be frozen.

Medicinally, rhubarb is still appreciated. Powdered rootstock in small doses will stimulate the appetite – rhubarb is an ingredient of several herb-based aperitifs popular in Europe – and larger doses are an effective laxative.

RHUBARB HAIR LIGHTENER

Simmer 3 tablespoons rhubarb root and 1 pint (550 ml) water in a stainless steel pan for 30 minutes. Leave to cool and steep for 6–8 hours, then strain.

Use as a rinse after shampooing, and leave the hair to dry naturally. You could use white wine instead of water which would be more expensive, but also good for the hair.

PERSIAN BEEF WITH RHUBARB SAUCE

An unusual combination of flavours.

2 ounces (50 g) butter
1 Spanish onion, finely chopped
1 pound (450 g) lean stewing beef, cubed
6–8 tablespoons chopped parsley, preferably flat-leaf
½–1 teaspoon ground cinnamon
Generous pinch of freshly grated nutmeg or ground mace
Salt and freshly ground black pepper
1 pound (450 g) washed and trimmed rhubarb
1–2 tablespoons lemon juice
Generous pinch of sugar

Melt half the butter in a heavy casserole and sauté the onion gently until transparent and golden. With a slotted spoon, transfer onion to a plate. Brown the cubed meat on all sides in the same fat. Mix in the sautéed onion, parsley and spices, and season to taste with salt and freshly ground black pepper. Add barely enough hot water to cover. Bring to simmering point; cover and cook gently for 1½–2 hours, or until meat is very soft.

Meanwhile, cut rhubarb stalks into 2 inch (5 cm) lengths. In a frying pan, sauté the rhubarb lightly in the remaining butter. Add lemon juice and sugar, and sauté for 2 or 3 minutes longer.

When beef is tender, add the rhubarb mixture to the simmering casserole and simmer, covered, for 5–10 minutes longer until the rhubarb is very soft and on the point of disintegrating.

Serve with rice.

Serves 4–6.

Note: Either chicken or one of the 'pale' meats such as pork or lamb can be substituted for the beef.

BAKED CHICKEN WITH RHUBARB SAUCE

Serve with a fluffy potato purée or a bowl of boiled or steamed Basmati rice. No other accompaniment is needed.

One 3 pound (1·4 kilo) roasting chicken
2 tablespoons melted butter
Salt
½ teaspoon ground cinnamon
½ teaspoon ground mace

Rhubarb sauce
4 stalks rhubarb (about 10 ounces or 275 g), washed and trimmed
5 tablespoons sugar, or to taste
Generous pinch of salt
1½ tablespoons cornflour
1 tablespoon butter
Lemon juice

Cut chicken into joints. Wipe them clean and fit them side by side, skin side up, in an ovenproof dish or roasting tin. Brush all over with melted butter and sprinkle with salt. Roast in a moderate oven (375°F, 190°C, Mark 5) for 30 minutes, turning joints over twice during this time and basting them with pan juices.

Meanwhile, prepare rhubarb sauce. Chop rhubarb stalks, and put in a pan with sugar, salt and ½ pint (300 ml) water. Bring to boiling point, cover and simmer for a few minutes until rhubarb is disintegrating. Blend cornflour smoothly with a little cold water. Stir into rhubarb and simmer, stirring, until sauce has thickened and is no longer cloudy, 2–3 minutes. Beat in butter and correct flavour of sauce with lemon juice and a little more sugar and salt if liked.

Spoon hot sauce over chicken joints to cover them generously. (Any sauce left over may be served with the chicken in a separate sauceboat.) Sprinkle chicken with cinnamon and mace, and return dish to the oven for 20 minutes longer, or until chicken is quite tender, basting frequently with sauce. Serve with rhubarb sauce and any buttery pan juices well mixed together and poured over the top.

Serves 4.

RHUBARB PIE

Maybe this is the reason why rhubarb used to be called the 'pie plant' and rhubarb pie was often referred to as 'pie plant pie'.

It is delicious eaten lukewarm with fresh thick cream, a dollop of ice cream or a vanilla-flavoured custard sauce.

The exact amount of sugar the pie needs will depend on the time of the year – rhubarb generally tends to need less as the season progresses.

1–1¼ pounds (450–550 g) washed and trimmed rhubarb
About 10 ounces (275 g) soft pale brown sugar (see above)
4 tablespoons plain flour
½–1 teaspoon finely grated orange rind
Generous pinch of salt
About 1 pound (450 g) rough puff pastry for a 2-crust, 8–9 inch (20–22·5 cm) pie (page 203)
1 ounce (25 g) butter
Caster sugar, to decorate

Chop rhubarb stalks. In a large bowl, blend sugar thoroughly with the flour, grated orange rind and salt. Add rhubarb and toss until well mixed.

Roll out about half of the pastry and cut out a lid for your pie dish, leaving a slight overhang all round. Put aside. Roll out remaining pastry and use it to line the pie dish, again with an overhang of about ½ inch (1·25 cm). Fill dish with prepared rhubarb and dot with flakes of butter. Moisten pastry rim with water. Place lid in position and press lightly all round edges with your fingertips to seal them. Flute or crimp edges neatly and cut a few gashes in pastry lid to allow steam to escape.

Bake pie in a hot oven (450°F, 230°C, Mark 8) for 10–15 minutes. Then turn oven down to moderate (350°F, 180°C, Mark 4) and continue to bake pie for about 30 minutes longer, or until pastry lid is well puffed, crisp and richly coloured. Cool to lukewarm with a dusting of caster sugar sifted over the top. To serve, see above.

Serves 6–8.

CREAMY RHUBARB PIE

This is made in the same way as the Rhubarb Pie on the left, but instead of using 4 tablespoons flour, cut it to 2 tablespoons and blend in 2 large, well-beaten eggs. Mix with the sugar, grated orange rind and generous pinch of salt. Fill the pastry-lined pie dish with rhubarb, dot with butter and pour over the egg mixture. Fit the pastry lid in position and continue as for Rhubarb Pie.

SPRING PUDDING

Adjust the amount of sugar to taste, depending on the acidity of the fruit and whether forced pink rhubarb or more mature stalks are used. This makes an excellent prelude to the summer pudding that will follow as soft fruits ripen.

1 pound (450 g) washed and trimmed rhubarb
About 4 ounces (100–125 g) sugar
Lemon juice (optional)
Stale white bread slices, about ¼ inch (6 mm) thick
Thick cream or custard sauce (page 205), to serve

Chop rhubarb stalks, and place in a pan with the sugar and 2 or 3 table-spoons water. Cover and stew gently until rhubarb is very soft but has not disintegrated completely. Cool slightly. Taste and add a little more sugar if necessary, or a squeeze of lemon if liked.

Meanwhile, trim crusts from bread slices. Cut a round to fit the bottom of the basin, then line the sides with fan-shaped pieces, butting them together as closely as possible. Spoon half of the rhubarb into the basin, followed by a layer of bread and the remaining rhubarb. Cover with another layer of bread. Cover with a flat plate that just fits inside the basin rim or with a thick cardboard template cut to measure and sealed in plastic wrap. Weight it down and chill for several hours or overnight if possible.

Turn out on to a shallow serving dish.

Serve the pudding with thick cream or a custard sauce.

Serves 6.

RHUBARB FOOL

A quick, simple sweet which allows the full flavour of rhubarb to come through, mellowed by cream. Young, pink rhubarb will need less sweetening and no stringing, whereas more mature stalks have a stronger flavour. Serve the fool accompanied by crisp, delicate biscuits.

1½ pounds (700 g) washed and trimmed rhubarb
Twist of orange peel
About 4 ounces (100–125 g) sugar
Lemon juice
¼ pint (150 ml) double cream
4 tablespoons single cream or creamy milk

Wash, prepare and chop rhubarb stalks, and put in a heavy pan with 2 tablespoons water and the twist of orange peel. Cover tightly and cook gently until rhubarb is pulpy and dis-integrating, shaking pan occasionally. Remove the orange peel and either crush the rhubarb up with a fork, purée it in an electric blender or rub it through a fine sieve. Sweeten to taste and sharpen flavour with a little lemon juice. The flavour should be quite pronounced as the cream is going to dilute it.

Leave until cold.

In a large bowl, beat the creams together lightly until thickened. Fold in the rhubarb and a little more sugar to taste if necessary. Chill well before serving.

Serves 4–6.

RHUBARB CRUMBLE

Serve with cream, a custard sauce or a dollop of plain yoghourt sweetened with brown sugar.

1 pound (450 g) washed and trimmed rhubarb
4 ounces (100–125 g) soft brown sugar
6 ounces (175 g) unbleached plain flour
1 teaspoon baking powder
3 ounces (75 g) soft margarine or butter

Chop rhubarb stalks, and put them in a large, ovenproof baking dish. Add half of the sugar and toss with a fork until well mixed.

Sift the flour and baking powder into a bowl. Rub in the margarine, not too finely, and stir in the remaining sugar. Stir in 2 or 3 tablespoons of this crumble mixture into the rhubarb. Then spoon the remainder over the surface, distributing it evenly but without pressing it down.

Bake in a moderate oven (350°F, 180°C, Mark 4) for 1 hour, or until the rhubarb feels soft when pierced with a skewer, and the crumble is crisp and golden. Serve hot, lukewarm or even cold.

Serves 4.

Note: For a slightly different flavour, the crumble may be spiced with a teaspoon of ground cinnamon, sifted in with the baking powder.

RHUBARB WITH OAT CRUMBLE

Serve with a light custard sauce, chilled pouring cream or plain yoghourt which you have sweetened lightly and into which you have folded a little whipped sweet cream, say a maximum of half and half.

1 pound (450 g) washed and trimmed
    rhubarb
3 tablespoons soft brown sugar
3 tablespoons orange juice

Topping
4 ounces (100–125 g) rolled oats
1 teaspoon ground cinnamon
2 ounces (50 g) soft margarine or
    butter
2 ounces (50 g) soft brown sugar

Chop rhubarb and lay in an oven-proof baking dish. Add sugar and orange juice, and mix with a fork until fruit is thoroughly coated.

Prepare topping. Mix oats with cinnamon. Work in margarine or butter (a large-tined fork will make this easy), then add sugar and continue to mash with the fork until all the ingredients are thoroughly mixed and crumbly.

Spoon the topping evenly over the fruit. Bake in a moderate oven (375°F, 190°C, Mark 5) for 35–40 minutes, or until the topping is crisp and the fruit underneath feels soft when pierced with a fork or skewer. Cool slightly.

Serves 4.

RHUBARB COMPOTE

Easy, quick and cheap, but no less delicious for all that. Serve with cream or yoghourt, or spooned over ice cream.

1 pound (450 g) washed and trimmed
    rhubarb
4 ounces (100–125 g) soft pale brown
    sugar

Chop rhubarb.

Heat sugar in ½ pint (300 ml) water, stirring until sugar has dissolved, and bring to boiling point. Immediately throw in rhubarb, lower heat and bring to simmering point once more. Cook gently for a few minutes with the lid half-on, swirling pan round occasionally, until pieces of rhubarb feel soft when pierced with a fork or skewer but have not disintegrated too much or gone mushy. Draw off the heat, cover and cool.

Serves 4.

Note: You can change the flavour of the compote quite appreciably by boiling a piece of orange peel, either fresh or dried, with the sugar, or by spicing the syrup with a cinnamon stick and 2 or 3 cloves. Leave them in the compote until just before serving.

RHUBARB MERINGUE TART

*One 8 inch (20 cm) rich shortcrust
    pastry case, pre-baked (page 203)*

Rhubarb filling
1 pound (450 g) washed and trimmed
    rhubarb
Strip of lemon rind
Sugar
2 egg yolks, lightly beaten
2 tablespoons melted butter

Meringue topping
2 egg whites
Pinch of salt
½ teaspoon cream of tartar
4 tablespoons caster sugar

Leave the pastry case in its baking tin on a baking sheet.

Prepare rhubarb filling. Chop rhubarb stalks and put them in a pan with the strip of lemon rind and a few tablespoons of water – just enough to cover bottom of pan. Cover pan tightly and simmer until rhubarb is quite soft and disintegrating. Then remove lemon rind. Sweeten rhubarb to taste, beating vigorously with a spoon to reduce it to a purée.

Cool to lukewarm, then blend in lightly beaten egg yolks and melted butter.

Pour rhubarb filling into pastry case and bake in a moderate oven (350°F, 180°C, Mark 4) until filling is set but not coloured, about 20 minutes. Cool slightly.

Meanwhile, prepare meringue topping. Beat egg whites until white and foamy. Add salt and cream of tartar, and beat to soft peak stage. Then beat in sugar, a tablespoon at a time, and continue to beat to a stiff, glossy meringue.

Pile meringue on top of rhubarb filling, spreading it right to the pastry edge so that filling is completely sealed in. With a knife blade, flick up surface of meringue decoratively. Return tart to the oven for 15–18 minutes until meringue is set on the surface and tips of flicks are tinged with brown. Leave to cool and serve lukewarm.

Serves 6.

Note: If you like the meringue to be hard and crisp all the way through, put it in a much cooler oven (300°F, 150°C, Mark 2) to dry out for 45–60 minutes. In this case, you could also beat another 2 tablespoons sugar into the meringue.

RHUBARB BURNT CREAM

1 pound (450 g) washed and trimmed
    rhubarb
Finely grated rind and juice of 1
    orange
Soft brown sugar
¼ pint (150 ml) double cream
¼ pint (150 ml) plain yoghourt

Chop rhubarb stalks, and put them in a pan with grated orange rind, orange juice and 2 ounces (50 g) soft brown sugar. Mix well, cover and cook gently until rhubarb is reduced to a pulp. Pour into a flameproof baking dish and allow to cool.

When ready to finish the dish, switch on grill so that it will be thoroughly hot when you come to use it.

Whip cream just until it has thickened. In another bowl, beat yoghourt until smooth. Beat yoghourt lightly into whipped cream until mixture is thoroughly blended and very thick again. Pile cream mixture over cooled rhubarb, spreading it out evenly with the back of the spoon. Sift a thick, even layer of brown sugar over entire surface.

Place dish under grill and grill steadily until sugar has melted to make a glassy coating for the cream. The grill should be turned up high but watch carefully that the sugar does not start to burn. Leave until quite cold and hard on top before serving.

Serves 4–6.

RHUBARB JAM

Green rhubarb stalks make a beautifully green jam, while the jam from red rhubarb is golden pink. In either case use thick, mature rhubarb, not thin, pink, forced stalks.

To every pound (450 g) of washed
*   and trimmed rhubarb:*
*   1 pound (450 g) sugar*
*   Finely grated rind of ½ lemon*

Chop rhubarb stalks, weigh them and put them in a preserving pan. Add sugar and grated lemon rind. The rhubarb may now be left overnight to allow sugar to draw out some of its juices. Or proceed immediately as follows. Place the pan over very low heat until sugar has dissolved, stirring frequently to prevent rhubarb or sugar scorching before the fruit has released some juice. Then boil over moderate heat until setting point is reached, skimming off scum as it rises to the surface, and stirring frequently.

Cool slightly, pot and cover.
See also page 198.

RHUBARB PICKLE SAUCE

4 pounds (1·8 kilos) washed and
*   trimmed rhubarb*
2 pounds (900 g) soft brown sugar
1 teaspoon ground cinnamon
1 teaspoon ground cloves
1 teaspoon ground mixed spice
½ teaspoon salt
½ teaspoon freshly ground black
*   pepper*
1 pint (550 ml) white wine or cider
*   vinegar*

Wash, prepare and chop rhubarb stalks, and put in a pan (preferably enamelled) with all the remaining ingredients, mix well and heat gently until sugar has dissolved. Then simmer over moderate heat until rhubarb has disintegrated and sauce is thick, stirring frequently to keep sauce from burning.

Cool sauce and pour into clean, dry bottles or jars.
See also page 200.

Fills about 5 jars.

RHUBARB AND GINGER PRESERVE

A good example of how inexpensive rhubarb makes an excellent foil for other more expensive ingredients such as ginger. Start the preserve the day before it is to be cooked so that the sugar has plenty of time to draw out juices from the rhubarb. It makes an unusual spread for warm, fresh scones and bread, as well as slices of buttered gingerbread.

2½ pounds (1·1 kilo) washed and
*   trimmed rhubarb*
2½ pounds (1·1 kilo) sugar
Juice and finely grated rind of 1 large
*   lemon*
A 1 ounce (25 g) piece of fresh ginger
*   root*
3–4 ounces (75–100 g) crystallized
*   ginger*

Chop rhubarb stalks. In a large bowl, layer rhubarb with sugar, lemon juice and rind. Cover bowl and leave overnight at room temperature.

The following day, turn contents of bowl into a preserving pan. Bruise the piece of fresh ginger root thoroughly all over. Tie it up in a square of muslin and drop it into pan. Over low heat, stir contents of pan frequently until sugar is quite dissolved and juices are running freely. Then raise heat and boil vigorously, stirring and mashing frequently with your spoon (or a potato masher) until rhubarb is very soft and pulpy, about 15 minutes.

Dice crystallized ginger finely. Remove bag of ginger root from pan, squeezing back as much of the juice from it as possible. Replace it with the diced ginger. Stir well, bring to a vigorous boil once more and boil until setting point is reached, about 7–10 minutes longer. Towards the end of cooking time, skim surface clear of scum.

Cool slightly, pot and cover.
See also page 198.

Fills about 5 jars.

RHUBARB ORANGE JAM

If you grow your own rhubarb, this is a very good and economical way of using up mature stalks before they turn fibrous.

2 pounds (900 g) washed and
*   trimmed rhubarb*
3 sweet oranges
Sugar

Chop rhubarb stalks, and weigh before putting them in a preserving pan. Rinse and dry oranges, and finely grate off the rind, stopping short of the white pith, which can be unpleasantly bitter. Peel off and discard every scrap of skin and pith from oranges. Slice them thickly crosswise, carefully picking out pips. Collect pips in a small bowl. Chop up slices of orange, picking out any tough pieces of skin and adding them to the pips. Cover pips with ¼ pint (150 ml) boiling water and put aside for at least 30 minutes. Weigh orange pulp and juices (12–16 ounces or 350–450 g on average).

Add grated orange rind, chopped pulp and juices to rhubarb, and mix well. Place pan over very low heat and cook slowly, stirring and mashing occasionally, until juices run and rhubarb is very soft and pulpy (contents will have reduced by about one-third).

Weigh out equivalent of rhubarb and oranges in sugar (original weight). Add to rhubarb. Strain in soaking water from pips. Stir over low heat until sugar has quite dissolved, then raise heat and boil briskly until setting point is reached. Towards the end of cooking time, skim surface clear of scum.

Cool slightly. Pot and cover.
See also page 198.

Fills about 5 jars.

Note: Instead of using chopped orange pulp, you may find it simpler and quicker to squeeze the oranges after grating off their rind and cook the rhubarb with orange juice instead.

STRAWBERRY

The appearance of the first strawberries is a sure sign that summer has arrived. According to the writings of Ovid, Pliny and Virgil, they were already well known in the Roman world. Much later, it was recorded that Henry VIII of England had paid 10 shillings for a 'pottle' of strawberries. But in spite of their obvious popularity, these fruits must have been rather miserable specimens compared with the cultivated ones we have today. Attempts were made to breed better strains, but the real breakthrough did not come about until the nineteenth century, when two species imported from the New World, *Fragaria chilensis* and *Fragaria virginiana*, met by accident in France. Since then, the strawberry has never looked back.

In addition to the usual garden varieties, there is also the alpine strawberry, a miniature plant that produces fruit throughout the summer. Although it has been cultivated for centuries, it has so far resisted all attempts to make it grow any bigger. Smallest of all are the wild strawberries which grow in grassy woods from the end of June to August, and have the sweetest and most highly flavoured berries of all.

When buying strawberries, look for fresh, clean fruit with bright green hulls and stems. As with other soft fruits, avoid washing if possible. If necessary, clean them lightly as follows. Lay the berries in a single layer on a cloth wrung out of cold water, roll the cloth up loosely and shake gently. Any grit or dust is transferred to the damp cloth, leaving the fruit clean. As a last resort, wash strawberries by floating a single layer in a large bowl of cold water. Swish the water gently with your hand, leave it for a minute to allow any grit to sink to the bottom, then quickly transfer the fruit to a colander to drain. Strawberries should always be cleaned or washed before they are hulled.

The only accompaniments recognized by purists are a jug of thick, chilled pouring cream and a bowl of fine sugar. But instead of cream, try using some fruit juice such as orange, lemon or even lime. Alternatively, bathe the berries in a thick purée of fresh raspberries or macerate them in orange liqueur, a little port or sweet white wine. Champagne can be quite sensational.

Make the most of strawberries while they last. Apart from jams, which are a great favourite, they do not make particularly good preserves. Unless you like crunching the berries in a semi-frozen state, freezing can be disappointing as the fruit turns flabby and loses its brightness when thawed. To avoid this, use small to medium-sized berries and freeze them in a thick raspberry purée so that the juices which the strawberries release as they thaw automatically blend with the purée. Alternatively, crush the strawberries to a pulp before freezing them, ready to use in other recipes.

A final warning. Strawberries have little natural pectin so more will have to be added in the form of lemon or redcurrant juice, or bottled pectin, if a jam is to set properly. This is especially important if frozen fruit is used.

Strawberries are both delicious and good for you. They are particularly high in Vitamin C and folic acid, and also have significant quantities of iron, calcium and phosphorus.

COSMETICS

Strawberries are universally recommended for the skin, especially the face. They have a mild astringent and bleaching effect, and are used in many masks and creams.

Masks made from strawberries cleanse and refresh the skin, reduce oiliness, and lighten freckles. Mash berries that are too over-ripe to serve, pat or smear them on your face, and leave on as long as possible.

Strawberry juice can also be used, on its own or with milk. Take a piece of linen or cotton roughly the size of your face, cut holes for eyes and mouth, soak it in the juice, wring out lightly and apply. As it dries, re-soak and re-apply.

FACE CREAM

This light, creamy but not greasy, cream softens and tones the skin.

Take 1 part lanolin, 3 parts oil (almond, avocado, peach or olive), and 2 parts strawberry juice. Melt the lanolin in the oil in the top half of a double boiler. Remove from the heat and add the strawberry juice gradually, beating all the time until cool.

To make a large quantity, substitute up to 10 per cent of the oil with wheatgerm oil, to preserve it. Add the contents of a Vitamin E capsule (200 I.U.) for extra nourishment.

REMEDIES

Fresh strawberries are excellent for invalids and have been recommended for sufferers from liver complaints, gout and rheumatism.

Strawberry leaves and roots are often used to make a tea: use 2 tablespoons to a pint (550 ml) water. They can also be boiled in wine. This relieves diarrhoea and dysentery, problems of the liver and urinary tract, and is recommended for heavy periods.

An infusion of strawberry leaves can be used as a mouthwash to strengthen gums and freshen the breath. It makes a good gargle for sore throats and mouth ulcers (and can be used as a compress for ulcers and sores anywhere).

The juice removes tartar from the teeth, and the leaves can be dried, powdered finely, sprinkled on a dry toothbrush and used, very effectively, as a toothpowder. The root may also be used; equal quantities of dried, powdered sage are a good addition. Brushing with this mixture stimulates and strengthens the gums.

WILD STRAWBERRY SOUP

These 'miniature' strawberries, which may either be cultivated or gathered in the wild, have so much sharp flavour of their own that they should be allowed to speak for themselves as much as possible. Serve this soup hot or cold.

1 pound (450 g) wild strawberries
About 4 ounces (100–125 g) sugar
2 egg yolks
¼ pint (150 ml) thick cream
Lemon juice (optional)
Sugared croûtons (page 205) or
*   puffed wheat cereal, to garnish*

Pick over and rinse strawberries if necessary. Mix them with the sugar and either purée in an electric blender or food processor, or crush to a purée with a fork. Dilute with 1¼–1¾ pints (about 1 litre) cold water. Pour into a pan and heat gently, stirring to dissolve any remaining sugar.

Beat egg yolks lightly with cream. Beat in a few tablespoons of the hot, puréed soup. Pour back into pan of soup and stir constantly over low heat until it thickens. Take great care not to let it boil or egg yolks will curdle. Taste soup and add a little more sugar or a squeeze of lemon juice if liked. Soup may be served either hot or cold; if the latter, cool and chill it lightly first. Serve garnished with sugared croûtons or puffed wheat cereal.

Serves 6.

HONEYED STRAWBERRIES

For about 1½ pounds (700 g) strawberries, which will serve 4–6, prepare the following syrup. In a wide saucepan, dissolve 4 tablespoons runny honey and 2 tablespoons sugar in ¼ pint (150 ml) water. (Use mild honey for this. A strong honey would get in the way of the flavour of the strawberries.) Add a strip of lemon peel and simmer for 5 minutes.

Add strawberries to the simmering syrup and cook gently for 5 minutes before switching off the heat. Allow to cool to lukewarm before serving.

STRAWBERRIES IN CREAM

1 pound (450 g) ripe, even-sized
*   strawberries, hulled*
Finely grated rind and juice of 1 small
*   sweet orange*
4–6 tablespoons caster sugar
1 large carton (about 8 fluid ounces or
*   225 ml) whipping cream*
1 small carton (about 5 fluid ounces or
*   150 ml) thick natural yoghourt*

In a bowl, sprinkle strawberries with orange rind and juice, and a tablespoon of sugar, and mix lightly.

Beat the cream until stiff but not buttery. In another bowl, beat yoghourt lightly until smooth. Fold whipped cream into yoghourt and sweeten with 3 tablespoons caster sugar. Fold strawberries and their juices into cream mixture, making sure they are individually coated, and sweeten with a little more sugar to taste if necessary. Spoon into a serving bowl and chill thoroughly.

Serves 4–6.

STRAWBERRIES IN LIME CREAM SAUCE

1 pound (450 g) strawberries
4 tablespoons fresh lime juice
About 2 tablespoons sifted icing
*   sugar*

Lime cream sauce
3 egg yolks
4 ounces (100–125 g) caster sugar
8 fluid ounces (225 ml) single cream
Thinly peeled rind of ½ lime
4 fluid ounces (100–125 ml) double
*   cream*

Start by preparing the sauce. In the top of a double saucepan (or a heatproof bowl that will fit snugly over a pan of simmering water), beat egg yolks and sugar together until fluffy. In a heavy pan, scald single cream with the lime-rind, peeled off with a potato peeler. Off the heat, pour gradually into the egg yolks and sugar, stirring vigorously with a wooden spoon. Fit top of pan or bowl over simmering water and cook, stirring,

until custard is thick enough to coat back of spoon. Take care not to let it boil, or egg yolks will curdle. Leave until quite cold, stirring ocasionally to prevent a skin forming on top. Finally, remove and discard the strip(s) of lime rind. Shortly before serving, beat double cream until thick and fold in lime custard sauce. Chill lightly.

Clean strawberries on a damp cloth or rinse them briefly if necessary. Hull them and halve or quarter any large ones so that they are all of the same size. In a bowl, toss strawberries gently with lime juice and sifted icing sugar, to taste. Cover bowl and chill lightly until ready to serve.

To serve, turn strawberries over in their juices once more and divide between 4 individual glass serving bowls. Spoon lime cream sauce over each bowl and serve immediately.

Serves 4.

STRAWBERRY MERINGUED CREAM

This is a glorious concoction of strawberries, cream and crushed meringues. For special occasions, flavour the cream with a little fruit liqueur – Grand Marnier, Kirsch or Framboise – or plain brandy. Alternatively, you can use just a little vanilla-flavoured sugar.

2 pounds (900 g) strawberries
About 8 tablespoons icing sugar
6 tablespoons fruit liqueur (optional, see above)
½ pint (300 ml) double cream, chilled
¼ pint (150 ml) single cream, chilled
6 meringues

Clean and hull strawberries. Pick out a dozen or so of the best specimens and put them aside for decoration. Chop remaining berries up roughly and put them in a bowl. Sift icing sugar, to taste, over the top. Sprinkle with liqueur or brandy if used. Mix lightly, cover and chill for 1 hour.

In another bowl, combine creams and beat until they hold their shape in soft peaks. Gently but thoroughly fold in chopped strawberries and all their juices. In the palm of your hand, crush each meringue into large pieces, dropping them on to strawberry cream. Fold into cream. Taste and add more sugar if necessary.

Pile cream into a glass serving bowl, dot with reserved whole strawberries and serve.

Serves 6–8.

FRAGOLE DAMA BIANCA
Italian Strawberries with Meringued Cream

1½ pounds (700 g) ripe, red strawberries
4 tablespoons orange liqueur
Caster sugar
2 egg whites
6 fluid ounces (175 ml) double cream
½–1 teaspoon vanilla essence

Clean or wash strawberries. Drain off any excess moisture and hull them. In a serving bowl, mix strawberries lightly with liqueur and sweeten to taste with about 2 tablespoons sugar. Cover bowl and chill thoroughly by placing bowl in refrigerator for about 3 hours.

About 30 minutes before serving, beat egg whites until they stand in soft peaks. Beat in 3 ounces (75 g) caster sugar, a little at a time, and continue to beat to a stiff, glossy meringue. In another bowl, using the same beaters, beat cream with vanilla until it is very thick and beginning to stand in soft peaks. Fold meringue and cream together lightly until well blended.

Pile cream on strawberries and return bowl to refrigerator to chill lightly for 30 minutes.

Serves 6.

STRAWBERRIES JUBILEE

A strawberry spectacular to serve with luxury ice cream. It also works beautifully with frozen berries. Whichever you choose, the final stage is most effective when it is carried out at the table.

2 pounds (900 g) strawberries, fresh or frozen
3–4 ounces (75–125 g) caster sugar
¼ pint (150 ml) Kirsch or Maraschino liqueur
About 1½–2 pints (900 ml–1.1 litres) ice cream

If using fresh berries, clean and hull them, keeping them as dry as possible. Sweeten to taste with sugar and put aside for 30 minutes. Frozen berries should be sweetened according to whether they were packed with sugar or not, and allowed to defrost only to the stage where they are still very chilly and firm to the touch.

When the ice cream has been unmoulded, ready to serve, bring the liqueur to haze point in a wide, shallow pan. Have a long match ready. Keeping the heat under the pan high, tip in the strawberries and shake them around in the hot liqueur until the juices have evaporated sufficiently for the alcohol to ignite. Let the flames get a good hold.

Tip the flaming contents of the pan over the ice cream and serve the dessert at once.

Serves 6–8.

SOYER'S STRAWBERRY SALAD

From Alexis Soyer's *Shilling Cookery for the People* (1855).

'A large pottle (basket) of ripe strawberries, picked (ie hulled) and put into a basin with two tablespoonfuls of sugar, a pinch of powdered cinnamon, a gill of brandy (or a few tablespoons liqueur, wine or fruit juice); stir gently, and serve.

'Currants and raspberries the same.'

STRAWBERRY AND CURRANT SALAD

From Mrs Bowman's *New Cookery Book* (1867).

'A pretty dessert dish may be made of mixed early fruits, strawberries, white or red currants, gooseberries and cherries, all carefully picked, placed in alternate layers strewed with sugar, and piled up with taste. Either simple cream, or wine or brandy cream, should be poured over the salad.'

FRESH STRAWBERRY FLAN

A flan made with fresh strawberries is quick and easy to make and always delicious.

Make a tart shell with rich shortcrust pastry (page 203) and when it is cool fill it with strawberries. Pack them tightly together with the pointed ends up. Make a glaze by melting 4 ounces (100–125 g) smooth strawberry jam with a little water. Strain the liquid, allow it to cool slightly, then spoon it over the fruit.

FRENCH STRAWBERRY ICE CREAM

1 pound (450 g) ripe red strawberries
Juice of 1 lemon
About 8 ounces (225 g) caster sugar
¼ pint (150 ml) double cream
Red food colouring (optional)
Whole strawberries or fresh puréed
*   raspberry sauce, to serve*

Clean and hull strawberries. In an electric blender or food processor, blend strawberries to a smooth purée. Blend in lemon juice, followed by enough sugar to give purée a strong, sweet flavour. (Remember that freezing will modify flavours, so use more lemon juice or sugar if necessary.)

In a bowl, beat cream until it thickens and begins to hold its shape softly. Gradually beat in strawberry purée. Add colouring if needed.

Pour into ice cube trays or a shallow plastic box. Cover with foil or a lid and freeze until ice cream has congealed around sides but is still soft and creamy in the middle.

Scrape mixture out into a bowl and beat vigorously until uniformly smooth and creamy once more (use an electric mixer for this if you have one).

Pour back into container(s). Cover and freeze until firm.

Transfer to main body of refrigerator for about 1 hour to soften slightly before serving.

Serve the ice cream with fresh whole strawberries, lightly sugared if necessary, or masked with a purée of fresh raspberries.

Serves 4–6.

HOT STRAWBERRY SAUCE

Use over-ripe fruit which is no longer quite suitable for serving fresh for this sauce which is delicious poured over fresh fruit, ice cream or sponge pudding.

1 pound (450 g) very ripe strawberries
12 ounces (350 g) sugar
3 tablespoons Kirsch

Clean and hull strawberries, and wash thoroughly in a colander under cold, running water. Make a purée by mashing the fruit with a fork or potato masher (or, ideally, use an electric blender). Leave the purée on one side.

In a thick-bottomed saucepan, heat the sugar and ½ pint (300 ml) water, stirring frequently, until boiling. Lower the heat and simmer, stirring occasionally, for about 20 minutes until the syrup thickens slightly. Leave to cool for a few moments before stirring in the strawberry purée and mixing thoroughly.

Just before serving, heat the mixture to desired temperature (do not boil). Remove from the heat, and stir in the Kirsch.

STRAWBERRY AND RASPBERRY ICE CREAM

Prepare as above, using 8 ounces (225 g) each strawberries and raspberries, and rubbing purée through a fine nylon sieve before sweetening it.

STRAWBERRY AND REDCURRANT ICE CREAM

Prepare as above, using 8 ounces (225 g) each strawberries and redcurrants, and rubbing purée through a fine nylon sieve before sweetening it.

COLONIAL STRAWBERRY SHORTCAKE

A scone filled with fresh strawberries and eaten warm with cream may not sound very exciting – more a way of spinning out the precious fruit – but this American favourite is remarkably good in its own right.

8 ounces (225 g) plain flour
3 teaspoons baking powder
Generous pinch of salt
2–3 tablespoons caster sugar
3 ounces (75 g) butter or white
*   vegetable fat*
Generous ¼ pint (150 ml) single
*   cream or creamy milk*

To finish
Softened butter
1½–2 pounds (700–900 g)
*   strawberries*
Caster sugar
Lemon juice (optional)
Lightly whipped cream

To make shortcake, sift flour, baking powder, salt and sugar into a bowl. Using your fingertips or 2 knives, work in butter or vegetable fat until mixture resembles fine breadcrumbs. Then, stirring with a knife blade, gradually pour in enough cream or milk to make a very soft dough that holds together. Turn it out on to a floured board and knead very briefly (literally, a few times only). Pat dough out into an 8 inch (20 cm) circle and place it on a buttered baking sheet, or fit it into a well-buttered layer cake tin that is 8 inches (20 cm) in diameter. Dot or spread surface with a tablespoon of softened butter.

Bake shortcake in a hot oven (450°F, 230°C, Mark 8) for about 15 minutes until well risen and nicely browned on top.

While shortcake is baking, clean and hull strawberries. Halve or slice half of them thickly, depending on size. Crush the remainder lightly with a fork. Sweeten the two portions of fruit with a little sugar and if liked add a few drops of lemon juice.

When shortcake is ready, turn it out on a cooling rack until it is just cool enough to handle. Then with a serrated knife, carefully split it in two horizontally. Spread cut surfaces generously with more softened butter.

Lay bottom half of shortcake, buttered side up, on a serving dish and cover with crushed strawberries and their juices. Cover with the other piece of shortcake, buttered side down. Pile sliced or halved berries on shortcake and top with a generous dollop of lightly whipped cream. Serve while still fresh and warm.

Serves 4.

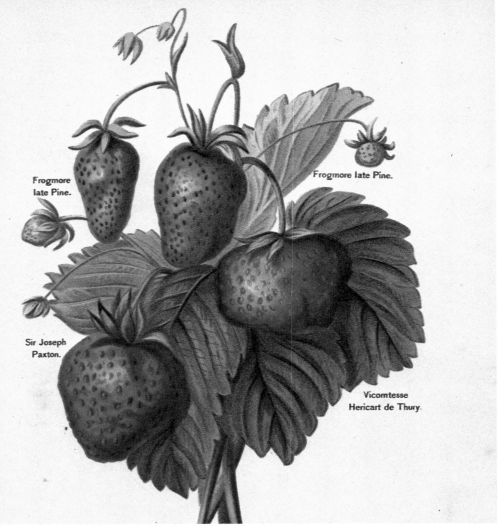

Frogmore late Pine.

Frogmore late Pine.

Sir Joseph Paxton.

Vicomtesse Hericart de Thury.

If this preserve is properly made, the strawberries remain whole, suspended in a clear, rosy syrup. The secret lies in never, at any point, stirring the fruit with a spoon which could bruise or mash the berries. Instead, lift the whole preserving pan by the handle, using both hands, and swirl the contents around gently. This will keep the jam well 'stirred' as it cooks, and also make all the scum collect at one point, where it can easily be skimmed off. Use firm, slightly under-ripe strawberries. Medium-sized are the best.

3 pounds (1.4 kilos) strawberries
3 pounds (1.4 kilos) sugar
Juice of 1 large or 2 small lemons,
  strained

Clean the strawberries if necessary and hull them. Lay them in a large, shallow dish and cover them evenly with 2 pounds (900 g) sugar. Leave until the next day to allow sugar to draw out as much juice as possible.

Next day, pour off strawberry juices into a preserving pan, together with as much of the sugar as possible. Add the remaining pound (450 g) of sugar. Place pan over low heat until all the sugar has completely dissolved, stirring frequently.

Bring the syrup to the boil and slide in the strawberries all at once. Bring to boiling point again and boil until strawberries are nearly ready and turning translucent, swirling pan round frequently and skimming off the scum with a large spoon as necessary (see above).

Then add the lemon juice and boil the jam until setting point is reached, shaking the pan frequently. Allow the jam to cool undisturbed in the preserving pan before potting and covering as usual.

See also page 198.

Fills about 5 jars.

Note: For a special luxury strawberry preserve, dip the hulled end of each strawberry into a saucerful of brandy as you prepare them. This is a favourite Middle Eastern trick.

CHOCOLATE STRAWBERRY JELLIES

These take both time and patience, so make a large batch in mid-summer when the fruit is plentiful and cheap. Box some as a gift or serve with coffee after a special meal.

2 pounds (900 g) fresh, ripe
  strawberries
1½ pounds (700 g) sugar
1 pound (450 g) dark dipping
  (couverture) chocolate

Clean and hull the strawberries, and wash in cold water, discarding any damaged berries. Purée by mashing or in an electric blender. Place the purée in a thick-bottomed saucepan. Stir in the sugar. Cook over a low heat, stirring constantly with a wooden spoon until the mixture is thick enough for a clean line to be left on the bottom of the pan when a spoon is drawn across it. Remove the pan from the heat.

Grease a large baking tray. Distribute the strawberry mixture in little mounds – about 1 heaped teaspoon of mixture in each – on the baking tray. Leave to set.

When each strawberry jelly is firm to touch, prepare the chocolate coating. Break the chocolate into small pieces and place in a bowl that will fit securely over a pan with hot water in it, without the water touching the bottom of the bowl.

Cover the bowl, and let the chocolate melt, stirring occasionally with a wooden spoon. When the chocolate has melted completely, beat until it is smooth and creamy. Place a sugar thermometer in the chocolate and leave it until the temperature has fallen to 110°F (43°C). At this temperature the chocolate should be of the right consistency for coating. A small amount picked up on a finger should set immediately.

Place the tray of strawberry jellies next to the bowl of chocolate. Line another, similar size, baking tray with waxed paper and place this on the other side of the bowl of chocolate. Drop the jellies, one at a time, into the chocolate. Use a fork to submerge and turn them. When well coated, lift out on the fork, tapping it on the side of the bowl to remove excess chocolate. Hold the fork over the tray lined with waxed paper and angle the fork so that the chocolate jelly rolls off. Make sure the jellies are well spaced. Leave for several hours until the chocolate is completely hard. Store between pieces of waxed paper in an air-tight container.

STRAWBERRY VINEGAR

This is a delicious accompaniment to hot sponge puddings. It also makes an unusual syrup for fresh fruit salads.

1 pound (450 g) strawberries
1 pint (550 ml) white wine vinegar

Put the strawberries and vinegar in a glass or china bowl. Cover with a clean cloth and leave for about 4 days. Stir the mixture occasionally.

Strain through a sieve and measure the liquid. For each pint (550 ml) allow 12 ounces (350 g) sugar. Combine the two in an enamel or stainless steel pan. Bring to the boil, stirring until the sugar has dissolved, and continue boiling for 10 minutes longer.

Pour into hot bottles and seal.
See also page 202.

SHERRIED STRAWBERRIES

2 pounds (900 g) fresh, ripe
*   strawberries, cleaned and hulled*
6–8 ounces (175–225 g) sugar
Sherry

Put alternate layers of strawberries and sugar in a wide-necked jar, filling the jar right up to the top. Pour in the sherry until the fruit is covered. Do this very slowly so that no air bubbles are formed.

If any bubbles remain trapped in the jar, release them by slipping a flat knife blade down the side of the jar. Be careful, though, not to pierce the fruit while doing so.

Seal tightly and store.

STRAWBERRY WINE

Making this sweet fragrant wine is an excellent way of using up the excess of fruit after a good harvest.

3 pounds (1·4 kilos) ripe strawberries
1 pound (450 g) ripe bananas
1 pound (450 g) raisins, chopped
½ ounce (15 g) citric acid
1 teaspoon Pectozyme
1 Campden tablet
Madeira yeast
3 pounds (1·4 kilos) demerara
*   sugar*

Clean and hull the strawberries and wash thoroughly under cold running water. Peel the bananas and chop coarsely. Heat 7 pints (4 litres) water to boiling point in a preserving pan. Put all the fruit including the raisins in the prepared mashing vessel and mash well together. Pour the hot water over the fruit, cover and allow to cool to 65°F (18°C). Then quickly stir in the citric acid, Pectozyme and Campden tablet. Cover the vessel. Leave for 24 hours.

Quickly, stir in the activated yeast (see manufacturer's instructions for quantity and method of use). No nutrient tablet is necessary in this recipe. Re-cover the vessel and leave in a warm place (65–75°F or 18–24°C) for 6 days. During this time, stir once a day to make sure the fruit is kept moist.

Using a fine sieve, strain off the liquid into a clean, sterile container. Put the fruit pulp into a linen bag. Seal the bag and squeeze out as much juice as possible into the strained liquid. Stir in the sugar. Quickly siphon into a fermentation vessel, filling to within 1 inch (2·5 cm) of the cork. Ferment in a warm, dark place 65–75°F or 18–24°C under an airlock. This will take about 4 weeks. When a deep layer of sediment has formed on the bottom of the vessel, rack until clear.

Store the wine in a dark place for 6 months, then bottle. Leave for 2 years before drinking.

See also page 205.

Makes 1 gallon (4·5 litres).

CHAMPAGNE COCKTAIL

6 strawberries
1 orange, peeled and sliced
3 tablespoons caster sugar
2 tablespoons lemon juice
¼ pint (100–125 ml) cognac
1 bottle champagne, well chilled

Chop the strawberries and orange very finely.

Sprinkle with the caster sugar and pour the lemon juice and cognac over the fruit.

Chill the mixture for a minimum of an hour.

Immediately before serving, divide the mixture between 6 chilled champagne glasses. Fill the glasses with champagne and serve.

Serves 6.

TANGERINE

The tangerine takes its name from Tangiers, and is thought to have reached Southern Europe from there. Its other common name, the mandarin (from the French *mandarine*), gives a clue as to its original cultivation in China and the Far East, where its delicately perfumed flowers are still used in scent-making. Like its close relatives the Japanese-sounding satsuma and the smooth-skinned clementine, the tangerine has a characteristic and inimitable flavour, and a loose skin that is quickly and easily peeled away. It is deliciously juicy, easy to segment and in today's highly bred versions even the few large pips it may have come as a surprise. Fresh tangerines should weigh well in the hand, have a sheen on the skin and a good, bright colour. Any signs of shrunken skin or spots of brown mean they've been on their way to market longer than is good for them.

Tangerines are fit companions for any other fruit in a salad and, because of their relatively low acid content, can be enjoyed by people with delicate digestions or sensitive stomachs. Their one drawback – often shared by the smaller satsumas – is that the tough white pith and membrane can be difficult to strip away before eating. To deal with this, carefully dip the segments into a bowl of almost-boiling water to soften the membrane for a few seconds. It should then be easy to release the flesh without breaking up the delicate juicy portions. Tangerines or mandarins take well to canning, while satsumas, being seedless, are ideal dessert fruits.

Tangerine skins are aromatic and full of oil. Extract this in the usual way by rubbing the wiped skin with a couple of cubes of sugar, then crush these and add them to the syrup for a fruit salad or sorbet. The skins of the larger varieties make effective containers for ices or sorbets made from citrus fruits, and can also be cut into strips and candied for use in cakes.

Tangerines can be used in any recipe which calls for oranges and freeze well for up to a year in a cold sugar syrup made from 8 ounces (225 g) sugar to 1 pint (550 ml) water; peel and segment them, and remove membrane.

SMOKED TANGERINE CHICKEN

This Chinese method of preparing chicken calls for a large steamer. Star anise, an essential ingredient, is the dried star-shaped fruit of an evergreen tree, native to China. It can be bought in specialist Chinese food stores.

3 pound (1·4 kilo) roasting chicken
1 tablespoon soya sauce
1 teaspoon salt
1 teaspoon white sugar
1 tablespoon sherry
Peel of 1 tangerine, sliced and dried
1 whole star anise
3 tablespoons brown sugar
Fresh coriander leaves (optional)

Wash the chicken, inside and out. In a large bowl, big enough to hold the chicken, mix a marinade of the soya sauce, salt, the white sugar and sherry. Place the chicken in the bowl and rub the marinade all over its inside and outside. Leave for 20 minutes. Then heat some water in the bottom half of a large steamer. Put the chicken in the top part and steam for 15 minutes.

Using a pestle and mortar or an electric grinder, grind the tangerine peel and star anise together as finely as possible. Mix this powder with the brown sugar. Take a large heavy casserole or pan, with a tightly fitting lid, and line with foil. Sprinkle the tangerine, anise and sugar mixture over the foil. Then place a trivet or wire rack in the casserole or pan and put the steamed chicken on this. Cover tightly.

Place the casserole or pan on a medium heat. When smoke starts to escape from under the lid, turn the heat down very low and allow the chicken to smoke for 20 minutes, until tender. Remove the pan from the heat, and allow to cool with the lid on. Then uncover and remove the chicken. Serve cold, with chicken slices arranged on a serving platter. Garnish with coriander leaves.

Serves 4.

HAND CREAM

Put some Vaseline (or any unscented cream like cold cream) into the top half of a double boiler. Add twice its weight of tangerine flowers and simmer for an hour, making sure the flowers are pressed into the cream. Strain.

CITRUS AND SYRUP DESSERT

This is a charming and quite unusual sweet. You can substitute any other small, thin-skinned citrus fruits such as mandarin oranges or clementines for the satsumas, or even kumquats, which are related to them, but satsumas are best because you can rely on them being seedless.

The fruits, glistening in their syrup, make an enchantingly pretty decoration for many other sweets, ranging from simple, light creams and cold, moulded rice puddings to yeast savarins and babas which have been saturated with some of the poaching syrup. Alternatively, pile them up in a pyramid in a glass dish, coat them with syrup, dust the pyramid with finely chopped green pistachio nuts, and serve the satsumas with plenty of unsweetened thick cream or portions of vanilla ice cream. Serve with dessert knives and forks as well as spoons.

1 pound (450 g) satsumas (about 6)
8 ounces (225 g) sugar

Rinse the satsumas. In a heavy pan into which the satsumas fit comfortably in one layer, dissolve the sugar in ½ pint (300 ml) water and simmer for a few minutes to make a syrup. Lower satsumas into it and adjust heat so that the syrup is barely simmering. Cook satsumas very gently for an hour or so until their skins are very soft and easily pierced with a skewer. Keep turning the satsumas over to ensure that they cook evenly, and after the first 30 or 35 minutes, pierce each fruit deeply in several places with a fork so that it absorbs plenty of syrup.

Cool in the syrup and chill lightly before serving.

Serves 6.

TANGERINES IN RUM AND CARAMEL SAUCE

This excellent, light winter dessert is very simple to prepare.

8 ounces (225 g) sugar
10 large tangerines
2 ounces (50 g) dates, stoned
2 ounces (50 g) walnuts, shelled and
  chopped
2 tablespoons dark rum
Unsweetened whipped cream

Place half the sugar in a thick-bottomed saucepan and heat gently until it melts, stirring occasionally to prevent burning. When it is deep brown and bubbling, gradually stir in 1 pint (550 ml) water. Do not lean over the pan, as this mixture will spit and bubble when the water is first added. When the bubbling has ceased, stir in the remaining sugar. Allow to boil and then simmer over a moderate heat, stirring frequently, until the syrup thickens. Remove from the heat and leave to cool.

Peel the tangerines, removing any pith, and divide into segments (discard any pips). Arrange the tangerine segments in a shallow glass serving dish. Chop the dates into small pieces and scatter these and the chopped nuts over the tangerines.

When the caramel is cool, stir in the rum. Mix well and pour this sauce over the fruit and nuts in the glass dish. Chill in the refrigerator for 30 minutes before serving with unsweetened whipped cream.

Serves 4.

TANGERINE PRESERVE

2 pounds (900 g) tangerines
2 thin-skinned lemons
2 pounds (900 g) sugar
Knob of butter or margarine (optional)

Quarter the tangerines and lemons. Pick out all the pips with the point of a knife. Tie the pips in a piece of muslin and put them in a preserving pan with about 1 pint (550 ml) water.

On a plate or board to catch all the juices, shred the fruit finely with a sharp knife. Add them to the pan and simmer, together with the pips, until the peels are tender.

Stir in the sugar and heat gently, stirring frequently, until sugar has dissolved. Then boil hard until setting point is reached. Skim scum from the surface as it accumulates and, if necessary, stir in a knob of butter at the end of cooking time to clear the preserve completely.

Cool slightly, pot and cover.
See also page 198.

Fills about 4 jars.

TANGERINE SALAD

This is a good alternative to Christmas pudding — rich but light, and refreshing.

4 large tangerines
2 large ripe pears
Juice of 1 large lemon
¼ pint (150 ml) double cream
2 ounces (50 g) preserved ginger,
  finely chopped

Peel the tangerines, and remove the pith. Divide into segments (removing the pips) and arrange in the centre of a flat serving dish.

Peel the pears and cut into thin slices, removing the core. Arrange the slices on top of the tangerines. Sprinkle with the lemon juice.

Beat the cream in a small bowl until stiff. Spoon or pipe all around the edge of the pile of fruit. Decorate with the chopped ginger, and chill in the refrigerator for at least 1 hour.

Serves 4.

WALNUT

Walnuts – dark, rich and unmistakable in flavour – were reputed to have been the favourite nut of the gods of ancient mythology. The magnificent, spreading deciduous trees with their rippling leaves and silvery grey bark are grown for their looks alone in parks and gardens all over the world. Though apparently native to south-west Europe and central Asia, walnut trees are cultivated commercially in Italy, France, Germany and California. To the French, a walnut is simply *le noix*, the nut, but we have aptly added the prefix *wal-* meaning 'foreign'.

Walnuts, shelled or unshelled, broken in pieces or halved, are readily available all year round. Many are kiln-dried in their shells to improve their keeping qualities and this process, together with the brown outer husk around the kernel, can make them taste bitter. If you blanch the whole nuts, without their shells, in boiling water for a minute or two, the brown husk will easily peel off.

Walnuts are rich in oil and protein and in France, particularly in the sunny south, their oil is a characteristic flavouring in salad dressings. It is very strongly flavoured and though far from cheap, very little is needed. (It will also remove white heat marks from the tops of polished tables, but try rubbing those with halved nuts and keep the oil for cooking.) Whole walnuts can be picked and pickled while still green, before the hard shells have had time to form; serve pickled walnuts with cold roast meats and poultry; once again, a little goes a long way. Walnuts are a deliciously different ingredient in soups, and also combine well with fish and poultry. The Italians scatter them over pasta and toss them with garlic, oil and parsley, while the Poles glaze halved nuts in a rich sugar syrup.

Walnuts are highly nutritious, and rich in Vitamin C when green.

MEXICAN WALNUT SOUP

1 potato, peeled and diced
1½ pints (900 ml) chicken stock
6–8 tablespoons finely chopped
  walnuts
¼ pint (150 ml) single cream
Salt and freshly ground black pepper

In a saucepan, simmer potato in stock until soft, about 20 minutes.

Stir in walnuts and continue to simmer for 10–15 minutes longer. Stir in cream and season as necessary with salt and freshly ground black pepper.

Reheat soup without allowing it to boil again and serve immediately.

Serves 6.

REMEDIES

Walnuts are recommended for a variety of complaints from gout to eczema, diabetes to loss of virility.

Traditionally, a paste made from crushed, stale walnuts was applied to wounds or sores to prevent infection and help healing.

HAIR TREATMENTS

Walnut oil, rubbed into the hair, will help cure split ends and is also good for dandruff.

Decoctions or infusions made from unripe green shells, the leaves or bark will dye hair brown or black — and are good for scalp and hair.

BALKAN TARATOR SOUP

1½–2 pints (900 ml–1·1 litres) natural
  yoghourt
1 medium-sized cucumber
Salt
Finely chopped fresh dill or parsley, to
  garnish

Walnut paste (tarator)
4 ounces (100–125 g) shelled
  walnuts
2–3 plump, fresh cloves garlic
3 tablespoons olive oil

Start by preparing the walnut paste. Whirl walnuts to a purée in an electric blender or food processor, or pound them in a mortar. Crush in the garlic cloves and continue to purée until well blended.

Beat in the olive oil a little at a time

to make a thick creamy paste.

In a large bowl, beat the yoghourt until smooth together with 6–8 tablespoons ice-cold water.

Dilute the walnut paste with a few tablespoons of the yoghourt to start with, then blend the two together very thoroughly.

Peel the cucumber. Cut it in half lengthwise and if the seeds are large, scrape them out with the tip of a small spoon. Cut the cucumber into small cubes and stir them into the soup. Season to taste with salt. Cover the bowl and chill the soup thoroughly. Serve the soup garnished with finely chopped dill or parsley.

Serves 6.

TROUT WITH WALNUT SAUCE

Just as the French have created trout with almonds, so the Georgian Russians are famous throughout the Middle East for cold poached trout with walnut sauce.

4 trout, about 8 ounces (225 g) each, gutted
Salt
3 black peppercorns
2 allspice berries
1 small bay leaf
2–3 tablespoons wine vinegar
Sprigs of parsley and fronds of fresh dill, to decorate
1 lemon, cut in wedges

Walnut sauce
2 ounces (50 g) walnuts
1 tablespoon wine vinegar
Reserved fish stock
1 tablespoon each finely chopped fresh dill and parsley
Salt and sharp (hot) paprika

Wash the fish thoroughly both inside and out. Pat off excess moisture with paper towels and gently rub fish all over with salt.

Half-fill a wide, shallow pan, preferably one which will take all the fish flat in at most two layers, with water. Bring it to boiling point with salt, peppercorns, allspice berries, and the bay leaf, and simmer for a few minutes. Stir in wine vinegar. Slip fish into simmering water, making sure they are just covered, and simmer for about 15 minutes, or until flesh can be prised away from backbone with a fork. Allow fish to cool to lukewarm before lifting them out of pan. Reserve fish stock.

Cool fish completely. Then carefully remove skins, leaving heads and tails intact. Arrange them side by side on a serving platter. Decorate with parsley and dill. Garnish with lemon wedges and serve with a bowl of walnut sauce.

To make sauce, pound walnuts to a creamy paste in a mortar, or whirl in an electric blender or food processor. Blend in vinegar and enough fish stock to give sauce a thick pouring consistency. Add finely chopped dill and parsley, a little more salt if necessary and a good pinch of hot red paprika, to taste. Chill lightly and serve in a separate bowl with cold trout.

Serves 4.

ÇERKEZ TAVUĞU
Circassian Chicken with Walnut Sauce

One of the finest dishes from the *haute cuisine* of the Ottoman Empire.

1 small roasting chicken, about 3 pounds (1.4 kilos)
1 large onion, quartered
1 large stalk celery, cut into chunks
1 medium-sized carrot, cut into chunks
Salt
1 bay leaf
3–4 black peppercorns
2 allspice berries
8 ounces (225 g) broken walnut kernels
3 slices day-old white bread
Sharp or sweet paprika
Finely chopped parsley, to garnish

Wash chicken and fit it into a large pot. Surround it with pieces of onion, celery and carrot. Sprinkle with a good teaspoon of salt, throw in the bay leaf, black peppercorns and allspice berries, and pour in water to cover chicken. Bring slowly to boiling point and simmer for 50 minutes, or until chicken is tender but not disintegrating.

Draw pan from heat. Skim surface clear of scum and leave chicken to cool in stock. When cold, remove chicken and strain stock through a sieve into a bowl. Allow stock to 'settle', then skim off fat and any remaining scum from surface once more.

Skin chicken and remove meat from bones. Dice meat and put aside in a covered bowl (to prevent it drying out) until needed.

Put walnuts twice through the fine blade of a meat mincer into a bowl. Each time, press the nut 'meal' firmly with the back of a metal spoon to extract any oil, and pour it off into a cup. Reserve this walnut oil.

Trim bread slices of crusts, soak them in a little of the chicken stock and gently squeeze out excess. Shred bread into bowl of walnuts. Mix them together with a generous pinch of paprika and put the whole through the meat mincer once more to blend ingredients thoroughly. With a wooden spoon, gradually work in enough chicken stock to make a thick, creamy sauce. Correct seasoning with a little more salt or paprika, if liked.

Gently mix diced chicken into sauce. Arrange in a serving bowl. Garnish with chopped parsley and sprinkle with reserved walnut oil. Serve cold with a selection of salads and chunks of fresh bread.

Serves 4–6.

CHINESE WALNUTS AND PEPPERS

This dish is intended to be served as part of a Chinese meal, but is delicious with almost any plain roasted or grilled meat or poultry.

4 ounces (100–125 g) shelled walnut halves
1 green pepper
1 red pepper
1 small mild onion
2 tablespoons cider vinegar
2 tablespoons sugar
2 tablespoons tomato ketchup
1 tablespoon soya sauce
½ teaspoon salt
Peanut or corn oil, for frying
1 teaspoon cornflour

Blanch and peel the walnuts, using the tip of a sharp knife to pick any pieces of skin out of the crevices. Halve the peppers lengthwise. Seed and core them. Cut the peppers and onion into ½ inch (1.25 cm) dice. Combine the next 5 ingredients in a small bowl with 3 tablespoons cold water. Put aside until needed. All this can be done in advance and the dish completed shortly before serving.

To cook the dish use a wok or a large, deep frying pan. In it heat 2 tablespoons oil and stir-fry the walnuts until golden on all sides. With a slotted spoon, transfer them to a dish and keep warm.

Add another 2 tablespoons oil to the pan and stir-fry the peppers and onion for about 30 seconds, just long enough to wilt them slightly without destroying their crisp texture. Pour over the vinegar mixture and bring to boiling point over high heat, stirring. Stir in the fried walnuts.

Blend cornflour smoothly with a tablespoon of cold water. Stir into the pan juices. Bring to boiling point again, stirring constantly, and simmer for a minute or two longer until sauce has thickened. Serve immediately.

Serves 4–6.

POTATO SALAD WITH WALNUTS

A delightfully different recipe from the Northern Caucasus. This salad goes well with cold meat and poultry dishes of all kinds, and is ideal for the cold buffet table. It is also very good with fried fish.

1 pound (450 g) waxy potatoes
Salt
2 ounces (50 g) walnuts
2 cloves garlic
Pinch of sharp (hot) paprika
2–3 shallots or 1 small mild onion, finely chopped
2 tablespoons finely chopped fresh dill and/or parsley
Juice of 1 lemon
2–3 tablespoons olive oil
Pinch of sugar

Scrub potatoes clean under cold running water. Boil them in their jackets in salted water until tender but not falling apart. As soon as they are cool enough to handle, peel and slice or cut potatoes into small (roughly ¾ inch or 2 cm) cubes.

While potatoes are cooking, prepare walnut dressing. Chop walnuts very finely, whirl them in an electric blender or food processor, or put them through the coarse blade of a meat mincer. Crush garlic to a purée with a teaspoon of salt, and mix into walnuts, together with paprika, chopped shallots and dill and/or parsley. Sprinkle with lemon juice and olive oil, adding a little more if necessary to bind ingredients into a creamy dressing. Add a pinch of sugar and taste for seasoning.

Pour dressing over potatoes, turning pieces to coat them. Give seasoning a final check and serve.

Serves 4–6.

Note: If dressing is thicker than you would like, it can be thinned down with a little cold water.

BEETROOT AND WALNUT RELISH

A side dish from Georgia in the Caucasus, which is usually served cold with cold meats.

1 pound (450 g) raw beetroots
1 ounce (25 g) walnuts
2 cloves garlic
Salt
3–4 sprigs fresh coriander, finely chopped
2–3 tablespoons wine or cider vinegar, or lemon juice
Pinch of sugar
Freshly ground black pepper
2–3 sprigs parsley, finely chopped

Scrub the beetroots clean under cold running water and boil them in their jackets until tender. Use a pressure cooker for this if available. When beetroots are cool, peel them and either dice them very finely or shred them coarsely on a grater.

Finely chop walnuts or whirl them to a coarse paste in an electric blender or food processor. Crush garlic to a paste with about ½ teaspoon salt. Blend pulp into walnuts, together with coriander. Moisten with vinegar or lemon juice.

Blend walnut sauce with beetroots. Correct seasoning with more salt if necessary, a pinch of sugar and freshly ground black pepper. Spoon into a serving dish. Scatter with parsley and serve.

Serves 4–6.

SAVOURY WALNUT OMELETTE

6–8 eggs
Salt and freshly ground black pepper
1 ounce (25 g) walnuts, finely chopped
Butter
Pinch of ground cinnamon
Green salad, to serve

Beat eggs very lightly, just enough to mix yolks into whites, adding a tablespoon of cold water and a good seasoning of salt and freshly ground black pepper. Stir in walnuts.

In a large omelette pan, melt about 1 ounce (25 g) butter and make an omelette in the usual way.

Fold omelette in half. Glaze it with a lump of butter speared on to the tip of a knife and sprinkle with cinnamon. Serve with a bowl of green salad.

Serves 2–3.

SWEET WALNUT AND APRICOT OMELETTE

This flat omelette is served in wedges like a cake. It makes a substantial snack or light supper dish. Serve it straight from the pan or turned out on to a lightly buttered plate.

6 ounces (175 g) plump dried apricots
Lemon juice
Sugar
4 eggs
Salt
Pinch of ground cinnamon
1 ounce (25 g) walnuts, finely
  chopped
Butter

Rinse apricots. Cover with warm water and leave to soak and soften for a couple of hours before proceeding. Drain and cut apricots into small pieces. Put them in a pan with barely enough water to cover, a good squeeze of lemon juice and 3 tablespoons sugar. Simmer, stirring frequently, until apricots have absorbed water and are thick and mushy. Beat in a little more lemon juice or sugar if liked and allow to cool.

Beat eggs lightly with a tiny pinch of salt and a little cinnamon. Do not make them too frothy. In the pan in which you are going to fry omelette (preferably one with a lid), sauté walnuts in 1 ounce (25 g) butter until crisp and golden brown. Stir in apricots and spread mixture evenly over bottom of pan. Pour eggs over surface, cover and cook gently until eggs have set. Failing a lid, cook over low heat until omelette starts setting. Then dot it with a few flakes of butter and finish the omelette off under a pre-heated hot grill.

Serves 4.

WALNUT MERINGUE BARS

These cakes are very rich so it is advisable to make individual portions rather small. The edible rice paper which is used instead of a pastry base can be bought from large food stores and some stationers.

Rice paper, for baking sheet
8 ounces (225 g) shelled
  walnuts
3½ ounces (90 g) softened butter
3 egg yolks
8 ounces (225 g) caster sugar
3½ ounces (90 g) plain flour, sifted
1 teaspoon vanilla essence
Juice of 1 lemon

Meringue
2 egg whites
5 ounces (150 g) caster sugar
½ teaspoon vanilla essence

Line a baking sheet with a single layer of rice paper, overlapping edges slightly where they meet.

Put aside a handful of the best walnut halves for decoration and mince the remainder.

Beat the butter until pale and fluffy. Beat in the egg yolks one at a time alternately with sugar, minced walnuts and sifted flour. Beat in vanilla essence and lemon juice. Taste mixture (it is quite delicious, even in its raw state) and sharpen flavour with a little more lemon juice if liked. Spread the walnut mixture evenly over the lined baking sheet.

To make meringue, beat the egg whites until they form soft, floppy peaks. Gradually beat in sugar and continue to beat to a stiff, glossy meringue, adding vanilla essence towards the end. Spread the meringue evenly over the walnut mixture and decorate the top with reserved walnut halves.

Bake in a moderate oven (350°F, 180°C, Mark 4) for 30 minutes, or until meringue feels firm to the touch. Allow to cool slightly before cutting the slab up into small rectangles or squares. For this operation use a serrated knife blade with a gently sawing motion so that meringue does not crumble.

TO PICKLE WALNUTS

The method of pickling walnuts has not changed over the years as the recipe below, which comes from Mrs Bowman's New Cookery Book of 1867 shows.

A drachm is an apothecary's measure weighing 60 grains or ⅛ ounce (or 4 g).

'The walnuts are in a proper state for pickling when a needle will easily pass through them. Lay them in a strong brine of boiled salt and water, poured over them cold for six days; then make a new brine, and leave them three days longer; leave them to dry; spread on a dish three days, when they will become black; then boil the vinegar (malt vinegar is best for this); to every quart add an ounce of ginger, an ounce of black peppercorns, two ounces of mustard seed, two ounces of eschalots (shallots), in which stick half a dozen cloves, a drachm of mace, a drachm of pimento, half an ounce of horseradish scraped (boil the vinegar and spices together for about 10 minutes before using it to release flavours); put the walnuts into the jars, filling them two-thirds; then pour over them the boiling vinegar and spices, and when quite cold, close the jars.'

Leave for a month.

SUGARED WALNUTS

1 pound (450 g) shelled walnut halves
1 pound (450 g) sugar

Blanch and peel the walnuts.

Dissolve the sugar in ½ pint (300 ml) water and boil hard until syrup has thickened. Drop in the walnuts and stir carefully over low heat for a few minutes until each nut is individually coated with syrup.

Lift nuts out with a slotted spoon on to a wire rack and leave to dry.

AKEBIA

A twining shrub, the akebia (left) is native to Japan, Korea and China, and although it will grow in temperate regions, sunlight and high temperatures are essential to ensure fruit with a good, pronounced flavour. Outside the Far East the akebia is grown mainly for decoration. The fruit is rarely exported.

Purple-grey, sausage-shaped akebia fruits are 2–5 inches (5–12·5 cm) long. As they ripen, the skin dries and becomes hard, finally splitting open to reveal soft, white flesh embedded with small, shiny, black seeds.

How to Use
The akebia's subtle flavour is best when it is eaten raw. Remove the seeds, sprinkle the flesh with a little lemon juice, and spoon straight from the fruit. For a quick, delicious dessert, blend the puréed flesh with an equal quantity of thick, double cream, the juice of a small lemon, and 2 tablespoons Kirsch. Akebia pulp is suitable for any recipe that uses an uncooked fruit purée, but the delicate flavour can easily be masked by that of other ingredients.

AKEE

The evergreen akee tree needs a subtropical or tropical climate to ensure healthy growth. A native of Guinea, West Africa, it was introduced to the West Indies by Captain Bligh of the *Bounty*, hence the plant's Latin name, *Blighia sapida*. Especially popular in Jamaica, akee arils are canned for export, and are now readily available in Afro-Caribbean speciality food shops.

The akee fruit (left), about the size of a small peach, has an outer casing which becomes hard as it ripens, changing in colour from yellow to a rich scarlet. When fully ripe, the casing splits open to reveal three large, black seeds, surrounded by white, fleshy arils. Only these arils are edible. The seeds are poisonous (and even the arils are difficult to digest when under-ripe).

How to Use
Akee can be eaten raw, but is more commonly cooked. To prepare a simple and delicious salad, boil fresh akees in salted water for about 15 minutes until tender and golden yellow. Drain. When cold, serve with a vinaigrette dressing. Simply drain canned akees and toss them in the vinaigrette.

Salt Cod with Akee

This is perhaps the most traditional use of akee in Jamaica – in combination with salt fish.

1 pound (450 g) dried salt cod
24 fresh akees, or 18 ounce (500 g)
   can akees
2 tablespoons groundnut oil
4 ounces (100–125 g) salt pork, diced
2 medium onions, finely chopped
1 small green pepper, seeded and
   finely chopped
1 red chilli, seeded and finely chopped
4 spring onions, chopped into 1 inch
   (2·5 cm) lengths
½ teaspoon dried thyme
3 medium tomatoes, peeled and
   coarsely chopped
Freshly ground black pepper
Parsley sprigs and 1 large tomato, to
   garnish

Place the fish in a bowl, cover with cold water, and leave overnight, until soft and fleshy. The next day, drain the fish, and wash well under cold, running water. Then pour about 2 inches (5 cm) of cold water into a fish kettle or casserole and place over a high heat. As soon as the water comes to the boil, lower the heat, add the fish, and allow to simmer gently until the fish is tender (about 30–45 minutes). If you are using fresh akees, add these to the casserole 15 minutes before the fish is done. If using canned akees, drain and set aside.

When the cod and akee are tender, remove the pan from the heat, drain off and discard the liquid. Remove the akees and set aside. Skin the fish, remove any bones, chop finely and leave with akees.

In a large frying pan, heat the oil until sizzling. Add the diced salt pork and cook until crisp and brown. Remove the pork and set aside with the fish and akees.

Lower the heat slightly. Add the onions and green pepper and fry until tender and lightly browned. Then add the chilli, spring onions, thyme and 3 chopped tomatoes to the pan. Stir well and cook for a further 5 minutes. Add the fish, akees and fried diced pork. Mix well together, then allow to heat through.

Stir and turn into a heated serving dish. Sprinkle over with freshly ground black pepper and garnish with the sprigs of fresh parsley and tomato wedges. Serve immediately, with hot jalapena chillis.

Serves 4.

ATEMOYA

The atemoya is one of the custard apples (page 192), a hybrid between the cherimoya and the sweet sop.

This new plant will grow under a broader range of climatic conditions than either of its parents, and is one of several hybrids which have been bred to improve their commercial potential. Several cultivars are now grown in Israel, Australia, South Africa, Central and South America and in the southern and south-west regions of the United States.

An increasing number of the custard apples found in shops are varieties of atemoya; Israel has developed a large, high quality one with few seeds, that crops twice a year.

How to Use
Atemoyas are best eaten raw. See custard apple, page 192.

BARBADOS CHERRY

Despite its name, the Barbados cherry (below) is a native of Brazil. The small tree – maximum height 10 feet (3 m) – was brought to Europe in 1757, principally for its decorative value, but in temperate regions it can only be grown under glass, or in an artificially heated environment. Plenty of sunshine is essential to produce good quality fruit.

The Barbados cherry is now found chiefly in Jamaica and Barbados, where several varieties have been developed; a popular garden fruit tree, it is exploited commercially. However, the fruit itself is rarely seen in markets or shops outside the West Indies.

The round, bright red, lobed berry or fruit is about the size of a cherry. The thin skin darkens as it ripens, sometimes becoming almost black. The Barbados cherry should be eaten only when the fruit is fully ripe, otherwise the normally sweet, juicy pink pulp can have a very slightly resinous taste.

The single seed is triangular and fluted.

How to Use
Barbados cherries are rich in Vitamin C, so are best eaten raw to obtain the full nutritional value as well as flavour.

However, they are also good in jams and pies; substitute for cherries in Cherry Jam (page 51) and Cherry Pie (page 50).

Barbados cherries can also be lightly stewed and served with whipped cream.

BERRIES

Although the following fruits are called berries, and can be treated in the same way, they are in fact berries, drupes or pomes.

A berry is a pulpy or fleshy fruit containing seeds but no true stone; barberries are an example.

Drupes are fruits in which the seeds are protected by a hard shell. Cherries are examples of one-seeded drupes but, confusingly, the fruits of some of the best-known 'berries' such as raspberries are in fact collections of drupelets on a single receptacle. Dewberries and wineberries are examples.

Pomes are technically fruits in which the seeds are collected in a core; the 'berries' of the juneberry are formed in this way.

Barberry

Once common, cultivated and wild, throughout Europe, the barberry bush has been eradicated from many farming areas, because it plays host to a common wheat parasite, black rust. However, with its bright yellow flowers and pendulous clusters of elongated, red or purple-blue berries, the barberry makes an attractive garden plant. The fruit is not sold commercially.

Most people find the flesh too acid to eat raw. However, barberries make good preserves.

Whole clusters were once candied, and the berries make an excellent jelly, traditionally eaten with mutton or venison (see Basic Jelly Recipe, page 199).

Bearberry

The name bearberry probably derives from the belief that bears feed on the bearberry shrub, an inhabitant of the colder regions of northern Europe.

Wild plants can be found in Canada, Ireland and in the extreme north of the British Isles, where the bearberry is sometimes confused with the cranberry.

It is usually cultivated for decorative reasons, though both the slimy, green leaves and the bright red berries can be harvested. (Arbutin, a drug used in the treatment of kidney disease is made from the leaves.)

Use bearberries instead of cranberries in Cranberry Tart (page 60), but remember to check the taste and add lemon juice or some other tart flavour if the berries are too sweet.

Boysenberry

The large, juicy, dark red boysenberry (below) is a hybrid (possibly of loganberry, raspberry and blackberry) created in California in the 1930s. It is mainly grown in the United States and only the canned variety is exported.

Similar in appearance to a giant loganberry, the success of this new fruit can be attributed to its ease of growth, few seeds and the lush, acidic but sweet, flesh.

The berries are delicious uncooked, sprinkled with a little sugar depending on taste, and topped with whipped cream. Use boysenberries like blackberries (page 34) or raspberries (page 162).

Boysenberry Summer Pudding

Summer pudding is traditionally made with early summer fruits — raspberries, redcurrants and, ideally, cherries. However, this version for later in the season, is equally delicious.

1½ pounds (700 g) boysenberries
2 medium cooking apples
2 ounces (50 g) sugar
White bread (see method)
Thick chilled cream, to serve

Wash and drain the berries and peel, core and slice the apples making sure you remove any bruised or damaged pieces.

Put the sugar in a saucepan with about ¾ pint (400 ml) water and bring to the boil. After about 5 minutes, add the prepared fruit and simmer, covered, until it is soft and pulpy. Strain, and set the juice aside.

Press the fruit through a fine nylon sieve to remove the seeds, and add half the juice to the purée. Keep the remaining juice to touch up pale patches when the pudding is turned out. Add more sugar if necessary.

Cut slices of bread a good ¼ inch (6 mm) thick, and trim off the crusts. Cut a round to fit the bottom of a basin, and line the sides with fan-shaped pieces, fitting them closely together.

Put the purée in the basin and cover with more slices of bread. Put a flat plate on top and weigh it down.

Chill overnight.

Just before serving turn out on to a plate and patch up any pale pieces of bread with reserved juice.

Serve accompanied by a jug of chilled cream.

Serves 4—6.

Cloudberry

The small, round, red or deep orange cloudberry grows in clusters on a creeping bramble which is native to the colder, northern regions of temperate zones.

Some cloudberries have even been found in the extreme arctic areas of Canada and Scandinavia. However, they are more abundant and accessible in the slightly milder, hilly areas of both countries, and also in similar parts of Wales and Scotland. Cloudberries are rarely cultivated.

The taste of these sweet, juicy berries has been likened to that of honey and sometimes baked apple. (In Canada, they are known as baked-apple berries.)

Cloudberries make an excellent pie filling; substitute for blackberries in Blackberry Tart (page 35).

Dewberry

The dewberry could easily be confused with the blackberry, and, indeed, in Europe it would be classified as such. In America the name is applied to blackberries that grow on trailing stems, rather than on upright bushes.

The trailing plants bear fewer berries, but mature earlier and the fruit is juicier than the bush-borne blackberry.

In America, several cultivars bearing especially large, lush fruit have been developed.

Use in the same way as blackberries (page 34).

Honeyberry

The honeyberry was originally native to most of tropical America, but wild and cultivated plants are now found mainly in the West Indies.

The oval, green berries grow in clusters, and grape-like bunches can be found on Caribbean market stalls. The thick, leathery skin is removed, revealing a large seed, surrounded by a thin band of yellow, juicy flesh that has a pleasant acid-sweet flavour when fully ripe. Unripe fruit can be extremely sour, which probably accounts for one of the honeyberry's common names – the Spanish lime.

The berries are rarely used in cooking. The seed can be cracked open, and the white kernel is roasted and then salted to be served as a snack with pre-dinner drinks.

Huckleberry

The huckleberry is a native of America. The lesser known, red huckleberry is found along the north-west coast of the United States, while the popular blue huckleberry inhabits the eastern regions, spreading west and south where conditions are cool enough. It flourishes in shaded woodland.

The small bushes are extremely attractive and, outside America, are sometimes grown as ornamental plants in gardens.

The huckleberry has not been as fully exploited for its fruit as two of its close relations – the cranberry and blueberry. Blue huckleberries are so similar to blueberries that no distinction is made by many Americans. Others claim they are superior in flavour.

Use in the same way as blueberries (page 40).

Juneberry

The juneberry is the fruit of the *Amelanchier* group of shrubs and small trees. This easily cultivated plant has a wide variety of species, and amelanchiers can be found in regions as different in climate as south-east Asia, northern Britain and North America (which has the largest number of native species).

Ease of growth and attractive white blossoms make it a popular garden plant. However, the juneberry is not grown commercially.

The fruit is similar in appearance to the blackcurrant, though the skin colour can vary from deep purple to dark red, depending on species. The common British variety is easily confused with the blackcurrant because of its blue-black skin.

Juneberries are especially popular in the United States, where they are still known by some of the early pioneer names: service berry, shad berry and swamp pear.

Use juneberries instead of apples in pies and puddings (pages 17–19). The berries are also good eaten raw.

Loganberry

A cross between a blackberry and a raspberry, the loganberry originated in California in 1881 – in the garden of Judge J. H. Logan.

The fruit looks like a large raspberry, and can be used instead of blackberries (page 34) and raspberries (page 162).

Wineberry

The wineberry is the fruit of an attractive garden shrub, native to Japan and north China. It can be grown in more temperate climates, but needs a light, well-drained soil, and plenty of water and sunlight while fruiting.

Wineberries are compound fruits, similar in appearance to blackberries (page 34) and raspberries (page 162). They can be used as an alternative to either. Whether you eat them raw or cooked, pick and use only when ripe.

Worcesterberry

The worcesterberry is an American hybrid of the gooseberry and the blackcurrant. It has the same blue-black skin as the latter, but is about midway in size between its two 'parents'. It is uncommon even in the United States.

Use in the same way as blackcurrants (page 37) and blueberries (page 40). The riper fruit is good eaten raw.

Youngberry

The youngberry is a hybrid of the dewberry and the loganberry, and looks like a large purple-black loganberry. Cultivation is still limited.

Eat raw or use as an alternative when a recipe calls for blackberries (page 34) or raspberries (page 162).

Youngberries and Bananas

1 pound (450 g) ripe youngberries
2–3 ripe bananas
Caster sugar
¼ pint (150 ml) whipping cream
Flaked or chopped toasted almonds

Pick over youngberries. Peel and slice bananas. In the bottom of 4 individual glass serving dishes put a few slices of banana. Cover with a layer of youngberries, sprinkle with a teaspoon or two of sugar to taste, and press lightly with the back of a fork. Arrange remaining banana slices on youngberries. Top with the rest of the berries and a sprinkling of sugar. Chill for a couple of hours before serving.

Serve decorated with lightly sweetened whipped cream and almonds.

Serves 4.

Note: Loganberries, boysenberries or wineberries can be used instead of youngberries.

BREADFRUIT

The breadfruit (below) is believed to be native to the Malay Archipelago, but for centuries has been widely cultivated in most tropical regions. Its main value stems from its high starch content, which makes it one of the great staple foods of the world. Captain Cook suggested its introduction to the West Indies as cheap nourishment for slaves.

Usually green skinned, but often tinged with yellow when fully ripe, this round fruit can be as large as 10 inches (25 cm) in diameter. The densely packed, seedless pulp is yellowish and sweet when ripe. Baked slices taste very similar to freshly baked bread.

Fresh breadfruit is sometimes available in markets specializing in tropical produce, but it is usually canned for export.

How to Use
Breadfruit can be cooked in much the same way as potatoes: boiled and then mashed with butter and milk, sautéed, cooked, diced and mixed with mayonnaise to make a salad, and added to stews.

BUTTERNUT

A member of the same *genus* as the walnut, the butternut is found in the eastern half of North America. The nuts are gathered locally, but are not important commercially.

How to use
Butternuts, with their soft, oily flesh, can be used in the same way as walnuts (page 182).

Breadfruit Pudding
1 pound (450 g) fresh breadfruit pulp, or 1½ pound (700 g) can breadfruit
4 ounces (100–125 g) demerara sugar
2 ounces (50 g) unsalted butter, melted
Grated rind of lemon or lime
2 tablespoons plain flour
½ teaspoon vanilla essence
¾ pint (400 ml) milk
2 eggs, beaten
5 tablespoons dark rum
½ pint (300 ml) whipping cream

Grease a large oven-proof dish with a little additional butter.

If using canned breadfruit, drain. If using fresh breadfruit, place the pulp in a large saucepan, sprinkle lightly with salt, and add enough water to cover. Bring the water to the boil over a high heat, then lower the heat and allow the breadfruit to simmer for 20 minutes until tender. Drain.

Place the drained fruit in a large bowl and mash until smooth. Using a wooden spoon, blend in the sugar, followed by the warm melted butter, grated rind and flour. Mix well. Add the vanilla essence, milk, beaten eggs and 3 tablespoons of the rum.

Beat the mixture until smooth and creamy, then turn into the prepared dish and bake in a moderate oven (350°F, 180°C, Mark 4) for about 45 minutes, until set. (A knife inserted in the pudding should come out clean.) Leave to cool slightly, and meanwhile blend the remaining rum with the cream and beat well until it begins to thicken. Serve warm with the flavoured cream poured over.

Serves 4–6.

CALAMONDIN ORANGE, PANAMA ORANGE

The calamondin is known in Europe as an exotic house plant and in the more tropical regions of the United States as an ornamental garden tree. Because it is grown largely for decoration, few people appreciate the culinary value of its fruit.

The calamondin orange (above) is similar in appearance to kumquats, though marginally larger.

How to Use
The flesh is sparse, but the peel makes an excellent marmalade.

The sharp acid juice is a good alternative to lemon juice in recipes. Like kumquats, calamondins are an ideal size to preserve whole.

Calamondin Oranges in Syrup
1 pound (450 g) calamondin oranges
2 pounds (900 g) sugar
3 tablespoons Kirsch

Wash the oranges thoroughly under cold running water, and pierce each fruit once with a fork.

Place the sugar and 1 pint (550 ml) water in a large thick-bottomed saucepan, over a medium heat. Stir constantly until the sugar has dissolved, then allow to boil. Simmer the syrup gently for 10 minutes. Add the prepared fruit to the syrup and continue to simmer for 30 minutes, until the fruit begins to soften. Remove the pan from the heat.

Allow the contents of the pan to cool slightly. Stir in the Kirsch, then transfer the oranges and syrup to warm, clean jars. Seal. Keep for at least a week before using.

CAPE GOOSEBERRY, GROUND CHERRY

The Cape gooseberry (above) and ground cherry, members of the tomato family, are so closely related as to be almost indistinguishable.

Both plants are native to South and Central America, but the former owes its name to the fact that it is cultivated around the Cape of Good Hope in South Africa. Many varieties of ground cherry grow wild in Mexico and the southern parts of the United States. The most familiar species is cultivated in the eastern and central areas of North America where it is also known as the husk tomato.

The round cherry-shaped berries are usually about 3 inches (7·5 cm) in diameter. They hang from bushes, enclosed in enlarged, hardened, grey-brown calyxes commonly known as 'Chinese lanterns'. The decorative value of the 'lanterns' makes the bushes popular garden plants.

Only ripe fruit should be eaten. The filled 'lantern' often falls to the ground before the fruit is ready, but the ripening process continues. All fruit, ripe or unripe, should be kept in the hardened 'lantern' until it is used.

Unripe berries are green, becoming increasingly golden-yellow as they mature. Some rarer varieties have a dark purple skin.

How to Use
The lightly seeded berries should be eaten whole. The distinctive sweet-sharp flavour is more pronounced if the fruit is gently stewed in syrup for about 10 minutes. The berries also make excellent jams and jellies (see Basic Recipes, pages 198, 199).

For a really superb finish to a meal, open the calyx and twist it without breaking. Using the calyx as a stem, dip the fully ripe berry into a vanilla fondant and dry.

CAROB

The tall, evergreen carob tree, a member of the pea family, is thought to be a native of the area once known as the Holy Land. Indeed, the carob fruit (below) is sometimes known as St John's bread, because it is believed the 'locusts' John the Baptist ate in the wilderness were carob pods. Prized as much for the shade it provides as for its fruit, this tree now grows, wild and cultivated, in the drier parts of the Mediterranean.

The fruits are dark brown, flattened pods 4—8 inches (10—12 cm) long and about 1—2 inches (2·5—5 cm) wide. The sweet flesh inside contains 4—12 extremely hard brown seeds, or 'beans'.

The quality of the fruit varies from species to species, and cultivation has been largely aimed at producing fleshier fruit. It can sometimes be difficult, however, to distinguish between wild and cultivated varieties; some of the fleshiest carob pods are found on wild, Sicilian species.

For centuries, the pods were harvested each September by shaking the branches of the tree with a long stick. They were then left to dry and used mainly as animal feed during the winter months. But the sweet chocolate-like flavour was also appreciated by humans and the dried pods were eaten as a confectionery. Because of their high sugar content, they were fermented to give a good yield of alcohol, and a medicinal syrup called 'carob molasses' was also manufactured. (The modern pharmaceutical industry uses carob in cough linctus.)

How to Use
Fresh whole pods are rarely seen outside the growing region, although sweet shops in Europe and the United States once sold the beans to chew. Now dried pods are often found in health food shops. Carob powder is a good substitute for cocoa, to which many people are allergic. Made by finely grinding the beans, it is used, exactly like cocoa, as a flavouring in drinks, puddings, ice cream and cakes. Many shops also stock carob 'chocolate' bars and carob-coated biscuits.

Carob Smoothie

This quickly made drink is rather thick and sweet, but should be a great favourite with children. (It is also highly nutritious.)

2 pints (1·1 litres) milk
3 tablespoons molasses
3 level tablespoons carob powder
1 ripe banana
2 ounces (50 g) peanuts, finely ground
3 tablespoons nutritional yeast

Put all the ingredients in an electric blender and process until smooth and creamy. Serve in tall, chilled glasses.

Serves 4.

CASHEW APPLE

Botanically, the cashew apple is not a fruit. It is the name given to the swollen, pear-shaped stem that bears the true fruit of the *Anacardium occidentale* tree – the cashew nut.

The plant is believed to be a native of tropical Africa, but is now grown in many tropical and subtropical parts of the world, including Central and South America, the warmer areas of Europe, and, especially, India and the East.

The cashew plant belongs to the same family as poison ivy, and even the smoke from its burning leaves can cause a rash.

Although the nuts are exported, few people outside the growing areas will be acquainted with the 'apple'. This glossy, bright red or yellow fruit matures early and can be ready to pick (along with its nut) while the tree is still flowering. The soft, juicy flesh is refreshing, but acid. Unless the fruit is fully ripe it may be too tart for most palates.

How to Use

In some countries cashew apples are used for wines and liqueurs, and they are also interesting in preserves and pies. Basic recipes for these are on pages 198–207. They can also be eaten raw, or lightly stewed and served with whipped cream.

CORNELIAN CHERRY

The small cornelian cherry tree is a native of the temperate parts of Europe. Today, the attractive, yellow, tassel-like flowers, which can appear as early as February if the frost is not too severe, make it a popular garden plant in many other parts of the world.

Since Greek and Roman times, the tree has been cultivated for its fruit, which was pickled in brine, in a similar way to olives, or made into a sharp beautifully pink preserve or jelly. Today, you are unlikely to find the small, bright red, oval berries unless you grow the tree in your own garden.

How to Use

Cornelian cherries can be eaten raw, and also make good preserves – whole in syrup (substitute for calamondin oranges, page 190), and in jams and jellies (see Basic Recipes, pages 198, 199).

CITRON

The small, evergreen citron tree grows, wild and cultivated, throughout the drier parts of the Mediterranean region. The Latin species name *medica* means 'coming from Medea'. However, the plant is believed to have been introduced to that area in about 500 BC from its native Far East, where the skin was used for perfuming rooms in Japan and China. There are also several American cultivars.

The citron looks like an odd lemon, and is, in fact, a close relative. It is prized for its green-yellow skin, much rougher and bumpier than that of the lemon. The flesh tastes like, and can be used in the same way as, the lemon's. However, there is much less of it as the rind covers an extremely thick layer of white pith. The whole skin, rind and pith, is used in the commercial production of candied peel. Most of the citron trees cultivated in Greece, Sicily and Corsica are for this small but lucrative industry. Sometimes the rind alone is distilled to extract an essential oil used for liqueurs, perfumes and medicines.

How to Use

If you are lucky enough to find imported citrons for sale in your local market or greengrocers, you can prepare your own candied peel; substitute for oranges in Candied Peel, page 123. The rind can also be used instead of lemon rind. It is especially good in preserves.

CUSTARD FRUITS

'Custard' is the common name given to a variety of tree fruits that belong to the genus *Annona*.

Custard Apple

A number of hybrids especially cultivated for ease of growth, large size, and lack of, or few, seeds are available in the shops. These include the atemoya, described on page 187.

The true custard apple (*A. reticulata*), the cherimoya (*A. cherimolia*) and the sweet sop (*A. squamosa*) are pure species. They are native to the tropical parts of America, although the cherimoya does better in slightly cooler, sub-tropical regions like Peru, its home.

All are borne on a small, attractive tree with a brownish down on its young branches and yellow-green flowers tinged with purple. It decorates gardens in Central America, India and most recently Australia. As early as 1690 custard apples were cultivated in the greenhouses of Europe. Now they are readily imported from the tropics.

Texture and skin colour vary with type. The true custard apple has a smooth, yellow to reddish-brown skin marked with a net-like pattern. The green skin of the cherimoya is rough and covered with scale-like bumps, like a cone, and the sweet sop is similar though often smaller and more yellow. All three fruits blacken as they become fully ripe.

Cherimoyas can weigh up to 14 pounds (6 kilos) though the others are usually between a half pound and 1½ pounds (225–700 g).

Their shape has led to some colourful common names – in the West Indies the custard apple is known as 'bullock's heart'.

How to Use

The fruits are picked before they are ready for eating, and should be kept until the skin has completely blackened. Then cut the fruit in half and spoon out the soft, creamy white and very sweet flesh. As the name suggests, it has a custard-like flavour. The best quality cherimoyas have a mild taste of strawberries.

You cannot really improve upon the raw fruit, spooned out from the shell, but the pulp does make a delicious ice cream (substitute for avocado pulp in Avocado Ice Cream, page 29).

Custard Banana

A native of the south-east corner of the United States, the custard banana is rarely exported. Confusingly, it is sometimes called a pawpaw – a label more correctly applied to the papaya fruit.

It is not in fact a banana, but a cylindrical berry 3–5 inches (7.5–12·5 cm) long. The thin, dark brown skin covers creamy, yellow flesh studded with small, black seeds.

How to Use

Like the custard apple, the banana must be allowed to ripen fully before it is eaten (the skin will be black), and, also like the apple, it is best eaten raw. The flesh tastes like a sweet blend of bananas and custard.

CRAB APPLE

More than twenty varieties of cultivated crab apple grow in Europe, Asia and North America, and large numbers of 'domestic' apples have seeded themselves in the wild and reverted to their original form or crossed with true crabs.

The crab apple tree is similar in size, flower and foliage to the domestic apple, and is often grown as an ornamental tree. The apples themselves are small and oval or slightly pear shaped.

How to Use
Crab apples make the clearest, most brilliant of jellies, and can also be used to make fruit cheese (see Basic Recipes, pages 199, 200).

ELDERBERRY

The common elder and the dwarf elder are both members of the genus *Caprifoliaceae* and grow wild in northern temperate zones. Said to be the tree on which Judas hanged himself, the elder is popularly associated with evil spirits – it was long thought that burning its wood allowed evil to enter the house down the chimney (although there are also records of using its branches and leaves as charms against witches).

Its tiny berries grow in clusters, changing from spring green through shades of red to glistening black in autumn.

The berries are ready for picking when the weight of the clusters of fruit pulls the stem down. The raw fruit is best eaten within twenty-four hours of picking.

How to Use
Elderberry wine is one of the most delicious of home-made wines. Made by fermenting the juice of the ripened fruit, it is a dark, purplish brew that looks rather like port. In fact, fraudulent use of it has been known when it was found to be mixed with port to make a deceptively cheaper 'fortified wine'. Information about wine-making is given on page 205.

The berries can also be used instead of blackberries (page 34), raspberries (page 162) and other soft fruits and the flowers add an aromatic flavour to gooseberry compotes and fools.

Remember to remove the stalks, and sieve the flesh to get rid of the numerous, hard pips.

FEIJOYA

The feijoya is native to Brazil, and was introduced into the warmer parts of Europe in 1890. Provided the climate is frost-free, the bushy, evergreen shrub will flourish and fruit abundantly in most soils. Because of this, it has become established in many subtropical areas of the world. It now grows wild in the South of France. Its appearance – the large flowers are milky purple with a red and yellow interior – make it a popular garden plant, especially in California, Australia, New Zealand, and on the Cornish Riviera in Britain.

The oval berry is about 2 inches (5 cm) long, with a tough but thin, waxy skin. It resembles a small passion fruit, but the juicy, yellow-green flesh, embedded with black seeds, tastes like a guava, with a slight strawberry and pineapple flavour – reason enough for its common name – 'pineapple guava'.

How to Use
The skin is easily peeled off and the flesh is delicious eaten raw, either alone or chopped into an exotic salad.

GOLDEN NARANJILLA

If you live in a temperate climate and wish to sample the golden naranjilla, you will need a greenhouse and a little patience. Under hothouse conditions, the plant – a tall, highly decorative shrub – is almost two years old before fruiting. Small, orange-like fruits will then appear every year.

The golden naranjilla is in fact a berry, but its resemblance to the orange probably accounts for one of its common names – the Quito orange.

How to Use
The best way to enjoy the sharp but delicious taste of the flesh is to eat it raw, though the abundance of tiny seeds can be annoying. The juice makes a refreshing drink.

GUAVA

The guava is a small deciduous tree, belonging to the myrtle family. In tropical America it can be seen growing both wild and cultivated. It was introduced to southern Europe by the Spanish.

The white or yellow-skinned guava, the most common and abundant species, has sweet but acidic flesh with a strong musky odour (present to some degree in any guava) that vanishes on cooking. There are several varieties; the guava pear is considered by the French to be the finest, although the Brazilians would contest this claim. Their 'strawberry guava', with its deep purplish-red skin and juicy flesh, has a flavour similar to that of a strawberry.

New cultivars are tried out regularly with a view to improving the guava's overall quality and commercial status.

Canned fruits labelled 'Guava Shells' have been deseeded and cooked before canning.

How to Use
Guavas are rich in Vitamin C. There is a thriving juice industry, and the fruits can be used in a wide variety of dishes that require a soft, pulpy flesh that purées easily.

Ripe guavas can be eaten raw. They can also be cooked by simmering gently until just pulpy. A little sugar (or preferably honey) is usually added to the cooked fruit.

Bastida Goiaba

This cocktail is from Brazil, the leading producer of Cachaca, a liqueur distilled from fermented sugar cane, but light rum may be used instead.

3 small or 2 large 'strawberry' guavas,
*   peeled and deseeded*
2 teaspoons sugar
3 tablespoons Cachaca or light rum
1 tablespoon crushed ice

Put all the ingredients in an electric blender and mix thoroughly. Pour into a tall, chilled glass and serve.

Makes 1 glass.

HICKORY NUT

A member of the same *genus* as the walnut, the hickory is a close relative of the pecan. Native to North America, the nuts have a strong flavour.

How to Use
Hickory nuts can be used in the same way as pecans (page 140).

JACKFRUIT

The jackfruit tree, with its lush, dark green, leathery leaves, can grow up to 65 feet (20 m) tall, and is therefore greatly appreciated for its decorative value. In its native India the prickly fruits grow to about the size of a large watermelon, weighing up to 50 pounds (22 kilos). The hard, prickly, light brown, outer rind of the jackfruit (above) encloses a surprisingly soft and juicy, yellow pulp, studded with large seeds. In Sri Lanka the seeds are more highly valued than the flesh; they are finely ground and sprinkled into many dishes. They can also be roasted and eaten like nuts.

Today, cultivation has spread to other parts of the world with a hot, humid climate – Africa, parts of America and, most recently, Australia. Once harvested, the jackfruit takes an extremely long time to ripen – six to eight months – and is therefore not commercially viable.

How to Use

Jackfruits are rarely found outside the tropics, and many people find the flesh unpalatable. The fruit is used raw or cooked: slices are lightly fried and served with curry, and it can be roasted or boiled and served as a vegetable.

LOQUAT

The loquat, also known as the Japanese medlar or Japanese loquat, is a subtropical relative of the apple and pear. Originally from China, it is now grown in many warm parts of the world and will even fruit freely in milder regions.

The golden fruits are shaped like eggs; about 1½ inches (4 cm) long, they hang in clusters of up to ten. The flesh varies from pale yellow or even white to rich gold. Some varieties have large pips and comparatively little flesh.

How to use

Ripe loquats are delicious when ripe, and best eaten raw. They can also be combined with other fruits in fruit salad or made into jelly (see Basic Jelly Recipe, page 199) but allow the fruit to stand in the water in which it was boiled for 24 hours before straining and measuring the juice.

JUJUBE

There are numerous varieties of the small, deciduous jujube tree in the Middle and Far East, along the Mediterranean, and in Australia and the United States. It is not readily available outside the countries where it is cultivated.

About the size and shape of a large olive, the fruit is initially green, changing to reddish-brown as the fruit ripens. The sweet, white flesh is rather slimy when the jujube is freshly picked, and the fruit is left to wither until the flesh is spongy, before being used or offered for sale.

How to Use

Rich in Vitamin C, jujubes soothe sore throats.

They are best either raw, or preserved: dried (when they taste like dates); and in jams and jellies (see Basic Recipes, pages 198, 199).

MACADAMIA

Native to Australia, macadamias or Queensland nuts are also grown in Hawaii and to some extent in California. The evergreen tree on which the nuts are borne is similar to the orange but has long, prickly leaves.

How to use

The nuts, which have a delectable, buttery taste, are roasted or can be eaten raw.

MANGOSTEEN

The mangosteen has only been successfully cultivated so far in its native Malaya and in the West Indies, although it is increasingly exported. Australian growers are working on its commercial potential, and closely related fruits are found in India and in the tropical regions of America and Africa.

The mangosteen is about the size and shape of a crab apple. A most attractive fruit, its thick, leathery rind is either dark red or purple on the outer surface and pale violet on the inside when the fruit is fully ripe. It contains five to seven snow-white arils, each surrounding a small seed.

How to Use

The fleshy arils, the edible part of the fruit, taste similar to a sweet ripe plum. They are best eaten raw.

MEDLAR

Of Central European origin, the medlar tree is often found wild in Britain and on the Continent.

Medlars (below) are about the size of a small plum, with tough, leathery skins that turn russet brown on ripening. They are best harvested in late autumn when the fruit is still hard. The flesh turns soft and mealy as the fruit ripens, and when it appears half-rotten or 'bletted' its pleasant, if rather acid, taste is quite palatable.

How to Use

The flesh of cooked medlars can be puréed and used in a fool (see Basic Fool Recipe, page 204) and the fruits also make good jams and jellies (see Basic Recipes, pages 198, 199) and cheeses (see Basic Cheese Recipe, page 200).

MULBERRY

There are about twelve species of mulberry tree, but the two most important are the black mulberry (*Morus nigra*) and the white mulberry (*Morus alba*). The fruits of the latter are not very well flavoured and the tree is best cultivated for its pale green leaves, a food for silk worms.

In 1608, James I issued an edict to encourage silk production in England. Large numbers of mulberry trees were planted in gardens throughout the country, but confusion led to the black rather than the white being cultivated. The silk trade did not flourish, but the black mulberry trees with their delicious fruit did.

Today the black mulberry is exploited for its large, luscious fruit. Iran and Turkestan produce an abundance of high quality, seedless varieties. However, production is not commercially viable — the fruit has to be fully ripe when picked, is best eaten immediately, and is easily squashed.

The berries look like inflated loganberries. Deep purple when fully ripe, the extremely juicy flesh has a sweet but acid flavour.

How to Use

Most people prefer to eat mulberries raw. Rinse the ripe berries gently, then sprinkle lightly with sugar, and serve with whipped cream. If you have a large crop, freeze some. Substitute them for blackberries (page 34) and raspberries (page 162).

Sopa de Amoras

This soup recipe comes from Brazil.

2 pounds (900 g) ripe black
    mulberries
½ bottle (about ¾ pint or 430 ml)
    white wine
1 teaspoon ground cinnamon
Sugar to taste

Wash the mulberries thoroughly in a colander under cold, running water, and place in a large saucepan. Add the wine and enough water to cover. Bring the contents to the boil over a moderate heat, and simmer gently until mushy. Stir well. Remove the pan from the heat and stir in the cinnamon and sugar. Return the pan to the heat and heat through, but do not boil. Serve immediately with fingers of dry toast.

Serves 4–6.

NATAL PLUM

The white blossom that covers the shrub *Carissa grandiflora* for most of the year, makes it an attractive and popular addition to subtropical gardens. Native to Africa, Australia and Asia, it was introduced into the southeastern part of the United States in the early twentieth century.

You are unlikely to encounter the scarlet, plum-like Natal plum outside its growing regions.

Although the plant is quite easy to grow, the fruit itself is not exploited commercially, perhaps because no matter how delicious, it is not especially distinctive.

How to Use

Use as you would plums (page 152). Only really ripe fruit should be eaten raw. Slightly under-ripe specimens are best for cooking and make a delicious jelly (see Basic Jelly Recipe, page 199).

PRICKLY PEAR

Many cacti produce delicious fruit, but those of the *Opuntia* species — prickly pears (below) — are probably the most abundant and the best known.

The Spaniards introduced the plant to Europe from Mexico in the sixteenth century. It has since spread all around the Mediterranean, where it grows easily. After being introduced into Australia, it spread so rapidly that it became an agricultural pest, and its growth is now controlled by law, and banned altogether in some regions.

Deliberate cultivation of the fruit is widespread, but the harvest from wild and semi-wild varieties is abundant enough for the 'pears' to be commonplace. Some are exported and are not too difficult to locate in specialist markets and greengrocers.

The so-called 'pear' is in fact a large berry, covered in spines; size and colour vary from species to species. They are shaped like an elongated apple (rather than a pear) and are all initially green, maturing to yellow or orange-red. Some are almost purple. Most are 1½–2 inches (3·75–5 cm) long, though one of the most commonly cultivated — also known as the Indian fig — can be up to 3 inches (7·5 cm) in length. Handle the pears with care — as their name suggests, the spine-covered skins are very prickly.

How to Use

Use the pulp in preserves or compotes if you wish, but remember to push it through a fine sieve to remove the numerous seeds. A few, less common cultivars are seedless. Most people prefer to eat the flesh raw. Carefully, take a fully ripe 'pear', slice it open lengthways and dig out the juicy sweet flesh (white, yellow or orange, depending on species), avoiding the spines. The seeds are harmless if eaten, but are usually discarded. A more elegant method would be to peel off the spiny skin, slice the flesh, sprinkle with lemon juice, then serve with cream.

RAMBUTAN

The tall rambutan tree is a native of the Malayan archipelago and is still most widely cultivated in Malaya. However, small plantations have been established in the Philippines, Australia and Central America. Despite the quality of the fruit, it is not exported in any significant quantity.

Ripe rambutans have a pinkish or orange-red outer casing, like that of a lychee, with soft spines or hair which give it's nickname 'hairy lychee'.

How to Use

The soft, grape-like flesh is best eaten raw, either alone or in fruit salads. Rambutans may be used as an alternative to lychees (page 98).

ROSELLA

The rosella is not a true fruit, but consists of an inner seed pod enclosed by swollen, fleshy sepals.

A native of the tropics, the rosella is valued for its leaves, which are used as a herb, as well as for its fruit. However, it is usually cultivated for the fruit, and fair-size crops are grown in Australia, the West Indies, Hawaii and parts of the Far East. Whole rosellas are not exported. Outside the tropics, only the dried sepals and a syrup used for flavouring can be found in specialist food stores.

How to Use

Rosellas should always be cooked. If fresh, separate the red sepals from the seed pods, then stew them lightly. The slightly tart pulp is traditionally used in jams and jellies (see Basic Recipes, pages 198, 199). You can also cook the seed pods, but remember to sieve the pulp before using, to remove the seeds. Dried rosella sepals must first be soaked in hot water to soften them.

ROSE HIP

The rose family is large, and although all species are native to the northern hemisphere many grow throughout the world. Cultivar roses are mainly cultivated for their flowers although the bright red hips are decorative. All are edible, although some have a better flavour than others.

Rose hips from the wild single rose are usually bright red, round to oval in shape and about ½–1 inch (1·25–2·5 cm) long. The shrivelled calyx from the flower is often still attached to the fruit. They can be easily gathered from hedgerows and in gardens.

How to Use

Only the fleshy, outer casing of the rose hip is used. Always cut the hip open, then remove and discard the hard, bristly seeds. The larger hips are good combined with other fruits – replace a proportion of the rhubarb with rose hips in Rhubard Pie (page 170) and Rhubarb Fool (page 171). The best-known use, however, is to make rose hip syrup, a traditional source of Vitamin C (see Basic Syrup Recipe, page 202).

ROWAN

The rowan or mountain ash is a slender tree, native to all parts of Europe and western Asia. It is easily grown and widely cultivated for its ornamental value. In late spring and early summer it bears almond-scented white blossom, and in autumn large bunches of tiny, bright orange rowanberries (left). Ancient myth claims that those who shelter under its branches will be protected from witches.

How to Use

If you have a mountain ash in your garden or know where to find a wild one, be sure to catch the berries early, as the birds are also fond of them. They are bitter raw, but are rich in pectin and frequently used in jelly (see Basic Jelly Recipe, page 199).

SAPODILLA

In the West Indies, the fruits of the sapodilla tree are known as naseberries, and in Central America the tree is usually cultivated for the white sap that is tapped from its bark and used to make chewing gum. However, the fruit has always been prized and trees can now be found all over the tropics, including parts of America and Australia. Sadly, exports are limited.

The round to oval fruits are the size of large plums or small lemons. The green rind changes to a deep red-brown when ripe.

How to Use

Sapodillas should be eaten only when they are ripe, with sweet, juicy, fragrant flesh.

They are best eaten raw. Be careful, however: each fruit contains several black seeds which should never be swallowed as their rough surface will scratch your throat. You can scoop the flesh straight from the halved fruit or chop it into salads (sweet or savoury). The pulp can also be puréed. Substitute for mango purée in Mango Mousse (page 101), leaving out the ground ginger; or use to make a fool (see Basic Fool Recipe, page 204).

SAPOTE

The name 'sapote' describes a number of fruits. Only two of these – the true sapote and the green sapote – are members of the same botanical family (Calocarpum), though the flavour of all the fruits is similar. The true sapote tree is indigenous to Central America, while the green sapote can fruit well in cooler climates.

The fruit known as the true sapote resembles a scruffy, misshapen brown ball. It is usually almost oval and 3–6 inches (8–15 cm) long, with thick rough, woody skin enclosing firm, reddish flesh and one large seed. The green sapote is about 5 inches (12 cm) in diameter and has thinner, pale green skin.

The flesh of the green sapote is invariably sweet and juicy, while that of the true sapote, at its best sweet and slightly spicy, can be rather insipid.

How to Use

Sapotes are usually cut up and eaten raw, though they lack acidity and many people find them too sweet to eat alone.

SLOE

A sprinkling of tiny, blue-black sloe berries (right) can be found growing wild in hedges in autumn every year. The small blackthorn tree which bears them is a member of the plum family and, botanically speaking, the sloe is a miniature plum. Growing wild in the temperate parts of Europe (not in the extreme north), the sloe's ancestry is obscure, though it appears to be native. Sloes are best picked after the first frost.

How to Use
The berries taste very bitter, but make a delicious jelly (see Basic Jelly Recipe, page 199).

Sloe Wine

Sloe gin is a traditional Christmas drink; this wine is less well known.

4 pounds (1·8 kilos) sloes, stalks removed
1 pound (450 g) raisins, chopped
1 Campden tablet
1 teaspoon Pectozyme
Burgundy yeast
1 nutrient tablet
3½ pounds (1·6 kilos) sugar

Wash the sloes thoroughly in a colander under cold, running water. Place in a large, sterilized preserving pan. Add 1 gallon (4·5 litres) cold water, then place the pan on a moderate heat and bring the contents to the boil. Lower the heat, simmering gently, until the fruit just starts to become pulpy. Remove the pan from the heat and pour the contents into a prepared mashing vessel. Stir in the chopped raisins. Cover the vessel and leave the contents to cool to a temperature of between 65–75°F (18–24°C). Uncover and stir in the Campden tablet and Pectozyme. Recover and leave for 24 hours.

Stir in the activated yeast (see manufacturer's instructions for quan-

tity and method of use) and the nutrient tablet. Leave the covered mashing vessel in a warm place (65–75°F or 18–24°C) for another 8 days. During this time, stir once a day to make sure the fruit is kept moist.

Using a fine sieve, strain off the liquid into a clean, sterile container. Place the fruit pulp in a linen bag. Seal the bag and squeeze it tightly over the bowl of strained liquid, to extract as much juice as possible. Stir the sugar into the bowl of liquid. Quickly siphon into a prepared fermentation vessel filling to within 1 inch (2·5 cm) of the cork. Allow to ferment in a warm, dark place (65–75°F or 18–24°C) under an air-lock. Leave until a good layer of sediment has formed on the bottom of the vessel. This will take about 4–5 weeks.

Rack until clear, store in a dark place for at least 6 months and finally pour into dark glass wine bottles and cork. Keep for at least a year, preferably longer, before drinking.

See also page 205.

Makes about 1 gallon (4·5 litres).

TREE TOMATO, TOMARILLO

Originally from Brazil, the tree tomato is a member of the tomato family and is cultivated in many tropical and subtropical parts of the world.

The plant grows quickly and easily, making it ideal for tropical fruit gardens. It can also be raised in a greenhouse, provided this is heated in winter. The oval fruits are about 2 inches (5 cm) long, with a tough yellow or red skin when ripe. Skin colour varies with type — there are

several — but the yellow variety is said to have the sweetest taste.

How to Use
Peel off the skin before eating. The fleshy interior, like that of the tomato, is divided into cells, each full of small, dark, edible seeds. The taste is reminiscent of a rather sweet tomato. You can eat tree tomatoes raw; or use them to make a delicious jam (see Basic Jam Recipe, page 198).

TAMARIND

The tall tamarind tree is related to the pea and grows in nearly all the tropical areas of the world. A native of East Africa, its economic viability — the wood, bark, leaves and flowers, as well as the fruit, are useful — account for its widespread cultivation.

The fruit is a thick, curved, brown pod, 3–6 inches (7·5–15 cm) long, containing up to about 10 black seeds embedded in an acid pulp. When fully ripe the pulp is rich brown and fairly sweet. Under-ripe tamarinds are extremely tart.

How to Use
The most common use is as a seasoning in savoury dishes such as curries and chutneys. Dried whole pods and seeds are exported, and should be easily obtainable in any good delicatessen or African or Asian speciality food store.

To make tamarind seasoning, steep 2 ounces (50 g) dried tamarind pods in ½ pint (300 ml) of hot water (just boiled) for 1 hour. When the pods are soft, mash them in with the water then strain this mixture through a fine sieve and use the liquid as directed.

In countries where the tamarind is grown, the sweet, mature pulp is eaten raw, scooped directly from the pod. The pulp can also be used in any recipe demanding a soft fruit purée.

Tamarinade

This refreshing drink comes from Jamaica.

6 fresh or dried tamarinds
2 ounces (50 g) sugar

Wash the tamarinds, then place in a bowl. Pour on ¾ pint (400 ml) water and leave for 30 minutes. If you are using dried tamarinds, boil the water first, then pour it over and leave until the fruit is soft and pulpy (about 1 hour).

Add the sugar and stir until it has dissolved. Then leave the liquid to stand for 5 minutes. Strain by pouring through a fine sieve. Serve chilled with ice, in tall, chilled glasses.

Serves 2.

PRESERVING

The word preserving probably conjures up visions of country kitchens, larders with serried rows of luscious jams and jellies, and rows of apple slices drying in airing cupboard. Nostalgic, perhaps, but very satisfying—and there is certainly no comparison between the flavour of a homemade preserve and its commercial counterpart.

On the next few pages you will find basic methods for the better-known processes, together with information on special equipment and ingredients.

JAMS, MARMALADES AND JELLIES

The basic principle is the same for all three preserves: fruit is cooked until soft, then combined with sugar and boiled until the mixture sets.

Jams and Marmalades

Marmalade normally describes a jam made from citrus fruit; shreds or chunks of peel are suspended in a clear jelly.

Equipment

Preserving pan, or any very large saucepan with a solid base and wide top. If possible, it should be enamel-lined, or stainless steel.

Scraps of sterilized muslin or *gauze* for holding pips and pith.

Jam jars. Any wide-mouthed glass jar can be used, provided it is unchipped. All jars must be scrupulously clean; wash them in warm, soapy water and dry with a clean towel. Then place in a moderate oven (350°F, 220°C, Mark 4) for about 5 minutes. Make sure the jars are still warm when you pour the jam or marmalade into them, or they may crack on contact with the hot preserve.

The jars referred to in the recipes are 1 pound (450 g) capacity.

Jam covers. Available from most good stationers, they consist of waxed discs (which should fit the surface of the jam exactly), and larger cellophane circles which are placed on top of the jar and secured round it with an elastic band. Screw-on lids, on used coffee jars, etc., can provide an alternative airtight seal together with the waxed disc, but make sure they are clean. Remember to remove the lid's cardboard lining.

Ingredients

Fruit. With the exception of apples (which should be fully ripe) and gooseberries (which should be half-ripe), it is best to use just-ripe or even slightly under-ripe fruit. This is because pectin, the mucilaginous substance which acts with sugar and acids to produce a set, is lowest in ripe and over-ripe fruits. Sweet fruits like peaches require the addition of citric acid or the juice of more acid fruits to enable the pectin to work effectively.

Some fruits are naturally low in pectin; this can be counteracted by the addition of:

(1) *The pips and pith of citrus fruits.* These contain pectin, and should be tied in a separate little muslin bag and cooked with the fruit. Use when making marmalade, but with other jams don't use too much or else the flavour of the jam will be affected.

(2) *Apple or lemon juice, or commercial pectin*. The usual ratio is ¼ pint (150 ml) apple juice or 2 tablespoons lemon juice to every 4 pounds (1.8 kilos) fruit. Follow the manufacturer's instructions if you use commercial pectin.

Fruits especially suitable for jams are listed on the left.

Sugar. Preserving sugar is the best choice, but lump or granulated are fine although they need more skimming to remove impurities.

Dark sugars are not really suitable as they can change the colour and flavour of the fruit.

Water. This is necessary to prevent dry fruit from scorching, and the amount used depends on the type of fruit. As a rough guide, very juicy soft fruits need no water, moderately juicy ones like plums and apples need half their weight, and dry fruits like pears need an equal weight.

Basic Jam Recipe

Wash, drain and dry the fruit immediately before cooking, otherwise the jam may develop mould. Very soft fruits should be placed, in very small quantities, in a colander and immersed in a pan or basin of cold water.

Slit the sides of stone fruit and put them into the pan – the stones will rise to the surface during cooking.

Put the fruit in a pan with water if necessary.

Always start cooking on a low heat, bring to the boil and simmer gently until the fruit is reduced to a pulp. Do

Fruits for Jams and Jellies

Excellent jams and jellies can be made with apples (especially green cooking ones), barberries, Cape gooseberries, cranberries, currants, damsons, grapes, gooseberries, jujubes, loganberries, medlars, quinces, rowans and sloes. Bearberries make good jams, while crab apples make a delicious jelly. All citrus fruits can be used to make marmalade.

Add additional pectin when making jams and jellies from the following: cherries, Natal plums, plums and rosellas. Jams made from apricots, figs, peaches, rhubarb, tree tomatoes, and all berries with the exception of those listed above will also need additional pectin, as will jellies made from guavas and rose hips.

Pectin Test

If you are in any doubt about the pectin content of the fruit you are cooking, apply the following simple test: place 1 teaspoon of cooked fruit pulp in a cup and add 3 teaspoons of methylated spirits. After about a minute a clot will have formed; if this is firm the pectin content of the pulp is high, but if the clot easily breaks up into smaller ones, you should add more pectin to your jam or jelly.

not stir. (If you are making marmalade, citrus fruits will require at least 1½–2 hours at this stage, as the peel is very tough.)

Meanwhile, warm the sugar separately (without dissolving it) in a low oven; this speeds up the process, as cold sugar slows the boiling.

Add the pectin required to the fruit, and then add the sugar. Stir the sugar gently with a wooden spoon as you add it, until it is completely dissolved.

Increase the heat, bring rapidly to boiling point, and keep at a vigorous rolling boil (less vigorous if making a whole fruit jam).

Do not stir, but occasionally draw a wooden spoon across the base of the pan in order to prevent the fruit from sticking.

Test the jam or marmalade for set when the mixture has begun to thicken, first lowering the heat. (Always test *before* you think setting point has been reached rather than *after*; once boiled too much, the preserve will become sticky and dark.)

To test for setting. The saucer test is the easiest method: put a little jam on a cold saucer, let it cool and gently push your finger against the top. A surface skin will wrinkle when the jam is ready.

If setting point has not been reached, bring the jam or marmalade to the boil and try again in 2–3 minutes.

Finally, remove any scum with a perforated spoon.

Potting. Jams and marmalades are generally bottled while very hot. Although preserves should never be bottled while they are just warm—mould may form—any with whole fruit or peel can be allowed to cool very slightly, before being stirred to distribute the pieces evenly throughout the jar.

Stand warm, clean, dry jars on several layers of newspaper and pour the jam or marmalade into them, using a funnel or wide-lipped jug. Fill each jar to within ½ inch (1.25 cm) of the top.

Wipe off any preserve from the outside of the jars, and cover the jam or marmalade immediately with a waxed disc, wax side down. Make sure the disc lies level, with no bumps, and that it fits exactly. Wipe the rims of the jars clean and fit the cellophane covers over the top (wet them first and they will dry to an airtight fit). Secure with an elastic band.

When completely cold, label and store in a cool, dry, dark place.

Jellies

Making jelly is simpler than making jam, although it is a more time-consuming process.

Unlike jams, which make use of whole fruits (or pieces of fruit), jellies are made from their juice.

A fruit, or combination of fruits, is cooked to extract as much juice as possible, which is then strained and combined with sugar.

A good fruit jelly is clear and bright and full of flavour. It should not be too firmly set.

Equipment
Preserving pan, jars and *sterilized muslin*, as for jam.

Jelly bag, or *colander* covered with 2 or 3 layers of thin muslin.

Ingredients
The same rules apply for fruit and sugar as with jams, but the minimum quantity of water is used.

See opposite page for especially suitable fruits.

Basic Jelly Recipe
It is generally unnecessary to peel and core fruit, unless specifically instructed. Just wash and remove stems, and cut larger fruit into pieces.

Put the fruit into a pan with just enough water to cover it, add lemon juice if needed, and simmer gently until the fruit is soft. Soft fruits like berries and black- or redcurrants are ready when the juice is running freely. You can help the process along by gently crushing with a potato masher or wooden fork. Hard fruits like apples and pears must be cut into pieces and cooked slowly until soft—about 30 minutes. Don't crush these—unlike soft, pulpy fruits they have tiny grains that will make the resulting jelly cloudy.

Prepare the jelly bag or colander lined with muslin and put a bowl underneath to catch the juice. Pour in the softened fruit and leave for several hours or overnight to allow the juice to drip through.

Never try to force the juice through by pushing the pulp or squeezing the jelly bag as this will make the jelly unattractively cloudy.

Measure the juice, and then measure out the correct proportion of sugar—normally 1 pound (450 g) for every pint (550 ml) of juice—warmed as for jam.

Place the juice in a clean preserving pan, add the sugar, and bring gently to the boil, stirring constantly until the sugar is dissolved. Then boil the mixture rapidly until setting point is reached. Don't overboil—the jelly will never set.

To test for setting. Take a small spoonful of jelly, allow it to cool, then turn the spoon on its side. If the jelly is setting it will drop in large flakes instead of running off the spoon.

Take the jelly off the heat and skim off the scum.

Potting. Using a funnel or wide-lipped jug, pour the hot jelly into clean, warm, dry jars, pouring it down the side of the tilted jar to avoid air bubbles.

Cover as for jam.

Move the jelly as little as possible, and store in a cool, dry, dark place.

FRUIT CHEESES AND BUTTERS

Fruit cheeses and butters are a traditional way of making use of windfalls and over-ripe fruit.

Fruit Cheeses

These can be served at the end of a meal instead of cheese, or eaten as a dessert.

Equipment
Preserving pan and *waxed discs*, as for jam (page 198).

Small jars or *individual moulds*. They must be warm, clean and dry.

Ingredients
Fruit. Most fruits make good cheeses.

Sugar. Use white granulated or preserving.

Method
Simmer the fruit in a pan with just enough water to cover, until it is fine enough to pass through a sieve to remove stones and skins.

Weigh the pulp and return it to the clean pan. (If the pulp is runny, boil fast until it is thick.)

Warm an equal weight of sugar in the oven, and add to the pulp.

Stir over a low heat until the sugar is dissolved, then simmer gently for about 1 hour, stirring constantly, until the mixture is so stiff and dry it will come away from the sides of the pan in a mass.

Potting. Press tightly into small, warm, clean, dry jars or individual moulds (brushed inside with a little glycerine), cover with waxed discs and seal with cellophane.

Store for at least 2 months.

Fruit Butters

These can be served with bread and scones, or on layer cakes, and are also delicious with cold desserts.

Equipment and ingredients are the same as for cheeses; however, less sugar is used.

Method
Follow instructions for fruit cheese, but add only 8 ounces (225 g) warmed sugar for every pound of pulp. Simmer until the water is absorbed and the mixture is thick and creamy.

Potting. Put in small, clean, dry, warm jars, cover with waxed discs and seal with cellophane.

Store for a few weeks and eat within days of opening.

PICKLES AND CHUTNEYS

Pickles and chutneys are a simple yet delicious way to preserve fruits, without the problem of setting that complicates jam- or jelly-making. The longer they are allowed to mature the better, so make them at least a month before you want to use them. If you can wait 3–4 months your patience will be rewarded.

A wide variety of fruit can be used for pickles and/or chutneys, including bananas, kiwi fruit, mangoes, papayas, tamarinds and watermelon, as well as stone fruit and tree fruit.

Pickles

The aim of this method is to preserve one or more fruits in sweetened, spiced vinegar so that it keeps its shape and appearance.

Equipment
Preserving pan, as for jam (page 198).

Preserving jars, or jars with plastic, screw-on lids – metal lids can corrode when they are in contact with vinegar. Jars and lids must be scrupulously clean.

The jars referred to in the recipes are 1 pound (450 g) capacity, unless otherwise stated.

Vinegar-proof paper for covering jars. Special paper is available, usually in rolls, and is secured to the jars by tying with string. Or put a disc of this paper on top of the pickle before screwing on the lids. Don't use ordinary paper or standard jam covers as these allow the vinegar to evaporate and the pickle to become dry.

Muslin bag for whole spices.

Muslin for straining vinegar if ground spices have been used.

Ingredients
Fruit. Use unblemished, just-ripe fruit.

Vinegar. White or red wine and malt or cider vinegars can be used, depending on the colour and flavour you want and the type of fruit. The quantity varies in individual recipes.

Sugar. The type you use – white, demerara, soft brown, etc. – is up to you. Proportions of sugar to vinegar vary with individual fruits.

Other ingredients, depending on the recipe, include *whole* or *ground* spices, *herbs* and *lemon rind*.

Water may be added to less juicy fruits.

Method
Chop or cube fruits if necessary. If you are pickling whole fruits, like cherries or apricots, prick the skins to make sure they don't shrivel. Keep stones in the fruit if you want them to look as attractive as possible.

Put vinegar (and water if used) in a saucepan with the sugar and spices, if any. Tie whole spices in muslin.

Bring to the boil, stirring until the sugar has dissolved. Add the fruit and cook gently, covered, until it is just tender. Put the fruit in clean, warm jars.

Return the vinegar to the pan and boil uncovered until it is syrupy. Strain the vinegar through muslin (twice if ground spices were used, to prevent the liquid from being cloudy) and pour over the fruit, covering it by about ½ inch (1·25 cm).

Potting. Cover with vinegar-proof paper and tie with string, or secure with a screw-on lid.

Keep for at least 1 month.

Chutneys

As with pickles, fruit for chutneys is cooked in a basic mixture of vinegar and sugar (with other ingredients, depending on the recipe). However, the solid ingredients are finely cut up or minced and the flavour depends on long, slow cooking.

Equipment
Jars and *preserving pan*, as for pickles.

Airtight covers. Ideally plastic, or metal coated with plastic.

Ingredients
Fruit. This need not be at its best. Remember, though, to remove all bad or blemished parts of the fruit.

Vinegar, sugar. The same rules apply as for pickles.

Other ingredients can include *strong-flavoured vegetables* like onions, *herbs*, *spices*, *mustard*, *raisins* and other *fruit*, etc.

Method
Peel and finely chop or mince the fruit (and other solid ingredients if necessary). Put in a pan with the rest of the ingredients including the vinegar and sugar, and bring to the boil, stirring until the sugar is dissolved. Then simmer gently, uncovered, for about 2 hours until the mixture is soft, individual ingredients are unrecognizable, and the chutney has thickened.

Potting. Pour the hot chutney into warm, clean jars, and seal with airtight covers while hot or cold.

Label, and keep in a cool, dark place for at least 2 months.

BOTTLING

Bottling is a cheap, quick and reliable way of preserving fruit and the only way, apart from freezing, in which the fruit and its taste and texture remain virtually intact.

Basically, the bottling process consists of packing fruit into sterile jars, covering it with syrup, and sterilizing it at a high temperature either on the top of the stove (the water-bath method) or in the oven (the oven method).

The jars are sealed while they are still hot, to prevent contamination by bacteria.

Equipment

Jars. It is best to use bottles or jars especially made for bottling. These have vacuum-seal glass or metal disc tops which are held on by spring-clips or screw-bands, and must be in perfect condition. The glass must not be chipped, the metal must not be scratched or damaged, and the rubber sealing-ring must not be flawed. Always use new rubber rings, and new metal discs if you are using screw-top jars.

It is possible to use glass jam jars, provided you can find lids that fit exactly (made by some manufacturers).

The jars referred to in the recipes are 1 pound (450 g) capacity, unless otherwise stated.

Large, deep container (for water-bath method). Special pans are available, but they are expensive and any deep vessel such as a preserving pan can be used. It must be large and deep enough to incorporate a false bottom (a rack or trivet, or wadded newspaper, to hold the bottles off the bottom of the pan) and to allow the jars to be covered by water during the sterilizing process.

Asbestos mat, thick sheet of cardboard, or several thicknesses of newspaper (for oven method).

Thermometer (for water-bath method). This is an essential piece of equipment; the best model, especially made for bottling and jam-making, registers up to 230°F (110°C).

Ingredients

Fruit. Must be fresh, just ripe, firm and clean.

A surprising number of fruits can be bottled successfully. They include most berries and citrus fruits, apples, apricots, cherries, figs, grapes, guavas, lychees, Natal plums and plums, nectarines, peaches, dessert pears, pineapples and quinces.

Syrup. Generally made from 8 ounces (225 g) sugar to 1 pint (550 ml) water, although very tart or tightly packed fruit may require more sugar. Put the water and sugar in a saucepan and bring to the boil, stirring until the sugar dissolves, and boil for 1 minute.

For luxurious preserves, add liqueur or brandy to the syrup.

Water can be used instead of syrup, but it is not as successful at preserving colour and flavour.

Method

Sterilizing jars. Wash very thoroughly in hot soapy water, scrubbing inside with a brush and paying particular attention to the bottom corners and to the tops. Rinse them equally thoroughly in hot water to remove all traces of detergent. Then, to be quite sure they are totally clean, boil the jars in a large vessel of boiling water for at least 5 minutes. They may crack if they touch each other or the bottom or sides of the pan, so put them on a trivet, rack, or wad of newspaper on the bottom of the pan and keep them apart by crumpling cloth or paper between them. Tops of jars must also be sterilized.

The jars need not be dried, as the fruit slips more easily into wet jars.

Use the same process to sterilize bottles (and corks).

Packing fruit into jars. Peel, core, stone, de-stalk or husk the fruit as appropriate. Depending on type and size, it can be bottled whole or it can be halved, sliced or cut into chunks; remember, though, that the pieces must be of uniform size.

Pack the fruit tightly into the prepared, still-wet jars, being careful not to bruise softer fruits. Tap or shake the jars to help the fruit settle.

Processing

Water-bath method. Pour cold syrup into the jars, to the brim, and insert a knife down the side of the jars to release any air bubbles. Place the lids on the jars and secure with spring-clips or screw-bands. If using screw-bands, slacken them a quarter of a turn to allow steam to escape during processing.

Place the jars on the false bottom of the large pan, and crumple paper or cloth between them to prevent their touching each other and the sides. Completely cover the jars with water and put the lid on the pan. Heat the water very gently, gradually raising the temperature until it reaches 130°F (55°C) in 1 hour, and the required temperature in 1½ hours.

The higher temperature depends on the type of fruit. Keep the water simmering at this temperature for the necessary length of time (an accurate thermometer is essential). Once again, this varies with individual fruits.

For example, apples, bananas, soft fruits like berries and kiwi fruit, passion fruit and rhubarb are held at 165°F (75°C) for 10 minutes; apricots, cherries, nectarines, peaches, pineapples, plums and citrus fruits must be held at 180°F (83°C) for 15 minutes; and figs and pears are held at 190°F (88°C) for 30 minutes.

Remove the jars from the container and secure the lids tightly. Leave to cool for 24 hours.

Oven method. Pack the jars with fruit and put on the lids, but not the bands or clips. Place the bottles in a low oven (300°F, 150°C, Mark 2) on an asbestos mat, a sheet of cardboard, or several thicknesses of newspaper, ensuring that they are not touching each other or the sides of the oven.

Process until the fruit looks cooked and has shrunk slightly. As with the water-bath method, the time needed will vary depending on the fruit and the number of jars in the oven.

For example, up to 4 jars containing apples, soft fruits, kiwi fruit or passion fruit must be heated for 30–40 minutes; the same quantity of whole cherries, plums, apricots or citrus fruit will need 40–50 minutes; and up to 4 jars of figs should be processed for 60–70 minutes.

Remove the jars, one by one, from the oven and fill with boiling syrup. Seal immediately, and leave for 24 hours to cool.

Storage

Test that the seal is complete before storing. Remove the screw-bands or clips with your fingertips, and hold each jar by the lid only. If the vacuum seal is complete, the lid will hold. Clips can then be washed, dried and set aside for future use; screw-bands can be washed, dried and greased with a little oil before they are replaced.

Label each jar with the name of the fruit and the date, and store in a cool, dry, dark place. Alternatively, wrap in heavy brown paper; this will prevent the fruit losing its colour.

Fruit Vinegars and Syrups

Fruit Vinegars

These taste wonderful in salad dressings, and with fruit salads.

Equipment

Preserving pan, as for jam (page 198).
   Fine, sterilized muslin or *gauze*.
   Hot, dry bottles with sterilized corks or screw-top lids. Warm in a moderate oven (350°F, 220°C, Mark 4) for about 5 minutes before using.

Ingredients

Fruit. Soft fruits like berries and currants give wonderful results, as do rose hips.
   Vinegar. White wine vinegar won't overpower the flavour of the fruit.
   White sugar.

Method

Put the fruit in a china or glass bowl, discarding any blemished or bad pieces. Bruise with a wooden spoon or kitchen fork and add 1 pint (550 ml) vinegar for every 1 pound (450 g) fruit. Put a cloth over the top of the bowl, and leave fo 3–5 days, stirring occasionally.
   Strain the liquid through a fine cloth or nylon sieve, and measure. Put in pan, add sugar in the ratio of 8 ounces (225 g) to 1 pint (450 g) liquid. Bring gently to the boil, stirring until the sugar is dissolved, and then boil for 10 minutes.
   Pour the hot vinegar into hot, dry bottles, to within ¾ inch (2 cm) of the top. Seal with screw-tops or corks.

Syrups

Syrups can be diluted with water or soda to make a refreshing drink, and can also be used as a sauce for puddings and desserts.

Equipment

Preserving pan and *hot, dry bottles,* as for fruit vinegars.
   Jelly bag or *colander* lined with 2 or 3 thicknesses of muslin, as for jelly (page 199).

Ingredients

Fruit. Soft fruits are best. They must be fresh, ripe and clean.
   Sugar. As for jam (page 198).
   Water. Very little is needed – just enough to start the juices flowing when the fruit is heated.

Method

Follow the instructions for making jelly (page 199), up to draining the juice through a jelly bag or colander. Unlike jellies, the fruit pulp can be pressed at the end of the process.
   Measure the juice and put in a pan with sugar in the ratio of 8–12 ounces (225–350 g) sugar for every 1 pint (550 ml) juice. Stir over gentle heat until dissolved.
   Strain again and pour into hot, dry bottles, filling to within 1 inch (2·5 cm) of the top. Loosely screw on the tops, or fix corks with insulating tape.
   Fit a trivet into the pan, or line its base with several thicknesses of newspaper, a folded cloth or thick cardboard. Stand the bottles side by side and fill the pan with water to about three-quarters of the way up bottles. Bring slowly to simmering point and simmer for 20 minutes.
   Remove bottles and screw on the tops tightly, or seal the corks with paraffin wax.
   Label and store in a cool, dark place for up to 6 months.
   Fruit juices can be processed in the same way.

Drying

One of the oldest methods of preserving food, drying is a simple but somewhat lengthy process.

Outdoor Drying

Sun drying is the most desirable method.
   To be successful, you will need special trays – stretch muslin across a wooden frame. Place the prepared fruit on the muslin, cover with another piece of muslin to protect the fruit from insects and dust, and put on a table in the sun until the fruit dries. This can take up to a week, so remember to bring the trays in at night. Always bring the fruit indoors, too, if there is any moisture in the air during the day.

Indoor Drying

Fruit can be successfully dried indoors provided you bear in mind that the basic principle of the process – to remove all moisture from the fruit, thus inhibiting growth of the enzymes which cause deterioration – is based on having the correct temperature, and also on plenty of ventilation.
   The warm air must circulate freely, so the fruit should be placed on a cake- or cooling-rack covered with cheesecloth or muslin.
   Fruit can be dried in a very cool electric oven—the ideal temperature is 120°–150°F (50°–65°C). If your oven does not have a low enough temperature, use the residual heat left after cooking when the oven is turned off. An airing cupboard containing a hot-water boiler can also be used. Leave the door ajar, whether you use an oven or cupboard.
   Whatever method you use, it is vital that the temperature is correct, otherwise the fruit will 'cook' and shrivel. Check the temperature with a thermometer.
   Drying times vary according to the moisture content of the fruit—as little as 4–6 hours for apples and pears, as much as 2 days for whole apricots and peaches. The process can be interrupted, and the total drying time spread over several days.
   When finally dry, fruit must be allowed to cool completely for about 12 hours in a cool, dark place before being stored in scrupulously clean containers. Allow some ventilation into containers or the fruit may become mouldy.

Individual Fruits

With the exception of citrus fruits and small soft fruits and berries (which become hard and shrivelled), most fruits can be dried. Common tree-growing fruits such as apples, pears and plums are especially suitable, as are grapes and bananas.
   Always use unblemished, just-ripe specimens.
   Apples and pears should be cored and thinly peeled, then sliced in rings and dropped into lightly salted water to prevent their going brown. Dry on kitchen paper, then either thread the rings on to canes cut to fit the width of the oven for indoor drying, or else place them in a single layer on muslin-covered racks. Pears can also be quartered and dried on racks, with the cut sides uppermost.
   Apricots, nectarines, peaches and plums can be dried whole but are better halved and stoned if large.
   Dry cherries, dates, figs and grapes whole—also persimmons, but skin them first. To dry lychees, remove the shell-like skins, cut in half, remove the stone, and lay the halves cut side uppermost. Peel bananas and cut into slices.

FREEZING

Provided it is properly prepared, fruit can be kept in a freezer for up to a year without loss of quality, flavour or colour. Choose top-quality specimens in just-ripe condition. Wash, drain and dry thoroughly (but unless it is absolutely essential do not wash soft fruit).

Though stoned fruit can be frozen whole, it is economical of space to peel and stone (or de-pip) them and cut them into segments or rings, for close packing.

Containers
Use heavy-duty polythene bags sealed with paper-covered wire ties, or moisture-proof plastic, aluminium foil or waxed cardboard containers. Square or rectangular boxes use less space than round ones.

Always make sure containers are scrupulously clean—freezing does not destroy bacteria.

Label each container not only with a description of its contents, but also with the date of freezing.

Methods
There are three methods of freezing.

Dry freezing. Place the prepared fruit on paper-covered trays in single layers, freeze overnight or until solidly frozen, and then pack into moisture-proof containers before returning to the freezer.

Sugar freezing. Pack the fruit straight into containers with a generous sprinkling of caster sugar between layers, in the proportion of 4 ounces (100–150 g) sugar to 1 pound (450 g) prepared fruit.

This method is particularly suitable for soft fruit.

Syrup freezing. Pack the prepared fruit into containers with a syrup made by dissolving 8 ounces to 1 pound (225–450 g) sugar in 1 pint (550 ml) water. The strength of the syrup varies with different fruits, but 8 ounces (225 g) sugar is generally used. Bring the syrup to the boil, and allow it to cool completely before pouring it over the fruit.

Leave a ½ inch (1.2 cm) space at the top of each container to allow for expansion during freezing.

Purées may be frozen, but they should not be kept in the freezer for longer than 8 months; fruit juices for up to 6 months.

Thaw fruit in the containers; this will take about 3 or 4 hours at room temperature.

BASIC RECIPES

The following pages contain detailed instructions on how to make the various kinds of pastry, mayonnaise and other sauces, garnishes, etc required for the recipes in this book. Basic methods for desserts are also included, as well as a section on wine- and liqueur-making.

PASTRY

The quantities given for the following recipes are enough to line, or cover, one 8 or 9 inch (20 or 22.5 cm) pie dish. If a greater quantity is needed, keep the same proportions between the ingredients.

Shortcrust Pastry
4 ounces (100–125 g) flour
Pinch of salt
1 ounce (25 g) lard or vegetable fat
1 ounce (25 g) butter or margarine

Sift flour and salt into a bowl. Cut fat and butter or margarine into small pieces and add to flour, rubbing together with the tips of the fingers until the mixture looks like fine breadcrumbs.

Add 1 or 2 tablespoons water and, using a round-bladed knife, mix to a stiff dough.

Leave in a cool place for about 30 minutes. Use as directed.

Rich Shortcrust Pastry
4 ounces (100–125 g) flour
2 ounces (50 g) butter or margarine
½ ounce (15 g) caster sugar
1 egg yolk

Combine flour and butter or margarine as for Shortcrust Pastry (above). Stir in caster sugar with a round-bladed knife. Beat the egg yolk together with a tablespoon of cold water and add to the mixture. Mix to a stiff dough.

Leave in a cool place for about 30 minutes. Use as directed.

Sweet Shortcrust Pastry
4 ounces (100–125 g) flour
3 ounces (75 g) butter or margarine
2 ounces (50 g) caster sugar
2 egg yolks
2–3 drops vanilla essence

Combine flour, butter or margarine and caster sugar as for Rich Shortcrust Pastry (above). Beat egg yolks with vanilla essence and add to the flour mixture. Mix to a stiff dough.

Leave for at least 30 minutes before rolling out. Use as directed.

Rough Puff Pastry
4 ounces (100–125 g) flour
1½ ounces (40 g) lard or vegetable fat
1½ ounces (40 g) butter or margarine
Lemon juice

Combine flour and fat and butter or margarine as for Shortcrust Pastry (left). Add a squeeze of lemon juice to about 3 fluid ounces (90 ml) water and mix with the flour mixture to form a soft dough.

Transfer to a floured board and roll to a rectangle of consistent thickness. Mark into thirds, then fold up the bottom third and fold down the top third to give 3 layers. Lightly seal the edges.

Turn the pastry through 90°, roll out into another rectangle and repeat the folding process.

Let the pastry rest in a cool place for 20 minutes, then repeat the rolling and folding process twice more. Allow it to rest a further 10 minutes. Use as directed.

Pre-baked Pastry Case
Use shortcrust, rich shortcrust or sweet shortcrust pastry made with 4 ounces (100–125 g) flour for an 8 or 9 inch (20 or 22.5 cm) tin.

Roll the pastry into a circle about ⅛ inch (3 mm) thick and about 2 inches (5 cm) wider than the tin.

Lift the pastry carefully on a rolling pin and transfer it to the tin. Don't stretch the pastry, but press it down gently on to the base and against the sides so that there are no gaps. Trim by rolling the rolling pin over the top of the tin to cut off any excess pastry.

Prick the pastry all over with a fork, and then line the base with a circle of foil. Alternatively, cover the base with greaseproof paper weighed down with dried beans.

Bake shortcrust and rich shortcrust pastry in a moderately hot oven (400°F, 200°C, Mark 6) for 15 minutes. Sweet shortcrust pastry is baked for the same length of time, but in a moderate oven (350°F, 220°C, Mark 4). After 15 minutes remove foil or greaseproof paper and beans, and bake for a further 5 or 10 minutes until lightly coloured.

DESSERTS

Fruit Tart

Use shortcrust, rich shortcrust or sweet shortcrust pastry for this recipe.

One 8 or 9 inch (20–22.5 cm) pastry case, pre-baked (page 203)
1 pound (450 g) fruit
Sugar
Arrowroot

Cook fruit gently in a saucepan with sugar to taste until it is tender but still keeps its shape. Drain fruit and arrange in the pastry case. Measure juice, add 1 tablespoon arrowroot for every ½ pint (300 ml) juice and bring to the boil. Pour over the fruit and leave to cool before serving.

Serves 6–8.

Note: Uncooked fruit may be arranged in the pastry case and covered with a glaze made from a suitably flavoured jam, melted and mixed with water or lemon juice.

Basic Fruit Fool

A fool is essentially a mixture of fruit purée and whipped cream or rich custard. Some fruits like bananas and ripe guavas can be puréed raw, while others like redcurrants must be cooked first with sugar and just enough water to cover.

½ pint (300 ml) double cream, or ¼ pint (125 ml) double cream and ¼ pint single cream, or ½ pint (300 ml) rich custard (see opposite page)
½ pint (300 ml) fruit purée
Sugar
Orange or lemon juice, vanilla essence or other flavouring

Whip the cream or creams and carefully fold in the fruit purée. If you are using custard, leave it to cool before adding the purée.
Add sugar and flavourings.
Chill and serve in individual glass dishes.

Serves 6.

Basic Fruit Cream

A cream is essentially the same as a fool, except that it is never made with custard and the fruit may be cut into small pieces (or even left whole) instead of being puréed.

Double-crust Pie

Use shortcrust or rich shortcrust pastry for this recipe.

8 ounces (225 g) pastry (see above)
1–½ pound (450–700 g) fruit
Sugar
Spices, lemon juice, etc (optional)
1–2 tablespoons cornflour or flour (optional)
Milk or beaten egg

Divide the pastry into 2 portions one slightly larger than the other. Roll out one portion into a circle about ⅛ inch (3 mm) thick and about 2 inches (5 cm) wider than pie dish.
Transfer the circle to the dish, lifting it on a rolling pin, and pressing it down gently on to the base and against the sides. Trim any overhanging pastry level with the top of the dish.
Slice fruit if necessary, and toss with sugar to taste, spices or other flavourings such as lemon juice, and cornflour or flour if necessary to thicken juices from the fruit. The filling should be piled high in the centre to allow for shrinkage during cooking.
Roll out the second portion of pastry into a circle about ⅛ inch (3 mm) thick and about 1 inch (2.5 cm) wider than the dish.
Moisten the edge of the pastry in the dish with water, then lift the second pastry circle and put it over the dish to form a lid.
Press the edges together to seal in the juices of the filling, and fold the overhang of the pastry lid under the dish's rim.
Cut a hole or slit in the centre of the pie, to allow steam to escape. Brush top with milk or beaten egg and bake in a moderately hot oven (400°F, 200°C, Mark 6) until golden.

Serves 6–8.

Note: For a single-crust pie put fruit directly into pie dish, and cover with shortcrust, rich shortcrust or rough puff pastry made with 4 ounces (100–125 g) flour.

Basic Ice Cream

Ice cream can be made in a freezer or in the ice-making compartment of a refrigerator. If you are using the latter, turn down to its lowest temperature a couple of hours before you prepare the ice cream.

½ pint (300 ml) fruit purée
4 ounces (100–125 g) caster sugar
1 teaspoon lemon juice
½ pint (300 ml) double cream, or ¼ pint (150 ml) double cream and ¼ pint (150 ml) single cream

Put the fruit purée, caster sugar and lemon juice in a bowl and mix well until smooth.
In another bowl beat the cream until thick but not so thick as to form peaks. Fold in the purée mixture, and transfer to an ice cube tray or shallow plastic box. Cover with foil and freeze until solid around the sides.
Scrape out into a bowl, beat until uniformly smooth, then return to the container. Freeze until firm. Transfer to the main compartment of the refrigerator about 30 minutes before serving.

Serves 6.

Note: The quantities of sugar and lemon juice will depend on the nature of the fruit, its sweetness or acidity.

Basic Water Ice

The proportion of fruit juice or fruit purée to syrup can vary, but they should combine to make about 1½ pints (900 ml).

4 ounces (100–125 g) sugar
1 pint (550 ml) fruit juice, or ½–¾ pint (300–400 ml) fruit purée
Juice of half a lemon
2 egg whites

Put the sugar in a saucepan with ½–1 pint (300–550 ml) water, depending on the quantity of fruit juice or purée (see above). Bring to the boil, stirring frequently, then simmer for about 10 minutes. Leave to cool.
Add lemon juice and fruit juice or purée to the syrup. Add more sugar if necessary.
Pour the mixture into a shallow tray, cover with foil, and put in the freezer or the ice-making compartment of the refrigerator.
When the water ice has a slushy consistency (after about an hour), turn it into a bowl and beat well to remove ice crystals. Beat egg whites and fold them into the water ice. Freeze again.
Transfer the water ice to the main compartment of the refrigerator about 30 minutes before serving.

Serves 6.

Basic Table Jelly
1 pint (550 ml) fruit juice
½ ounce (10–15 g) gelatine
Sugar

Put about 3 tablespoons fruit juice in a small bowl and sprinkle with gelatine. Leave gelatine to soften for about 10 minutes.

Meanwhile, put the remaining fruit juice in a saucepan and add enough sugar to sweeten it if necessary. Heat gently, stirring, until the sugar is dissolved and put aside to cool.

Place the bowl containing the softened gelatine over a pan of hot (not boiling) water until the gelatine dissolves. Add to the fruit juice, and stir gently.

Pour juice into a mould that has been rinsed with cold water, and chill until set.

To turn out the jelly, hold the mould in a basin of hot water for a few seconds.

Serves 6.

Note: For a jelly made with fruit purée instead of juice, sweeten the purée to taste with sugar and make up to 1 pint (550 ml) with water. Dissolve gelatine with water and proceed as above.

GARNISHES

Croutons
Cut slices of stale white bread into very small cubes. Fry in shallow or deep fat until golden brown. Drain well and salt lightly before serving.

Sugared Croutons
Cut slices of sweet milk bread and spread them thinly on both sides with butter. Bake them in a moderately hot oven (400°F, 200°C, Mark 6) for 15–20 minutes until crisp and golden. Dice the baked bread and toss the cubes in sugar.

Cinnamon Croutons
Follow instructions for sugared croutons, but toss cubes in a mixture of ground cinnamon and sugar.

VANILLA SUGAR
Put 1 pound (450 g) of caster or granulated sugar in a jar with a vanilla pod. Close the jar and store. The vanilla flavour will permeate the sugar.

SAUCES
Thick Custard Sauce
Double the quantities given below for 1 pint (550 ml) of custard.

½ pint (300 ml) milk
½ vanilla pod
2 eggs
1 generous tablespoon sugar

Heat the milk very gently in a saucepan with the vanilla pod. Do not allow to boil. Remove the pan from the heat, cover and stand in a warm place to infuse for 10 minutes.

Cream eggs and sugar together in a bowl. Remove the vanilla pod from the milk and gradually pour the milk on to the egg mixture, whisking all the time. Strain the mixture into a saucepan and heat very gently, over hot water or very low heat, until the custard is creamy, and stays separated if you run your finger through it on the back of a wooden spoon.

Rich Custard
Use ½ pint (300 ml) double or single cream instead of milk, and 3 egg yolks instead of 2 eggs.

Orange or Lemon Custard
Stir in 2 tablespoons orange juice or 1 tablespoon lemon juice when the custard thickens. Stir gently until the juice is blended with the custard.

Mayonnaise
1 egg yolk
½ teaspoon dry mustard
½ teaspoon salt
Freshly ground black pepper
¼ pint (150 ml) olive or salad oil
1 tablespoon white wine vinegar

Beat the egg yolk in a bowl until it is thick.

Add the mustard, salt and pepper, beating well.

Add the oil drop by drop to start with, whisking hard after every drop so that it is completely absorbed before the next drop is added. When the mixture is thick and shiny you can add the rest of the oil in a steady trickle, whisking all the time. Finally, add the vinegar and blend in well.

Makes ¼ pint (150 ml).

Lemon Mayonnaise
Use 1 tablespoon lemon juice instead of white wine vinegar.

WINES AND LIQUEURS
The most important point to remember when making wine is to make sure that all the equipment is clean and rinsed in a sterilizing solution, usually 2 Campden tablets and ½ teaspoon of citric acid dissolved in 1 pint (550 ml) cold water.

Wines also need a warm atmosphere (65–75°F or 18–24°C) for fermentation to take place successfully. Always store at about 55°F (12°C).

Wines
Equipment
Specialized equipment is available from winemakers' supply shops and some large chemist shops.

Mashing vessel. This is a large container in which the fruit is prepared for fermentation. It must have a close-fitting lid and be easy to keep scrupulously clean. A 4½ gallon (20.5 litre) plastic dustbin with a lid is ideal. If you are going to make smaller quantities use a plastic bucket, again with a close fitting lid. Never use a metal mashing vessel (fermentation can only take place in an acidic solution which reacts with metals).

Fermentation vessel. The main fermentation occurs in this container, which should have a narrow neck and also be easy to keep scrupulously clean. A glass carboy satisfies these requirements and you will also be able to see the wine and check its progress. The standard 1 gallon (4.5 litre) size is ideal for most recipes.

Fermentation lock (air-lock). This should be fitted into the narrow neck of the fermentation vessel.

Siphon. In its simplest form this is a length of tubing about 4 feet (1.2 metres) long. Plastic tubing is popular, although more sophisticated siphons can be bought.

Storage vessel. This can also be a corked glass carboy. If you are making a deep red wine, it is advisable to cover a clear glass vessel with a brown paper 'jacket' to exclude light and preserve the rich colouring of the wine. A large glazed earthenware jar, which can be tightly sealed, also makes an excellent storage vessel.

Wine bottles. These must be thoroughly cleaned and sterilized before use.

Cylindrical corks.

Corking gun. This is essential for inserting corks into bottles.

Linen bag. A large bag about 2 foot by 1 foot (60 cm by 30 cm), which can be securely sealed, is useful for squeezing fruit pulp in order to extract the maximum juice.

With hard fruits, such as apples, *a small press* or even an *electric juice extractor* is a good investment, especially if you are sure you are going to make wine regularly.

Ingredients
Specialized ingredients are available from winemakers' supply shops and some large chemist shops.

Fruit. Always use good quality, undamaged fruit. It should be washed thoroughly and stoned if necessary. There is no need to remove skin or peel. Hard fruits like apples should be crushed before placing in the mashing vessel.

Water should be pure. British tap-water satisfies this requirement.

Sugar. White granulated sugar is suitable for most wine recipes. Brown sugar gives a slight caramel flavour to the wine.

Sugar should always be added in the form of a syrup, made up of 2 pounds (900 g) sugar to 1 pint (550 ml) water, unless the recipe calls for it to be added before the yeast.

Yeast. Use a proper wine yeast. It comes in several forms, usually as tablets or a liquid. Follow manufacturer's instructions for activation and use.

Nutrient tablet. Yeast, like any other living organism, needs nutrients if it is to grow and cause fermentation. Only grapes provide the natural food for wine yeast. When using other fruits, nutrients must be added.

Citric acid. The yeast cannot ferment sugar, turning it into alcohol, unless it is in an acid solution. Although some fruits provide enough acid, it is sometimes necessary to add extra acid.

Tannin. This is necessary to give a wine 'bite'. As with citric acid, some fruits contain enough tannin. The cheapest way to provide extra is in the form of cold, strong tea.

Pectozyme. This is an artificial pectin-destroying enzyme. It is found in many fruits, and will cause haze in wine if not removed.

Campden tablets. A form of sulphur dioxide, these are used for sterilizing. Sterile conditions are necessary to prevent growth of unwanted moulds and bacteria.

Sultanas/raisins. Most recipes include sultanas or raisins to give the wine true vinosity.

Basic wine recipe
All equipment must be thoroughly washed, dried and sterilized. Sterilization is essential to prevent the growth of moulds and bacteria which will inhibit or even stop fermentation.

A standard sterilizing solution consists of 2 Campden tablets and ½ teaspoon citric acid dissolved in 1 pint (550 ml) cold water. Rinse everything—vessels, bottles, corks, spoons, siphon—in this solution.

Preparing a must. The fruit mixture on which fermentation takes place is known as a must.

Put the prepared fruit in a clean, sterile mashing vessel. Add the chopped sultanas or raisins, water, Campden tablet(s), Pectozyme and citric acid (if required).

Cover the vessel and leave for at least 24 hours, in a warm place (65–75°F or 18–24°C).

Fermenting on the pulp. This preliminary fermentation improves the colour and flavour of most fruit wines. Not all recipes include this stage.

Quickly uncover the mashing vessel and stir in the crushed nutrient tablet and activated yeast. Manufacturer's instructions should be followed for the amount of yeast to use and method of activation.

Replace the lid and leave for the time recommended in the recipe in a warm place (65–75°F or 18–24°C).

This fermentation gives off carbon dioxide which lifts the fruit up. It must be pushed down and stirred into the liquid, at least once a day, to keep it moist.

Do this quickly and be sure to keep the vessel closely covered at all other times.

Extracting the juice (young wine). Strain the fruit mixture through a fine sieve, taking out a jugful at a time, into a clean sterilized container.

Put the pulp into a linen bag or cloth. Close in the pulp tightly and squeeze out the rest of the juice into the sterilized container.

A small press or electric juice extractor is useful for large quantities of hard fruits.

Fermentation. Stir in the sugar syrup. (Some recipes ask for sugar to be added before the yeast.) Add tannin if necessary, in the form of cold strong tea – ½ teacup to 1 gallon (4.5 litres) wine. Stir well, then siphon the young wine into a clean, sterilized fermentation vessel, filling to within 1 inch (2.5 cm) of the cork. Do all this quickly so that the young wine is not left uncovered for too long, to prevent bacteria entering and inhibiting fermentation.

Seal the fermentation vessel with a clean, sterile, tight-fitting air-lock.

When siphoning, place the fermentation vessel so that its top is below the level of the bottom of the container being emptied. Put one end of the siphon tube in the container of young wine and the other well into the fermentation vessel.

Leave the sealed fermentation vessel in a warm place (65–75°F or 18–24°C) until fermentation is complete and bubbling in the air-lock has ceased.

A layer of sediment (the lees) will appear on the bottom of the vessel as the wine clears from the top downwards. Leave until there is a good layer of lees, then rack.

Racking. This helps to produce a clear, bright wine. It is usual to rack at least 3 times. All but the final racking should be into a clear vessel of similar type and size to the fermentation vessel—a glass carboy is ideal. Like all winemaking equipment it should be cleaned and sterilized in the Campden tablet solution. The final racking is into the storage vessel. It need not be clear, but should be of a size to be filled almost exactly with the quantity of wine produced.

Racking consists of siphoning off the clear wine, above the lees in the fermentation vessel, into a new vessel. Make sure the end of the siphon tube is above the lees when doing this. If necessary top up with cold water to fill the vessel and keep air out of the wine. (The size of the receiving vessel should not be such that a large quantity of water needs to be added.)

Seal the vessel and leave in a cool, dark place (55°F or 12°C) until another layer of lees has formed (no longer than 10 weeks), then repeat the process until no lees form. Rack once more into a storage vessel keeping the end of the siphon tube just above the bottom of the vessel the wine is being racked from. Seal the storage vessel tightly.

Storage. Leave the storage vessel in a cool dark place (55°F or 12°C) for 2 months. Then check for haze by pouring off some of the wine into a glass. This is unlikely to form, but if it has, rack the wine again and store for a further 2 months. Check again for haze. If the wine is not clear, add a teaspoon of Pectozyme and continue to store. The total storage time must be at least the minimum time stated in the recipe.

Bottling. Prepare the corks by soaking them for 30 minutes in hot water, then rinsing in the Campden tablet solution to sterilize them.

Siphon the wine into clean, sterilized wine bottles to within 1¾ inches (3 cm) of the top. Cork using the corking gun. Fit a foil cap over the cork, to prevent bacteria entering the bottle. Label each bottle with the name of the wine and date of bottling.

Store the bottles on their sides (in a wine rack) in a cool, dark place (55°F or 12°C). Keep at least 6 months before drinking.

Liqueurs

Fruit liqueurs are prepared by steeping the fruit in a commercially produced alcohol to extract the flavour, aroma and colour.

No special equipment is needed, but all bottles, etc, must be scrupulously clean. If you want to make doubly sure that equipment is clean, rinse in the sterilizing solution given for wines.

Ingredients

Fruit Liqueurs can be made from most fruits, although those with a strongly distinctive flavour give the best results.

Alcohol. Choice of spirits is optional. Vodka is popular, and there are certain traditional combinations like cherries and brandy.

Sugar. White or demerara sugar can be used, depending on the fruit and type of spirit.

Basic Liqueur Recipe

2 pounds (900 g) fruit
2 pounds (900 g) sugar
2½ pints (1.4 litres) spirits

Wash the fruit and remove stones if necessary. Pack fruit into a large wide-necked, screw-top glass jar, covering each layer of fruit with a generous layer of sugar. Berries should be crushed and mixed with the sugar before they are placed in the jar.

Fill the jar with spirits, tightly screw on the lid, and leave to mature for up to 6 months at room temperature.

Strain off the liqueur, and pour or siphon it into clean dry bottles.

Makes about 2½ pints (1.4 litres).

MEASUREMENTS

Quantities have been given in both imperial and metric measures in this book. However, many foodstuffs are now available only in metric quantities; the list below gives metric measures for weight and liquid capacity, and their imperial equivalents used in this book.

Weight

25 g	1 ounce
50 g	2 ounces
75 g	3 ounces
100–125 g	4 ounces
150 g	5 ounces
175 g	6 ounces
200 g	7 ounces
225 g	8 ounces
250 g	9 ounces
275 g	10 ounces
300 g	11 ounces
350 g	12 ounces
375 g	13 ounces
400 g	14 ounces
425 g	15 ounces
450 g	1 pound
500 g (½ kilo)	17½ ounces
1 kilo	2 pounds 3 ounces
1.5 kilos	3 pounds 5 ounces
2 kilos	4 pounds 6 ounces
2.5 kilos	5 pounds 8 ounces
3 kilos	6 pounds 10 ounces
3.5 kilos	7 pounds 11 ounces
4 kilos	8 pounds 13 ounces
4.5 kilos	9 pounds 14 ounces
5 kilos	11 pounds

Liquid Capacity

150 ml	¼ pint
300 ml	½ pint
425 ml	¾ pint
550–600 ml	1 pint
900 ml	1½ pints
1000 ml (1 litre)	1¾ pints
1.2 litres	2 pints
1.3 litres	2¼ pints
1.4 litres	2½ pints
1.5 litres	2¾ pints
1.9 litres	3¼ pints
2 litres	3½ pints
2.5 litres	4½ pints

Oven Temperatures

Very low	130°C, 250°F, Mark ½
Low	140°C, 275°F, Mark 1
Very slow	150°C, 300°F, Mark 2
Slow	170°C, 325°F, Mark 3
Moderate	180°C, 350°F, Mark 4
	190°C, 375°F, Mark 5
Moderately hot	200°C, 400°F, Mark 6
Fairly hot	220°C, 425°F, Mark 7
Hot	230°C, 450°F, Mark 8

NUTRITION

Any normal diet (unless you are restricted for medical reasons) should include at least two servings of fruit a day. One of the easiest ways to manage this is to have fruit juice or sliced fruit at breakfast, and fresh fruit (instead of cake or pudding) as a lunchtime or dinner dessert.

RAPID-ACTION DIETS

Fruit is the basis of many 'wonder diets' or 'crash diets' – the sort that, typically, are taken up by the press and gain an international following until superseded by some even newer formula for rapid weight loss.

If you have the willpower to embark on one of these semi-starvation diets – and are prepared to cope with an essentially monotonous succession of mini-meals comprising only one or two ingredients – you will undoubtedly lose weight!

But it is certainly inadvisable to pursue such a diet for more than two or three days at a stretch without your doctor's approval.

This is because a 'wonder diet' is unlikely to be a well-balanced diet, and therefore it cannot supply your body with all the essential nutrients in the right amounts and proportions. Some crash diets aim specifically to reduce the body's calorific intake; be very careful of these if the recommended intake falls below 1,000 calories a day and you take regular physical exercise.

Another thing to consider – and be prepared for – is that some all-fruit diets are inclined to have a laxative effect. Indeed, for some people on normal diets, a sudden switch to a fruit-only regimen may wreak havoc with the digestion; if the symptoms persist or cause any real pain, switch immediately to a more varied diet that includes fruit.

Older people are likely to find large quantities of rhubarb or stewed apples difficult to digest; they too should keep to milder forms of restricted fruit diet, including fruit juices.

Once you are down to your target weight you will still have to take care to prevent it from creeping up again. So when you have completed the crash diet change to a well-balanced maintenance one.

All in all, it is a good idea to talk to your doctor before embarking on any diet involving the loss of more than 5–10 pounds (2·3–4·6 kilos).

Single-fruit Diets

The theory about single-fruit — or any single-food — diets is simply that the appetite is diminished by boredom. An appetizer of sliced oranges or melon can be a delightful start to a meal; but when the main course is also sliced oranges or melon, and the dessert is sliced oranges or melon, it takes a determined food freak to continue eating huge quantities even if no limit is placed on the amount of fruit permitted.

This effect is important; if you in fact went on eating voraciously you would ingest an enormous number of calories.

As it is, a day a week on a restricted fruit diet can be added to your dieting programme (unless your doctor advises otherwise).

Apples

A single good-sized apple, cored but unskinned, 4 times a day. It can be raw, puréed, baked or stewed, with spices but no sugar. To drink: water and pure unsweetened apple juice.

Bananas

2 medium-sized bananas and 1 glass of skimmed milk at breakfast, lunch and supper. To ring the changes you can liquidize the milk and bananas in a blender — adding a sprinkling of cinnamon, nutmeg or other spice — to make a creamy drink. Bananas are one of the high-calorie fruits, so don't add anything else to this diet.

Grapefruit

1 large grapefruit 3 times a day — with added spices sprinkled on, if you wish, but no sugar. If you really find grapefruit too sour on its own, add just a dab of honey. To drink: either grapefruit juice or else pure lemon juice diluted in hot water.

The theory that grapefruit is able to destroy fats in the system is without foundation but — like apricots, berries, lemons, melon, rhubarb and tangerines — it is low in calories.

A less spartan diet that includes grapefruit is as follows:

Breakfast: half a grapefruit, unsweetened; 2 eggs, cooked as you wish; 2 slices bacon; coffee or tea, without milk or sugar (but add an artificial sweetener if necessary).

Lunch: half a grapefruit; one small portion of meat or fish, with either a green-leaf vegetable like spinach, or a salad with lemon-juice dressing; coffee or tea, as at breakfast.

Dinner: the same as lunch.

Grapes

4 pounds (1·8 kilos) fresh grapes, to be eaten at any time during the course of a day. Wash them well but don't skin them; in fact eat them whole.

To drink: a selection of herbal teas (sweetened if necessary with a dash of honey) and water.

Oranges

2 medium-sized oranges, 3 times a day. To drink: orange juice, up to 5 times a day — or water.

Once again, a sprinkling of spices like ground cloves — or a fragrant dried herb such as oregano — will ring the changes.

Pineapples

This fruit is the basis of the original 'Beverly Hills Diet' created by ex-actress Judy Mazel. During an initial weight-loss period lasting 9 days, dieters are instructed to eat pineapples, papayas, grapes, kiwi fruit, bananas and watermelon in a given order prescribed by Miss Mazel.

After this period they then return gradually to a balanced diet or 'normal' food.

Judy Mazel's book is available in hard cover and paper-back.

Watermelon

As much watermelon as you like — but nothing else — each day. Watermelon is filling and satisfying, especially when it is absolutely ripe. Its calorie count is low.

Mixed fruit diet

Breakfast: either half a grapefruit or else a whole orange.

Lunch: a fresh fruit salad, unsweetened but spiced if you wish; or an assortment of whole fresh fruits such as apples, mangoes, melons, papayas, pineapples, various berries, cherries.

Dinner: as for lunch.

Nuts

You can relieve the monotony of an all-fruit diet with modest amounts of nuts (fresh, not roasted in oil). Remember though that nuts are not only very high in protein but have a particularly high calorific content — higher, weight for weight, than fried streaky bacon, cream cheese or fudge!

Brazil nuts, cashews and coconuts are especially high in calories, chestnuts comparatively low.

Orange Health Drink Diet

This is a good experiment for a long weekend, and will give your system a change from solid foods. If you keep to it for 2 to 3 days you will lose up to 5 pounds (2·3 kilos) but don't stay on it for more than 4 days.

Make sure, too, that this is a relatively quiet, inactive period; you will need a reasonable amount of sleep and leisure.

2 pints (1·1 litres) skimmed milk
8 ounces (225 g) natural yoghourt
2 eggs
Juice of 3 freshly squeezed oranges
1 tablespoon sunflower oil (or pure corn oil)
2 tablespoons honey
½ teaspoon vanilla essence

Mix all the above ingredients in a blender and chill. This will give you a day's requirement. Drink a glass at each mealtime, seasoning the drink with cinnamon, coriander or extra vanilla if you wish for the second day.

You can also drink water, mineral water and herbal teas as often as you like — but eat no solids at all.

If you find the diet a bit too spartan, make up an extra formula and drink up to an extra glassful each day.

HIGH-FIBRE FRUIT DIET

When you are concentrating on adding bulk and roughage to your diet, fruit can be a useful addition to make bran and its derivatives more palatable.

Serve bran cereals with fresh fruit, sliced before the meal so that their juices can help to absorb and flavour the grains.

Add bran to cooked fruits — for example to apricot fluff puddings or hot apple sauce.

Berry dishes — those made with raspberries and blackberries in particular — are high in fibre. Make fruit crumbles with oat-flakes added to the crumbs.

When you roast chicken or turkey, add chestnuts and fresh cranberries to the stuffing along with some bran- or oat-flakes.

Beans of all kinds are extremely high in fibre. You can make marvellous salads with crisp apples, chopped nuts and cooked beans, all mixed with a vinaigrette dressing.

Vegetarian Diets

Fruits and nuts feature prominently in all vegetarian diets, as they are the major source of many minerals and vitamins for vegetarians.

Recent medical research has come to the conclusion that we actually need far less protein than we used to think was necessary; nevertheless protein from nuts, cheese and eggs are very important to vegetarians. Mixed nuts are often used in vegetarian restaurants as a kind of minced meat.

Brazil nuts, hazelnuts, cashews and sunflower seeds ground up together can be stored in a refrigerator or freezer, and used whenever needed to make nut rissoles, meatless loaves, or crumbles for topping vegetables, stewed fruits, salads and puddings. This particular mixture is very high in methionine and lysine, and rich in unsaturated fatty acids.

Vegetarian diets usually have a high fruit content, as most people recognize that fruit is essential, but are sometimes too low in protein – so make use whenever possible of nuts as well.

Low Blood Sugar Diet

When the pancreas underproduces insulin, the sugar content in the blood rises and diabetes develops. But when the pancreas produces too much insulin the level of sugar in the blood is kept abnormally low – a condition that may cause a feeling of general physical weakness, depression and nervous irritability.

Confusingly, one of the reasons why the pancreas secretes insulin in excess is that it is over-stimulated when we eat too *much* sugar! So the cure for a low blood sugar condition is to cut back on sugar in your diet.

Among other things that means keeping away from the high-sugar fruits such as raisins, dates, figs, plums, bananas, grapes, pineapples, persimmons, avocados and olives. It is also necessary to avoid fruit canned in syrup.

However, you can eat grapefruit, oranges, lemons, tangerines, all kinds of berries, apples, pears, melons, kiwi fruit, mangoes, pomegranates, passion fruit, and also nuts. Natural unsweetened fruit juices are also permitted.

Fruit in Children's Diets

We have come a long way in the past decade from the theory that chubby children are automatically healthy and happy.

We now know that over-fed children are all too likely to grow into over-fed, and often unhealthy, adults, starting a battle with the bulge which may last all their lives.

So do your children a favour and be as sensible with them as you are with yourself. Of course children are growing fast and need extra nourishment and carbohydrates, but they don't need the 'empty' calories that come with junk foods and excessive amounts of processed and fried snacks.

Bananas are among the easiest foods for young children to digest; learn to use them fresh. They are nice served mashed, but don't add sugar – a ripe banana has plenty of natural sugar, and filling carbohydrates as well.

Apples, plums and pears are all popular with older children as they can be held in the hand and munched during tea-time or as dessert. Try to give children a wide variety of fresh fruit, so that there is something delicious to eat all through the year.

Children love working when the results of that work are obvious. Picking blackberries and gathering nuts – the fruits of the countryside – will provide enjoyable afternoons for all the family.

If you have a garden, see how many useful, versatile fruits you can grow. Don't forget crab apples, nor the many new thornless berries and vines with improved cropping for the table.

Make fruit dishes that you can pack into lunch-boxes, and add raisins, dried prunes and nuts for between-class nibbles.

Older children can explore cooking with fruit and nuts. Remember to be around, though, even if it's in the background, to guard against over-heated ovens, overflowing saucepans, and sharp knives clumsily handled. If there is any caramel or boiling syrup involved, you can unobtrusively take over.

Some children have allergies – to, among other things, certain fruits – or other conditions which necessitate special attention to their diets, and it can be difficult for the active, sociable child to remember these limitations. It is best to explain what the diet is for, and what foods will make him or her ill; there is then less chance of the child accepting the wrong food because it is not polite to complain or make a fuss in someone else's house.

Few children are allergic to every kind of fruit; and any child on a restricted diet needs extra quantities of acceptable fruits and nuts to keep temptation at bay.

Have a talk with your doctor about this before exploring some of the new fruits now easily available from supermarkets and greengrocers. An allergy to, say, strawberries is seldom transferred to loganberries or blackberries, or for that matter to lychees or kiwi fruits.

Buying and Preparing Fruit

For proper nutrition the emphasis is on *fresh* fruit; bottled or preserved fruit is likely to have large quantities of sugar in the syrup, and in any case most of the vitamin and mineral content will have gone long before it is served.

A recent test showed the horrifying speed with which vitamins disappear even from freshly squeezed oranges: within half an hour, 25 per cent of the vitamin content had gone, within an hour another 20 per cent – and this without any cooking, which would reduce the vitamin level even further.

So make an effort to find a place to buy fruit at its best – newly picked where possible, or properly stored to conserve nutrients when it is ripened off the tree or bush.

Don't peel fruit before you have to, and eat the skins when you can; they contain really high proportions of essential nutrients.

Do remember, though, that some fruits are high in calories and carbohydrates. A large apple contains as many calories as a small piece of caramel or chocolate – but then, of course, it is full of many other good things that cooked sugars and chocolates lack.

Learn to include fruit in savoury meals too. Remember how delicious cranberry sauce is with turkey, or prunes with pork.

Choose from among the recipes throughout this book to find new and exciting ways to serve fruit throughout a meal.

VITAMIN AND MINERAL CHART

The chart below and on the pages that follow lists fruits and nuts that are relatively rich in nutrient minerals and one or more vitamins. It also indicates which has a relatively high fibre content, and gives a calorie count for each.

The calorie count refers to a quantity of 4 ounces (100–125 g) of fruit but only 1 ounce (25 g) of nuts. Most nuts – chestnuts are an exception – have a much higher calorific content than fresh fruits, weight for weight.

Vitamins

The full range of vitamins, in small but constant quantities, is necessary to a well-balanced diet. Fruit and nuts can supply many of these vitamins but not all of them; Vitamins B12 and D, for example, are not found at all in products of plant origin, but adequate quantities of them are contained in dairy products such as milk and butter, as well as in eggs.

Vitamin A

Vitamin A protects the body's epithelial tissue: the skin, and the mucous membranes lining internal organs including the stomach and intestines.

It is also necessary to ensure healthy eyes, hair and nails, and for resistance to infection.

Apricots, cherries, cantaloup melons and rose hips are among fruits rich in Vitamin A.

Vitamin B

The B complex of vitamins embraces twelve different sub-groups. Among these are thiamin (Bl), needed for the metabolism of carbohydrates; riboflavin (B2), necessary for the metabolism of proteins; and folic acid, which is essential for the formation of the blood, and without which a form of anaemia results. Peanuts are rich in folic acid.

Vitamin C

Vitamin C (ascorbic acid) is present in many fruits, and especially in blackcurrants, rose hips, strawberries and citrus fruits. It is well known that scurvy is caused by Vitamin C deficiency.

This vitamin is also needed for the correct functioning of the adrenal glands. And extra amounts of it help to counteract the effects of the common cold and other debilitating infections.

Vitamin E

All sorts of extravagant claims have been made for Vitamin E, which is present in many kinds of nut. It is not, in fact, a cure for coronary heart disease, nor have its alleged rejuvenating properties been proved.

However, Vitamin E does assist the normal development of the reproductive functions.

Minerals

In the same way as we need a balanced intake of vitamins we also require a regular diet of minerals, essential for the building of the body and for the metabolism of food. Some of these minerals – copper, zinc and selenium for example – are necessary in only very small quantities; these are known as the 'trace elements'.

Calcium and Phosphorus

Both calcium and phosphorus play a decisive part in the formation of bones and teeth. We need these minerals even when we are fully grown, for our bone tissue is constantly being renewed.

Magnesium

Magnesium also plays an important, if lesser role, in the formation of bones and teeth. It also assists in such essential functions as the regulation of the body's temperature and the healthy performance of the muscles and nerves.

Iron

A deficiency of iron, a constituent of haemoglobin, leads to loss of energy and anaemia. Iron is essential in early childhood and puberty, as well as in pregnancy.

Nuts in particular are rich in iron, which is also present in certain exotic fruits such as avocados and tamarinds.

Sodium and Potassium

In a healthy body the two minerals sodium and potassium are present in balanced proportions; if they are not, the functions of muscles and nerves will be impaired and the body's powers of resistance and regeneration will be lowered.

Both sodium and potassium are contained in fruits and nuts, though the proportion of potassium is much higher.

Fruit	Quantity	Calories	Nutrients
ALMONDS, *shelled*	1 oz/25 g	140	Vitamins B, E; calcium, iron, magnesium, phosphorus, potassium, sodium; fibre
APPLE	1 small (4 oz/100–125 g)	35	Vitamin B; potassium
APRICOT	4 medium (4 oz/100–125 g)	30	Vitamins A, B, C; phosphorus, potassium
dried	4 oz/100–125 g	200	+ calcium, magnesium; fibre
AVOCADO	½ medium (4 oz/100–125 g)	225	Vitamins A, B, C; iron, magnesium, phosphorus, potassium
BANANA	1 small (4 oz/100–125 g)	80	Vitamins B, C; magnesium, phosphorus, potassium

Fruit	Quantity	Calories	Nutrients
BLACKBERRY	4 oz/100–125 g	30	Vitamins C, E; calcium, magnesium, phosphorus, potassium
BLACKCURRANT	4 oz/100–125 g	30	Vitamin C; calcium, phosphorus; fibre
BLUEBERRY	4 oz/100–125 g	30	Vitamin C; fibre
BRAZIL NUTS, *shelled*	1 oz/55 g	125	Vitamins B, E; calcium, iron, magnesium, phosphorus, potassium; fibre
CASHEW NUTS	1 oz/25 g	160	Vitamins B, E; iron, magnesium, phosphorus, potassium; fibre
CHERRY	4 oz/100–125 g	45	Vitamins A, B, C; potassium; fibre
CHESTNUTS, *shelled*	1 oz/25 g	40	Vitamin B; calcium, magnesium, phosphorus, potassium
COCONUT, *fresh*	1 oz/25 g	90	Vitamin B; magnesium, phosphorus, potassium; fibre
desiccated	1 oz/25 g	150	+ sodium
CRANBERRY	4 oz/100–125 g	15	Vitamin C; potassium
DATE, *stoned*	4 oz/100–125 g	250	Vitamin B; calcium, magnesium, phosphorus, potassium
FIG, *fresh*	4 medium (4 oz/100–125 g)	40	Vitamin B; calcium, magnesium, potassium
dried	4 oz/100–125 g	240	+ phosphorus, sodium; fibre
GOOSEBERRY, *ripe*	4 oz/100–125 g	40	Vitamin C; potassium
GRAPE, *white*	4 oz/100–125 g	65	Vitamin B; phosphorus, potassium; fibre
black	4 oz/100–125 g	60	Vitamin B; phosphorus, potassium; fibre
dried (currants, raisins, sultanas)	4 oz/100–125 g	250	+ calcium, magnesium, sodium
GRAPEFRUIT	½ medium (4 oz/100–125 g)	20	Vitamins B, C; potassium; fibre
GUAVA	4 oz/100–125 g	60	Vitamins A, C; potassium
HAZELNUTS, *shelled*	1 oz/25 g	95	Vitamins B, E; calcium, magnesium, phosphorus, potassium, sodium; fibre
LEMON	1 medium (4 oz/100–125 g)	15	Vitamin C; calcium, phosphorus, potassium
LOGANBERRY	4 oz/100–125 g	20	Vitamin C; calcium, magnesium, phosphorus, potassium
LYCHEE	4 oz/100–125 g	65	Vitamin C; potassium
MANGO	4 oz/100–125 g	60	Vitamins A, C; potassium; fibre
MEDLAR	4 oz/100–125 g	40	potassium
MELON, *cantaloup*	small slice (4 oz/100–125 g)	25	Vitamins A, B, C; magnesium, phosphorus, potassium
casaba/honeydew	small slice (4 oz/100–125 g)	20	Vitamins B, C; potassium, sodium
watermelon	small slice (4 oz/100–125 g)	20	potassium

Fruit	Quantity	Calories	Nutrients
MULBERRY	4 oz/100–125 g	40	Vitamin C; calcium, phosphorus, potassium
NECTARINE	1 small (4 oz/100–125 g)	50	Vitamins A, B, C; phosphorus, potassium; fibre
OLIVE, *stoned green* *stoned black* *in brine*	1 oz/25 g 1 oz/25 g 1 oz/25 g	30 35 100	potassium; fibre + calcium, magnesium, sodium
ORANGE	1 small (4 oz/100–125 g)	25	Vitamin C; calcium, potassium
PAPAYA/PAW PAW	4 oz/100–125 g	65	Vitamin C; potassium
PASSION FRUIT	1 large (4 oz/100–125 g)	15	Vitamin C; phosphorus, potassium
PEACH	1 medium (4 oz/100–125 g)	30	Vitamins A, B; potassium; fibre
PEANUTS, *fresh* *roasted & salted*	1 oz/25 g 1 oz/25 g	140 140	Vitamins B, E; calcium, iron, magnesium, phosphorus, potassium; fibre + chlorine, sodium
PEAR	1 small (4 oz/100–125 g)	30	Vitamin B; potassium; fibre
PECAN	1 oz/25 g	196	Vitamin A; magnesium, phosphorus, potassium; fibre
PERSIMMON	4 oz/100–125 g	88	Vitamins A, C; potassium; fibre
PINEAPPLE	4 oz/100–125 g	45	Vitamin C; potassium
PISTACHIO	4 oz/100–125 g	170	Vitamins B, E; iron, magnesium, phosphorus, potassium; fibre
PLUM, *dried (prune)*	2 medium (4 oz/100–125 g) 8 medium (4 oz/100–125 g)	40 150	Vitamin B; potassium; fibre + calcium, magnesium, phosphorus
POMEGRANATE	4 oz/100–125 g	90	Vitamin C; potassium
QUINCE	4 oz/100–125 g	25	potassium
RASPBERRY	4 oz/100–125 g	25	Vitamins B, C, E; calcium, magnesium, phosphorus, potassium; fibre
REDCURRANT	4 oz/100–125 g	20	Vitamin C; calcium, phosphorus, potassium
RHUBARB	4 oz/100–125 g	5	Vitamin C; calcium, phosphorus, potassium; fibre
SAPODILLA	4 oz/100–125 g	98	potassium
STRAWBERRY	4 oz/100–125 g	25	Vitamins B, C; calcium, phosphorus, potassium; fibre
TAMARIND	4 oz/100–125 g	230	Vitamin B; calcium, iron, phosphorus, potassium, sodium
TANGERINE	1 large (4 oz/100–125 g)	25	Vitamins B, C; calcium, potassium; fibre
WALNUTS, *shelled*	1 oz/25 g	130	Vitamin B; calcium, magnesium, phosphorus, potassium

HOW TO GROW FRUITS & NUTS

Even in a tiny garden it is worth reserving some space to grow your own fruit – a few raspberry canes, a blackcurrant bush, even a grape vine. Not only will you ensure that you enjoy the freshest of fresh fruit, you can also have the enormous pleasure of growing a variety or type that is too unusual, or not commercial enough, to be sold in shops.

Happily, many fruits and nuts have more than one appeal. Trees can provide delightful flowers and sometimes scent, bushes can be used to screen a rather mundane vegetable patch, and perennials provide colour and ground cover for months at a time.

Some tropical and subtropical plants can be grown indoors if the outdoor climate is unsuitable, and will still bear fruit.

There are specialized and more technical books for the enthusiast, but we hope the brief paragraphs that follow will start you off in the right direction, making you aware how easy and rewarding it can be to harvest your own fruit.

BUSH FRUIT

The *Ribes* family of fruits – blackcurrants, red- and whitecurrants, goose-berries and Worcesterberries – does best in cooler climates – indeed, gooseberries positively like the cold and will grow up to the Arctic Circle.

All are native to the northern hemisphere, found wild from Scandinavia to the Himalayas. They are now cultivated in many other parts of the world. Because they are the host of a fungus which causes white pine blister rot (a very serious disease) growing currants and gooseberries is forbidden in parts of the United States and strongly discouraged in others.

Currants and gooseberries make quite attractive, compact, even dense, deciduous bushes, up to 6 feet (just under 2 metres) high and about the same across. They are not really ornamental enough to be grown as specimen bushes (flowering currants, with showy crimson, pink or scarlet blooms, are a different species, originating in North America), but they are not difficult to grow and will fruit very well in tubs. All *Ribes* are self-compatible, so only a single bush need be grown. They can easily be propagated from cuttings.

CULTIVATION AND MANAGEMENT

Spring frosts will damage the flowers and fruit buds, so protect the plants at blossom time. Netting may also be necessary against birds.

Generally, cultivation is the same for all of the species. They have shallow root systems which dislike being disturbed. Once planted they will live and bear prolifically for up to thirty years, and in some cases even longer. This means that the ground must be very well prepared, not only thoroughly dug over and free of weeds, but given plenty of manure or compost. Beds for blackcurrants, which are greedy feeders, would be particularly enriched. Once planted, the bushes will need regular fertilizing, mulching and watering. Potash is essential for redcurrants and gooseberries.

BLACKCURRANTS

Blackcurrants like rich, damp, slightly acid soil; they will stand wet and shady conditions better than almost any other fruit, but set a much better crop if grown in full sun, as long as the position is not too hot and dry.

Cultivation

Blackcurrant bushes have several shoots or stems growing from below ground level. Plants bought from a nursery are generally planted to a few inches extra depth to encourage the stems. After planting, cut down all shoots to just above ground level. This means no fruit in the first season, but the strong new shoots will need little or no pruning and can be left to bear fruit the following summer. The plants need generous feeding.

Pruning

As blackcurrants bear fruit on wood formed the previous year, pruning is aimed at stimulating strong new growth. Cut back wood (easily distinguished from young shoots by its much darker colour) hard each year, by about a third. This is usually done immediately after fruiting, but not later than early winter. You can combine pruning with harvesting by cutting out the older stems with their last crop of fruit.

Pests and Diseases

The most serious pest is blackcurrant gall mite, which spreads reversion disease. Buy only stock certified free from the disease. If any bushes do become affected they must be dug up and burnt.

Varieties

Not all varieties are suitable for small gardens; the popular Boskoop Giant and the later Blacksmith, though excellent varieties, make spreading bushes. Mendip Cross (a hybrid of Boskoop Giant Research Station) and the very late Amos Black make smaller, more compact plants, suitable for pots and tubs.

Harvesting and Storage

Blackcurrants ripen from midsummer onwards, depending on the variety. Shiny and swollen currants should be picked before they begin to shrivel. If you are making juice or jelly there is no need to remove all the little stalks.

REDCURRANTS AND WHITECURRANTS

Whitecurrants are a blander variety of redcurrant.

Both types thrive in similar conditions to blackcurrants, but are hardier, and more resistant to pests and diseases, indeed, less troubled by them than almost any fruit. They will also grow in much drier and poorer soil, though they do like plenty of humus and potash.

Cultivation
Red- and whitecurrants are usually grown as bushes on a short stem or leg, but they can also be grown as taller standards.

Pruning
They fruit on old wood as well as on one-year-old shoots. In the first few years the aim is to build a strong permanent framework of branches, growing away from the centre, which should be kept open. In early winter, prune back the leaders and any laterals required for the framework. Mature plants will not need so much winter pruning. Summer pruning is very beneficial; shortening back the laterals by about half will let light and air into the bush, encourage the wood and fruit to ripen, and lessen the chances of infection with mildew.

Red- and whitecurrants are quite often grown as cordons, and sometimes as fans, making the most of restricted space. They will fruit on a sunless wall but not develop their best flavour. When grown as cordons, prune the leader back by about half each year and cut the laterals back hard. Summer-prune new growths to about four or five leaves.

Varieties
Both Laxton's No. 1, a well-flavoured, all-round redcurrant which does well on most soils, and the mid-season Red Lake, which has huge fruits are good, reliable varieties. The latter is also suitable for small gardens.

Harvesting and Storage
The fruit ripens in late summer, becoming clear, and almost translucent-looking. It is usually picked in whole bunches to avoid damage. All the fruit on a bush may not ripen at the same time. Preserve by cooking or freezing.

GOOSEBERRIES

The gooseberry is much loved in England, where the British have been more percipient and appreciative of a good food than the French.

Gooseberries tolerate much cooler conditions than currants. They will do well in shade and can be grown on a sunless wall; some varieties will even survive frost pockets. They are often grown with redcurrants and strawberries, both of which like the same balance of nitrogen and potash. They make dense bushes, often with a distinctive drooping habit; sharp thorns can make picking a painful task.

They can be grown as cordons – a method which can make it much easier to pick the fruit without getting impaled on the thorns. They do not, however, like too hot a wall; the heat will tend to scorch the fruit.

Cultivation
Gooseberries are cultivated in much the same way as red- and whitecurrants.

Pruning
Careful pruning will encourage more upright growth to make harvesting easier. They bear fruit on older wood and on the previous year's growth.

Pests and Diseases
American gooseberry mildew seems to affect only European strains of gooseberries, not American ones. Regular spraying with an appropriate fungicide will control it, but diseased shoots should be cut out and burnt.

Varieties
The best varieties are: the popular Keepsake, with pale, green-tinged fruit (although it ripens late the fruit can be picked very early for cooking); the delectable Early Sulphur; the mid-season small, white Langley Gage, winner of an Award of Merit for its flavour; and the later Leveller.

The berry can be hairy or smooth, and when ripe, it can be white, green, yellow, amber or even deep red. Size and colour are not necessarily related to flavour, but on the whole red varieties tend to be less sweet.

Harvesting and Storage
Depending on the variety, gooseberries ripen over a long period, all through the summer. Fruit for cooking can be picked before the rest of the crop is ripe to encourage the fruit that is left to grow succulent for desserts.

Gooseberries can be bottled, frozen or made into preserves or wines.

WORCESTERBERRIES
Worcesterberries have sometimes been considered hybrids, but are now generally accepted as being a form of a North American species of the genus *Ribes*. They bear fruit which looks rather like a cross between a gooseberry and a blackcurrant. It would not perhaps be the first choice where space is limited – it is very thorny and the fruit acid – but it makes delicious jam and is hardy and resistant to disease.

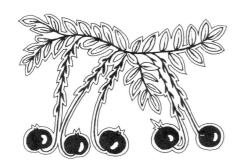

BLUEBERRIES AND CRANBERRIES
Various species of blueberry are grown in North America; the bilberry is found wild over much of northern Europe and Asia. The cranberries, too, of which the best known is the American cranberry, are all part of the genus Vaccinium.

The lowbush blueberry grows widely over much of the north-eastern United States; it is not so much cultivated as managed by burning over the ground in rotation, which destroys unwanted weeds and stimulates new growth. Highbush blueberries are more suited to cultivation and are grown along much of the eastern seaboard of the United States. They vary in height from 4–20 feet (1–6 metres).

Blueberries and cranberries are members of the heather family and need acid, damp soil as well as a particular fungus found only in such soils. Their natural habitat may be mountainous moorland, peat bog or the edge of coniferous woods where decaying pine needles provide ideal conditions. The average garden, therefore, is not the best environment.

Cultivation and Management
Land in which rhododendrons and heathers grow well should be ideal. They like plenty of sun and abundant water, but the drainage must be good. In swamps they are often found growing on tussocks. If your drainage is bad, make raised beds. Use moisture-conserving mulches, such as sawdust or peat. Tubs or pots are excellent settings, and blueberries are attractive shrubs. They should be protected from frost at blossom time.

Plant out blueberry bushes in spring or autumn, about 5 feet (1.5 metres) apart, with 6 feet (2 metres) or more between rows. They are shallow-rooting, so don't disturb the soil once the plants are in. De-blossoming in the first year encourages formation of a healthy system. For the first two years pruning is not necessary. After that, each winter, cut back weak or unwanted wood to vigorous shoots at ground level. The object is to encourage plenty of new wood, because they fruit on one-year-old growth. Birds are often a bother, but in Europe the berries are not much troubled by pests and diseases.

Blueberries are not self-pollinating, so you must grow at least two.

Cranberries thrive in similar, but even damper conditions, and can be useful if you have a problem piece of land where nothing else will grow. They are planted 2 feet (60 centimetres) apart and immediately flooded ideally with rainwater, which contains no chalk, and will keep the soil acid. Creating the necessary conditions is only really practicable in small areas. Another method is to dig a trench, line it with plastic sheeting, and fill it with peat. Cranberries need no pruning.

Both are still fairly new to garden cultivation so the choice of varieties may be limited. In America, cranberry fruit-worm and blueberry maggot can sometimes be a nuisance. Spray two or three times after the petals fall.

Harvesting and Storage
Both blueberries and cranberries are best picked ripe, and keep well in the refrigerator. They also freeze well in punnets or plastic bags.

CANE FRUIT

Raspberries, blackberries and other brambles are all part of the genus *Rubus*. Most species bear edible fruit, but a few are simply ornamental plants.

RASPBERRIES

Raspberries are perhaps the most delicious of all fruits, and among the earliest to come into bearing, after only eighteen months; only the strawberry fruits in less time. As they crop far more prolifically than most soft fruit, they are very well worth the extra work involved in feeding, spraying and tying-in.

Plant canes about 18–24 inches (45–60 centimetres) apart, with 5–6 feet (1.5–2 metres) between rows. These should ideally run north to south so that no row shades, or is shaded by, another.

Red raspberries like plenty of moisture and do well in the soft climates of Scotland, the west of England and Ireland. American varieties include the native black raspberry, called the Blackcap, as well as yellow- and purple-fruited varieties, some of which have a particularly fine flavour but all of which are sadly susceptible to the serious disease verticillium wilt.

Cultivation and Management

Plant the young raspberry shoots or canes in late autumn, usually just below the surface at a depth of not more than 2 or 3 inches (5–7 centimetres). They like a rich, well-drained soil; if the soil is poor to start with, generous manuring and feeding will solve the problem. Good drainage is absolutely essential; if the soil is waterlogged the canes will die. Because raspberry canes have shallow roots, the ground must be thoroughly cleared beforehand.

Left to grow naturally, raspberry canes will trail on the ground under the weight of fruit, so they should always be supported, either by a single or double wire fence, individual stakes for each plant, or even a trellis.

In the spring of their first year cut the canes to the ground. This will encourage a strong, healthy system of young canes. As these develop they can be tied upright onto wires, about 4 inches (10 centimetres) apart.

The following spring, cut out the weakest canes leaving a few of the most vigorous on each stool. At this stage they can also be tipped back – a few inches are removed from the end of the main shoots, to encourage fruit-bearing laterals to form; keep the leaders to a manageable length, and eliminate any end growth which may have suffered damage during the winter.

New canes (to bear the next year's crop) will now be growing up and will need to be tied in at intervals through the summer. Take care to avoid damaging these when the time comes to pick the ripe berries. As soon as fruiting is over, in late autumn, cut down all the canes which have borne fruit to just above ground level, and thin the new ones, leaving about six of the strongest canes per plant (or stool).

Autumn-fruiting varieties fruit on the current year's growth, in the tips of the canes, and although the flavour is not always as good they do extend the season, and the canes may go on bearing until midwinter. Some will fruit twice, in summer and again later, but to encourage a good autumn crop at the expense of the summer one, all these canes should be cut down to ground level in winter or early spring.

Propagation is easy; the stools are divided immediately after fruiting.

Pests and Diseases

Raspberries are unfortunately susceptible to disease, and used to succumb quickly to air- or insect-borne viral or fungal infections. Nowadays, provided certified virus-free canes are planted, they will usually survive for about seven years before some disease inevitably creeps in and they need replacing.

One of the most common viral diseases is the Mosaic virus. There is no cure; infected plants must be dug up and burnt. Fungal diseases can be controlled with regular spraying with fungicides.

A tar oil spray in winter will kill aphid eggs. Spraying with malathion when the flowers open will kill insects, including the raspberry beetle. Birds will happily strip the canes if they are not netted.

Varieties

Malling Jewel has an excellent flavour, is fairly resistant to virus, and flowers late; it is both a suitable variety for planting in frosty areas and a good plant for a small garden. Other Malling strains are bred to be disease-resistant. Golden Everest is a delicious yellow-fruited variety which fruits over a long period in summer. Fallgold, another yellow variety with an excellent flavour, fruits in the autumn until stopped by frost. Zeva, from Switzerland, is an autumn-fruiting variety; it bears large, succulent dark red fruit.

Harvesting and Storage
Leave hulls and stems on raspberries when picking – the fruit will slip easily off the cane if ripe. Raspberries are best eaten the day you pick them.

BLACKBERRIES

The straggling, thorny wild blackberry is a familiar sight but hybrids are also quite widely cultivated. Some varieties are ornamental, and thornless varieties have also been developed.

Cultivated plants yield fruit within two or three years, are much hardier than raspberries, flower later, will stand up to frost, and are not particularly fussy about soil. Feed with plenty of manure or compost.

They dislike changeable, extreme climates with very cold winters and arid summers, and will not tolerate hot, dry winds. They thrive in partial shade.

Cultivation and Management
Blackberries fruit on laterals of the previous year's growth, and crop to some extent on old wood, which may sometimes be left in for more than one season. For the best crops cut out all old wood in early spring.

Blackberry canes are usually planted at least 8 feet (2.5 metres) apart, and twice that in the case of a vigorous variety such as Himalaya Giant. Rows of canes should be 6 feet (just under 2 metres) apart, or more. Unsupported canes will arch down and take root where the tip touches the ground, and soon become a dense untidy thicket, so young canes should be carefully woven or trained along wires or trelliswork. They are self-fertile.

Pests and Diseases
All brambles are susceptible to the same diseases as raspberries. Some varieties succumb to orange rust; spray regularly for protection.

Varieties
One of the best-known of the widely available varieties is Himalaya Giant. It bears heavily, with fruits which have a real blackberry flavour, but is too vigorous to be suitable for a small garden, where Oregon Thornless is probably the best. This is mercifully free from spines, has a good flavour, and is both easy to contain and ornamental, with pretty, parsley-shaped leaves. One of the most delicious varieties, Darrow, is resistant to orange rust.

Harvesting and Storage
Pick blackberries when they are well and truly ripe. They are best preserved in the form of superb jams and jellies.

OTHER BRAMBLES

Dewberries are very similar to blackberries, but fruit later and make low, trailing plants, more like vines than canes.

The loganberry has large, fine-flavoured berries, with an upright habit, and is a little more tender than the blackberry. A thornless form is available. Loganberries are not self-fertile, so at least two plants must be grown.

Another related species is the wineberry, usually grown for its ornamental value; the canes turn reddish in winter and the fruits develop from golden-yellow to rich red. The raw flavour is not outstanding.

The youngberry or young dewberry, is unanimously regarded as one of the finest flavoured berries.

The Boysenberry is also a cross with a special taste. Though very rampant, it will grow in dryish conditions, and there is a thornless variety.

VINES
GRAPES

For thousands of years the grape has been grown around the Mediterranean where it gets the long, warm, dry summer and the cool winter it needs in order to flourish.

Grapevines will tolerate snow and frost in winter. But once new growth has started in spring they should not be exposed to frosts or strong winds, and all through the summer they should have as much sun as they can get.

The vines are very easy to grow. Given favourable conditions, even completely neglected specimens have been known to thrive and fruit quite prolifically.

They will grow on almost any soil, from chalk to clay, as long as the drainage is good; this is essential, because waterlogged ground can cause root rot. Though poor soil is sometimes recommended, they do excellently in rich soil, which can encourage lush leaf growth but may also produce plump, sweet fruit.

Cultivation

Cuttings are planted in the dormant season. If you are going to support them on a trellis or post, erect the prop first; the roots are easily damaged and should not be disturbed. Gently spread out the roots in the planting hole, firm them in well, and give the soil a good mulch of manure or compost. Grapevines are very long-lived so it pays to do whatever is necessary to get them off to a good start. The ground must be kept clean and weed-free.

They can be trained to ramble over a trellis or pergola, or against a sunny wall – ideal if you have restricted space and do not wish to spend too much time on them. Because they respond well to having their roots restricted they will grow very happily in pots or tubs. They can be planted in rows in the open (usually as cordons) and kept to a manageable height by rigorous pruning and training; vines can be pruned more drastically than any other plant. They can be grown as espaliers and bushes as well as cordons and fans, and trained into almost any shape.

In cooler climates the extra protection of cloches is often necessary. This is easy when the vines are kept low, as in the Guyot system (below), or trained on a wall, and can mean the luxury of fresh grapes at Christmas.

Pruning

Although they will grow and bear fruit even if not given much attention, careful pruning is needed for a very heavy crop of good quality fruit. They bear on two-year-old wood, so fruiting spurs on the previous year's wood must be encouraged, mostly by pinching off any non-productive shoots and superfluous leaves which compete for nourishment. At the same time at least one replacement shoot or cane must be grown on, which will bear the next year's fruit.

This principle applies whether you let a permanent trunk or rod grow, to produce spurs which in their turn produce fruiting wood, or whether you cut the canes right back after bearing.

If you want to make wine, grapes need not be thinned, but for the table, thinning is very important. Using special blunt-ended scissors, when the grapes are the size of small peas, remove all misshapen and overcrowded ones. Do not be afraid of over-thinning; to improve the quality, you can safely take out half to two-thirds of each bunch. You may also need to reduce the actual number of bunches. Leave a foot between each spur.

Pests and Diseases

Grapevines are not often afflicted by any serious diseases. You may get mildew, which can be prevented by regular spraying. But beware of hormone weed-killers, which can cause serious spray damage and distort the plants. The ripening fruit will probably need to be netted against birds.

Varieties

Two varieties, mostly suitable for wine making, have a good reputation for growing sturdily outdoors. The Riesling Sylvoner is a light tawny grape which ripens in autumn, and makes a pleasant, Alsatian type wine. Siegerrebe has a fine muscat-type flavour, and also ripens in autumn.

Harvesting and Storage

Eating fruit should not be picked before it is fully ripe, and may even be left on the vine after the first frosts, when it is extra sweet. Some grapes can be dried, but they do not freeze well; conserve by cooking or making them into juices or wines.

See Greenhouse Cultivation.

MELONS

Melon plants are annuals, with a life span of only four months from seed to fruit.

They thrive in warm, airy climates with night temperatures of at least 60–65°F (15–18°C), but very hot and humid climates are actually not suitable since melons are particularly susceptible to fungoid diseases. In cooler areas they grow very well under cloches. Melons from the cantaloup and casaba groups respond best to cloche cultivation, and also to being grown in tunnels or in unheated greenhouses. Musk melons are usually considered to be the best for hothouse cultivation.

Watermelons belong to a different genus, but are of the same family and require much the same basic cultivation.

Cultivation

Melons can be started indoors, in peat fibre pots, or in a cold frame; where the climate is suitable, the seed can be sown outdoors in spring. Plant in clean, fertile ground and give them abundant water. They can be grown on the level, in pits, or on mounds, and sometimes in the curious combination of a depression (to collect water) circling a mound to keep the plant itself clear. They are very susceptible to stem rot so water must never be directed straight at the stem. For the same reason, when seedlings are set out, they are often planted with 1 inch (2.5 centimetres) of the soil ball above ground.

For the best growing conditions, each melon should be pollinated on the same day so that they all develop equally. Otherwise, one fruit may grow at the expense of the others. The growing point is pinched out to first encourage production of laterals; four of the strongest are usually selected and trained out in the form of a cross. Remove any flowers that appear alone and prematurely. You will probably have to pollinate the flowers with a brush.

Another method of artificial pollination is to strip the petals from a male flower and push the exposed centre into firm contact with a female flower. Female flowers can be identified by the embryo fruit behind the petals, which will swell soon after pollination. When the fruits are about the size of a large walnut, concentrate on the four best specimens (one on each lateral). Remove all other flowers and fruit, pinch out the tips of main shoots and any new growths, and stop the bearing shoots at two or three leaves beyond the chosen bud. Watermelons are an exception – the shoots are not pinched out, but left to trail.

Put a piece of wood or tile or an upturned flowerpot under each fruit, to keep it dry. Do not give the ripening fruits too much water or they will split.

Harvesting and Storage

Melons are ripe when the end nearest the stalk begins to show signs of circular cracking and parts easily from the stalk and/or when the end furthest from the stalk gives gently under thumb pressure. The flavour of a melon ripened on the plant is far superior to that of one picked unripe. Winter (casaba) melons may be picked before they are fully ripe, but even they are better if left on the vine. Melons are best fresh – they can be pared, cut up and frozen, but the flavour will be poor. They can also be used to make chutneys and pickles – use the almost-ripe fruits before they are soft.

See Greenhouse Cultivation.

KIWI FRUIT (CHINESE GOOSEBERRY)

The kiwi fruit is a rampant perennial twining climber, with attractive heart-shaped leaves and fragrant creamy flowers. It will happily cover quite large spaces and is suitable for growing over pergolas or trellises.

Although the plant itself is hardy (it can even stand some frost) the fruit needs a long warm summer to ripen. A sunny wall gives it the extra warmth it needs in cooler climates.

Cultivation

Year-old grafted seedlings (or cuttings) of a known variety are best planted in the dormant season (not too deep, because the roots are shallow) in almost any well-drained soil. A deep sandy loam is ideal, well dug, with lots of organic matter and plenty of water. Put in any supports beforehand, and shelter the site from strong wind. Male and female plants are separate, so you will need at least two, about 10–15 feet (3–4.5 metres) apart; one male will pollinate up to seven females. The females can be identified by the embryo fruit just behind the flower. Prune to 12 inches (30 centimetres) after planting.

Kiwis take some years to bear, but are long-lived.

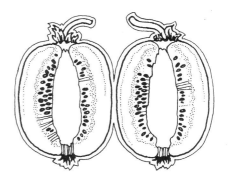

Pruning

They crop on the current year's growth. Production of laterals is stimulated by cutting back growing tips; pinch back fruiting shoots to seven leaves beyond the last fruit and barren shoots to five leaves. They are very vigorous and need regular pruning and cutting back of unwanted growth. The fruit may also need thinning.

Harvesting and Storage

Kiwis ripen in late autumn and should be picked while still firm but not too hard. The fruit can be stored for six to eight weeks.

Kiwi fruit do very well in pots or tubs.

See Greenhouse Cultivation.

PASSION FRUIT

This tropical climber produces fragrant white flowers and delicious purple or yellow fruit; the yellow variety is much grown in Hawaii for its acid juice, but the purple variety is slightly easier to cultivate because pollination is simpler.

The passion fruit likes as much sun as possible and will not stand frost or cold wind. It will grow easily from seed, but does not always come true and may be self-sterile.

Cultivation

Seedlings or cuttings may be planted, 2 feet (60 centimetres) apart, in fertile, well-drained, not too heavy soil in early spring. The roots should be restricted or too much leaf growth will be made at the expense of the flowers.

Several shoots are usually sent up, but if there is only one, encourage it to branch by pinching out the tip. Laterals should appear after about 3 or 4 feet (90–120 centimetres); if not, pinch out the growing tips. Train the shoots along supports; passion fruit climbs by means of its tendrils, and will rapidly cover a pergola or trellis. It may also be used as ground cover. There will be very little fruit the first year.

Pruning

Very little pruning is needed; cut out dead and unwanted growth, remove canes that have fruited (it bears on current wood) and generally keep the plant tidy. If necessary, prune while the plant is dormant by shortening back strong shoots by about one-third to encourage new growth. Leave a spur at the base of each cane for a replacement. It is an easy plant to grow and look after, though sometimes too much leaf growth results if it is too harshly pruned or overfed.

Harvesting and storage

The fruit is picked when fully ripe; it parts easily from the vine.

PERENNIALS
Temperate Climate Fruits
STRAWBERRIES

The strawberry, unlike most fruit, is a herbaceous perennial. There are three main types: summer-fruiting strawberries; perpetual or remontant varieties, sometimes known as everbearers; and pretty, small-fruited alpine strawberries. All are short lived.

Remontants and alpines are usually grown for no more than two years, since the crop deteriorates both in quality and quantity after the first year. Summer-fruiting varieties are usually left for slightly longer – three or at the most four years.

Strawberries like a medium or light moisture-retaining loam; they prefer it slightly acid, but will grow on most soils as long as the drainage is good. In damp soils, mound the earth into ridges about 3 inches (7 centimetres) high, and plant the strawberry crowns on top.

They should have plenty of sun, especially the perpetual varieties. Since they fruit best in their first year they are greedy for everything they can get; sun, water, food. Summer-fruiting varieties will tolerate a little shade and alpines actually prefer partial shade.

Cultivation and Management

The bed must be really well prepared; the plants have surface roots so that the ground around them cannot be dug over again during their life. The soil must be completely weed-free, with plenty of manure and compost dug in. The crowns should be at the right depth, with the earth half-way up the crown.

Summer-fruiting strawberries are usually planted in early or late summer to crop the next year; they are the quickest-bearing of all fruit. If they are not planted until the autumn they will still bear a crop the next year, but pick off the blossom in order to build up healthy, well-established plants which will crop heavily the next year.

Perpetual varieties can be planted from spring until autumn to bear the following year. They bear flowers and fruit continuously from spring until the frosts come. Some gardeners pick off the first flush of blossom. This eliminates the first crop of fruit, which would ripen at the same time as the summer-fruiting kinds, and encourages more prolific autumn crops.

Strawberries are surprisingly easy and undemanding to grow. Protect the ripening berries from damp, dirt and pests with straw or plastic. Also protect against frost at blossom-time (late spring onwards) since frost-damaged flowers will set no fruit. Because they are so low growing, the plants are particularly susceptible, but in a small garden it is quite practicable to cover them with straw or sacking at night, and remove it during the day.

Alpines, which carry their fruit on taller stalks, do not need unsightly layers of straw. They are worth growing for their ornamental value alone, quite apart from the delicate flavour of their berries, which is usually considered finer than that of their bigger cousins. They are almost evergreen in milder climates, and make excellent ground cover plants in borders, and edgings for herb beds.

While all strawberries are growing they need plenty of water, but must not be allowed to get damp as botrytis (grey mould) may develop. When they begin to swell (but not before, as the flowers need the heat from the earth), place straw or polythene under the plants to keep the berries from getting dirty. Slug pellets will probably also be needed, and some form of protection against birds is essential. Many commercial growers grow the plants from scratch through holes in black polythene sheeting. This prevents weeds, discourages pests, and keeps the fruit clean and warm. The polythene sheeting should slope away from the plants on both sides so that rain water does not collect around them.

The strawberry bed usually has three rows; one of new plants, one of two- and one of three-year-olds. Each year a row is dug in fresh soil, while the oldest row is taken out and the soil dug over and used for something completely different, often a vegetable; soil rotation is essential for strawberries.

Strawberry plants are usually planted 12–15 inches (30–38 centimetres) apart, depending on whether they will be left in for one year only or longer, and also on whether runners will be encouraged to root in the spaces between. Rows should be 30–36 inches (76–90 centimetres) apart.

Propagate from runners, except in the case of alpines, which are grown from seed sown in autumn to fruit the following year. Some growers do not allow their plants to produce both fruit and runners, and remove all the runners from the fruiting plants while keeping a separate group of plants to propagate. Others prefer to take runners from plants that have proved themselves healthy croppers. The runners are pegged down and will quickly take root. If the runners are pegged directly into pots buried in the earth, when the new plants are large enough, in about four to six weeks, they are easily separated and transplanted. Some perpetuals do not produce runners and can only be divided, usually in early autumn. Alpines can also be divided, but are less vigorous than when grown from seed.

Because they are ideal for a small space, pots and barrels have become increasingly popular in recent years. The fruit is easily protected against frost and birds, and there is no need for straw or polythene. Line the bottom of a large container, usually of clay or wood, with openings around it in which the plants are placed, and drainage holes in the bottom, with shards or stones to help drainage. Then gradually fill the container with a suitable compost. As each opening is reached insert the plants from the outside. Plant the top as well. Then simply keep them well watered and feed them occasionally with liquid manure.

Pests and Diseases
As soon as possible after fruiting (so as not to damage the new shoots) all the old leaves are cut off and burnt, together with the straw. This removes a potential source of pests and disease, to which strawberries are unfortunately vulnerable. Birds and children are probably the worst pests, but slugs, snails and mice also love the berries. Aphids can be very troublesome, as well as carrying virus diseases, and insecticide should be sprayed on the plants at the first sight of the pests. Only certified virus-free stock (available from specialist nurserymen) should be bought.

Varieties
Royal Sovereign is one of the oldest and still one of the best varieties of strawberry, suitable for all purposes, including pot cultivation, but rather prone to disease. The summer-fruiting Grandee and the perpetual Gento are both delicious. Of the alpines, Baron Solemacher and Alexandria have an excellent flavour and are recommended for pot cultivation.

Harvesting and Storage
Pick strawberries with their hulls and calyxes — and eat right away.

See Greenhouse Cultivation; also Indoor Cultivation (alpine strawberries).

RHUBARB
Rhubarb is, strictly speaking, not a fruit at all; it has however been valued as a winter subsitute and is generally cooked and treated as a fruit. The edible part is the leaf stalk. Never eat the leaves — they contain a high level of poisonous oxalic acid.

Rhubarb does best in a cool climate, and indeed will go dormant when it is too hot. It grows from roots or crowns; plants grown from seed are often feeble. Plant in good soil in an open, sunny position, and with plenty of feeding and watering.

Cultivation
Dig the ground deeply before planting, and work in about two buckets of compost per square yard (metre), and a sprinkling of wood ash and bone meal. Otherwise the plants need almost no attention.

Plant crowns when dormant, in autumn or spring, with the bud or eye 2 to 3 inches (5–7 centimetres) below soil level. Make sure that each root has at least one eye or bud. The ground should be moist but not wet. Space the plants 3 feet (90 centimetres) apart.

Cut off the flower heads as soon as they appear, in order to concentrate strength in the leaves. Rhubarb is pulled from spring until summer, but not later. When pulling is over it is a good idea to mulch the crowns with manure. After four years the plants can be lifted and divided.

Varieties

Some reliable varieties are: The Sutton, a large main-crop variety, and Hawke's Champagne. Timperly Early, which matures early, is suitable for forcing, and Victorian is a good bet for raising from seed.

Harvesting and Storage

The stalks are pulled out whole, never cut or broken off the first year, so the plant will have time to establish itself. In the second year, pull a few stems, as you need them; not too many, or the plant will give a poor crop next year. Always leave at least three or four strong stems on each plant. Do not pull any at all if you want to force them later on.

Rhubarb can be frozen, bottled, or made into pickles, jams and wines.

Forcing

Rhubarb for forcing is usually grown from three-year-old roots, which can be lifted and divided in late autumn or early spring. Add some more manure to the soil before replacing the plants.

Outdoors, cover each plant with an upturned container which excludes all light (a bucket is a good idea), and cover it with straw and manure or compost for warmth. The stems will be ready in three weeks or so and will be a lovely brilliant pink. The plants will have lost most of their strength and are usually thrown away after all the stems have been gathered.

For indoor forcing, lift the plants in late autumn or early winter and leave them on the ground until after the first frost; this makes them grow faster when brought indoors. Put them in a box, cover lightly with soil, water well and put in a warm, dark place; 60°F (15°C) is good. Water when necessary to keep the roots moist but not wet, and in five or six weeks the stalks will be ready.

Warm Climate Fruits

BANANAS

Though they look like trees, bananas are herbaceous perennials. What seems to be a trunk is technically a pseudostem, formed by the expanded leaf bases; the true stem is underground. What appear to be leaves are actually bracts.

There are hundreds of different varieties of banana, most of which have come a long way from the original seed-filled, unpalatable fruit — the result of years of intensive cultivation. Some are known as plantains. Bananas and plantains vary from small to large, short and stubby to long and slender, and yellow to green or reddish. The flavour also varies, from sweet and fragrant fruit, usually eaten raw, to types used only for cooking, that are not necessarily very palatable even then. They are one of the most important of all tropical food crops, and grow up to 20 feet (6 metres) high.

Cultivation and Management

The only kind really suitable for the amateur to grow is the Cavendish banana. This is popular all over the world and will grow in subtropical conditions. It is disease-resistant and only grows to about 8 feet (2 metres) high. One variety, the Dwarf Cavendish, can be grown in a very small space. The size of the plants can be further controlled if only one sucker at a time is allowed to grow up and bear. The leaf sheaths which form the trunk unroll at the top into large, pale green leaves. The flowers appear above them and later curve downwards. Since both male and female flowers are carried on the same plant only one plant is needed; the male flowers develop in the bell at the bottom (originally the top) of the flower stem, and the female flowers develop into the upward-pointing hands of fruit.

They are not difficult for an amateur to grow, as long as a humid climate with a minimum temperature of 65°F (18°C) can be provided. They will grow happily in hothouses and are suitable for growing in bigger pots. They like well-drained soil and as much sun as possible, with plenty of water during the growing season.

Harvesting and Storage

Bananas should be harvested while still green as they will ripen off the plant — or they will develop an unpleasantly strong flavour. The stem dies back after fruiting. Cut it out and allow a healthy shoot to take its place.

Well-known varieties of the Cavendish (or Chinese) banana are Lady Finger, a comparatively tall plant with small and very sweet fruit, Red Fig, and Silk Fig.

See Greenhouse Cultivation.

PAPAYAS

Also known as tree melons or paw paws, papayas are herbaceous perennials, but are usually thought of as trees. The papaya 'tree' is palm-like, with a soft, unbranched stem and a crown of large, deeply lobed leaves.

These tropical plants have spread to the subtropics and will even tolerate cooler conditions, which may however have an adverse effect on the taste of the fruit. They have a short life, about four years, but grow fast and bear fruit in twelve to eighteen months; they can reach 30 feet (9 metres), but are kept lower in cultivation.

Papayas have a complicated sex life: plants can be male, female, or hermaphrodite (bisexual); they can be a mixture; they can even change sex during their short lifetime; and some males produce bisexual flowers and eventually fruit. In the tropics they tend to be hermaphrodite. In cooler climates the monosexual kinds do better. As one male will pollinate up to ten females, unwanted males are generally removed.

Papayas are known for their tenderizing qualities, which are also thought to help digestion.

Cultivation and Management

Papayas, like bananas, like deep, rich, well-drained soil, but they will tolerate much drier climates, especially in winter. While too much humidity may impair their flavour, they need plenty of water during hot dry summers. The temperature should not drop much below 60°F (16°C).

The fruit looks like a large melon, often pear-shaped, and is carried in a cluster just below the leaf crown. As it ripens it turns from green to yellow or orange-yellow, sometimes reddish. The juicy, refreshing flesh is golden or pinkish, and it is best eaten raw, like a melon.

Harvesting and Storage

Papayas may be picked when unripe and left to ripen in warmth. If left on the tree till fully ripe the fruit becomes sweet, but its weight may tear it away from the stem and damage it. The fruit is usually cut, not pulled, off the tree. It can also be preserved, used for ice cream, candies, etc.

See Greenhouse Cultivation.

PINEAPPLE

One of the most delicious and popular of tropical fruits, the pineapple is grown commercially in many countries including Australia, Brazil (its original home), Malaysia, South Africa and, especially, Hawaii. It is, in fact, a multiple fruit – when individual flowers are fertilized they make small, succulent fruits which join together to form the flesh of the pineapple. The fruit is borne on a stem, 2–4 feet (60–120 centimetres) high, surrounded by long, sharp leaves. The spiky crown on top of the pineapple is a continuation of the stem, which also forms the hard core of the fruit.

Pineapples are divided into three main groups: the Spanish type (said to have been brought to Spain by Christopher Columbus), the Queen with small, juicy fruit, and the Cayenne or Kew Giant originally introduced for greenhouse cultivation in the mid-nineteenth century.

Cultivation and Management

Pineapples are easy to grow, given the right conditions: warmth, moisture and freedom from frost. Plant them in rich, well-drained soil in a sunny position and water freely during their growing period. Make sure they are allowed to dry out between waterings. The plants bear fruit within about eighteen months.

Harvesting and Storage

Although pineapples taste best if picked when fully ripe, unripe fruit will ripen off the plant. Cut the pineapple from the stem – do not twist or break it off – and store in a cool, dark place.

See Indoor Cultivation.

STONE FRUIT

The genus *Prunus* includes a variety of delectable fruit: peaches and nectarines, almonds and plums, apricots and cherries. Most make attractive trees, and are often grown for the beauty of the flowers alone. The sight of almond orchards in blossom on Etna's southern slope is a spectacular feature of the early Sicilian spring. The Japanese have long found the contemplation of flowering cherries a rewarding occupation, and Chekhov's Madame Ranevskaya was deeply attached to her cherry orchard.

Prunus are all deciduous, hardy in temperate zones, and require much the same basic cultivation. Most grow up to 20 or 30 feet (6 or 9 metres), but a dwarfing or semi-dwarfing rootstock (usually St. Julien A) will keep them much smaller, and make them very suitable for cultivation in pots. The exception is the sweet cherry tree, which grows up to 60 feet (18 metres), and for which no effective dwarfing rootstock is widely available.

Prunus trees grow best in moisture-retaining but well-drained, deep, neutral to slightly alkaline soil, and in a warm, sunny position with protection from frost and wind. Acid cherries will grow happily on a sunless wall, and some plums if well protected from frost will grow on east or west walls. Most need plenty of water, especially in the growing season, but hate being waterlogged. Nor do they take kindly to rapid changes from dust-dry to swamps. All the *Prunus* need a little more care than the hardier apple and pear trees.

CULTIVATION

In colder climates, although the tree itself is hardy, an early flowering period may mean frost-killed buds. Protect them by planting on a slope which will allow cold air to drain away, or by training as a fan or a bush near a sunny wall. Netting will add extra protection but should be removed as soon as the risk of frost is over to allow pollination to take place. Net the trees again later to protect ripening fruit from birds.

Too warm a climate eliminates the risk of frost, but all stone fruits need a cold dormant period to bear fruit. Plant at the beginning of the dormant season after harvesting and leaf fall, but before the real frosts begin.

Trees prefer growing in the open as bushes or standards, but, except for sweet cherries and almonds, will also thrive as fans or espaliers on a sunny wall.

PRUNING

Prune only in spring; in winter trees become susceptible to silverleaf disease, sometimes called fireblight or peach curl.

Apricots, cherries and plums do not need severe pruning. Peaches on the other hand fruit on the previous year's wood; after fruiting, the old wood must be cut out and new growth encouraged to replace it. Unwanted new wood should be cut back in spring, leaving some to grow on for the next year.

COMMON PESTS AND DISEASES

The most troublesome pests are red spider mites and aphids which can be controlled by spraying, usually with malathion. Brown rot can affect the fruits of cherries, plums and nectarines; the diseased fruit must be picked off and burnt.

Silverleaf disease is a serious fungoid disease for which there is no cure: infected wood must be cut out and burnt. Bacterial canker is another threat, the risk of which increases if the trees are pruned in winter. It can be controlled by regular spraying with Bordeaux mixture.

Treat peach leaf curl by spraying with Bordeaux mixture when the buds begin to swell; unfortunately this may not always be entirely effective. If only a few leaves are affected the spread of the disease may be arrested by picking off and burning the diseased leaves.

APRICOTS

Among the first fruit trees to bloom, their name means 'the early one', an Arab-Greek mixture of *al* and *praecox* which survives in modern Portuguese as *albricoque*.

The fruit also ripens early, and, as there are often not enough insects around, may need to be hand-pollinated. Brush the flowers one after the other with a soft rabbit tail or thick, soft brush as they come into bloom.

Cultivation and Management

Apricots are self-compatible and do not need much pruning. They crop heavily on the short spurs of two- to three-year-old wood. In cooler regions they are nearly always grown as fans or cordons. They will grow up to about 8 feet (2.5 metres), on rootstock St. Julien A and are suitable for growing in containers. Follow general instructions for stone fruit for cultivation, pruning, and pests and diseases.

A good all-round variety is Moor Park, grown outside on a wall, or in a cool greenhouse.

Harvesting and Storage

Apricots are best harvested when they are fully ripe; the fruit will come off the spur easily, without tearing. They make good jams and other preserves.

See Greenhouse Cultivation.

CHERRIES

There are sour or acid cherries, sometimes called Morellos, and sweet cherries, which include Dukes, an old-fashioned cross between sweet and acid cherries that is no longer very popular. The two types are very different in habit, but are cultivated similarly. Both kinds will grow as fans, standards or bushes, and will do well even in poor soil as long as they are given enough nitrogen and potash. In blossom, they are perhaps the most beautiful of all fruit trees; every inch of bare bark appears covered with white flowers.

Cultivation

Because sweet cherries normally grow to 60 feet (18 metres) or more, and no effective dwarfing rootstock has been found despite intensive research, they are definitely *not* suitable for the small garden. But acid cherries will grow happily on a sunless wall. The trees are hardy, but because the blossom is easily killed if warm spells are followed by a sharp drop in temperature, you will need to protect them with netting. They are self-compatible (and will pollinate sweet cherries) and are inherently dwarfing, even on vigorous stock, so they are very suitable for small gardens. They fruit mainly on the previous year's growth. It is normally about seven years before a tree bears a good crop.

Follow general instructions for pruning, pests and diseases.

The best-known variety of acid or sour cherries is the Morello which has given its name to the type. The Amarelle is lighter in colour and slightly less acid in flavour.

Harvesting and Storage

Keep the stalks on the fruit when you pick them. Cherries can be frozen and make excellent jams.

See Greenhouse Cultivation.

PEACHES, NECTARINES & ALMONDS

Nectarines are simply smooth-skinned peaches, with a delicate flavour, but they are slightly less hardy, and their smooth skins make them more susceptible to brown rot. Take special care in spraying and bird protection — in a temperate climate grow in a greenhouse or conservatory.

Almonds are closely related to peaches and are cultivated in the same way but often grown only for their blossom. There are flowering almonds which bear little or bitter fruit — make sure you buy the correct variety. Almonds are only partly self-fertile and may need pollinating like the apple.

Cultivation and Management

The soil should be well dug over and free of weeds. Some bonemeal and fertilizer is useful in poor soil. A mulch of compost, peat or well-rotted manure will help retain moisture, essential while the fruits are growing, and also discourages weeds. Peaches and nectarines will crop in the fourth year, and will often survive for only another seven to ten years. The available dwarf peaches are even shorter lived. Peaches are eminently suitable for greenhouse cultivation, which yields luscious fruit.

Starting in late spring when peaches and nectarines are about the size of small cherries, and continuing gradually, thin the fruit to ensure a crop of good-sized fruit. Peaches should be about a foot (30 centimetres) apart (less for nectarines), on the upper, sunny, side of the branch if possible. Follow general instructions for pests and diseases.

Harvesting and Storage

Peaches and nectarines are ready to be picked when they come off the tree easily if lifted and very gently twisted. The fresh fruit does not store for long.

Almonds need not be thinned. They are harvested in autumn when they fall from the tree, and should be husked and left to dry in airy surroundings.

See Greenhouse Cultivation (peaches and nectarines).

PLUMS

Plums include the gages as well as the little golden Mirabelles and the myrobalan or cherry plums. Damsons, bullaces and Mirabelles are all small compact trees usually between 10 and 20 feet (3–6 metres) high. They are hardier than other stone fruit, and also used for making delicious preserves. Damsons, with their tart individual flavour, are especially popular for jams and pies. Strongly-scented Mirabelles are excellent to eat, and are also used to flavour the world-famous white fruit brandies from Alsace. Myrobalan plums are a different species often used as rootstocks for other plums. Very good jam can be made from their early ripening, cherry-like fruit.

Cultivation and Management

Plums are not difficult to grow; they do well as bushes or standards and also take easily to being trained as fans. A climate of cold winters and warm dry summers suits them, provided they are well protected from frost at blossom time. They need sun and warmth to bring out their full flavour.

Most plums will grow to 15–30 feet (4.5–9 metres) but can be kept to a much smaller size. The semi-dwarfing St. Julien A, compatible with all plums, peaches and nectarines is a widely-used rootstock. For even smaller plants there is the new rootstock Pixy for plums (but not peaches).

Many plums, including cherry plums and damsons, are self-compatible, but others need a pollinator, and will set heavier crops if a pollinator is available.

Prunes are simply dried plums; those dried in the sun have the best flavour. Varieties for drying are produced extensively in California and around the Mediterranean. Not all plums are suitable; some ferment before drying out.

Follow general instructions for pests and diseases.

Plums begin to bear about the fourth or fifth year. Pruning to keep the tree open must be done in summer, not winter, to avoid silverleaf disease.

Harvesting and Storage

The fruit ripens from late summer to early autumn and should be picked fully ripe, and generally eaten or processed fairly quickly.

See Greenhouse Cultivation.

CITRUS FRUIT

Most citrus fruits are native to tropical or semi-tropical countries, but have taken well to cultivation. There are now vast groves in the Mediterranean region, Australia, California, the southern United States, South Africa, Latin America, Israel and elsewhere. They are excellent container plants; most of them make pretty, ornamental trees and bushes, both small and large with glossy evergreen leaves, fragrant white flowers, and decorative fruit which can appear at the same time as the flowers, since the fruit may take up to a year to mature. Indeed, grapefruit can take far longer and sometimes bears two crops simultaneously.

Citrus fruits are not particularly fussy about soil type, but it should be well-drained. Apart from warmth, they need air and sunshine, and a moist atmosphere in the growing season. Frost and drought are the worst enemies.

Cultivation

Citrus trees must never be allowed to dry out in hot weather. They are self-fertile and do not need pollinators, but they must be well nourished with nitrogen if the fruit is to ripen well. Apply general fertilizer in spring and a heavy mulch of organic matter in autumn.

Oranges in particular are very susceptible to frost damage. Ironically, because frost comes so seldom in warmer climates it is all the more difficult to protect the trees. If you have a tree or tub in your garden, protect it with thin netting. (Commercial growers use smoke pots to prevent damage to blossom.)

Pruning
Pruning is mostly straightforward; the plant is kept neat by removing shoots which are too low-growing or too vigorous. Very little pruning is needed once the trees mature.

Harvesting and Storage
The fruit is ripe when it feels heavy with juice. Most citrus fruits store well in a cool dark place.

Types of Citrus Fruit
Oranges are thought to derive originally from the Seville orange, now used for marmalade. The bergamot, a sub-species of the Seville, is a beautiful small tree with very fragrant flowers. Another sub-species is the blood-orange, thin-skinned with deliciously sweet rich crimson flesh. Other sweet oranges include the ever popular navel. Orange trees grow to 20 or 30 feet (6–9 metres) but can be kept much smaller.

Lemons and limes grow mainly in the Mediterranean basin, though they are now also cultivated in California, Florida, Australia, Israel, etc and are the tenderest of the citrus fruits. They have a more weeping habit than the orange, and grow to about 12 or 14 feet (3.5–4 metres). Lemon trees can be quite thorny. The fruit varies considerably in size. Limes make slightly bushier trees; the thin-skinned fruit may be green or yellow, but the acid flesh is always green.

Tangerines, also known as mandarins or mandarin oranges, are basically small, thin-skinned, very sweet, juicy, easily-peeled oranges.

The name tangerine is sometimes kept for the more strongly coloured varieties. Clementines are a variety of mandarin; so are satsumas, which have the advantage of being almost or completely seedless. They are the hardies of the citrus fruits, and will grow in slightly cooler conditions than oranges.

Grapefruits and pomelos are generally considered identical, although some authorities say the grapefruit is a hybrid between the pomelo and orange. Other names commonly used, sometimes as separate species, sometimes as synonyms for grapefruit are pummelo or shaddock. This does little to sort out the confusion, which was originally caused in part by a Captain Shaddock who introduced a fruit called pummelo to the West Indies.

However, taking grapefruit to cover all the related species, they are smallish trees of up to 18 feet (5.5 metres), which bear large fruit in bunches, not unlike grape clusters. Some varieties have pink flesh; others are seedless. They need even less pruning than orange or lemon trees, and are a little hardier than lemons.

Citrons, one of the earliest known species, are the sacred fruit used by the Jews in the Feast of Tabernacles. They have very thick skins and little flesh, and are used mainly for candied peel.

Kumquats are close relatives of the citrus species and will interbreed with them. They make excellent tub plants, very sweetly scented.

Kumquats are hardier than oranges and mandarins, and grow only to 6 or 8 feet (2–2.5 metres). In a temperate winter, they will need some protection from frost, and tubs should be moved indoors or under glass.

Hybrids
Intergeneric breeding is very easy, so it is not always possible to tell if a particular form is a species or a hybrid. Some hybrids, however, are well documented. Among them are the tangelo and the uglifruit, both tangerine/grapefruit crosses; the name of the latter speaks for itself. The calamondin is believed to be a lime/kumquat cross, although it has been classed as a separate species. It is much used as a rootstock for grafting, since it makes a small, disease-resistant tree. It is an attractive houseplant, suitable for cooler climates, and the fruit, though acid, is palatable. The peel is also edible.

See Greenhouse Cultivation, Indoor Cultivation.

OTHER TREE FRUITS
Temperate Climate Fruits
APPLES AND PEARS

Apples and pears require similar conditions, with a fair amount of sun, and a period of cold weather so that the fruiting buds mature in a dormant state. Apples always taste best when the winters are crisp and the summers are not too hot, but pears need more warmth.

Both apples and pears tolerate a wide range of soils as long as the drainage is good; but they grow and fruit best on a medium loam. Above all, the site should not be too susceptible to spring frosts, which will damage the blossom and prevent fruit from setting. In temperate climates, a north slope helps drain away frosty air, and retards flowering until the worst of the winter weather is past. For flat land or warmer climates, simply choose from the later-flowering apple cultivars. There are no late pears available; they all bloom about a month before the apple trees, so protect them if possible by planting them near a wall — this will also add reflected warmth later so the fruit ripens well. If you have long hot summers, pears are best grown in the open — otherwise the reflected heat will simply burn the leaves and the swelling fruit. Young stock will need watering in dry conditions, and fruiting trees must get enough moisture to swell the young growth. Make sure there is water nearby, or at the end of a hose — each tree can absorb two or three gallons a day in drought conditions.

Cultivation

Except for cider and crab apples which are grown on their own roots and in their natural forms, dessert and cooking apples are grown in a variety of ways, from huge commercial orchards to back garden tubs. They are propagated on special rootstocks by grafting or budding, so the rootstock is very important; it determines the size (of the tree and fruit) and how soon the tree will bear.

A great deal of work has been done at the Royal Horticultural Society's research stations at East Malling and Malling Merton in Kent. Dwarfing apple rootstocks such as M (for Malling) 7, 9 and 26 and MM (for Malling Merton) 106 are known and used throughout the world for trees which are small and sturdy, yet bear abundant and tasty fruit.

The traditional orchard of standards is rarely planted today even by commercial farmers. Dwarfing stocks seem to have almost every possible advantage — they are easier to protect from wind and frost, easier to cultivate, prune and harvest, and come into bearing much earlier (often in the second or third year). There are a few disadvantages: some varieties require permanent staking, and if the tree is neglected, spurs from the roots may grow and gradually take over the entire tree.

An extremely dwarfing rootstock, M27, is now available, and produces trees only about 4 feet (1.2 metres) high, small enough to be grown in a tub or pot and ideal for a restricted space — even on a small balcony. Remember, however, that apples are not self-fertile; at least two varieties must be grown for fruit, unless you can buy a tree with three or more varieties budded on one stock.

Pear trees are usually grafted on one of two quince stocks. Quince A will bear fruit after about four years and grows to between 10 and 15 feet (3—4.5 metres), depending on the cultivar. Quince C is more dwarfing but unfortunately also more succeptible to virus infection.

Forms of Tree

Most trees can be trained into a variety of shapes. Forms grown in the open include: the old standard trees; spindle-bushes (also known as central leader trees) which are cone-shaped and crop heavily; dwarf bushes, grafted onto dwarfing stock, which fruit early and are easy to look after, but require a fertile soil; and bush trees, which are rather taller, with a stem of between 2 and 3 feet (60—90 centimetres).

Very restricted forms include the cordon, yielding about 10—12 pounds (4.5 kilos) of fruit per tree, and the fan and the espalier, yielding 20—30 pounds (9—13 kilos); these are all very decorative against fences or walls. For intensive cultivation cordons are grown in rows usually about 6 feet (just under 2 metres) apart and with about 3 feet (90 centimetres) between each plant,

though at East Malling experiments with the new M27 have had them in rows 4½ feet (1.4 metres) apart with 20 inches (50 centimetres) between plants.

Another restricted form is the dwarf pyramid; this grows to about 7 feet (2 metres) high and is, as the name implies, cone-shaped. It is a heavy cropper and forms a compact tree, but in a garden setting remember it needs staking, or supporting with wires, which can be unsightly.

Pruning

Prune the trees to obtain a high-quality crop of good appearance, size and flavour, on trees which are easy to look after. This means encouraging a framework of robust, well-spaced branches, generally in the shape of a vase or a pyramid so that light and air can circulate. Neglected trees will still bear fruit, but pests and diseases will flourish where too many branches, too close together, create damp, humid conditions.

In its early years a tree is pruned in winter, to stimulate wood growth. Remove superfluous or weak branches and encourage robust ones growing in an appropriate direction. Once mature (generally after about four years, or rather longer with pears) the tree is pruned only to encourage fruiting. With free-growing forms (standards and bushes) this is still done in the winter, but with restricted forms the main pruning is done in the summer to check vigour, encourage fruit formation, and keep the trees a manageable size. Dwarf varieties, once established, often need hardly any pruning, though some weak-growing varieties may need continued pruning to stimulate growth. Some thinning is also often necessary to prevent a too-heavy crop — not all the blossom should be allowed to fruit. Keep about 6 inches (15 centimetres) between spurs, and the growing clusters may also be thinned by removing the central or king fruits as soon as they have formed. This will give more nourishment and vigour to the remaining fruits.

Pests and Diseases

A large number of pests affect apples and pears. Luckily many of them can be controlled by spraying with pesticides, some of which are compatible and may be applied together, such as malathion (for aphids, capsids, apple sawfly, red spider mite and pear sucker) and captan (for scab). Netting will provide some protection against birds.

The most troublesome pest with apples is codling moth. Spray with fenitrothion (which controls all caterpillars) or tie bands of sacking around the trunks soon after midsummer. The caterpillars will spin their cocoons and pupate in it, and the sacking and cocoons can be burnt together in late autumn.

The most serious problem for pears is fireblight, a highly infectious bacterial disease. Control by spraying or, better still, prevent it by planting resistant varieties.

Shoots or fruit affected by mildew, canker, apple sawfly, scab or brown rot should always be cut out and burnt. A tar oil spray against aphids can be applied in winter, about every two or three years.

Varieties

Choosing which varieties to plant is mainly a matter of personal taste; some are very vigorous, even when grown on dwarfing stocks. At least two varieties must be planted; virtually all apples and pears need to be cross-pollinated. Even 'self-compatible' trees will set a much better crop if pollinated by another variety. Two compatible varieties — which flower at the same time — can be planted; for example, Lord Lambourne and Beauty of Bath, or the later-flowering Golden Delicious and Laxton's Superb. Although most varieties have a normal number of chromosomes, some have little pollen and therefore are not good pollinators; others do not flower regularly, or will only pollinate certain other varieties. In such cases a third tree must be planted to ensure pollination.

You can avoid unsatisfactory pollinators altogether, but some are very desirable, such as the apple Ribston Pippin or the pear Jargonelle. And, of course, the great advantage of growing your own trees is to have unusual varieties which are delicious but may be too difficult or too irregular for the commercial grower.

Most breeders/growers provide lists of the varieties they carry, and some larger growers have apple and pear tastings in the autumn.

Harvesting and Storage

Apples and pears are ready to pick over a period from late summer to late autumn. Early-ripening varieties can be eaten as soon as they are ready, but autumn fruits may need up to two months after picking before they are ripe. Both apples and pears can be kept in a cool place until ripe, and some will keep all winter.

Storage for long-term winter keeping needs a cool dry cellar or spare room without heat but with sufficent ventilation. Wrap each piece of fruit in a separate square of wax paper, and examine them every few weeks to remove any over-ripe or diseased pieces.

See Greenhouse Cultivation.

MEDLARS

The medlar, a relative of the pear and quince, and a native of south-eastern Europe and Asia, is happiest in a cool, temperate climate and now grows throughout much of northern Europe.

It was once a valuable winter fruit, but today there is such a wide choice of other fruits it is not nearly so popular. However, medlars have great ornamental value. Slow-growing, smallish trees which will reach 20–25 feet (6–7.5 metres), they can be kept to half that without much trouble, and are rather like quinces, with a distinctive gnarled, crooked habit, sometimes pendulous, and very pretty in flower.

Medlars are very undemanding; they thrive in most soils, including even damp, heavy ground where not much else will grow, although drainage is helpful. Quite hardy in cool temperate zones, they need some shelter from winds, with as much sun as possible, and have few pests or diseases. Garden cultivars are thornless, although the wild species has thorns.

Cultivation and Management

A named variety is grafted onto rootstock, which may be another medlar or a related pear, hawthorn or quince. A quince is the best for dwarf forms. Standards may need the support of a stake in their early years. The trees are pruned to spread outwards, leaving a fairly uncrowded centre, and once mature (after three or four years) need little further pruning beyond that required to keep them a manageable size. They can also be grown as pyramids.

Harvesting and Storage

Traditionally, medlars are picked after the first frosts, but even then they are still hard and bitter and need a period of maturing, known as bletting, to become palatable. For this they are stored, stalks up, in a cool, well-ventilated place, without touching each other, for about three weeks, or until they turn soft and brown, rather like over-ripe pears. The stalks may be dipped in brine to help prevent rotting. Although they may look unattractive and semi-rotten they have finally acquired their characteristic slightly sweet yet acid taste and soft, buttery consistency.

In warm climates the fruit will ripen on the tree and does not need to be bletted. Ripe medlars are traditionally eaten with port. Slightly unripe fruit is used to make a delicious orange jelly with a quince-like taste.

The Mediterranean medlar, or azorole, although related, actually belongs to the hawthorn genus *Crataegus*. Some of the hawthorns are cultivated in different parts of the world, including China; the fruit often resembles small apples but seldom has a particularly noteworthy taste.

MULBERRIES

The mulberry most often grown for its fruit is the black mulberry, as opposed to the white mulberry which provides food for silkworms. Very widely cultivated at one time, it is very long-lived and many of the original trees still survive. It is slow-growing and takes many years to achieve its characteristic gnarled spreading shape. In old age it often needs support for its drooping branches. The trees are very ornamental, with pretty leaves and loganberry-like dark red fruit ripening to purplish-black. The fruit is borne while the trees are still small and young.

The mulberry tree is found throughout Europe and Asia, but it does like shelter from cold winds and as much sun as possible. It is also cultivated in the United States. The native American mulberry, the red mulberry, is larger and hardier.

Mulberries are not fussy about soil as long as it is well drained, but do best in rich, slightly acid soil. Although often grown in grass, for the best crops the soil around the trees should be kept clean. In colder areas they will do well trained on wires against a sunny wall.

Cultivation and Management

The ground should be thoroughly cleared of weeds before planting (they have brittle roots and, once planted, do not like the surounding ground to be disturbed), and a supporting stake driven in. When free-standing they are usually grown as standards but can also be grown as pyramids. They are self-fertile.

Mulberry trees need little pruning. On standards, cut back unwanted branches in winter and protect the cuts with wound paint. On pyramids and wall-trained plants cut back all the side-shoots in summer to about 6 inches (15 centimetres), which will encourage fruit-bearing spurs to form. Mulberry trees will bear fruit while still quite young.

They will grow very well in pots, usually as dwarf bushes or pyramids, but need repotting each year in winter. They must never be allowed to dry out; regular watering in dry weather is essential, for mulberries in open ground as well as in pots. Red mulberries are particularly fond of damp places, like the banks of streams.

They are not much affected by pests and diseases, except for birds, which love them; the ripening fruit should be netted.

Harvesting and Storage

The fruit ripens from late summer. While still red it may be picked and used for tarts, pies and jams. When it turns almost blue (purplish in the red mulberry) it is fully ripe and can be eaten raw. The taste is distinctive and delicious. With older, taller trees gather the fruit by spreading a sheet on the ground and shaking the tree gently to dislodge the ripe berries. Do this every few days; the fruit ripens irregularly over about three weeks. Mulberries are seldom available commercially.

They cannot be stored, and lose some of the flavour when frozen; eat them fresh, or make into juice, jam or jelly.

Warm Climate Fruits

AVOCADO (ALLIGATOR) PEARS

Many people have started to grow an avocado plant from its pit, which will root very easily in a glass of water; planted out in a temperate climate it will be killed by the first cold spell. Given the right conditions, however, the avocado is an easy tree to grow and can fruit within seven years. Most species are natives of central and southern America but some come from South-East Asia and the Canary and Azores islands. They are spreading, evergreen trees, usually about 30 feet (9 metres) high though they can grow to 60 feet (17 metres). At least 55°F (13°C) is necessary in winter, more in summer although they will not tolerate too high a heat; about 80°–85°F (27°–29°C) is ideal. Avocados need high humidity and plenty of water, especially in summer.

The trees grow successfully in many subtropical areas: the southern United States, California and the Caribbean; parts of South Africa; Australia and Israel.

Cultivation and Management

They like a rich, acid soil and hate extremes of either waterlogged ground or drought. For growing in milder temperate zones, the Mexican variety is the hardiest and therefore the most suitable for the garden.

The fruit does not always set even in suitable conditions. This may be due, in part at least, to problems of pollination. Although each tree bears both male and female flowers, they do not open at the same time, so that at least two trees may be needed.

Pruning will keep them lower and more manageable. To achieve a neat plant, pinch out the central shoot after three or four leaves have broken.

Harvesting and Storage

One reason for the fruit's popularity is that it ripens off the tree, and so can be picked while unripe. It will travel long distances and still arrive in good condition. If you have your own tree, the fruit can be left until it is just ready to drop.

See Greenhouse Cultivation.

DATES

The date palm is one of the oldest cultivated plants, going back at least 5,000 years. It will grow to 100 feet (30 metres) or more and live for about eighty years. The palms are too big for all but colossal greenhouses, and to grow them outside you will need a dry subtropical climate, with water available. They are tolerant of wind and seaside conditions, and are often found on bay shores. They grow widely in North Africa and the Middle East, as well as Israel and the south-western United States. Fruiting starts five to six years after planting, but maximum crops are produced after fifteen years.

The stem supports a spreading cluster of evergreen leaves with painfully sharp tips. The fruit hangs in clusters below the leaves, ripens from green to yellow, and then turns dark brown.

There are several different varieties, of which much the best known is Deglet Nour. The care and management of date palms is not difficult but they are so tall that they are not recommended for the garden.

FIGS

The handsome glossy fig is related to the mulberry and has been domesticated since ancient times. Smyrna figs have been famous since 1000 BC. Though probably from Asia, the fig has naturalized over the warmer parts of the world, and is happiest in warm temperate climates.

The tree needs sun and warmth if it is to produce ripe, succulent fruit, and in cool areas it is best as a fan against a sunny wall, or in a cold greenhouse.

Varieties grown in the warmer areas, which include California, Texas, the Mediterranean, South Africa and Australia, are, with one important exception, pollinated exclusively by means of an insect called the fig wasp which breeds only in the wild fig, or caprifig. So a few caprifigs are always interspersed with the others though their fruit is unpalatable. Happily, the common or Adriatic fig sets fruit without the wasp; it and its hybrids can be grown in colder climates, although most connoisseurs would say that the Smyrna fig (which also dries well) has the finest flavour.

Cultivation and Management

Figs grow well provided the soil is well drained and not too rich; the roots should not be allowed free rein, or the result will be a large elegant plant with luxuriant foliage but sparse fruit. It is best to restrict the root run with a special trench, about 3 feet (90 centimetres) deep and 3 by 6 feet (90 centimetres by 2 metres). Pack the bottom with rubble or chalk, so that it blocks the main roots but is porous enough to allow good drainage. Pot cultivation in a large tub is ideal for restricting root growth.

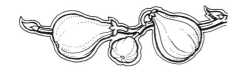

The fig will produce two crops a year, on both one- and two-year-old wood. One crop starts developing at the end of the summer, over-winters as small, pea-sized embryos, and ripens the following summer, unless killed by winter cold. The next crop is produced on the current season's wood to ripen in the autumn, with smaller and less juicy fruit. The second crop will not ripen in cool climates and should be removed.

In hot countries, the tree buds in early winter after a very brief dormant period, so three crops may be obtained: one in spring from the previous year's crop; one in summer; and another in autumn on the current year's growth. This may, however, exhaust the tree and needs considerable management. Watering is always required during the growing season, especially for tub plants.

Pruning in the first three or four years is aimed simply at shaping the tree. Fan-trained trees are pruned much like peaches. Prune standards to make a strong framework of sturdy shoots with an uncrowded centre.

Once the tree is mature, simply pinch out the tips of about half the young shoots, in order to encourage them to produce more strong young shoots which will carry a good crop of embryo figs. In cool areas the embryo-bearing shoots must be protected right through the winter to avoid frost damage. Old bare branches may be shortened right back to encourage new growth.

Pests and diseases are rarely a problem.

Harvesting and Storage

Figs are ripe when they are soft, the skin is on the verge of splitting, and nectar collects in the 'eye' of the fruit. Colour is no guide either to ripeness or taste, as figs vary widely from palest yellow-green to dark green, and from reddish-brown to purple and almost black; the colour of the flesh can be almost transparent, yellowish-green, pink, red or purple.

Figs are only at their best when tree-ripened so commercially sold figs seldom represent the peak of perfection. It is worth growing your own tree, even in a balcony tub, just for the experience of tasting a ripe fresh fig still warm from the sun.

Best eaten fresh, figs can be dried, bottled or preserved in jams or jellies.

The Indian fig is actually a large cactus, also called prickly pear. It probably came from South America, but it is naturalized all over the Mediterranean.

See Greenhouse Cultivation.

LOQUATS

Sometimes known as Japanese medlar or Japanese plum, the loquat is from the apple-pear-quince family (the *Rosaceae*) and looks rather like a medlar. A native of central China, it has long been cultivated both there and in Japan, as well as in India. It is by nature a subtropical plant, but is now also grown in California, Australia, the West Indies and the Mediterranean, where it is very popular as an ornamental tree – it was first brought to Europe for the beauty of its foliage rather than for its fruits. It will not fruit in cooler climates, though the tree itself is hardy.

At full height it is a shady, evergreen tree of about 10 or 12 feet (3–4 metres), but can be kept lower. The white flowers, carried throughout the winter, are intensely fragrant, and the pretty, golden-yellow fruits ripen early, in spring. Loquats make ideal pot plants, both in warm countries and in cooler areas where they are easily protected in the winter.

Loquats like most soils, but prefer a deep, light, not too alkaline loam, with plenty of water in the growing season. They can be grown from seed, but are generally grafted or budded, often on to quince stock for a dwarfing effect.

Cultivation and Management

The trees can bear so much one year that they have little or no fruit the next. Thin to prevent this biennial pattern from establishing itself. Cutting the flowers for indoor display may have the desired effect, although not all flowers will set fruit.

The trees need little pruning, but unfortunately the loquats themselves are vulnerable to fruit fly when ripe.

Harvesting and Storage

Pick loquats as soon as they mature, and never let them hang on the tree unless you want to keep it for ornamental purposes only. The fruit is sweet, juicy and refreshing, and although it is at its best eaten raw, can also be made into a delicious jelly.

LYCHEES

The lychee or litchi is another tropical plant which will grow in subtropical conditions: a hot, humid summer and a damp, cooler but not too cold winter. A handsome, slow-growing tree, up to 40 feet (12 metres), it has narrow, shiny leaves, often pinkish or coppery when young, and profuse whitish flowers in spring.

Lychees have always been highly thought of in China and India and their cultivation is now spreading to Australia, parts of New Zealand, Florida and South Africa, as well as Japan.

Cultivation and Management

The lychee will grow in many kinds of soil, but prefers a rich, deep, acid loam. It will tolerate damp soil, provided it is well drained, but not dried out.

The trees are particularly pretty when the fruit is ripening from pinkish to dark reddish brown. The brittle shell is covered with little bumps or tubercles and is easily peeled off.

Harvesting and Storage

The fruit will not ripen off the tree. Picking whole clusters or branches at a time prunes out old growth which will not fruit again and also helps to avoid damage to the fruit.

MANGOES

One of the longest-lived of all fruit trees, the mango has been cultivated in the tropics, especially India, for over 4,000 years. It probably originates in Malaya and the East Indies, and is now grown in tropical Asia, Africa, Central America and the Caribbean, as well as in many other parts of the tropics and sub-tropics, and in Israel.

Mangoes are attractive, shady, evergreen trees with lovely foliage and flowers – the Buddha is traditionally believed to have been given a mango grove for meditation.

The fruits hang on long, stiff stalks below the leaves. Depending on the variety, they ripen from dark green to soft orange, golden or reddish-gold and one colour is often flushed with another.

Mango trees grow to 60 or 70 feet (18–21 metres) and are therefore generally only grown where the outdoor climate is suitable. Although young plants need adequate water, they do not like too much rain, preferring a dry spring and summer. Mangoes grown in too humid a climate produce inferior fruit. Deep, rich, well-drained soil is ideal, but the plants are not fussy and will grow provided there is room for the roots.

Cultivation and Management

Mangoes can be grown from seed, but it is usually more satisfactory to buy a grafted tree which will come into bearing after about three years. Flowers appearing earlier should be removed to prevent premature fruiting and ensure strong young growth.

The size of a mango tree can be controlled to some extent by pinching out the top of the central shoot when it is about 3 feet (90 centimetres) high, in order to encourage a lower, more spreading habit. Apart from this very little pruning is needed.

Harvesting and Storage
Pick the fruit when the colour has turned, but before it becomes soft; the taste improves if the fruit is kept for a few days to ripen.

The sap or oil contained in the peel can be toxic or irritating to some people; take care when picking the fruit.

See Greenhouse Cultivation.

OLIVES
Although few people would consider growing olives, it is in fact quite possible – olives can even be grown in pots. They have been cultivated over more than 5,000 years, often in the most unpromising ground. The tree does not usually grow very tall – about 30 feet (9 metres) on average – but with age (and it is extremely long-lived) it becomes thick and densely branched, often with the trunk split into three or more sections. The branches are covered with greyish, evergreen leaves. The flowers are white and usually inconspicuous, but about once every seven years they will put on a show.

Although the olive tree is hardy enough to withstand several degrees of frost, it needs Mediterranean conditions to bear fruit: a cool, but not too cold, period in winter to encourage flower buds to form, and hot summers to set good quality fruit.

Cultivation and Management
Though the tree survives in poor conditions and shallow soils, the best crops require a rich, well-drained soil with plenty of water in the growing season. Olive trees are not fully productive for fifty to seventy-five years.

To keep the trees a manageable size, remove over-vigorous shoots as necessary. Several varieties can be grafted onto one tree, which also eliminates the need for two trees to pollinate each other.

Harvesting and Storage
The main disadvantage of growing olives in your garden is that the crop is not edible right from the tree. Raw olives are bitter and need to be soaked in a caustic soda solution before they can be eaten. Olives for pickling may be picked still green or when ripe and purplish-black, depending on the variety.

Olive oil is the most important product apart from the fruit. If you live in an olive-growing area you can probably arrange to take your crop (picked when ripe, or collected as the olives fall) to the local oil-press.

See Greenhouse Cultivation.

PERSIMMONS
Persimmons are natives of Asia and North America, and have become very popular around the Mediterranean and, more recently, in Australia.

Persimmon trees are comparatively hardy and will fruit as far north as Peking in China and the Great Lakes in North America. Very ornamental, they are evergreen in some climates and deciduous in others (the leaves turn to glowing colours in the autumn) with large, golden-orange or reddish fruit. They are not fussy about soil provided it is alkaline and well watered. They will even grow in wet soils, though they prefer a medium loam.

Cultivation and Management
Persimmons can be budded or grafted onto a dwarfing rootstock to make a more manageable tree. Pruning is very simple: to keep the tree low and a good shape, cut back the central shoot when it is about 2 feet (60 centimetres) high, and encourage about four or five buds above 1 foot (30 centimetres) high to sprout and form a well-spaced framework of outward-facing branches; remove the other buds. The only pruning necessary once the tree is formed is to remove unwanted growth and keep the centre uncrowded and open to light and air. Persimmons can be trained as fans or espaliers. Only one tree is necessary; the female flowers need not be pollinated to set fruit.

The fruit is borne within two or three years, and must be fully ripe before eating or it will be astringent. It will ripen off the tree if kept in a warm place, so it can be picked while hard and unripe. Placing an apple nearby will hasten the ripening process because of the ethylene gas the apple gives off.

Harvesting and Storage

Persimmons are often left on the tree until the first frost. This is thought to improve their taste, which some people find unexciting at the best of times — others consider it delicious. Much depends on the climate. The best and sweetest fruit is found in the warmest and sunniest areas.

The fruit is best raw, but it can be made into ice cream or fruit sauce; it will not bottle, dry or freeze well.

POMEGRANATES

Always pretty, the pomegranate tree is especially eyecatching when its brilliant red flowers are in bloom. It grows naturally around the Mediterranean and Middle East. The soft yellow or red fruit is also decorative. It is now also cultivated in the tropics, where it is evergreen, in many subtropical climates, and even in some cool temperate areas, where it becomes deciduous.

In hardiness the pomegranate is much like the peach, and will flower in areas too cool for it to fruit unless protected under glass. It likes well-drained soil and hot, dry conditions. Apart from the water needed for the fruit to set, it should not be over-watered.

Cultivation and Management

The trees should be pruned to encourage low, spreading growth. Suckers and side-shoots should be removed or the tree will become bushy. They can be kept to below 15 feet (4.5 metres), ideal for growing in pots.

Pomegranates begin to bear in about their fifth or sixth year and continue until they are about thirty years old.

Harvesting and Storage

The fruit ripens about six months after the blossom appears; it turns a dull yellowish-pinkish-brown, and will keep for some months; this actually improves the flavour and the seeds become more tender. The pith and seed kernels are always very bitter, and should never be eaten.

QUINCES

The quince is closely related to apples, pears and medlars. Although it will grow in cool temperate zones, it is happiest in Mediterranean climates, and known from Portugal to Yugoslavia, as well as in Australia, central America, parts of the United States, and southern Africa.

The quince tree grows in most soils and does particularly well in heavy, moisture-retaining ground, even in the wet conditions found beside streams. It has also been known to flourish in much drier conditions, but it must be well watered during the growing season.

Cultivation and Management

Quinces do not take kindly to pruning and training, and although they can be grown against a sunny wall in the north they are more usually found free-standing. The attractive smaller trees have distinctive, crooked branches, and both flowers and fruit are ornamental. They are easy to grow, long-lived and need little pruning once mature (four to five years). The trees bear fruit in about five years.

The roots are shallow, so the ground should be kept weed-free to avoid undue competition for food and water.

Harvesting and Storage

It is not always easy to know when quinces are ready to be harvested. Their flavour develops on the tree, so they should not be picked too soon; some older books recommend waiting until one fruit falls to the ground. They should be stored separately because of their very distinctive, powerful fragrance which will affect other fruit.

Quinces are sometimes confused with their near relatives, the ornamental or Japanese quinces, more commonly known as japonicas.

Japonicas are grown for their showy flowers rather than their fruit, which although edible, especially if cooked, has nothing like the fine flavour of the true quince.

NUT TREES

Temperate Climate Nuts

The temperate regions produce three well-known kinds of nut trees: the walnut family, chestnuts, and hazelnuts or filberts. All these trees have been cultivated for centuries; their nuts provide valuable food in winter and they have many other uses. Walnuts yield a uniquely flavoured oil, once commonly used for cooking but now expensive and highly prized. Chestnuts can be made into the flour which is a traditional staple food in parts of France and Italy. Both are valuable timber trees as well.

WALNUTS

The most widely grown American walnut, the eastern black walnut (*Juglans nigra*), is one of the hardiest of nut trees. It is cultivated all over the eastern and central United States for its excellent timber as well as for its nuts. The Old World walnut (*Juglans regia*) – also known as the English or Persian walnut, native to central Asia and south-west Europe – is smaller and not quite so hardy, because the flowers are easily killed by spring frosts. Though the nuts are generally considered finer, the timber is inferior. It is grown in parts of the western United States.

Walnuts need a deep, rich, well-drained soil to which some lime should be added if necessary. They are slow growers, and do not bear for the first six to ten years, but in time they will become magnificent trees of 70 feet (21 metres) or more so they are not suitable for small gardens.

Cultivation and Pruning

When walnuts are cultivated they are usually grown as bushes, half-standards or standards. They may be shaped to make a central-leader tree, but otherwise need very little pruning. Indeed they should not be severely pruned; there is a risk that the wood will die back and cause rotting. All wounds should be painted over. Avoid spring pruning; the trees are likely to bleed and become infected.

Pests and Diseases

Walnuts are susceptible to honey fungus, for which there is no cure. Infected plants must be dug up and burnt, roots and and all; the soil must then be sterilized to stop the disease from spreading.

Varieties

Walnuts carry both male and female flowers on the same tree, but not always at the same time, so check which variety you have and plant a complementary tree if necessary. The English or Old World walnut always needs a pollinator, but the American or black walnut does not.

Since the quality of the nuts varies with different varieties, buy a young tree of a known variety. Two of the best flavoured are Franquette and Mayette, the latter with a taste slightly reminiscent of hazelnuts or filberts. Both are late-flowering, so they are suitable for areas where spring frosts might endanger early flowering plants.

Harvesting and Storage

Walnuts are picked as soon as they begin to fall to the ground, though some authorities say they should be picked just before, as soon as the leaves start to fall. In any case they should not be left on the tree. As soon as they are picked, remove the husks, scrub them gently and let them dry in a well-ventilated place. They will store, in containers between layers of sand or sprinkled with salt, for up to six months.

Other Members of the Walnut Family: Pecans, Hickory Nuts and Butternuts

Pecans are also members of the walnut family, native to North America, cultivated to a considerable extent in the south eastern United States, from Texas to Georgia. They are now also grown in Australia, Israel and South Africa. The pecan is universally acknowledged to be one of the best flavoured of all nuts, and makes a most delicious pie.

They can become huge trees of up to 160 feet (49 metres) high, but when grown in orchards they are often kept to 30 or 40 feet (9–12 metres). One of the most widely-grown varieties is Success.

The hickory nut is closely related to the pecan, and is also a native of North America. The nuts have a very strong, aromatic flavour and are much used in cooking as well as eaten raw. The best nuts are considered to be those of the shagbark hickory. The trees grow best in a humid climate and are found wild on both upland slopes and in lower country near streams and other damp places. They are not widely cultivated; they do not transplant well, and are slow to come into bearing. The nuts will store for up to two years.

The butternut is a popular tree which comes into bearing relatively early (two to three years after planting) and produces delicious nuts not often found on the market. Its cultivation is similar to that of other walnuts.

The hardiest walnut of all is the Carpathian walnut, grown in Canada and parts of the northern United States. It is a smaller tree, only 30 or 40 feet (9–12 metres) high, producing fine-flavoured nuts.

Yet another type of walnut is the Japanese walnut or heartnut, with a flavour more like that of its cousin the butternut.

CHESTNUTS

The sweet or Spanish chestnut is one of the hardiest nut trees, native to southern Europe. Large wild chestnut forests can still be found in Corsica, mainland France and Italy. The trees eventually grow to a huge size – up to 115 feet (35 metres) high. A single specimen in parkland looks superb.

If you have lots of room and a sandy, acid, even dry soil with good drainage, you can grow a magnificent tree that will produce in late autumn an abundant crop which only needs to be picked up off the ground as soon as possible after the nuts fall.

In the United States the equivalent tree is the Chinese chestnut, which has replaced the native American chestnut killed by blight. It is a much smaller tree, only about 35 feet (10 metres) high, but a bad pollinator so at least two trees should be planted. It is grown in eastern and central states and is flower-bud hardy to 10 degrees below zero (−23°C).

Cultivation and Pruning

Little pruning is required. The trees will grow happily with only the over-crowded shoots, if any, needing to be cut out. They often make trees with two or more trunks, so if you want a central-leader standard (ie with one trunk only) cut back the lower laterals by half in spring, then, in late autumn or early winter, prune them back level with the stem, until you have the desired length of stem. The roots can be lightly pruned to restrict growth.

Pests and Diseases

The trees are very seldom troubled by disease. Leaf spot sometimes occurs, but feeding the trees well can help prevent it.

Harvesting and Storage

Pick the nuts as soon as they fall. They may be stored between layers of sand for up to six months.

HAZELNUTS (FILBERTS)

Hazelnuts (or filberts) are native to both America and Europe. There are two species: *Corylus maxima*, which is narrow with the husk longer than the nut; and *Corylus avellana*, which is round, with the husk shorter than the nut. *Corylus maxima* is known as the giant filbert in America and filbert or hazelnut in England; *Corylus avellana* is called filbert in America and cobnut in England, though hazelnut and filbert are also used generally. Just to add to the confusion the Kentish cob is not a cob but a filbert—ie, long-husked.

Both species make small trees, up to about 15 feet (4.5 metres) high, and are often found wild in hedgerows. They will grow in most soils and under varying conditions, including shade and damp, but, like so many fruit and nut trees, they will produce a much better crop if they can have good drainage, plenty of sun, and clean, weed-free soil, preferably not too rich. They tolerate a fair amount of lime, and like protection from strong winds.

Each plant bears both female flowers and male catkins, so pollination is not usually a problem, except in some species which bear few or no catkins and therefore need another variety as pollinator. The flowers are small and red, usually borne on the weaker shoots; the decorative catkins vary from pale yellow to bright red.

Cultivation and Pruning

When cultivated, hazelnut trees can be grown as open-centred bushes and kept at a height of about 6 or 7 feet (2–2.5 metres). Young trees (two or three year olds) are usually planted in winter, in ground which has been cleared of weeds and had lime added if necessary. Before planting the tree, drive in a supporting stake. Space the trees about 15 feet (4.5 metres) apart.

In early spring, cut back the leaders by about half to an outward-facing bud to encourage the formation of an open-centred bush with half a dozen or so branches. To keep the tree at a manageable height, cut back any too-vigorous laterals, but not if they are bearing flowers which will turn into nuts. Any suckers, often found around the base, should be pulled out or twisted off. Follow the same process every spring and as the tree matures cut out at the same time any branches liable to cause disease or overcrowding.

In August, a type of pruning known as 'brutting' is carried out. This consists of breaking off some of the stronger laterals, by hand, to about half their length. They are not broken right off, but left hanging on the tree. As with most summer pruning, this lets in light and air to ripen the fruit buds. These 'brutted' laterals are shortened back another inch or so in winter or early spring, usually at pollination time, in order to disturb the pollen and encourage fertilization. Help is often needed for pollination – shake the tree gently once a day.

Pests and Diseases

Diseases are not usually much of a problem with filberts. Nut weevil and winter moth caterpillar sometimes appear, but both can be quite easily controlled by spraying.

Varieties

One of the best-known varieties, the Kentish Cob (or Lambert's Filbert) bears few catkins, but is still widely grown for the sake of its abundantly produced, well-flavoured nuts. Cosford is a delicious variety with plenty of yellow catkins. Another good variety is the Purple Filbert: not a very heavy cropper, but an attractive tree with long red catkins. The Red Filbert, also an attractive tree with fine-flavoured nuts, is one of the best varieties for smallish gardens, but its dark red catkins are sparse and it does need a pollinator.

Harvesting and Storage

Hazelnuts should be picked when the shells are hard and brown and then left to dry before the husk is removed. They will store for up to six months if kept in layers of salt.

Warm Climate Nuts
BRAZIL NUTS

The equatorial forests along tributaries of the Amazon and the Rio Negro, and parts of Venezuela, Chile and Africa, are home to a handsome tree, whose trunk may reach 160 feet (49 metres). It is not cultivated.

CASHEW NUTS

Although cashews originated in the tropics, they also enjoy subtropical conditions, and are found in Central and South America, the West Indies, India and East Africa. They are even grown sometimes in the warmer part of southern Europe and supposedly can withstand a very light frost.

Cashews grow in various soils, but thrive best in rich, well-drained ground. They need little attention and are attractive trees, especially when the fruit and flowers overlap; the flowers are small and sweet-smelling, and the cashew apples are bright red and yellow. These apples are actually the stems, swollen into a pear shape; the true fruit is the kidney-shaped nut underneath. Though they taste a little tart, the apples are succulent when ripe.

The trees grow to between 15 and 30 feet (4.5–9 metres) sometimes to 40 feet (12 metres); each one may yield from 67 to 133 pounds (30–60 kilograms) of nuts a year, and yields of 200 pounds (about 100 kilograms) have been known. Unhappily for gardeners there is one large snag: the cashew is a member of the poison ivy family; the shell of the nut contains a highly irritant oil which can blister the skin and inflame the eyes painfully.

COCONUTS

As a cultivated crop the coconut is grown mostly on small plantations, but the palms are also often seen in gardens in southern Florida. The trees thrive in sandy soil, near the sea but a little above high water, and plenty of rain. The tall trunks (up to 80 feet (24 metres) high or more) are topped by a feathery crown. They take five or six years to fruit and another ten to come into full bearing, but continue until they are about fifty years old. A good yield is fifty fruit per tree, and some will produce up to a hundred a year. The fruits need a year to ripen, and a strong wind will bring down the harvest.

PEANUTS

Also known as groundnuts or monkey nuts, peanuts are not nuts at all, but beans, or legumes; the shell is in fact a dry, fibrous seed-pod. New pods form above the ground, then work through the soil and develop underground.

Peanuts probably originated in tropical Brazil, but are now widely grown throughout the tropics and subtropics as well as in parts of the Mediterranean and the southern United States.

The plant needs a light soil, and will tolerate dry and sandy areas. It spreads like a vine, and produces a rewarding yield on good soil with a reasonable amount of water. It can be grown from seed. In spring, plant nuts 1 inch (2·5 cm) below the surface. In autumn the entire plant is harvested.

PINE NUTS

Also known as pine kernels (and sometimes in the United States as Indian nuts) pine nuts originally come from the stone pine, that lovely tree so characteristic of the Mediterranean coastline. In North America they can be obtained from the piñon or nut pine, as well as from various other species of pine, but the quality and flavour varies considerably.

The stone pine grows freely in a wild state all round the Mediterranean and needs little cultivation as such, though in parts of Spain and Italy specially planted belts of pines fringe the shoreline. The cones are collected during the winter and kept until early the following summer, when they are spread out in the sun until they open enough for the seeds to be removed. The pine nut itself is actually the kernel of the seed.

PISTACHIOS

A member of the cashew family, the green pistachio probably originated in Syria or Iran, and quickly spread throughout the Mediterranean region and the Middle East, where it has been cultivated for at least 3,000 years. It reached Italy during the reign of Tiberius. The tree takes well to fairly dry conditions and will grow in the same climate as almonds and olives. It is not difficult to manage and becomes an attractive small tree about 30 feet (9 metres) high, with spreading branches, bearing its flowers and fruit in clusters. Male and female trees are distinct, so at least one of each must be planted.

Nowadays pistachios are also cultivated in India (which has become one of the leading exporters), Africa and parts of the United States.

Prune the tree only to keep an open shape and cut out broken or diseased branches. Keep watered and mulched in drought, and reasonably free of weeds. The nuts should be harvested when ripe; they can be salted and dried in the sun, when the shells will open naturally.

See Greenhouse Cultivation.

GREENHOUSE CULTIVATION

There are various reasons for growing fruit under glass. You can have fruit earlier than normal and the crops are better flavoured and of higher quality than those cultivated outside. And of course there is the opportunity to grow fruit indigenous to warmer climates, which would not otherwise be possible.

Greenhouses and glasshouses or conservatories range from unheated glassed-in lean-tos to highly elaborate structures, but certain basic requirements are common to all. The site should be protected from cold winds and get as much sun as possible, even during winter when the sun is low and might be obstructed by buildings which present no problem in summer. Light as well as warmth is crucial to the proper development of fruit. If there is too much sun during the summer, the house can always be shaded: for example, by using blinds.

Even a simple, glassed-in shed or lean-to can provide ideal conditions for growing the most luscious peaches, nectarines, grapes, figs, passion fruit and citrus fruit.

However simple the house, adequate ventilation is extremely important. Aim for a 'buoyant' atmosphere: freely moving air without draughts. The air in a greenhouse should never feel stuffy. Always open windows or ventilators gradually, to avoid those suddenly fluctuating conditions of temperature and atmosphere which most plants cannot tolerate. Automatic ventilators are now inexpensive and respond to temperatures both inside and outside the house. Many gardeners prefer fan heaters, which will keep the air moving gently even if they are not used to heat it. Proper ventilation also reduces the risk of grey mould and other mildews.

Humidity is the other crucial ingredient. Although some plants need less than others, no fruit should ever be allowed to dry out entirely and all require abundant moisture while developing. Many fruits, especially the tropical varieties, need very generous watering and a high humidity. If you are serious about fruit growing you may want to divide the greenhouse in two, with cooler and less humid conditions in one half. Daily spraying in spring and summer not only benefits fruit but is good for the foliage; simply watering the soil may not create or maintain a moist enough atmosphere. It is of course also important to have efficient drainage; few plants like soggy soil.

The best way to manage and use a greenhouse properly is to visit it regularly. There is a constant interplay of heat, temperature and ventilation. Spray less if the day is overcast, and be careful not to overwater if a cold night is expected. Opening the ventilators on a windy day will bring the temperature down much more quickly than on a calm day. Thermostats and time-switches, automatic watering devices and the like, are all useful for holidays and working hours, but there is no substitute for keeping an eye on things personally.

Most gardeners who have grown fruit successfully would agree that it is also extremely rewarding.

Pests and diseases need not be a great problem, especially if you maintain the correct atmosphere. Good ventilation discourages mildew, and red spider mite will not flourish in a humid atmosphere. The greenhouse, including the woodwork, should be kept clean and free of any decaying matter. Keep the glass clean too; dirty glass will keep out an astonishing amount of light.

Indeed the most important aspect of fruit production is cleanliness – make sure your tools are clean and sterile so that the precious melons or avocado pears do not develop diseased spots or virus infections passed from one to another.

Good soil is very important. The usual soil is a suitably enriched John Innes No 2 compost (7 parts of loam to 3 of peat and 2 of grit).

If you decide you want to grow different fruits with differing soil requirements in the same house, this need not be a problem since so many fruit trees will grow happily in tubs.

While additional heat is not always necessary, it must be provided for some varieties and a little is useful if you want early crops. A cool greenhouse is one which can be kept at a minimum temperature of 45° to 50°F (7–10°C) in winter. With protection from wind and frost, this will suit many kinds of fruit, including some whose natural climate is ordinarily somewhat warmer. In the old days, the so-called 'stove houses' for tropical plants were kept permanently heated to a minimum 65°F (18°C). This is not usually considered necessary nowadays, since it has been found that a minimum of 55°F (12°C) is enough even for many of the tropical fruit.

Many different kinds of fruit can be grown successfully in an unheated greenhouse, and the quality is sometimes even better than that of outdoor crops. Peaches, nectarines, apricots, grapes, cantaloup and casaba melons, figs and strawberries all respond well, although a little extra heat may be necessary when they are first starting into growth.

Apples and *pears* can be potted in autumn and brought into a cold greenhouse in early spring, or when the buds are just beginning to swell. They will then crop earlier and the fruit will be of much better quality. Hand pollination will be necessary – remember to make sure that the varieties are compatible. (Poor pollinators often fruit better in greenhouse conditions.) Once the fruit has been harvested, plunge the trees outside again.

Alternate them with melons to make full use of the greenhouse all year round.

Apricots like similar conditions to peaches and nectarines (opposite) but be careful not to exceed a temperature of 45°F (7°C) at night during the early stages of growth, or the blossom may drop off. A good variety for the greenhouse is the self-fertile Moorpark.

Avocado pears are notoriously difficult to grow as fruit under glass, but if you want to try, they need a minimum winter temperature of 55°F (12°C), and up to 85°F (29°C), with abundant watering in summer.

Bananas will grow in the same conditions as papayas (opposite), except that they must have adequate humidity at all times. The warmer the house the better, and the temperature should not be allowed to fluctuate too much.

Cherries require the same treatment as apples and pears.

Citrus fruits need a minimum winter temperature of 40°–50°F (4°–10°C) and a summer minimum of 55°–65°F (about 15°C). The most tender varieties are limes and lemons, and the hardiest are kumquats. All kinds of citrus fruit must have plenty of ventilation, and can be stood outdoors from June to September.

Figs will usually yield only one crop in an unheated greenhouse. In a heated house, with skilled management, they can give three crops, but the usual aim is for two, the first in summer and a second, generally better crop, in autumn.

When starting into growth they like a minimum temperature of 50°F (10°C) or more, and need not be ventilated until after the first crop has been harvested and the temperature reaches 80° or 90°F (26°–32°C). While the crops are ripening they should not be fertilized or over-watered. Stop feeding them when the second crop has been picked, but continue watering just enough to prevent the soil from drying out: remember that the embryos of next year's first crop are already there.

Figs should have about two months of cool dormancy, ideally above 40°F (4°C). Outdoor figs in tubs may benefit from being brought in for the winter; if the weather is very cold, all ventilators should be closed.

Grapes grow extremely well indoors and this is an excellent way of producing delicious fruit in cooler climates. Hothouse cultivation is really only for specialists, but there are many varieties suited to cold greenhouses. The roots often grow outside the house so that only the fruiting wood gets protection from cold and wind. This usually gives very good results, and it means there is more room inside the greenhouse for other plants, as long as they also like a moist but well-ventilated atmosphere in summer and a cold winter.

The roots can be enclosed in beds or borders, restricted to start with but increased in size later on; for example, a 3 foot (90 centimetre) border the first year may be increased by a foot or two (30–60 centimetres) the next year, and so on to an eventual width of 8 or 10 feet (2.5 to 3 metres). One advantage of having the roots outside is that they need less watering; vines, whether indoor or outdoor, are greedy for both food and water.

Indoor vines can grow to an impressive size and survive for centuries. In a restricted space they can of course be stopped at whatever length is appropriate. They may be grown vertically or horizontally, or trained into whatever shape is required. A simple method of growing vines in a greenhouse is to train the plants along wires which have been strung the length of the house and attached to it by eye-bolts at 10 foot (3 metre) intervals. The wires should be at least a foot apart and set 6 inches (15 centimetres) in from the glass.

Correct ventilation is vital. There should be plenty of air movement but not a through draught. Good ventilation will help prevent mildew, and a suitably moist atmosphere discourages red spider mite. The important thing is to be consistent; don't suddenly increase or decrease ventilation or humidity. If you do heat the greenhouse it should be done gradually, and of course all heating must be turned off in winter. This is the time to prune the vine, and also give it another mulch.

At least four varieties of grape have proved suitable for greenhouse cultivation. 'Black Hamburgh' is hardy and prolific; it is sweet, soft-fleshed and blue-black, and ripens in mid-season. 'Muscat of Alexandria' ripens late in the season and has a lovely flavour, but needs high night temperatures during flowering. 'Buckland Sweetwater' is an early ripener, with green juicy berries. 'Madresfield Court' is an early black grape with a good flavour; it is particularly suitable for pot culture, but needs warm conditions.

Ripe fruit should be cut off with scissors; bunches will keep for a little while if their stems are put in water.

Kiwi fruit are not usually grown under glass, but they can do exceptionally well in large containers. A heated house is not necessary. They will need hand-pollinating and regular liquid feeding.

Mangoes are not a first choice for greenhouse cultivation, partly because of the size of the tree, but also because for best results they like rather special conditions: a comparatively dry period while in flower and fruit, but high humidity for about four months in between. Fairly constant high temperatures are necessary.

Melons grow well in greenhouses, especially the cantaloup variety, which can be grown under cloches or in cold frames – the simplest method of growing under glass. Sow the seed in spring in a greenhouse heated to 65°F (18°C). Some four to six weeks later plant the seedlings out, one in the middle of each frame, and then keep them closed for a week to ten days and shaded if the sun is strong. Train the plants with one lateral to each corner of the frame. Increase the ventilation gradually and remove the shading. A dry atmosphere is necessary for pollination: if the weather is warm enough, remove the covers during the day, but replace them at night. Provide plenty of ventilation while the fruits are swelling, with shading if necessary in late summer.

Cantaloup melons are also suitable for unheated houses, as are casaba or winter melons. The more delicately flavoured musk melons need a heated house. Well-rooted seedlings can be set out, often on a 'hot-bed' over a base of horse manure. Train the plants up wires and tie the laterals to horizontal wires or netting. Pollinate by hand when at least four female flowers on separate laterals are open; if all the fruits set, thin them out to three or four per plant. The ripening fruit can be supported by special nets, like mini-hammocks, available from garden centres. The atmosphere should be humid but buoyant, with ventilation if the temperature goes over 70°F (21°C) – the ideal constant temperature.

Olives should have a minimum winter temperature of 40° (4°C), and must not be exposed to frost. If grown in containers, they can be stood outside in summer and brought in for the winter.

Pistachios like similar conditions.

Papayas like a warm house with a minimum winter temperature of 60°F (15°C). They need little watering in winter, but they must have plenty during summer heat.

Peaches and *nectarines* like a cool dormant period, during which they will withstand even below-freezing temperatures, so it is not necessary to heat the greenhouse at all unless you want very early crops. Too little heat is better than too much. Sun, good drainage and an area of up to 15 by 10 feet (4.5 by 3 metres) per tree are essential.

During the dormant period the house should have as much ventilation as possible. To encourage flowering and early good-quality fruit, close the ventilators when the buds begin to swell and heat the house to a minimum of 45°F (7°C). Only open the ventilators if the temperature goes over 65°F (18°C). Keep the atmosphere humid, preferably by daily spraying, with regular soakings in warm weather to prevent the soil drying out. Regular fertilizing is also important.

Do not spray the trees while the fruit is actually ripening; keep the atmosphere humid and ventilate as much as possible – this will improve the flavour, as well as help to prevent mildew. After harvesting, leave the ventilators open to cool the house down for the dormant season – if the plants are in tubs they can be placed outside during the winter.

Although peaches and nectarines are self-fertile they will need hand-pollinating under glass, as few if any insects will be able to get into the house at blossom time when ventilation is minimal. Two recommended varieties for growing under glass are the peach Peregrine and the nectarine Pine Apple.

A great advantage of growing peaches under glass is that they seldom suffer from the most serious of peach diseases, peach leaf curl, although they are sometimes susceptible to mildew.

Plums should be treated like apples and pears.

Strawberries respond well to greenhouse culture. New plants which have been potted on can be left outside in late autumn to go dormant, in a cold frame covered with straw or peat to protect them from frost. Don't cover them before late winter or early spring or they will make too much leaf growth. In midwinter (about the end of December in the northern hemisphere), bring them into a cold greenhouse – the temperature should be just above freezing. After about two or three weeks gradually raise the temperature to 45°F (7°C). The earlier they are started, the earlier they will crop (in about three months' time), but it is easier to achieve successful crops if you leave them till February. When the flowers begin to appear (about a month later), gradually increase the temperature to 55°F (12°C) and ventilate at 75°F (23°C). Hand-pollinate daily to ensure fruit.

When the fruit is swollen and begins to change colour, stop the weekly feed or you will have soft insipid berries. Spraying can also be stopped, and the strawberries should have as much ventilation as possible. If you have been growing them in a vinery or peach house, the conditions so far will have suited both, but at this stage strawberries should ideally be moved some-where drier and airier.

Ripe strawberries for Christmas can sometimes be achieved by bringing year-old plants into a warm house (55°F or 12°C minimum) in November. The Royal Sovereign variety is usually recommended for warm houses, as the only one worth forcing, but it is essential to acquire a healthy strain.

In an unheated greenhouse the procedure is exactly the same, but bring the plants in a little later – about February. They will ripen ahead of outdoor plants.

INDOOR CULTIVATION

Although growing fruit indoors does not always produce the best quality, as conditions tend to vary too much, it is perfectly possible to do so, given plenty of light and water. A humidifier is a great help, both for the fruit and for maintaining a healthy atmosphere in a centrally-heated house. Alternatively, stand the plant pots in a larger container with peat or some other substance which can be kept damp. Daily syringing is also helpful.

The following selection of plants will look attractive indoors, as well as producing fruit.

Akebia is an unusual trailing plant with fragrant purple flowers and interest-ing, sausage-shaped fruits, lavender or pale violet, which are a little insipid but much liked in their native China, where the plant is also valued for its medicinal properties.

Alpine strawberries will do very well indoors, grown in a strawberry pot or an ordinary 6 inch (15 centimetre) pot. If the young plants are potted in early winter and brought into the house about two months later, they should bear fruit by late spring.

Citrus fruits do well in pots indoors, provided they get enough light and water, and plenty of ventilation in hot weather, preferably by being stood outside.

One of the most suitable is the calamondin orange, a small, very ornamental tree that bears fruit when still young. One-year-old trees are sometimes available, but the plant can be grown from cuttings, or from seed, which usually takes up to a month to germinate. Both flowers and fruit are usually prolific. It is disease-resistant and one of the hardiest of the citrus family.

The calamondin orange likes to feel a distinct contrast in the seasons and does not need too hot a room in winter. It should have a humid atmosphere, plenty of water, and some liquid manure during the summer. In winter it needs less watering, but the soil should never be allowed to dry out.

Pick the fruit by cutting it off cleanly. Pulling it off may tear the plant and leave a raw area in which fungoid diseases are likely to develop.

Some mandarin oranges are also suitable for growing indoors.

Feijoya is an unusual fruit which is also known as the pineapple guava—no relation to either of these, it has a taste reminiscent of both. Although it can grow into a tree it is easy to keep it pruned to the shape of a bushy shrub. The plant is very ornamental, with evergreen leaves, abundant, slightly fuchsia-like flowers, and attractive green fruit resembling passion fruit in appearance. The flower petals are also edible, either in salads or crystallized.

The feijoya will germinate in two or three weeks from seed sown in spring, or can be propagated from cuttings in summer—if possible over bottom heat, like pineapples. It will fruit when three or four years old. Hand-pollinate indoor plants to ensure fertilization.

The fruit falls when ripe, and should be eaten or cooked at once. It can also be picked while still a little unripe and allowed to mature off the tree; some people consider that this method improves the flavour. All the fruit is edible, except the thin outer skin.

Pineapples have been successfully grown indoors as pot plants. Although they need plenty of water while the fruit is developing, they can stand up to occasional periods of dry conditions better than most fruit. They need high temperatures and even in winter should be kept at 65°F (18°C).

Choose a deep pot and weight the bottom well with plenty of stones, rubble or other heavy material which will allow good drainage; even a small pineapple can weigh 3 pounds (1.4 kilos), and such a fruit growing at the top of a 3 or 4 foot (about 1 metre) plant will make the plant very top-heavy. Fill up the pot with a sandy loam.

If you cannot get a slip or sucker from an existing plant it is possible to grow pineapples by rooting the crown, or top. Cut it off cleanly and remove the lower leaves. To prevent the crown from rotting, let it dry for at least a day before planting it head down. Setting the plant over bottom heat will encourage rooting. A radiator shelf or storage heater is ideal, but the soil *must* be kept moist. Once the plant has rooted, the soil should still be kept moist—not over-watered, but never allowed to dry out. Pineapples like lots of light, so put it as near the window as you can, though preferably not at eye level; the sharp edges of the leaves are aggressive enough, but the tips can do serious damage.

The plant should fruit in about 18 months or so. Feed it with liquid manure while the fruits are developing. When they are full grown but still unripe the plants will not need so much water. The sweetest pineapples are those allowed to ripen fully on the plant. Pick them by cutting cleanly through the stalk an inch or two (3—5 centimetres) below the fruit. The same plant can produce two or more fruit in subsequent seasons on branches or suckers sprouting from the leaf axils. Alternatively these can be removed and used to form new plants. Another sort of shoot, called a slip, grows from the base of the fruit, and this too can be used for propagation.

Variegated pineapples are very decorative houseplants, though their flavour, should the plant fruit, is not always as good as that of the ordinary pineapple.

MENU PLANNER

The recipes on these pages have been divided into various categories to help you make use of the widest possible variety of fruits and nuts when planning meals.

APPETIZERS AND SAVOURIES

SOUPS

MAIN COURSES

SIDE DISHES

VEGETARIAN DISHES

Some of these dishes can be used as main courses, others are more suitable as side dishes.

Hot

Fried Papaya (page 126)
Chinese Aubergines in Peanut Sauce
  (page 133)
Gado Gado (peanuts) (page 133)
Curried Pears (page 136)
Italian Spinach with Pine Nuts
  (page 149)
Chinese Walnuts and Peppers
  (page 184)

Cold

Salade Parisienne (apples) (page 16)
Waldorf Salad (apples) (page 15)
Avocado Salad (page 28)
Banana Waldorf (page 31)
Watercress, Brazil Nut and Orange
  Salad (page 44)
Moroccan Date Salad (page 62)
Grapefruit and Carrot Salad (page 82)
Hazelnut and Cherry Salad (page 84)
Lemon and Artichoke Salad (page 92)
Melon and Cucumber Salad
  (page 105)
Amargoso Salad (watermelon)
  (page 109)
Orange Onion Salad (page 118)
Orange and Carrot Salad (page 118)
Orange and Date Salad (page 119)
Mexican Orange Salad (page 119)
Pistachio Rice Salad (page 150)
Redcurrant and Carrot Salad
  (page 166)
Potato Salad with Walnuts (page 184)

DESSERTS

Apple Jellies (page 21)
Apple Snow (page 18)
Baked Apples (page 17)
Baked Rice and Apple Pudding
  (page 18)
Barbecued Apples (page 18)
Hot Apple Charlotte (page 19)
Italian Apple Pancake (page 17)
Sherried Apples with Spiced Nuts
  (page 19)
Apricot Cream (page 23)
Apricot Ice Cream (page 24)
Avocado Ice Cream (page 29)
Avocado Lime Cream (page 29)
Banana Cheese (page 32)
Banana Ice Cream (page 33)
Bananas with Raspberry Sauce
  (page 32)
Bananes Brûlées (page 32)
Grilled Bananas (page 32)
Blackberry Orange Mousse (page 35)
Blackcurrant Yoghourt Ice Cream
  (page 36)
Polish Blackcurrant Kisiel (page 37)
Spiced Blackcurrant Pudding
  (page 37)
Witches' Foam (blackcurrants)
  (page 38)
Blueberry Buckle (page 42)
Blueberry Cinnamon Toasts (page 41)
Blueberry Cream (page 42)
Blueberry Custard Flan (page 41)

Steamed Blueberry Pudding
  (page 41)
Breadfruit Pudding (page 190)
Cherry Breadcrumb Pudding
  (page 49)
Cherry Compote (page 49)
Clafoutis (cherries) (page 50)
Coconut Pudding (page 57)
Cranberry Fluff (page 59)
Cranberry Layer Dessert (page 60)
Cranberry Orange Compote
  (page 59)
Cranberry Parfait (page 60)
Cranberry Sorbet (page 60)
Chinese Date Pancakes (page 64)
Dates with Cream (page 63)
Steamed Date Pudding (page 63)
Figgy Pudding (page 67)
Figs and Apple Crispy Bake (page 68)
Figs and Ice Cream (page 68)
Figs and Orange Compote
  (page 67)
Figs and Peaches in Cream (page 68)
Figs in Brandy (page 68)
Khoshaf (figs) (page 67)
English Gooseberry Fool (page 71)
Gooseberry Charlotte (page 71)
Gooseberry Compote with Ice Cream
  (page 72)
Gooseberry Orange Fool (page 71)
Gooseberry Soufflé (page 72)
Grapes in Sour Cream (page 77)
Swedish Grape Jelly with Vanilla
  Cream (page 76)
Gertie's Christmas Pudding (raisins)
  (page 79)
Cranberry Grapefruit Compote
  (page 83)
Minted Grapefruit Sorbet (page 83)
Hazelnut Soufflé (page 85)
Grace's Pavlova (kiwi fruit) (page 87)
Kiwi Fritters (page 87)
Kiwi Ice Cream (page 87)
Baked Lemon Pudding (page 92)
Fresh Lemon Jelly (page 94)
Lemon Ice Cream (page 94)
Lemon Pancakes (page 92)
Lemon Soufflé (page 94)
Sussex Pond Pudding (lemons)
  (page 93)
Syllabub (lemons) (page 94)
Lime Sorbet (page 97)
Tropical Fruit Salad (lychees)
  (page 99)
Mango and Ginger Ice Cream Tart
  (page 101)
Mango Cream (page 102)
Mango Fool Créole (page 102)
Mango Mousse (page 101)
Mango Sorbet (page 101)
Mangoes in Syrup (page 102)
Baked Melon Alaska (page 108)
Baked Spiced Melon (page 106)
Melon à la Scheherezade (page 107)
Melon Stuffed with Fruits (page 106)
Melon Water Ice (page 107)
Melon with Blackcurrants (page 107)

Melon with Port (page 107)
Melon with Raspberries (page 106)
Guyanan Watermelon (page 109)
Baked Nectarines (page 111)
Flambéed Nectarines (page 111)
Boodle's Orange Fool (page 120)
Crêpes Suzette (oranges) (page 121)
Orange Soufflé Pudding (page 120)
Oranges in Marsala (page 121)
Petits Pots de Chocolat à l'Orange
  (page 191)
Dulce de Papaya Verde (page 126)
Passion Whip (page 127)
Grilled Peaches (page 130)
Italian Stuffed Peaches (page 130)
Peach Dumplings (page 129)
Peach Parfait (page 130)
Peach Salad (page 129)
Baked Pears with Orange (page 138)
Pears in Butterscotch Sauce
  (page 137)
Pears in Chocolate Sauce (page 137)
Pears in Cream (page 136)
Pears in Red Wine (page 138)
Persimmon Fluff (page 142)
Persimmon Ice Cream (page 143)
Persimmon Water Ice (page 143)
Trader Vic's Persimmons with Rum
  (page 143)
Fruit in a Blanket (pineapple)
  (page 145)
Pineapple Ambrosia (page 146)
Pineapple Cream (page 145)
Pineapple Jelly (page 146)
Pine and Apple Salad (page 145)
Roast Pineapple (page 145)
Pistachio Ice Cream (page 151)
Fresh Plum Compote (page 153)
Plum Compote with Red Wine Syrup
  (page 153)
Plums in Cream (page 153)
Steamed Prune Pudding (page 157)
Pomegranate Water Ice (page 159)
Frozen Raspberry Cream (page 163)
Raspberry Almond Meringue
  (page 164)
Raspberry Mousse (page 164)
Raspberry Orange Cream (page 163)
Raspberry Yoghourt Ice Cream
  (page 164)
Summer Pudding (raspberries)
  (page 163)
Redcurrant and Honey Fool
  (page 166)
Redcurrant Water Ice (page 167)
Rodgrod Med Flode (redcurrants)
  (page 167)
Rhubarb Burnt Cream (page 172)
Rhubarb Compote (page 172)
Rhubarb Crumble (page 171)
Rhubarb Fool (page 171)
Rhubarb with Oat Crumble (page 172)
Spring Pudding (rhubarb) (page 171)
Fragole Dama Bianca (strawberries)
  (page 176)
French Strawberry Ice Cream
  (page 177)

PIES AND TARTS

BIBLIOGRAPHY

Berry, C. J. J., 130 NEW WINE MAKING RECIPES, Amateur Winemaker, 1967

Bowen, Carol, A TO Z OF HEALTH FOODS, Hamlyn, 1979

Bon Viveur, 365 PUDDINGS, Daily Telegraph Publications, 1975

Boyd, Lizzie, BRITISH COOKERY, B.T.A., 1976

Chu, Grace Zia, THE PLEASURES OF CHINESE COOKING, Faber, 1974

Dinnage, Paul, THE BOOK OF FRUIT & FRUIT COOKERY, Sidgwick & Jackson, 1981

Dixon, Pamela, NEW WAYS WITH FRESH FRUIT & VEGETABLES, Faber, 1973

Fitzgibbon, Theodora, THE FOOD OF THE WESTERN WORLD, Hutchinson, 1976

Foster, Charles, HOME WINEMAKING, Ward Lock, 1969

Good Housekeeping's World Cookery, Ebury Press, 1962

Good Housekeeping Cookery Book, Ebury Press, 1976

Graham, Winifred, CHOCOLATES & CANDIES FOR PLEASURE & PROFIT, White Lion Publishers Ltd, 1977

Heath, Ambrose, THE PENGUIN BOOK OF SAUCES, Penguin, 1970

Hunter, Beatrice Trum, THE NATURAL FOODS COOKBOOK, Faber, 1975

Innes, Francesca, & Lincoln, Frances, THE COUNTRY KITCHEN, Weidenfeld & Nicholson, 1979

Johns, Leslie, & Stevenson, Violet, THE COMPLETE BOOK OF FRUIT, Angus & Robertson, 1979

Kaufman, William I., THE NUT COOKERY BOOK, Faber, 1966

Lo, Kenneth, THE CHINESE COOKERY ENCYCLOPEDIA, William Collins, 1974

Mabey, David, & Mabey, Rose, JAMS, PICKLES & CHUTNEYS, Penguin, 1976

Maxwell Hudson, Claire, THE NATURAL BEAUTY BOOK, Macdonald & Jane, 1976

Maxwell Hudson, Claire, YOUR HEALTH & BEAUTY BOOK, Macdonald General Books, 1979

Nilson, Bee, PENGUIN COOKERY BOOK, Penguin, 1952

Olsen, Gloria Preston, CULINARY CLASSICS, Charter House Publishers, Tennessee, 1978

Orsini, Elizabeth, BOOK OF PIES, Pan, 1981

Ortiz, Elisabeth, CARIBBEAN COOKING, Penguin, 1977

Reekie, Jennie, NO NEED TO COOK, Pelham, 1977

Richardson, Rosamund, HEDGEROW COOKERY, Penguin, 1980

Sass, Lorna, TO THE QUEEN'S TASTE, John Murray, 1971

Singh, Dharamjit, INDIAN COOKERY, Penguin, 1970

Solomon, Charmaine, THE COMPLETE ASIAN COOKBOOK, Summit Books, Paul Hamlyn, Sydney, 1976

Tayleur, W. H. T., THE PENGUIN BOOK OF HOME BREWING & WINE MAKING, Penguin, 1973

The Complete Guide to the Art of Modern Cookery, translated by H. L. Cracknell & R. J. Kaufman, Heinemann, 1979

The Feill Cookery Book, MacNaughtan & Sinclair, 1907

The World Atlas of Food, Mitchell Beazley, 1974

Walker, Michael, CINZANO COCKTAIL BOOK, Queen Anne Press, 1980

Watt, Ruth Mulvey, & Alvarez, Luisa Maria, GOOD FOOD FROM MEXICO, Macmillan, New York, 1962

INDEX